SUPERCHARGED GRAPHICS

GRAPHICS

A PROGRAMMER'S SOURCE CODE TOOLBOX

Lee Adams

TAB BOOKS Inc.

Blue Ridge Summit, PA

FIRST EDITION
FIRST PRINTING

Copyright © 1988 by Lee Adams
Printed in the United States of America

Library of Congress Cataloging in Publication Data

Adams, Lee.
Supercharged graphics : a programmer's source code toolbox / by
Lee Adams.
p. cm.
Bibliography: p.
Includes index.
ISBN 0-8306-0659-9.   ISBN 0-8306-2959-9 (pbk.)
1. Computer graphics Computer programs. I. Title.
T385.A34 1988   88-2307
006.6′869—dc19   CIP

Questions regarding the content of this book
should be addressed to:

Reader Inquiry Branch
TAB BOOKS Inc.
Blue Ridge Summit, PA 17294-0214

Notes on the Photographs and Illustrations

The color photographs on the cover are examples of graphics produced by the
demonstration programs included inside this book. Exposure was ¼ second at
f2.8 using Kodak Ektachrome 100 daylight color slide film. The camera was a
standard 35mm Pentax K1000, fitted with a 2× teleconverter to reduce distortion,
using a 1:2 50mm lens. A tripod and remote shutter cable release were used
to suppress camera vibration. The computer graphics were generated by an IBM
PC on an IBM Enhanced Color Display monitor using a Quadram QuadEGA+
enhanced graphics adapter.

The black and white photographs are halftones taken from b/w prints produced
with Kodak Plus-X Pan film. Exposure was ¼ second at f2.8.

The line drawings are stats of ink drawings created on Bienfang Ad Art Layout
paper. The technical pens were Staedtler Mars-700 nib widths 3, 2, and 00. The
drawing ink was Pelikan no. 50 black.

The graphics print-outs were generated on a Panasonic KX-P1091 dot-matrix
printer using the Pizazz software package from Application Techniques, Inc. The
screen dump was made from a QuadEGA+ enhanced graphics adapter.

Contents

—— PART ONE: THE SOFTWARE ENVIRONMENT ——

Choosing a Programming Language   1

Manipulating the Hardware   11

___ PART THREE: INTERACTIVE 2D GRAPHICS ___

_____ PART FOUR: INTERACTIVE 3D GRAPHICS _____

Acknowledgments

The material in this book was made possible in part by insight which I derived from a variety of superb texts, manuals, journals, and user's guides. These sources are fully annotated in the bibliography.

I am grateful to Quadram Corporation for generously providing a Quadram ProSync enhanced graphics adapter and a Quadram QuadEGA+ enhanced graphics adapter for my use during preparation of the demonstration programs in the book.

Appreciation is extended to the fine people who organized and prepared IBM's BASIC Version 3.21 Reference manual, which sets the standard by which other BASIC manuals are judged. Their diligent attention to detail is an achievement which should not go unheralded.

Thanks to Leo Scanlon, who is a distinguished author of microcomputer books in his own right, for his helpful and forthright advice concerning writing, programming, and career.

Special thanks is extended to Victoria Adams, for constantly bringing to my attention various magazine articles and books relating to computer graphics programming. Appreciation is also owed to Warren Szkolnicki, for his healthy skepticism and constructive criticism of my programming ventures.

Notices

Introduction:
How to Use This Book

This book provides you with the hands-on knowledge you need to create high-performance interactive graphics software. Using your personal computer, you will be able to write graphics programs with features that rival those of packaged software. Simply stated, *SUPERCHARGED GRAPHICS* is an advanced graphics text that starts where other introductory books stop short.

The book contains over 8,000 lines of valuable source code. You will learn many of the closely guarded secrets of professional graphics programmers. The text gives you the theory in no-nonsense language; the program listings show you how to translate the theory into fast-running code. Included in the book are complete program listings for a drafting program, a paintbrush program, a 3D CAD modeling program, an interactive arcade-style animation program, and more. All the demonstration programs are also available on a companion disk (see the order form in the back of this book).

Supercharged Graphics is filled with the vital algorithms and time-saving routines you need. You will learn how to control the display screen, the keyboard, the disk, data files, a mouse, and more. You will see first-hand how to plan, develop, test, and polish a variety of advanced graphics programs. Whether you prefer to program in Turbo C, QuickC, QuickBASIC, Turbo BASIC, Turbo Pascal, assembly language, Modula-2, or BASIC, you will find the advanced graphics techniques that you need in the BASICA listings in this book.

WHO SHOULD USE THIS BOOK?

If you use a personal computer and you are interested in computer graphics, then you will want to read this book. If you are a beginner to high-performance computing, then the exciting field of computer-generated graphics is waiting for you to discover! If you are an experienced programmer, this book will show you some graphics techniques that you may have thought possible only with expensive packaged software. If you are a professional programmer or software author, you will learn some useful techniques for enhancing your graphics applications programming.

ABOUT THE BOOK

Supercharged Graphics has been designed as a learning tool. If you want to turn back the corners of pages which interest you so you can quickly find them again, go right ahead. You might find it helpful to highlight the text with a marker pen. Writing your own observations into the margins can be helpful, too.

What The Book Strives To Do

Supercharged Graphics teaches you how to write full-length, interactive graphics programs on IBM-compatible personal computers in the context of a modular programming environment. The book employs the learn-by-example style of teaching. Four major program listings are provided, supplemented by a rich assortment of shorter programs and important here-is-how-to-do-it code fragments.

Emphasis is placed on helping you understand the concepts behind the programs. Once you learn what makes a program perform, you will find it easy to write your own interactive graphics programs. Using the information presented in *Supercharged Graphics*, you will be able to generate fully-interactive graphics programs which use 2D displays, 3D displays, and even animated displays. The list of possible applications is limited only by your imagination. Because a modular, structured programming approach is used throughout the book, you will find it easy to convert the routines to other programming languages such as QuickC, Turbo C, Turbo Pascal, Modula-2, assembly language, and others.

SPECIAL FEATURES OF THE BOOK

Supercharged Graphics is organized in a step one, step two, step three linear format. Important fundamentals which are discussed near the beginning of the text become the building blocks for advanced applications later in the book. Using a modular programming philosophy, independent routines which perform specific tasks are called by a master routine to create spectacular graphics on your personal computer.

When an important graphics concept is discussed, it is also provided to you as a here-is-how-to-do-it program listing or code fragment. Major program listings for 3D CAD, drafting, paintbrush, arcade-style animation, and others give you the routines you need to write your own high-performance programs.

Every major program listing is presented in a ready-to-run stand-alone format. Simply type it in, and it is ready to run on your IBM PC, XT, AT, PCjr, PS/2, or compatible. In many instances, if the graphics functions are hardware-specific, separate listings are provided for the EGA and for the color/graphics adapter. A selection of program listings have been provided for the PCjr, too. If you are using a PS/2 computer, your VGA will run the EGA programs as-is. Your PS/2 MCGA will run the CGA programs as-is.

Each program listing in *Supercharged Graphics* is accompanied by a photograph of an actual monitor display, so you can verify the graphics generated on your own personal computer. A rich selection of artwork provides the background information you need in order to understand how each program works. A robust discussion of each program gives you a modular description of the programming logic involved.

Every 3D CAD, drafting, and paintbrush program is accompanied by a powerful Mini-User's Guide; a here-is-how-to-use-it Sample Sessions Tutorial; and a here-is-how-it-works Program Analysis.

If you wish to select only topics of specific interest to your programming needs, a comprehensive table of contents at the beginning of the book and a detailed index at the end of the book will quickly direct you to the pages which contain the information you seek.

HOW THE BOOK IS ORGANIZED

The material in the book is organized into five sections for your easy reference.

Part One—The Software Environment

Part One introduces the programming environment. You will learn about different hardware and software capabilities. You will discover useful programming tools and, more important, you will learn good programming skills. You will see how to manage your graphics project from start to finish. You will learn different methods for protecting your original software.

Part Two—The Hardware Environment

Part Two introduces the hardware environment. You will see how to manage the keyboard and the display screen. You will explore control algorithms for managing a mouse. Also discussed are the light pen, track ball, tablet, and touch-screen. Reliable techniques for managing disk files and data files are provided. You will see how to fold machine code subroutines into your graphics programs in order to provide a wider performance envelope.

Part Three—Interactive 2D Graphics

Part Three introduces interactive 2D graphics. The source code for a full-function, interactive paintbrush program is provided and analyzed. An interactive 2D drafting program with multiple drawing layers is provided. You will learn first-hand how to handle advanced keyboard controls, code overlays, and data manipulation.

Part Four—Interactive 3D Graphics

Part Four introduces interactive 3D graphics. After a detailed discussion of 3D algorithms and shading routines, two advanced interactive 3D CAD program listings are provided. First, you will learn how to generate 3D wire-frame models. Then you will see how to produce fully shaded solid models on your personal computer by using an illumination matrix.

Part Five—Interactive Animation Graphics

Part Five introduces three different techniques for high-speed animation on your personal computer. Plenty of source code is provided, including a prototype for an arcade-style applications program and a ready-to-run listing that demonstrates frame animation of a 3D object.

Appendices

The appendices contain time-saving information about mathematics and algorithms for computer graphics. Programs already adapted for QuickBASIC, Turbo BASIC, the color/graphics adapter, and the PCjr are provided. A comprehensive glossary helps you discover the exciting field of advanced graphics.

WHAT YOU NEED TO USE THE BOOK

You probably already have everything you need to get the most out of *Supercharged Graphics*.

Software Requirements

You can work in any language, but if you have BASIC, then you have all the software you need. The programs are written in IBM BASICA. Conversion to GW-BASIC, COMPAQ BASIC, and compatible interpreters is straightforward. You can also readily convert many of the demonstration programs for QuickBASIC and Turbo BASIC. Two fully-converted program listings for these compilers are provided in Appendix E. If you program in Turbo C, QuickC, Turbo Pascal, Modula-2, Ada, or assembly language, you can easily translate the graphics concepts into your preferred language.

Hardware Requirements

If you have access to an IBM-compatible personal computer, then you have all the hardware you need. The programs are written for the IBM PC, the IBM PC XT, the IBM AT, the IBM RT, the IBM PCjr, and the IBM Personal System/2 series. Any microcomputer which is compatible with these models will run the demonstration programs. The graphics adapter installed in your personal computer and the version of BASIC you are using will affect program compatibility, of course.

Color/Graphics Adapter

If you have a color/graphics adapter in your personal computer, the converted programs will run in the 320×200 four-color mode and the 640×200 two-color mode. Refer to Appendix G for the program listings which have been converted for the color/graphics adapter, including a sophisticated 3D CAD editor which you can use to create wire-frame models.

EGA

If you have an EGA, the programs run in the 640×200 16-color mode. You can easily adapt the programs to run in the 320×200 16-color mode or the 640×350 16-color mode. You will need a version of BASIC that supports EGA graphics, such as IBM BASICA 3.21 and newer, Microsoft QuickBASIC 2.x and newer, or Borland Turbo BASIC 1.x and newer. The notation x is intended to represent assorted version numbers. Program listings for the EGA appear throughout the main body of the book.

Personal System/2

If you have a VGA as found on the 80286-based and 80386-based models of the IBM PS/2 series, the programs run in the 640×200 16-color EGA mode. Programs for the VGA appear in the main body of the book. If you have a MCGA as found on the 8086-based models of the IBM PS/2 series, the programs run in the same modes as the Color/Graphics Adapter. Refer to Appendix G for the program listings which have been converted for the MCGA. You will need IBM BASICA 3.3x or newer with your PS/2 personal computer, or any other BASIC interpreter or compiler which supports VGA and MCGA graphics functions, such as Turbo BASIC 1.x and QuickBASIC 4.0, and others.

PCjr

If you have an IBM PCjr or a Tandy 1000 SX, the demonstration programs run in the 640×200 four-color mode and the 320×200 four-color mode. Refer to Appendix H for the program listings which have been converted for the PCjr, including a 3D CAD editor which you can use to create wireframe models.

THE COMPANION DISK

The companion disk for *Supercharged Graphics* contains the demonstration programs from the main body of the book. Using the companion disk, you can begin immediately to explore the high-performance graphics routines discussed in the book. The disk can save you hours of debugging time trying to track down the keyboard errors that always seem to infiltrate a program while it is being typed in.

The companion disk is a what-you-see-is-what-you-get item. It is not copy-protected and there are no hidden files. You can load and run the programs. You can display the source code on your display screen. You can print out the program listings on your printer. The companion disk is a powerful graphics tool kit from which you can select fully tested subroutines for use in your own programs.

The programs on the companion disk use BASIC's compressed tokenized format. You get over 8,000 lines of valuable source code, providing real value for your investment. The order coupon is at the back of the book.

THE HARDWARE AND SOFTWARE USED TO CREATE THE GRAPHICS

The demonstration programs in *Supercharged Graphics* were developed on an IBM PC using IBM DOS 3.20, IBM BASICA 3.21, an IBM Enhanced Color Display monitor, and a Quadram QuadEGA+ enhanced graphics adapter. Additional testing was performed on a Quadram QuadEGA ProSync adapter. The programs for the color/graphics adapter were created using IBM DOS 2.10 and IBM BASICA 2.10. In addition, IBM DOS 2.10 and IBM Cartridge BASIC J1.00 were used on an IBM PCjr to adapt some of the programs for junior.

Microsoft QuickBASIC 2.0 and Borland Turbo BASIC 1.0 were employed to create and test the sample adapted programs for each compiler. IBM DOS 3.20 was used in each instance.

The assembly language subroutines used for page flipping on the Color/Graphics Adapter were developed using IBM Macro Assembler 2.0. The link and debug utilities from IBM DOS 2.10 were also used in this context.

The demonstration programs will run on virtually all personal computers which claim IBM-compatibility. A discussion of various BASIC interpreters and compilers which run on these compatibles may be found in Appendix D and Appendix E.

IF YOU INTEND TO ADAPT MATERIAL FROM THIS BOOK

If you intend to adapt any material from this book for your own purposes, or if you intend to use the information in this book to write commercial software, shareware, or freeware, then you should read the next three paragraphs.

I have done my best to prepare the material and the program listings which appear in *Supercharged Graphics*. These efforts include the development, research, and thorough testing of the demonstration programs to determine their effectiveness and accuracy.

However, in recognition of the wide diversity of applications which exist in the microcomputer environment, I am unable to make any absolute guarantees to you that the information and program listings in this book will solve your particular design, engineering, simulation, CAD, or animation problems.

You will find many powerful programming techniques in *Supercharged Graphics*, but if you intend to adapt the material for your own purposes, you must thoroughly test the programs before you rely upon their performance.

HOW TO CONTACT THE AUTHOR

I welcome your observations and will reply to all letters. You can write to me in care of Reader Inquiry Branch, Editorial Department, TAB BOOKS Inc., P.O. Box 40, Blue Ridge Summit, PA, USA 17294-0214. Please allow three weeks for your correspondence to reach me. Include your telephone number and area code if you wish a verbal reply.

SUGGESTED READING

The text occasionally makes reference to my previous books. You might find the detailed background information provided in these references helpful, although you will gain considerable graphics expertise by using *Supercharged Graphics* as a stand-alone text. My other books include *High-Speed Animation & Simulation for Microcomputers* (TAB book 2859) and *High-Performance Interactive Graphics: Modeling, Rendering & Animating for IBM PCs and Compatibles* (TAB book 2879).

List of
Demonstration Programs

You will find over 8,000 lines of valuable source code in this book. Major program listings for 3D CAD, drafting, paintbrush, arcade-style animation, and other programs give you the routines you need to write your own high-performance software.

In this list of programs EGA means enhanced graphics adapter; CGA means color/graphics adapter; VGA means the video graphics array on PS/2 computers; MCGA means the multicolor graphics array on PS/2 computers. The logical line-length and size in bytes of each major program is given in parentheses.

PROGRAM LISTINGS SPECIFICALLY FOR THE EGA AND VGA

MENU.BAS—interactive menu system. (253 lines-10612 bytes)

SKETCH-A.BAS—start-up module: interactive paintbrush program. (226 lines-12703 bytes)

SKETCH-B.BAS—runtime module: interactive paintbrush program. (846 lines-35393 bytes)

CADD-1.BAS—start-up module: interactive drafting program. (249 lines-12762 bytes)

CADD-2.BAS—runtime module: interactive drafting program. (649 lines-26007 bytes)

CAD-1.BAS—interactive 3D CAD wireframe editor. (561 lines-23607 bytes)

CAD-2.BAS—interactive 3D CAD solid model editor. (687 lines-31187 bytes)

FRAME.BAS—frame animation manager.

ARCADE.BAS—interactive arcade animation prototype.

PROGRAM LISTINGS COMPATIBLE WITH ALL GRAPHICS ADAPTERS

MENU-CGA.BAS—interactive menu system. (253 lines-10726 bytes)

MOUSE.BAS—mouse initializer.

MENUMOUS.BAS—interactive menu system for mouse. (241 lines-12040 bytes)

AREAFILL.BAS—demonstration of advanced area fill algorithm for complex irregular polygons.

PROGRAM LISTINGS SPECIFICALLY FOR THE CGA AND MCGA

CAD-CGA1.BAS—interactive 3D CAD wireframe editor. (600 lines-24293 bytes)

ARCADE1.BAS—interactive arcade animation prototype.

FRAME1.BAS—frame animation manager.

PROGRAM LISTINGS SPECIFICALLY FOR THE PCJR AND TANDY

CAD-JR1.BAS—interactive 3D CAD wireframe editor. (561 lines-22565 bytes)

ARCADEJR.BAS—interactive arcade animation prototype.

FRAMEJR.BAS—frame animation manager.

PROGRAM LISTINGS SPECIFICALLY FOR QUICKBASIC AND TURBO BASIC

QB-001.BAS—interactive 3D CAD solid model editor for QuickBASIC. (687 lines-35611 bytes ASCII)

TB-001.BAS—interactive 3D CAD wireframe editor for Turbo BASIC. (600 lines-27698 ASCII)

HERE-IS-HOW-TO-DO-IT CODE FRAGMENTS

A-01.BAS—keyboard input controller.

A-02.BAS—light pen input controller.

A-03.BAS—BSAVE and BLOAD screen images for EGA and VGA.

A-04.BAS—using MID$ to alter disk file names during runtime.

A-05.BAS—reading and writing .CDF data files.

A-06.BAS—high speed page moves on the Color/Graphics Adapter with the PCOPY machine code subroutine.

A-07.BAS—assembly language listing for PCOPY emulator.

A-08.BAS—3D perspective formulas.

A-09.BAS—hidden surface formulas for 3D modeling.

A-10.BAS—formulas and algorithm for computer-controlled shading of 3D models.

A-11.BAS—halftoning codes and dithering matrix for computer-controlled shading on the EGA and VGA in the 640×200 16-color mode.

A-12.BAS—halftoning codes and dithering matrix for computer-controlled shading on the EGA and VGA in the 640×350 16-color mode.

A-13.BAS—halftoning codes and dithering matrix for computer-controlled shading on the Color/Graphics Adapter and PCjr in the 320×200 4-color mode.

A-14.BAS—window mapping utility.

A-15.BAS—viewport mapping utility.

A-16.BAS—reprise 3D perspective formulas.

A-17.BAS—cubic parametric curve formulas.

A-18.BAS—reprise BSAVE/BLOAD EGA and VGA modes.

A-19.BAS—palette environments for 3D shading on EGA and VGA.

Choosing a
Programming Language

If you are interested in creating finished, full-length, interactive graphics programs for the IBM PC and compatibles, you may be surprised to learn that you can work in almost any programming language.

Because the principles of graphics programming are universal, you can write your original programs in C, Pascal, Modula-2, Ada, BASIC, or assembly language. This means you can use popular languages such as QuickC, Turbo C, Turbo Pascal, QuickBASIC, Microsoft C, Turbo Modula-2, IBM Macro Assembler, Turbo Prolog, Microsoft Macro Assembler, Turbo BASIC, GW-BASIC, IBM BASICA, ZBasic, True BASIC, BetterBASIC, and many others.

The other side of the coin is that not all languages are created equal. Each language offers distinct advantages and disadvantages when used for high-performance graphics programming. The more you understand these advantages and disadvantages, the easier it will be for you to select a programming language for developing your own original interactive graphics programs.

The following discussion assumes that you have already reviewed the section entitled "Introduction: How to Use This Book."

CHOOSING A LANGUAGE

When choosing a programming language, you should take into consideration four factors. These factors are: (a) the graphics capabilities of the language, (b) ease of use during program development, (c) runtime speed of the finished product, and (d) distribution potential.

Your choice will often mean sacrificing one feature in order to obtain other features which are important to you. In fact, professional graphics programmers often create their rough prototypes in one language before writing the finished code in a second language. The prototyping language usually offers ease of development and experimentation, while the finishing language often provides improved runtime speed and a more secure format for distribution.

FACTOR 1: GRAPHICS CAPABILITIES

The built-in graphics capabilities of various languages adhere to no standard. Some languages offer extensive graphics routines, while others provide no routines whatsoever. The graphics routines provided by a programming language usually reflect its level. High-level languages usually, but not always, tend to offer more built-in graphics functions than middle-level languages or low-level languages.

What is the difference between high-level, middle-level, and low-level languages? Refer to Fig. 1-1. A high-level language is one that places more emphasis on communicating efficiently with you than on communicating with the microprocessor. High-level languages are generally easy to use. The resulting program, however, is not as efficient as it could be.

A middle-level language makes some sacrifices in ease of use in order to provide more efficient use of the microprocessor. Source code written in a middle-level language is often a bit more difficult to read and understand than a program written in a high-level language. The payoff is that a middle-level language gives you more direct control over the microprocessor. That means you have more power and control; you can create specialized and efficient routines within the broad limitations of the language.

A low-level language has no limitations whatsoever. It gives top priority to efficient use of the microprocessor; the language syntax is often terse and mnemonic. In return for source code which is difficult to read and understand, onerous to test and debug, and which forces you to provide your own graphics routines, your payback is a superpower-class programming language that provides absolute control over the computer. You can push the display hardware to its maximum potential only with a low-level language.

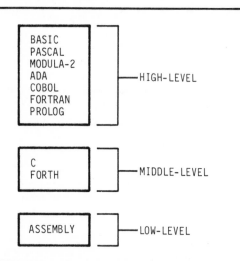

Fig. 1-1. Categorization of common programming languages. A high-level language such as IBM BASICA 3.21 contains over 160 instructions, including many complex graphics and math functions. A middle-level language such as Turbo C 1.0 contains 32 instructions. Many math and text functions are provided in the standard library of subroutines, but users must create their own graphics functions. A low-level language such as IBM Macro Assembler 2.0 contains 75 instructions (mnemonics), but the user must create all functions and subroutines from scratch.

BASIC is often considered the highest of the high-level languages. Assembly language is often considered the most powerful low-level language. C is usually considered a middle-level language. ADA and Modula-2 are considered to have some features of all levels.

Graphics Capabilities of BASIC

BASIC interpreters such as IBM BASICA, GW-BASIC, and others provide a robust selection of built-in graphics routines. Advanced graphics features such as page flipping and graphic arrays allow you to construct highly sophisticated animation programs, simulations, and 3D displays. The everyday syntax used by IBM-compatible BASIC interpreters makes it easy to grasp the purpose of the graphics functions being used.

BASIC compilers such as Microsoft QuickBASIC and Borland Turbo BASIC also provide a rich repertory of built-in graphics. Refer to Fig. 1-2. The primary differences between compilers and interpreters concern functions collateral to graphics programming, such as using runtime code overlays, conventions for CALLing assembly language subroutines, and buffer manipulation. Turbo BASIC 1.0, for example, provides no PCOPY instruction for moving graphics data from one page location to another. (An explanation of pages, buffers, and graphics instructions is provided in coming chapters.) Other BASIC compilers such as True BASIC, BetterBASIC, and ZBasic are available, but they do not generally adhere to the standard established by IBM syntax rules.

Graphics Capabilities of C

As a general rule, most versions of the C programming language do not come with built-in graphics functions. In these instances, you must either write your own graphics subroutines with assembly language or you must purchase a separate library of graphics routines such as MetaWINDOW or Essential Graphics. These are available from independent software publishers. Writing your own routines costs time; buying a library of routines costs cash. You must decide for yourself which you have more of.

A welcome trend towards the inclusion of built-in graphics functions is overtaking the C market. Beginning with version 5.0 of Microsoft C and with QuickC, an extensive collection of graphics routines has been provided with the C compiler. Other C language publishers are following suit, making C an attractive choice for learning graphics concepts and for writing advanced graphics programs.

Graphics Capabilities of Assembly Language

The advantages of using assembly language to create interactive graphics programs can be enormous if you already have a full understanding of intricate graphics programming concepts, especially if you also have a full understanding of the hardware. You can produce the fastest runtime code with assembly language, even quicker than the code produced by compilers. You have full access to the hardware's potential with assembly language. However, if you are still learning and experimenting with graphics concepts, assembly language can exact a harsh price from you in terms of time and effort.

Graphics Capabilities of Other Languages

Turbo Pascal is provided with no built-in graphics functions, although separate libraries of routines are readily available for purchase. You are limited to the graphics capabilities

	IBM BASICA	Microsoft QuickBASIC	Borland TURBO BASIC	Microsoft GW-BASIC
CGA GRAPHICS	yes	yes	yes	yes
EGA GRAPHICS	3.21+	2.0+	yes	3.21+
VGA GRAPHICS	3.30+	NO	yes	NO
CLS	yes	yes	yes	yes
LINE	yes	yes	yes	yes
CIRCLE	yes	yes	yes	yes
AREA FILL	yes	yes	yes	yes
HALFTONE FILL	yes	yes	yes	yes
LINESTYLING	yes	yes	yes	yes
FLIP PAGES	3.21+	3.0+	yes	yes
DRAW HIDDEN PAGE	3.21+	3.0+	NO	yes
CLS HIDDEN PAGE	3.30+	3.0+	NO	yes
PALETTE	3.21+	2.0+	yes	yes
WINDOW	yes	yes	yes	yes
VIEW	yes	yes	yes	yes
GET/PUT	yes	yes	yes	yes
PCOPY	3.21+	2.0+	NO	yes
CALL	yes	*yes	*yes	yes
CODE OVERLAY	yes	.EXE	.TBC	yes
SEQUENTIAL FILES	yes	yes	yes	yes
RANDOM FILES	yes	yes	yes	yes
BSAVE/BLOAD	yes	yes	yes	yes
MAX. SOURCE CODE	64K	>64K	64K	64K
MATH COPROCESSOR	NO	3.0+	yes	NO

* QuickBASIC requires special routine in library to
redirect call back to your assembly language routine.
TURBO BASIC uses CALL ABSOLUTE syntax.

Fig. 1-2. Comparison of graphics-related features of different versions of BASIC. At time of comparison, highest version numbers available were IBM BASICA 3.30, Microsoft QuickBASIC 3.0, Borland Turbo BASIC 1.0, and Microsoft GW-BASIC 3.2. Other products such as True BASIC, BetterBASIC, and ZBasic do not adhere to the BASICA syntax standard.

provided by the library unless you create your own routines with assembly language.

Prolog, which is an artificial intelligence-based language useful for decision-making functions, can be easily interfaced to C. This means you can readily use the graphics functions which are available to you through your C compiler. Turbo Prolog, for example, is specifically designed by its manufacturer, Borland International, to be used with Turbo C.

Modula-2 is a high-level/middle-level language which is useful for systems programming and real-time programming. You can access high-performance graphics functions by interfacing Modula-2 to routines which you have created with assembly language.

Fortran is a high-level language used mainly for scientific and engineering applications. Although third-party graphics libraries are available, you can also write your own graphics routines in assembly language for use with your Fortran compiler.

Graphics Capabilities: A Summary

For the no-nonsense convenience of built-in graphics routines, BASIC and C are the clear choices. However, other programming languages can implement a rich selection of graphics routines through third-party libraries such as MetaWINDOWS and Essential Graphics, or through your own assembly language subroutines.

FACTOR 2: EASE OF USE

The ability to run a program, observe the graphics output, and then return to the source code to make minor changes is very important during development of graphics programs. The faster this feedback can occur, the quicker the program can be developed and perfected. Feedback is an essential element of the experimental process that characterizes graphics programming.

Compilers VS. Interpreters

In general, interpreters are better suited to preliminary graphics prototype development than compilers. What is the difference between an interpreter and a compiler? An interpreter executes your source code one line at a time. Refer to Fig. 1-3. It reads a line, translates the BASIC instructions into machine code, and then executes the machine code. It then begins work on the next line. It does not—and it cannot—check ahead to figure out ways to optimize loops or subroutines. It plods along methodically and reliably one line at a time. Lines found inside loops are translated on each pass through the loop, even though they have been translated previously!

Although runtime speed is not as fast as it could be, an interpreter allows immediate start-up of the program. Once the program is running, you can stop at any time and return to the editor. This means you can get quick feedback while you are building your program.

On the other hand, a compiler reads and translates your entire source code into machine language before it begins executing the program. Refer to Fig. 1-4. Because translation occurs only once, runtime performance is fast and efficient. During compilation (translation), the compiler will often figure out innovative ways to optimize loops and subroutines, making for even more efficient runtime output.

Even with today's interactive editor-driven compilers, there is a substantive delay caused by the translation of the entire source code into assembly language. The delay is

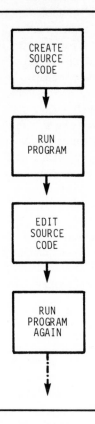

Fig. 1-3. Interpreted BASIC provides immediate runtime feedback while a programmer is developing, testing, and debugging a graphics program.

aggravated if you must link your program to other modules. You are compensated for this delay by improved runtime speed, of course.

Examples of BASIC interpreters are IBM BASICA, GW-BASIC, COMPAQ BASIC, and others. BASIC compilers include QuickBASIC, Turbo BASIC, and others.

Nearly all versions of C are compilers. Examples of interactive editor-driven compilers include QuickC and Turbo C. You must provide your own editor if you are using larger compilers such as Microsoft C.

Error Reporting

A BASIC interpreter will stop immediately and it will display an error message when it encounters an error in the source code. Simply stated, the program runs up to the first point it encounters a syntax error or illegal instruction. If you enjoy dealing with errors one at a time, then a BASIC interpreter is the best tool for you. Being able to observe a program's performance up to the error can be of assistance in understanding what is happening.

A compiler usually reports errors during compilation. A list of errors is provided, allowing you to correct all oversights before the next compilation. A compiler will often not permit you to run a program until all syntax errors and illegal instructions have been corrected. Interactive editor-driven BASIC compilers such as QuickBASIC and Turbo BASIC provide extensive error-checking to help you avoid locking up or crashing your personal

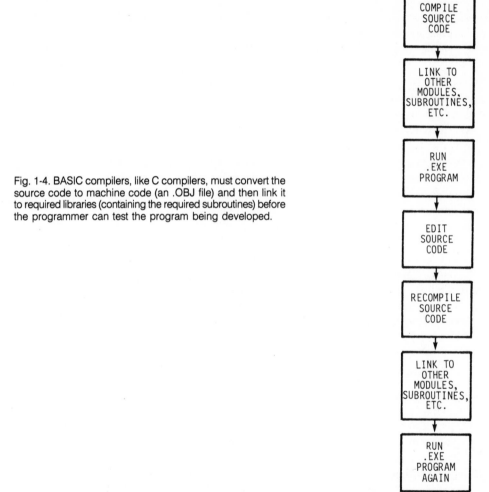

Fig. 1-4. BASIC compilers, like C compilers, must convert the source code to machine code (an .OBJ file) and then link it to required libraries (containing the required subroutines) before the programmer can test the program being developed.

computer. Interactive editor-driven C compilers such as Quick C and Turbo C provide fewer error checks, so there is greater opportunity for you to inadvertently lock up the computer. Larger C compilers such as Microsoft C provide very limited error-checking; you are on your own in this instance.

The best error-checking is provided by BASIC interpreters. The next best error-checking is provided by interactive BASIC compilers, although even then many errors are not caught until runtime. Good error-checking is performed by editor-driven C compilers. If you are learning to program advanced graphics programs, you might wish to limit your language choices to these options.

Debugging

Debugging is mainly the process of searching for and correcting performance errors. Performance errors are errors which occur even though no syntax errors or illegal instructions are present in the source code. Needless to say, these are the most difficult errors to locate.

Debugging can occur at two levels: at the source code level and at the object code level. BASIC interpreters allow you to make changes to the source code and then re-run the program. This is debugging at the source code level.

When you are using an interactive editor-driven compiler such as QuickBASIC, Turbo BASIC, Quick C, or Turbo C, you can debug at the source code level. If the compiler encounters an error during runtime, it returns you to the source code. After you make the required changes to the source code, you simply recompile the code and run the program again.

If, however, you have compiled your source code to an .EXE file or a .COM file on disk, you often must debug it at the object code level. This can be difficult and time consuming, because hexadecimal opcodes are usually much more difficult to understand than the source code instructions.

Clearly, BASIC interpreters offer the quickest and most interactive debugging capabilities during preliminary program development. The debugging capabilities of interactive editor-driven compilers, both BASIC and C, come close to matching those of interpreted BASIC. Debugging at the object code level should not be considered as a realistic option when source code level choices are available.

Ease of Use: A Summary

BASIC interpreters offer the most responsive features for feedback, error reporting, and debugging, but runtime speeds can be disappointing. Interactive editor-driven compilers for both BASIC and C provide acceptable levels of feedback, error reporting, and source level debugging, in addition to offering fast runtime performance.

FACTOR 3: RUNTIME SPEED

If runtime speed is the overriding factor—and it usually is after you have completed the preliminary prototype—then using a compiler is usually your best choice. As described earlier, a BASIC interpreter simply cannot produce the fastest code possible because of its insistence on re-translating lines of code which occur in loops.

A compiler gives you the best of both worlds. You can write your source code using familiar syntax; the compiler does all the work of translating your source code into fast-running machine code. In addition, if runtime performance still does not meet your expectations, you can rewrite important graphics loops in assembly language, thereby giving you the fastest speed possible.

FACTOR 4: DISTRIBUTION POTENTIAL

Clearly, a program written in interpreted BASIC is not a serious candidate for use on a distribution disk. A distribution disk is the medium you distribute as commercial software, shareware, or freeware. First, interpreted BASIC provides only minimal protection against users inspecting your source code. (After spending months developing original fast-running routines, you would normally want to keep your proprietary programming methods confidential.) Second, interpreted BASIC is not a stand-alone environment: the end-user must have a BASIC interpreter in order to run your program. Combine these disadvantages with less-than-ideal runtime speeds, and BASIC interpreters do not lend themselves to distribution.

Compilers, on the other hand, provide good security against browsers who would like to inspect your source code (and possibly use your original routines in their own programs). The object code produced by compilers, whether in .EXE or .COM format, is extremely difficult to unravel, even by experts using professional debuggers. In addition, compilers can produce stand-alone code which requires only the presence of an operating system on the end-user's personal computer. Combine these advantages with good runtime speeds, and compiler seems to be a strong candidate for producing distribution code.

Licenses

If you intend to produce professional software, you must consider the issue of licenses. If you use a graphics library from a third-party publisher, you often must pay a license fee if you wish to include parts of the graphics library on your distribution disk. On the other hand, if you write your own graphics routines with assembly language, you can freely include the routines as part of your program. Interactive, editor-driven compilers that include built-in graphics routines usually provide for distribution of the resulting program without any additional licensing requirements.

WHICH LANGUAGE IS BEST?

Simply stated, whichever language you choose is the language which is best for you. Just be sure that you have carefully considered the advantages and disadvantages of each possibility. BASIC interpreters provide ideal learning environments, but runtime performance is sometimes disappointing, although you may be surprised by the speed of the innovative graphics code in this book. BASIC compilers provide very good runtime speeds, but the delay caused by recompilation during program development and debugging can annoy some programmers. Interactive C compilers provide lots of power and versatility, but do not always come with built-in graphics routines. In addition, C is a more challenging language with which to write code.

When all is said and done, you can create high-performance interactive graphics software with any language. If your language does not come with built-in graphics, simply use a graphics library from a third-party publisher, or write your own specialized graphics routines using assembly language.

THE DEMONSTRATION PROGRAMS

Supercharged Graphics contains complete program listings for a CADD drafting program, a paintbrush program, a 3D CAD wireframe editor, a 3D CAD solid model editor, an arcade-style animation manager, and more. These polished, fast-running demonstration programs are provided as IBM BASICA listings for the following reasons:

- Nearly everyone is familiar with BASIC. Many popular magazines and journals regularly use BASIC to demonstrate short utilities and routines. BASIC is a good teaching language.
- Nearly everyone has BASIC. It is bundled as part of the original purchase price of most personal computers.
- BASIC includes a first-class library of graphics routines, especially versions of BASIC which support the EGA and VGA.
- BASIC code is relatively easy to translate into C, Pascal, Ada, Modula-2, and assembly language because BASIC code is relatively easy to read. The converse is not always true.
- BASICA listings can be run under GW-BASIC, COMPAQ BASIC, QuickBASIC, and Turbo BASIC with few, if any, changes required.
- Because BASIC is a relatively straightforward, simple language, it allows you to concentrate on learning the graphics concepts, rather than struggling with the syntax and idiosyncracies of the language itself.
- Once you have earned a full understanding of graphics concepts, you will find it easy to transpose your source code into C, Pascal, or assembly language. You will also find it easy to write sophisticated graphics applications in C, Pascal, or assembly language.
- Because of the high-performance, innovative programming concepts used in the program listings throughout this book, even BASIC interpreters can generate surprisingly quick runtime speeds.

SUMMARY

In this chapter you studied the advantages and disadvantages of using different languages for the development of advanced graphics programs. You learned about the differences between compilers and interpreters.

The next chapter discusses the graphics capabilities of different display monitors and graphics adapters on IBM-compatible personal computers.

2
Manipulating the Hardware

Unlike other forms of programming, graphics programming requires you to possess at least a general understanding of the hardware's capabilities. At a minimum, you should understand the potential and the limitations of your own computer system. At best, you should be familiar with the broad spectrum of different graphics modes available on all IBM-compatible personal computers.

Three factors control the quality of the graphics which can be generated on any particular personal computer system. These factors are the graphics adapter, the display monitor, and the programming language. Of the three components, the graphics adapter is the most important.

THE GRAPHICS ADAPTER

The particular graphics adapter which is installed in your microcomputer determines the maximum graphics capabilities of your system. In general, five main types of graphics adapters are commonly used on personal computers. These are the VGA, the EGA, the MCGA, the CGA, and the PCjr video subsystem. Combined together, these five graphics adapters can generate a dazzling selection of graphics modes. Refer to Fig. 2-1.

The CGA

If there is a common denominator in the world of IBM-compatible personal computers, it is the CGA, more commonly called the color/graphics adapter. The CGA can generate a 320×200 four-color screen and a 640×200 two-color screen. The notation 320×200

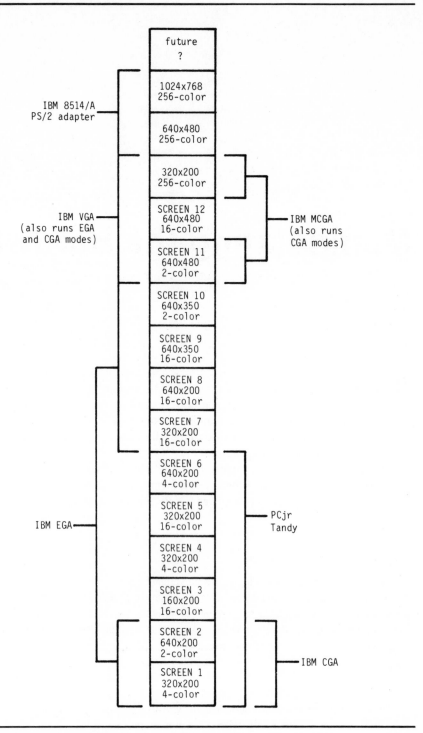

Fig. 2-1. Graphics modes available with assorted IBM-compatible graphics adapters.

means 320 pixels across by 200 raster lines down. A pixel is the smallest element or dot which can be controlled on the display screen. It is called a pel by IBM.

Although the CGA is a superb general-purpose graphics adapter, the coarse resolution in the four-color mode and the severely limited choice of colors in the 640×200 mode makes it less than ideal for advanced graphics programming. The CGA is a fine graphics adapter for learning purposes, however. Only one graphics page is available on the color/graphics adapter.

The MCGA

MCGA is an acronym for multicolor graphics array. The MCGA is the graphics adapter found on the 8086-based models of the IBM Personal System/2 series, such as the Model 30 and the Model 25. (8086 refers to the Intel microprocessor used in these systems.) The MCGA is essentially an extension of the CGA. In addition to the standard 320×200 four-color mode and the 640×200 two-color mode, the MCGA provides a 640×480 two-color mode and a 320×200 256-color mode. The 256-color mode has attracted the attention of many professional programmers and computer users. Multiple graphics pages are available on the MCGA.

The EGA

EGA is an acronym for enhanced graphics adapter. The EGA provides the 320×200 four-color and the 640×200 two-color modes of the CGA, in addition to four enhanced graphics modes: a 320×200 16-color mode, a 640×200 16-color mode, a 640×350 16-color mode, and a 640×350 two-color mode. The EGA is considered by many to be the new graphics standard for IBM-compatible personal computers. Multiple graphics pages are available on the EGA.

The VGA

The VGA is the video graphics array found on the 80286-based and the 80386-based models of the IBM Personal System/2 series, such as the Model 50 and the Model 60. (80286 and 80386 refer to the Intel microprocessors found in these systems.) The VGA provides all the modes of the EGA, the CGA, and the MCGA, as well as one additional graphics mode: the 640×480 16-color mode. Multiple graphics pages are available on the VGA.

The PCjr Video Subsystem

The PCjr video subsystem is part-CGA and part-EGA. You might wish to think of the PCjr as a superset of the CGA and a subset of the EGA. In addition to the standard CGA modes, the PCjr can generate the 160×200 16-color mode, an enhanced 320×200 four-color mode, a 320×200 16-color mode, and a 640×200 four-color mode. The 320×200 16-color mode and the 640×200 four-color mode are the most useful for advanced graphics programming. Multiple graphics pages are available on the PCjr video subsystem.

GRAPHICS MODES

Figure 2-2 illustrates the range of graphics modes officially recognized by IBM. Although all the modes depicted in Fig. 2-2 are supported by BIOS routines, not all graphics modes are supported by IBM BASICA or by other BASIC interpreters and compilers. BIOS is an acronym for basic input/output services. Simply stated, BIOS is a collection of assembly language subroutines permanently stored in read-only memory in your personal computer. BIOS subroutines typically provide functions such as setting a pixel, reading a pixel, setting the graphics mode, and so forth. Many programming languages and many commercial software packages call upon the BIOS routines to set the graphics modes and even generate the graphics themselves.

The BIOS source code listings for the CGA can be found in the Technical Reference for the IBM PC and in the Technical Reference for the IBM Personal Computer XT. The BIOS source code listings for the EGA can be found in the Technical Reference for the IBM Enhanced Graphics Adapter (sometimes found in the IBM Options and Adapters Man-

IBM GRAPHICS MODES								
BIOS MODE	BASIC MODE	RESO LUTION	COLOR	BITS PER PIXEL	PAGE SIZE	MEMORY LAYOUT	GRAPHICS ADAPTER
4H	4	1	320x200	4	2 bpp	16,000	2 banks	CGA
6H	6	2	640x200	2	1 bpp	16,000	2 banks	CGA
DH	13	7	320x200	16	4 bpp	32,000	4 planes	EGA
EH	14	8	640x200	16	4 bpp	64,000	4 planes	EGA
10H	16	9	640x350	16	4 bpp	112,000	4 planes	EGA
FH	15	10	640x350	2	1 bpp	28,000	2 planes	EGA
11H	17	11	640x480	2	1 bpp	38,400	2 planes	MCGA
12H	18	12	640x480	16	4 bpp	153,600	4 planes	VGA
13H	19	--	320x200	256	8 bpp	64,000	4 planes	MCGA/VGA
--	--	--	640x480	256	8 bpp	307,200	4 planes	8514/A
--	--	--	1024x768	256	8 bpp	786,432	4 planes	8514/A

Fig. 2-2. An overview of different graphics modes on IBM-compatible personal computers.

ual). These manuals are (or were) available for purchase, often identified by differing parts numbers in different countries. By studying these texts you can learn a lot about writing your own assembly language routines to control the CGA and the EGA.

Regrettably, other hardware manufacturers have opted not to publish source code listings of their BIOS. Even IBM discontinued the practice with the introduction of the VGA and the MCGA on the Personal System/2 series.

GRAPHICS ADAPTER STANDARDS

Most graphics adapters are purchased from manufacturers other than IBM. The EGA provides a illuminating example of how third-party manufacturers have adopted and expanded the capabilities of a graphics adapter standard originally introduced by IBM.

CASE STUDY: QUADRAM CORPORATION

Quadram Corporation is a typical example of a third-party manufacturer who provides graphics adapters for use in IBM-compatible personal computers. Quadram's range of products has kept pace with—and often surpassed—the graphics standards endorsed by IBM. A brief overview of Quadram's graphics adapters will demonstrate the fierce competition present in the personal computer industry that drives third-party manufacturers to deliver boards with better performance and more features.

Quadram QuadEGA+

The QuadEGA+ is a full-function EGA card with 256K display memory. Refer to Fig. 2-3. The QuadEGA+ is 100% compatible at the hardware level and 100% compatible

Fig. 2-3. QuadEGA+ enhanced graphics adapter.

at the BIOS level with the genuine IBM EGA. The 256K standard display memory is typical of third-party EGAs; it is four times the 64K provided on an IBM EGA.

The QuadEGA+ can generate the 320×200 four-color mode and the 640×200 two-color mode of the CGA, in addition to the EGA graphics modes: the 320×200 16-color mode, the 640×200 16-color mode, the 640×350 16-color mode, and the 640×350 2-color mode. As an added feature, the QuadEGA+ also provides emulation of the IBM Monochrome Text Adapter (MA) and the Hercules Graphics Adapter (HGA).

The QuadEGA+ provides eight different graphics pages in the 320×200 16-color mode, four graphics pages in the 640×200 16-color mode, and two pages in the 640×350 mode. Multiple graphics pages are useful for a number of advanced graphics functions, including animation and menu systems, as you will learn later in this book.

The QuadEGA+ is a half-length card. It comes with detailed installation and operating instructions.

Quadram QuadEGA ProSync and QuadVGA

The QuadEGA ProSync produced by Quadram Corporation is an enhancement of their QuadEGA+. Refer to Fig. 2-4. In addition to the modes found on the QuadEGA+, the

Fig. 2-4. QuadEGA ProSync enhanced graphics adapter.

ProSync offers a 640×480 16-color mode and a 752×410 16-color mode. Like the QuadEGA+, the ProSync provides smooth, flicker-free horizontal and vertical scrolling of graphics images.

Quadram's QuadVGA board is typical of third-party manufacturers who are providing VGA emulation. The QuadVGA ProSync is VGA-compatible at the BIOS level, providing to owners of IBM or IBM-compatible personal computers an alternative to purchasing an IBM Personal System/2 in order to get VGA graphics.

The QuadVGA ProSync is a half-length card. It comes with detailed installation and operating instructions.

Quadram QuadHPG

Quadram Corporation is one among a number of third-party manufacturers who are pushing graphics standards to higher and higher levels. The QuadHPG board is a high-performance, high-end graphics adapter intended to compete with IBM's Professional Graphics Controller (PGC). Refer to Fig. 2-5.

The QuadHPG is available in three different configurations. Series 1 is for presentation graphics and CAD applications needing 640×480 256-color resolution. Series 2 provides

Fig. 2-5. QuadHPG high-performance graphics adapter.

a 1600×1200 two-color mode to meet the specialized needs of desktop publishers. Series 3 offers a 1280×960 256-color mode for graphics workstations.

Of particular interest is the Intel 82786 graphics coprocessor used in the QuadHPG. This microprocessor is specifically assigned the task of performing all graphics operations, thereby relieving the computer's main microprocessor from these time-consuming chores. The improvement in graphics speed is dramatic. A 2500 percent jump is typical. It seems reasonable to predict that graphics coprocessors are a growing trend that will soon influence the average EGA and VGA graphics adapter.

The QuadHPG is a full-length card. It comes with a complete set of installation and operating instructions.

HOW GRAPHICS ADAPTERS WORK

The way in which the display memory is organized and the way in which the hardware displays that memory on the monitor is different for the CGA modes and the EGA/VGA/MCGA modes.

Multiplane-per-pixel Display Memory

The EGA employs a strategy called multiplane-per-pixel graphics memory (mpp). Refer to Fig. 2-6. Four separate graphics images are stored in display memory. Each image is called a bit plane. Each bit plane stores the complete image, but as only one of the four primary color codes used by the EGA: red, green, blue, and intensity level.

The display controller of the EGA reads the corresponding bits from each bit plane simultaneously and uses them to determine which of 16 colors should be displayed at that location on the display screen. Because each bit plane can exhibit a 0 or a 1 value at a particular point, adding all four bit planes together yields a range of 0000 binary to 1111 binary, or a range from 0 to 15: 16 choices. In concept, the four bit planes are sandwiched together to yield the full-color display image.

Although the multiplane-per-pixel technique permits a wider selection of display colors, faster graphics, and limits the amount of memory required, the numerous registers of the EGA are considered by some programmers to be complicated and difficult to program.

Multibit-per-pixel Display Memory

On the other hand, the CGA uses a strategy called multibit-per-pixel display memory (mbp). Refer to Fig. 2-7. Only a single bit plane is used, commonly called a bit map. For four-color graphics, two bits per pixel are required. Two bits can express four different color attributes: 00, 01, 10, and 11. Therefore, one byte in the bit map controls four pixels on the display screen.

Although the CGA is easier to program than the EGA, it is more restricted in terms of resolution and colors.

DISPLAY MONITORS

The display monitor which is connected to a particular graphics adapter will provide a physical limitation on the output of the graphics adapter. There are four main types of display monitors being used with IBM-compatible personal computers. These are the stan-

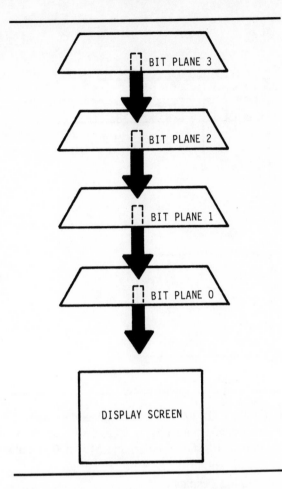

Fig. 2-6. Conceptual representation of multiplane-per-pixel graphics memory. The corresponding bits from each bit plane are simultaneously read by the hardware to determine the four-bit software color (in the range 0 to 15).

dard color display (SCD), the enhanced color display (ECD), the analog display, and the variable frequency display.

Standard Color Display

The SCD provides a maximum screen resolution of 640×200 pixels and it can generate a maximum of 16 colors. If a standard color display is used with a CGA, both the 320×200 four-color mode and the 640×200 two-color mode can be displayed. If a standard color display is used with an EGA, the additional 320×200 16-color mode and the 640×200 16-color mode can be displayed. The 640×350 16-color mode cannot be displayed on a standard color display because only 200 raster lines are available on the SCD.

Enhanced Color Display

The ECD provides a maximum screen resolution of 640×350 pixels and it can generate a maximum of 16 colors. However, unlike the SCD, the ECD can choose those 16 displayable colors from a palette of 64 colors! If an enhanced color display is used with

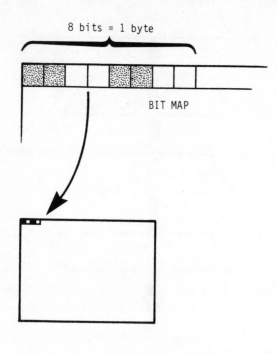

8 bits = 1 byte

BIT MAP

Fig. 2-7. Conceptual representation of multibit-per-pixel graphics memory. Four-color graphics require two bits per pixel in order to define software colors in the range 0 to 3. One byte will control four pixels.

a CGA the 320×200 four-color mode and the 640×200 two-color mode can be displayed. If an enhanced color display is used with an EGA, the additional modes of 320×200 16-color, 640×200 16-color, and 640×350 16-color can be displayed.

Analog Display

Whereas the SCD and the ECD use digital technology to display colors, analog displays like those found on the IBM Personal System/2 series of microcomputers use a continuously variable signal capable of generating more colors and more subtle gradations between those colors.

When used with a VGA, an analog display can display all the CGA and EGA graphics modes. An impressive 320×200 256-color mode can also be displayed, as well as a 640×480 16-color mode.

Variable Frequency Displays

Variable frequency displays offer the best of both worlds: they can display digital video signals and analog video signals. The ''multi'' name used by some manufacturers refers to the ability of the monitor to scan the variable output signal of the graphics adapter to determine which graphics mode is being used. Displays such as the NEC Multisync and the Sony Multiscan can display all of the EGA, CGA, MCGA, and VGA modes. They can even display non-standard modes such as the 752×410 16-color mode of the QuadEGA ProSync adapter.

THE PROGRAMMING LANGUAGE

No matter which graphics adapter and display monitor you have connected to your personal computer, you still must rely upon a programming language to create graphics. Because the programming language used in the demonstration programs in *Supercharged Graphics* is BASIC, a discussion of the graphics capabilities of different versions of BASIC will be useful to you. (If you are using C, refer to your version's reference manual. If you are using assembly language, there are no restrictions on what you can do.)

IBM BASICA 2.00, 2.10, 3.00, 3.10

The common denominator graphics modes of 320×200 four-color and 640×200 two-color are supported by all versions of BASIC which claim IBM-compatibility. Refer to Fig. 2-8. IBM BASICA versions 2.00 through 3.10 support these modes, but do not support any of the higher modes. IBM Cartridge BASIC J1.00 supports these modes as well as the graphics modes unique to the PCjr (look back at Fig. 2-1). GW-BASIC as found on Tandy microcomputers is virtually identical to IBM Cartridge BASIC as found on the PCjr.

IBM BASICA 3.21, QuickBASIC, Turbo BASIC

The full range of graphics modes available on the EGA are supported by IBM BASICA 3.21. Refer to Fig. 2-9. These EGA modes are also supported by Microsoft QuickBASIC 2.0 and newer, and by Borland Turbo BASIC 1.0 and newer. If you are using an EGA, you should consider using one of these three versions of BASIC if you want to harness the full potential of your enhanced graphics adapter. Otherwise, only the minimal modes of the CGA can be generated by your EGA.

IBM BASICA 3.30

IBM BASICA 3.30, introduced with the VGA of the IBM Personal System/2 series of microcomputers, supports all EGA and CGA functions, but it does not support any of the new MCGA or VGA graphics modes. It is interesting to note that Borland Turbo BASIC 1.0 was the first popular version of BASIC to support the VGA modes of 640×480 two-color and 640×480 16-color. QuickBASIC 4.0 supports VGA and EGA modes.

MEMORY MAPPING

As a graphics programmer, you might find it useful to be apprised of memory allocation

Fig. 2-8. Graphics capabilities of early versions of IBM BASICA. Many versions of COMPAQ BASIC, GW-BASIC, and Microsoft BASICA offer identical graphics modes.

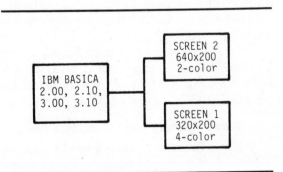

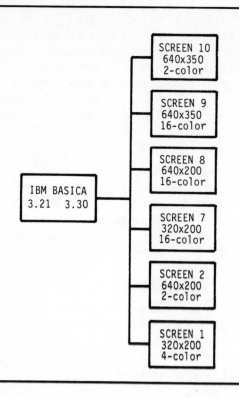

Fig. 2-9. Graphics capabilities of recent versions of IBM BASICA. Microsoft QuickBASIC 2.0, 3.0, and newer supports these modes. Borland Turbo BASIC 1.0, 2.0, and newer supports these modes, in addition to the 640 × 480 2-color and 16-color modes.

during runtime. Two types of memory mapping are involved here: the overall system memory (RAM) and the display memory (bit maps and bit planes).

System Memory Map: Interpreters

When an IBM-compatible personal computer is used with a BASIC interpreter, the memory allocation is similar to that illustrated in Fig. 2-10. At the bottom of memory are the vectors which contain the addresses of the DOS interrupts and BIOS interrupts. These interrupts are low-level subroutines that perform hardware control tasks.

The next section of memory holds the operating system (DOS). Above the operating system resides your BASICA, BASIC, or GW-BASIC interpreter. The original source code that you create with the interpreter is placed just above the interpreter in memory. Your original program cannot exceed 64K in length. The 64K module starts at approximately 125K, depending upon the version of DOS and the version of BASIC you are using.

The area of memory set aside for display memory begins at the 640K mark and continues until 896K, where the built-in ROM BIOS begins. The amount of display memory which is available for your use is contingent upon the particular graphics adapter you are using. A CGA uses only 16K; an EGA can use the full 256K. A VGA uses 256K.

System Memory Map: Compilers

When a BASIC compiler is used with your IBM-compatible personal computer, the assignment of memory is similar to that illustrated in Fig. 2-11.

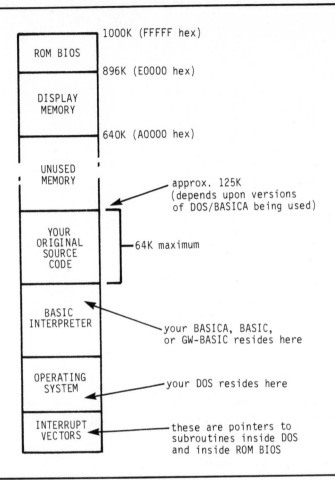

Fig. 2-10. Memory map of an IBM-compatible personal computer using a BASIC interpreter.

Again, lowest memory holds the interrupt vectors and the operating system. Your QuickBASIC, Turbo BASIC, or similar interactive editor-driven compiler sits just above DOS in memory. The original source code that you create with the editor is a part of this section of memory.

At roughly the 150K mark your compiled program is located. This is the runtime code generated by the compiler. Because both your original source code and the resultant compiled code must reside simultaneously in memory, a compiler requires more RAM than an interpreter.

The display memory is still located at 640K and runs until the BIOS begins at 896K.

Display Memory Map

The 256K of memory which has been set aside for display purposes is depicted in Fig. 2-12. If a color/graphics adapter is present, it uses 16K of memory beginning at address B8000 hex (736K). If an enhanced graphics adapter is present, its display memory begins

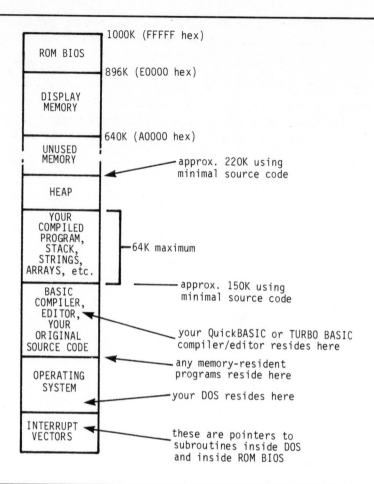

Fig. 2-11. Memory map of an IBM-compatible personal computer using a BASIC compiler such as Microsoft QuickBASIC or Borland Turbo BASIC.

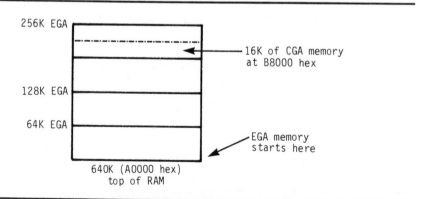

Fig. 2-12. Assignment of display memory on IBM-compatible personal computers.

at A0000 hex (640K). An EGA with 256K of display memory will use all the memory reserved for graphics; an EGA with 64K (such as IBM's EGA) will only use one quarter of memory actually reserved for display purposes.

The multiplane-per-pixel strategy used by the EGA and VGA is represented in Fig. 2-13. In the 640×200 16-color mode, four graphics pages are available, but they are not contiguous. (Only one graphics page is available on a CGA.)

The first 64K of EGA display memory holds only bit plane 0 of each of the four graphics pages. The next bit plane for each page is found in the next 64K segment of

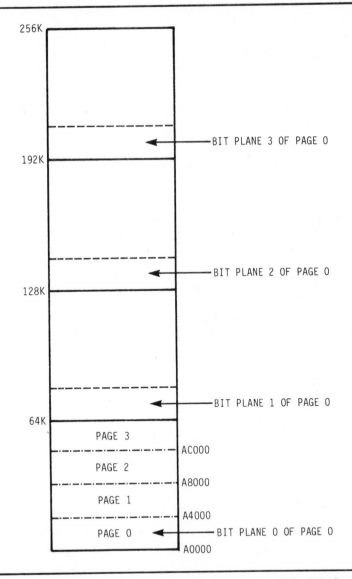

Fig. 2-13. Assignment of display memory in a 256K EGA operating in the 640×200 16-color mode (as used by the EGA demonstration programs in this book).

memory. It is interesting to note that only the first 64K segment of display memory can be directly accessed by your program; you must use the latching registers of the EGA to write graphics to the bit planes which reside in the higher segments. Versions of BASIC and C which support the EGA perform this latching for you, of course. (For further discussion of EGA display memory mapping refer to one of my other books, *High-Performance Interactive Graphics: Modeling, Rendering & Animating for IBM PCs and Compatibles*, TAB book 2879, available through your favorite bookstore or direct from TAB BOOKS.)

An EGA and a CGA cannot be installed at the same time, although an EGA which is running in the CGA modes will use the 16K of display memory beginning at B8000 hex.

SUMMARY

In this chapter you learned about the different graphics adapters and display monitors which are commonly used with IBM-compatible personal computers. You considered the various graphics modes which are available for your programs.

The next chapter discusses the programming tools you will find helpful when writing advanced interactive graphics programs.

3

Using Good
Programming Tools

Perhaps more than most languages, BASIC provides a set of efficient high-level programming tools that you can use to create advanced graphics programs. These tools include statements, numeric expressions, numeric operators, and the algorithms which these tools can generate.

A statement is an instruction. A numeric expression is a number. A numeric operator can be a relation operator, an arithmetic operator, a logical operator, or a function operator. An algorithm is a method for producing a specific desired result. Statements are sometimes called instructions or keywords in other languages. Operators are used universally throughout different programming languages.

The discussion in this chapter is presented as an overview. It assumes that you have a general understanding of programming tools. Most programmers have successfully developed their programming skills by trial and error without necessarily understanding the concepts involved. Delving into those abstracts can often hone your coding skills, but if you already feel comfortable with your grasp of the concepts behind BASIC programming, you can skip past this material.

Eight programming tools provided by BASIC deserve discussion here.

PROGRAMMING TOOL NO. 1: NUMERIC EXPRESSIONS

Graphics is math-oriented. If you understand mathematics, then you will find it easy to understand computer graphics; it is as simple as that.

A numeric expression is simply another name for a number. It can be a numeric constant such as 256, −528, 6.28319, or 32767. It can be a numeric variable such as X or

Y or SR1. A numeric expression can be either an integer value or a floating point value. BASIC will use floating point values for all calculations unless you tell it otherwise.

An integer is a whole number that does not contain any decimal point. Because BASIC uses two bytes of memory to store an integer, the number cannot exceed +32767 and it cannot be smaller than −32768. Calculations performed with integers are very fast.

A floating point number is a number that contains a decimal point. BASIC uses scientific notation to store floating point numbers in memory. This means a floating point number can be very large or very small. BASIC uses floating point numbers which are accurate to six digits, which means a floating point number can be as tiny as $10E-38$ or as huge as $10E+38$. (This is simply a scientist's way of describing the number 10 with 38 zeros appended.) BASIC uses four bytes of memory to store a single-precision floating point number. Calculations performed with floating point numbers are not as quick as calculations performed with integers.

The 3D demonstration programs in *Supercharged Graphics* use floating point numbers. Integer math would be much faster, of course, but the accuracy provided by floating point numbers is required by the 3D formulas for crisp CAD displays. If you are using C or assembly language, you can scale the numbers up, perform integer math, then scale the numbers back down.

In your graphics programs, numeric expressions are often manipulated by programming tools called numeric operators.

PROGRAMMING TOOL NO. 2: NUMERIC OPERATORS

The numeric operators provided by BASIC (and other programming languages) fall into four categories: relational operators, arithmetic operators, logical operators, and function operators.

Relational Operators

Relational operators, also called relation operators, express the relationship between two values. Relation operators are used to make decisions. They are often used in concert with IF . . . THEN statements. The less-than symbol (<), the greater-than symbol (>), and the equals symbol (=) are relation operators. For example, the statement **IF A>B THEN GOSUB 500** means that the program will jump to line 500 if A is greater than B. Relation operators need not be used singly; they can be combined. The symbol < = means less than or equal to.

Arithmetic Operators

Arithmetic operators are mathematical. For example, the addition symbol (+) is an arithmetic operator. Other common arithmetic operators include −, *, and /, which stand for subtraction, multiplication, and division, respectively.

Function Operators

Function operators are closely related to arithmetic operators. Function operators are trigonometric or geometric or mathematical functions such as sine, cosine, square, tangent, square root, and others. A function is simply a group of arithmetic operators designed to produce a specific result. BASIC has a number of useful function operators already built in as a part of the language, including SIN and COS for sine and cosine, respectively. C compilers often provide function operators in the form of subroutines in the library.

Logical Operators

Logical operators, also called boolean operators, are used in order to check for true and false conditions. Logical operators are useful for making decisions about program flow, in addition to controlling the results of graphic array manipulation. The logical operators available in BASIC include NOT, AND, OR, XOR, and others. The demonstration programs in *Supercharged Graphics* use the XOR logical operator to manipulate a crosshair cursor in the interactive drafting, CAD, and paintbrush environments. Chapter 16 describes how to employ multiple logical operators with graphic arrays to move or copy graphics entities to different parts of the screen. (Advanced techniques for moving multicolor graphic arrays over multicolor backgrounds can be found in another of my books, *High-Speed Animation & Simulation for Microcomputers*, TAB book 2859, available through your favorite bookstore or direct from TAB BOOKS.)

PROGRAMMING TOOL NO. 3: STATEMENTS

A statement is an instruction or a combination of instructions. IBM BASICA, IBM Cartridge BASIC, GW-BASIC, COMPAQ BASIC, Microsoft QuickBASIC, and Borland Turbo BASIC each possess a robust repertory of powerful graphics statements and, of course, general statements. IBM BASICA 3.21 offers over 160 statements. Microsoft QuickBASIC 2.0 features over 150 different statements. Borland Turbo BASIC 1.0 provides over 170 statements. By contrast, Borland Turbo C 1.0 offers 38 statements; all other functions are provided as subroutines in the library.

You can find further discussion of graphics-related BASIC statements in Chapter 5 and Chapter 6.

PROGRAMMING TOOL NO. 4: LOOPS

A loop is a part of your program which is repeated until a certain condition is met. Refer to Fig. 3-1. Loops are vital ingredients of keyboard routines and of animated displays. The demonstration programs in *Supercharged Graphics* are filled with loops, as you will soon discover.

Loops are relatively easy to understand, although the logic flow in nested loops can often become tricky to trace. As Fig. 3-1 illustrates, a nested loop will perform a complete series of repetitions (iterations) on each pass through the larger loop. In any language, including BASIC, you must take care to cleanly exit a running loop. Every FOR is assigned a NEXT in BASIC; if you exit the loop prematurely and leave a NEXT hanging, your program can produce erratic behavior at a later point during runtime.

Two tools in BASIC are available for controlling loops. They are the FOR . . . NEXT construct and the WHILE . . . WEND construct. A FOR . . . NEXT loop will continue to execute until a previously non-existing condition occurs. A WHILE . . . WEND loop will continue to execute only while a pre-existing condition continues to exist. A FOR . . . NEXT loop will always execute at least once. The execution of the first iteration of a WHILE . . . WEND loop, on the other hand, depends upon whether or not the WHILE

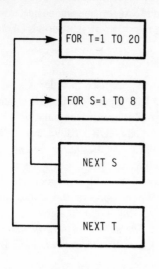

Fig. 3-1. Nested loops are loops inside loops. The T loop will execute for 20 occurrences. Because the S loop will execute 8 times on each of 20 passes through the T loop, the S loop will execute a total of 160 occasions.

condition pre-exists the approach to the loop. Examples of both techniques are used in the demonstration programs later in the book. The program in this book called *YOUR MICROCOMPUTER 3D CAD DESIGNER* uses the WHILE . . . WEND construct to control the creation of a drawing grid. The program *YOUR MICROCOMPUTER DRAFTING TABLE* uses the FOR . . . NEXT construct to control preparation of the on-screen icon display.

PROGRAMMING TOOL NO. 5: DECISION-MAKING ALGORITHMS

The IF . . . THEN construct is often used to control program flow in interactive graphics programming, especially in keyboard control subroutines and mouse control subroutines. It is important to optimize these algorithms because they are used repeatedly. An inefficient decision-making routine in a loop can slow down runtime performance considerably. Refer to Fig. 3-2.

By testing for the likeliest condition first, you can save your program the trouble of having to test for unlikely conditions. If the first condition tested is true, then your program can continue with graphics execution without having to test the other conditions.

This time-saving approach is especially beneficial in keyboard control routines. Refer to Fig. 3-3. If you first test for a no-keystroke condition, then you can avoid the delay involved in checking for a variety of keys if no key at all has been pressed by the user.

PROGRAMMING TOOL NO. 6: ADVANCED BOOLEAN OPERATORS

Boolean operators, often called logical operators, can be used in decision-making algorithms. They can also be used instead of mathematical decision-makers (often called flags or toggles). Refer to Fig. 3-4. The XOR operator is particularly useful for alternating between two conditions, such as often encountered in animation which flips between two pages. Although very efficient and quick, advanced boolean decision-making techniques

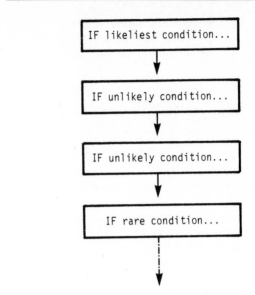

Fig. 3-2. Runtime performance can be improved by testing for the likeliest conditions first in decision-making algorithms. If the condition is met, then other less-likely conditions need no testing, thereby saving time.

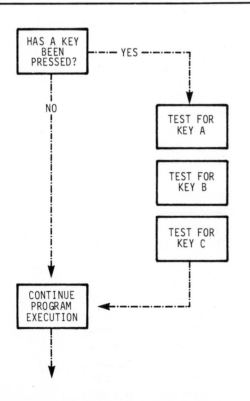

Fig. 3-3. Runtime performance of interactive keyboard routines can be improved by bypassing the decision-making routine if no key has been pressed.

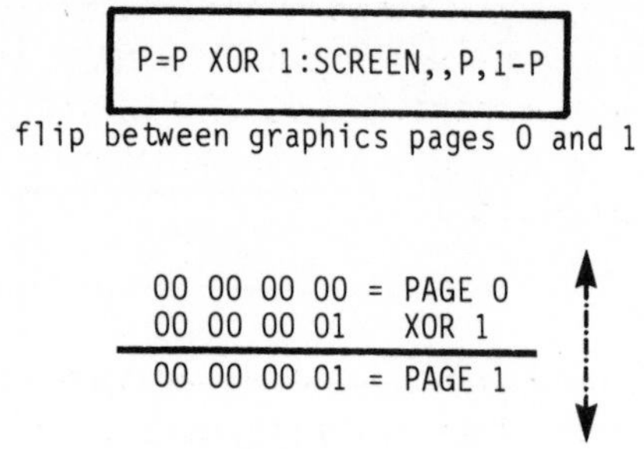

```
P=P XOR 1:SCREEN,,P,1-P
```
flip between graphics pages 0 and 1

```
00 00 00 00 = PAGE 0
00 00 00 01   XOR 1
00 00 00 01 = PAGE 1
```

Fig. 3-4. Boolean operators can often be used instead of math. The above code would be written as P=1−P:SCREEN,, P,1−P if ordinary math were used. The XOR operator is quicker at runtime, but the source code is more difficult to understand.

are not used in the demonstration programs in *Supercharged Graphics*. Why? Only because the resulting source code tends to be difficult to read and understand. They are perfectly sound from a logical point of view, however, and can be especially useful when programming in C or assembly language.

PROGRAMMING TOOL NO. 7: RUNTIME FLAGS

A runtime flag, sometimes called a toggle, is a variable which is set to a certain value when a certain condition exists during runtime. Other subroutines can base their actions on the value of this flag. The ability to easily set and modify runtime flags is a tremendous asset in the programming of interactive graphics software.

A global variable is a variable which is accessible to all routines in a program. Because BASIC uses primarily global variables, it is a straightforward task to manage runtime flags. Simply assign a value to the runtime flag and any other subroutine in your BASIC program can check the status of the runtime flag. A static variable, on the other hand, is a variable which is only known by a particular subroutine. Other parts of the program can neither use nor modify the static variable. Interactive editor-driven compilers such as QuickBASIC and Turbo BASIC can be configured to use global and/or static variables. BASIC interpreters use only global variables. C usually uses static variables and must specifically pass the value of a runtime flag to any subroutines which are called.

The efficient and effective use of runtime flags is demonstrated by the drawing function switchers in the drafting, paintbrush, and 3D CAD program listings in *Supercharged Graphics*.

PROGRAMMING TOOL NO. 8: ERROR TRAPPING

The ON ERROR statement in BASIC provides a powerful method for configuring your advanced graphics programs to run on different computer systems. If you set the ON ERROR statement and then attempt to initialize a graphics mode which is not supported by the graphics adapter being used, you can control what happens after the error, including an attempt to initialize a different graphics mode. (For a detailed discussion of automatic self-configuration of your software refer to another of my books, *High-Performance Interactive Graphics: Modeling, Rendering & Animating for IBM PCs and Compatibles*, TAB book 2879, available through your favorite bookstore or direct from TAB BOOKS.)

You can also invoke the ON ERROR statement to provide a polished way for dealing with attempted disk reads or writes that go sour. If your program attempts to save an image on disk, for example, and encounters an empty disk drive, your ON ERROR statement can gently advise the user of his/her oversight. When the disk is loaded, normal program execution continues. If no ON ERROR error-trapping is used, the program crashes, of course. See Chapter 19 for further discussion of this.

SUMMARY

In this chapter you learned about different programming tools available to you when writing advanced graphics software. You read about statements, numeric expressions, numeric operators, and the algorithms they can create. You considered an overview of different techniques for optimizing certain decision-making routines.

The next chapter provides tips on supercharging your code with modular programming.

4

Supercharging Your Code
With Modular Programming

Any advanced graphics program can be conceived, written, tested, and debugged quicker if you use modular programming techniques. The final program will always be more compact, easier to read, easier to revise, and will almost always produce higher quality graphics. It would have been impossible to create the full-length drafting, paintbrush, and 3D CAD demonstration programs in this book without using a modular programming approach. Simply stated, modular programming can take a very complex piece of code and make it easy to understand. It is a realistic way to attack a large project one step at a time. As the philosopher says, even a journey of a thousand miles begins with one step.

WHAT IS MODULAR PROGRAMMING?

What is modular programming? It is an attitude towards writing computer programs. In addition, it is a set of skills that you use while you are writing programs. So in essence, modular programming is two things at the same time: it is attitude and it is technique.

Modular programming means invoking separate subroutines, sometimes called modules, to accomplish separate tasks. Refer to Fig. 4-1. A modular program often consists of one main routine which calls upon a number of separate subroutines to get the job done. A subroutine may in turn call upon another subroutine to help it accomplish its assigned objective.

The opposite of modular code is inline code. Refer to Fig. 4-2. Instead of calling separate subroutines to accomplish specific tasks, the code which produces the desired result is written right into the main routine. This approach to writing code inevitably leads to spaghetti code.

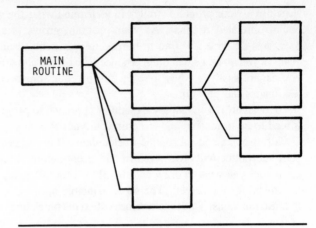

Fig. 4-1. Conceptual representation of modular programming.

Although you can obtain good results with either inline code or modular code, you will find yourself using a lot more time and effort if you insist on the inline code approach. Inline coding may be an exciting way to first learn and experiment with programming, but just like the training blocks on your first bicycle it must be soon discarded if you expect to reach higher goals.

Inline code is a seductive trap. And it snares many beginner and intermediate programmers. It is easy to simply turn on the computer and start writing code, but without a modular plan the program soon becomes disorganized. It is difficult to keep the logical

Fig. 4-2. Conceptual representation of inline programming.

structure of your program straight in your mind when the program is a convoluted melting pot of unrelated routines. As your program grows in size, as all interactive graphics programs do, you will find it increasingly difficult to make changes to your code. The changes you do make will often produce unexpected and erratic results. This occurs because you cannot easily see how one section of your source code is logically linked to other sections of the program.

However, if you employ a modular approach to programming, you are automatically forced to be organized and structured in your thinking and in your code writing. If you use a self-contained subroutine to calculate 3D coordinates, for instance, you know that your subroutine will always return consistent output. You input the world coordinates of the model you wish to draw and the 3D subroutine gives you the display coordinates of the image for the screen. The same principle applies to subroutines that perform other specific functions. This is sometimes called the black box model of modular programming.

VARIABLE TYPES

The global variables used by BASIC interpreters lend themselves easily to modular programming. Refer to Fig. 4-3. Because all the variables in a BASIC program can be accessed by all the subroutines in the program, it is an effective way to pass values between the main program and the subroutine and between the subroutines themselves. Variable passing is virtually automatic, and therein lies the rub.

There are two important pitfalls to avoid when using global variables. First, it is importance of this quagmire when you consider that both IBM Macro Assembler and a lengthy program, otherwise you may inadvertently use the same variable name twice. Duplicate variable naming is a particularly difficult bug to locate. You can judge the importance of this guagmire when you consider that both IBM Macro Assembler and Microsoft Macro Assembler include built-in error-checking for duplicate label names. BASIC just looks the other way while these oversights sneak into your program, however.

Second, it is important to remember that if a subroutine changes the value of a variable, then the variable has been changed for all subsequent usage anywhere in your code. So

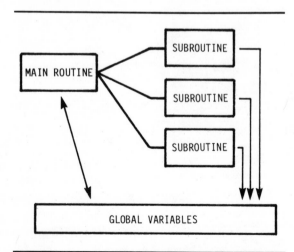

Fig. 4-3. Global variables can be used by—and changed by— any routine or subroutine in the program. A subroutine must deal with a variable which may have been altered by other subroutines. All variables in interpreted BASIC are global variables.

if you want to preserve a variable for a particular use, store it temporarily in another variable before passing control to a subroutine which will alter the first variable.

QuickBASIC and Turbo BASIC can use static variables as well as global variables. A static variable, also called a local variable, is a variable that is unique to the subroutine in which it is found. Refer to Fig. 4-4. Needless to say, this reduces the chances of accidental name duplication, but it raises other concerns. There is no free lunch.

A program which uses static variables does not run on "cruise-control," so to speak. As the program's author, you must specifically make arrangements to pass variable values to a subroutine each time you call it. The subprograms used by QuickBASIC and Turbo BASIC require that parameters (also called arguments) be passed by the caller. The converse also holds true. If your subroutine changes a variable which is used by other subroutines, you must specifically pass the changed value back to the main routine.

THE NINETY-TEN RULE

Successful programmers have an old saying. They say that 10% of the program code usually performs 90% of the computing load during runtime. This is especially true for graphics programming.

Using a modular approach to programming means that you will have a separate subroutine for each separate graphics function. If you make heavy use of a particular subroutine, you can work on optimizing that routine, perhaps even rewriting it in assembly language. Because it is a separate stand-alone subroutine, you can revise it and edit it without worrying about inadvertently changing other parts of your program. If unexpected bugs begin to appear, you know exactly where the problem originates: in the subroutine you are tinkering with.

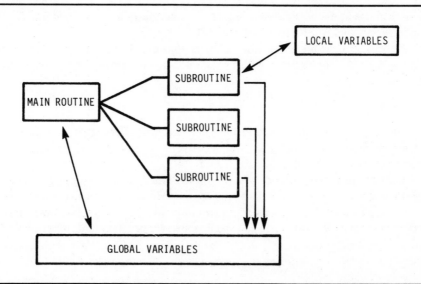

Fig. 4-4. Local variables may be used or changed only by a particular routine. Other subroutines do not have access to the local variables of a particular subroutine. Local variables are also called static variables. BASIC compilers such as QuickBASIC and Turbo BASIC permit local variables as well as global variables.

The MERGE statement in interpreted BASIC also means that you can insert previously-written subroutines into your current project. Simply save the subroutine as a separate ASCII file using the **SAVE** *filename*.**BAS,A** command. You can then merge it into the program on which you are currently working, a particularly time-saving benefit of modular programming.

FORMATTING YOUR PROGRAMS

Modular programming makes it easy to correctly format your programs. Formatting refers to the layout of the program when the source code is displayed on the screen or printed on your printer.

Proper program formatting yields two important benefits. First, a properly formatted graphics program runs faster, especially with interpreted BASIC. Second, a properly formatted program is easier to read and maintain.

Refer to any of the program listings in this book. Notice how remark lines have been employed to visually separate the various subroutines of each program. These remark lines make it easier to read the program. It is important to the BASIC interpreter that these remark lines are never encountered during runtime. It takes time for the interpreter to determine that a particular line is in fact only a remark line. The compiler encounters remark lines only during compilation, never during runtime, of course.

Note that more than one statement is included on one line. In fact, many statements have been placed on each line. This makes interpreted BASIC run faster, and it makes the code easier to read because logically connected statements are grouped tightly together. Notice also that no spaces have been left between individual statements. Separate statements are butted up against one another, separated only by the obligatory colon.

In each program listing in *Supercharged Graphics*, line numbers increment by ten. This makes it easier to read the wraparounds where multiple statements extend onto the next physical line of the listing. Line numbers are mandatory in interpreted BASIC; they are optional in QuickBASIC and Turbo BASIC.

Some programmers prefer the tab and indent approach to formatting. This technique is also a noteworthy approach; its only limitation is that it uses up a lot of space during screen display or print-out.

OPTIMIZED CODE

Modular programming tends to foster optimized code. Because it is so easy to dip into a subroutine and make changes without adversely affecting the remainder of the program, optimization becomes second nature.

Optimized code is program code which has been crafted to run as efficiently as possible. For high-performance graphics, that usually means code which has been designed to run as quickly as possible. The interactive demonstration programs in this book use a number of optimizing techniques which you can use in your own programming, whether you use QuickC, Turbo C, QuickBASIC, Turbo BASIC, GW-BASIC, IBM BASICA, Ada, Modula-2, Turbo Pascal, or assembly language.

Optimizing the Math

Some arithmetic operations are much quicker than others. This holds true for any programming language. If you want to square a number, it will happen faster if you simply multiple the number by itself. In BASIC, for example, X*X is much quicker than X^2. Any type of division executes very slowly on a 8088, 8086, 80286, or 80386 microprocessor. If you need to divide a number by two it makes more sense to multiple it by 0.5. Various bit shift instructions are available in C and assembly language which can provide lightning-quick multiplication and/or division by two, four, eight, etc.

Integer math often executes 100 times quicker than floating point math. If you program in assembly language, you can easily scale the 3D formulas in this book. Use the shift instructions to bump the numbers up to integer range, perform the necessary math, then use shift instructions to bump the numbers back down.

Optimizing the Decisions

The IF . . . THEN construct is the most often-used method for making a decision. If a number of conditions are being tested, you should always test the most likely condition first. Why waste valuable time checking rare conditions? Simply check the likeliest one first. If it is positive, you can skip the other tests altogether. This coding strategy is especially useful in keyboard control loops, which occur often in interactive graphics programming. (Refer back to Chapter 3 for further discussion on this.)

Optimizing the Subroutines

A compiler such as QuickBASIC or Turbo BASIC is unaffected by the positioning of a subroutine in the source code. It does not matter how close the caller is to the called subroutine. Surprisingly, the same is true in interpreted BASIC. On the first occasion that a subroutine is called by a GOSUB statement, BASIC must search through the program until it finds the subroutine. But on every subsequent call, BASIC simply jumps right to the subroutine. So there is no excuse for not writing modular programs, even with BASIC interpreters such as IBM BASICA, GW-BASIC, COMPAQ BASIC, and so on.

STUBS

Modular programming makes it easy to build complicated graphics programs in stages, one step at a time. By inserting a do-nothing subroutine, often called a stub by professional programmers, your main routine can be developed without the necessity of having to finish each and every function in the program. You will see stubs in action in the 3D solid model CAD editor, where a few program functions are inactive (waiting for a sharp graphics programmer like you to polish them off).

OVERLAY MODULES

Modular programming puts you in the right frame of mind for using overlays. What is an overlay? An overlay is a new module of runtime code which is usually loaded from disk into memory which is already occupied by existing runtime code. The overlay is laid over the previous code. This technique is a noteworthy way of conserving memory.

For example, if you use 10K of source code to initialize a program (setting up the menu system, drawing opening graphics, and so on), there is no need to keep that code hanging around if you never use it again. It makes much more sense to simply load the next module of runtime code right over the start-up code. This advanced technique is particularly useful for both BASIC interpreters and BASIC compilers, where program length is often limited to 64K.

The demonstration programs *YOUR MICROCOMPUTER SKETCH PAD* in Chapter 17, and *YOUR MICROCOMPUTER DRAFTING TABLE* in Chapter 21, each use a start-up module which is then overwritten by a runtime module downloaded from disk. Because the event occurs when the program pauses for user input, the CHAINing of the overlay is seamless. (*Seamless* means that no apparent break in program execution is seen by the end-user.)

The concept of separate start-up and runtime modules is a natural extension, of course, of the philosophy of modular programming.

SUMMARY

In this chapter you explored the potential advantages of using modular programming techniques in your graphics programming. You learned a few ways to optimize your code.

The next chapter introduces fundamental graphics instructions.

5

Using Fundamental
Graphics Instructions

$\mathcal{S}$urprisingly, only a modest handful of BASIC instructions is required in order to write highly sophisticated graphics programs, as the demonstration programs in this book prove. These graphics statements must be well-understood and well-used, but a huge repertoire of language instructions is not necessary.

The BASIC instructions used for the advanced demonstration programs in *Supercharged Graphics* fall into four broad categories. First, *initialization statements* are used to set up the screen mode, the display colors, and window and viewport mapping. Second, *graphics primitives* are employed to draw lines, circles, polygons, and to fill areas. Third, *bitblt statements* (also called *block graphics*) are used to move graphics entities. Fourth, *alphanumeric statements* are used to display text readouts and to provide labels. A fifth category, advanced graphics instructions, is discussed in the next chapter. The discussion in this chapter presumes that you are familiar with alphanumeric statements such as LOCATE and PRINT.

The assessment of available graphics instructions which is provided in this chapter is by no means a complete or exhaustive description. Rather, it is intended as a discussion of the most vital parts of your graphics tool kit.

INITIALIZATION STATEMENTS

INITIALIZATION INSTRUCTION: **SCREEN**

PURPOSE: The SCREEN statement sets the graphics mode. Depending upon your hardware and the version of BASIC which you are using, you can select from up to six graphics modes on an EGA, up to nine graphics modes on a VGA, up to eight graphics modes on an MCGA, up to two graphics modes on a CGA, and up to six graphics modes with a PCjr. Refer to Chapter 2 for more information about screen modes. The SCREEN statement is also used to set the written-to page and the displayed page, which do not have to be the same page. IBM BASICA 3.21 (and newer), QuickBASIC 2.0 (and newer), and Turbo BASIC 1.0 (and newer) have this capability, although an EGA or VGA is required.

SYNTAX: **SCREEN mode, color on/off, written-to page, displayed page**

EXAMPLE: **SCREEN 1** establishes the 320×200 four-color mode on a CGA.

EXAMPLE: **SCREEN 8,,0,0** sets up the 640×200 16-color mode on an EGA or VGA with page 0 as the written-to page and page 0 as the displayed page.

EXAMPLE: **SCREEN 8,,1,0** would change the written-to page to page 1 (which would be hidden because page 0 is still being displayed by the hardware). You can omit any of the arguments for the SCREEN statements, but you must include the commas before any argument which you do include.

WARNINGS: If the screen mode which you request is not supported by your hardware configuration, BASIC will display an error message and the program will crash.

COMMENTS: Microsoft, Borland, and IBM refer to the written-to page as the a-page (for *active page*). They call the displayed page the v-page (for *visual page*).

INITIALIZATION INSTRUCTION: **COLOR**

PURPOSE: The COLOR statement establishes the colors which will be used by graphics primitives and by alphanumerics. The COLOR statement also establishes the background color. Refer to Fig. 5-1 for an overview of the standard colors which are available on IBM-compatible personal computers. Unfortunately, the syntax for the COLOR statement is not uniform between the EGA modes and the CGA modes.

0	BLACK	8	GRAY
1	BLUE	9	INTENSE BLUE
2	GREEN	10	INTENSE GREEN
3	CYAN	11	INTENSE CYAN
4	RED	12	INTENSE RED
5	MAGENTA	13	INTENSE MAGENTA
6	BROWN	14	YELLOW
7	WHITE	15	INTENSE WHITE

Fig. 5-1. The standard palette of hardware colors for IBM-compatible personal computers.

Syntax for CGA Modes: **COLOR background, palette number**

Syntax for EGA and VGA Modes: **COLOR foreground, background**

Example: **SCREEN 1,0:COLOR 0,1** sets up the 320×200 four-color mode. The COLOR statement sets color 0 (black) as the background and palette 1 as the foreground. Palette 1 defines 0 as black, 1 as cyan, 2 as magenta, and 3 as white. There are only two palettes available in SCREEN 1.

Example: **SCREEN 8,,0,0:COLOR 7,0** establishes the 640×200 16-color mode on an EGA or VGA. The 7 argument invokes color 7 (white) as the foreground color. Alphanumerics will be displayed in this color. Any graphics statements whose color is not specified will be drawn in this color. The 0 argument defines black as the background color.

Comments: The arguments used with the COLOR statement must fall within legal hardware limits. When using a CGA, for example, you can choose from 16 background colors (0 to 15), but only two palette choices are available as foreground colors. In normal EGA modes you can select from 16 background colors and 16 foreground colors. In the 640×350 16-color EGA and VGA mode, you can choose your 16 colors from 64 available hardware colors.

Initialization Instruction: **PALETTE**

Purpose: The PALETTE statement is used to choose which hardware colors will be assigned to the software color codes. Refer to Fig. 5-2. On an EGA a maximum of 16 software colors are available, numbered as colors 0 to 15. In addition, if you are using the 640×350 16-color mode, you can use the PALETTE statement to assign any of the 64 available hardware colors to the 16 software colors. Only 16 hardware colors are available in the 640×200 16-color and 320×200 16-color modes on an EGA or VGA. On a CGA running in the 320×200 four-color mode, only four hardware colors are available, numbered as software colors 0 to 3. Two arrangements of hardware colors are provided by BASIC, which are invoked by the COLOR statement, as described previously.

Syntax: **PALETTE software color, hardware color.**

Example: You could use **PALETTE 1,14** to assign hardware color yellow (14) to software color 1 (which is blue by default). Whenever you draw a graphic using color 1 you would actually receive yellow.

Warnings: Only versions of BASIC which provide EGA or VGA capabilities support the PALETTE statement, whether or not you have an EGA or VGA in your system.

Comments: An EGA or VGA can use the PALETTE statement to change the selection of colors available in the 320×200 four-color mode. A CGA cannot. IBM and Microsoft insist on calling a software color a *color attribute*, which is no great assistance in trying to understand an already confusing situation.

Initialization Instruction: **WINDOW SCREEN**

Purpose: The WINDOW SCREEN statement allows you to redefine the logical coordinates of the display screen. These new coordinates are called world coordinates.

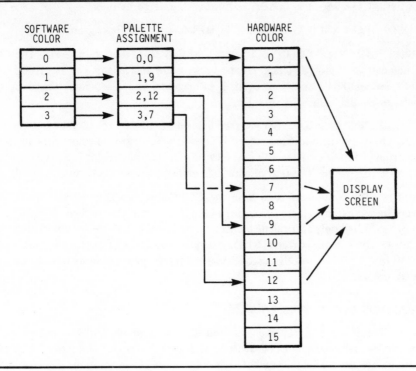

Fig. 5-2. The PALETTE instruction assigns new hardware colors to the software colors (color attributes) used by any graphics screen mode.

They are mapped (or fitted) onto the display screen, whose actual coordinates are called physical coordinates. Refer to Fig. 5-3. BASIC provides these built-in mapping routines. If you are using another language such as C, Pascal, Modula-2, Ada, or assembly language, you may wish to refer to Appendix B for source code for window mapping routines.

SYNTAX: **WINDOW SCREEN (upper left xy coordinates)-(lower right xy coordinates).**

EXAMPLE: **WINDOW SCREEN (−399,−299)-(400,300)** establishes a world coordinate system 800 units across by 600 units down. Point 0,0 would be located at the physical center of the display screen. As Fig. 5-3 illustrates, WINDOW SCREEN mapping would scale the entire graphic to fit the actual display screen. Using the WINDOW statement (without the SCREEN argument) will invert the y coordinates.

COMMENTS: When using with 3D world coordinates, the size of the WINDOW SCREEN statement must preserve the 4:3 aspect ratio of the display monitor, otherwise the 3D model will appear distorted. The drafting, paintbrush, and 3D CAD programs in *Supercharged Graphics* use the WINDOW SCREEN statement to clip the drawing area on the display screen. Some versions of BASIC, such as True BASIC and ZBasic, make it mandatory to use world coordinates (in order to make their graphics more portable between different computer systems).

INITIALIZATION INSTRUCTION: **VIEW**

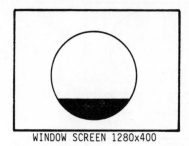

WINDOW SCREEN 1280x400

Fig. 5-3. The graphics scaling ability of
BASIC's WINDOW SCREEN instruction.

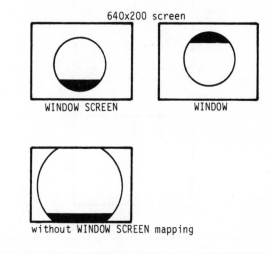

640x200 screen

WINDOW SCREEN   WINDOW

without WINDOW SCREEN mapping

PURPOSE: The VIEW statement is used for installing viewports on the display screen. A viewport is merely a window within the overall window of the display screen itself. Refer to Fig. 5-4. The VIEW routine in BASIC will map world coordinates into a specified rectangle of the display screen, the size of which you predefine.

SYNTAX: **VIEW (upper left coordinates, lower right coordinates).**

EXAMPLE: **VIEW (0,0)-(320,100)** would map graphics into a logical rectangle which is located in the upper left quadrant of the 640×200 display screen. As Fig. 5-4 illustrates, the VIEW statement will map the entire graphic to the viewport, whereas the VIEW SCREEN variant will clip the graphic to fit the viewport.

WARNINGS: The size of the viewport must be expressed as actual physical coordinates on the display screen, even if you have used WINDOW SCREEN to establish world coordinates. An example provided in many versions of IBM's BASIC manual is mistaken in its explanation of this point. In addition, a CLS instruction will only blank the viewport if a VIEW mode is active.

COMMENTS: Use VIEW without any arguments to disable the viewport and return to the entire display screen. The VIEW statement is used in the 3D CAD programs in

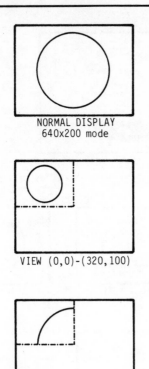

NORMAL DISPLAY
640x200 mode

VIEW (0,0)-(320,100)

VIEW SCREEN (0,0)-(320,100)

Fig. 5-4. Differences in viewport mapping between the VIEW and VIEW SCREEN instructions.

Supercharged Graphics to set up a separate 2D viewport for drawing and a separate 3D viewport for displaying the finished 3D model. If you are using C, Pascal, Modula-2, Ada, or assembly language, you will find a useful viewport-mapping algorithm in Appendix B.

GRAPHICS PRIMITIVES

GRAPHICS PRIMITIVE INSTRUCTION: **PSET**

PURPOSE: The PSET statement is used to place a single point on the display screen. It activates one pixel.

SYNTAX: **PSET (x-coordinate, y-coordinate),color.**

EXAMPLE: **PSET (320,100),7** will place a white dot at the center of the 640×200 graphics screen.

WARNINGS: If you omit the color parameter, then BASIC will use the foreground color established by the COLOR statement to draw the pixel.

GRAPHICS PRIMITIVE INSTRUCTION: **LINE**

PURPOSE: The LINE statement draws a straight line between any two points on the display screen. By using the styling options described in Chapter 6, you can create dotted and dashed lines in a range of colors.

SYNTAX: **LINE (starting coordinates)-(ending coordinates),color**

EXAMPLE: **LINE (0,0)-(320,100),7** draws a white line from the upper left corner of the display screen to the center of the display screen in the 640×200 16-color graphics mode on the EGA and VGA. For the 640×200 two-color mode, you would use **LINE (0,0)-(320,100),1.**

EXAMPLE: **LINE-(639,0),7** would continue from the endpoint of the previous example and draw a line to the upper right corner of the display screen. The previous endpoint is called the *last-referenced point*.

WARNINGS: Be aware that if you were to draw a circle and then use the LINE-(x,y) option, BASIC considers the center of the circle to be the last-referenced point.

COMMENTS: BASIC automatically clips lines which extend past the physical boundaries of the display screen. Variations of the LINE statement will create a rectangle and fill it, providing extremely quick erasing functions.

GRAPHICS PRIMITIVE INSTRUCTION: **PAINT**

PURPOSE: The PAINT instruction fills a polygon with a color selected by you. Area fill is sometimes called region fill or flood fill. You can use PAINT to fill any rectangle, circle, oval, or irregular polygon.

SYNTAX: **PAINT (x-seed, y-seed),fill color, boundary color.** (The name seed refers to the point where area fill is to begin.)

EXAMPLE: **PAINT (320,100),12,3** would begin the area fill procedure at the center of the 640×200 16-color screen. The software color 12 would be used to fill the polygon. The fill would stop whenever it encountered software color 3.

WARNINGS: Refer to Fig. 5-5. If the starting point for the area fill occurs on a point exhibiting the boundary color, then no fill will occur. If the graphic to be filled is not a closed polygon, then the fill will spill out of the graphic and corrupt other parts of the screen. The area fill algorithm used by IBM, Microsoft, and Borland exhibits the following quirk: if the fill routine encounters a complete horizontal line where no fill is required, then the routine will not continue past that line, even though additional fill may be required on other lines.

COMMENTS: Efficient fill routines employ a first-in first-out queue construct to keep track of seed points. A high-performance algorithm for filling complex, random polygons with multiple islands and peninsulas is provided in Appendix A. Users of C, Pascal, Ada, Modula-2, and assembly language will find this algorithm useful.

GRAPHICS PRIMITIVE INSTRUCTION: **CIRCLE**

PURPOSE: The CIRCLE statement draws an oval. By default the oval is circular, but you can use parameters of the CIRCLE statement to create oblong ovals and even portions of ovals.

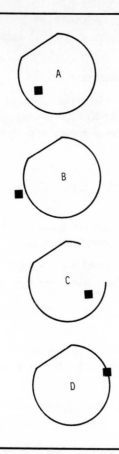

Fig. 5-5. Area fill using BASIC's PAINT instruction. In example A, the area fill will operate correctly. In example B, the background (but not the polygon) will be filled. In example C, the area fill will spill out onto the background. In example D, no area fill will occur.

SYNTAX: **CIRCLE (xy center coordinates),radius,color,start,end,shape.**

EXAMPLE: **CIRCLE (320,100),50,7** will create a circle at the center of the 640×200 16-color screen. The circle will have a radius of 50 units, measured as x units. (The BASIC routine will calculate the appropriate number of y units while it is drawing the circle.) The circle will be drawn in color 7.

COMMENTS: The start and end parameters define the points where the circle is to start and end, providing for partial ovals. The drawing routines in *YOUR MICROCOMPUTER SKETCH PAD*, provided as a complete listing in Chapter 17, provide a precise example of these parameters. The shape parameter defines the distortion of the oval, which, by default, is a perfect circle. The CIRCLE statement provides a reliable method of checking the aspect ratio of your display monitor. Use the tweaking knobs at the rear of the chassis to make the necessary adjustments if a circle looks more like an oval.

BITBLT STATEMENTS

Bitblt is an acronym for *bit boundary block transfer*. Bitblt is also called block graphics.

BITBLT INSTRUCTION: **GET**

PURPOSE: The GET statement captures a rectangle of graphics data from a bit map (usually the display screen) and stores it in memory as a graphic array. When used for animation or for menu management, this use of graphic arrays is called bitblt or block graphics. Refer to Fig. 5-6.

SYNTAX: **GET (upper left corner)-(lower right corner), array name.**

EXAMPLE: **GET (10,20)-(160,100),ARRAY1** would save the image inside a rectangle whose upper left corner is at 10,20 and whose lower right corner is at 160,100. The array's name is ARRAY1.

WARNINGS: GW-BASIC insists that the coordinates provided as parameters to a GET statement must be actual physical coordinates. Most other versions of BASIC permit you to use world coordinates previously defined by a WINDOW SCREEN statement.

COMMENTS: A DIM statement must be used to set aside memory space to hold the array before any GET statement is used. The menu systems used through *Supercharged Graphics* use graphic arrays to provide pull-down menus, as you will soon see.

BITBLT INSTRUCTION: **PUT**

PURPOSE: The PUT instruction retrieves the data from a graphic array stored in memory and places it into a bit map (usually the display screen).

SYNTAX: **PUT (upper right coordinates), array name, logical operator.**

EXAMPLE: **PUT (160,100),ARRAY1,PSET** would place the array named ARRAY1 at position 160,100 on the display screen. The PSET logical operator means that the array will be written over any existing graphics. Other logical operators such as OR, AND, XOR can be used singly or in combination with one another to produce assorted special effects.

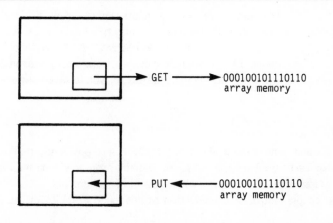

Fig. 5-6. BASIC's GET and PUT instructions operate on graphic arrays. Similar functions in other languages are called block graphics or bitblt (bit boundary block transfer).

WARNINGS: See the warnings for the GET instruction.

COMMENTS: Manipulation of the logical operators can produce a rich selection of special effects. The crosshair cursor used in many of the demonstration programs in this book is placed on the screen using the XOR logical operator. A second placement erases the cursor, providing a simple but effective method for cursor management.

BITBLT INSTRUCTION: **PCOPY**

PURPOSE: The PCOPY statement copies the contents of one graphics page to another graphics page. Simply put, PCOPY transfers the binary contents from one bit map to another bit map.

SYNTAX: **PCOPY source page, target page.**

EXAMPLE: **PCOPY 1,0** would transfer the contents of page 1 to page 0. The contents of page 1 would not be damaged during the transfer, of course.

COMMENTS: PCOPY is extremely useful for interactive graphics programming with an EGA and a VGA. Because only one graphics page is supported on the CGA, however, this book uses a short assembly language subroutine to emulate PCOPY, establishing simulated graphics pages in RAM memory. If you are using a CGA, you can find a full-length 3D wireframe CAD program in Appendix G which uses this technique.

BITBLT INSTRUCTION: **BSAVE**

PURPOSE: The BSAVE statement saves a display image on disk as a binary image file. Simply stated, the BSAVE routine stores the contents of the bit map on disk. Saving the four bit planes of the EGA and VGA is a tricky, but manageable, process. A comprehensive discussion of BSAVE techniques for EGA, VGA, MCGA, CGA, and PCjr graphics adapters is found in Chapter 13.

BITBLT INSTRUCTION: **BLOAD**

PURPOSE: The BLOAD statement retrieves a display image from disk and loads it into a bit map. The bit map may be the display page or it may be a hidden page. A comprehensive discussion of BLOAD techniques for EGA, VGA, MCGA, CGA, and PCjr graphics adapters is found in Chapter 13. All the major demonstration programs in *Supercharged Graphics* provide BSAVE and BLOAD mechanisms for you to save your drawings to disk for later retrieval and editing.

SUMMARY

In this chapter you learned about the modest, yet powerful, toolkit of graphics instructions that can be used to create advanced graphics programs. You studied initialization statements, graphics primitives statements, and bitblt statements.

The next chapter introduces a selection of advanced graphics instructions.

6

Using Advanced
Graphics Instructions

A variety of very advanced techniques for computer graphics is provided by the optional parameters used by standard BASIC graphics instructions. These techniques include dithering, halftoning, page flipping, color cycling, and frame grabs. Many of these impressive-sounding names are simply programmer's jargon for straightforward functions.

ADVANCED GRAPHICS TECHNIQUE #1: DITHERING

When a 3D model is shaded by a microcomputer, two adjacent flat surfaces may have a hard edge which appears unrealistic. A patterned line is used to subdue the harsh difference between the two surfaces. The creation of any patterned line is called linestyling. When linestyling is used to create smoother images in solid 3D models it is called dithering. (Professional programmers call this the removal of discontinuities.)

The syntax for BASIC's line statement is **LINE (start)-(end), color, box, style**.

The style parameter consists of a binary code expressed as a four-digit hexadecimal number. The on/off nature of the binary number determines whether a particular pixel is set or not set during the drawing of the line. Refer to Fig. 6-1.

Simple dotted lines and dashed lines can be easily created. Hex code &HAAAA is 10101010 10101010 in binary, which is a dotted line, for example. Longer dashes can be produced with hex code &HFEFE, which is 11111110 11111110 in binary. A typical statement in BASIC might appear thus: **LINE (10,20)-(320,100),3,,&HEOEO**. This line would be drawn in color 3 using the pattern 11100000 11100000.

In its standard usage, the linestyling is simply placed over the existing screen graphics. However, if a colored line is drawn first and then a second line drawn over the first line using linestyling, an almost infinite number of dithering possibilities become available.

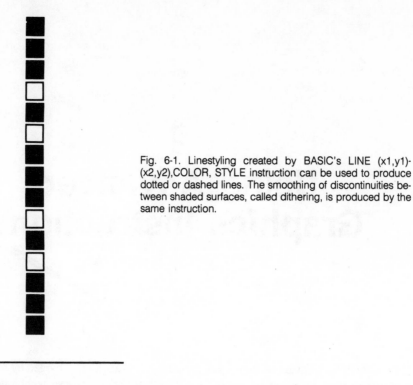

Fig. 6-1. Linestyling created by BASIC's LINE (x1,y1)-(x2,y2),COLOR, STYLE instruction can be used to produce dotted or dashed lines. The smoothing of discontinuities between shaded surfaces, called dithering, is produced by the same instruction.

Style 10101010 10101010 looks much different when drawn over black than it does when drawn over blue, for instance.

The program listing for *YOUR MICROCOMPUTER DRAFTING TABLE* in Chapter 21 provides a comprehensive set of dashed and dotted line examples. A set of dithering codes is provided as code fragments in Chapter 24. The program listing for *YOUR MICROCOMPUTER 3D CAD MODELER* in Chapter 29 can be used to create fully shaded 3D models. It provides a working example of line dithering at work.

ADVANCED GRAPHICS TECHNIQUE #2: HALFTONING

The PAINT statement in BASIC can be used to create patterns using a programming technique called *bit tiling*. Refer to Fig. 6-2. The pattern to be used in the area fill is expressed as a string using CHR$. A comprehensive discussion of how bit tiling can be invoked on an EGA or VGA and on a CGA is provided in Chapters 24 and 25.

When an area fill pattern is used to simulate the effect of illumination on a surface, the technique is called *halftoning*. Simply stated, a mixture of different colored pixels will blend into a shaded tone when viewed by the human eye from a reasonable distance. This is exactly the same technique used by newspapers and magazines to reproduce black-and-white photographs and color photographs. In fact, black-and-white photos are called halftone photos. Carefully inspect any photograph in your favorite daily newspaper and you can readily pick out the individual dots which make up the halftone, even without resorting to a magnifying glass.

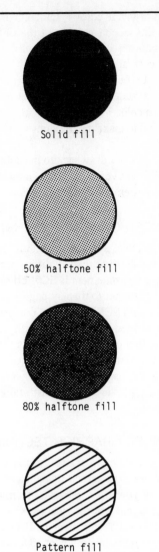

Fig. 6-2. BASIC's bit tiling capabilities.

The program listing for *YOUR MICROCOMPUTER DRAFTING TABLE* in Chapter 21 provides numerous examples of patterning, including crosshatching and parallel lines. The program listing for *YOUR MICROCOMPUTER 3D CAD MODELER* in Chapter 29 provides a set of halftoning patterns suitable for rendering a wide range of illumination levels on the surfaces of 3D models.

ADVANCED GRAPHICS TECHNIQUE #3: COLOR CYCLING

The PALETTE statement in BASIC can be used to produce extremely high-speed animation using an advanced technique called color cycling. Assume, for example, that a white object is drawn against a black background. If a subsequent version of the same object is drawn in color 1, but color 1 has been defined by a PALETTE statement as color 0, then the second version of the object will be invisible (because it is being drawn in black against a black background).

By careful use of the PALETTE statement, you could draw five different versions of the same object by using software colors 1 through 5, each defined as color 0 by a PALETTE statement. Then, by selectively using PALETTE to swap the value of software color 1 to color 7 (white), you can instantaneously animate the object. You must also use PALETTE to make the previous version of the object disappear into the black background, of course.

The primary drawback to the color cycling technique is the complications which arise when different versions in the animation sequence overlap each other. Color cycling can produce extremely quick animation, but it requires meticulous planning in advance.

ADVANCED GRAPHICS TECHNIQUE #4: PAGE FLIPPING

On graphics adapters which provide more than one graphics page, the microprocessor can be instructed to display different pages using the SCREEN statement in BASIC. The syntax for this statement is **SCREEN mode, color burst, written-to page, displayed page**.

For example, to display page 1 you could use SCREEN,,,1. You could instantly flip to page 2 with SCREEN,,,2. (You are still writing graphics to page 0, of course. To flip both the written-to page and the displayed page to page 1 you could use SCREEN,,1,1.)

Page flipping is available on the EGA, the VGA, and the PCjr video subsystem (which is virtually identical to the graphics adapter of the Tandy). Chapter 15 provides a short assembly language routine which you can use to invoke simulated page flipping on a CGA. Chapter 33 provides a demonstration program which uses page flipping to create frame animation.

ADVANCED GRAPHICS TECHNIQUE #5: FRAME GRAB

Simply stated, a frame grab is the storage of a complete screen image in memory for later use. The screen image can be one which has been generated by your program, created by your user, retrieved from a disk's binary image file, or even captured as the digitized signal from a videocamera.

The PCOPY statement in BASIC provides frame grab capabilities on your IBM-compatible personal computer. Because multiple graphics pages are available on the EGA, the VGA, and the PCjr video subsystem, frames of graphics data can be stored on these unused pages.

PCOPY 0,1 would move the image from page 0 into the bit map for page 1. The original image in page 0 is not affected by the data transfer.

When a color/graphics adapter is being used, a short assembly language subroutine must be used to store frames in dynamic RAM. See Chapter 15 for more information on this technique.

ADVANCED GRAPHICS TECHNIQUE #6: VIRTUAL SCREEN

Under normal circumstances, the bit map containing the data to be displayed on the screen is the same size as the screen buffer. The bit positions in the screen buffer are read by the hardware and must directly correspond to pixel positions on the display moni-

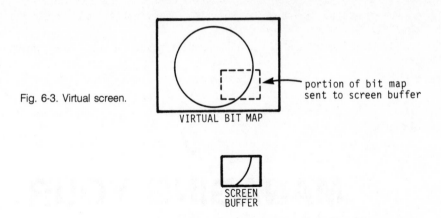

Fig. 6-3. Virtual screen.

VIRTUAL BIT MAP

portion of bit map
sent to screen buffer

SCREEN
BUFFER

tor, of course. As you probably already know, the screen buffer for the color/graphics adapter is located at memory address B8000 hex. The screen buffer for an EGA using page 0 is located at memory address A0000 hex.

However, if you are using C or assembly language graphics drivers to draw your graphics, there is nothing preventing you from drawing on a bit map which is much larger than the screen buffer. Refer to Fig. 6-3. This virtual bit map can be located anywhere in free RAM.

To display a portion of the virtual bit map on the display screen, a rectangle which is the same size as the screen buffer is moved into the screen buffer from the virtual bit map. By changing the location of this rectangle and moving subsequent graphics data in the screen buffer, high-speed pans and scrolls can be invoked.

Unfortunately, the graphics drivers which are built into BASIC are designed to create graphics on bit maps which are exactly the same dimensions as the screen buffer. Virtual bit maps are sometimes called virtual screens.

SUMMARY

In this chapter you learned about a variety of advanced graphics techniques which are useful for interactive graphics programming.

The next chapter discusses important considerations for successfully managing your graphics project from start to finish.

7

MANAGING YOUR GRAPHICS PROJECT

If you plan to write serious software using interactive graphics, you will improve your productivity if you adopt a project plan. Simply stated, what is needed is a specific objective and a plan for achieving that objective. After all, if you don't have a road map, how will you know if you are still on course? And if you don't know where you are going, how will you know when you get there?

DEFINING YOUR PROJECT

Like most things in life, there is more than one way of looking at a serious program-ming project. However, in interactive graphics programming, you must consider two points of view: yours and the end-user's.

When you are defining the project and planning your coding strategy it is all too easy to overlook the most important element . . . the end-user. It is vital to keep asking the essential question: who is this program being developed for, the programmer or the end-user?

Because the end-user is not watching over your shoulder while you write the program, you must discipline yourself to act as a watchdog for the end-user's interests. At numerous stages during program development you will find yourself faced with important decisions. If you take the easy way out—if you choose a coding solution that is convenient from a programming point of view—then you are probably forcing serious compromises upon the end- user. In the long run, these compromises invariably mean fewer software sales. The end-user, after all, usually cares about only one thing: how easy is it for me to get good results?

YOUR MASTER PLAN

The master plan is a long-term plan to help you manage the development of a complicated graphics program. A good master plan covers a lot of ground, including the initial concept, objectives, logic flowchart, pseudocode, source code, testing and debugging, outsider testing, and preparation of the finished distribution disk. Refer to Fig. 7-1. Other, equally important, considerations include preparation of the user's manual, marketing, advertising, and distribution. Often these factors are not the responsibility of the programmer.

Depending upon your philosophy towards programming, you may wish to assign target completion dates for each of the components of your master plan. If you are working alone, you may feel more comfortable with only a few vague deadlines. If you are part of a team, specific deadlines are essential in order to keep different parts of the team in harmony.

THE CONCEPT

The starting point for any programming project is always the same: the establishment of a viable concept. The concept is the idea from which the rest of the project emerges.

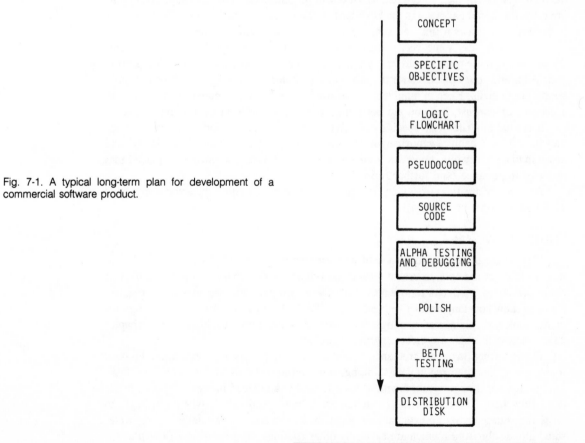

Fig. 7-1. A typical long-term plan for development of a commercial software product.

A good concept can usually be summarized in a single sentence such as: We want to design a menu-driven 3D CAD editor which will allow users to create accurate wireframe models using their keyboard and a CGA or EGA.

From this single concept can be derived a few paragraphs of related thoughts. Your 3D CAD program might provide mouse support, for example. Or you might have some original ideas about the design of the on-screen menus which will make your 3D CAD editor vastly superior to others on the market.

The concept is loosely akin to a marketing plan. It articulates your idea of your niche in the market. It defines your program's reason for being. It gives you a general sense of purpose and direction. Do not proceed any further with your project—no matter how ambitious—until you have successfully identified a formal concept.

SPECIFIC OBJECTIVES

After you have identified a concept, your next step should be to write down a series of specific objectives. You might like to think of objectives as program functions. In other words, what will your program actually do? How many pull-down menus will be needed? Will it permit the user to save images on disk? Will it provide a graphics print-out? Will it display a 3D view while the 2D plan view is being created by the user? . . . or must the plan view be finished before the 3D view will be generated? Will the program support input from a digital pad, or will the keyboard be the primary input device? What happens if the end-user draws a line and subsequently wishes to undo the line?

Needless to say, some very complicated questions can emerge from your concept. By answering these questions as best you can at this early stage, you are in effect setting your goals and your objectives for the project as a whole. At this stage, don't be too timid about setting goals. Keep in mind that if you reach for the sky you may not come up with a handful of stardust, but you are not going to end up with a handful of mud either.

It is vital to write these specific objectives down on paper. Good ideas are fleeting; they have a nasty habit of vaporizing if not captured on paper. Once they have been nailed down in black and white, however, your specific objectives can be reworked, placed into order of importance, and further refined.

As lawyers are fond of saying, if you don't have it in writing then you don't have it. So get it down in writing.

LOGIC FLOWCHART

If you have done a thorough job of itemizing your specific objectives, you will find it a straightforward task to create a logic flowchart. A flowchart is simply a series of connected boxes. Each box represents a part of your program, and the lines which connect the parts show how they interact with each other. Each of the major demonstration programs in this book is supplemented by a logic flowchart. You might want to skip ahead to Chapter 23 to browse through a typical program flowchart.

Flowcharting has some tremendous advantages for you as a programmer. First, it forces you to be organized in your thinking. It encourages you to think in a modular fashion because separate program functions usually tend to be placed in separate boxes in the logic flowchart. The result is an improvement in your productivity when you begin to write the source code. You can, for example, write the code for a number of separate, stand-alone subroutines which are called by other routines. By preparing a flowchart for the project, you will have already seen the need for these subroutines. On the other hand, if you had merely jumped right into the codewriting process, you likely would have written a number of these functions right into a routine . . . only to discover later that other sections of your code could use the same function.

YOUR PSEUDOCODE

Once you have prepared a logic flowchart for your graphics program, you can begin to write pseudocode. What is pseudocode? It is a series of statements written in everyday English which describe what various parts of the program do from the point of view of the application program, the operating system, and the hardware. Whereas the concept and the objectives were written from the end-user's point of view, the pseudocode is written from the programmer's point of view.

If you are working on the menu system, for example, you could write this:

save the existing screen image and then display the Options pull-down menu

This is English for the following:

PCOPY 0,1:PUT (320,60),A6,PSET

Your next pseudocode statement might be this:

use scrolling cursor to select choice from menu.

The Programmer's Dilemma

Using pseudocode frees you from the programmer's traditional dilemma of trying to do two things at once. Pseudocode separates the programming goals from the syntax tasks. Rather than thinking: "What do I do next and how am I going to do it?", you will be able to focus your attention on using the programming language. Because you have already written your program in pseudocode, you already know exactly what you are going to do next (ie save the current screen image, pop the pull-down menu onto the screen, install the scrolling cursor for the menu, et cetera).

The segregation of what-am-I-trying-to-do from how-am-I-going-to-do-it is the mark of a well-organized, professional graphics programmer. Pseudocode is the what-am-I-trying-to-do component. Writing the source code is the how-am-I-going-to-do-it component. Pseudocode will save you time, effort, and quite likely money.

Some programmers write the pseudocode for the entire program before starting to write source code. Other programmers write only the pseudocode for the particular routine or subroutine upon which they are currently working. Provided that you have a reasonably detailed logic flowchart to follow, you can use either approach with great success. If you are developing new routines and learning as you go, so to speak, you will be forced into writing pseudocode on a piecemeal basis, of course.

YOUR SOURCE CODE

After writing the relevant portions of the pseudocode, you can begin to create the source code. What is source code? It is the program code written in the syntax of whatever programming language you are using.

A typical approach to writing source code runs something like this: first, create the portions of the program which set up the starting display screen. Next, you might choose to write a few of the subroutines which will be used by higher level routines. A subroutine which puts a particular pull-down menu on the screen is a good candidate for early source code. The subroutine which provides a clean exit from the program should also be coded early.

Because you have spent some time preparing a logic flowchart, you will be able to leave pockets in your source code for subroutines that you choose to write at a later time. This approach is superior to having to go back later and insert a subroutine where you had made no allowance for one. In addition, you can easily create a do-nothing subroutine for inactive functions; this allows you to build more important parts of your program while maintaining a semi-finished effect on the display screen. The solid model 3D CAD editor in Chapter 29, called YOUR MICROCOMPUTER 3D CAD MODELER, provides a hands-on example of do-nothing routines (often called stubs).

While you are working on your source code, always save your code on disk before running the program. Even better, save once on your working disk and save an additional copy on your back-up disk. Computing history is littered with programmers who were confident that the code they had just written was bullet-proof . . . unfortunately their computer did not share their enthusiasm and locked up on the first trial run. Remember, you can't save anything meaningful on disk after a reboot.

TESTING AND DEBUGGING

Development of source code involves repeated testing and debugging. You add a bit more code, test the program, add a bit more code (or go back and correct a few bugs) and test the program again. This incremental process enables you to eventually complete a very complex, high-performance graphics program. There are, however, many dangerous pitfalls for the unwary.

On each occasion when you are about to add some major new portions to your source code, be certain to save the existing version first. Then, rename the program before you begin to add the new code. This ensures that your original version—which is probably the only correctly working version—will not be lost forever if your new code turns out to be a dead end. This redundant approach gobbles up a lot of disk space, but any other approach is like playing with live hand grenades.

As your program grows in size—as your investment of time and effort grows—you should set up a secure back-up system. You might wish to consider using a working disk and a primary back-up disk for current work. You would also be wise to consider a secondary back-up disk. The secondary back-up is used to save your work at the end of the day. Some programmers even use a third back-up disk to save work at the end of each week. These third back-ups are often stored at a site away from the work area, or carried in a personal attache case, or locked in a fire-resistant safe.

Is all this redundancy overkill? Probably. But many programmers simply cannot sleep at night without the peace of mind that only multiple back-ups provide. During final debugging, this author inadvertently destroyed the only copies of the CADD drafting program on his working disk, on the primary back-up disk, and on the secondary back-up disk. The onerous chore of typing in 650 lines of source code from the program print-out was averted only by the third back-up disk which this author keeps in his attache case.

POLISHING

Once you have a working version of your interactive graphics program, it is time to go back and correct all those little things that you promised yourself you would fix later. (You did keep a list of those runtime idiosyncrasies, didn't you?) Sometimes this polishing takes real willpower, but it often spells the difference between a ho-hum program and an award-winner.

The first major demonstration program in this book is a full-function interactive paintbrush program called *YOUR MICROCOMPUTER SKETCH PAD*. This program provides a good example of the need for polishing. As you will learn in Chapter 19, the subroutines which create the graphics for the pull-down menus are very inefficient, almost to the point of embarrassment. They slow down the start-up process considerably. These subroutines were optimized in the subsequent drafting and 3D CAD programs, but because the paintbrush program is intended as a teaching program, the inefficient subroutines were left intact in *YOUR MICROCOMPUTER SKETCH PAD*. If you were developing a similar program for commercial distribution, shareware distribution, or freeware distribution, you would go back and rewrite the offending sections of code. There is no reason for any programmer to turn a blind eye to sloppy graphics code. Laziness is not a reason, it is an excuse, and a poor one at that.

OUTSIDE TESTING

As soon as you have polished your program, it is time for outside testing. After nurturing your program for weeks or even months, you have come to accept its idiosyncrasies and its quirks. You need an unbiased opinion. By submitting your program to an outsider for testing and appraisal, you are getting a fresh point of view. Outside testing is often called beta testing by professional programming shops.

Outside testing can be a painful process for the programmer. The beta tester is not emotionally attached to the program like you are and is unlikely to overlook the quirks and bugs that you have opted to leave in place (or perhaps that you are not even aware of). But outside testing sure beats the alternative, which is the school of hard knocks. With outside testing, you get a second chance: you can correct the bugs, eliminate the quirks, overcome the idiosyncrasies—you are rewarded with a vastly improved program ready for the marketplace. On the other hand, if you choose to skip outside testing and deliver a potentially defective product to the marketplace, the program's reputation will be ruined, making later versions doomed to failure too, even though they may have been improved.

Use some judgment in your selection of outside testers. Do not provide the source code to the tester. The runtime modules produced by any compiler will usually yield all the protection your code requires at this stage, although you may wish to invest in some serious software protection. See Chapter 8 for more on this topic.

WHAT DOES THE END-USER REALLY WANT?

Software engineering involves much more than merely writing efficient code. It means careful consideration of the end-user's needs. And that means good design.

Studies show that end-users have trouble with software because of four reasons. These reasons are: too much jargon, overly fine distinctions, non-obvious design, and design inconsistencies. By avoiding these traits in your original programs you can make your software easier to use.

Too Much Jargon

Sometimes its difficult to remember that not everyone enjoys computing just for the sake of computing. Many individuals are using your program in order to accomplish a specific task. They neither need to understand nor do they want to understand all the jargon, catchphrases, and acronyms used by the computer gurus. If your program starts off by calling a diskette a disk, then stick with that name throughout the session. Don't occasionally call it a ''floppy'' or ''flippy'' or ''mass storage device'' or ''magnetic media''. Say ''restart'' instead of ''reboot''. Say ''personal computer'' instead of ''micro''.

Overly Fine Distinctions

Fine distinctions include keystrokes or menu commands which accomplish similar results, but which must be used only in specific situations. Fine distinctions also include identical keystrokes that produce wildly different results, depending upon when the keystrokes are used.

These fine distinctions are almost always the result of quirks in the source code. Rather than make the effort to rewrite the offending sections of code, the programmer has taken the easy way out and shunted the problem onto the end-user's lap.

Non-Obvious Design

Non-obvious design means elements that are not intuitive. The result of a keystroke should be immediate, obvious, and visible on the display screen—especially in an interactive graphics program! What is an end-user supposed to think when a keystroke has apparently produced no result? Even a simple beep is better than no response at all. And how is an end-user to learn your program when you have used the Backspace key to implement a function instead of the Enter key?

Design Inconsistency

Design inconsistency infests both software and user's manuals. The concept of design inconsistency can best be illustrated by a few examples. Design inconsistency is calling the same function by different names: using SAVE and KEEP interchangeably, using WRITE and LIST to mean the same thing.

Design inconsistency means that you have burdened your end-user with the unsavory task of memorizing extra names, instead of naturally (and enjoyably) learning how to use your program. You have turned your easy-to-use graphics program into something that requires rote memorization. Design inconsistency equals confusion.

WHAT POORLY DESIGNED PROGRAMS REALLY DO

If your original program suffers from poor design, then without fail it will produce the following results: confusion, frustration, boredom, and eventually abandonment of the program itself.

If the program's menu system is peppered with fine distinctions and redundant labels, then the end-user has difficulty seeing meaningful patterns and becomes confused.

If your end-user cannot see what really happened after a keystroke, or if there is no way to undo undesired actions, or if long response times bog down the user interface, then frustration will occur.

If you have forced your end-user to perform simple tasks over and over again rather than having your program automatically perform the tasks, boredom is likely to set in.

The end result of all these shortcomings will likely be the abandonment of your program by the end-user, but probably the saddest effect of a poorly designed program is that the program will never be used to its fullest potential. With all the fun taken out of computing, who can blame the end-user to using the program only when absolutely necessary? Or, even worse, the end-user may modify his or her goals, making them match the capabilities of the program. This is definitely not the way to ensure repeat software sales.

HOW TO WRITE A GOOD USER'S GUIDE

If you can write a good user's guide, then often you have already won the battle. A strong user's guide can often alleviate many of the shortcomings and quirks in a program (although it is no excuse for not eliminating those bugs in the first place).

Generally speaking, a good user's guide will contain seven distinct elements. These elements are: a table of contents, a general description of the program, the system requirements, a description of how to start and how to exit the program, at least one sample session, a reference section containing keywords and error messages, and a detailed index. Refer to Fig. 7-2.

Although other features may be found in a good user's guide, you will not miss the mark if you ensure that these seven elements are present in your user's guide—especially if it is written in everyday English. The drafting, paintbrush, and 3D CAD programs in this book are each accompanied by a concise user's guide. Although occasionally panned by the pundits, the manuals provided with QuickBASIC, Turbo BASIC, QuickC, and Turbo C are examples of good user's guides.

Table of Contents

An accurate table of contents enables your end-user to locate topics of interest to him/her. A good table of contents is characterized by the detail of topics listed under each heading. More is better.

General Description

The general description of the program tells the end-user (in a conversational way) about the performance of the program. It describes the features of the program. It talks about the uses to which the program can be put. It describes the benefits of the program. (Benefits are what you describe when the end-user asks you, ''But what is in it for me?'')

As a general rule of thumb, it is usually also wise to clarify what the program cannot do. Honesty is the best policy in the long run.

System Requirements

The system requirements section tells the end-user what hardware and what operating system is required in order to run your program. Be specific. There is, for example, a world of difference between IBM DOS 3.1 and IBM DOS 3.2.

How To Start/How To Exit

A step-by-step description is vital. You should assume that a small percentage of your

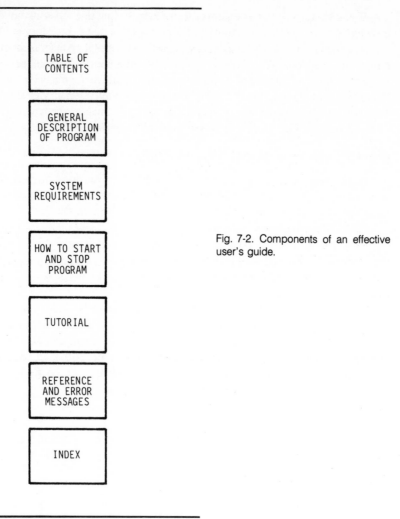

Fig. 7-2. Components of an effective user's guide.

end-users will be first-time computer users. If you treat them kindly at this stage, they will respond with repeat business for other programs bearing your name. Even weathered computer users appreciate a simple, straightforward explanation of how to start up the program and how to cleanly exit. Be sure to caution your end-users to create back-up copies of the program disk before using it. (If you are using copy protection, you should provide a back-up.)

Tutorials

Tutorials are also called *sample sessions*. As you probably recall from your earlier schooling, the quickest way to learn is to learn by doing. Simply stated, sample sessions are learning by doing, learning by example. A sample session is your chance to instill some good work habits in your end-user so that he/she will use your program the way you intended it to be used. It also gives you the opportunity to show the end-user how to handle some of the more common error situations that may arise during the use of your program.

A good sample session can occur simply in the user's guide, or it can require that the end-user actually use a computer to follow along. Hands-on is always the best, of course.

Reference

The reference section of your user's guide is an alphabetized listing of keywords, mnemonics, and error messages. Including this information as part of other sections in the user's guide is not enough. Only an alphabetical arrangement gives the end-user the ability to look up a particular item on short notice without the necessity of wading through unneeded adjacent material.

Index

The index is an alphabetized list of topics found throughout the user's guide. The more extensive the index, the better.

SUMMARY

In this chapter you learned about using a master plan to manage your graphics programming project. You read about creating a viable concept and defining specific objectives. You learned the difference between pseudocode and source code. You considered the end-user's point of view, and you discovered the essential components of a good user's guide.

The material touched upon by this chapter could easily be expanded to fill an entire book. If this chapter started you thinking, then your time here was well-spent.

The next chapter discusses methods for protecting your original software.

8

Protecting Your
Original Software

After investing many hours in the creation and testing of your interactive graphics program, you will likely want to protect your investment. Some form of protection is necessary no matter whether you circulate your program by commercial distribution, shareware distribution, or freeware distribution.

What is commercial distribution, shareware distribution, and freeware distribution; and what do these terms mean to you, the programmer?

COMMERCIAL DISTRIBUTION

Commercial distribution means the ordinary sale of packaged software. More precisely, commercial distribution usually means sale of a license to use the software. The purchaser is buying the right to use your program, not ownership of the program itself. This market concept can best be illustrated by an example. When a traveller buys a ticket from an airline, the traveller is purchasing the right to fly on the aircraft; ownership of the airplane has not changed hands.

Commercial distribution of software usually implies that the full purchase price is paid before the goods are taken by the buyer. The software package usually includes the right to use the product (the license), the program disks (the physical media), user's guides (the documentation), and a limited warranty (the guarantee).

SHAREWARE DISTRIBUTION

Shareware distribution, on the other hand, usually implies that only a nominal fee (if any) is paid when the prospective buyer acquires the program disk. The shareware concept is based upon the premise of try-it-before-you-buy-it. The programmer is betting that after the buyer has tried out the software, the user will want to pay additional voluntary fees to acquire the official user's guides, improved versions of the software (product updates), and so on. Some shareware programs, particularly word processing applications, have become very successful using this method of distribution.

Even shareware programs which are distributed gratis are not without strings attached, however. The author is still the lawful owner of the program, and has merely granted a temporary license to use the software. Technically, the prospective user has been granted the right to test and appraise the software for a reasonable period of time. The user incurs an obligation to pay the additional fees for documentation and updates when the user makes the decision to use the product on a regular basis. Shareware is not freeware.

FREEWARE DISTRIBUTION

Freeware distribution implies that the program has been placed in the public domain. The author has relinquished all rights of ownership and has given the program to the public at large. Public domain programs belong to everyone and anyone. As a programmer and as an end-user, you can copy, revise, use, and merge any portion of a program which is in the public domain. You cannot, however, claim that it is yours, because it belongs to everyone. But you can otherwise use it as if it were yours.

PROTECTING YOUR SOFTWARE

The protection of computer programs falls into two broad categories: intellectual protection and physical protection. Both categories raise complex challenges and issues. The responses to these challenges are remedies for the groups of persons who either enforce or benefit from the protection. These software protection remedies usually are classified as lawyers' remedies and programmers' remedies. However, you do not have to be a lawyer to use the lawyers' remedies.

LAWYERS' REMEDIES

A lawyer's approach to protection includes copyright, trademarks, patents, trade secrets, license agreements, non-disclosure agreements, and non-competition agreements.

Copyright

Copyright refers to the legal right to make copies of an intellectual work. An intellectual work is a product that is generally the result of creative labor, including but not limited to paintings, books, television dramas, musical recordings, video recordings, and computer programs. For example, when you purchase a painting from an art gallery you are usually purchasing only the physical painting itself; seldom do you receive ownership of copyright. The physical painting and copyright are two separate entities. The right to take possession of a property and the right to make copies of the property are two separate legal entities. You have the right to display the painting in your home or office; you do not have the right to make lithographic prints of the painting and sell them for a profit (unless you have specifically purchased the copyright from the artist).

As soon as you have created an intellectual work, copyright begins to exist. In other words, as soon as you have created your computer program (or significant portions of it), your copyright begins to take effect.

Notice of Copyright

You must, however, provide notice of your ownership of copyright. The usual means for doing so is the copyright symbol shown in Fig. 8-1. If you publish or distribute your program without a message announcing your ownership of copyright, then your program runs the risk of falling into the public domain. The message is called the copyright notice.

All countries who adhere to copyright conventions recognize the word "copyright." Not all countries, however, recognize the © symbol. To be safe, you should use the phrase "© Copyright 1988 by *Your Name*," inserting the appropriate date and your name, and omitting the quotation marks, of course. Although "© 1988 *Your Name*" is a reasonable substitute which is often used throughout North America, it is not recognized by some other countries.

In addition, a few countries (particularly in South America, for example) insist that the phrase "All rights reserved" be included as a part of the copyright notice. If you do not clearly state that you are reserving all rights for yourself, then the laws of these countries assume that you are specifically not reserving all rights for yourself. To be prudent, a safe notice would take one of the following formats:

© **Copyright 1988 by** *Your Name*. **All rights reserved.**
Copyright © **1988 by** *Your Name*. **All rights reserved.**
© **Copyright 1988** *Your Name*. **All rights reserved.**
Copyright © **1988** *Your Name*. **All rights reserved.**

How to Copyright a Computer Program

If you are protecting a computer program, your notice of copyright should appear in three places. First, the copyright notice should be placed in some prominent location in your source code. Second, it should also appear on the display screen during program start-up. Third, the notice of copyright should be displayed on the disk jacket. Failure to display the notice in all three locations could place your ownership of copyright at risk in some jurisdictions.

Formal registration of your copyright with the federal Copyright Office is not necessary, although it may be helpful in proving that you were the first originator of the material in the event of a later lawsuit. Many major programming shops are reluctant to register their copyright because major portions of source code must be provided to the registrar (and the registrar's records are open to the public!).

Trademarks

A trademark is simply a symbol (which can take the form of a mark, a logo, a name,

---

Fig. 8-1. The internationally-recognized copyright symbol, the mark of intellectual property ownership. The syntax "Copyright" and "All rights reserved" are necessary adjuncts.

or a phrase) under which business (trade) is conducted. Hence, "trademark" means business symbol. The logo "IBM," for example, is a trademark of International Business Machines Corporation. The product name "QuickBASIC" is a trademark of Microsoft Corporation.

Once it has been properly registered with the government, a trademark may only be used in the marketplace by the owner of the trademark. This legal convention ensures that consumers will not be duped by imitators who use identical or similar names, hoping to cash in upon the hard-won reputation of the trademark owner. The real value of a trademark resides, after all, in the *public goodwill* associated with the symbol.

You are free to use almost any trademark that is not being used by someone else, but your rights may be severely limited if you have not applied for formal registration of the trademark. This application is usually filed through your lawyer.

In some countries, you acquire rights to a trademark as soon as you begin to use the trademark in the marketplace. In England, for example, if you were the first to use the trademark, no one else can use it, even if you have not registered it. In the United States, however, it is necessary to formally register your trademark once you have started to use it in the marketplace. If you stop using your trademark in the marketplace, your competitors (or the trademark registrar) can apply to have your registration revoked.

Like a copyright, a trademark notice must accompany the symbol or phrase which it protects. The symbol illustrated in Fig. 8-2 is recognized in North America. The proper phrase to use in conjunction with the symbol is "Trademark" or "Registered Trademark."

Patents

Whereas a copyright protects intellectual property, a patent protects physical property. The design and method of operation of a computer part such as IBM's microchannel architecture is protected by a patent. There is nothing preventing competitors from using different means to achieve the same output, but they cannot use the means which are protected by the patent.

Patents are generally enforced by governments in order to allow manufacturers to recover the research and development costs associated with new inventions. As a graphics programmer, you will probably not need a patent.

Trade Secrets

If you are working with partners during the development of your program, you might want to protect your confidential information. This information is sometimes called *proprietary information* or *trade secrets*. It represents your expertise and your experience, often acquired at considerable time, effort, and expense. The law recognizes the value of trade secrets. Clearly, if you know something your competitors do not know, then you have a business advantage in the marketplace.

Fig. 8-2. Notices of a commercial trademark, as used in the USA. The syntax "Trademark" or "Registered Trademark" is often a necessary adjunct.

TM **®**

Your right to claim a trade secret disappears the instant that you make your proprietary information known to the public. Provided you have formally advised your partners or subcontractors that the information you are sharing with them is a trade secret, you can obtain legal recompense from them if they allow your trade secrets to become known to others.

Non-Disclosure Agreements

Propriety information is usually protected by using a non-disclosure agreement. A non-disclosure agreement is simply a civil contract whereby the other person promises not to disclose any confidential information which you provide while the two of you are cooperating on a particular project.

License Agreements

Nearly all commercial software is sold on the basis of a license agreement. Specifically, the user is buying the right to use the program, not ownership of the program itself.

A lot of software is sold using the shrinkwrap approach to licensing. In essence, the software distributor is saying that if you open the shrinkwrap of the package then you have accepted the terms of the license agreement. This approach to a legal contract is dubious at best, coercive at worst, and many software publishers include a formal license agreement inside the package which they ask you to sign and return to them under the flimsy guise of "registering" your package. There is, after all, nothing ambiguous about your signature on an agreement. It is interesting to note that musical recordings, whether LPs or cassettes, are not cluttered with such nuisances either on the shrinkwrap or inside the product itself.

Non-Competition Clauses

If you have hired programmers to help you develop your program, you might want to protect yourself from the unpleasant effects of your employees taking the knowledge you taught them and using that information to compete against you in the marketplace.

A non-competition agreement is a legally binding civil contract wherein the other party agrees not to compete directly against you for a reasonable period of time, say two years. Provided that you have in fact disclosed proprietary information to the employee or subcontracted programmer, the law recognizes such an agreement.

PROGRAMMERS' REMEDIES

As a programmer, there are a number of steps you can take during program development to help protect your rights. It is assumed, of course, that you have inserted copyright and trademark notices where appropriate, and that you have used either a compiler or assembly language to make your source code difficult to unravel.

Embedded Serial Numbers

First, you can use embedded serial numbers in your distribution disk. For example, if your original interactive graphics program can be used to save image files on disk, you might want to use a subroutine which includes the serial number of the distribution disk as part of the header for each image file created by the program. Some BASIC compilers seed the resulting runtime code with serial numbers. The one you are using probably does. One popular word processing program places the distribution disk's serial number into the documents created by the user.

Stonewalling

Second, you can pepper your code with INT 3. Normally, this interrupt is a do-nothing routine used by the Debug program provided on your DOS disk, but a number of professional debugging utilities also use this interrupt to set break-points during their debugging sessions. By planting plenty of INT 3s in your program, you can bog down the actions of any individual who wishes to browse through your code with a debug utility. You might find it interesting to use the Debug which came with your DOS to wander through some of the code generated by your favorite BASIC compiler. As you will see, the compiler distributor is playing hardball, even though the INT 3 stonewalling technique slows down runtime speed for the honest end-user.

Hidden Files

Third, you can use hidden files. By using assembly language, you can create files which the DOS copy commands cannot find. Often, a simple adjustment to the disk directory will suffice. By fragmenting the file across noncontiguous sectors on the disk, you can make it very difficult for the casual browser to piece together your source code. One popular word processing program loads the hidden file (which contains the runtime module) into high memory, merging it down into the low memory runtime code only after the copy protection and computer ID code have successfully executed.

Encrypted Files

Fourth, you can use the rotate instructions in assembly language to encrypt key portions of the files on your distribution disk. (*Advanced Assembly Language*, by Steven Holzer, provides explicit guidance. Refer to the bibliography at the end of this text.)

Serious Copy Protection

Fifth, you can purchase a copy protection system from a third-party developer. Expensive, nearly foolproof copy protection schemes involve laser-generated holes on the disk itself and/or a hardware plug that the end-user must attach to the back of the computer before the program will run. In the first case, your program checks to make certain that data is not there; in the second case, your program checks to ensure that data is there.

Other protection schemes are based upon the *weak bit theory*. Special recording equipment is used to encode weak bits on the distribution disk. These bits are not fully on and not fully off. Sometimes your computer will fail to read these bits and the software will hence fail to run. A reboot or two is all that is needed, of course, since the laws of chance assure that the computer will eventually read the ambiguous bit. However, because a disk copy function reads the bit only once (whereas the boot code might attempt to read the bit a dozen times), the chances of the disk being successfully copied are much reduced.

Some protection schemes involve the dynamic creation of batch files to load and run the necessary files. Others involve the dynamic renaming of files.

A BETTER WAY

When all is said and done, copy protection is a major inconvenience for the end-user. The end-user clearly needs a method for ensuring that back-ups of the program disk are readily available. This is because all media will fail sooner or later. Anything you do not have backed up, you will eventually lose.

As a prudent programmer, you might find it more businesslike to make your user's guide an essential part of using your program. After all, a thick user's guide is much more difficult to copy than a disk. This explains why so many popular programs insist on using non-intuitive keystroke combinations that keep you delving into the user's guide for help.

SUMMARY

In this chapter you learned about commercial distribution, shareware distribution, and freeware distribution. You explored the concepts of copyright, trademarks, trade secrets, and license agreements. You learned that a variety of methods are available to protect your original programs.

The next chapter discusses the keyboard and introduces techniques for managing the keyboard during runtime.

9

Managing The Keyboard

Your interactive graphics program should respond to the user's input by changing the image currently being displayed on the monitor. Likewise, the user can respond to that image by either accepting the display or by requesting further changes. Interactivity of high-performance graphics programs is a dynamic, reciprocal process. It is a two-way street.

An exciting variety of useful input devices is available for interacting with your programs. These include the keyboard, mouse, light pen, track balls, tablets, and touch-screens. This chapter focuses on interacting with the keyboard. Subsequent chapters address the other input devices.

KEYBOARD MANAGEMENT

The ability to manage the keyboard gives you a powerful tool in writing advanced graphics programs. It gives you the ability to develop smooth, seamless user interfaces for both graphics programs and non-graphics programs.

Managing the keyboard while an interactive graphics program is running presents a substantive programming challenge, even for professional programmers. A good keyboard routine is like a sieve, filtering out and discarding unacceptable keystrokes gracefully. A good keyboard routine is also like a net, effortlessly capturing keystrokes which fall within parameters of acceptance.

The conceptual structure which describes the physical interaction between end-user, keyboard, screen, and computer is often called the user interface. It is the user interface that shields the inner workings of your source code from the end-user. As you will learn in later chapters, there is often a significant difference between what is really happening in your program and what the end-user sees apparently happening on the display screen. In any case, the user often does not really want to know what algorithms are at work; he or she is usually interested only in results.

THE KEYBOARD BUFFER

The central utility which makes keyboard control possible is the keyboard buffer. Refer to Fig. 9-1. The keyboard buffer is sometimes called a *first-in first-out queue* (FIFO) or a *circular event queue*.

The hardware and the BIOS of your personal computer take care of capturing keystrokes while your program is running. As a key is struck, the microprocessor inside the keyboard itself generates a *scan code* and transmits this scan code to the microprocessor in the computer. The operating system (DOS) and BIOS work in concert to translate this scan code into an ASCII code.

Keystroke ASCII codes are stored in a buffer in low memory. This buffer is called the keyboard buffer, as illustrated in Fig. 9-1. Working on the first-in first-out principle, the buffer has enough room to store 15 keystrokes. The computer beeps if any additional keystrokes are generated after the keyboard buffer is full, and the additional keystrokes are discarded.

The first-in first-out principle means that if the user presses keys A-B-C-D-E, then the first key to be retrieved from the keyboard buffer will be A. If another key is struck by the user, it will be placed in the buffer after the E code. The next key to be retrieved from the keyboard buffer would, of course, be the B code.

Even special keys such as Enter, Alt, Ctrl, and Ins can be stored in the keyboard buffer. It is easy for the end-user to enter these special keys; simply use the keyboard. It is a bit trickier for the programmer to retrieve these special characters from the keyboard buffer. Fortunately, BASIC provides some powerful tools to help you manage the keyboard.

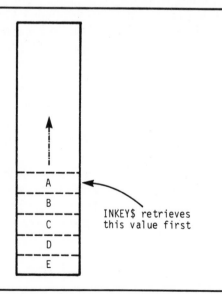

INKEY$ retrieves
this value first

Fig. 9-1. The keyboard buffer on IBM-compatible personal computers is a first-in, first-out queue capable of holding 15 keystrokes.

THE INKEY$ INSTRUCTION

The INKEY$ instruction in both interpreted BASIC and compiled BASIC will retrieve one keystroke from the keyboard buffer. When you use the instruction **K$=INKEY$**, for example, the top character in the keyboard buffer is assigned to the variable K$. It is at this specific point in your code that a keystroke is retrieved from the keyboard buffer. After this point you can use a variety of algorithms to determine the identity of the variable to which the keystroke has been assigned. The procedure occurs very quickly and can be used dynamically while your program is generating graphics output. (K$ is used arbitrarily here; you could use A$ or KEYSTROKE$ or any other string variable name.)

The most useful algorithm is the IF . . . THEN construct. The algorithm **K$=INKEY$:IF K$="A" THEN** . . . checks if the character A is present. This simple statement can be used to check for any standard uppercase character from A to Z, any standard lowercase character from a to z, any standard numerical character from 0 to 9, and other characters (such as =, +, (, ?, $, and so on). You could also check to determine if the spacebar was pressed by using the statement, **K$=INKEY$:IF K$=" " THEN** . . . provided that you place a space between the quotation marks.

THE PAUSE

If you want your program to pause while awaiting input from the user, there are a number of algorithms you can employ. The following example will pause until the user presses any key.

```
590 K$=INKEY$
600 IF K$="" THEN 590
```

Line 590 retrieves a keystroke from the keyboard buffer. Line 600 checks the identity of the keystroke. If it is *null* (i.e., no key has been struck), then the program loops back to line 590 and checks for another keystroke. Note that there is no space between the two sets of quotation marks. This loop continues until a non-null condition is encountered—a non-null condition being any keystroke, of course.

If you prefer to use WHILE . . . WEND constructs, you could accomplish the same effect with the following example:

```
590 K$=INKEY$:WHILE K$="":K$=INKEY$:WEND
```

If you want a specific key to be pressed before your program will continue, you might want to use the following algorithm:

```
590 K$=INKEY$
600 IF K$< >"G" THEN 590
```

In the above example, line 600 will loop back to line 590 if any keystroke other than G is found in the keyboard buffer.

HOW TO PURGE THE BUFFER

The INKEY$ instruction can also be used to empty the keyboard buffer. This is sometimes called *purging the buffer*. Unless you specifically retrieve keystrokes from the buffer, they will remain there (even after your program has ended!). An unexpected character in the keyboard buffer could send your program into an unexpected routine if the user has been striking the keyboard when you did not expect it. Unexpected characters in the keyboard buffer could produce illegal strings if your program is asking the user for input to create a file name.

To empty the keyboard buffer before you ask the user for input, you might use the following algorithm:

590 K$=INKEY$
600 IF K$< >"" THEN 590

In this example, line 600 will loop back to line 590 if it finds any character other than null in the keyboard buffer. In other words, it will keep retrieving characters from the keyboard buffer until the buffer is empty.

KEYSTROKE CONVENTIONS

Over the years, a number of keyboard conventions have become established in commercial software packages. Refer to Fig. 9-2.

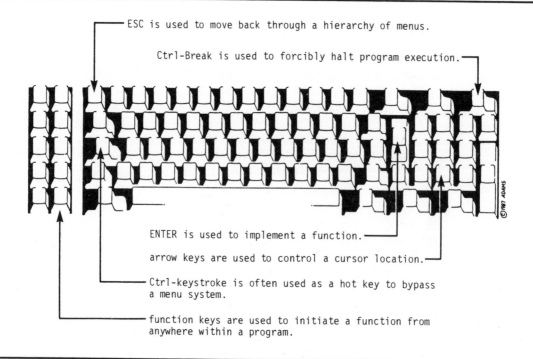

ESC is used to move back through a hierarchy of menus.

Ctrl-Break is used to forcibly halt program execution.

ENTER is used to implement a function.

arrow keys are used to control a cursor location.

Ctrl-keystroke is often used as a hot key to bypass a menu system.

function keys are used to initiate a function from anywhere within a program.

Fig. 9-2. Keyboard conventions.

Enter is often used to implement a command. Esc is often used to cancel a command or to discard a pull-down menu and return to the main menu bar (see the next chapter for more on this). The arrow keys are often used to control cursor movement. Interesting keystroke combinations such as Ctrl-A and others are often used to provide keyboard shortcuts (*hot keys*) which bypass normal multistep keyboard actions.

ASCII CHARACTER CODES

Keystrokes are stored in the keyboard buffer as ASCII character codes. The alphanumeric character A would be stored as ASCII character 75. In BASIC, you can code this as either ''A'' or CHR$(75) or CHR$(075).

The ability to reference characters by their ASCII codes is very helpful when dealing with special keystrokes. The following example checks for the Enter key:

600 K$=INKEY$:IF K$=CHR$(13) THEN . . .

The following example detects the Esc key:

600 K$=INKEY$:IF K$=CHR$(27) THEN . . .

The next example looks for the Backspace key:

600 K$=INKEY$:IF K$=CHR$(8) THEN . . .

The following example checks for the spacebar:

600 K$=INKEY$:IF K$=CHR$(32) THEN . . .

Here is how to look for the Tab key:

600 K$=INKEY$:IF K$=CHR$(9) THEN . . .

EXTENDED ASCII CODES

The keystroke combinations such as Ctrl-A and so on are comprised of not one, but two, ASCII codes (called *extended ASCII codes*). Refer to Fig. 9-3. Retrieving these keystroke combinations from the keyboard buffer is a two-step process. First, you must check to determine if the character string retrieved by INKEY$ is composed of one or two ASCII codes. Second, if two codes are present, you must determine the identity of the second code. The first ASCII code in a two-code string is normally CHR$(0).

By referring to Fig. 9-3, you can determine the extended ASCII codes for many useful keystroke combinations, including the arrow keys and function keys. Your BASIC manual also contains a table of single ASCII codes and extended ASCII codes. Using these advanced keystrokes in your original programs can introduce a flavor of real professionalism into your work.

Suppose you want to designate the keystroke combination of Alt-Q for a particular function in your program, perhaps as a hot key shortcut to the exit routine. Alt-Q is a

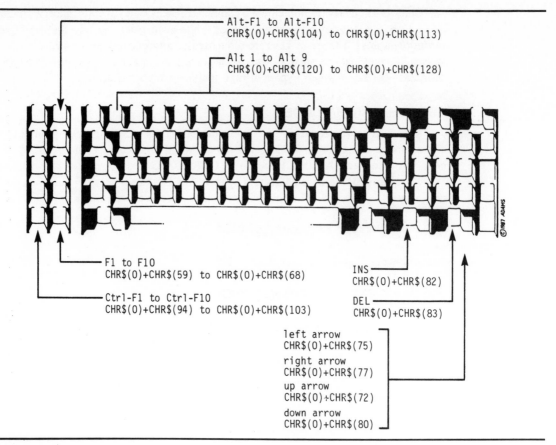

Fig. 9-3. Extended keyboard codes.

sensible choice of characters, because Q is intuitively associated with Quit, and because the two-key combination of Alt and Q is unlikely to be accidentally struck by the user.

If the Alt-Q keystroke combination were struck by the user, it would show up in the keyboard buffer as a two-character string composed of CHR$(0) and CHR$(16). To check for this set of ASCII codes in the buffer, you would first determine if a two-code character set is present by using the following algorithm:

```
580 K$=INKEY$
590 IF LEN(K$)=2 THEN K$=RIGHT$(K$,1)
```

Line 590 first checks the length of the K$ variable. If the length equals two, then the value of K$ is defined as the first offset into an array whose address is the location of the variable. This offset is the second component of the two-code ASCII set.

To determine the identity of this second ASCII code, you would then use the standard algorithm to check for the presence of Q:

```
600 IF K$=CHR$(16) THEN . . .
```

SAMPLE SOURCE CODE

The code fragment in Fig. 9-4 is an excerpt from *YOUR MICROCOMPUTER SKETCH PAD* in Chapter 17. Similar source code is employed in the drafting and 3D CAD demonstration programs. This code fragment illustrates the dynamic keyboard control of a roaming crosshair cursor during program runtime. The keyboard input controller provides a method for the user to control the movement of a crosshair cursor by using the arrow keys.

```
100 'Code fragment A-01.BAS   Keyboard input controller.
110 'Copyright (c) 1988 by Lee Adams and TAB Books Inc.
120 'All rights reserved.
130 '_____
140 '
150 'module:  interactive control of plastic polyline
160   SOUND 250,.7:VIEW SCREEN (J6,J7)-(J8,J9)  'clip canvas edges
170   PUT (SX,SY),A12,XOR  'install crosshair cursor
180   T6=0  'reset polyline flag
190   T3=0  'reset line flag
200   K$=INKEY$
210   IF LEN(K$)=2 THEN K$=RIGHT$(K$,1) ELSE 380
220   IF K$=CHR$(77) THEN PUT (SX,SY),A12,XOR:SX=SX+J ELSE 250
230   IF SX>XR THEN SX=XR:SOUND 250,.7
240   PUT (SX,SY),A12,XOR:GOTO 200
250   IF K$=CHR$(75) THEN PUT (SX,SY),A12,XOR:SX=SX-J ELSE 280
260   IF SX<XL THEN SX=XL:SOUND 250,.7
270   PUT (SX,SY),A12,XOR:GOTO 200
280   IF K$=CHR$(72) THEN PUT (SX,SY),A12,XOR:SY=SY-J ELSE 310
290   IF SY<YT THEN SY=YT:SOUND 250,.7
300   PUT (SX,SY),A12,XOR:GOTO 200
310   IF K$=CHR$(80) THEN PUT (SX,SY),A12,XOR:SY=SY+J ELSE 340
320   IF SY>YB THEN SY=YB:SOUND 250,.7
330   PUT (SX,SY),A12,XOR:GOTO 200
340   IF K$=CHR$(71) THEN PUT (SX,SY),A12,XOR:SX=85:SY=19:PUT (SX,SY),A12,XOR:GOT
0 200
350   IF K$=CHR$(73) THEN PUT (SX,SY),A12,XOR:SX=594:SY=19:PUT (SX,SY),A12,XOR:GO
TO 200
360   IF K$=CHR$(81) THEN PUT (SX,SY),A12,XOR:SX=594:SY=180:PUT (SX,SY),A12,XOR:G
OTO 200
370   IF K$=CHR$(79) THEN PUT (SX,SY),A12,XOR:SX=85:SY=180:PUT (SX,SY),A12,XOR:GO
TO 200
380   IF K$=CHR$(27) THEN PUT (SX,SY),A12,XOR:VIEW:SOUND 250,.7:RETURN  '<ESC>
390   IF K$=CHR$(13) THEN PUT (SX,SY),A12,XOR:GOSUB 420:PUT (SX,SY),A12,XOR ELSE
400   '<Enter> to implement command
400 GOTO 200
410 'submodule:  plastic polyline function
420   IF T6=0 THEN SXC=SX+7:SYC=SY+3:PSET (SXC,SYC),C:T6=1:SXP=SXC:SYP=SYC:RETURN
 ELSE 430
430   SXC=SX+7:SYC=SY+3:LINE (SXP,SYP)-(SXC,SYC),C:SXP=SXC:SYP=SYC:RETURN
440 '_____
450 '
460   END
```

Fig. 9-4. A code fragment which demonstrates keyboard control algorithms.

Line 200 starts the loop by retrieving a keystroke from the keyboard buffer. Line 210 checks to determine if the keystroke is an extended ASCII code (a two-code set). If so, program execution continues with line 220. If not, program flow jumps ahead to line 380 where single ASCII codes are inspected.

Line 220 checks for CHR$(77), which is the right arrow key. Refer to Fig. 9-3 for keystroke ASCII definitions. If CHR$(77) is found, then the crosshair cursor is moved one unit to the right by the SX=SX+J algorithm. If CHR$(77) is not found, then program flow immediately jumps to line 250, where the algorithm attempts to find CHR$(75), which is the left arrow key.

Although it is not necessary to fully understand the other graphics-related components in this code fragment at this point, you can readily see how lines 280 and 310 search for the up and down arrow keys. Lines 340, 350, 360, and 370 check for the diagonal arrow keys. Line 380 checks for the single ASCII code of Esc. Line 390 checks for the single ASCII code of Enter.

What is important about this code fragment is the logic flow. First, the program checks the length of the keystroke. If it is single, program execution jumps down to line 380, where only single ASCII codes are checked. When a particular keystroke has been found by the algorithm, program flow is cleanly rerouted back to the start of the keyboard loop.

It would be a serious mistake to simply let the program fall down through the code until it hits line 400, because of possible confusion between the values of second ASCII codes and single ASCII codes. Your program could easily misinterpret the identity of a code if it mistakenly assumed it was looking at the second part of an extended ASCII code when in fact it was inspecting only a single ASCII code.

USING THE KEYBOARD WITH OTHER INPUT DEVICES

As a graphics programmer, you can design your program to accept input from alternative devices, such as a mouse, for example. Two approaches can be used: first, your program can ask the user which input device is preferred, and then load a version of the program which supports only that device. (Overlay loading is described in Chapter 15 and Chapter 19). Alternatively, your source code can contain routines for both keyboard and mouse input. By setting a runtime flag during program start-up, you can control which input routine is to be used by checking the value of the flag during runtime. (Runtime flags are discussed in Chapter 3 and are used in the major drafting, paintbrush, and 3D CAD demonstration programs in this book.)

HOT KEYS

Hot keys are keystroke shortcuts to activate functions from any location within your program. Two methods are available to you to incorporate hot keys into your original interactive graphics programs. Both methods are used in the major drafting, paintbrush, and 3D CAD demonstration programs in this book.

First Method

You can use the standard **K$=INKEY$:IF K$=** . . . **THEN** algorithm to check for the presence of the hot key in the keyboard buffer. This approach involves two drawbacks. First, you must insert the IF . . . THEN code, or at least a GOSUB to jump to the subroutine containing the IF . . . THEN code, into many locations throughout your program. Second, if other keystrokes are already present in the keyboard buffer, the hot key character will not be retrieved until after the other keystrokes have been retrieved. This delay might be unacceptable.

Second Method

By using the ON KEY instruction in BASIC, you can automatically check for a hot key after each and every instruction is executed by the computer. The instruction **ON KEY(2) GOSUB 1000:KEY(2) ON** would cause the program to jump to a subroutine at line 1000 if key F2 is pressed at any point during runtime.

The ON KEY technique is easy to code and makes it possible to invoke a hot key routine at literally any point during program execution. The disadvantage is that runtime performance is slower by a substantial factor, which is especially critical during interactive graphics programs using graphics cursors.

STRINGS

The INKEY$ instruction in BASIC can also be used to accept string input, such as names for files, and so on. Although the INPUT$ instruction accepts whole strings, it is extremely difficult to trap errors gracefully using INPUT$. By accepting strings one character at a time using INKEY$, you can exercise precise control over the user's input and can trap errors with your own messages.

Chapter 13 provides a code fragment which demonstrates file name manipulation by accepting input from the keyboard. Also refer to each of the major drafting, paintbrush, and 3D CAD demonstration programs for examples of source code to handle changing file names caused by user input.

SUMMARY

In this chapter you learned how to accept input from the user via the keyboard. You saw how to use professional-looking keystrokes such as Ctrl-Q, Alt-A, function keys, and others.

The next chapter discusses techniques for managing the display screen.

10

Managing the Screen: Menu Systems

A vital part of the user interface is the display screen. Because the video display usually represents the computer's primary method of providing feedback to the user, efficient techniques for managing the screen are useful for writing high-performance interactive graphics programs.

The major demonstration programs in this book use a screen management system composed of pull-down menus. Refer to Fig. 10-1. This approach to managing the screen provides uniform visual cues to the user. In addition, it is easy to organize the program's functions into logical groups by simply placing the function's routine under the control of a particular pull-down menu.

MENU SYSTEMS

In addition to menu systems which utilize pull-down menus, as a graphics programmer you can opt to use pop-up menus. *Pull-down menus* are so named because they are written onto the screen in a location which makes it appear as if they had been pulled down from the top of the screen. As Fig. 10-1 shows, a main menu bar across the top of the screen provides the cursor choices which activate particular pull-down menus.

Pop-up menus, on the other hand, are written onto the screen in a location unconnected with other graphics. Pop-up menus appear to pop up onto the screen. As a graphics programmer, you can arbitrarily select the location where your pop-up menus appear.

Both pull-down menus and pop-up menus use the same programming logic: bitblt graphics. Nested menus, illustrated by Fig. 10-3, are simply a combination of pull-down menus and pop-up menus. Program logic makes it necessary to pass through one menu

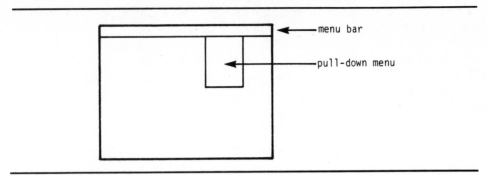

Fig. 10-1. Pull-down menu.

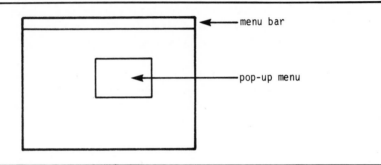

Fig. 10-2. Pop-up menu.

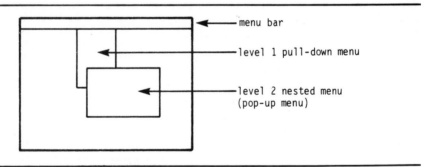

Fig. 10-3. Nested menus.

before reaching a secondary menu. The secondary menu is, in effect, one of the choices available for selection from the earlier menu.

BITBLT GRAPHICS

Bitblt is an acronym for *bit b*oundary *bl*ock *t*ransfer. Other names for this programming technique are *graphic arrays* and *sprites*.

Bitblt is the driving force behind pull-down menus for graphics programs. By saving the menu's image in a graphic array, the menu can be installed on the screen at any time by merely writing the graphic array onto the screen. If you have taken the precaution of saving the previously existing screen, you can easily erase the menu by simply restoring the previous screen.

If you are using interpreted BASIC or compiled BASIC to write your interactive graphics programs, you can use either of two techniques to manage your menu system—which is, in effect, the same as managing the screen. Broadly speaking, these two approaches are the bitblt technique and the page technique.

BITBLT-DRIVEN MENUS

Figure 10-4 shows the bitblt technique for controlling pull-down menus. First, the portion of the screen where the menu will be displayed is saved as a graphic array in memory. This image will be needed when the time comes to restore the original graphics on the screen. Second, the menu is placed on the screen. In this book, the menu graphics are created and saved in graphic arrays during program start-up. In programs which are intended for distribution, it would be wiser to store the menu graphics as binary image files on disk, ready for downloading at program start-up. (Chapter 13 discusses binary image files.)

At this stage, your program is free to permit the user to scroll a cursor within the confines of the pull-down menu, perhaps selecting choices. When the time comes to erase the pull-down menu, the graphic array containing the original graphics for that portion of the screen is simply written back to its original location, thereby overwriting the pull-down menu.

This technique is especially quick for the 640x200 two-color mode. Runtime performance drops a little as additional colors are used, because of the larger number of bytes which must be written to the screen in the 640x200 16-color screen, for example. (The memory requirements of different multibit-per-pixel screen modes are discussed in Chapter 2.)

Because graphic arrays are stored inside the BASIC workspace (which is limited to 64K), programs which require large menu systems are better off using a page-driven approach.

PAGE-DRIVEN MENUS

Figure 10-5 shows the concepts used in page-driven pull-down menus. This approach is especially useful when the graphics adapter being used is an EGA or a VGA, both of which offer multiple graphics pages. Conversely, bitblt-driven pull-down menus are especially suited to the CGA and MCGA, where only one graphics page is normally available on the graphics card.

As Fig. 10-5 illustrates, the original screen graphics are saved in their entirety by copying them into a separate graphics page. (In BASIC this is accomplished with the PCOPY instruction.) Next, the graphic array containing the pull-down menu is written onto the screen in the appropriate location. After the user has made a selection, the pull-down menu is disposed of by simply copying the contents of the hidden graphics page back into the visible graphics page.

The main advantage of the page-driven approach is its simplicity. Because the entire screen is saved no matter which pull-down menu is to be invoked, writing the program is a little easier. Surprisingly, the size of the image to be saved is not a critical factor

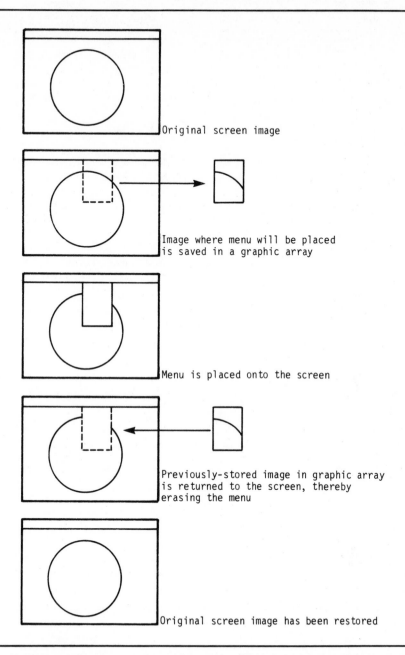

Original screen image

Image where menu will be placed
is saved in a graphic array

Menu is placed onto the screen

Previously-stored image in graphic array
is returned to the screen, thereby
erasing the menu

Original screen image has been restored

Fig. 10-4. The bitblt technique for managing a menu system. Bitblt is the same as graphic array and block graphics.

from a performance point of view, because the bit map address calculations necessary to save a rectangular graphic array often mean that an entire screen can be copied to a hidden page just as quickly as a small graphic array can be saved into memory.

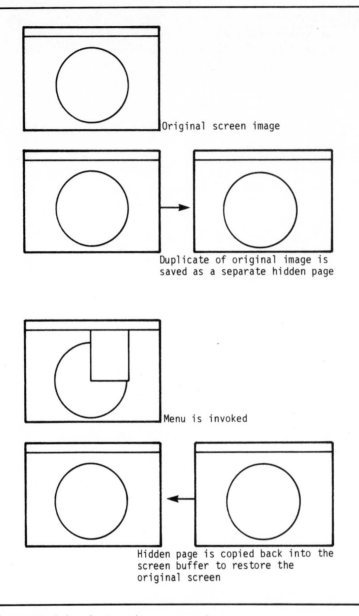

Original screen image

Duplicate of original image is
saved as a separate hidden page

Menu is invoked

Hidden page is copied back into the
screen buffer to restore the
original screen

Fig. 10-5. The page technique for managing a menu system.

SCREEN DESIGN

A logical, orderly screen design is an essential ingredient of a properly managed screen, especially in a menu system. Usually, the screen continually displays the program's title, the current file name, and a main menu bar. Refer to Fig. 10-6.

By moving a *panning cursor* across the main menu bar, the user can choose which pull-down menu is to be displayed. The panning cursor is usually designed so that it wraps

Fig. 10-6. Menu manager user interface.

around onto the other end of the menu bar rather than forcing the user to ''ping pong'' back and forth when either end is reached.

The Enter key is usually used to call up a menu. Refer to Fig. 10-7. The pull-down menu is customarily written to the screen just beneath its namesake on the menu bar. A cursor which scrolls up and down is used to give the user the power to make choices from the pull-down menu. When a mouse is used instead of the keyboard, the user employs a point-and-shoot technique rather than scrolling with a cursor.

CURSOR DESIGN

As a graphics programmer, you can use your judgment in designing the panning cursor, the scrolling cursor, and the roaming cursor. A *panning cursor* usually exhibits only horizontal left-right movement. A *scrolling cursor* normally only moves vertically: up and down. A *roaming cursor* can move in any direction, including diagonally.

The cursor which is used to control the graphics (lines, curves, etc.) on the screen is often a crosshair cursor. Refer to Fig. 10-8. Other popular styles include a gunsight, solid arrow, simulated pencil, rectangle, and an alphanumeric greater-than arrow. You

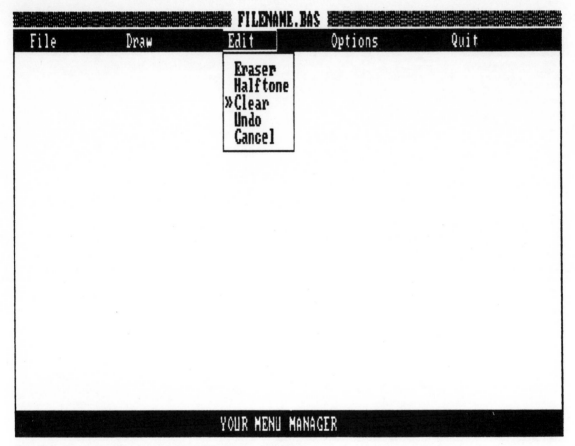

Fig. 10-7. A typical editing menu in a menu manager interface.

can easily change the cursors in the drafting, paintbrush, and 3D CAD demonstration programs in this book to suit your own preferences.

In general, the smaller the cursor, the better the runtime performance. Cursors are implemented by writing and erasing small graphic arrays to and from the display screen. The smaller the graphic array, the faster the action can occur.

MENU DESIGN

A wide range of design options can be applied to menu arrangement. Most menu systems use vertical lists of options, which have been shown to be more easily absorbed by the user than horizontal lists. The pull-down menu manager used throughout this book uses the vertical list approach.

The selections contained in a pull-down menu can be portrayed by alphanumeric characters or by stylized icons. The CADD drafting program and the paintbrush program in this book demonstrate on-screen icons. The 3D CAD programs in the book use only alphanumeric-based pull-down menus.

A menu which requires a string input from the user is often called a *dialog box*. If, for example, you want the user to provide a file name, you would likely use a dialog box

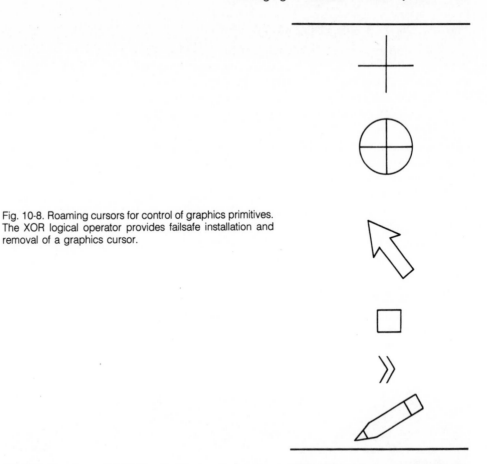

Fig. 10-8. Roaming cursors for control of graphics primitives. The XOR logical operator provides failsafe installation and removal of a graphics cursor.

like the function used by the drafting, paintbrush, and 3D CAD programs in this book. A dialog box usually displays the characters as the user is entering them on the keyboard.

AUDITORY CUES

Sound is a helpful adjunct to a properly controlled menu system. If the user presses an illegal key, for example, a short beep should be used to provide immediate feedback. You may also decide to use a beep to provide feedback when a particular function does not provide obvious graphic feedback on the display screen. As you will later see, the major demonstration programs in this box announce the successful completion of an image file save to disk with a short chirp.

POLLED TRACKING

Once a pull-down menu has been invoked, the program normally enters a loop while it awaits the user's input. The program keeps checking and rechecking the keyboard buffer (or mouse driver) to see if a selection has been made or if the scrolling cursor is to be moved. This looping procedure is called polled tracking. Many third-party graphics libraries, such as MetaWINDOWS from MetaGraphics Software, can perform other graphics tasks while they are in the polled tracking loop.

MENU CONTROL VS. PROGRAM CONTROL

It is important to realize that controlling the menu is a task separate from controlling the program's assorted graphics functions. The menu system is a switchpoint. It accepts the user's input and calls the appropriate subroutines to perform the desired functions. The core functions are those substantive functions which give the program its reason for being. The interface functions are merely part of the method for the user to access the core functions.

A properly designed menu system can be run as an independent entity, as the demonstration program in this chapter shows. This independence is an important quality, because you can use the same generic menu system to control programs which produce entirely different graphic results. By simply changing the itemized contents inside each pull-down menu, you have a new user interface, without the necessity of recoding the entire menu system.

A menu system can be visualized as a program driver. In essence, the user drives the menu system. The menu system then in turn drives the program.

DEMONSTRATION PROGRAM: MENU MANAGER

The photograph in Fig. 10-9 illustrates the video output of the demonstration program. The photograph in Fig. 10-10 shows the program in action.

Two demonstration programs are provided in this chapter to demonstrate menu management techniques on your personal computer. The program listing in Fig. 10-11

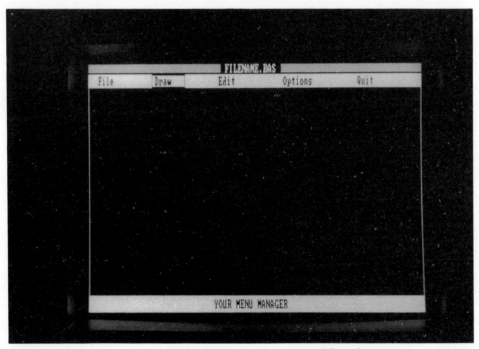

Fig. 10-9. The display image produced by the user interface provided by the demonstration program listing in Fig. 10-11 and Fig. 10-12. The panning cursor on the menu bar can be moved with the left-arrow and right-arrow keys.

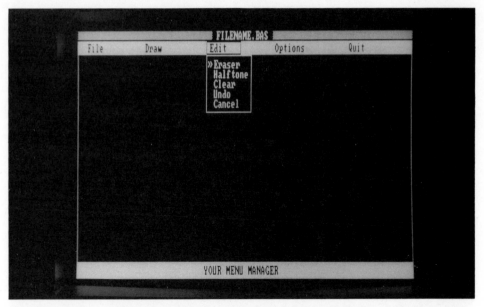

Fig. 10-10. The display image generated by the demonstration program listing in Fig. 10-11 and Fig. 10-12. Pressing <Enter> will invoke the pull-down menu which corresponds to the location of the panning cursor. The scrolling cursor in the pull-down menu can be moved with the arrow-down key.

is intended for use with an EGA or a VGA. The program listing in Fig. 10-12 is for a personal computer using a CGA or an MCGA (although it will also run with an EGA or VGA). If you are using the companion disk to this book, (see the last page for ordering information) you can run the appropriate program by entering **LOAD MENU.BAS,R** if you are using an EGA or VGA. Enter **LOAD MENU-CGA.BAS,R** if you are using a CGA or MCGA. (If you are using a PCjr, use **LOAD MENU-CGA.BAS,R**.)

MENU.BAS utilizes the page approach to pull-down menu management, because multiple graphics pages are available on both EGAs and VGAs using the 640x200 16-color mode. MENU-CGA.BAS uses the bitblt approach to menu management, because only one graphics page is available on a CGA or MCGA using the 640x200 2-color mode.

Program Compatibility

Both program listings use the same line numbers. The substantive difference between the programs can best be illustrated by line 1010. In MENU.BAS, the existing screen graphics are saved by the PCOPY instruction. In MENU-CGA.BAS, the existing screen graphics are saved by the GET instruction. The PCOPY instruction uses the page-driven approach; the GET instruction uses the bitblt-driven approach to pull-down menus.

Using the Program

The menu manager program is intuitive in design. Simply press the left-arrow and right-arrow keys to move the menu bar cursor to the left or to the right. Then press Enter to activate a pull-down menu.

```
100 'Program MENU.BAS:  a pull-down menu manager
110 'Copyright (c) 1987 by Lee Adams and TAB Books Inc.
120 'All rights reserved.
130 'This program demonstrates a menu bar with panning cursor and pull-down menu
s with scrolling cursors.
140 'EGA version.  640x200 16-color mode.
150 '_____     _._____
160 '
170  KEY OFF:CLS:CLEAR:SCREEN 0,0,0,0:WIDTH 80:COLOR 7,0,0:CLS:LOCATE 10,20,0:PR
INT "Assigning memory space for graphic arrays"
180 '_____  _____
190 '
200 'module:  data assignments
210  DEFINT A,C,T
220  DIM A1(325):DIM A2(150):DIM A3(150):DIM A4(150):DIM A5(150):DIM A6(150)  't
emporary arrays for screen template
230  DIM A7(177)  'array for panning cursor
240  DIM A8(1121)  'array for Quit menu
250  DIM A9(21)  'array for scrolling cursor
260  DIM A10(969)  'array for File menu
270  DIM A13(1035)  'array for Edit menu
280  DIM A14(2131)  'array for Options menu
290  C0=1:C1=2:C2=9:C3=7:C4=11:C5=5:C6=6:C7=4:C8=8:C9=3:C10=10:C12=12:C13=13:C14
=14:C15=15  'software color codes
300  T1=2  'selection flag for menu bar
310  T8=1  'selection flag for menus
320 '_____
330 '
340 'module:  set up runtime environment
350  CLS:SCREEN 8,,0,0:COLOR C7,0:CLS  '640x200 16-clr mode
360  PALETTE 1,0:PALETTE 2,1:PALETTE 3,9:PALETTE 4,7:PALETTE 5,5:PALETTE 6,6:PAL
ETTE 7,3:PALETTE 8,8:PALETTE 9,2:PALETTE 10,10:PALETTE 11,4:PALETTE 12,12:PALETT
E 13,13:PALETTE 14,14:PALETTE 15,15
370  ON KEY(2) GOSUB 2500:KEY(2) ON  'install hot key
380  COLOR,0  'restore hardware color for background
390 '_____
400 '
410 'module:  set up screen template
420  GOSUB 2070  'save alphanumeric graphic arrays
430  GOSUB 2220  'create pull-down menus
440  LINE (0,8)-(639,199),C8,B  'border
450  LINE (0,187)-(639,187),C8:PAINT (320,190),C8,C8:PUT (240,189),A1,OR  'banne
r
460  LINE (0,0)-(639,6),C1,B:PAINT (320,3),C1,C1:LOCATE 1,33:PRINT " FILENAME.BA
S "  'filename bar
470  LINE (1,8)-(639,18),C8,B:PAINT (320,10),C8,C8  'menu bar
480  PUT (18,9),A2,OR:PUT (130,9),A3,OR:PUT (250,9),A4,OR:PUT (370,9),A5,OR:PUT
(510,9),A6,OR  'selections for menu bar
490  LOCATE 10,19:PRINT "Reclaiming memory used by temporary arrays":ERASE A1,A2
,A3,A4,A5,A6  'free up array memory
500  LOCATE 10,19:PRINT "                                                      "
```

Fig. 10-11. Complete source code for a fully-interactive, keyboard-controlled, menu-driven program manager. This version is for the EGA and VGA.

```
510   PUT (126,8),A7,XOR  'panning cursor for menu bar
520   PCOPY 0,1  'establish refresh buffer
530   LOCATE 9,33:COLOR C12:PRINT "SAMPLE MENU MANAGER":LOCATE 12,25:COLOR C7:PRI
NT "Copyright (c) 1987 by Lee Adams and":LOCATE 13,25:PRINT "TAB Books Inc.  All
 rights reserved."
540   LINE (212,60)-(450,60),C12:LINE (212,74)-(450,74),C12
550   COLOR C15:LOCATE 19,29:PRINT "Press <Enter> to continue...":SOUND 250,.7:CO
LOR C7
560   K$=INKEY$:IF K$<>CHR$(13) THEN 560  'wait for <Enter>
570   PCOPY 1,0:SOUND 250,.7:GOTO 610
580   '_____
590   '
600   'main module:  interactive control of menu bar
610   K$=INKEY$
620   IF LEN(K$)=2 THEN K$=RIGHT$(K$,1) ELSE 660
630   IF K$=CHR$(77) THEN T1=T1+1:GOSUB 720:GOTO 610
640   IF K$=CHR$(75) THEN T1=T1-1:GOSUB 820:GOTO 610
650   IF K$=CHR$(16) THEN GOSUB 2500  'Alt-Q to quit
660   IF K$=CHR$(13) THEN GOSUB 920  '<Enter> key
670   GOTO 610
680   GOTO 680  'bulletproof code barrier
690   '_____
700   '
710   'module:  pan right on menu bar
720   IF T1>5 THEN T1=1
730   ON T1 GOTO 740,750,760,770,780
740   PUT (506,8),A7,XOR:PUT (14,8),A7,XOR:RETURN  'File
750   PUT (14,8),A7,XOR:PUT (126,8),A7,XOR:RETURN  'Draw
760   PUT (126,8),A7,XOR:PUT (246,8),A7,XOR:RETURN  'Edit
770   PUT (246,8),A7,XOR:PUT (366,8),A7,XOR:RETURN  'Options
780   PUT (366,8),A7,XOR:PUT (506,8),A7,XOR:RETURN  'Quit
790   '_____
800   '
810   'module:  pan left on menu bar
820   IF T1<1 THEN T1=5
830   ON T1 GOTO 840,850,860,870,880
840   PUT (126,8),A7,XOR:PUT (14,8),A7,XOR:RETURN  'File
850   PUT (246,8),A7,XOR:PUT (126,8),A7,XOR:RETURN  'Draw
860   PUT (366,8),A7,XOR:PUT (246,8),A7,XOR:RETURN  'Edit
870   PUT (506,8),A7,XOR:PUT (366,8),A7,XOR:RETURN  'Options
880   PUT (14,8),A7,XOR:PUT (506,8),A7,XOR:RETURN  'Quit
890   '_____
900   '
910   'module:  execute menu bar choices
920   ON T1 GOTO 930,940,950,960,970
930   GOSUB 1240:RETURN  'invoke File menu
940   SOUND 250,.7:RETURN  'invoke on-screen Draw menu
950   GOSUB 1490:RETURN  'invoke Edit menu
960   GOSUB 1750:RETURN  'invoke Options menu
970   GOSUB 1010:RETURN  'invoke Quit menu
980   '_____
990   '
1000 'module:  interactive control of Quit menu
```

Fig. 10-11. (Continued from page 92.)

```
1010   PCOPY 0,1  'save existing graphics
1020   PUT (505,19),A8,PSET  'place menu on screen
1030   PUT (507,25),A9,XOR  'place cursor >> on menu
1040   T8=1  'reset flag
1050   K$=INKEY$
1060   IF LEN(K$)=2 THEN K$=RIGHT$(K$,1) ELSE 1130
1070   IF K$=CHR$(80) THEN T8=T8+1:GOTO 1080 ELSE 1050
1080   IF T8>3 THEN T8=1
1090   ON T8 GOTO 1100,1110,1120
1100   PUT (507,41),A9,XOR:PUT (507,25),A9,XOR:GOTO 1050   'Quit
1110   PUT (507,25),A9,XOR:PUT (507,33),A9,XOR:GOTO 1050   'Save and quit
1120   PUT (507,33),A9,XOR:PUT (507,41),A9,XOR:GOTO 1050   'Cancel
1130   IF K$=CHR$(13) THEN 1160  '<Enter> to implement
1140   IF K$=CHR$(27) THEN 1200  '<ESC> to cancel
1150   GOTO 1050
1160   ON T8 GOTO 1170,1180,1190
1170   GOTO 2500  'implement quit
1180   SOUND 250,.7:GOTO 1050  'implement save and quit
1190   PCOPY 1,0:RETURN  'implement cancel
1200   PCOPY 1,0:RETURN  'restore previous graphics and return to menu bar level
1210   '_____
1220   '
1230   'module:  interactive control of File menu
1240   PCOPY 0,1  'save existing graphics
1250   PUT (14,19),A10,PSET  'place menu on screen
1260   PUT (16,25),A9,XOR  'place cursor >> on menu
1270   T8=1  'reset flag
1280   K$=INKEY$
1290   IF LEN(K$)=2 THEN K$=RIGHT$(K$,1) ELSE 1370
1300   IF K$=CHR$(80) THEN T8=T8+1:GOTO 1310 ELSE 1280
1310   IF T8>4 THEN T8=1
1320   ON T8 GOTO 1330,1340,1350,1360
1330   PUT (16,49),A9,XOR:PUT (16,25),A9,XOR:GOTO 1280 'Save
1340   PUT (16,25),A9,XOR:PUT (16,33),A9,XOR:GOTO 1280 'Load
1350   PUT (16,33),A9,XOR:PUT (16,41),A9,XOR:GOTO 1280 'Name
1360   PUT (16,41),A9,XOR:PUT (16,49),A9,XOR:GOTO 1280  'Cancel
1370   IF K$=CHR$(13) THEN 1400  '<Enter> to implement
1380   IF K$=CHR$(27) THEN 1450  '<ESC> to cancel
1390   GOTO 1280
1400   ON T8 GOTO 1410,1420,1430,1440
1410   SOUND 250,.7:GOTO 1280  'implement save
1420   SOUND 250,.7:GOTO 1280  'implement load
1430   SOUND 250,.7:GOTO 1280  'implement name change
1440   PCOPY 1,0:RETURN  'implement cancel
1450   PCOPY 1,0:RETURN  'restore previous graphics and return to menu bar level
1460   '_____
1470   '
1480   'module:  interactive control of Edit menu
1490   PCOPY 0,1  'save existing graphics
1500   PUT (246,19),A13,PSET  'place menu on screen
1510   PUT (248,24),A9,XOR  'place cursor >> on menu
1520   T8=1  'reset flag
1530   K$=INKEY$
```

Fig. 10-11. (Continued from page 93.)

```
1540   IF LEN(K$)=2 THEN K$=RIGHT$(K$,1) ELSE 1630
1550   IF K$=CHR$(80) THEN T8=T8+1:GOTO 1560 ELSE 1530
1560   IF T8>5 THEN T8=1
1570   ON T8 GOTO 1580,1590,1600,1610,1620
1580   PUT (248,56),A9,XOR:PUT (248,24),A9,XOR:GOTO 1530 'Eraser
1590   PUT (248,24),A9,XOR:PUT (248,32),A9,XOR:GOTO 1530 'Halftone
1600   PUT (248,32),A9,XOR:PUT (248,40),A9,XOR:GOTO 1530 'Clear
1610   PUT (248,40),A9,XOR:PUT (248,48),A9,XOR:GOTO 1530 'Undo
1620   PUT (248,48),A9,XOR:PUT (248,56),A9,XOR:GOTO 1530 'Cancel
1630   IF K$=CHR$(13) THEN 1660  '<Enter> to implement
1640   IF K$=CHR$(27) THEN 1710  '<ESC> to cancel
1650   GOTO 1530
1660   ON T8 GOTO 1670,1680,1690,1700,1710
1670   SOUND 250,.7:GOTO 1530  'implement eraser
1680   SOUND 250,.7:GOTO 1530  'implement halftone
1690   SOUND 250,.7:GOTO 1530  'implement clear
1700   SOUND 250,.7:GOTO 1530  'implement undo
1710   PCOPY 1,0:RETURN  'implement cancel
1720   '_____
1730   '
1740   'module:  interactive control of Options menu
1750   PCOPY 0,1 'save existing graphics
1760   PUT (366,19),A14,PSET  'place menu on screen
1770   PUT (368,24),A9,XOR  'place cursor >> on menu
1780   T8=1  'reset flag
1790   K$=INKEY$
1800   IF LEN(K$)=2 THEN K$=RIGHT$(K$,1) ELSE 1920
1810   IF K$=CHR$(80) THEN T8=T8+1:GOTO 1820 ELSE 1790
1820   IF T8>8 THEN T8=1
1830   ON T8 GOTO 1840,1850,1860,1870,1880,1890,1900,1910
1840   PUT (368,80),A9,XOR:PUT (368,24),A9,XOR:GOTO 1790 'Active color
1850   PUT (368,24),A9,XOR:PUT (368,32),A9,XOR:GOTO 1790 'Fill color
1860   PUT (368,32),A9,XOR:PUT (368,40),A9,XOR:GOTO 1790 'Brush color
1870   PUT (368,40),A9,XOR:PUT (368,48),A9,XOR:GOTO 1790 'Halftone %
1880   PUT (368,48),A9,XOR:PUT (368,56),A9,XOR:GOTO 1790 'Boundary
1890   PUT (368,56),A9,XOR:PUT (368,64),A9,XOR:GOTO 1790 'Snap +/-
1900   PUT (368,64),A9,XOR:PUT (368,72),A9,XOR:GOTO 1790 'Brush +/-
1910   PUT (368,72),A9,XOR:PUT (368,80),A9,XOR:GOTO 1790 'Cancel
1920   IF K$=CHR$(13) THEN 1950  '<Enter> to implement
1930   IF K$=CHR$(27) THEN 2030  '<ESC> to cancel
1940   GOTO 1790
1950   ON T8 GOTO 1960,1970,1980,1990,2000,2010,2020,2030
1960   SOUND 250,.7:GOTO 1790  'change active color
1970   SOUND 250,.7:GOTO 1790  'change fill color
1980   SOUND 250,.7:GOTO 1790  'change brush color
1990   SOUND 250,.7:GOTO 1790  'change halftone %
2000   SOUND 250,.7:GOTO 1790  'change boundary color
2010   SOUND 250,.7:GOTO 1790  'implement snap +/-
2020   SOUND 250,.7:GOTO 1790  'implement brush +/-
2030   PCOPY 1,0:RETURN  'implement cancel
2040   '_____
2050   '
```

Fig. 10-11. (Continued from page 94.)

```
2060 'module: create alpha arrays for screen template
2070   COLOR C15:LOCATE 10,20:PRINT "YOUR MENU MANAGER"
2080   GET (150,71)-(290,79),A1:LOCATE 10,20:PRINT "
     "
2090   LOCATE 10,20:PRINT "File":GET (150,71)-(210,79),A2
2100   LOCATE 10,20:PRINT "Draw":GET (150,71)-(210,79),A3
2110   LOCATE 10,20:PRINT "Edit":GET (150,71)-(210,79),A4
2120   LOCATE 10,20:PRINT "Options":GET (150,71)-(210,79),A5
2130   LOCATE 10,20:PRINT "Quit   ":GET (150,71)-(210,79),A6
2140   COLOR C7:LOCATE 10,20:PRINT "         "
2150   LINE (150,70)-(212,80),C3,B:GET (150,70)-(212,80),A7   'create panning curs
or for menu bar
2160   LINE (150,70)-(212,80),0,B
2170   RETURN
2180 '_____
2190 '
2200 'module:  create pull-down menus
2210 'submodule:  create Quit menu
2220   COLOR C12:LOCATE 10,20:PRINT "Quit":LOCATE 11,20:PRINT "Save and quit":LOC
ATE 12,20:PRINT "Cancel":COLOR C7
2230   LINE (138,67)-(264,101),C7,B
2240   GET (138,67)-(264,101),A8:PAINT (200,70),C2,C7:PAINT (200,70),0,C7:LINE (1
38,67)-(264,101),0,B   'save Quit menu
2250   LOCATE 10,20:COLOR C15:PRINT CHR$(175):COLOR C7   'menu cursor >>
2260   GET (151,73)-(159,77),A9:LOCATE 10,20:PRINT " "
2270 '
2280 '_____
2290 'submodule:  create File menu
2300   COLOR C12:LOCATE 10,20:PRINT "Save":LOCATE 11,20:PRINT "Load":LOCATE 12,20
:PRINT "Name":LOCATE 13,20:PRINT "Cancel":COLOR C7
2310   LINE (138,67)-(220,110),C7,B
2320   GET (138,67)-(220,110),A10:PAINT (200,70),C2,C7:PAINT (200,70),0,C7:LINE (
138,67)-(220,110),0,B  'save File menu
2330 '
2340 '_____
2350 'submodule:  create Edit menu
2360   COLOR C12:LOCATE 4,20:PRINT "Eraser":LOCATE 5,20:PRINT "Halftone":LOCATE 6
,20:PRINT "Clear":LOCATE 7,20:PRINT "Undo":LOCATE 8,20:PRINT "Cancel"
2370   LINE (138,20)-(220,66),C7,B
2380   GET (138,20)-(220,66),A13:PAINT (200,30),C2,C7:PAINT (200,30),0,C7:LINE (1
38,20)-(220,66),0,B   'save Edit menu
2390 '_____
2400 '
2410 'submodule:  create Options menu
2420   LOCATE 4,20:PRINT "Active color":LOCATE 5,20:PRINT "Fill color":LOCATE 6,2
0:PRINT "Brush color":LOCATE 7,20:PRINT "Halftone %":LOCATE 8,20:PRINT "Boundary
":LOCATE 9,20:PRINT "Snap +/-":LOCATE 10,20:PRINT "Brush +/-"
2430   LOCATE 11,20:PRINT "Cancel"
2440   LINE (138,20)-(254,90),C7,B
2450   GET (138,20)-(254,90),A14:PAINT (200,30),C2,C7:PAINT (200,30),0,C7:LINE (1
38,20)-(254,90),0,B:COLOR C7   'save Options menu
2460   RETURN
2470 '_____
```

Fig. 10-11. (Continued from page 95.)

```
2480 '
2490 'module:  exit routine
2500  CLS:SCREEN 0,0,0,0:WIDTH 80:COLOR 7,0,0:CLS:LOCATE 1,1,1:COLOR 2:PRINT "YO
UR MENU MANAGER":LOCATE 2,1:PRINT "is finished.":COLOR 7:SOUND 250,.7:END
2510 '_____
2520 '
2530  END 'of menu manager
```

Fig. 10-11. (Continued from page 96.)

```
100 'Program MENU-CGA.BAS:  a pull-down menu manager
110 'Copyright (c) 1987 by Lee Adams and TAB Books Inc.
120 'All rights reserved.
130 'This program demonstrates a menu bar with panning cursor and pull-down menu
s with scrolling cursors.
140 'CGA version.  640x200 2-color mode.
150 '_____
160 '
170  KEY OFF:CLS:CLEAR:SCREEN 0,0,0,0:WIDTH 80:COLOR 7,0,0:CLS:LOCATE 10,20,0:PR
INT "Assigning memory space for graphic arrays"
180 '_____
190 '
200 'module:  data assignments
210  DEFINT A,C,T,J
220  DIM A1(82):DIM A2(37):DIM A3(37):DIM A4(37):DIM A5(37):DIM A6(37)  'tempora
ry arrays for screen template
230  DIM A7(45)  'array for panning cursor
240  DIM A8(281)  'array for Quit menu
250  DIM A9(6)  'array for scrolling cursor
260  DIM A10(243)  'array for File menu
270  DIM A13(260)  'array for Edit menu
280  DIM A14(534):DIM A14C(534)  'array for Options menu, screen-saver
290  C0=0:C1=1:C2=1:C3=1:C4=1:C5=1:C6=1:C7=1:C8=1:C9=1:C10=1:C12=1:C13=1:C14=1:C
15=1  'software color codes
300  T1=2  'selection flag for menu bar
310  T8=1  'selection flag for menus
311  J6=85:J7=19:J8=608:J9=186  'viewport
312  A$=CHR$(&HAA)+CHR$(&H55)  '50% shading
320 '_____
330 '
340 'module:  set up runtime environment
350  CLS:SCREEN 2:CLS:GOTO 370  '640x200 2-color mode
360 'PALETTE 1,0:PALETTE 2,1:PALETTE 3,9:PALETTE 4,7:PALETTE 5,5:PALETTE 6,6:PAL
ETTE 7,3:PALETTE 8,8:PALETTE 9,2:PALETTE 10,10:PALETTE 11,4:PALETTE 12,12:PALETT
E 13,13:PALETTE 14,14:PALETTE 15,15
370  ON KEY(2) GOSUB 2500:KEY(2) ON  'install hot key
380  SOUND 250,.7
390 '_____
400 '
410 'module:  set up screen template
```

Fig. 10-12. Complete source code for a fully-interactive, keyboard-controlled, menu-driven program manager. This version, for the CGA, will run on all graphics adapters (including VGA, EGA, MCGA, and PCjr).

```
420   GOSUB 2070  'save alphanumeric graphic arrays
430   GOSUB 2220  'create pull-down menus
440   LINE (0,8)-(639,199),C8,B  'border
450   LINE (0,187)-(639,187),C8:PAINT (320,190),C8,C8:PUT (240,189),A1,XOR  'bann
er
460   LINE (0,0)-(639,6),C1,B,&H5555:PAINT (320,3),A$,C1:LOCATE 1,33:PRINT " FILE
NAME.BAS "  'filename bar
470   LINE (1,8)-(639,18),C8,B:PAINT (320,10),C8,C8  'menu bar
480   PUT (18,9),A2,XOR:PUT (130,9),A3,XOR:PUT (250,9),A4,XOR:PUT (370,9),A5,XOR:
PUT (510,9),A6,XOR  'selections for menu bar
490   LOCATE 10,19:PRINT "Reclaiming memory used by temporary arrays":ERASE A1,A2
,A3,A4,A5,A6  'free up array memory
500   LOCATE 10,19:PRINT "                                            "
510   PUT (126,8),A7,XOR  'panning cursor for menu bar
520   VIEW SCREEN (J6,J7)-(J8,J9):CLS:VIEW  'clip drawing area
530   LOCATE 9,33:PRINT "SAMPLE MENU MANAGER":LOCATE 12,25:PRINT "Copyright (c) 1
987 by Lee Adams and":LOCATE 13,25:PRINT "TAB Books Inc.  All rights reserved."
540   LINE (212,60)-(450,60),C12:LINE (212,74)-(450,74),C12
550   LOCATE 19,29:PRINT "Press <Enter> to continue...":SOUND 250,.7
560   K$=INKEY$:IF K$<>CHR$(13) THEN 560  'wait for <Enter>
570   VIEW SCREEN (J6,J7)-(J8,J9):CLS:VIEW:SOUND 250,.7:GOTO 610
580   '———————————————————————————————————————————
590   '
600   'main module:  interactive control of menu bar
610   K$=INKEY$
620   IF LEN(K$)=2 THEN K$=RIGHT$(K$,1) ELSE 660
630   IF K$=CHR$(77) THEN T1=T1+1:GOSUB 720:GOTO 610
640   IF K$=CHR$(75) THEN T1=T1-1:GOSUB 820:GOTO 610
650   IF K$=CHR$(16) THEN GOSUB 2500  'Alt-Q to quit
660   IF K$=CHR$(13) THEN GOSUB 920  '<Enter> key
670   GOTO 610
680   GOTO 680  'bulletproof code barrier
690   '
700   '————
710   'module:  pan right on menu bar
720   IF T1>5 THEN T1=1
730   ON T1 GOTO 740,750,760,770,780
740   PUT (506,8),A7,XOR:PUT (14,8),A7,XOR:RETURN  'File
750   PUT (14,8),A7,XOR:PUT (126,8),A7,XOR:RETURN  'Draw
760   PUT (126,8),A7,XOR:PUT (246,8),A7,XOR:RETURN  'Edit
770   PUT (246,8),A7,XOR:PUT (366,8),A7,XOR:RETURN  'Options
780   PUT (366,8),A7,XOR:PUT (506,8),A7,XOR:RETURN  'Quit
790   '
800   '————
810   'module:  pan left on menu bar
820   IF T1<1 THEN T1=5
830   ON T1 GOTO 840,850,860,870,880
840   PUT (126,8),A7,XOR:PUT (14,8),A7,XOR:RETURN  'File
850   PUT (246,8),A7,XOR:PUT (126,8),A7,XOR:RETURN  'Draw
860   PUT (366,8),A7,XOR:PUT (246,8),A7,XOR:RETURN  'Edit
870   PUT (506,8),A7,XOR:PUT (366,8),A7,XOR:RETURN  'Options
880   PUT (14,8),A7,XOR:PUT (506,8),A7,XOR:RETURN  'Quit
890   '
```

Fig. 10-12. (Continued from page 97.)

```
900  '_____
910  'module:  execute menu bar choices
920   ON T1 GOTO 930,940,950,960,970
930   GOSUB 1240:RETURN  'invoke File menu
940   SOUND 250,.7:RETURN  'invoke on-screen Draw menu
950   GOSUB 1490:RETURN  'invoke Edit menu
960   GOSUB 1750:RETURN  'invoke Options menu
970   GOSUB 1010:RETURN  'invoke Quit menu
980  '_____
990  '
1000 'module:  interactive control of Quit menu
1010  GET (505,19)-(631,53),A14C  'save existing graphics
1020  PUT (505,19),A8,PSET  'place menu on screen
1030  PUT (507,25),A9,XOR  'place cursor >> on menu
1040  T8=1  'reset flag
1050  K$=INKEY$
1060  IF LEN(K$)=2 THEN K$=RIGHT$(K$,1) ELSE 1130
1070  IF K$=CHR$(80) THEN T8=T8+1:GOTO 1080 ELSE 1050
1080  IF T8>3 THEN T8=1
1090  ON T8 GOTO 1100,1110,1120
1100  PUT (507,41),A9,XOR:PUT (507,25),A9,XOR:GOTO 1050  'Quit
1110  PUT (507,25),A9,XOR:PUT (507,33),A9,XOR:GOTO 1050  'Save and quit
1120  PUT (507,33),A9,XOR:PUT (507,41),A9,XOR:GOTO 1050  'Cancel
1130  IF K$=CHR$(13) THEN 1160  '<Enter> to implement
1140  IF K$=CHR$(27) THEN 1200  '<ESC> to cancel
1150  GOTO 1050
1160  ON T8 GOTO 1170,1180,1190
1170  GOTO 2500  'implement quit
1180  SOUND 250,.7:GOTO 1050  'implement save and quit
1190  PUT (505,19),A14C,PSET:RETURN  'implement cancel
1200  PUT (505,19),A14C,PSET:RETURN  'restore previous graphics and return to me
nu bar level
1210  '_____
1220  '
1230 'module:  interactive control of File menu
1240  GET (14,19)-(96,62),A14C  'save existing graphics
1250  PUT (14,19),A10,PSET  'place menu on screen
1260  PUT (16,25),A9,XOR  'place cursor >> on menu
1270  T8=1  'reset flag
1280  K$=INKEY$
1290  IF LEN(K$)=2 THEN K$=RIGHT$(K$,1) ELSE 1370
1300  IF K$=CHR$(80) THEN T8=T8+1:GOTO 1310 ELSE 1280
1310  IF T8>4 THEN T8=1
1320  ON T8 GOTO 1330,1340,1350,1360
1330  PUT (16,49),A9,XOR:PUT (16,25),A9,XOR:GOTO 1280 'Save
1340  PUT (16,25),A9,XOR:PUT (16,33),A9,XOR:GOTO 1280 'Load
1350  PUT (16,33),A9,XOR:PUT (16,41),A9,XOR:GOTO 1280 'Name
1360  PUT (16,41),A9,XOR:PUT (16,49),A9,XOR:GOTO 1280  'Cancel
1370  IF K$=CHR$(13) THEN 1400  '<Enter> to implement
1380  IF K$=CHR$(27) THEN 1450  '<ESC> to cancel
1390  GOTO 1280
1400  ON T8 GOTO 1410,1420,1430,1440
1410  SOUND 250,.7:GOTO 1280  'implement save
```

Fig. 10-12. (Continued from page 98.)

```
1420   SOUND 250,.7:GOTO 1280   'implement load
1430   SOUND 250,.7:GOTO 1280   'implement name change
1440   PUT (14,19),A14C,PSET:RETURN   'implement cancel
1450   PUT (14,19),A14C,PSET:RETURN   'restore previous graphics and return to men
u bar level
1460   '_____
1470   '
1480   'module:  interactive control of Edit menu
1490   GET (246,19)-(328,65),A14C   'save existing graphics
1500   PUT (246,19),A13,PSET   'place menu on screen
1510   PUT (248,24),A9,XOR   'place cursor >> on menu
1520   T8=1   'reset flag
1530   K$=INKEY$
1540   IF LEN(K$)=2 THEN K$=RIGHT$(K$,1) ELSE 1630
1550   IF K$=CHR$(80) THEN T8=T8+1:GOTO 1560 ELSE 1530
1560   IF T8>5 THEN T8=1
1570   ON T8 GOTO 1580,1590,1600,1610,1620
1580   PUT (248,56),A9,XOR:PUT (248,24),A9,XOR:GOTO 1530 'Eraser
1590   PUT (248,24),A9,XOR:PUT (248,32),A9,XOR:GOTO 1530 'Halftone
1600   PUT (248,32),A9,XOR:PUT (248,40),A9,XOR:GOTO 1530 'Clear
1610   PUT (248,40),A9,XOR:PUT (248,48),A9,XOR:GOTO 1530 'Undo
1620   PUT (248,48),A9,XOR:PUT (248,56),A9,XOR:GOTO 1530 'Cancel
1630   IF K$=CHR$(13) THEN 1660   '<Enter> to implement
1640   IF K$=CHR$(27) THEN 1710   '<ESC> to cancel
1650   GOTO 1530
1660   ON T8 GOTO 1670,1680,1690,1700,1710
1670   SOUND 250,.7:GOTO 1530   'implement eraser
1680   SOUND 250,.7:GOTO 1530   'implement halftone
1690   SOUND 250,.7:GOTO 1530   'implement clear
1700   SOUND 250,.7:GOTO 1530   'implement undo
1710   PUT (246,19),A14C,PSET:RETURN   'implement cancel
1720   '_____
1730   '
1740   'module:  interactive control of Options menu
1750   GET (366,19)-(482,89),A14C   'save existing graphics
1760   PUT (366,19),A14,PSET   'place menu on screen
1770   PUT (368,24),A9,XOR   'place cursor >> on menu
1780   T8=1   'reset flag
1790   K$=INKEY$
1800   IF LEN(K$)=2 THEN K$=RIGHT$(K$,1) ELSE 1920
1810   IF K$=CHR$(80) THEN T8=T8+1:GOTO 1820 ELSE 1790
1820   IF T8>8 THEN T8=1
1830   ON T8 GOTO 1840,1850,1860,1870,1880,1890,1900,1910
1840   PUT (368,80),A9,XOR:PUT (368,24),A9,XOR:GOTO 1790 'Active color
1850   PUT (368,24),A9,XOR:PUT (368,32),A9,XOR:GOTO 1790 'Fill color
1860   PUT (368,32),A9,XOR:PUT (368,40),A9,XOR:GOTO 1790 'Brush color
1870   PUT (368,40),A9,XOR:PUT (368,48),A9,XOR:GOTO 1790 'Halftone %
1880   PUT (368,48),A9,XOR:PUT (368,56),A9,XOR:GOTO 1790 'Boundary
1890   PUT (368,56),A9,XOR:PUT (368,64),A9,XOR:GOTO 1790 'Snap +/-
1900   PUT (368,64),A9,XOR:PUT (368,72),A9,XOR:GOTO 1790 'Brush +/-
1910   PUT (368,72),A9,XOR:PUT (368,80),A9,XOR:GOTO 1790 'Cancel
1920   IF K$=CHR$(13) THEN 1950   '<Enter> to implement
1930   IF K$=CHR$(27) THEN 2030   '<ESC> to cancel
```

Fig. 10-12. (Continued from page 99.)

```
1940   GOTO 1790
1950   ON T8 GOTO 1960,1970,1980,1990,2000,2010,2020,2030
1960   SOUND 250,.7:GOTO 1790   'change active color
1970   SOUND 250,.7:GOTO 1790   'change fill color
1980   SOUND 250,.7:GOTO 1790   'change brush color
1990   SOUND 250,.7:GOTO 1790   'change halftone %
2000   SOUND 250,.7:GOTO 1790   'change boundary color
2010   SOUND 250,.7:GOTO 1790   'implement snap +/-
2020   SOUND 250,.7:GOTO 1790   'implement brush +/-
2030   PUT (366,19),A14C,PSET:RETURN   'implement cancel
2040   '_____
2050   '
2060   'module: create alpha arrays for screen template
2070   LOCATE 10,20:PRINT "YOUR MENU MANAGER"
2080   GET (150,71)-(290,79),A1:LOCATE 10,20:PRINT "
     "
2090   LOCATE 10,20:PRINT "File":GET (150,71)-(210,79),A2
2100   LOCATE 10,20:PRINT "Draw":GET (150,71)-(210,79),A3
2110   LOCATE 10,20:PRINT "Edit":GET (150,71)-(210,79),A4
2120   LOCATE 10,20:PRINT "Options":GET (150,71)-(210,79),A5
2130   LOCATE 10,20:PRINT "Quit   ":GET (150,71)-(210,79),A6
2140   LOCATE 10,20:PRINT "            "
2150   LINE (150,70)-(212,80),C3,B:GET (150,70)-(212,80),A7   'create panning curs
or for menu bar
2160   LINE (150,70)-(212,80),0,B
2170   RETURN
2180   '_____
2190   '
2200   'module:  create pull-down menus
·2210   'submodule:  create Quit menu
2220   LOCATE 10,20:PRINT "Quit":LOCATE 11,20:PRINT "Save and quit":LOCATE 12,20:
PRINT "Cancel"
2230   LINE (138,67)-(264,101),C7,B
2240   GET (138,67)-(264,101),A8:LINE (138,67)-(264,101),0,BF   'save Quit menu
2250   LOCATE 10,20:PRINT CHR$(175)   'menu cursor >>
2260   GET (151,73)-(159,77),A9:LOCATE 10,20:PRINT " "
2270   '_____
2280   '
2290   'submodule:  create File menu
2300   LOCATE 10,20:PRINT "Save":LOCATE 11,20:PRINT "Load":LOCATE 12,20:PRINT "Na
me":LOCATE 13,20:PRINT "Cancel"
2310   LINE (138,67)-(220,110),C7,B
2320   GET (138,67)-(220,110),A10:LINE (138,67)-(220,110),0,BF   'save File menu
2330   '_____
2340   '
2350   'submodule:  create Edit menu
2360   LOCATE 4,20:PRINT "Eraser":LOCATE 5,20:PRINT "Halftone":LOCATE 6,20:PRINT
"Clear":LOCATE 7,20:PRINT "Undo":LOCATE 8,20:PRINT "Cancel"
2370   LINE (138,20)-(220,66),C7,B
2380   GET (138,20)-(220,66),A13:LINE (138,20)-(220,66),0,BF   'save Edit menu
2390   '_____
2400   '
2410   'submodule:  create Options menu
```

Fig. 10-12. (Continued from page 100.)

```
2420  LOCATE 4,20:PRINT "Active color":LOCATE 5,20:PRINT "Fill color":LOCATE 6,2
0:PRINT "Brush color":LOCATE 7,20:PRINT "Halftone %":LOCATE 8,20:PRINT "Boundary
":LOCATE 9,20:PRINT "Snap +/-":LOCATE 10,20:PRINT "Brush +/-"
2430  LOCATE 11,20:PRINT "Cancel"
2440  LINE (138,20)-(254,90),C7,B
2450  GET (138,20)-(254,90),A14:LINE (138,20)-(254,90),0,BF   'save Options menu
2460  RETURN
2470  '_____
2480  '
2490  'module:  exit routine
2500  CLS:SCREEN 0,0,0,0:WIDTH 80:COLOR 7,0,0:CLS:LOCATE 1,1,1:COLOR 2:PRINT "YO
UR MENU MANAGER":LOCATE 2,1:PRINT "is finished.":COLOR 7:SOUND 250,.7:END
2510  '_____
2520  '
2530  END 'of menu manager
```

Fig. 10-12. (Continued from page 101.)

Press the down-arrow key to scroll down through the selections in a pull-down menu. The cursor automatically wraps back to the top selection when the bottom selection is passed. The up-arrow key has no effect, although you can easily modify the source code if you wish to enable scrolling in both directions.

Many of the selections in the pull-down menus are not active. When you press Enter to implement an inactive selection, the program simply beeps.

Program Analysis

Lines 100 through 140 are informative comments. Program execution begins at line 170, where the system is initialized to the appropriate screen mode. The notice which is displayed on the screen is used to mitigate the delay encountered during data assignment and graphic array space initialization.

Space is set aside in memory for the graphic arrays by lines 220 through 280. For example, DIM A3(150) sets aside space for 150 array elements in an array named A3.

Lines 290 through 310 assign values to variables used by the menu manager.

The module located at line 340 sets up the runtime environment. Line 350 invokes the appropriate graphics screen mode. Line 370 initializes F2 as a hot key which can be used to cleanly exit the program at any time. Hot keys are useful during program development, although they slow down runtime performance somewhat. The exit subroutine is located at line 2500.

The module which begins at line 410 calls subroutines which create the pull-down menus and then creates the main menu display. Lines 530 through 560 provide the program title and copyright notice (refer to Chapter 8). Notice line 520, which saves the menu display before the title is invoked, and line 570, which restores this clean display.

The main routine for this demonstration program is located at lines 600 through 680. This loop calls upon subroutines at line 720 and line 820 to move the panning cursor. Note the use of the T1 flag to keep track of the location of the panning cursor. The ON . . . GOTO instruction in each subroutine uses the value of the T1 flag to determine where to place the panning cursor. The ON . . . GOTO is a switchpoint.

The XOR operator is used to place the panning cursor on the screen. When the cursor is XOR'd onto the same location a second time, the cursor is effectively erased, providing an easy method of moving the cursor.

Line 660 is used to test if the user has pressed the Enter key. If so, program control jumps to line 920, where the T1 flag is again used to jump to a line which calls the appropriate pull-down menu subroutine. For example, if the cursor were resting upon the Edit selection of the menu bar when Enter was pressed, program control would jump from line 660 to line 920 to line 950 to the subroutine at line 1490.

Interactive keyboard control for the Quit menu is located at lines 1000 through 1200. Control for the File menu is located at lines 1230 through 1450. Control for the Edit menu is located at lines 1480 through 1710. Interactive keyboard control for the Options menu is located at lines 1740 through 2030.

Interactive Menu Control

The Edit menu controls at lines 1480 through 1710 provide a good example of general pull-down menu management. Line 1490 saves the existing graphics. Line 1500 writes the pull-down menu onto the screen. Line 1510 places the scrolling cursor onto the first selection. Line 1520 resets a flag which is used to keep track of the location of the scrolling cursor.

Line 1530 checks the keyboard buffer to see if the user has pressed a key. Line 1540 checks to see if an extended ASCII code was found in the buffer. If not, program flow jumps to the single ASCII character checks at line 1630.

Line 1560 inhibits the range of the flag. In this case, only five selections are available on the Edit menu, so the flag cannot be permitted to exceed five. Line 1570 uses the value of the flag to jump to an appropriate line to erase the previous scrolling cursor and to install the new scrolling cursor. Program control then loops back to line 1530 to repeat the scrolling cycle.

If Enter is pressed, line 1630 sends the program to the switcher at line 1660. Using the value of T8 as a runtime flag, program control is then transferred to the appropriate function. In this case, none of the functions are action, so the program merely issues a beep (lines 1670 through 1700).

If Esc is pressed, line 1640 sends the program to line 1710, which restores the original screen and returns control back to the main menu bar. Note that this escape mechanism can be invoked by either pressing Esc, or by selecting the Cancel option from the Edit menu. In this respect, the Esc key is a hot key.

Program Concept

The important lesson to learn from this demonstration program is the concept of using runtime flags to control program execution. By setting a program flag (as in line 1550, for example) and by using a switcher to redirect program flow according to the value of that flag (as in line 1570, for example), you can create fast-running and highly effective menu management programs. The flag makes it easy to develop pull-down menus of different sizes with a minimum of programming effort.

SUMMARY

In this chapter you experimented with a keyboard-driven menu management demonstration program. You learned about the main components of typical menu systems.

The next chapter discusses techniques for managing a mouse in cooperation with a menu system.

Managing A Mouse

A mouse can make your original graphics program run three times faster than a keyboard-controlled program. The mouse makes it possible for the end-user to simply point and shoot, rather than using scrolling cursors to select a function from the menu system. A point-and-shoot strategy is much quicker than a scrolling strategy; it is also much more intuitive.

Adapting your source code to accept input from a mouse is not as difficult as you might think. In fact, the sections of code which provide mouse control are no more complex than the INKEY$ routines which provide keyboard control.

HOW A MOUSE WORKS

Using a mouse is not difficult at all for the end-user. As you move the mouse around on your desktop, you will observe the screen cursor moving in a corresponding fashion. Refer to Fig. 11-1. When the cursor is located where you wish it to be, simply press the appropriate button on the mouse to implement the function you have selected.

To select an option from a pull-down menu, for example, move the mouse to place the cursor on (or near) the desired selection, and press the button on the mouse to implement the function.

From the programmer's point of view, the mouse automatically takes care of moving the cursor for you. Sensors inside the mouse chassis interpret the relative movement of the mouse over the desk surface and calculate the appropriate movement for the cursor. Some mouses (*mice* are animals, *mouses* are computer peripherals) use a ball apparatus to enable smooth movement on the desktop; others use wheels; still others use a light sensor

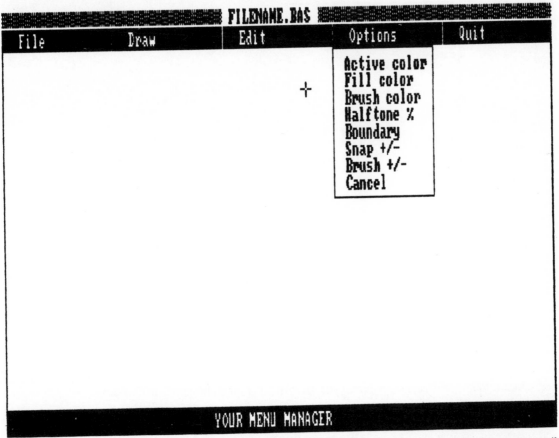

Fig. 11-1. The roaming cursor generated by a mouse can be used to control a menu manager. The programmer must specify proximity sensitivity in order to determine how near to the icon the cursor must be before the requested function will be implemented.

to detect movement of the mouse over a reflective grid. As a graphics programmer, an understanding of the mechanical innards of a mouse is helpful, but not essential.

Microsoft's mouse, which is recognized as the industry standard in North America, is available in a serial version and a bus version. The *serial mouse* simply attaches to the serial port of your personal computer. The *bus mouse* is driven by an adapter card which must be installed inside your computer in one of the expansion slots. If you are already using your serial port for communications, you will probably wish to use a bus mouse; otherwise, the serial mouse is a good choice. Both versions require special software in order to run properly. This software is called the *mouse driver*. It is usually included on the disk which accompanies your mouse as MOUSE.SYS of MOUSE.COM.

THE MOUSE DRIVER

The software which controls the mouse must be installed as a memory-resident program. Refer to Fig. 11-2. Before your graphics program is loaded—and before your BASIC interpreter or compiler is loaded—you must instruct DOS to load the mouse driv-

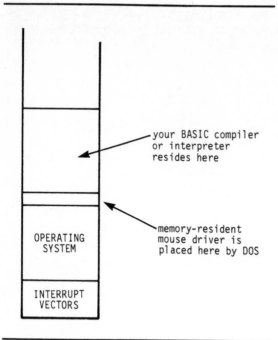

your BASIC compiler
or interpreter
resides here

memory-resident
mouse driver is
placed here by DOS

OPERATING
SYSTEM

INTERRUPT
VECTORS

Fig. 11-2. Location of the memory-resident mouse driver.

er. You must follow this same procedure if you are writing graphics programs in C, Pascal, or assembly language which use the mouse.

The mouse driver provides a convenient interface between the graphics programmer and the mouse. By making CALLs to the mouse driver, you can read the location of the cursor, check whether a mouse button has been pressed or not, and perform other important functions. Once you know the number codes which control the various mouse functions, you will find it a manageable task to work with a mouse at the source code level. MOUSE.COM can be run by DOS. MOUSE.SYS needs a CONFIG.SYS file.

THE CONFIGURATION FILE

When you first turn on your personal computer, DOS automatically looks for a file called CONFIG.SYS. It uses the instructions that it finds in this file to logically configure your system. To instruct DOS to load the mouse driver software, the following statement must be in the CONFIG.SYS file:

DEVICE=MOUSE.SYS

Setting up this configuration file is probably the trickiest part of using a mouse. Once you are past this hurdle, the path is clear. After the CONFIG.SYS file has been created, programming the mouse is more like fun than work.

To create the CONFIG.SYS file on your boot disk, use the following script after you have loaded DOS. The boot disk is the diskette you use to start up your computer. If you are using a diskette drive system, your personal computer usually boots from a disk in drive A. If you are using a hard disk system, your computer will boot from the hard disk drive C if drive A is empty.

Make certain your boot disk is the active drive and then type:

COPY CON A:CONFIG.SYS (press Enter)
DEVICE=**MOUSE.SYS** (press Enter)

Strike F6 and press Enter, then you will see the prompt:

A>

The instruction COPY CON tells DOS to accept input (COPY) from the keyboard (CON) and make it into a file called CONFIG.SYS. The instruction F6 is actually an end-of-file marker which tells DOS that you have finished typing the contents of the file. If these DOS instructions are new to you, you might want to read an introductory text about DOS. Refer to the bibliography for guidance.

The preceding script assumes that the boot disk is loaded in drive A. If you normally start your personal computer from drive C (using a hard disk), change the A to C and be sure you are writing to the appropriate subdirectory on your hard disk.

If you already have a configuration file on your diskette or hard disk, merely add the statement **DEVICE**=**MOUSE.SYS** to the existing contents of the file. In addition, be sure that the file MOUSE.SYS is present on your boot disk. Copy it over from the disk that came with your mouse.

CALLING CONVENTIONS

While your graphics program is running, the memory-resident mouse software will automatically take care of moving the cursor around on the screen. However, if you want to discover the xy coordinates, or if you want to test if a mouse button has been pressed, your program must take steps to access the status byte inside the mouse driver.

To access the mouse status during runtime, you CALL the mouse driver subroutine by sending four variables to it. **CALL MOUSE (M1,M2,M3,M4)** is the format to use, although the names of the variables are not mandatory. (You could just as easily use the syntax **CALL A1(A,B,C,D)** if you wished.) In the first example, M1 is the number of the mouse function which you want to invoke. The other variables represent parameters which you are either passing to or receiving from the mouse driver software.

For example, the syntax **M1**=**4:M2**=**0:M3**=**320:M4**=**100: CALL MOUSE (M1,M2,M3,M4)** would set the cursor to position 320,100 on the display screen. M1 represents mouse function 4. M2 is unused. M3 is the x-coordinate. M4 is the y-coordinate.

To correctly execute this call in BASIC, you must define the mouse driver's segment address with a DEF SEG instruction. The variable MOUSE defines the driver's offset into the segment address.

A complete listing of mouse function numbers is found in the user's guide which accompanies your mouse. The parameters which you must send to the mouse driver and the parameters which the mouse drivers return to you are also indicated.

THE MOUSE CURSOR

The mouse cursor is simply a graphic array which is placed into the screen buffer (i.e., onto the display screen). Although a graphics cursor can be controlled using only the XOR logical operator, a mouse usually uses two graphic arrays in order to provide more flexibility.

The first array uses the AND logical operator to set up a template on the screen. This template is also called a *key matte*. The second array uses the XOR logical operator to place the cursor itself on the screen. This double-array approach provides more precise control over the resulting color of the cursor in the 4-color and 16-color modes. (For a more detailed discussion of the placement of multicolor graphic arrays on multicolor backgrounds using key mattes, refer to *High-performance Interactive Graphics: Modeling, Rendering & Animating for IBM PCs and Compatibles*, TAB book 2879, available through your favorite bookstore or direct from TAB BOOKS Inc.)

In the 320×200 four-color mode, the mouse cursor is actually a rectangle comprised of 8 horizontal pixels by 16 vertical lines. In the 640×200 two-color and 16-color modes the cursor is sized 16 pixels by 16 lines.

GETTING THE MOUSE READY

Before you can use the mouse in your interactive graphics program, the mouse cursor must be designed, its location must be set, and the mouse itself must be initialized. These general housekeeping functions can be accomplished by including an initialization routine in your original graphics program.

The program listing in Fig. 11-3 demonstrates mouse initialization and cursor control for the 640×200 two-color mode. The program will run on all graphics adapters, including the EGA, VGA, MCGA, CGA, and PCjr. If you are using the companion disk to this book, you can load and run the program by entering the following:

LOAD "MOUSE.BAS",R.

As described earlier, the mouse driver must be loaded as a memory resident program during the boot process.

MOUSE MANAGEMENT: PROGRAM ANALYSIS

The module at lines 290 through 360 is a bullet-proof method of checking for the presence of the mouse driver (MOUSE.SYS) in low memory. Because any CALLs to the mouse driver will lock up the computer if the driver is not present, it is essential to include a module to check for the presence of the mouse software before you CALL it.

Line 300 sets BASIC's extra segment address to the start of RAM memory. Line 310 then determines the segment address of the mouse driver. Line 320 determines the offset address of the driver, expressed relative to the segment address, and assigns it to the variable MOUSE. Line 330 uses boolean logic to compare the value of two bytes within the mouse driver code. If the test is false, the mouse driver is not present. If the test is true, it is highly likely that the driver is present (although there is also the remote possibility that, through mere coincidence, the bytes being tested are the values being sought, even though the driver is missing).

```
100 'Program MOUSE.BAS:  mouse initializer
110 'Copyright (c) 1987 by Lee Adams and TAB Books Inc.
120 'All rights reserved.
130 'Demonstrates how to initialize Microsoft Mouse.  The mouse-driver MOUSE.SYS
 must be installed by DOS at boot time via a CONFIG.SYS file.
140 'Generic version:  640x200 2-color SCREEN 2
150 '_____
160 '
170  KEY OFF:CLS:SCREEN 2:CLS:LOCATE 25,25:PRINT "SCREEN 2: 640x200 2-color mode
"
180  ON KEY (2) GOSUB 610:KEY (2) ON  'install hot key
190 '_____
200 '
210 'module:  data assignments
220  DEFINT A,C,M
230  DIM A15(15,1)  'graphic array for mouse cursor
240  MSEG=0  'variable to contain mouse driver seg address
250  MOUSE=0 'variable to contain mouse driver offset
260  M1=0:M2=0:M3=0:M4=0  'syntax: CALL MOUSE(M1,M2,M3,M4)
270 '_____
280 '
290 'module:  determine if mouse driver is present
300  DEF SEG=0  'set to start of physical memory
310  MSEG=256*PEEK(51*4+3)+PEEK(51*4+2)  'driver segment
320  MOUSE=256*PEEK(51*4+1)+PEEK(51*4)+2 'driver offset
330  IF MSEG OR (MOUSE-2) THEN 350  'is driver there?
340  DEF SEG:CLS:SCREEN 0,0,0,0:WIDTH 80:COLOR 7,0,0:CLS:LOCATE 1,1,1:COLOR 28:P
RINT "MOUSE DRIVER NOT FOUND!":COLOR 4:LOCATE 2,1:PRINT "Program terminated.":LO
CATE 4,1:COLOR 7:SOUND 200,18:END  'exit program because mouse driver not found
350  DEF SEG=MSEG 'set mouse driver segment
360  IF PEEK(MOUSE-2)=207 THEN 340  'if a default value is at that address, then
 jump to exit routine
370 '_____
380 '
390 'module:  initialize the mouse
400  M1=0:M2=0:M3=0:M4=0:CALL MOUSE(M1,M2,M3,M4)  'initialize mouse
410  M1=15:M2=0:M3=4:M4=8:CALL MOUSE(M1,M2,M3,M4)  'set mouse sensitivity
420 '_____
430 '
440 'module:  define shape of mouse cursor
450  A15(0,0)=&HFFFF:A15(1,0)=&HFFFF:A15(2,0)=&HFFFF:A15(3,0)=&HFFFF:A15(4,0)=&H
FFFF:A15(5,0)=&HFFFF:A15(6,0)=&HFFFF:A15(7,0)=&HFFFF:A15(8,0)=&HFFFF:A15(9,0)=&H
FFFF
460  A15(10,0)=&HFFFF:A15(11,0)=&HFFFF:A15(12,0)=&HFFFF:A15(13,0)=&HFFFF:A15(14,
0)=&HFFFF:A15(15,0)=&HFFFF
470  A15(0,1)=&H100:A15(1,1)=&H100:A15(2,1)=&H100:A15(3,1)=&H7C7C:A15(4,1)=&H100
:A15(5,1)=&H100:A15(6,1)=&H100:A15(7,1)=&H0:A15(8,1)=&H0:A15(9,1)=&H0:A15(10,1)=
&H0
480  A15(11,1)=&H0:A15(12,1)=&H0:A15(13,1)=&H0:A15(14,1)=&H0:A15(15,1)=&H0
490  M1=9:M2=7:M3=3:M4=0:CALL MOUSE(M1,M2,M3,A15(0,0))  'invoke mouse cursor sha
pe and define hot spot
```

Fig. 11-3. Demonstration program listing for mouse initialization and cursor handling. The version is for all graphics adapters, including VGA, EGA, MCGA, CGA, and PCjr.

```
500 '_____
510 '
520 'install mouse cursor on screen
530   M1=4:M2=0:M3=320:M4=100:CALL MOUSE(M1,M2,M3,M4)  'set cursor location at 32
0,100 on 640x200 virtual screen
540   M1=1:M2=0:M3=0:M4=0:CALL MOUSE(M1,M2,M3,M4):SOUND 250,.7  'activate mouse
550 '
560 '_____
570   GOTO 570  'do nothing
580 '
590 '_____
600 'module:  exit routine
610   DEF SEG=MSEG:M1=2:M2=0:M3=0:M4=0:CALL MOUSE (M1,M2,M3,M4):DEF SEG  'erase m
ouse cursor from screen
620   SCREEN 0,0,0,0:WIDTH 80:COLOR 7,0,0:CLS:LOCATE 1,1,1:COLOR 2:PRINT "MOUSE I
NITIALIZATION ROUTINE finished.":COLOR 7:SOUND 250,.7:END
630 '
640 '_____
650   END 'of mouse control routines.
```

Fig. 11-3. (Continued from page 109.)

Line 340 contains the abort routine to be executed if the driver has not been found by the boolean test. Line 350 resets BASIC's extra segment to the mouse segment address, then line 360 performs a second boolean test to test that the expected code is indeed at that address.

The mouse is turned on by line 400, which uses mouse function 0 in the M1 variable. The sensitivity of the mouse to lateral movement is set by line 410, using mouse function 15.

Designing the Cursor

The module at lines 440 through 490 determines the design of the mouse cursor on the display screen. This particular module creates a simple crosshair design. By changing the hexadecimal values in this module to binary numbers and stacking them on top one another, you can see the crosshair design. Refer to your mouse user's guide for further guidance in creating other shapes, such as arrows, hands, hourglasses, and so on.

Line 490 initializes the cursor design and sets the *hot spot*. The hot spot is the single pixel position within the overall cursor that represents the pointer of the cursor. It is the position of the hot spot that is tested when your program makes a decision based upon the location of the cursor.

Line 530 installs the mouse cursor on the display screen, using mouse function 4. In this particular example, the cursor is placed at position 320,100. Line 540 activates the mouse. From this point on, the cursor will move when you slide the mouse across the desktop.

A Clean Exit

Note line 610, which uses mouse function 2 to erase the mouse cursor from the screen. In addition, the DEF SEG instruction returns the BASIC extra segment to its default value before line 620 exits the program. If you leave the mouse cursor on the screen, or if you fail to return BASIC's extra segment to its default, you could run into intermittent problems with both video and data values. You should always strive to leave the entire system as you found it prior to invoking the mouse.

Mouse-Driven Menus

The program listing in Fig. 11-4 demonstrates a pull-down menu system controlled by a mouse. The program runs in the 640×200 two-color mode and is compatible with EGA, VGA, MCGA, CGA, and PCjr graphics systems. If you are using the companion disk for this book, you can load and run the demonstration program by typing **LOAD "MENUMOUS.BAS",R.**

The program listing is very similar to the listing in Fig. 10-12 found in Chapter 10. The menu management system in this chapter is virtually identical to the menu management system found in Chapter 10, with the exception of the code required to read the mouse status.

Note line 380, which installs the mouse. All mouse initialization has been moved to a subroutine at the end of the program. This strategy keeps the general housekeeping functions out of the way when you are building a complex graphics program.

```
100 'Program MENUMOUS.BAS:  mouse control of a menu manager
110 'Copyright (c) 1987 by Lee Adams and TAB Books Inc.
120 'All rights reserved.
130 'This program demonstrates mouse control of a menu bar with pull-down menus.
    Mouse driver MOUSE.SYS must be loaded during DOS boot.
140 'CGA version.  640x200 2-color mode.
150 '_____
160 '
170  KEY OFF:CLS:CLEAR:SCREEN 0,0,0,0:WIDTH 80:COLOR 7,0,0:CLS:LOCATE 10,20,0:PR
INT "Assigning memory space for graphic arrays"
180 '_____
190 '
200 'module:  data assignments
210  DEFINT A,C,J,M,T
220  DIM A1(82):DIM A2(37):DIM A3(37):DIM A4(37):DIM A5(37):DIM A6(37)  'tempora
ry arrays for screen template
230  DIM A8(281)  'array for Quit menu
240  DIM A10(243)  'array for File menu
250  DIM A13(260)  'array for Edit menu
260  DIM A14(534):DIM A14C(534)  'array for Options menu, screen-saver
270  DIM A15(15,1)  'graphic array for mouse cursor
280  MSEG=0 'variable to contain mouse driver seg address
290  MOUSE=0 'variable to contain mouse driver offset
300  M1=0:M2=0:M3=0:M4=0  'arguments for mouse CALL
310  C0=0:C1=1:C2=1:C3=1:C4=1:C5=1:C6=1:C7=1:C8=1:C9=1:C10=1:C12=1:C13=1:C14=1:C
15=1  'software color codes
320  J6=85:J7=19:J8=608:J9=186  'viewport
330  A$=CHR$(&HAA)+CHR$(&H55)  '50% shading
340 '_____
350 '
360 'module:  set up runtime environment
```

Fig. 11-4. Complete source code for a mouse-driven menu system. This version is for all graphics adapters, including VGA, EGA, MCGA, CGA, and PCjr.

```
370  CLS:SCREEN 2:CLS  '640x200 2-color mode
380  GOSUB 2120  'install mouse cursor
390  '_____
400  '
410  'module:  set up screen template
420  GOSUB 1730  'save alphanumeric graphic arrays
430  GOSUB 1860  'create pull-down menus
440  LINE (0,8)-(639,199),C8,B  'border
450  LINE (0,187)-(639,187),C8:PAINT (320,190),C8,C8:PUT (240,189),A1,XOR  'bann
er
460  LINE (0,0)-(639,6),C1,B,&H5555:PAINT (320,3),A$,C1:LOCATE 1,33:PRINT " FILE
NAME.BAS "  'filename bar
470  LINE (1,8)-(639,18),C8,B:PAINT (320,10),C8,C8  'menu bar
480  PUT (18,9),A2,XOR:PUT (146,9),A3,XOR:PUT (274,9),A4,XOR:PUT (402,9),A5,XOR:
PUT (530,9),A6,XOR  'selections for menu bar
490  LINE (128,8)-(128,18),0:LINE (256,8)-(256,18),0:LINE (384,8)-(384,18),0:LIN
E (512,8)-(512,18),0  'dividers on menu bar
500  LOCATE 10,19:PRINT "Reclaiming memory used by temporary arrays":ERASE A1,A2
,A3,A4,A5,A6  'free up array memory
510  LOCATE 10,19:PRINT "                                                  "
520  VIEW SCREEN (J6,J7)-(J8,J9):CLS:VIEW  'clip drawing area
530  LOCATE 9,33:PRINT "SAMPLE MENU MANAGER":LOCATE 12,25:PRINT "Copyright (c) 1
987 by Lee Adams and":LOCATE 13,25:PRINT "TAB Books Inc.  All rights reserved."
540  LINE (212,60)-(450,60),C12:LINE (212,74)-(450,74),C12
550  LOCATE 19,29:PRINT "Press <Enter> to continue...":SOUND 250,.7
560  K$=INKEY$:IF K$<>CHR$(13) THEN 560  'wait for <Enter>
570  VIEW SCREEN (J6,J7)-(J8,J9):CLS:VIEW  'clear canvas
580  M1=4:M2=0:M3=320:M4=100:CALL MOUSE(M1,M2,M3,M4)  'set mouse cursor location
 to center of screen
590  M1=1:M2=0:M3=0:M4=0:CALL MOUSE(M1,M2,M3,M4)  'display the mouse cursor
600  SOUND 250,.7:GOTO 640
610  '_____
620  '
630  'main module:  interactive mouse control of menu bar
640  M1=3:CALL MOUSE(M1,M2,M3,M4)  'read mouse location
650  IF M2 AND 1 THEN 660 ELSE 720  'loop if no button has been pressed
660  IF (M4<19) AND (M4>7) THEN 670 ELSE 720  'loop if cursor is not positioned
on the menu bar
670  IF (M3>0) AND (M3<128) THEN M1=2:CALL MOUSE(M1,M2,M3,M4):GOSUB 790:M1=1:CAL
L MOUSE(M1,M2,M3,M4):GOTO 640  'pull down File menu
680  IF (M3>128) AND (M3<256) THEN M1=2:CALL MOUSE(M1,M2,M3,M4):GOSUB 800:M1=1:C
ALL MOUSE(M1,M2,M3,M4):GOTO 640  'invoke Draw menu
690  IF (M3>256) AND (M3<384) THEN M1=2:CALL MOUSE(M1,M2,M3,M4):GOSUB 810:M1=1:C
ALL MOUSE(M1,M2,M3,M4):GOTO 640  'pull down Edit menu
700  IF (M3>384) AND (M3<512) THEN M1=2:CALL MOUSE(M1,M2,M3,M4):GOSUB 820:M1=1:C
ALL MOUSE(M1,M2,M3,M4):GOTO 640  'pull down Options menu
710  IF (M3>512) AND (M3<639) THEN M1=2:CALL MOUSE(M1,M2,M3,M4):GOSUB 830:M1=1:C
ALL MOUSE(M1,M2,M3,M4):GOTO 640  'pull down Quit menu
720  K$=INKEY$:IF LEN(K$)=2 THEN K$=RIGHT$(K$,1) ELSE 640
730  IF K$=CHR$(16) THEN GOSUB 2370  'Alt-Q to quit
740  GOTO 640  'loop
750  GOTO 750  'bulletproof code barrier
```

Fig. 11-4. (Continued from page 111.)

```
760  '_____
770  '
780  'module:  execute menu bar choices
790   GOSUB 1050:RETURN   'invoke File menu
800   SOUND 250,.7:RETURN   'invoke on-screen Draw menu
810   GOSUB 1250:RETURN   'invoke Edit menu
820   GOSUB 1460:RETURN   'invoke Options menu
830   GOSUB 870:RETURN   'invoke Quit menu
840  '_____
850  '
860  'module:  interactive control of Quit menu
870   GET (512,19)-(638,53),A14C  'save existing graphics
880   PUT (512,19),A8,PSET  'place menu on screen
890   M1=1:CALL MOUSE(M1,M2,M3,M4)   'restore cursor
900   M1=3:CALL MOUSE(M1,M2,M3,M4)   'read mouse location
910   IF M2 AND 1 THEN 920 ELSE 960   'loop if no button has been pressed
920   IF (M3>512) AND (M3<638) THEN 930 ELSE 960   'loop if cursor is not position
ed inside the menu
930   IF (M4>39) AND (M4<47) THEN 1000  'cancel
940   IF (M4>31) AND (M4<39) THEN 990  'save and quit
950   IF (M4>23) AND (M4<31) THEN 980  'quit
960   K$=INKEY$:IF K$=CHR$(27) THEN 1010  '<ESC> to cancel
970   GOTO 900  'loop
980   GOTO 2370  'implement quit
990   SOUND 250,.7:GOTO 900  'implement save and quit
1000   M1=2:CALL MOUSE(M1,M2,M3,M4):PUT (512,19),A14C,PSET:RETURN  'implement can
cel
1010   M1=2:CALL MOUSE(M1,M2,M3,M4):PUT (512,19),A14C,PSET:RETURN  'restore previ
ous graphics and return to menu bar level
1020  '_____
1030  '
1040  'module:  interactive control of File menu
1050   GET (14,19)-(96,62),A14C  'save existing graphics
1060   PUT (14,19),A10,PSET  'place menu on screen
1070   M1=1:CALL MOUSE(M1,M2,M3,M4)   'restore cursor
1080   M1=3:CALL MOUSE(M1,M2,M3,M4)   'read mouse location
1090   IF M2 AND 1 THEN 1100 ELSE 1150   'loop if no button has been pressed
1100   IF (M3>14) AND (M3<96) THEN 1110 ELSE 1150   'loop if cursor is not positio
ned inside the menu
1110   IF (M4>23) AND (M4<31) THEN 1170  'save
1120   IF (M4>31) AND (M4<39) THEN 1180  'load
1130   IF (M4>39) AND (M4<47) THEN 1190  'name change
1140   IF (M4>47) AND (M4<55) THEN 1200  'cancel
1150   K$=INKEY$:IF K$=CHR$(27) THEN 1210  '<ESC> to cancel
1160   GOTO 1080  'loop
1170   SOUND 250,.7:GOTO 1080  'implement save
1180   SOUND 300,.7:GOTO 1080  'implement load
1190   SOUND 350,.7:GOTO 1080  'implement name change
1200   M1=2:CALL MOUSE(M1,M2,M3,M4):PUT (14,19),A14C,PSET:RETURN  'implement canc
el
1210   M1=2:CALL MOUSE(M1,M2,M3,M4):PUT (14,19),A14C,PSET:RETURN  'restore previo
us graphics and return to menu bar level
```

Fig. 11-4. (Continued from page 112.)

```
1220 '
1230 '_____
1240 'module:  interactive control of Edit menu
1250 GET (256,19)-(338,65),A14C  'save existing graphics
1260 PUT (256,19),A13,PSET  'place menu on screen
1270 M1=1:CALL MOUSE(M1,M2,M3,M4)  'restore cursor
1280 M1=3:CALL MOUSE(M1,M2,M3,M4)  'read mouse location
1290 IF M2 AND 1 THEN 1300 ELSE 1360  'loop if no button has been pressed
1300 IF (M3>256) AND (M3<338) THEN 1310 ELSE 1360  'loop if cursor is not posit
ioned inside the menu
1310 IF (M4>23) AND (M4<31) THEN 1380   'eraser
1320 IF (M4>31) AND (M4<39) THEN 1390   'halftone
1330 IF (M4>39) AND (M4<47) THEN 1400   'clear
1340 IF (M4>47) AND (M4<55) THEN 1410   'undo
1350 IF (M4>55) AND (M4<63) THEN 1420   'cancel
1360 K$=INKEY$:IF K$=CHR$(27) THEN 1420  '<ESC> to cancel
1370 GOTO 1280
1380 SOUND 250,.7:GOTO 1280  'implement eraser
1390 SOUND 300,.7:GOTO 1280  'implement halftone
1400 SOUND 350,.7:GOTO 1280  'implement clear
1410 SOUND 400,.7:GOTO 1280  'implement undo
1420 M1=2:CALL MOUSE(M1,M2,M3,M4):PUT (256,19),A14C,PSET:RETURN  'implement can
cel
1430 '_____
1440 '
1450 'module:  interactive control of Options menu
1460 GET (384,19)-(500,89),A14C  'save existing graphics
1470 PUT (384,19),A14,PSET  'place menu on screen
1480 M1=1:CALL MOUSE(M1,M2,M3,M4)  'restore cursor
1490 M1=3:CALL MOUSE(M1,M2,M3,M4)  'read mouse location
1500 IF M2 AND 1 THEN 1510 ELSE 1600  'loop if no button has been pressed
1510 IF (M3>384) AND (M3<500) THEN 1520 ELSE 1600  'loop if cursor is not posit
ioned inside the menu
1520 IF (M4>23) AND (M4<31) THEN 1620   'active color
1530 IF (M4>31) AND (M4<39) THEN 1630   'fill color
1540 IF (M4>39) AND (M4<47) THEN 1640   'brush color
1550 IF (M4>47) AND (M4<55) THEN 1650   'halftone %
1560 IF (M4>55) AND (M4<63) THEN 1660   'boundary clr
1570 IF (M4>63) AND (M4<71) THEN 1670   'snap +/-
1580 IF (M4>71) AND (M4<79) THEN 1680   'brush +/-
1590 IF (M4>79) AND (M4<87) THEN 1690   'cancel
1600 K$=INKEY$:IF K$=CHR$(27) THEN 1690  '<ESC> to cancel
1610 GOTO 1490
1620 SOUND 250,.7:GOTO 1490   'change active color
1630 SOUND 300,.7:GOTO 1490   'change fill color
1640 SOUND 350,.7:GOTO 1490   'change brush color
1650 SOUND 400,.7:GOTO 1490   'change halftone %
1660 SOUND 450,.7:GOTO 1490   'change boundary color
1670 SOUND 500,.7:GOTO 1490   'implement snap +/-
1680 SOUND 550,.7:GOTO 1490   'implement brush +/-
1690 M1=2:CALL MOUSE(M1,M2,M3,M4):PUT (384,19),A14C,PSET:RETURN  'implement can
cel
```

Fig. 11-4. (Continued from page 113.)

```
1700 '_____
1710 '
1720 'module: create alpha arrays for screen template
1730   LOCATE 10,20:PRINT "YOUR MENU MANAGER"
1740   GET (150,71)-(290,79),A1:LOCATE 10,20:PRINT "
     "
1750   LOCATE 10,20:PRINT "File":GET (150,71)-(210,79),A2
1760   LOCATE 10,20:PRINT "Draw":GET (150,71)-(210,79),A3
1770   LOCATE 10,20:PRINT "Edit":GET (150,71)-(210,79),A4
1780   LOCATE 10,20:PRINT "Options":GET (150,71)-(210,79),A5
1790   LOCATE 10,20:PRINT "Quit   ":GET (150,71)-(210,79),A6
1800   LOCATE 10,20:PRINT "           "
1810   RETURN
1820 '_____
1830 '
1840 'module:  create pull-down menus
1850 'submodule:  create Quit menu
1860   LOCATE 10,20:PRINT "Quit":LOCATE 11,20:PRINT "Save and quit":LOCATE 12,20:
PRINT "Cancel"
1870   LINE (138,67)-(264,101),C7,B
1880   GET (138,67)-(264,101),A8:LINE (138,67)-(264,101),0,BF   'save Quit menu
1890 '
1900 '_____
1910 'submodule:  create File menu
1920   LOCATE 10,20:PRINT "Save":LOCATE 11,20:PRINT "Load":LOCATE 12,20:PRINT "Na
me":LOCATE 13,20:PRINT "Cancel"
1930   LINE (138,67)-(220,110),C7,B
1940   GET (138,67)-(220,110),A10:LINE (138,67)-(220,110),0,BF   'save File menu
1950 '
1960 '_____
1970 'submodule:  create Edit menu
1980   LOCATE 4,20:PRINT "Eraser":LOCATE 5,20:PRINT "Halftone":LOCATE 6,20:PRINT
"Clear":LOCATE 7,20:PRINT "Undo":LOCATE 8,20:PRINT "Cancel"
1990   LINE (138,20)-(220,66),C7,B
2000   GET (138,20)-(220,66),A13:LINE (138,20)-(220,66),0,BF   'save Edit menu
2010 '
2020 '_____
2030 'submodule:  create Options menu
2040   LOCATE 4,20:PRINT "Active color":LOCATE 5,20:PRINT "Fill color":LOCATE 6,2
0:PRINT "Brush color":LOCATE 7,20:PRINT "Halftone %":LOCATE 8,20:PRINT "Boundary
":LOCATE 9,20:PRINT "Snap +/-":LOCATE 10,20:PRINT "Brush +/-"
2050   LOCATE 11,20:PRINT "Cancel"
2060   LINE (138,20)-(254,90),C7,B
2070   GET (138,20)-(254,90),A14:LINE (138,20)-(254,90),0,BF   'save Options menu
2080   RETURN
2090 '_____
2100 '
2110 'module:  determine if mouse driver is present
2120   DEF SEG=0  'set to start of physical memory
2130   MSEG=256*PEEK(51*4+3)+PEEK(51*4+2)   'driver segment
2140   MOUSE=256*PEEK(51*4+1)+PEEK(51*4)+2 'driver offset
2150   IF MSEG OR (MOUSE-2) THEN 2170   'is driver there?
```

Fig. 11-4. (Continued from page 114.)

```
2160  DEF SEG:CLS:SCREEN 0,0,0,0:WIDTH 80:COLOR 7,0,0:CLS:LOCATE 1,1,1:COLOR 28:
PRINT "MOUSE DRIVER NOT FOUND!":COLOR 4:LOCATE 2,1:PRINT "Program terminated.":L
OCATE 4,1:COLOR 7:SOUND 200,18:END  'exit program because mouse driver not found
2170  DEF SEG=MSEG  'set mouse driver segment
2180  IF PEEK(MOUSE-2)=207 THEN 2160  'if a default value is at that address, th
en jump to exit routine
2190  ON KEY(2) GOSUB 2370:KEY (2) ON  'redefine hot key
2200  '_____
2210  '_____
2220  'module:  initialize the mouse
2230  M1=0:M2=0:M3=0:M4=0:CALL MOUSE(M1,M2,M3,M4)  'initialize mouse
2240  M1=15:M2=0:M3=4:M4=8:CALL MOUSE(M1,M2,M3,M4)  'set mouse sensitivity
2250  '_____
2260  '_____
2270  'module:  define shape of mouse cursor
2280  A15(0,0)=&HFFFF:A15(1,0)=&HFFFF:A15(2,0)=&HFFFF:A15(3,0)=&HFFFF:A15(4,0)=&
HFFFF:A15(5,0)=&HFFFF:A15(6,0)=&HFFFF:A15(7,0)=&HFFFF:A15(8,0)=&HFFFF:A15(9,0)=&
HFFFF
2290  A15(10,0)=&HFFFF:A15(11,0)=&HFFFF:A15(12,0)=&HFFFF:A15(13,0)=&HFFFF:A15(14
,0)=&HFFFF:A15(15,0)=&HFFFF
2300  A15(0,1)=&H100:A15(1,1)=&H100:A15(2,1)=&H100:A15(3,1)=&H7C7C:A15(4,1)=&H10
0:A15(5,1)=&H100:A15(6,1)=&H100:A15(7,1)=&H0:A15(8,1)=&H0:A15(9,1)=&H0:A15(10,1)
=&H0
2310  A15(11,1)=&H0:A15(12,1)=&H0:A15(13,1)=&H0:A15(14,1)=&H0:A15(15,1)=&H0
2320  M1=9:M2=7:M3=3:M4=0:CALL MOUSE(M1,M2,M3,A15(0,0))  'invoke mouse cursor sh
ape and define hot spot
2330  RETURN
2340  '·_____
2350  '_____
2360  'module:  exit routine
2370  DEF SEG=MSEG:M1=2:M2=0:M3=0:M4=0:CALL MOUSE (M1,M2,M3,M4):DEF SEG  'erase
mouse cursor from screen
2380  SCREEN 0,0,0,0:WIDTH 80:COLOR 7,0,0:CLS:LOCATE 1,1,1:COLOR 2:PRINT "MOUSE/
MENU PROGRAM finished.":COLOR 7:SOUND 250,.7:END
2390  '_____
2400  '_____
2410  END 'of mouse/menu program.
```

Fig. 11-4. (Continued from page 115.)

The Mouse Loop

The control loop at lines 640 through 740 is the workhorse of this program. Line 640 checks the location of the cursor by using mouse function 3. Line 650 uses boolean logic to test if no button has been pressed. If a button has been pressed by the user, program flow continues with line 660, otherwise the program loops back up to line 640 and checks the mouse again.

Line 660 checks the y-coordinate of the mouse cursor. Clearly, the mouse cursor must be positioned somewhere on the main menu bar before the user can request that a menu be pulled down. The whole trick to mouse programming is using IF . . . THEN instructions to determine if the cursor is within a certain space on the display screen.

Lines 670 through 710 check the cursor's x-coordinate to determine which pull-down menu is being targetted. Program flow then jumps to the appropriate subroutine to install the pull-down menu. Note how mouse function 2 is used to erase the cursor before the menu is installed. Mouse function 1 is used to restore the cursor when control returns from the menu subroutine.

Lines 720 and 730 provide for a keyboard hot key. If Alt-Q is pressed, then program flow jumps to the exit routine. As this module demonstrates, both keyboard and mouse can be used concurrently, provided that algorithms for both sets of controls are included in your source code.

It is well worth your while to carefully study this module. All polled tracking (closed loops) for mouse control adheres to similar logic. You might find it helpful to refer back to Chapter 10, where the logic for the menu system itself is discussed.

MOUSE MENUS VS. MOUSE GRAPHICS

The algorithms for using a mouse to create graphics (such as lines, circles, and paint) are identical to the routines used in the two demonstration programs in this chapter. CALLs to the mouse driver are used in order to determine the location of the cursor and to check if a button on the mouse has been pressed. If the status of the mouse meets the requirements of your program, program flow can then be directed to any subroutine you choose. Provided that you erase the mouse cursor before you construct the graphics and then restore it after the graphics have been drawn, there is no great mystery to creating mouse-driven graphics. In fact, using a mouse to drive a menu system is far more complex than using a mouse to create graphics.

SUMMARY

In this chapter you learned how your graphics program can initialize a mouse. You experimented with source code that provides complete mouse control over a menu management system.

The next chapter discusses light pens, track balls, tablets, and touch-screens.

12

Managing Light Pens, Track Balls, Tablets, and Touch-Screens

In addition to the mouse, a number of other popular input devices can be used with your original graphics program. These devices include light pens, track balls, tablets, and touch-screens. Although none of these devices is as popular as the mouse, each has advantages and disadvantages which you should consider when writing your programs.

TRACK BALLS

A track ball is essentially an upside-down mouse. By stroking your palm across the exposed ball, you control the cursor movement on the display screen. For track balls which are supplied with memory-resident drivers, you simply CALL the track ball driver in much the same way you would CALL the mouse driver. (See Chapter 11 for more on this.)

The main advantage which a track ball offers over a mouse concerns precision and space. The human hand seems to adapt more readily to the track ball concept. Subtle control of the ball is easier when only the palm is being moved, as opposed to when both the hand and the mouse are being moved. This translates into more precise control over the cursor. In addition, a track ball requires far less desk space than a mouse, because its chassis is stationary. A mouse, on the other hand, is a free-roaming tool, and the user is often required to lift the mouse and return it to a more convenient position on the desktop.

Despite its ergonomic advantages, the track ball has never become as widely accepted as the mouse.

TOUCH-SCREENS

Touch-screens are aptly named. You use your finger to touch the screen in order to make your selection. In most cases, a prewired frame has been attached to the monitor chassis surrounding the display screen. The logical electronic grid established by the electrical current in the frame can be used to determine where your finger has been placed on the screen.

Touch-screens are useful in applications where choices are limited and where the user's computer expertise is not high. Needless to say, not much precision can be expected from a stubby fingertip being pointed at the display screen. A lot of pixels can be covered by that finger. In addition, the display screen soon becomes littered with greasy smudges from repeated finger touches.

You should consider using touch-screen input in your original graphics program only if it is a specialized program, and only after investigating the software driver and documentation available from the manufacturer of the touch-screen. Touch-screen programs are not serious candidates for mass-market distribution at this point.

TABLETS

A tablet is a flat plastic surface across which you stroke an electronic pen or stylus. The position of the pen on the tablet is translated into cursor movement (or other graphics output) on the display screen. Tablets are widely used in top-end drafting and 3D CAD programs, but are rarely found in mass-market applications, where the mouse is more prevalent.

Tablets are very precise and versatile. Many fit on a standard desktop, but others can be as large as a drafting table. When compared to the standard mouse, however, tablets are expensive.

The electronic or magnetic tablet has a fine wire mesh grid implanted in the plastic surface. This grid acts as an antenna. The pen or stylus is actually a mini-transmitter whose location can be determined by comparing the signal strength on the horizontal and vertical antennae of the grid.

The resistive touch-pad tablet uses two sandwiched surfaces. The electrical current which results when you press the top surface down against the bottom surface can be used to determine the xy position of the contact point.

The acoustic tablet uses a number of microphones, located around the perimeter of the tablet, to identify the location of the pen transmitter on the surface of the tablet.

Of these three types of tablets, the electronic tablet is the most widely used.

The strongest advantage of a tablet is its ability to use templates. By placing a template guide on the surface of the template, the user can readily see the program functions which are available. The display screen is free to display only graphical output; the menu has been transferred to the template resting on the surface of the tablet. In addition, templates can be easily changed by simply lifting one off the tablet and laying down the next.

A further advantage enjoyed by tablets is the ability to use physical cursors. Instead of using a pen-like stylus, users can employ a mouse-shaped utensil which contains a built-in crosshair cursor. This chassis design is extremely efficient and precise. Like a mouse, a button is pressed when the physical cursor has been located at the desired position on the tablet.

Because many tablets use drivers which are fully compatible with Microsoft's mouse driver (the industry standard), you can readily incorporate tablet compatibility into your original graphics programs. You may wish to investigate driver availability and documentation before you purchase a tablet system.

LIGHT PENS

When a light pen is pressed up against the display screen, it uses a lens at its tip to detect phosphor excitation caused by the passing electron beam. It passes this information to the computer, which can calculate the pen's xy coordinates from the timing of the phosphor's glow.

Light pens are very inexpensive, but somewhat difficult to use. The user's hand and arm suffer from fatigue as the pen is lifted repeatedly. In addition, the light pen's cord has a nasty habit of becoming tangled with other objects on your desktop.

On the plus side, the software driver for the light pen is built into IBM's BIOS in ROM. Even using BASIC, you can easily control your graphics programs with a light pen. The code fragment in Fig. 12-1 illustrates a sample routine for this purpose.

Despite their reasonable price, light pens have never enjoyed mass popularity. A mouse is a better choice for your original graphics programs at this point.

SUMMARY

In this chapter you learned that a mouse is not the only input device which you can use with your original graphics programs. Track balls, touch-screens, tablets, and light pens each offer a different way of accomplishing graphics input, but often at the expense of other advantages. You learned that the mouse is still the most widely accepted input device besides the keyboard.

The next chapter discusses graphics management of the disk.

```
100 'Code fragment A-02.BAS   Light pen input controller.
110 'Copyright (c) 1988 by Lee Adams and TAB Books Inc.
120 'All rights reserved.
130 '_____
140 '
150 'module:  install light pen trapping environment
160  ON PEN GOSUB 250  'identify light pen subroutine
170  PEN ON  'activate the trapping mechanism
180  K$=INKEY$  'read the keyboard buffer
190  IF K$=CHR$(13) THEN GOSUB 3000  'if <Enter> is pressed then jump to appropr
iate subroutine
200  IF K$=CHR$(27) THEN CLS:SCREEN 0,0,0,0:WIDTH 80:COLOR 7,0,0:CLS:PEN OFF:END
    'if <Esc> is pressed then quit the program
210  GOTO 180  'keyboard loop
220 '
230 '_____
240 'module:  pen subroutine
250  X=PEN(1)  'pen function #1, read x-coordinate
260  Y=PEN(2)  'pen function #2, read y-coordinate
270  PSET (X,Y),1  'set pixel at light pen location
280  RETURN  'return to main routine
290 '
300 '_____
310  END
```

Fig. 12-1. A code fragment which demonstrates light pen control algorithms.

13

Managing the Disk

Managing the disk for interactive graphics programs usually means managing image files, data files, and code overlays. Image files contain binary maps of the display image. Data files contain numerical and string values. Code overlays are replacement modules of runtime code. This chapter discusses image files. Data files are discussed in Chapter 14. Code overlays are discussed in Chapter 15.

THE DISK

Most personal computers use a floppy disk-based system. The 5.25-inch disk is the most popular medium, although a general trend towards the 3.5-inch disk is well under way. Another way of saying disk is *diskette* or *floppy*. An internal disk is usually called a *hard disk*.

The 5.25-inch disk is protected by a flexible jacket. Refer to Fig. 13-1. A read/write access opening in the jacket permits the magnetic read/write heads inside the computer to touch the diskette while it spins. To facilitate spinning of the disk, a clamp grabs the disk by the reinforced hub. An index hole in the jacket permits the disk drive to watch a hole on the disk itself spin by, thereby providing a reference point for reading and writing on the disk.

Information is stored on the disk in physical spaces called sectors. Each sector holds 512 bytes of data. The sectors are arranged in rings called *tracks*. (IBM calls them cylinders.) A typical 5.25-inch disk contains 40 tracks on each side of the disk. Refer to Fig. 13-2. Even if only a few bytes are being saved in a file on disk, an entire sector of 512 bytes is used. DOS will not break up a sector.

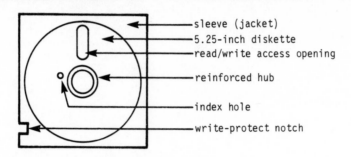

Fig. 13-1. The physical components of a 5.25 inch disk.

SAVING IMAGE FILES

An image file is often called a *binary image file,* and sometimes carries the .BIF extension. Other common extensions are .PIC (for PICture) and .SLD (for SLiDE).

When the binary contents of the CGA's screen buffer are saved to disk, the image is saved as two separate banks of data. Bank 0, which contains the even raster lines, is saved first. Then bank 1, which holds the odd raster lines is saved. Refer to Fig. 13-3.

BASIC provides a straightforward method for saving CGA binary image files to disk: the BSAVE instruction. To save the screen image in the 320×200 four-color mode, use the following syntax: **DEF SEG=&HB800: BSAVE "filename.ext",0,&H4000: DEF SEG.** To retrieve the image from disk and display it on the screen, use **DEF SEG=&HB800:BLOAD "filename,ext",0:DEF SEG.** Images in the 640×200 two-color mode can be saved and retrieved using the same syntax. Both the 320×200 four-color mode and the 640×200 two-color mode use 16,000 bytes of data to store an image in the screen buffer. These 16,000 bytes are arranged in a physical space of 16384 bytes, which equals 4000 hex. Refer back to Chapter 2 for a memory map of the CGA graphics mode.

A 360K diskette can hold 22 full-screen images from either the 320×200 four-color mode or the 640×200 two-color mode.

EGA AND VGA MODES

A more complex method is required to save the multiplane-per-pixel graphics modes of the EGA and the VGA. Unless the latching registers of the EGA and VGA are modified,

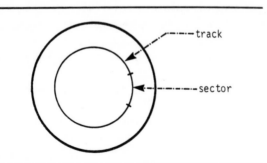

Fig. 13-2. The logical components of a 5.25 inch disk.

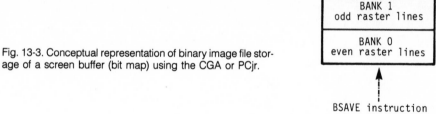

Fig. 13-3. Conceptual representation of binary image file storage of a screen buffer (bit map) using the CGA or PCjr.

BASIC's BSAVE and BLOAD instructions will only read and write the first bit plane. The result of a retrieval from disk will always be a monochrome image, despite the 16-color capabilities of the EGA and VGA. Refer to Fig. 13-4.

The multiple registers of the EGA and VGA can pose substantive challenges even for experienced programmers. Fortunately, however, an intricate understanding of the internal workings of the registers is not needed in order to save and retrieve graphic images, because only one register requires alteration in order to read from or write to different bit planes (Fig. 13-5).

The program listing in Fig. 13-6 demonstrates modules which save and retrieve full-screen images in the EGA's 640×200 16-color mode. You can use this module in any of your original graphics programs to save an image. The OUT instructions in each module are used to address the different bit planes in the EGA. The F2$ variable should contain a legal file name.

In the BSAVE module, the value 16000 is used to represent the 16,000-byte length of each bit plane in the 640×200 16-color mode. If you wished to save the 320×200 16-color mode, you would change the 16000 value to 8000, because each bit plane occupies 8,000 bytes. Change the value to 28000 if you are saving the 640×350 16-color mode. If you have a version of BASIC that supports the 640×480 16-color mode, change the value to 38400.

For your reference, remember that the 640×200 16-color mode requires a total of 64,000 bytes of display memory; the 320×200 16-color mode needs 32,000 bytes; the

Fig. 13-4. Conceptual representation of binary image file storage of a screen buffer (consisting of four bit planes) using the EGA or VGA.

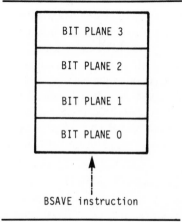

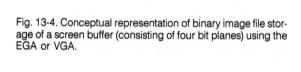

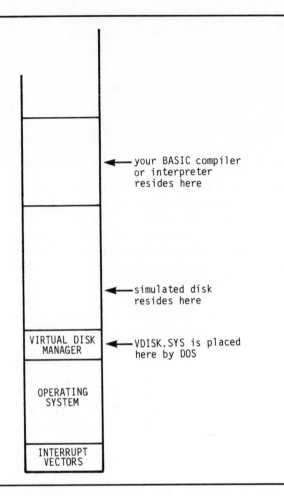

Fig. 13-5. Memory map of an IBM-compatible personal computer using a simulated disk in RAM, often called a RAMdisk or a virtual disk.

640×350 16-color mode requires 112,000 bytes; the 640×480 16-color mode takes 153,600 bytes. Dividing each of these figures by four yields the length of each of the four bit planes used in the EGA and VGA modes. Refer back to Chapter 2 for a memory map of an EGA mode. (If you wish to save from a page other than page 0, you must adjust the DEF SEG instruction to the memory address of the desired page, of course. Page 0 always begins at A0000 hex. See Appendix C for further discussion.)

A 360K diskette can hold five screen images from the 640×200 16-color mode, eleven images from the 320×200 16-color mode, three images from the 640×350 16-color mode, and two images from the 640×480 16-color mode.

SIMULATED DISKS

You can improve runtime performance of image saves and retrievals by using a simulated disk in memory. Simulated disks are also called logical disks, virtual disks,

```
100 'Code fragment A-03.BAS    BSAVE/BLOAD EGA-VGA graphics.
110 'Copyright (c) 1988 by Lee Adams and TAB Books Inc.
120 'All rights reserved.
130 '_____
140 '
150 'module: save 640x200 16-color image to disk
160 SOUND 250,.7:DEF SEG=&HA000 'set up segment
170 OUT &H3CE,4:OUT &H3CF,0:BSAVE "B:"+F2$+".BLU",0,16000 'bsave bit plane 0
180 OUT &H3CE,4:OUT &H3CF,1:BSAVE "B:"+F2$+".GRN",0,16000 'bsave bit plane 1
190 OUT &H3CE,4:OUT &H3CF,2:BSAVE "B:"+F2$+".RED",0,16000 'bsave bit plane 2
200 OUT &H3CE,4:OUT &H3CF,3:BSAVE "B:"+F2$+".INT",0,16000 'bsave bit plane 3
210 OUT &H3CE,4:OUT &H3CF,0:DEF SEG 'restore regs
220 SOUND 250,.7:RETURN
230 '_____
240 '
250 'module: load 640x200 16-color image from disk
260 SOUND 250,.7:DEF SEG=&HA000 'set up segment
270 OUT &H3C4,2:OUT &H3C5,1:BLOAD "B:"+F2$+".BLU",0 'bload bit plane 0
280 OUT &H3C4,2:OUT &H3C5,2:BLOAD "B:"+F2$+".GRN",0 'bload bit plane 1
290 OUT &H3C4,2:OUT &H3C5,4:BLOAD "B:"+F2$+".RED",0 'bload bit plane 2
300 OUT &H3C4,2:OUT &H3C5,8:BLOAD "B:"+F2$+".INT",0 'bload bit plane 3
310 OUT &H3C4,2:OUT &H3C5,&HF:DEF SEG 'restore regs
320 SOUND 250,.7:RETURN
330 '_____
340 '
350 END
```

Fig. 13-6. A code fragment which demonstrates the BSAVE and BLOAD instructions for the EGA and VGA multiplane-per-pixel graphics modes.

or RAM disks. Versions of IBM DOS and MS-DOS after version 3.0 contain a simulated disk driver called VDISK.SYS or RAMDRIVE.SYS. In order to set up a simulated disk in RAM, place the following instruction in the CONFIG.SYS file on your boot disk:

DEVICE=A:VDISK.SYS 360 512 16.

This particular instruction sets up a disk of 360K bytes, with sectors sized at 512 bytes, and room for 16 entries in the disk directory. You can change any of these parameters, of course. Refer to your DOS manual for a complete explanation. Refer back to Chapter 11 for more discussion about CONFIG.SYS files. You must, of course, ensure that the VDISK.SYS file is present on your DOS boot disk.

If your personal computer has two disk drives, then the simulated disk will be called drive C. If you have a hard disk, then the simulated disk will be called drive D. The simulated disk always assumes a drive ID which is one greater than the actual number of physical disks installed in your system.

A simulated disk is also very helpful when dealing with code overlays. Code overlays are discussed in Chapter 15. The CADD drafting program and paintbrush demonstration programs in this book can be given improved runtime performance by a simulated disk, as you will learn in Chapter 19 and Chapter 23.

Figure 13-5 contains a memory map of a personal computer which is using a simulated disk. The disk driver is installed as a memory-resident program immediately above the operating system in memory. You might be surprised to learn that the simulated disk itself is installed immediately above this location, pushing your BASIC interpreter or your BASIC compiler upward in memory. If you are using a BASIC compiler such as QuickBASIC or Turbo BASIC, you may wish to limit the size of the simulated disk to less than 100K in order to leave enough memory for the compiler to work with programs of reasonable size.

FILE NAMES

The ability to save screen images to disk is a helpful programming skill, but by itself it is not a very professional adjunct to interactive graphics programming. What is needed is the ability to allow the user to create and change file names.

The code fragment in Fig. 13-7 demonstrates a module which allows manipulation of a string. This string can later be used as a file name, of course, as illustrated in the BSAVE/BLOAD code fragment discussed earlier. The code fragment assumes that a legal file name already exists in the string.

Note line 170, which saves the existing file name in a dummy variable before beginning the manipulation. This provides for an abort by the user if a decision is made to keep the original file name intact.

Lines 220 and 230 inhibit the range of legal characters to uppercase letters from A to Z. You can easily modify these IF . . . THEN statements to create a different range, if you wish.

```
100 'Code fragment A-04.BAS   Amend file names.
110 'Copyright (c) 1988 by Lee Adams and TAB Books Inc.
120 'All rights reserved.
130 '_____
140 '
150 'module:  interactive control of file name
160 T2=25  'echo position flag
170 F1$=F$  'temporary save of existing filename
180 FOR T=1 TO 8 STEP 1
190 K$=INKEY$
200 IF K$="" THEN 190  'wait for keystroke
210 IF K$=CHR$(27) THEN F$=F1$:T=8:GOTO 250  '<ESC> to cancel instructions and
restore previous filename
220 IF K$<"A" THEN SOUND 250,.7:GOTO 190  'must be A-Z
230 IF K$>"Z" THEN SOUND 250,.7:GOTO 190  'must be A-Z
240  T2=T2+1:LOCATE 8,T2:PRINT K$:MID$(F$,T,1)=K$  'echo user input and insert c
haracter into F$
250  NEXT T
260  LOCATE 8,26:PRINT F$
270  K$=INKEY$:IF K$<>CHR$(13) THEN 270
280 '_____
290 '
300  END
```

Fig. 13-7. A code fragment which demonstrates how to accept user-defined changes to file names during runtime.

Line 240 is the workhorse of this module. The MID$ instruction is used to insert one new character into the file name at position T. The variable T is used to step across each of the file name positions from 1 to 8, as indicated by line 180.

Each of the drafting, paintbrush, and 3D CAD demonstration programs in this book provides the user with the ability to define and change file names for the purpose of saving and retrieving image files.

SUMMARY

In this chapter you learned how to save full-screen images to disk. You inspected a module which permits the user to create and change file names during runtime.

The next chapter discusses ways of managing data files, which are an important support process for drafting and 3D CAD programs.

14

Managing Data Files

If primitive data about graphic entities is saved in data files, then drawings can be regenerated. This redrawing is often called a *regen function*. The amount of memory required to save graphics data (such as xy coordinates, paint colors, and so on) is much less than the amount of memory required to save an entire screen image. In addition, saving data elements is much quicker than saving images. Data files are also useful for saving keystrokes for replay modes in entertainment software.

DATA FILE TYPES

BASIC provides two methods for storing and retrieving data elements: *sequential files* and *random files*. In a sequential file, every piece of data that you add to the file is merely appended to the end of the file. When you read a sequential file, you must begin from the start of the file. In a random file, you can add a piece of data to any location within the file; you are not restricted to writing in a sequential manner. In addition, you can retrieve a piece of data from any location within the file.

If you use a sequential file, BASIC keeps track of the active location within the file. If you use a random file, you must keep track of the active location yourself. This means incrementing or decrementing a separate variable (runtime flag) on each occasion when you access the file. Sequential files are simpler to program than random files, but in many instances random files provide quicker access to the contents of the file.

Comma Delimited Files

Data files are often called comma delimited files, because the pieces of data are separated by commas. Data files can carry the file name extension .CDF. Some packaged

Fig. 14-1. The three steps involved in managing a sequential data file during runtime. First-in, first-out design means that data will be retrieved in the same order it was stored.

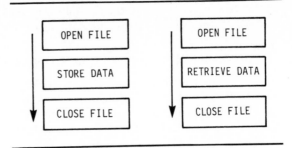

graphics programs use the extension .DXF, which is an acronym for data interchange format. (Autodesk, Inc. claims DXF as a trademark.)

FILE MANAGEMENT

There are three steps involved in reading and writing a sequential file. Refer to Fig. 14-1. First, the file must be opened for writing. Second, the data is written to the file or read from the file. Third, the file must be closed.

There are four steps involved in reading and writing a random file. Refer to Fig. 14-2. First, the file must be opened for writing. Second, you must specifically identify the active location within the file. Third, the data is written to the file or read from the file. Fourth, the file must be closed.

A group of related entries in a file is called a *record*. All the data pertaining to the graphical attributes of a straight line on the display screen would be a record, for example. Each of those separate attributes, including the xy coordinates, color, and style, is called a *field*. Each record, therefore, contains a number of fields.

BASIC and DOS require information to help them deal with the data file. The file *number* is the ID that BASIC uses to find the file in memory. The file *name* is the ID that DOS uses to find the file on disk. Note that BASIC merely reads and writes the data to and from a buffer in low memory. DOS, on the other hand, is responsible for transferring

Fig. 14-2. The four steps involved in managing a random-access data file during runtime. The programmer is responsible for keeping track of the current location inside the data file.

the contents of that buffer to and from disk, no matter whether that disk is in drive A, drive B, a hard disk as drive C, or a simulated disk in RAM.

CODE FRAGMENT: DATA FILE MANAGEMENT

The code fragment in Fig. 14-3 demonstrates modules for writing and reading sequential .CDF data files. The algorithm presented is used throughout the major drafting and 3D CAD demonstration programs in this book.

Line 170 opens the data file. The syntax **APPEND** means that new data will be appended to existing data if the file already exists. Otherwise, opening the file would destroy previous data. The syntax **#1** is the ID by which BASIC will identify this particular file buffer in memory. The syntax **B:FILENAME.BAS** is the name of the physical file on disk which will be manipulated by DOS.

Data Storage

The WRITE instruction in line 170 writes the individual graphical attributes to the data file. In this case, SXP and SYP are the starting points of the line. SXC and SZC are the endpoints of the line. C is the color of the line. SYP and SYC represent elevation values for the line in the event it is drawn in 3D space. As you can see, it is a relatively straightforward process to save data to a sequential data file using BASIC. Other languages are often not so easy, unfortunately.

```
100 'Code fragment A-05.BAS   Read/write data files.
110 'Copyright (c) 1988 by Lee Adams and TAB Books Inc.
120 'All rights reserved.
130 '
140 '_____DATA FILE INPUT/OUTPUT_____
150 '
160 'module:  storage of graphics attributes in data file
170  OPEN "B:FILENAME.BAS" FOR APPEND AS #1:WRITE #1,SXP,SZP,SXC,SZC,C,SYP,SYC:C
LOSE #1:RETURN
180 '_____
190 '_____
200 'module:  retrieval of graphics attributes from data file
210  OPEN "C:FILENAME.BAS" FOR INPUT AS #1
220  INPUT #1,SXP,SZP,SXC,SZC,C,SYP,SYC   'dummy pass
230  IF EOF(1) THEN CLOSE #1:RETURN
240  INPUT #1,SXP,SZP,SXC,SZC,C,SYP,SYC:GOSUB 280:GOTO 230
250 '_____
260 '_____
270 'module:  regen function for 2D/3D modes
280  LINE (SXP,SZP)-(SXC,SZC),C:RETURN   'polyline regen
290 '_____
300 '_____
310  END
```

Fig. 14-3. A code fragment which demonstrates an algorithm for storing and retrieving data to and from a sequential data file.

Data Retrieval

Line 210 opens the file for reading. Note how the file name and the file number are again identified for the benefit of DOS and BASIC. Line 220 retrieves a set of dummy values from the data file (for reasons relating to interactive control which will be explained in Chapter 23). Line 230 checks to see if the end-of-file marker has been found. If so, program flow aborts the read function.

Lines 240 and 230 form a loop which continues to retrieve items from the data file until the end-of-file marker is encountered. In order to use a loop like this, each record in the data file must contain the same number of fields. Therefore, it becomes necessary to use a different data file ID for different types of graphics primitives. One data file should be established to hold data for lines, another data file will contain data for curves, and so on. This multiple data file technique is used in the drafting and 3D CAD demonstration programs in this book. By alternating the order in which these data files are read during regen, the file management system contains the best benefits of both sequential and random files.

Line 240 uses the INPUT instruction to retrieve the data items from the file and assign their values to the appropriate variables. Program control then jumps to a short subroutine at line 280, which uses the retrieved data values to recreate the graphic, which is in this case a line from SXP,SZP to SXC,SYC in color C.

DISK MANAGEMENT

In a dual-disk system, drive B is often designated as the data file drive. This means that program performance will only be as fast as the read/write performance of the disk drive, which is not optimum performance, regrettably.

In a hard disk system, runtime performance can be increased substantively by instructing the program to use drive C for data file reads and writes.

The fastest approach, however, is to use a simulated disk for data file management. Even live-action, real-time programs can manipulate data files with no adverse performance during runtime. This makes it easy to save keystrokes for replay modes, of course. Refer back to Chapter 13 for guidance in setting up a simulated disk. Each of the major demonstration programs in this book can be easily modified to use a lightning-quick simulated disk for data file storage and retrieval.

MULTIPLE DATA FILES

In its default mode, interpreted BASIC is ready to manage up to three data files. As a graphics programmer, you will often wish to handle more than three sets of data. You can increase BASIC's capabilities when you first start up the interpreter by using the following DOS command line syntax to load BASICA: **BASICA/F:**n, where n is the number of files you wish to use during your session. For example, the CADD drafting program in this book requires four data files during runtime in order to accommodate four different drawing levels. If you were running the drafting program under a BASIC interpreter such as IBM BASICA, GW-BASIC, COMPAQ BASIC, or similar interpreter, you would first load BASIC as follows from the DOS prompt by typing: **BASICA/F:4**.

When DOS is used to start your personal computer, DOS uses a default value to decide the maximum number of files which may be open at any one time. Naturally, the number of files used by your program cannot exceed this DOS value. You can change the DOS files value by using a FILES=*n* instruction in the CONFIG.SYS file.

QuickBASIC and Turbo BASIC will allocate the appropriate number of data files during the compilation of the program. QuickBASIC and Turbo BASIC permit up to 255 data files (subject to DOS permission, of course).

SUMMARY

In this chapter you learned how to save individual graphical attributes in sequential data files. You saw how to retrieve data elements for the purposes of regeneration or replay.

The next chapter discusses the use of performance boosters in your interactive graphics programs.

15

Managing
Performance Boosters

Because of the immediate feedback available from BASIC—especially interpreted BASIC—you can maximize your productivity by creating and testing your initial graphics programs prototypes in BASIC. However, BASIC is hamstrung by two limitations.

First, your program source code cannot exceed 64K. Second, runtime performance is sometimes less than ideal. Even high-performance BASIC compilers like QuickBASIC and Turbo BASIC sometimes suffer from poor runtime speeds, often caused by less-than-ideal disk I/O (input and output). You can alleviate some of these performance concerns by using performance boosters.

This chapter discusses three types of performance boosters for interpreted BASIC and compiled BASIC: code overlays, simulated disks, and machine code routines. If you use BASIC to build your advanced interactive graphics programs, or if you use BASIC to build your initial prototypes, and then recode them in C, Ada, Pascal, Modula-2 or assembly language, you might find these performance boosters very helpful.

CODE OVERLAYS

Using a code overlay is an effective countervail to the 64K space limitation imposed by the BASIC interpreter. The interactive paintbrush program in this book uses such a code overlay. (The source code is listed in Chapter 17; the program's algorithms are analyzed in Chapter 19.) The interactive CADD drafting program also uses this technique. (The source code is listed in Chapter 21; the program's algorithms are analyzed in Chapter 23.)

Many interactive graphics programs rely heavily upon graphic arrays. Unfortunately, these arrays are stored inside BASIC's workspace, where they quickly gobble up available memory. During preliminary development of the paintbrush program, for example, it rapidly became apparent that a major portion of the 64K available memory would be monopolized by the menu system.

In particular, the graphic arrays used to store the assorted pull-down menus were using over 20K of memory—a whopping one-third of available workspace! The start-up code which prepared the menus, created the on-screen display, and assigned various data values consumed another 10K bytes. The addition of the menu system routines and the pull-down menu controls left a very limited workspace indeed. There was hardly any room left in BASIC's workspace for the core functions which would perform the actual drawing and painting for the paintbrush program!

The solution was to break up the source code into two separate modules. The first module would be used to set up the environment, create the pull-down menus and store them in graphic arrays, assign various data values to variables, and create the on-screen graphics. The second module would contain the code to run the menu system and to generate the various graphics which would be implemented by the user.

At runtime, the start-up module would perform its functions and then use BASIC's CHAIN instruction to download the runtime module from disk. The runtime module would be loaded into the same memory space occupied by the start-up module, thereby erasing the start-up module. Because the start-up module would never again be needed by the program, this strategy caused no harm, while recovering valuable space for reuse. Control was passed to the runtime module, which could function correctly because all data variables had already been established and because the graphic arrays containing the pull-down menus had already been created.

SYNTAX

The instruction **CHAIN "B:SKETCH-B.BAS",160,ALL** will load a code overlay named SKETCH-B.BAS from drive B. (You can select any drive you wish.) The overlay will be loaded into the same memory occupied by the current runtime code. Program control will be passed directly to the instruction at line 160 of the overlay code. (You can select any line number you wish.) The syntax **ALL** ensures that all variables and arrays will be passed to the overlay (meaning that their existence in memory will not be corrupted when the overlay is loaded).

When using interpreted BASIC, the overlay must have been previously saved as an ASCII file on disk. In this example, **SAVE "B:SKETCH-B.BAS",A** will do the trick. (The ''A'' at the end instructs BASIC to save the file in ASCII, rather than the usual tokenized format.) If a BASIC compiler such as QuickBASIC or Turbo BASIC is being used, the overlay must have been previously compiled and saved on disk as an .EXE file. (Refer to Appendix E for more discussion about compilers.)

Many other variations on the merging effect of the CHAIN instruction are available. Refer to your BASIC manual.

COMPILERS

Using a compiler like QuickBASIC 2.0 or Turbo BASIC does not forever free you from memory limitations. Although graphic arrays are stored outside the runtime code space, QuickBASIC still limits the runtime code segment to 64K. If you are preparing a complex graphics program, its length can easily exceed 64K bytes (although the programs in this book are optimized not to exceed 64K).

To overcome lengthy source code, you can use the CHAIN instruction to load new overlays (but remember that the target overlays must have been previously compiled as .EXE files on disk). You can even "ping pong" back and forth between overlays, loading and reloading them from disk, if you wish. The size of your program, therefore, is limited only by the size of your storage medium (the disk), meaning that a graphics program 400K in length could be run on a personal computer with only 256K of RAM!

DISK I/O

Although code overlays are a wonderful way to manage memory in your personal computer, they can suffer from sluggish delays, especially if you are loading the overlay from a 5.25-inch disk drive. There are two remedies to this delay, which often exceeds 10 seconds' duration.

First, you can camouflage the delay by presenting some text material to be read and a "Press any key to continue" interface to the user. Most of the overlay will have been loaded by the time the user reads the text and presses a key. This approach, however, is a second-best solution, although it makes disk-based overlays a manageable task for your original graphics programs (especially in compiled BASIC). Alternatively, you can use a simulated disk in RAM to store your code overlay(s).

SIMULATED DISKS

If you are using DOS version 3.0 or newer, you can create a simulated disk in RAM memory when you start your personal computer using a DOS boot disk. Simply ensure that the instruction **DEVICE=VDISK.SYS 360 512 16** appears in a CONFIG.SYS file on your boot disk. Refer back to Chapter 13 for further discussion of setting up this file and for a memory map showing the location of the simulated disk in memory. (Check the bibliography for Wolverton's fine book which provides detailed guidance on this and other DOS functions.)

Reading and writing files to and from a simulated disk is lightning fast. A 20K code overlay can be loaded and starting to execute in less than one second on a standard PC. The same material takes nearly thirty seconds using a 5.25-inch disk drive, and can take over eight seconds using a hard disk. Clearly, a simulated disk is the best solution for runtime performance when passing program control to an overlay.

MACHINE CODE ROUTINES

You can easily add assembly language subroutines to your BASIC programs, whether you are using interpreted BASIC or compiled BASIC. In some instances, it is mandatory that you use assembly language assistance. If your system uses the standard color/graphics adapter (CGA), you must use an assembly language routine if you wish to create simulated graphics pages in RAM memory. There is no other easy way to invoke hidden pages when a CGA is being used for an advanced graphics program.

The simplest assembly language subroutine merely takes control, performs some task, and returns control to the BASIC program. If variables must be passed to the assembly language subroutine, then the addresses of these values are passed on the stack by BA-

SIC. If variables must be changed by the assembly language subroutine, then it simply writes the new values into the addresses passed by BASIC on the stack. In the most complicated cases, the assembly language subroutine must set up its own stack to handle complex algorithms, because the stack passed by BASIC contains room for only eight PUSHes.

MACHINE CODE DEMONSTRATION

The program listing in Fig. 15-1 demonstrates the use of an assembly language performance booster. The program illustrates the use of a hidden graphics page when a color/graphics adapter is being used. If you use a CGA, you should carefully study the program listing in Fig. 15-1, because this technique can vastly enhance the graphics capabilities of your color/graphics adapter. (EGA, VGA, and PCjr users already possess many advanced graphics features like this, and more.)

The demonstration program in Fig. 15-1 first loads the *hex opcodes* into a scalar array in BASIC's workspace. The hex opcodes are the actual machine instructions which were generated by the Macro Assembler. These opcodes can be derived from the .LST file generated by the assembler. The original .ASM source code for this assembly language subroutine is in Fig. 15-2. "Hex opcodes" is an abbreviation for "*hex*adecimal *op*erational codes."

Note line 420, which uses the VARPTR (variable pointer) instruction to locate the address of the array A99 in memory. Line 430 uses a FOR . . . NEXT loop to load 35 opcodes into this array.

The database of hexadecimal opcodes is located in lines 480 through 510. Note line 410, which resets BASIC's data pointer to this database before the module attempts to retrieve the hex values.

During program runtime, the machine code subroutine is first called by line 320. Because BASIC sometimes moves various data and variables during runtime, the VARPTR instruction is used each time the subroutine is CALLed. When using a BASIC compiler, the code does not move during runtime, so only one VARPTR instruction is needed.

Note the POKE instructions in line 320. These are used to change the values of the target address and source address used by the machine code subroutine, which moves 16384 bytes of data from one graphics page to another.

Line 320 moves the screen image into a hidden page at memory address 3C000 hex in RAM (at the 240K position). You can change this address if you wish. Line 350 adjusts the target and source address used by the machine code subroutine, and then moves the image back onto the display screen.

This particular assembly language subroutine is extremely useful for general graphics programming. The ability to move graphics to and from hidden pages makes it possible to invoke "undo" functions and other algorithms of professional caliber. The high-speed frame animation of a 3D model in Chapter 34 uses exactly this technique. (The CGA version of the program listing for frame animation may be found in Appendix G.) Using short subroutines like the listing in Fig. 15-2, you can mimic on your CGA many of the multiple page capabilities of the EGA and VGA! (For a detailed discussion about modifying your BASIC interpreter to actually draw graphics on a hidden page, see *High-Speed Animation & Simulation for Microcomputers*, TAB book 2859.)

```
100 'Program A-06.BAS   CGA PCOPY prototype.
110 'Copyright (c) 1988 by Lee Adams and TAB Books Inc.
120 'All rights reserved.
130 '_____
140 '
150 'module:  data assignments
160  DEFINT A,H,P,T
170  DIM A99(18)  'reserve space in memory for scalar array
180  HEX=0 'variable to migrate contents of database
190  T=0  'counter
200  PCOPY=0  'address of machine code subroutine
210 '_____
220 '
230 'module:  set up runtime environment
240  KEY OFF:CLS:SCREEN 1,0:COLOR 0,1
250  ON KEY(2) GOSUB 260:KEY(2) ON:GOTO 270
260  CLS:SCREEN 0,0,0,0:WIDTH 80:COLOR 7,0,0:CLS:LOCATE 1,1,1:COLOR 2:PRINT "Col
or/Graphics Adapter PCOPY demonstration is finished.":COLOR 7:SOUND 250,.7:LOCAT
E 3,1:END
270  GOSUB 410  'load machine code opcodes into memory
280  LOCATE 10,1:PRINT "PCOPY has been loaded.":LOCATE 13,1:PRINT "Press <Enter>
 to create graphics.":SOUND 860,2:SOUND 800,2
290  K$=INKEY$:IF K$<>CHR$(13) THEN 290
300  CLS:PAINT (160,0),1,3:CIRCLE (160,100),51,0:CIRCLE (160,100),50,3:PAINT (16
0,100),2,3:LOCATE 3,2:PRINT "Press <Enter> to move to hidden page.":SOUND 250,.7
310  K$=INKEY$:IF K$<>CHR$(13) THEN 310
320  PCOPY=VARPTR(A99(0)):POKE (PCOPY+8),&HB8:POKE (PCOPY+13),&H3C:CALL PCOPY
330  CLS:LOCATE 10,1:PRINT "Press <Enter> to move graphics from":LOCATE 11,1:PRI
NT "hidden page back to screen buffer...":SOUND 250,.7
340  K$=INKEY$:IF K$<>CHR$(13) THEN 340
350  PCOPY=VARPTR(A99(0)):POKE (PCOPY+8),&H3C:POKE (PCOPY+13),&HB8:CALL PCOPY
360  LOCATE 3,2:PRINT " Page move done.  Press F2 to exit.  "
370  GOTO 370
380 '_____
390 '
400 'module:  load hex opcodes into scalar array A99 inside BASIC's workspace
410  RESTORE 480  'set data pointer
420  PCOPY=VARPTR(A99(0))  'define PCOPY as address of array
430  FOR T=0 TO 34 STEP 1:READ HEX:POKE (PCOPY+T),HEX:NEXT T  'move hex opcode v
alues from database into array A99
440  RETURN
450 '_____
460 '
470 'module:  database of hex opcodes for PCOPY machine code routine to move gra
phics page from 3C000 hex to B8000 hex
480  DATA  &H51,&H1E,&H06,&H56,&H57,&H9C,&HB9,&H00,&H3C
490  DATA  &H8E,&HD9,&HB9,&H00,&HB8,&H8E,&HC1,&HFC
500  DATA  &HBE,&H00,&H00,&HBF,&H00,&H00,&HB9,&H00,&H40
510  DATA  &HF3,&HA4,&H9D,&H5F,&H5E,&H07,&H1F,&H59,&HCB
520 '_____
530 '
540  END
```

Fig. 15-1. A code fragment which demonstrates an assembly language subroutine to provide page move capabilities on a standard CGA (color/graphics adapter).

```
                    ;Code fragment A-07.ASM
                    ;Copyright (c) 1988 by Lee Adams
                    ;and TAB Books Inc.
                    ;All rights reserved.
                    ;--for interface with BASICA--
                    ;moves graphics page from
                    ;    3C00H to B800H
                    ;_____
                    ;
                    PAGE 50  ;set length of print-out
                    ;_____
                    ;
                    CODE SEGMENT PUBLIC
                    ASSUME CS:CODE,DS:CODE
                    PUBLIC PCOPY
                    PCOPY PROC FAR
                    ;
                    PUSH CX
                    PUSH DS
                    PUSH ES
                    PUSH SI
                    PUSH DI
                    PUSHF    ;save registers
                    ;
                    MOV CX,3C00H  ;source buffer
                    MOV DS,CX ;load DS with source address
                    MOV CX,0B800H ;target buffer
                    MOV ES,CX ;load ES with target address
                    CLD ;set flag to incremental count
                    MOV SI,0  ;start of source bank 0
                    MOV DI,0  ;start of target bank 0
                    MOV CX,16384  ;count 16384 bytes
                    REP MOVSB  ;move 16384 bytes
                    ;
                    POPF
                    POP DI
                    POP SI
                    POP ES
                    POP DS
                    POP CX ;restore registers
                    RET    ;return to BASICA program
                    ;
                    PCOPY ENDP
                    CODE ENDS
                        END
```

Fig. 15-2. Demonstration program listing which illustrates high-speed graphics page move on a standard CGA. This BASIC program loads and CALLs an assembly language subroutine to implement the page transfer.

ASSEMBLY LANGUAGE INTERFACING

There are a number of different methods you can use to interface assembly language subroutines with your BASIC programs.

Your first task, of course, is to create the subroutine itself. The simplest way is to use IBM Macro Assembler, or Microsoft Macro Assembler, or a compatible assembler.

Alternatively, you can use the Debug which came with your DOS disk to create the subroutine.

How do you get the assembly language subroutine into memory so BASIC can use it? Two major approaches are available. These are the hex opcode poke technique and the MASM/BLOAD technique.

THE HEX OPCODE POKE TECHNIQUE

The .LST listing generated by the assembler provides the hex opcodes for each instruction in the source code. By using these opcodes as your database, you can load them into memory as a ready-to-run subroutine.

When creating your database, each element in the database must be one byte: &HB8, for example. If you encounter a word in the opcodes, such as B800, you must enter this as **&H00,&HB8** in your database. Be sure to split it up into two bytes—and ensure that the data is entered backwards to account for the "backwords" storage that the CPU expects to encounter in memory.

Where do you put your machine code subroutine? Anywhere you want. You can pick a random location in high memory, if you wish. This is called *hardcoding*. Just be sure that other code will not need the address. Alternatively, you can use the technique demonstrated in Fig. 15-1 to place your subroutine inside BASIC's workspace. This frees you from the worry of memory conflict, because BASIC now accepts responsibility for managing this chunk of code.

The main advantage of the hex opcode poke technique is that you can easily modify portions of the machine code during runtime. By using BASIC's POKE instruction, you can insert new opcodes into the routine. This technique is used in the hidden page demonstration program in Fig. 15-1.

The main disadvantage of the hex opcode poke technique is that it is very time-consuming and error-prone if your subroutine is a lengthy one. Keying in 300 opcodes can be a nitpicking experience!

THE MASM/BLOAD TECHNIQUE

The MASM/BLOAD technique is a more efficient method for dealing with long, complex assembly language subroutines. In essence, here is how the technique works. First, use MASM to create the subroutine. Then, use BASIC to BSAVE the subroutine on disk as a binary image file. Finally, during runtime, use BLOAD to download the assembly language routine from disk.

There are a few tricks of which you should be aware, however. The subroutine must be placed in high memory before you first load BASIC, otherwise BASIC will overwrite the routine before you have a chance to BSAVE it. But the routine cannot be placed so high that the transient portion of DOS will overwrite it when you return to DOS to load BASIC. The following steps provide a detailed script that will work with any assembly language subroutine, no matter how long or complicated.

Step One: Use EDLIN (or your favorite text editor) to create the source code. Save this file as **B:*filename*.ASM** on drive B.

Step Two: Use MASM to assemble the program. Place your MASM disk in drive A.

Ensure your .ASM source code is in drive B. Now type A > A:MASM B:filename.ASM. Respond to the MASM prompts as follows:

Object filename [filename.OBJ]:   B:filename.OBJ
Source listing [NUL.LST]:   B:filename.LST
Cross reference [NUL.CRF]:   (press Enter)

MASM will generate an .OBJ file and a .LST file on drive B. The .LST file can be used to obtain the opcodes for the hex opcode poke method, if you wish. Otherwise, the .OBJ file must be linked before you can use it in the MASM/BLOAD method.

Step Three: Use LINK to link the .OBJ file. Ensure that the DOS LINK program is in drive A and that your .OBJ file is in drive B. Then type **LINK B:filename.OBJ/H**.

The /H parameter tells LINK to ensure that the resulting .EXE file will be loaded in high memory (so that BASIC will not overlay it when BASIC is loaded later).

Respond to the LINK prompts as follows:

Run File [filename.EXE]:   B:filename.EXE
List File [NUL.MAP]:   (press Enter)
Libraries [.LIB]:   (press Enter)

LINK will create a ready-to-run .EXE file in drive B. This .EXE file is the file that you want BASIC to BSAVE. It will be the file you use during runtime of your BASIC graphics programs.

Step Four: Load Debug with the command line **DEBUG B:filename.EXE**. Debug will load the .EXE file from drive B. This file is loaded at highest memory, however. You must move it down a bit to ensure that the DOS transient code does not overwrite it when you return to DOS to load BASIC.

Type **R** <ENTER>. Note the contents of the DS register. The length of the subroutine is in CX. Type **R DS** <ENTER>. Change DS to **8000** hex by typing 8000 <ENTER>. Move the subroutine to a safe location at 8000 hex by entering **M CS:0000 nnnn 0000** <ENTER>. (Note that nnnn is the length of the subroutine previously found in the CX register). Then, type **R DS** <ENTER> to restore the DS register. Finally, type **Q** <ENTER> to return to DOS.

Now load BASICA. Save the subroutine at 8000 hex on disk by using **DEF SEG=&H8000:BSAVE "filename",0,length:DEF SEG**. The assembly language subroutine is now on disk, ready to be used by your BASIC programs. To load it into memory, set DEF SEG to a safe memory location and use BLOAD. You can CALL the subroutine by setting DEF SEG to that same address, of course.

SUMMARY

In this chapter you learned about three performance boosters for your graphics programs: code overlays, simulated disks, and machine code subroutines.

The next chapter discusses the components of interactive paintbrush programs.

16

Components of
Paintbrush Programs

Most paintbrush programs employ buffer-based algorithms, as opposed to entity-based algorithms. In particular, the graphics which are generated by a paintbrush program are dealt with on a full-screen basis. It is not the individual lines, ovals, area fill, and graphic arrays which are important, but rather the overall screen image (which is the image held in the screen buffer in memory).

Paintbrush programs are useful for creating, saving, and editing illustrations for business slide show presentations, for desktop publishing applications, for educational environments, and for recreational entertainment (art for art's sake). Many of the advanced functions available in packaged paintbrush software programs can be readily encoded by you on your personal computer, especially if you use an EGA.

The photograph in Fig. 16-1 shows the start-up image produced by the paintbrush demonstration program listing in the next chapter. The program is entitled *YOUR MICROCOMPUTER SKETCH PAD*. It is capable of generating, saving, and editing complex graphics illustrations. Functions include polylines, circles, ovals, smooth curves, sketching, paintbrush, eraser, and more. A full range of halftone fill is available, in addition to a full range of hues.

A complete User's Guide for *YOUR MICROCOMPUTER SKETCH PAD* appears in the chapter immediately following the program listing.

MENU MANAGEMENT

Paintbrush programs are often driven by menu systems. The program listing for *YOUR MICROCOMPUTER SKETCH PAD* in the next chapter utilizes five menus to access the full range of graphics functions afforded by the program.

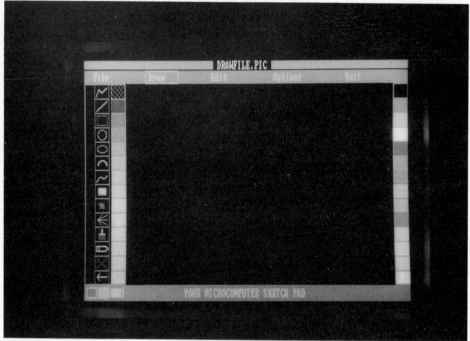

Fig. 16-1. The start-up display image generated by the paintbrush program listing in Chapter 17.

Paintbrush programs often provide mouse support, where the intuitive nature of the mouse can be brought to bear on the creative nature of computer artwork. Because most personal computers are used without a mouse, however, the program listing for *YOUR MICROCOMPUTER SKETCH PAD* uses keyboard controls. By referring back to Chapter 11 you can easily add the mouse control routines which would be needed to make this a completely mouse-driven paintbrush program.

The menu system for *YOUR MICROCOMPUTER SKETCH PAD* is based upon the programming algorithms introduced in Chapter 10. Five menus are used, including File, Draw, Edit, Options, and Quit. Of the five, Draw is an on-screen menu consisting of icons. The other four are pull-down menus which use text selections.

FILE MENU

The File menu provides the following selections for the user: Save, Load, Name, and Cancel. The selections are presented in text format in the pull-down menu and are accessed by a scrolling cursor.

The Save selection saves the current screen image on disk.

The Load selection loads a previously saved image from disk and displays it on the screen for further editing, if desired.

The Name selection uses a dialog box to enable you to specify file names for saving or loading.

The Cancel selection discards the File pull-down menu and returns you the main menu bar at the top of the screen.

Other file-related functions which could be easily added to this pull-down menu are Rename and Erase. The Rename function could be used to rename existing files on disk. The Erase function could be used to erase existing files. See Chapter 19 for further discussion.

DRAW MENU

The on-screen Draw menu for *YOUR MICROCOMPUTER SKETCH PAD* presents a selection of icons which correspond to the following functions: Plastic Polyline, Rubber Polyline, Rubber Rectangle, Rubber Circle, Rubber Ellipse, Rubber Arc, Freeform Curve, Area Fill, Spray, Rubber Burst, Brush, Sketch, Undo, and Return. The functions are selected by means of a scrolling cursor. Each icon represents one function. Refer to Fig. 16-1 to see how the icons are arranged along the left side of the screen.

The Plastic Polyline and Rubber Polyline functions can create either a single line or a long series of seamless connected lines. Each function draws a line from the last-referenced point to the current location of the crosshair cursor. Refer to Fig. 16-2. The Rubber Polyline displays a tentative line which is erased and moved until you press Enter to implement the line in the current color. The Plastic Polyline does not display any tentative line while you are moving the crosshair cursor around the drawing surface.

The Rubber Rectangle function creates a rectangle of any size. A tentative rectangle is displayed on the screen as you move the crosshair cursor. Refer to Fig. 16-3. This allows you to see what the rectangle will look like before you press Enter to draw the entity on the screen.

The Rubber Circle function creates a circle of optional size at any location on the display screen. Again, a tentative circle is displayed as you experiment with size and location. Refer to Fig. 16-4.

The Rubber Ellipse function creates an ellipse of optional size, shape, and location. A tentative ellipse is presented while you move the cursor about the screen and adjust the size and shape attributes. Refer to Fig. 16-5.

The Rubber Arc function allows you to select portions of a circle. It is useful for rounded corners. You can adjust the length of the arc, its location on the circumference, and the radius of the circle upon which the arc is based. Refer to Fig. 16-6.

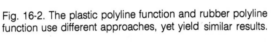
Fig. 16-2. The plastic polyline function and rubber polyline function use different approaches, yet yield similar results.

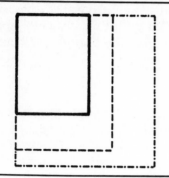

Fig. 16-3. The rubber rectangle displays a tentative shape which is not stored in the screen buffer until <Enter> is pressed.

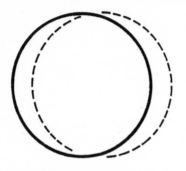

Fig. 16-4. The rubber circle operates on the same principle as the rubber rectangle.

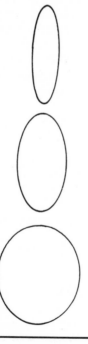

Fig. 16-5. The rubber ellipse provides a means to change the aspect ratio and the radius of the entity.

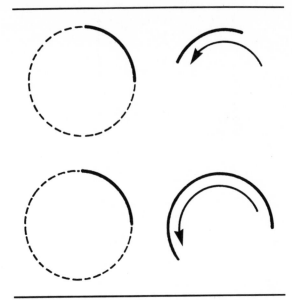

Fig. 16-6. The rubber arc can be lengthened, shortened, and rotated around its center. The radius of the logical circle can be altered.

The Freeform Curve function uses parametric curve formulas to allow you to create smooth curves. By entering a start point, an end point, and two magnetic control points on the screen, you can create smooth curves of infinite shape.

The Area Fill function will fill any polygon with a solid color. By referring to the Options menu (discussed later), you can change the fill color and boundary color. By invoking the Edit menu (discussed later), you can use halftone shading to create subtle differences in coloring.

The Spray function can be used to create a spatter-like airbrush effect in any color. Refer to Fig. 16-7.

The Rubber Burst function can be implemented to create starburst-like effects.

The Brush function can be used for calligraphic writing or for filling unique shapes in a solid color. Refer to Fig. 16-8. The thickness of the brush can be varied by using the Options menu (discussed later).

The Sketch function lets you draw an infinitely variable line on the display screen. The color of the sketch line can be changed by the Options menu (discussed later).

The Undo function permits you to erase your most recent graphics activity. On each occasion when you select an icon from the Draw menu, the existing graphics are saved on a hidden page before you begin to draw. When you select the Undo function from the

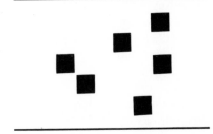

Fig. 16-7. The rudimentary splatter function uses a predefined graphic array to spray dots onto the screen.

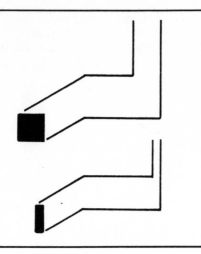

Fig. 16-8. The brush shape can be changed to permit calligraphic strokes.

the Draw menu, this hidden page is copied back into the visible screen buffer, thereby restoring the original image. The Undo function enhances the creative versatility of *YOUR MICROCOMPUTER SKETCH PAD*, in addition to compensating for fill functions which corrupt the rest of the screen when the chosen polygon was not completely closed.

The Return function simply returns program control to the main menu bar, from which any of the other four pull-down menus can be invoked.

EDIT MENU

Five functions are provided by the Edit pull-down menu. These functions are accessed via a scrolling cursor. The five Edit selections are Eraser, Halftone Fill, Clear Screen, Undo, and Cancel.

The Eraser Function uses a brush-like routine to permit you to erase selected portions of existing graphics. The eraser brush uses color black.

The Halftone Fill function operates in a manner similar to the Area Fill function discussed in the Draw menu. The density of the fill shading and the boundary color can be chosen from the Options menu (discussed later).

The Clear Screen function restores the screen to black, ready to start another drawing. This function can be aborted by the Undo function, even after the screen has been cleared.

The Undo function is used to cancel the effects of any graphics function in the Edit pull-down menu. It will restore the previously existing graphics which were affected by either the Eraser, Halftone Fill, or Clear Screen functions.

The Cancel function discards the Edit pull-down menu and returns you to the main menu bar, from which you can select any of the other four menus.

A Pattern Fill function could easily be added to this pull-down menu. See Chapter 19 for further discussion of this. (A Pattern Fill function is fully implemented in the CADD drafting program listing in Chapter 21.)

OPTIONS MENU

The functions provided by the Options pull-down menu include Active Color, Fill Color, Brush Color, Halftone Shade, Boundary Color, Snap Size, Brush Width, and Cancel.

These functions are used mainly as parameters for the drawing functions contained in the on-screen Draw menu icons.

The Active Color function uses the hue swatches along the right side of the screen to select the current drawing color. Any line, circle, oval, or sketching will be implemented in the current drawing color. A scrolling cursor is used to select the active color.

The Fill Color function selects the color to be used for area fill. A scrolling cursor is used to select the active fill color from the hue swatches along the right side of the screen.

The Brush Color function selects the active color of the drawing brush from the hue swatches along the right side of the screen.

The Halftone Shade function uses the halftone swatches along the left side of the screen to set the Halftone Fill function (in the Edit pull-down menu). A scrolling cursor is used to make the selection.

The Snap Size function is used to modify the amount of crosshair cursor movement which will be generated by a single strike of one of the arrow keys. Increasing the amount of snap means that the crosshair cursor will jump a larger distance. Decreasing the amount of snap means that the crosshair cursor will move a smaller distance on each occasion when an arrow key is pressed.

The Brush Width function will adjust the size of the brush utility. The brush can be made wider or narrower. The color of the brush can be changed by the Brush Color function (discussed previously).

The Cancel function discards the Options pull-down menu and returns you to the main menu bar. The Options menu contains no Undo function because the menu itself permits you to change any parameters with which you are not satisfied. The Options menu produces no immediate changes in the image of your current drawing; it merely alters parameters which are used by the drawing functions present in the other menus found in the program.

A wide variety of other options could easily be added to this pull-down menu, including line grid, dot grid, visible coordinates, select input device (mouse or keyboard), line style, splatter pattern, and others. Refer to Chapter 19 for further discussion.

QUIT MENU

Three functions are provided in the Quit pull-down menu. These functions are Quit, Save and Quit, and Cancel.

The Quit function simply terminates the program and returns control to the BASIC editor (if an interpreter or interactive compiler editor is being used) or to DOS (if the program has been compiled as an .EXE file). The Quit function does not save your current drawing before terminating the program. Your drawing is irrevocably lost.

The Save and Quit function saves your drawing on disk before terminating the program. The image will be written to disk under the file name currently defined by the name function in the File menu. At program start-up, the default file name is DRAWFILE.PIC.

The Cancel function discards the Quit pull-down menu and places you back in the main menu bar, from which you can select any of the program's pull-down menus.

POTENTIAL ENHANCEMENTS

Although *YOUR MICROCOMPUTER SKETCH PAD* provides a rich selection of drawing tools (see the tutorial sessions in Chapter 18 for photographs of drawings created by this program), you might want to add even more functions.

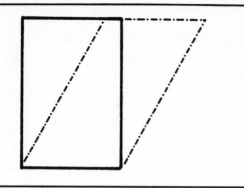

Fig. 16-9. Shear is usually accomplished by matrix math.

Shear functions are often provided by packaged paintbrush programs. Refer to Fig. 16-9. By using a pixel-by-pixel analysis of the contents of a graphic array, the image can be stretched in any direction.

Rotation is a function often present in paintbrush software. Refer to Fig. 16-10. By using standard rotation matrix formulas and pixel-by-pixel analysis of a section of the screen, any image can be rotated about an axis. This function is also often used in CADD drafting programs to allow the user to create and manipulate multiple copies of the same component in a technical drawing.

Closely related to the shear and rotation functions is the *zoom function*. By performing a pixel-by-pixel analysis of a graphic entity, simple math can be used to enlarge or shrink the entity on the display screen.

COPYING AN ENTITY

Copying and moving of graphic entities is an exciting attribute present in many paintbrush programs. As Fig. 16-11 illustrates, it is not difficult to add such a routine to your original graphics programs.

By using graphic arrays, any rectangle on the display screen can be copied to another part of the screen. First, use BASIC's PCOPY instruction to save the current screen image on a hidden page. Next, draw a rectangle around the entity to be copied. Then paint the

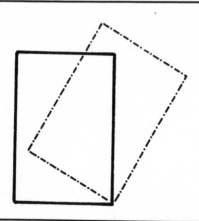

Fig. 16-10. Rotation of an entity requires sine and cosine math.

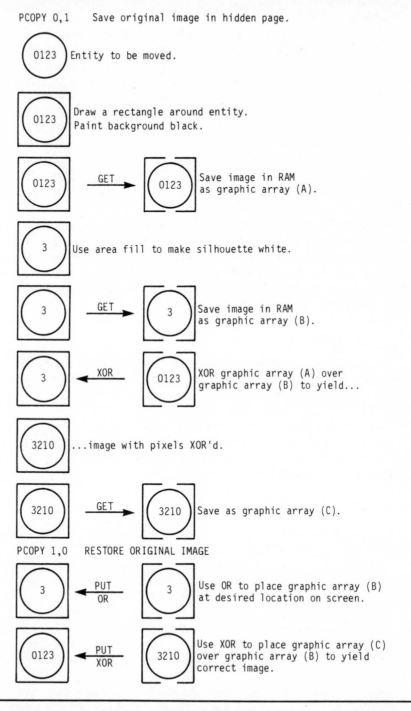

Fig. 16-11. A graphic entity can be copied or moved from one location to another on the display screen by using successive block graphic (graphic array) operations.

background inside the rectangle black. Use BASIC's GET instruction to save this rectangle as graphic array A.

Next, use BASIC's PAINT instruction to paint the entity white. You are now left with a white silhouette against a black background. Save the rectangle as graphic array B.

Next, use the XOR logical operator to place the previously saved graphic array A over the entity on the screen. This will yield an entity with the colors inverted (XOR'd) on a black background. Save this as graphic array C.

Now use the PCOPY instruction to restore the original screen image. This will clean up the minor mess created by the various rectangles and area fills which have been used up to this point.

Next, select the location where you wish to copy the entity. It can be anywhere on the screen, even overlapping the original entity, if you wish. Use BASIC's PUT instruction with the OR logical operator to place graphic array B at that location. A template consisting of a white silhouette has been written to the screen.

Finally, use BASIC's PUT instruction with the XOR instruction to place graphic array C over graphic array B at that location. The entity has now been accurately copied to the new location! The spectacular copying effect which looks so magical on packaged paintbrush software is really just a clever manipulation of graphic array boolean logic, which you can readily add to your graphics programs, no matter whether you use BASIC, C, Ada, Modula-2, Pascal, or assembly language.

INSERTING AN ENTITY

There is nothing preventing you from saving graphic arrays A, B, and C as image files on disk. By using BASIC's VARPTR instruction, you can use BSAVE to create an image file of each array. (Refer back to Chapter 15 for more discussion concerning VARPTR.)

This technique gives to you the ability to insert the array into any future drawings you create with *YOUR MICROCOMPUTER SKETCH PAD*. It also gives you the ability to create and save libraries of graphics for use in future drawings. The insertion technique is merely a spinoff of the copying technique, of course.

OTHER ENHANCEMENTS

Other functions which could easily be added to the program listing in Chapter 17 are virtual screen and pan/scroll screen.

As discussed in Chapter 6, a virtual screen is an oversized buffer in memory from which selected portions are copied to the screen buffer. By carefully choosing which portion of the virtual screen is to be placed into the screen buffer, you can invoke impressive effects such as scrolling and panning.

Even advanced techniques such as airbrushing a pattern fill can be invoked by using the same key matte technique discussed previously for copying of entities. The shape of the key matte silhouette will determine which portions of the pattern fill array will appear on the screen.

Once you have studied and experimented with the routines and algorithms in the paintbrush demonstration program, you will be in a position to add enhancements of your own.

SUMMARY

In this chapter you learned about the multitude of graphics functions present in typical paintbrush programs, and you discovered the functions which have been incorporated into the program listing for *YOUR MICROCOMPUTER SKETCH PAD*.

The next chapter contains the complete source code listing for a multifunction paintbrush program, ready to run on your personal computer.

17

Program Listing—Your Microcomputer Sketch Pad

This chapter contains the complete source code for *YOUR MICROCOMPUTER SKETCH PAD,* a multifunction paintbrush and drawing program. The photograph in Fig. 17-1 illustrates the start-up display produced by the program.

YOUR MICROCOMPUTER SKETCH PAD is composed of two modules. The program listing for SKETCH-A.BAS is the start-up module. The program listing for SKETCH-B.BAS is the runtime module which is loaded as an overlay by SKETCH-A.BAS. (Refer to Chapter 15 for further discussion of code overlays.)

The start-up module creates and saves the graphic arrays which contain the various pull-down menus which the paintbrush program uses during runtime. This module also assigns values to various variables, including the halftone area fill patterns. In addition, the start-up module creates the on-screen graphical user interface which the program uses.

After the start-up module has completed its tasks, it downloads SKETCH-B.BAS from disk. You should, therefore, ensure that SKETCH-B.BAS is present on a disk in drive A. If you are using a hard disk as drive C for this purpose, be sure to change the drive assignment in line 1150 of the SKETCH-A.BAS. (Refer to Chapter 19 for further guidance on modifying this program.)

The runtime module (SKETCH-B.BAS) contains the menu management system and the subroutines which implement the various graphics functions. The program is keyboard-controlled, although you can easily modify it to accept mouse input by applying the algorithms discussed in Chapter 11.

The program listing for the start-up module (SKETCH-A.BAS) is contained in Fig. 17-2. The program listing for the runtime module, SKETCH-B.BAS, is contained in Fig. 17-3. If you are using the companion disk to this book, all you need do to run *YOUR*

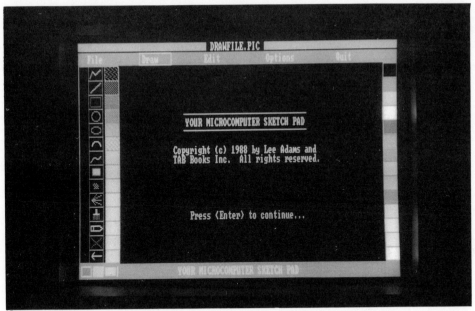

Fig. 17-1. The opening title generated by the paintbrush program listing in Fig. 17-2.

MICROCOMPUTER SKETCH PAD is enter **LOAD** *"*:**SKETCH-A.BAS***"*,**R**. (You should have the companion disk loaded in drive A.) If you are keying in the program listings from the book, be sure to key in and save the listings as two separate programs, of course.

YOUR MICROCOMPUTER SKETCH PAD is designed to run on IBM-compatible personal computers equipped with an EGA or a VGA graphics adapter. The program runs in the 640×200 16-color mode. Because of the generous range of colors used by the program, it must be modified before it can be run on a CGA, MCGA, or PCjr. Refer to Appendix G for guidance concerning CGA and MCGA conversions. Refer to Appendix H for guidance concerning PCjr conversions.

If you are using a CGA and are anxious to skip ahead to programs which can be run on a CGA, you might want to move directly ahead to Chapter 26, where a 3D CAD program is presented which has already been adapted in the appendices for both the CGA and the PCjr.

User's Guide

A detailed User's Guide for *YOUR MICROCOMPUTER SKETCH PAD* is contained in the chapter following the program listings. The User's Guide contains sample sessions which include photographs of advanced drawings produced by the program listing in this chapter. A detailed analysis of how the program's algorithms work is provided in Chapter 19.

HARDWARE/SOFTWARE COMPATIBILITY

The program listings in this chapter have been developed and tested on an IBM PC equipped with an EGA, using IBM BASICA 3.21. The program will run on a VGA-equipped PS/2 using IBM BASICA 3.30. The program will run on an IBM-compatible personal computer equipped with an EGA and which uses a BASIC interpreter which provides EGA graphics.

If you are using QuickBASIC or Turbo BASIC with your EGA, you should read Appendix E.

If you are using another BASIC interpreter which provides only CGA graphics, such as GW-BASIC or COMPAQ BASIC, you should read Appendix D.

If you are using a Color/Graphics Adapter (CGA) or a MCGA, you should read Appendix G.

If you are using a PCjr or Tandy, you should read Appendix H.

```
100 'Program SKETCH-A.BAS:  YOUR MICROCOMPUTER SKETCH PAD
110 'Copyright (c) 1988 by Lee Adams and TAB Books Inc.
120 'All rights reserved.
130 'Start-up module:  creates menus and saves in graphic arrays;  creates scree
n template with Draw menu, halftone palette, hue palette;  calls overlay program
 SKETCH-B.BAS which provides full-function menu management and drawing functions
.
140 'Version for EGA and VGA.  640x200 16-color mode.
150 '
160 '_____INITIALIZE SYSTEM_____
170 '
180  KEY OFF:CLS:CLEAR:SCREEN 0,0,0,0:WIDTH 80:COLOR 7,0,0:CLS:LOCATE 10,20,0:PR
INT "Assigning memory space for graphic arrays"
190 '
200 '_____DATA ASSIGNMENTS_____
210 '
220 'module:  data assignments
230  DEFINT A,C,T,J
240  DIM A1(560):DIM A2(150):DIM A3(150):DIM A4(150):DIM A5(150):DIM A6(150)  't
emporary arrays for screen template
250  DIM A7(177) 'array for panning cursor
260  DIM A8(1121)  'array for Quit menu
270  DIM A9(21) 'array for scrolling cursor
280  DIM A10(969)  'array for File menu
290  DIM A11(953):DIM A11C(953)  'for Name dialog box
300  DIM A12(29)  'array for roaming crosshair cursor
310  DIM A13(1035) 'array for Edit menu
320  DIM A14(2131)  'array for Options menu
330  C0=1:C1=2:C2=9:C3=7:C4=11:C5=5:C6=6:C7=4:C8=8:C9=3:C10=10:C12=12:C13=13:C14
=14:C15=15  'software color codes
340  C=C7:CF=C6:CB=C7:CE=C7  'drawing, fill, brush, boundary colors
350  C16=C4  'temporary storage for color switcher
360  T1=2  'selection flag for menu bar
370  T2=25  'flag for echo position of file menu input
380  T3=0  'iterative flag for rubber functions
390  T5=0  'flag for function switcher
400  T6=0  'iterative flag for plastic functions
410  T7=1  'selection flag for Draw on-screen command menu
```

Fig. 17-2. Complete source code for the start-up module for a menu-driven, keyboard-controlled paintbrush program. This version is for the EGA and VGA.

```
420  T8=1  'selection flag for menus
430  T9=0  'function flag for color changer
440  T9X=612:T9Y=23  'location of color changer cursor
450  T9F=23  'erase position for color changer cursor
460  T10=1  'switcher for color changer
470  J1=40  'radius for rubber circle, ellipse, arc
480  J2=4   'increment/decrement radius for rubber circles
490  J3=14:J4=6  'size of brush, eraser
500  J=5:JS=J  'snap, temporary storage of snap value
510  J6=85:J7=19:J8=608:J9=186  'viewport dimensions for active drawing surface
on 640x200 screen
520  H1=.16  'aspect ratio for rubber ellipse
530  H2=.04   'increment/decrement aspect ratio
540  H3=0:H4=1.57079  'start/end for rubber arc
550  H5=.39269  'increment/decrement rubber arc length
560  H6=1.57079  'length of rubber arc
570  SX=100:SY=40  'crosshair array location
580  XL=85:XR=594:YT=19:YB=180  'left, right, top, bottom range of roaming cross
hair cursor
590  SXC=SX+7:SYC=SY+3  'center of crosshair cursor
600  SXP=0:SYP=0  'last referenced drawing point
610  SXM=100:SYM=40  'erase position for crosshair cursor for rubber functions
620  TX=7:TY=23  'location of Draw menu scrolling cursor
630  TYF=23  'erase position for Draw cursor
640  F$="DRAWFILE.PIC":F1$=F$:F2$="DRAWFILE"  'strings used to manipulate filena
me when saving images
650  V=0  'size of free memory in BASICA workspace
660  V1=1024  'threshold memory flag
670  B=0:B2=0:B3=0:D1=0:D2=0:D3=0:D4=0:X1=0:X2=0:X3=0:X4=0:Y1=0:Y2=0:Y3=0:Y4=0
'used in freeform curve routine
680  A1$=CHR$(&HDF)+CHR$(&H20)+CHR$(&HO)+CHR$(&HO)+CHR$(&HFD)+CHR$(&H2)+CHR$(&HO
)+CHR$(&HO)+CHR$(&H7F)+CHR$(&H80)+CHR$(&HO)+CHR$(&HO)+CHR$(&HF7)+CHR$(&H8)+CHR$(
&HO)+CHR$(&HO)
690  A2$=CHR$(&HBB)+CHR$(&H44)+CHR$(&HO)+CHR$(&HO)+CHR$(&HEE)+CHR$(&H11)+CHR$(&H
0)+CHR$(&HO)
700  A3$=CHR$(&HAA)+CHR$(&H55)+CHR$(&HO)+CHR$(&HO)+CHR$(&H55)+CHR$(&HAA)+CHR$(&H
0)+CHR$(&HO)
710  A4$=CHR$(&H44)+CHR$(&HBB)+CHR$(&HO)+CHR$(&HO)+CHR$(&H11)+CHR$(&HEE)+CHR$(&H
0)+CHR$(&HO)
720  A5$=CHR$(&H20)+CHR$(&HFF)+CHR$(&HO)+CHR$(&HO)+CHR$(&H2)+CHR$(&HFF)+CHR$(&HO
)+CHR$(&HO)+CHR$(&H80)+CHR$(&HFF)+CHR$(&HO)+CHR$(&HO)+CHR$(&H8)+CHR$(&HFF)+CHR$(
&HO)+CHR$(&HO)
730  A6$=CHR$(&H44)+CHR$(&HFF)+CHR$(&HO)+CHR$(&HO)+CHR$(&H11)+CHR$(&HFF)+CHR$(&H
0)+CHR$(&HO)
740  A7$=CHR$(&H55)+CHR$(&HFF)+CHR$(&HO)+CHR$(&HO)+CHR$(&HAA)+CHR$(&HFF)+CHR$(&H
0)+CHR$(&HO)
750  A8$=CHR$(&HBB)+CHR$(&HFF)+CHR$(&HO)+CHR$(&HO)+CHR$(&HEE)+CHR$(&HFF)+CHR$(&H
0)+CHR$(&HO)
760  A9$=CHR$(&HDF)+CHR$(&HDF)+CHR$(&H20)+CHR$(&HO)+CHR$(&HFD)+CHR$(&HFD)+CHR$(&
H2)+CHR$(&HO)+CHR$(&H7F)+CHR$(&H7F)+CHR$(&H80)+CHR$(&HO)+CHR$(&HF7)+CHR$(&HF7)+C
HR$(&H8)+CHR$(&HO)
770  A10$=CHR$(&HBB)+CHR$(&HBB)+CHR$(&H44)+CHR$(&HO)+CHR$(&HEE)+CHR$(&HEE)+CHR$(
&H11)+CHR$(&HO)
```

Fig. 17-2. (Continued from page 154.)

```
780  A11$=CHR$(&HAA)+CHR$(&HAA)+CHR$(&H55)+CHR$(&HO)+CHR$(&H55)+CHR$(&H55)+CHR$(
&HAA)+CHR$(&HO)
790  A12$=CHR$(&H44)+CHR$(&H44)+CHR$(&HBB)+CHR$(&HO)+CHR$(&H11)+CHR$(&H11)+CHR$(
&HEE)+CHR$(&HO)
800  A$=A6$  'halftone fill
810  AT$=A$  'temporary storage for color switcher
820  '
830  '_____SET UP RUNTIME ENVIRONMENT_____
840  '
850  'module:  set up runtime environment
860  CLS:SCREEN 8,,0,0:COLOR C7,0:CLS  '640x200 16-clr mode
870  PALETTE 1,0:PALETTE 2,1:PALETTE 3,9:PALETTE 4,7:PALETTE 5,5:PALETTE 6,6:PAL
ETTE 7,3:PALETTE 8,8:PALETTE 9,2:PALETTE 10,10:PALETTE 11,4:PALETTE 12,12:PALETT
E 13,13:PALETTE 14,14:PALETTE 15,15
880  ON KEY(2) GOSUB 1950:KEY(2) ON  'install hot key
890  COLOR,0  'restore hardware color for background
900  '
910  '_____SET UP USER INTERFACE_____
920  '
930  'module:  set up screen template
940  GOSUB 1210  'save alphanumeric graphic arrays
950  GOSUB 1390  'create level 1 pull-down menus
960  LINE (0,8)-(639,199),C8,B  'border
970  LINE (0,187)-(639,187),C8:PAINT (320,190),C8,C8:PUT (198,189),A1,XOR  'bann
er
980  LINE (0,0)-(639,6),C1,B:PAINT (320,3),C1,C1:LOCATE 1,33:PRINT " FILENAME.BA
S ":LOCATE 1,34:PRINT F$  'filename bar
990  LINE (1,8)-(639,18),C8,B:PAINT (320,10),C8,C8  'menu bar
1000  PUT (18,9),A2,XOR:PUT (130,9),A3,XOR:PUT (250,9),A4,XOR:PUT (370,9),A5,XOR
:PUT (510,9),A6,XOR  'selections for menu bar
1010  LOCATE 10,19:PRINT "Reclaiming memory used by temporary arrays":ERASE A1,A
2,A3,A4,A5,A6  'free up array memory
1020  LOCATE 10,19:PRINT "                                           "
1030  GOSUB 1740  'create on-screen command menu for Draw
1040  GOSUB 2000  'create on-screen menu for halftones
1050  GOSUB 2090  'create on-screen menu for hues
1060  GOSUB 2180  'create icons for default colors
1070  PUT (126,8),A7,XOR  'panning cursor for menu bar
1080  PCOPY 0,1:PCOPY 1,2  'establish refresh buffers
1090  LOCATE 9,28:COLOR C12:PRINT "YOUR MICROCOMPUTER SKETCH PAD":LOCATE 12,25:C
OLOR C7:PRINT "Copyright (c) 1988 by Lee Adams and":LOCATE 13,25:PRINT "TAB Book
s Inc.  All rights reserved."
1100  LINE (212,60)-(450,60),C12:LINE (212,74)-(450,74),C12
1110  LOCATE 19,29:PRINT "Press <Enter> to continue...":SOUND 250,.7
1120  K$=INKEY$:IF K$<>CHR$(13) THEN 1120  'wait for <Enter>
1130  PCOPY 1,0:SOUND 250,.7  'restore screen
1140  LOCATE 10,24:PRINT "Loading overlay code for menu manager"
1150  CHAIN "A:SKETCH-B.BAS",160,ALL  'load menu manager and drawing functions
1160  GOTO 1160  'bulletproof code barrier
1170  '
1180  '_____CREATE DISPLAY LABELS_____
1190  '
1200  'module: create alpha arrays for screen template
```

Fig. 17-2. (Continued from page 155.)

```
1210   COLOR C12:LOCATE 10,20:PRINT "YOUR MICROCOMPUTER SKETCH PAD"
1220   GET (150,71)-(392,79),A1:LOCATE 10,20:PRINT "
   "
1230   LOCATE 10,20:PRINT "File":GET (150,71)-(210,79),A2
1240   LOCATE 10,20:PRINT "Draw":GET (150,71)-(210,79),A3
1250   LOCATE 10,20:PRINT "Edit":GET (150,71)-(210,79),A4
1260   LOCATE 10,20:PRINT "Options":GET (150,71)-(210,79),A5
1270   LOCATE 10,20:PRINT "Quit   ":GET (150,71)-(210,79),A6
1280   COLOR C7:LOCATE 10,20:PRINT "          "
1290   LINE (150,70)-(212,80),C12,B:GET (150,70)-(212,80),A7   'create panning cur
sor for menu bar
1300   LINE (150,70)-(212,80),0,B
1310   LINE (323,44)-(337,44),C7:LINE (330,41)-(330,47),C7:LINE (329,44)-(331,44)
,0 'create roaming crosshair cursor
1320   GET (323,41)-(337,47),A12:LINE (323,41)-(337,47),C2,B:PAINT (330,44),C1,C2
:PAINT (330,44),0,C2:LINE (323,41)-(337,47),0,B
1330   RETURN
1340   '
1350   '_____CREATE PULL-DOWN MENUS_____
1360   '
1370   'module:  create pull-down menus
1380   'submodule:  create Quit menu
1390   COLOR C12:LOCATE 10,20:PRINT "Quit":LOCATE 11,20:PRINT "Save and quit":LOC
ATE 12,20:PRINT "Cancel":COLOR C7
1400   LINE (138,67)-(264,101),C7,B
1410   GET (138,67)-(264,101),A8:PAINT (200,70),C2,C7:PAINT (200,70),0,C7:LINE (1
38,67)-(264,101),0,B  'save Quit menu
1420   LOCATE 10,20:COLOR C7:PRINT CHR$(175)  'menu cursor >>
1430   GET (151,73)-(159,77),A9:LOCATE 10,20:PRINT " "
1440   '_____
1450   '
1460   'submodule:  create File menu
1470   COLOR C12:LOCATE 10,20:PRINT "Save":LOCATE 11,20:PRINT "Load":LOCATE 12,20
:PRINT "Name":LOCATE 13,20:PRINT "Cancel":COLOR C7
1480   LINE (138,67)-(220,110),C7,B
1490   GET (138,67)-(220,110),A10:PAINT (200,70),C2,C7:PAINT (200,70),0,C7:LINE (
138,67)-(220,110),0,B  'save File menu
1500   '
1510   '_____
1520   'submodule:  create Name dialog box
1530   COLOR C2:LOCATE 10,20:PRINT "Enter new filename:              ":COLOR C7
1540   LINE (144,69)-(413,82),C7,B
1550   GET (144,69)-(413,82),A11:PAINT (200,72),C3,C7:PAINT (200,72),0,C7:LINE (1
44,69)-(413,82),0,B  'save Name dialog box
1560   '_____
1570   '
1580   'submodule:  create Edit menu
1590   COLOR C12:LOCATE 4,20:PRINT "Eraser":LOCATE 5,20:PRINT "Halftone":LOCATE 6
,20:PRINT "Clear":LOCATE 7,20:PRINT "Undo":LOCATE 8,20:PRINT "Cancel"
1600   LINE (138,20)-(220,66),C7,B
1610   GET (138,20)-(220,66),A13:PAINT (200,30),C2,C7:PAINT (200,30),0,C7:LINE (1
38,20)-(220,66),0,B  'save Edit menu
1620   '_____
```

Fig. 17-2. (Continued from page 156.)

```
1630 '
1640 'submodule:  create Options menu
1650   LOCATE 4,20:PRINT "Active color":LOCATE 5,20:PRINT "Fill color":LOCATE 6,2
0:PRINT "Brush color":LOCATE 7,20:PRINT "Halftone %":LOCATE 8,20:PRINT "Boundary
":LOCATE 9,20:PRINT "Snap +/-":LOCATE 10,20:PRINT "Brush +/-"
1660   LOCATE 11,20:PRINT "Cancel"
1670   LINE (138,20)-(254,90),C7,B
1680   GET (138,20)-(254,90),A14:PAINT (200,30),C2,C7:PAINT (200,30),0,C7:LINE (1
38,20)-(254,90),0,B:COLOR C7  'save Options menu
1690   RETURN
1700 '
1710 '_____CREATE DRAW ICONS_____
1720 '
1730 'module:  create icons for Draw on-screen menu
1740   LINE (1,19)-(50,186),C8,B:LINE (21,20)-(21,185),C8  'border around active
drawing area
1750   FOR T=31 TO 186 STEP 12:LINE (22,T)-(49,T),C8:NEXT T 'compartments
1760   LINE (24,29)-(30,23),C3:LINE-(35,26),C3:LINE-(46,22),C3  'plastic polyline
 compartment 1
1770   LINE (25,41)-(46,33),C5  'rubber polyline compartment 2
1780   LINE (25,45)-(46,53),C4,B  'rubber rectangle compartment 3
1790   CIRCLE (36,61),9,C2,,,.44  'rubber circle compartment 4
1800   CIRCLE (36,73),10,C6,,,.3  'rubber ellipse compartment 5
1810   CIRCLE (36,87),9,C3,0,3.14159,.44  'rubber arc compartment 6
1820   LINE (24,101)-(30,97),C5:LINE-(34,97),C5:LINE-(38,98),C5:LINE-(40,98),C5:L
INE-(45,96),C5  'freeform curve compartment 7
1830   LINE (28,106)-(43,112),C4,B:PAINT (35,109),C7,C4:LINE (27,106)-(27,112),C4
:LINE (44,106)-(44,112),C4  'area fill compartment 8
1840   PSET (35,121),C7:PSET (31,121),C7:PSET (39,121),C7:PSET (33,120),C7:PSET (
37,120),C7:PSET (33,122),C7:PSET (37,122),C7:PSET (35,119),C7:PSET (35,123),C7:P
SET (31,123),C7:PSET (39,123),C7:PSET (31,119),C7:PSET (29,120),C7  'spray compa
rtment 9
1850   LINE (26,133)-(46,133),C6:LINE (26,133)-(46,129),C6:LINE (26,133)-(46,137)
,C6:LINE (26,133)-(34,129),C6:LINE (26,133)-(34,137),C6:PSET (26,133),C7:PSET (2
7,133),C7:PSET (36,128),C6  'rubber burst compartment 10
1860   LINE (29,149)-(29,145),C2:LINE (32,149)-(32,145),C2:LINE (35,149)-(35,145)
,C2:LINE (38,149)-(38,145),C2:LINE (41,149)-(41,145),C2:LINE (34,144)-(34,141),C
7:LINE (36,144)-(36,141),C7:LINE (29,145)-(41,145),C7  'brush compartment 11
1870   LINE (24,155)-(42,155),C7:LINE (24,159)-(42,159),C7:LINE-(48,157),C7:LINE-
(42,155),C7:LINE (24,155)-(24,159),C7:LINE (29,155)-(29,159),C7  'sketch compart
ment 12
1880   LINE (25,165)-(46,173),C4:LINE (25,173)-(46,165),C4  'undo compartment 13
1890   LINE (26,180)-(46,180),C3:LINE (26,180)-(31,177),C3:LINE (26,180)-(31,183)
,C3  'return to menu bar compartment 14
1900   RETURN
1910 '
1920 '_____QUIT_____
1930 '
1940 'module:  exit routine
1950   CLS:SCREEN 0,0,0,0:WIDTH 80:COLOR 7,0,0:CLS:LOCATE 1,1,1:COLOR 2:PRINT "YO
UR MICROCOMPUTER SKETCH PAD":LOCATE 2,1:PRINT "is finished.":COLOR 7:SOUND 250,.
7:END
1960 '
```

Fig. 17-2. (Continued from page 157.)

```
1970 '_____CREATE HALFTONE SWATCHES_____
1980 '
1990 'module:  create on-screen menu for halftones
2000  LINE (55,20)-(55,186),C8:LINE (83,20)-(83,186),C8:FOR T=31 TO 186 STEP 12:
LINE (55,T)-(83,T),C8:NEXT T:LINE (50,19)-(83,19),C8:LINE (50,186)-(83,186),C8:L
INE (84,20)-(84,186),C8  'compartments
2010  Y=26:PAINT (65,Y),A1$,C8:Y=Y+12:PAINT (65,Y),A2$,C8:Y=Y+12:PAINT (65,Y),A3
$,C8:Y=Y+12:PAINT (65,Y),A4$,C8:Y=Y+12:PAINT (65,Y),C1,C8:Y=Y+12:PAINT (65,Y),A5
$,C8
2020  Y=Y+12:PAINT (65,Y),A6$,C8:Y=Y+12:PAINT (65,Y),A7$,C8:Y=Y+12:PAINT (65,Y),
A8$,C8:Y=Y+12:PAINT (65,Y),C9,C8:Y=Y+12:PAINT (65,Y),A9$,C8:Y=Y+12:PAINT (65,Y),
A10$,C8
2030  Y=Y+12:PAINT (65,Y),A11$,C8:Y=Y+12:PAINT (65,Y),A12$,C8
2040  RETURN
2050 '
2060 '_____CREATE HUE SWATCHES_____
2070 '
2080 'module:  create on-screen menu for hues
2090  LINE (610,19)-(639,186),C8,B:LINE (609,19)-(609,186),C8:FOR T=31 TO 186 ST
EP 12:LINE (611,T)-(638,T),C8:NEXT T  'compartments
2100  Y=26:PAINT (620,Y),0,C8:Y=Y+12:PAINT (620,Y),C8,C8:Y=Y+12:PAINT (620,Y),C7
,C8:Y=Y+12:PAINT (620,Y),C15,C8:Y=Y+12:PAINT (620,Y),C4,C8:Y=Y+12:PAINT (620,Y),
C1,C8
2110  Y=Y+12:PAINT (620,Y),C2,C8:Y=Y+12:PAINT (620,Y),C3,C8:Y=Y+12:PAINT (620,Y)
,C5,C8:Y=Y+12:PAINT (620,Y),C6,C8:Y=Y+12:PAINT (620,Y),C12,C8:Y=Y+12:PAINT (620,
Y),C9,C8
2120  Y=Y+12:PAINT (620,Y),C10,C8:Y=Y+12:PAINT (620,Y),C14,C8
2130  RETURN
2140 '
2150 '_____DISPLAY DEFAULT COLORS_____
2160 '
2170 'module:  display default color icons
2180  LINE (79,189)-(79,197),C:LINE (80,189)-(80,197),C  'display active color
2190  LINE (5,189)-(25,197),CE,B:LINE (30,189)-(50,197),CE,B  'display boundary
color
2200  PAINT (20,193),CF,CE  'display fill color
2210  PAINT (45,193),A$,CE  'display halftone color
2220  LINE (55,190)-(75,196),CB,BF  'display brush color
2230  RETURN
2240 '_____
2250 '
2260  END 'of start-up module
```

Fig. 17-2. (Continued from page 158.)

```
100 'Program SKETCH-B.BAS:  YOUR MICROCOMPUTER SKETCH PAD
110 'Copyright (c) 1987 by Lee Adams and TAB Books Inc.
120 'All rights reserved.
130 'Overlay module:  called by program SKETCH-A.BAS.  This overlay provides a f
ull-function menu manager, file functions, quit functions, drawing functions, ed
iting functions, options, and undo facility.
```

Fig. 17-3. Complete source code for the runtime module for a menu-driven, keyboard-controlled paintbrush program. This version is for the EGA and VGA.

```
140 'I/O Notes:  Read/write disk functions are not error-trapped.  Aspect ratio
in rubber ellipse is not error-trapped. User is alerted if available memory in B
ASIC workspace drops below 1024 bytes.
150 '_____
160 '
170  DEFINT A,C,T,J  'reassign integer status
180  PCOPY 1,0  'restore screen
190  SOUND 250,.7:ON KEY(2) GOSUB 560:KEY(2) ON  'restore trap
200 '
210 '_____MENU BAR CONTROL_____
220 '
230 'main module:  interactive control of menu bar
240  K$=INKEY$:GOSUB 610
250  IF LEN(K$)=2 THEN K$=RIGHT$(K$,1) ELSE 290
260  IF K$=CHR$(77) THEN T1=T1+1:GOSUB 350:GOTO 240
270  IF K$=CHR$(75) THEN T1=T1-1:GOSUB 450:GOTO 240
280  IF K$=CHR$(16) THEN GOSUB 560  'Alt-Q to quit
290  IF K$=CHR$(13) THEN GOSUB 730  '<Enter> key
300  GOTO 240
310  GOTO 310  'bulletproof code barrier
320 '
330 '_____
340 'module:  pan right on menu bar
350  IF T1>5 THEN T1=1
360  ON T1 GOTO 370,380,390,400,410
370  PUT (506,8),A7,XOR:PUT (14,8),A7,XOR:RETURN  'File
380  PUT (14,8),A7,XOR:PUT (126,8),A7,XOR:RETURN  'Draw
390  PUT (126,8),A7,XOR:PUT (246,8),A7,XOR:RETURN  'Edit
400  PUT (246,8),A7,XOR:PUT (366,8),A7,XOR:RETURN  'Options
410  PUT (366,8),A7,XOR:PUT (506,8),A7,XOR:RETURN  'Quit
420 '
430 '_____
440 'module:  pan left on menu bar
450  IF T1<1 THEN T1=5
460  ON T1 GOTO 470,480,490,500,510
470  PUT (126,8),A7,XOR:PUT (14,8),A7,XOR:RETURN   'File
480  PUT (246,8),A7,XOR:PUT (126,8),A7,XOR:RETURN  'Draw
490  PUT (366,8),A7,XOR:PUT (246,8),A7,XOR:RETURN  'Edit
500  PUT (506,8),A7,XOR:PUT (366,8),A7,XOR:RETURN  'Options
510  PUT (14,8),A7,XOR:PUT (506,8),A7,XOR:RETURN   'Quit
520 '
530 '_____QUIT_____
540 '
550 'module:  exit
560  CLS:SCREEN 0,0,0,0:WIDTH 80:COLOR 7,0,0:CLS:LOCATE 1,1,1:COLOR 2:PRINT "YOU
R MICROCOMPUTER SKETCH PAD":LOCATE 2,1:PRINT "is finished.":COLOR 7:SOUND 250,.7
:END
570 '
580 '_____CHECK BASICA WORKSPACE_____
590 '
600 'module:  check if user is running out of memory
610  V=FRE(0):IF V>V1 THEN RETURN
620  V1=256  'lower threshold to permit return to pgm
```

Fig. 17-3. (Continued from page 159.)

```
630   PCOPY 0,1:CLS:COLOR C12:LOCATE 10,32:PRINT "W A R N I N G":COLOR C7:LOCATE
12,23:PRINT "Out of memory in BASIC workspace."
640   LOCATE 13,27:PRINT "Save your drawing on disk!":LOCATE 15,21:PRINT "Press <
Enter> to return to SKETCH PAD."
650   FOR T=1 TO 4 STEP 1:SOUND 250,3:SOUND 450,3:SOUND 650,3:NEXT T
660   K$=INKEY$:IF K$<>CHR$(13) THEN 660   'wait for <Enter>
670   K$=INKEY$:IF K$<>"" THEN 670   'empty keyboard buffer
680   PCOPY 1,0:SOUND 250,.7:RETURN
690   '
700   '_____MENU BAR SWITCHER_____
710   '
720   'module:  execute menu bar choices
730   ON T1 GOTO 740,750,760,770,780
740   GOSUB 1070:RETURN   'invoke File menu
750   GOSUB 1740:RETURN   'invoke on-screen Draw menu
760   GOSUB 6390:RETURN   'invoke Edit menu
770   GOSUB 6660:RETURN   'invoke Options menu
780   GOSUB 830:RETURN   'invoke Quit menu
790   '
800   '_____QUIT MENU CONTROL_____
810   '
820   'module:  interactive control of Quit menu
830   PCOPY 0,1  'save existing graphics
840   PUT (505,19),A8,PSET  'place menu on screen
850   PUT (507,25),A9,XOR  'place cursor >> on menu
860   T8=1  'reset flag
870   K$=INKEY$
880   IF LEN(K$)=2 THEN K$=RIGHT$(K$,1) ELSE 950
890   IF K$=CHR$(80) THEN T8=T8+1:GOTO 900 ELSE 870
900   IF T8>3 THEN T8=1
910   ON T8 GOTO 920,930,940
920   PUT (507,41),A9,XOR:PUT (507,25),A9,XOR:GOTO 870   'Quit
930   PUT (507,25),A9,XOR:PUT (507,33),A9,XOR:GOTO 870   'Save and quit
940   PUT (507,33),A9,XOR:PUT (507,41),A9,XOR:GOTO 870   'Cancel
950   IF K$=CHR$(13) THEN 980   '<Enter> to implement
960   IF K$=CHR$(27) THEN 1020   '<ESC> to cancel
970   GOTO 870
980   ON T8 GOTO 990,1000,1010
990   GOTO 560   'implement quit
1000   PCOPY 1,0:GOSUB 1320:GOTO 560   'implement save and quit
1010   PCOPY 1,0:RETURN   'implement cancel
1020   PCOPY 1,0:RETURN   'restore previous graphics and return to menu bar level
1030   '
1040   '_____FILE MENU CONTROL_____
1050   '
1060   'module:  interactive control of File menu
1070   PCOPY 0,1  'save existing graphics
1080   PUT (14,19),A10,PSET  'place menu on screen
1090   PUT (16,25),A9,XOR  'place cursor >> on menu
1100   T8=1  'reset flag
1110   K$=INKEY$
1120   IF LEN(K$)=2 THEN K$=RIGHT$(K$,1) ELSE 1200
1130   IF K$=CHR$(80) THEN T8=T8+1:GOTO 1140 ELSE 1110
```

Fig. 17-3. (Continued from page 160.)

```
1140   IF T8>4 THEN T8=1
1150   ON T8 GOTO 1160,1170,1180,1190
1160   PUT (16,49),A9,XOR:PUT (16,25),A9,XOR:GOTO 1110 'Save
1170   PUT (16,25),A9,XOR:PUT (16,33),A9,XOR:GOTO 1110 'Load
1180   PUT (16,33),A9,XOR:PUT (16,41),A9,XOR:GOTO 1110 'Name
1190   PUT (16,41),A9,XOR:PUT (16,49),A9,XOR:GOTO 1110  'Cancel
1200   IF K$=CHR$(13) THEN 1230  '<Enter> to implement
1210   IF K$=CHR$(27) THEN 1280  '<ESC> to cancel
1220   GOTO 1110
1230   ON T8 GOTO 1240,1250,1260,1270
1240   PCOPY 1,0:GOSUB 1320:RETURN  'implement save
1250   PCOPY 1,0:GOSUB 1430:GOSUB 8120:RETURN  'implement load
1260   GOSUB 1540:PCOPY 1,0:LOCATE 1,34:PRINT F$:RETURN  'implement name change
1270   PCOPY 1,0:RETURN  'implement cancel
1280   PCOPY 1,0:RETURN  'restore previous graphics and return to menu bar level
1290   '
1300   '————————
1310   'module: save 640x200 16-color image to disk
1320   MID$(F2$,1,8)=F$  'strip extension from file name
1330   SOUND 250,.7:DEF SEG=&HA000 'set up segment
1340   OUT &H3CE,4:OUT &H3CF,0:BSAVE "B:"+F2$+".BLU",0,16000 'bsave bit plane 0
1350   OUT &H3CE,4:OUT &H3CF,1:BSAVE "B:"+F2$+".GRN",0,16000 'bsave bit plane 1
1360   OUT &H3CE,4:OUT &H3CF,2:BSAVE "B:"+F2$+".RED",0,16000 'bsave bit plane 2
1370   OUT &H3CE,4:OUT &H3CF,3:BSAVE "B:"+F2$+".INT",0,16000 'bsave bit plane 3
1380   OUT &H3CE,4:OUT &H3CF,0:DEF SEG 'restore regs
1390   SOUND 250,.7:RETURN
1400   '
1410   '————————
1420   'module: load 640x200 16-color image from disk
1430   MID$(F2$,1,8)=F$  'strip extension from file name
1440   SOUND 250,.7:DEF SEG=&HA000 'set up segment
1450   OUT &H3C4,2:OUT &H3C5,1:BLOAD "B:"+F2$+".BLU",0 'bload bit plane 0
1460   OUT &H3C4,2:OUT &H3C5,2:BLOAD "B:"+F2$+".GRN",0 'bload bit plane 1
1470   OUT &H3C4,2:OUT &H3C5,4:BLOAD "B:"+F2$+".RED",0 'bload bit plane 2
1480   OUT &H3C4,2:OUT &H3C5,8:BLOAD "B:"+F2$+".INT",0 'bload bit plane 3
1490   OUT &H3C4,2:OUT &H3C5,&HF:DEF SEG 'restore regs
1500   SOUND 250,.7:RETURN
1510   '
1520   '————————
1530   'module:  interactive control of Name dialog box
1540   GET (34,53)-(303,66),A11C  'save existing graphics
1550   PUT (34,53),A11,PSET  'display Name dialog box
1560   T2=25  'echo position flag
1570   F1$=F$  'temporary save of existing filename
1580   FOR T=1 TO 8 STEP 1
1590   K$=INKEY$
1600   IF K$="" THEN 1590  'wait for keystroke
1610   IF K$=CHR$(27) THEN F$=F1$:T=8:GOTO 1650  '<ESC> to cancel instructions an
d restore previous filename
1620   IF K$<"A" THEN SOUND 250,.7:GOTO 1590  'must be A-Z
1630   IF K$>"Z" THEN SOUND 250,.7:GOTO 1590  'must be A-Z
1640   T2=T2+1:LOCATE 8,T2:PRINT K$:MID$(F$,T,1)=K$  'echo user input and insert
character into F$
```

Fig. 17-3. (Continued from page 161.)

```
1650   NEXT T
1660   LOCATE 8,26:PRINT F$
1670   K$=INKEY$:IF K$<>CHR$(13) THEN 1670
1680   LOCATE 1,34:PRINT F$:SOUND 250,.7  'display on filename bar
1690   PUT (34,53),A11C,PSET:RETURN  'restore previous graphics
1700   '
1710   '_____DRAW MENU CONTROL_____
1720   '
1730   'module:  interactive controls for Draw menu
1740   PUT (TX,TY),A9,XOR  'install scrolling cursor
1750   K$=INKEY$:GOSUB 610
1760   IF LEN(K$)=2 THEN K$=RIGHT$(K$,1) ELSE 1840
1770   IF K$=CHR$(80) THEN TY=TY+12:T7=T7+1 ELSE 1750   'if cursor-down key
1780   IF TY>179 THEN TY=23  'inhibit scrolling range
1790   IF T7>14 THEN T7=1  'inhibit flag
1800   PUT (TX,TYF),A9,XOR  'erase previous cursor
1810   PUT (TX,TY),A9,XOR   'new cursor position
1820   TYF=TYF+12:IF TYF>179 THEN TYF=23  'update previous flag
1830   GOTO 1750
1840   IF K$=CHR$(13) THEN 1850 ELSE 1870   '<Enter>
1850   IF T7<>13 THEN PUT (TX,TY),A9,XOR:PCOPY 0,1:PUT (TX,TY),A9,XOR:GOTO 1890 E
LSE 1860
1860   IF T7=13 THEN 2020  'jump to undo function
1870   IF K$=CHR$(27) THEN PUT (TX,TY),A9,XOR:SOUND 250,.7:RETURN   '<ESC>
1880   GOTO 1750
1890   ON T7 GOTO 1900,1910,1920,1930,1940,1950,1960,1970,1980,1990,2000,2010,202
0,2030  'jump to appropriate drawing function
1900   T5=1:GOSUB 2070:GOTO 1750  'plastic polyline
1910   T5=2:GOSUB 3880:GOTO 1750  'rubber polyline
1920   T5=3:GOSUB 2380:GOTO 1750  'rubber rectangle
1930   T5=4:GOSUB 2690:GOTO 1750  'rubber circle
1940   T5=5:GOSUB 3040:GOTO 1750  'rubber ellipse
1950   T5=6:GOSUB 3410:GOTO 1750  'rubber arc
1960   T5=7:GOSUB 5240:GOTO 1750  'freeform curve
1970   T5=8:GOSUB 4500:GOTO 1750  'area fill
1980   T5=9:GOSUB 6020:GOTO 1750  'spray
1990   T5=10:GOSUB 4190:GOTO 1750  'rubber burst
2000   T5=11:GOSUB 5560:GOTO 1750  'brush
2010   T5=12:GOSUB 4780:GOTO 1750  'sketch
2020   PCOPY 1,0:PUT (TX,TY),A9,XOR:SOUND 250,.7:GOTO 1750  'undo
2030   PUT (TX,TY),A9,XOR:SOUND 250,.7:RETURN  'return to menu bar
2040   '_____
2050   '
2060   'module:  interactive control of plastic polyline
2070   SOUND 250,.7:VIEW SCREEN (J6,J7)-(J8,J9)  'clip canvas edges
2080   PUT (SX,SY),A12,XOR  'install crosshair cursor
2090   T6=0  'reset polyline flag
2100   T3=0  'reset line flag
2110   K$=INKEY$
2120   IF LEN(K$)=2 THEN K$=RIGHT$(K$,1) ELSE 2290
2130   IF K$=CHR$(77) THEN PUT (SX,SY),A12,XOR:SX=SX+J ELSE 2160
2140   IF SX>XR THEN SX=XR:SOUND 250,.7
2150   PUT (SX,SY),A12,XOR:GOTO 2110
```

Fig. 17-3. (Continued from page 162.)

```
2160  IF K$=CHR$(75) THEN PUT (SX,SY),A12,XOR:SX=SX-J ELSE 2190
2170  IF SX<XL THEN SX=XL:SOUND 250,.7
2180  PUT (SX,SY),A12,XOR:GOTO 2110
2190  IF K$=CHR$(72) THEN PUT (SX,SY),A12,XOR:SY=SY-J ELSE 2220
2200  IF SY<YT THEN SY=YT:SOUND 250,.7
2210  PUT (SX,SY),A12,XOR:GOTO 2110
2220  IF K$=CHR$(80) THEN PUT (SX,SY),A12,XOR:SY=SY+J ELSE 2250
2230  IF SY>YB THEN SY=YB:SOUND 250,.7
2240  PUT (SX,SY),A12,XOR:GOTO 2110
2250  IF K$=CHR$(71) THEN PUT (SX,SY),A12,XOR:SX=85:SY=19:PUT (SX,SY),A12,XOR:GO
TO 2110
2260  IF K$=CHR$(73) THEN PUT (SX,SY),A12,XOR:SX=594:SY=19:PUT (SX,SY),A12,XOR:G
OTO 2110
2270  IF K$=CHR$(81) THEN PUT (SX,SY),A12,XOR:SX=594:SY=180:PUT (SX,SY),A12,XOR:
GOTO 2110
2280  IF K$=CHR$(79) THEN PUT (SX,SY),A12,XOR:SX=85:SY=180:PUT (SX,SY),A12,XOR:G
OTO 2110
2290  IF K$=CHR$(27) THEN PUT (SX,SY),A12,XOR:VIEW:SOUND 250,.7:RETURN   '<ESC>
2300  IF K$=CHR$(13) THEN PUT (SX,SY),A12,XOR:GOSUB 2330:PUT (SX,SY),A12,XOR ELS
E 2310   '<Enter> to implement command
2310  GOTO 2110
2320  'submodule:   plastic polyline function
2330  IF T6=0 THEN SXC=SX+7:SYC=SY+3:PSET (SXC,SYC),C:T6=1:SXP=SXC:SYP=SYC:RETUR
N ELSE 2340
2340  SXC=SX+7:SYC=SY+3:LINE (SXP,SYP)-(SXC,SYC),C:SXP=SXC:SYP=SYC:RETURN
2350  '
2360  '─────────────────────────────────────────────
2370  'module:   interactive control of rubber rectangle
2380  PCOPY 0,2  'use page 2 as refresh buffer
2390  SOUND 250,.7:VIEW SCREEN (J6,J7)-(J8,J9)   'viewport
2400  PUT (SX,SY),A12,XOR   'install crosshair cursor
2410  T3=0   'reset iteration flag
2420  K$=INKEY$
2430  SXM=SX:SYM=SY
2440  IF LEN(K$)=2 THEN K$=RIGHT$(K$,1) ELSE 2590
2450  IF K$=CHR$(77) THEN SX=SX+J ELSE 2480
2460  IF SX>XR THEN SX=XR:SOUND 250,.7
2470  GOTO 2560
2480  IF K$=CHR$(75) THEN SX=SX-J ELSE 2510
2490  IF SX<XL THEN SX=XL:SOUND 250,.7
2500  GOTO 2560
2510  IF K$=CHR$(72) THEN SY=SY-J ELSE 2540
2520  IF SY<YT THEN SY=YT:SOUND 250,.7
2530  GOTO 2560
2540  IF K$=CHR$(80) THEN SY=SY+J ELSE 2580
2550  IF SY>YB THEN SY=YB:SOUND 250,.7
2560  IF T3=1 THEN SXC=SX+7:SYC=SY+3:PCOPY 2,0:LINE (SXP,SYP)-(SXC,SYC),C7,B:PUT
 (SX,SY),A12,XOR:GOTO 2420
2570  IF T3=0 THEN PUT (SXM,SYM),A12,XOR:PUT (SX,SY),A12,XOR:GOTO 2420
2580  SOUND 250,.7:GOTO 2420
2590  IF K$=CHR$(27) THEN PCOPY 2,0:VIEW:SOUND 250,.7:RETURN   '<ESC> to return t
o Draw menu
2600  IF K$=CHR$(8) THEN T3=0:PCOPY 2,0:PUT (SX,SY),A12,XOR:GOTO 2420   '<BKSPC>
```

Fig. 17-3. (Continued from page 163.)

```
to reset start point
2610  IF K$=CHR$(13) THEN PUT (SX,SY),A12,XOR:PCOPY 2,0:GOSUB 2630:PCOPY 0,2:PUT
 (SX,SY),A12,XOR:GOTO 2420
2620  GOTO 2420
2630  IF T3=0 THEN SXC=SX+7:SYC=SY+3:T3=1:SXP=SXC:SYP=SYC:RETURN ELSE 2640  'set
 start point
2640  IF T3=1 THEN SXC=SX+7:SYC=SY+3:LINE (SXP,SYP)-(SXC,SYC),C,B:RETURN  'imple
ment rectangle
2650  SOUND 250,.7:RETURN
2660  '_____
2670  '
2680  'module:  interactive control of rubber circle
2690  PCOPY 0,2  'use page 2 as refresh buffer
2700  SOUND 250,.7:VIEW SCREEN (J6,J7)-(J8,J9)  'viewport
2710  SX=320:SY=100  'reset position of cursor
2720  PUT (SX,SY),A12,XOR  'install crosshair cursor
2730  J1=40  'reset radius
2740  SXC=SX+7:SYC=SY+3
2750  CIRCLE (SXC,SYC),J1,C7  'install rubber circle
2760  K$=INKEY$
2770  SXM=SX:SYM=SY
2780  IF LEN(K$)=2 THEN K$=RIGHT$(K$,1) ELSE 2920
2790  IF K$=CHR$(77) THEN SX=SX+J ELSE 2820
2800  IF SX>XR THEN SX=XR:SOUND 250,.7
2810  GOTO 2900
2820  IF K$=CHR$(75) THEN SX=SX-J ELSE 2850
2830  IF SX<XL THEN SX=XL:SOUND 250,.7
2840  GOTO 2900
2850  IF K$=CHR$(72) THEN SY=SY-J ELSE 2880
2860  IF SY<YT THEN SY=YT:SOUND 250,.7
2870  GOTO 2900
2880  IF K$=CHR$(80) THEN SY=SY+J ELSE 2910
2890  IF SY>YB THEN SY=YB:SOUND 250,.7
2900  SXC=SX+7:SYC=SY+3:PCOPY 2,0:CIRCLE (SXC,SYC),J1,C7:PUT (SX,SY),A12,XOR:GOT
0 2760
2910  SOUND 250,.7:GOTO 2760
2920  IF K$=CHR$(27) THEN PCOPY 2,0:VIEW:SOUND 250,.7:RETURN  '<ESC> to return t
o Draw menu
2930  IF K$="L" THEN J1=J1+J2:PCOPY 2,0:CIRCLE (SXC,SYC),J1,C7:PUT (SX,SY),A12,X
OR:GOTO 2760  'increment radius
2940  IF K$="S" THEN J1=J1-J2 ELSE 2970
2950  IF J1<8 THEN J1=8:SOUND 250,.7
2960  PCOPY 2,0:CIRCLE (SXC,SYC),J1,C7:PUT (SX,SY),A12,XOR:GOTO 2760  'decrement
 radius
2970  IF K$=CHR$(13) THEN PUT (SX,SY),A12,XOR:PCOPY 2,0:GOSUB 2990:PCOPY 0,2:PUT
 (SX,SY),A12,XOR:GOTO 2760
2980  GOTO 2760
2990  SXC=SX+7:SYC=SY+3:CIRCLE (SXC,SYC),J1,C:RETURN  'implement circle
3000  SOUND 250,.7:RETURN
3010  '_____
3020  '
3030  'module:  interactive control of rubber ellipse
3040  PCOPY 0,2  'use page 2 as refresh buffer
```

Fig. 17-3. (Continued from page 164.)

```
3050    SOUND 250,.7:VIEW SCREEN (J6,J7)-(J8,J9)  'viewport
3060    SX=320:SY=100  'reset position of cursor
3070    PUT (SX,SY),A12,XOR  'install crosshair cursor
3080    J1=40:H1=.24  'reset radius, aspect ratio
3090    SXC=SX+7:SYC=SY+3
3100    CIRCLE (SXC,SYC),J1,C7,,,H1  'install rubber ellipse
3110    K$=INKEY$
3120    SXM=SX:SYM=SY
3130    IF LEN(K$)=2 THEN K$=RIGHT$(K$,1) ELSE 3270
3140    IF K$=CHR$(77) THEN SX=SX+J ELSE 3170
3150    IF SX>XR THEN SX=XR:SOUND 250,.7
3160    GOTO 3250
3170    IF K$=CHR$(75) THEN SX=SX-J ELSE 3200
3180    IF SX<XL THEN SX=XL:SOUND 250,.7
3190    GOTO 3250
3200    IF K$=CHR$(72) THEN SY=SY-J ELSE 3230
3210    IF SY<YT THEN SY=YT:SOUND 250,.7
3220    GOTO 3250
3230    IF K$=CHR$(80) THEN SY=SY+J ELSE 3260
3240    IF SY>YB THEN SY=YB:SOUND 250,.7
3250    SXC=SX+7:SYC=SY+3:PCOPY 2,0:CIRCLE (SXC,SYC),J1,C7,,,H1:PUT (SX,SY),A12,XO
R:GOTO 3110
3260    SOUND 250,.7:GOTO 3110
3270    IF K$=CHR$(27) THEN PCOPY 2,0:VIEW:SOUND 250,.7:RETURN  '<ESC> to return t
o Draw menu
3280    IF K$="L" THEN J1=J1+J2:PCOPY 2,0:CIRCLE (SXC,SYC),J1,C7,,,H1:PUT (SX,SY),
A12,XOR:GOTO 3110  'increment radius
3290    IF K$="S" THEN J1=J1-J2 ELSE 3320
3300    IF J1<8 THEN J1=8:SOUND 250,.7
3310    PCOPY 2,0:CIRCLE (SXC,SYC),J1,C7,,,H1:PUT (SX,SY),A12,XOR:GOTO 3110  'decr
ement radius
3320    IF K$="=" THEN H1=H1+H2:PCOPY 2,0:CIRCLE (SXC,SYC),J1,C7,,,H1:PUT (SX,SY),
A12,XOR:GOTO 3110  'increase aspect ratio
3330    IF K$="-" THEN H1=H1-H2:PCOPY 2,0:CIRCLE (SXC,SYC),J1,C7,,,H1:PUT (SX,SY),
A12,XOR:GOTO 3110  'decrease aspect ratio
3340    IF K$=CHR$(13) THEN PUT (SX,SY),A12,XOR:PCOPY 2,0:GOSUB 3360:PCOPY 0,2:PUT
 (SX,SY),A12,XOR:GOTO 3110
3350    GOTO 3110
3360    SXC=SX+7:SYC=SY+3:CIRCLE (SXC,SYC),J1,C,,,H1:RETURN  'implement circle
3370    SOUND 250,.7:RETURN
3380    '_____
3390    '_____
3400    'module:  interactive control of rubber arc
3410    PCOPY 0,2  'use page 2 as refresh buffer
3420    SOUND 250,.7:VIEW SCREEN (J6,J7)-(J8,J9)  'viewport
3430    SX=320:SY=100  'reset position of cursor
3440    PUT (SX,SY),A12,XOR  'install crosshair cursor
3450    J1=40:H6=1.57079:H3=0:H4=H3+H6  'reset radius, length, start point, end po
int
3460    SXC=SX+7:SYC=SY+3
3470    CIRCLE (SXC,SYC),J1,C7,H3,H4  'install rubber arc
3480    K$=INKEY$
3490    SXM=SX:SYM=SY
```

Fig. 17-3. (Continued from page 165.)

```
3500   IF LEN(K$)=2 THEN K$=RIGHT$(K$,1) ELSE 3640
3510   IF K$=CHR$(77) THEN SX=SX+J ELSE 3540
3520   IF SX>XR THEN SX=XR:SOUND 250,.7
3530   GOTO 3620
3540   IF K$=CHR$(75) THEN SX=SX-J ELSE 3570
3550   IF SX<XL THEN SX=XL:SOUND 250,.7
3560   GOTO 3620
3570   IF K$=CHR$(72) THEN SY=SY-J ELSE 3600
3580   IF SY<YT THEN SY=YT:SOUND 250,.7
3590   GOTO 3620
3600   IF K$=CHR$(80) THEN SY=SY+J ELSE 3630
3610   IF SY>YB THEN SY=YB:SOUND 250,.7
3620   SXC=SX+7:SYC=SY+3:PCOPY 2,0:CIRCLE (SXC,SYC),J1,C7,H3,H4:PUT (SX,SY),A12,X
OR:GOTO 3480
3630   SOUND 250,.7:GOTO 3480
3640   IF K$=CHR$(27) THEN PCOPY 2,0:VIEW:SOUND 250,.7:RETURN  '<ESC> to return t
o Draw menu
3650   IF K$="L" THEN J1=J1+J2:PCOPY 2,0:CIRCLE (SXC,SYC),J1,C7,H3,H4:PUT (SX,SY)
,A12,XOR:GOTO 3480  'increment radius
3660   IF K$="S" THEN J1=J1-J2 ELSE 3690
3670   IF J1<8 THEN J1=8:SOUND 250,.7
3680   PCOPY 2,0:CIRCLE (SXC,SYC),J1,C7,H3,H4:PUT (SX,SY),A12,XOR:GOTO 3480  'dec
rement radius
3690   IF K$="R" THEN H3=H3+H5:H4=H3+H6 ELSE 3720
3700   IF H4>6.28318 THEN H4=6.28318:H3=H4-H6:SOUND 250,.7
3710   PCOPY 2,0:CIRCLE (SXC,SYC),J1,C7,H3,H4:PUT (SX,SY),A12,XOR:GOTO 3480  'rot
ate arc counterclockwise
3720   IF K$="=" THEN H6=H6+H5 ELSE 3770
3730   IF H6>6.28318 THEN H6=6.28318:SOUND 250,.7
3740   H4=H3+H6
3750   IF H4>6.28318 THEN H4=6.28318:SOUND 250,.7
3760   PCOPY 2,0:CIRCLE (SXC,SYC),J1,C7,H3,H4:PUT (SX,SY),A12,XOR:GOTO 3480  'len
gthen arc
3770   IF K$="-" THEN H6=H6-H5 ELSE 3810
3780   IF H6<.39628 THEN H6=.39629:SOUND 250,.7
3790   H4=H3+H6:IF H4>6.28318 THEN H4=6.28318
3800   PCOPY 2,0:CIRCLE (SXC,SYC),J1,C7,H3,H4:PUT (SX,SY),A12,XOR:GOTO 3480  'sho
rten arc
3810   IF K$=CHR$(13) THEN PUT (SX,SY),A12,XOR:PCOPY 2,0:GOSUB 3830:PCOPY 0,2:PUT
 (SX,SY),A12,XOR:GOTO 3480
3820   GOTO 3480
3830   SXC=SX+7:SYC=SY+3:CIRCLE (SXC,SYC),J1,C,H3,H4:RETURN  'implement circle
3840   SOUND 250,.7:RETURN
3850   '_____
3860   '
3870   'module:  interactive control of rubber line
3880   PCOPY 0,2  'use page 2 as refresh buffer
3890   SOUND 250,.7:VIEW SCREEN (J6,J7)-(J8,J9)  'viewport
3900   PUT (SX,SY),A12,XOR  'install crosshair cursor
3910   T3=0  'reset iteration flag
3920   K$=INKEY$
3930   SXM=SX:SYM=SY
3940   IF LEN(K$)=2 THEN K$=RIGHT$(K$,1) ELSE 4090
```

Fig. 17-3. (Continued from page 166.)

```
3950    IF K$=CHR$(77) THEN SX=SX+J ELSE 3980
3960    IF SX>XR THEN SX=XR:SOUND 250,.7
3970    GOTO 4060
3980    IF K$=CHR$(75) THEN SX=SX-J ELSE 4010
3990    IF SX<XL THEN SX=XL:SOUND 250,.7
4000    GOTO 4060
4010    IF K$=CHR$(72) THEN SY=SY-J ELSE 4040
4020    IF SY<YT THEN SY=YT:SOUND 250,.7
4030    GOTO 4060
4040    IF K$=CHR$(80) THEN SY=SY+J ELSE 4080
4050    IF SY>YB THEN SY=YB:SOUND 250,.7
4060    IF T3=1 THEN SXC=SX+7:SYC=SY+3:PCOPY 2,0:LINE (SXP,SYP)-(SXC,SYC),C7:PUT (
SX,SY),A12,XOR:GOTO 3920
4070    IF T3=0 THEN PUT (SXM,SYM),A12,XOR:PUT (SX,SY),A12,XOR:GOTO 3920
4080    SOUND 250,.7:GOTO 3920
4090    IF K$=CHR$(27) THEN PCOPY 2,0:VIEW:SOUND 250,.7:RETURN   '<ESC> to return t
o Draw menu
4100    IF K$=CHR$(8) THEN T3=0:PCOPY 2,0:PUT (SX,SY),A12,XOR:GOTO 3920   '<BKSPC>
to reset start point
4110    IF K$=CHR$(13) THEN PUT (SX,SY),A12,XOR:PCOPY 2,0:GOSUB 4130:PCOPY 0,2:PUT
(SX,SY),A12,XOR:GOTO 3920
4120    GOTO 3920
4130    IF T3=0 THEN SXC=SX+7:SYC=SY+3:T3=1:SXP=SXC:SYP=SYC:RETURN ELSE 4140   'set
 start point
4140    IF T3=1 THEN SXC=SX+7:SYC=SY+3:LINE (SXP,SYP)-(SXC,SYC),C:SXP=SXC:SYP=SYC:
RETURN   'implement solid line
4150    SOUND 250,.7:RETURN
4160    '_____

4170    '
4180    'module:   interactive control of rubber burst
4190    PCOPY 0,2   'use page 2 as refresh buffer
4200    SOUND 250,.7:VIEW SCREEN (J6,J7)-(J8,J9)   'viewport
4210    PUT (SX,SY),A12,XOR   'install crosshair cursor
4220    T3=0   'reset iteration flag
4230    K$=INKEY$
4240    SXM=SX:SYM=SY
4250    IF LEN(K$)=2 THEN K$=RIGHT$(K$,1) ELSE 4400
4260    IF K$=CHR$(77) THEN SX=SX+J ELSE 4290
4270    IF SX>XR THEN SX=XR:SOUND 250,.7
4280    GOTO 4370
4290    IF K$=CHR$(75) THEN SX=SX-J ELSE 4320
4300    IF SX<XL THEN SX=XL:SOUND 250,.7
4310    GOTO 4370
4320    IF K$=CHR$(72) THEN SY=SY-J ELSE 4350
4330    IF SY<YT THEN SY=YT:SOUND 250,.7
4340    GOTO 4370
4350    IF K$=CHR$(80) THEN SY=SY+J ELSE 4390
4360    IF SY>YB THEN SY=YB:SOUND 250,.7
4370    IF T3=1 THEN SXC=SX+7:SYC=SY+3:PCOPY 2,0:LINE (SXP,SYP)-(SXC,SYC),C7:PUT (
SX,SY),A12,XOR:GOTO 4230
4380    IF T3=0 THEN PUT (SXM,SYM),A12,XOR:PUT (SX,SY),A12,XOR:GOTO 4230
4390    SOUND 250,.7:GOTO 4230
```

Fig. 17-3. (Continued from page 167.)

```
4400  IF K$=CHR$(27) THEN PCOPY 2,0:VIEW:SOUND 250,.7:RETURN  '<ESC> to return t
o Draw menu
4410  IF K$=CHR$(8) THEN T3=0:PCOPY 2,0:PUT (SX,SY),A12,XOR:GOTO 4230  '<BKSPC>
to reset start point
4420  IF K$=CHR$(13) THEN PUT (SX,SY),A12,XOR:PCOPY 2,0:GOSUB 4440:PCOPY 0,2:PUT
 (SX,SY),A12,XOR:GOTO 4230
4430  GOTO 4230
4440  IF T3=0 THEN SXC=SX+7:SYC=SY+3:T3=1:SXP=SXC:SYP=SYC:RETURN ELSE 4450  'set
 start point
4450  IF T3=1 THEN SXC=SX+7:SYC=SY+3:LINE (SXP,SYP)-(SXC,SYC),C:RETURN  'impleme
nt solid burst
4460  SOUND 250,.7:RETURN
4470  '_____
4480  '
4490  'module:  interactive control of area fill
4500  SOUND 250,.7:VIEW SCREEN (J6,J7)-(J8,J9)  'clip canvas edges
4510  PUT (SX,SY),A12,XOR  'install crosshair cursor
4520  K$=INKEY$
4530  IF LEN(K$)=2 THEN K$=RIGHT$(K$,1) ELSE 4700
4540  IF K$=CHR$(77) THEN PUT (SX,SY),A12,XOR:SX=SX+J ELSE 4570
4550  IF SX>XR THEN SX=XR:SOUND 250,.7
4560  PUT (SX,SY),A12,XOR:GOTO 4520
4570  IF K$=CHR$(75) THEN PUT (SX,SY),A12,XOR:SX=SX-J ELSE 4600
4580  IF SX<XL THEN SX=XL:SOUND 250,.7
4590  PUT (SX,SY),A12,XOR:GOTO 4520
4600  IF K$=CHR$(72) THEN PUT (SX,SY),A12,XOR:SY=SY-J ELSE 4630
4610  IF SY<YT THEN SY=YT:SOUND 250,.7
4620  PUT (SX,SY),A12,XOR:GOTO 4520
4630  IF K$=CHR$(80) THEN PUT (SX,SY),A12,XOR:SY=SY+J ELSE 4660
4640  IF SY>YB THEN SY=YB:SOUND 250,.7
4650  PUT (SX,SY),A12,XOR:GOTO 4520
4660  IF K$=CHR$(71) THEN PUT (SX,SY),A12,XOR:SX=85:SY=19:PUT (SX,SY),A12,XOR:GO
TO 4520
4670  IF K$=CHR$(73) THEN PUT (SX,SY),A12,XOR:SX=594:SY=19:PUT (SX,SY),A12,XOR:G
OTO 4520
4680  IF K$=CHR$(81) THEN PUT (SX,SY),A12,XOR:SX=594:SY=180:PUT (SX,SY),A12,XOR:
GOTO 4520
4690  IF K$=CHR$(79) THEN PUT (SX,SY),A12,XOR:SX=85:SY=180:PUT (SX,SY),A12,XOR:G
OTO 4520
4700  IF K$=CHR$(27) THEN PUT (SX,SY),A12,XOR:VIEW:SOUND 250,.7:RETURN  '<ESC>
4710  IF K$=CHR$(13) THEN PUT (SX,SY),A12,XOR:GOSUB 4740:PUT (SX,SY),A12,XOR ELS
E 4720  '<Enter> to implement command
4720  GOTO 4520
4730 'submodule:  area fill function
4740  SXC=SX+7:SYC=SY+3:PAINT (SXC,SYC),CF,CE:RETURN
4750  '_____
4760  '
4770  'module:  interactive control of sketch
4780  SOUND 250,.7:VIEW SCREEN (J6,J7)-(J8,J9)  'clip canvas edges
4790  PUT (SX,SY),A12,XOR  'install crosshair cursor
4800  T3=0  'reset toggle flag
4810  JS=J:J=1  'save current snap, set to 1
4820  K$=INKEY$
```

Fig. 17-3. (Continued from page 168.)

```
4830   IF LEN(K$)=2 THEN K$=RIGHT$(K$,1) ELSE 5000
4840   IF K$=CHR$(77) THEN PUT (SX,SY),A12,XOR:SX=SX+J ELSE 4870
4850   IF SX>XR THEN SX=XR:SOUND 250,.7
4860   GOSUB 5120:PUT (SX,SY),A12,XOR:GOTO 4820
4870   IF K$=CHR$(75) THEN PUT (SX,SY),A12,XOR:SX=SX-J ELSE 4900
4880   IF SX<XL THEN SX=XL:SOUND 250,.7
4890   GOSUB 5120:PUT (SX,SY),A12,XOR:GOTO 4820
4900   IF K$=CHR$(72) THEN PUT (SX,SY),A12,XOR:SY=SY-J ELSE 4930
4910   IF SY<YT THEN SY=YT:SOUND 250,.7
4920   GOSUB 5120:PUT (SX,SY),A12,XOR:GOTO 4820
4930   IF K$=CHR$(80) THEN PUT (SX,SY),A12,XOR:SY=SY+J ELSE 4960
4940   IF SY>YB THEN SY=YB:SOUND 250,.7
4950   GOSUB 5120:PUT (SX,SY),A12,XOR:GOTO 4820
4960   IF K$=CHR$(71) THEN PUT (SX,SY),A12,XOR:SX=SX-J:SY=SY-J:GOSUB 5180:GOSUB 5
120:PUT (SX,SY),A12,XOR:GOTO 4820
4970   IF K$=CHR$(73) THEN PUT (SX,SY),A12,XOR:SX=SX+J:SY=SY-J:GOSUB 5180:GOSUB 5
120:PUT (SX,SY),A12,XOR:GOTO 4820
4980   IF K$=CHR$(81) THEN PUT (SX,SY),A12,XOR:SX=SX+J:SY=SY+J:GOSUB 5180:GOSUB 5
120:PUT (SX,SY),A12,XOR:GOTO 4820
4990   IF K$=CHR$(79) THEN PUT (SX,SY),A12,XOR:SX=SX-J:SY=SY+J:GOSUB 5180:GOSUB 5
120:PUT (SX,SY),A12,XOR:GOTO 4820
5000   IF K$=CHR$(27) THEN PUT (SX,SY),A12,XOR:J=JS:VIEW:SOUND 250,.7:RETURN  '<E
SC> and restore snap
5010   IF K$=CHR$(13) THEN PUT (SX,SY),A12,XOR:GOSUB 5060:PUT (SX,SY),A12,XOR ELS
E 5020  '<Enter> to implement command
5020   GOTO 4820
5030  '_____
5040  '
5050  'submodule:   toggle on/off sketch flag
5060   IF T3=0 THEN T3=1:RETURN ELSE 5070
5070   IF T3=1 THEN T3=0:RETURN
5080   RETURN  'failsafe barrier
5090  '
5100  '_____
5110  'submodule:   sketch function
5120   IF T3=1 THEN SXC=SX+7:SYC=SY+3:PSET (SXC,SYC),C:RETURN ELSE 5130
5130   IF T3=0 THEN RETURN
5140   RETURN  'failsafe barrier
5150  '
5160  '_____
5170  'submodule:   inhibit diagonal movement of cursor
5180   IF SX>XR THEN SX=XR:SOUND 250,.7 ELSE IF SX<XL THEN SX=XL:SOUND 250,.7
5190   IF SY>YB THEN SY=YB:SOUND 250,.7 ELSE IF SY<YT THEN SY=YT:SOUND 250,.7
5200   RETURN
5210  '
5220  '_____
5230  'module:   interactive control of freeform curve
5240   SOUND 250,.7:VIEW SCREEN (J6,J7)-(J8,J9)  'clip canvas edges
5250   PUT (SX,SY),A12,XOR  'install crosshair cursor
5260   X1=100:X2=130:X3=160:X4=190:Y1=40:Y2=100:Y3=140:Y4=70  'reset default cont
rol points for freeform curve
5270   K$=INKEY$
5280   IF LEN(K$)=2 THEN K$=RIGHT$(K$,1) ELSE 5410
```

Fig. 17-3. (Continued from page 169.)

```
5290   IF K$=CHR$(77) THEN PUT (SX,SY),A12,XOR:SX=SX+J ELSE 5320
5300   IF SX>XR THEN SX=XR:SOUND 250,.7
5310   PUT (SX,SY),A12,XOR:GOTO 5270
5320   IF K$=CHR$(75) THEN PUT (SX,SY),A12,XOR:SX=SX-J ELSE 5350
5330   IF SX<XL THEN SX=XL:SOUND 250,.7
5340   PUT (SX,SY),A12,XOR:GOTO 5270
5350   IF K$=CHR$(72) THEN PUT (SX,SY),A12,XOR:SY=SY-J ELSE 5380
5360   IF SY<YT THEN SY=YT:SOUND 250,.7
5370   PUT (SX,SY),A12,XOR:GOTO 5270
5380   IF K$=CHR$(80) THEN PUT (SX,SY),A12,XOR:SY=SY+J ELSE 5410
5390   IF SY>YB THEN SY=YB:SOUND 250,.7
5400   PUT (SX,SY),A12,XOR:GOTO 5270
5410   IF K$=CHR$(27) THEN PUT (SX,SY),A12,XOR:VIEW:SOUND 250,.7:RETURN   '<ESC>
5420   IF K$="1" THEN X1=SX+7:Y1=SY+3:PUT (SX,SY),A12,XOR:PSET (X1,Y1),C:PUT (SX,
SY),A12,XOR:GOTO 5270
5430   IF K$="2" THEN X2=SX+7:Y2=SY+3:PUT (SX,SY),A12,XOR:PSET (X2,Y2),C:PUT (SX,
SY),A12,XOR:GOTO 5270
5440   IF K$="3" THEN X3=SX+7:Y3=SY+3:PUT (SX,SY),A12,XOR:PSET (X3,Y3),C:PUT (SX,
SY),A12,XOR:GOTO 5270
5450   IF K$="4" THEN X4=SX+7:Y4=SY+3:PUT (SX,SY),A12,XOR:PSET (X4,Y4),C:PUT (SX,
SY),A12,XOR:GOTO 5270
5460   IF K$=CHR$(13) THEN PUT (SX,SY),A12,XOR:GOSUB 5500:SX=100:SY=40:PSET (X1,Y
1),C0:PSET (X2,Y2),C0:PSET (X3,Y3),C0:PSET (X4,Y4),C0:PUT (SX,SY),A12,XOR:K$=CHR
$(27):GOTO 5410 ELSE 5470   '<Enter> to implement command
5470   GOTO 5270
5480 '_____
5490 '
5500 'submodule:  freeform curve driver
5510   B=0:B2=B*B:B3=B*B*B:GOSUB 5520:PSET (SX,SY),C:FOR B=0 TO 1.01 STEP .05:B2=
B*B:B3=B*B*B:GOSUB 5520:LINE-(SX,SY),C:NEXT B:RETURN
5520   D1=X1*(-B3+3*B2-3*B+1):D2=X2*(3*B3-6*B2+3*B):D3=X3*(-3*B3+3*B2):D4=X4*B3:S
X=D1+D2+D3+D4:D1=Y1*(-B3+3*B2-3*B+1):D2=Y2*(3*B3-6*B2+3*B):D3=Y3*(-3*B3+3*B2):D4
=Y4*B3:SY=D1+D2+D3+D4:RETURN
5530 '_____
5540 '
5550 'module:  interactive control of brush function
5560   SOUND 250,.7:VIEW SCREEN (J6,J7)-(J8,J9)   'clip canvas edges
5570   PUT (SX,SY),A12,XOR   'install crosshair cursor
5580   T3=0   'reset toggle flag
5590   JS=J:J=1   'save current snap, set to 1
5600   K$=INKEY$
5610   IF LEN(K$)=2 THEN K$=RIGHT$(K$,1) ELSE 5780
5620   IF K$=CHR$(77) THEN PUT (SX,SY),A12,XOR:SX=SX+J ELSE 5650
5630   IF SX>XR THEN SX=XR:SOUND 250,.7
5640   GOSUB 5900:PUT (SX,SY),A12,XOR:GOTO 5600
5650   IF K$=CHR$(75) THEN PUT (SX,SY),A12,XOR:SX=SX-J ELSE 5680
5660   IF SX<XL THEN SX=XL:SOUND 250,.7
5670   GOSUB 5900:PUT (SX,SY),A12,XOR:GOTO 5600
5680   IF K$=CHR$(72) THEN PUT (SX,SY),A12,XOR:SY=SY-J ELSE 5710
5690   IF SY<YT THEN SY=YT:SOUND 250,.7
5700   GOSUB 5900:PUT (SX,SY),A12,XOR:GOTO 5600
5710   IF K$=CHR$(80) THEN PUT (SX,SY),A12,XOR:SY=SY+J ELSE 5740
5720   IF SY>YB THEN SY=YB:SOUND 250,.7
```

Fig. 17-3. (Continued from page 170.)

```
5730  GOSUB 5900:PUT (SX,SY),A12,XOR:GOTO 5600
5740  IF K$=CHR$(71) THEN PUT (SX,SY),A12,XOR:SX=SX-J:SY=SY-J:GOSUB 5960:GOSUB 5
900:PUT (SX,SY),A12,XOR:GOTO 5600
5750  IF K$=CHR$(73) THEN PUT (SX,SY),A12,XOR:SX=SX+J:SY=SY-J:GOSUB 5960:GOSUB 5
900:PUT (SX,SY),A12,XOR:GOTO 5600
5760  IF K$=CHR$(81) THEN PUT (SX,SY),A12,XOR:SX=SX+J:SY=SY+J:GOSUB 5960:GOSUB 5
900:PUT (SX,SY),A12,XOR:GOTO 5600
5770  IF K$=CHR$(79) THEN PUT (SX,SY),A12,XOR:SX=SX-J:SY=SY+J:GOSUB 5960:GOSUB 5
900:PUT (SX,SY),A12,XOR:GOTO 5600
5780  IF K$=CHR$(27) THEN PUT (SX,SY),A12,XOR:J=JS:VIEW:SOUND 250,.7:RETURN  '<E
SC> and restore snap
5790  IF K$=CHR$(13) THEN GOSUB 5840 ELSE 5800  '<Enter> to implement command
5800  GOTO 5600
5810  '_____
5820  '
5830  'submodule:  toggle on/off paint flag
5840  IF T3=0 THEN T3=1:RETURN ELSE 5850
5850  IF T3=1 THEN T3=0:RETURN
5860  RETURN  'failsafe barrier
5870  '
5880  '_____
5890  'submodule:  paint function
5900  IF T3=1 THEN LINE (SX,SY)-(SX+J3,SY+J4),CB,BF:RETURN
5910  IF T3=0 THEN RETURN
5920  RETURN  'failsafe barrier
5930  '_____
5940  '
5950  'submodule:  inhibit diagonal movement of cursor
5960  IF SX>XR THEN SX=XR:SOUND 250,.7 ELSE IF SX<XL THEN SX=XL:SOUND 250,.7
5970  IF SY>YB THEN SY=YB:SOUND 250,.7 ELSE IF SY<YT THEN SY=YT:SOUND 250,.7
5980  RETURN
5990  '_____
6000  '
6010  'module:  interactive control of spray
6020  SOUND 250,.7:VIEW SCREEN (J6,J7)-(J8,J9)  'clip canvas edges
6030  PUT (SX,SY),A12,XOR  'install crosshair cursor
6040  K$=INKEY$
6050  IF LEN(K$)=2 THEN K$=RIGHT$(K$,1) ELSE 6220
6060  IF K$=CHR$(77) THEN PUT (SX,SY),A12,XOR:SX=SX+J ELSE 6090
6070  IF SX>XR THEN SX=XR:SOUND 250,.7
6080  PUT (SX,SY),A12,XOR:GOTO 6040
6090  IF K$=CHR$(75) THEN PUT (SX,SY),A12,XOR:SX=SX-J ELSE 6120
6100  IF SX<XL THEN SX=XL:SOUND 250,.7
6110  PUT (SX,SY),A12,XOR:GOTO 6040
6120  IF K$=CHR$(72) THEN PUT (SX,SY),A12,XOR:SY=SY-J ELSE 6150
6130  IF SY<YT THEN SY=YT:SOUND 250,.7
6140  PUT (SX,SY),A12,XOR:GOTO 6040
6150  IF K$=CHR$(80) THEN PUT (SX,SY),A12,XOR:SY=SY+J ELSE 6180
6160  IF SY>YB THEN SY=YB:SOUND 250,.7
6170  PUT (SX,SY),A12,XOR:GOTO 6040
6180  IF K$=CHR$(71) THEN PUT (SX,SY),A12,XOR:SX=SX-J:SY=SY-J:GOSUB 6320:PUT (SX
,SY),A12,XOR:GOTO 6040
6190  IF K$=CHR$(73) THEN PUT (SX,SY),A12,XOR:SX=SX+J:SY=SY-J:GOSUB 6320:PUT (SX
```

Fig. 17-3. (Continued from page 171.)

```
,SY),A12,XOR:GOTO 6040
6200  IF K$=CHR$(81) THEN PUT (SX,SY),A12,XOR:SX=SX+J:SY=SY+J:GOSUB 6320:PUT (SX
,SY),A12,XOR:GOTO 6040
6210  IF K$=CHR$(79) THEN PUT (SX,SY),A12,XOR:SX=SX-J:SY=SY+J:GOSUB 6320:PUT (SX
,SY),A12,XOR:GOTO 6040
6220  IF K$=CHR$(27) THEN PUT (SX,SY),A12,XOR:VIEW:SOUND 250,.7:RETURN  '<ESC>
6230  IF K$=CHR$(13) THEN PUT (SX,SY),A12,XOR:GOSUB 6280:PUT (SX,SY),A12,XOR ELS
E 6240  '<Enter> to implement command
6240  GOTO 6040
6250  '_____
6260  '
6270  'submodule:  spray function
6280  PSET (SX+1,SY),C:PSET (SX+7,SY+3),C:PSET (SX+14,SY+4),C:PSET (SX+3,SY+5),C
:PSET (SX+10,SY+1),C:RETURN
6290  '_____
6300  '
6310  'submodule:  inhibit diagonal movement of cursor
6320  IF SX>XR THEN SX=XR:SOUND 250,.7 ELSE IF SX<XL THEN SX=XL:SOUND 250,.7
6330  IF SY>YB THEN SY=YB:SOUND 250,.7 ELSE IF SY<YT THEN SY=YT:SOUND 250,.7
6340  RETURN
6350  '
6360  '_____EDIT MENU CONTROL_____
6370  '
6380  'module:  interactive control of Edit menu
6390  PCOPY 0,1  'save existing graphics
6400  PUT (246,19),A13,PSET  'place menu on screen
6410  PUT (248,24),A9,XOR  'place cursor >> on menu
6420  T8=1  'reset flag
6430  K$=INKEY$
6440  IF LEN(K$)=2 THEN K$=RIGHT$(K$,1) ELSE 6530
6450  IF K$=CHR$(80) THEN T8=T8+1:GOTO 6460 ELSE 6430
6460  IF T8>5 THEN T8=1
6470  ON T8 GOTO 6480,6490,6500,6510,6520
6480  PUT (248,56),A9,XOR:PUT (248,24),A9,XOR:GOTO 6430 'Eraser
6490  PUT (248,24),A9,XOR:PUT (248,32),A9,XOR:GOTO 6430 'Halftone
6500  PUT (248,32),A9,XOR:PUT (248,40),A9,XOR:GOTO 6430 'Clear
6510  PUT (248,40),A9,XOR:PUT (248,48),A9,XOR:GOTO 6430 'Undo
6520  PUT (248,48),A9,XOR:PUT (248,56),A9,XOR:GOTO 6430 'Cancel
6530  IF K$=CHR$(13) THEN 6560  '<Enter> to implement
6540  IF K$=CHR$(27) THEN 6610  '<ESC> to cancel
6550  GOTO 6430
6560  ON T8 GOTO 6570,6580,6590,6600,6610
6570  PCOPY 1,2:PCOPY 1,0:GOSUB 7260:PCOPY 0,1:GOTO 6400   'implement eraser
6580  PCOPY 1,2:PCOPY 1,0:GOSUB 6980:PCOPY 0,1:GOTO 6400   'implement halftone
6590  PCOPY 1,2:VIEW SCREEN (J6,J7)-(J8,J9):CLS:VIEW:SOUND 250,.7:PCOPY 0,1:GOTO
 6400  'implement clear
6600  PCOPY 2,1:PCOPY 1,0:SOUND 250,.7:RETURN  'implement undo
6610  PCOPY 1,0:RETURN  'implement cancel
6620  '
6630  '_____OPTIONS MENU CONTROL_____
6640  '
6650  'module:  interactive control of Options menu
6660  PCOPY 0,1  'save existing graphics
```

Fig. 17-3. (Continued from page 172.)

```
6670   PUT (366,19),A14,PSET   'place menu on screen
6680   PUT (368,24),A9,XOR   'place cursor >> on menu
6690   T8=1   'reset flag
6700   K$=INKEY$
6710   IF LEN(K$)=2 THEN K$=RIGHT$(K$,1) ELSE 6830
6720   IF K$=CHR$(80) THEN T8=T8+1:GOTO 6730 ELSE 6700
6730   IF T8>8 THEN T8=1
6740   ON T8 GOTO 6750,6760,6770,6780,6790,6800,6810,6820
6750   PUT (368,80),A9,XOR:PUT (368,24),A9,XOR:GOTO 6700   'Active color
6760   PUT (368,24),A9,XOR:PUT (368,32),A9,XOR:GOTO 6700   'Fill color
6770   PUT (368,32),A9,XOR:PUT (368,40),A9,XOR:GOTO 6700   'Brush color
6780   PUT (368,40),A9,XOR:PUT (368,48),A9,XOR:GOTO 6700   'Halftone %
6790   PUT (368,48),A9,XOR:PUT (368,56),A9,XOR:GOTO 6700   'Boundary
6800   PUT (368,56),A9,XOR:PUT (368,64),A9,XOR:GOTO 6700   'Snap +/-
6810   PUT (368,64),A9,XOR:PUT (368,72),A9,XOR:GOTO 6700   'Brush +/-
6820   PUT (368,72),A9,XOR:PUT (368,80),A9,XOR:GOTO 6700   'Cancel
6830   IF K$=CHR$(13) THEN 6860   '<Enter> to implement
6840   IF K$=CHR$(27) THEN 6940   '<ESC> to cancel
6850   GOTO 6700
6860   ON T8 GOTO 6870,6880,6890,6900,6910,6920,6930,6940
6870   T9=1:GOSUB 7720:GOTO 6700   'change active color
6880   T9=2:GOSUB 7720:GOTO 6700   'change fill color
6890   T9=3:GOSUB 7720:GOTO 6700   'change brush color
6900   T9=4:GOSUB 7720:GOTO 6700   'change halftone %
6910   T9=5:GOSUB 7720:GOTO 6700   'change boundary color
6920   GOSUB 8210:GOTO 6700   'implement snap +/-
6930   GOSUB 8340:GOTO 6700   'implement brush +/-
6940   PCOPY 1,0:GOSUB 8120:RETURN   'implement cancel
6950   '_____
6960   '
6970   'module:   interactive control of halftone fill
6980   SOUND 250,.7:VIEW SCREEN (J6,J7)-(J8,J9)   'clip canvas edges
6990   PUT (SX,SY),A12,XOR   'install crosshair cursor
7000   K$=INKEY$
7010   IF LEN(K$)=2 THEN K$=RIGHT$(K$,1) ELSE 7180
7020   IF K$=CHR$(77) THEN PUT (SX,SY),A12,XOR:SX=SX+J ELSE 7050
7030   IF SX>XR THEN SX=XR:SOUND 250,.7
7040   PUT (SX,SY),A12,XOR:GOTO 7000
7050   IF K$=CHR$(75) THEN PUT (SX,SY),A12,XOR:SX=SX-J ELSE 7080
7060   IF SX<XL THEN SX=XL:SOUND 250,.7
7070   PUT (SX,SY),A12,XOR:GOTO 7000
7080   IF K$=CHR$(72) THEN PUT (SX,SY),A12,XOR:SY=SY-J ELSE 7110
7090   IF SY<YT THEN SY=YT:SOUND 250,.7
7100   PUT (SX,SY),A12,XOR:GOTO 7000
7110   IF K$=CHR$(80) THEN PUT (SX,SY),A12,XOR:SY=SY+J ELSE 7140
7120   IF SY>YB THEN SY=YB:SOUND 250,.7
7130   PUT (SX,SY),A12,XOR:GOTO 7000
7140   IF K$=CHR$(71) THEN PUT (SX,SY),A12,XOR:SX=85:SY=19:PUT (SX,SY),A12,XOR:GO
TO 7000
7150   IF K$=CHR$(73) THEN PUT (SX,SY),A12,XOR:SX=594:SY=19:PUT (SX,SY),A12,XOR:G
OTO 7000
7160   IF K$=CHR$(81) THEN PUT (SX,SY),A12,XOR:SX=594:SY=180:PUT (SX,SY),A12,XOR:
GOTO 7000
```

Fig. 17-3. (Continued from page 173.)

```
7170  IF K$=CHR$(79) THEN PUT (SX,SY),A12,XOR:SX=85:SY=180:PUT (SX,SY),A12,XOR:G
OTO 7000
7180  IF K$=CHR$(27) THEN PUT (SX,SY),A12,XOR:VIEW:SOUND 250,.7:RETURN  '<ESC>
7190  IF K$=CHR$(13) THEN PUT (SX,SY),A12,XOR:GOSUB 7220:PUT (SX,SY),A12,XOR ELS
E 7200  '<Enter> to implement command
7200  GOTO 7000
7210  'submodule:  area fill function
7220  SXC=SX+7:SYC=SY+3:PAINT (SXC,SYC),A$,CE:RETURN
7230  '_____
7240  '
7250  'module:  interactive control of eraser function
7260  SOUND 250,.7:VIEW SCREEN (J6,J7)-(J8,J9)  'clip canvas edges
7270  PUT (SX,SY),A12,XOR  'install crosshair cursor
7280  T3=0  'reset toggle flag
7290  JS=J:J=1  'save current snap, set to 1
7300  K$=INKEY$
7310  IF LEN(K$)=2 THEN K$=RIGHT$(K$,1) ELSE 7480
7320  IF K$=CHR$(77) THEN PUT (SX,SY),A12,XOR:SX=SX+J ELSE 7350
7330  IF SX>XR THEN SX=XR:SOUND 250,.7
7340  GOSUB 7600:PUT (SX,SY),A12,XOR:GOTO 7300
7350  IF K$=CHR$(75) THEN PUT (SX,SY),A12,XOR:SX=SX-J ELSE 7380
7360  IF SX<XL THEN SX=XL:SOUND 250,.7
7370  GOSUB 7600:PUT (SX,SY),A12,XOR:GOTO 7300
7380  IF K$=CHR$(72) THEN PUT (SX,SY),A12,XOR:SY=SY-J ELSE 7410
7390  IF SY<YT THEN SY=YT:SOUND 250,.7
7400  GOSUB 7600:PUT (SX,SY),A12,XOR:GOTO 7300
7410  IF K$=CHR$(80) THEN PUT (SX,SY),A12,XOR:SY=SY+J ELSE 7440
7420  IF SY>YB THEN SY=YB:SOUND 250,.7
7430  GOSUB 7600:PUT (SX,SY),A12,XOR:GOTO 7300
7440  IF K$=CHR$(71) THEN PUT (SX,SY),A12,XOR:SX=SX-J:SY=SY-J:GOSUB 7660:GOSUB 7
600:PUT (SX,SY),A12,XOR:GOTO 7300
7450  IF K$=CHR$(73) THEN PUT (SX,SY),A12,XOR:SX=SX+J:SY=SY-J:GOSUB 7660:GOSUB 7
600:PUT (SX,SY),A12,XOR:GOTO 7300
7460  IF K$=CHR$(81) THEN PUT (SX,SY),A12,XOR:SX=SX+J:SY=SY+J:GOSUB 7660:GOSUB 7
600:PUT (SX,SY),A12,XOR:GOTO 7300
7470  IF K$=CHR$(79) THEN PUT (SX,SY),A12,XOR:SX=SX-J:SY=SY+J:GOSUB 7660:GOSUB 7
600:PUT (SX,SY),A12,XOR:GOTO 7300
7480  IF K$=CHR$(27) THEN PUT (SX,SY),A12,XOR:J=JS:VIEW:SOUND 250,.7:RETURN  '<E
SC> and restore snap
7490  IF K$=CHR$(13) THEN GOSUB 7540 ELSE 7500  '<Enter> to implement command
7500  GOTO 7300
7510  '_____
7520  '
7530  'submodule:  toggle on/off eraser flag
7540  IF T3=0 THEN T3=1:RETURN ELSE 7550
7550  IF T3=1 THEN T3=0:RETURN
7560  RETURN  'failsafe barrier
7570  '
7580  '_____
7590  'submodule:  erase function
7600  IF T3=1 THEN LINE (SX,SY)-(SX+J3,SY+J4),0,BF:RETURN
7610  IF T3=0 THEN RETURN
7620  RETURN  'failsafe barrier
```

Fig. 17-3. (Continued from page 174.)

```
7630 '_____
7640 '
7650 'submodule:  inhibit diagonal movement of cursor
7660  IF SX>XR THEN SX=XR:SOUND 250,.7 ELSE IF SX<XL THEN SX=XL:SOUND 250,.7
7670  IF SY>YB THEN SY=YB:SOUND 250,.7 ELSE IF SY<YT THEN SY=YT:SOUND 250,.7
7680  RETURN
7690 '
7700 '_____
7710 'module:  interactive color changer
7720  IF T9=4 THEN T9X=56 ELSE T9X=612  'determine horizontal location of cursor
7730  T10=1  'reset flag
7740  T9Y=23:T9F=23  'reset vertical position of cursor
7750  PUT (T9X,T9Y),A9,XOR  'install scrolling cursor
7760  K$=INKEY$
7770  IF LEN(K$)=2 THEN K$=RIGHT$(K$,1) ELSE 7850
7780  IF K$=CHR$(80) THEN T9Y=T9Y+12:T10=T10+1 ELSE 7760  'if cursor-down key
7790  IF T9Y>179 THEN T9Y=23  'inhibit scrolling range
7800  IF T10>14 THEN T10=1  'inhibit flag range
7810  PUT (T9X,T9F),A9,XOR  'erase previous cursor
7820  PUT (T9X,T9Y),A9,XOR  'new cursor position
7830  T9F=T9F+12:IF T9F>179 THEN T9F=23  'update and inhibit
7840  GOTO 7760  'loop
7850  IF K$=CHR$(13) THEN 7880 ELSE 7860  '<Enter>
7860  IF K$=CHR$(27) THEN PUT (T9X,T9Y),A9,XOR:SOUND 250,.7:RETURN '<ESC>
7870  GOTO 7760  'loop
7880  ON T10 GOTO 7890,7900,7910,7920,7930,7940,7950,7960,7970,7980,7990,8000,80
10,8020
7890  C16=0:AT$=A1$:GOTO 8030
7900  C16=C8:AT$=A2$:GOTO 8030
7910  C16=C7:AT$=A3$:GOTO 8030
7920  C16=C15:AT$=A4$:GOTO 8030
7930  C16=C4:AT$=CHR$(&HO)+CHR$(&HFF)+CHR$(&HO)+CHR$(&HO):GOTO 8030
7940  C16=C1:AT$=A5$:GOTO 8030
7950  C16=C2:AT$=A6$:GOTO 8030
7960  C16=C3:AT$=A7$:GOTO 8030
7970  C16=C5:AT$=A8$:GOTO 8030
7980  C16=C6:AT$=CHR$(&HFF)+CHR$(&HFF)+CHR$(&HO)+CHR$(&HO):GOTO 8030
7990  C16=C12:AT$=A9$:GOTO 8030
8000  C16=C9:AT$=A10$:GOTO 8030
8010  C16=C10:AT$=A11$:GOTO 8030
8020  C16=C14:AT$=A12$:GOTO 8030
8030  IF T9=1 THEN C=C16:LINE (79,189)-(79,197),C:LINE (80,189)-(80,197),C:GOTO
8080  'change and display active color
8040  IF T9=2 THEN CF=C16:LINE (5,189)-(25,197),C13,BF:LINE (5,189)-(25,197),CE,
B:PAINT (20,193),CF,CE:GOTO 8080  'change and display fill color
8050  IF T9=3 THEN CB=C16:LINE (55,190)-(75,196),CB,BF:GOTO 8080  'change and di
splay brush color
8060  IF T9=4 THEN A$=AT$:LINE (30,189)-(50,197),C13,BF:LINE (30,189)-(50,197),C
E,B:PAINT (45,193),C13,CE:PAINT (45,193),A$,CE:GOTO 8080  'change and display ha
lftone color
8070  IF T9=5 THEN CE=C16:LINE (5,189)-(25,197),CE,B:LINE (30,189)-(50,197),CE,B
:GOTO 8080  'change and display boundary color
8080  PUT (T9X,T9Y),A9,XOR:SOUND 250,.7:RETURN
```

Fig. 17-3. (Continued from page 175.)

```
8090 '_____
8100 '
8110 'module:  refresh color icons
8120  LINE (79,189)-(79,197),C:LINE (80,189)-(80,197),C  'display active color
8130  LINE (5,189)-(25,197),CE,B:LINE (30,189)-(50,197),CE,B  'display boundary
color
8140  LINE (5,189)-(25,197),C13,BF:LINE (5,189)-(25,197),CE,B:PAINT (20,193),CF,
CE  'display fill color
8150  LINE (30,189)-(50,197),C13,BF:LINE (30,189)-(50,197),CE,B:PAINT (45,193),A
$,CE  'display halftone color
8160  LINE (55,190)-(75,196),CB,BF  'display brush color
8170  RETURN
8180 '_____
8190 '
8200 'module:  change snap factor
8210  LOCATE 9,58:PRINT J
8220  K$=INKEY$
8230  IF K$="=" THEN J=J+1 ELSE 8260
8240  IF J>9 THEN J=9:SOUND 250,.7
8250  LOCATE 9,58:PRINT J:RETURN
8260  IF K$="-" THEN J=J-1 ELSE 8290
8270  IF J<1 THEN J=1:SOUND 250,.7
8280  LOCATE 9,58:PRINT J:RETURN
8290  IF K$=CHR$(13) THEN RETURN ELSE 8300
8300  GOTO 8220  'keyboard loop
8310 '_____
8320 '
8330 'module:  change brush/eraser width
8340  LOCATE 10,57:PRINT J3
8350  K$=INKEY$
8360  IF K$="=" THEN J3=J3+1 ELSE 8390
8370  IF J3>20 THEN J3=20:SOUND 250,.7
8380  LOCATE 10,57:PRINT J3:RETURN
8390  IF K$="-" THEN J3=J3-1 ELSE 8420
8400  IF J3<1 THEN J3=1:SOUND 250,.7
8410  LOCATE 10,57:IF J3<10 THEN PRINT J3" ":RETURN ELSE PRINT J3:RETURN
8420  IF K$=CHR$(13) THEN RETURN ELSE 8430
8430  GOTO 8350  'keyboard loop
8440 '_____
8450 '
8460  END 'of runtime module
```

Fig. 17-3. (Continued from page 176.)

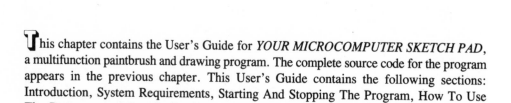

18

Sketch Pad Documentation
—A User's Guide

This chapter contains the User's Guide for *YOUR MICROCOMPUTER SKETCH PAD*, a multifunction paintbrush and drawing program. The complete source code for the program appears in the previous chapter. This User's Guide contains the following sections: Introduction, System Requirements, Starting And Stopping The Program, How To Use The Program, and Sample Sessions.

INTRODUCTION

YOUR MICROCOMPUTER SKETCH PAD gives you the drawing tools you need to create colorful illustrations and artwork with your personal computer. A rich selection of built-in functions give you complete control over your creativity and talent. The comprehensive User's Guide gets you started right away by providing tutorial sessions complete with photographs of sample drawings created by the program.

Drawing tools include lines, rectangles, circles, ellipses, arcs, smooth curves, solid area fill, halftone area fill, spray, burst, brush, eraser, and much more. Editing features include a powerful undo function and a useful clear screen function. A comprehensive set of Options features gives you the ability to change the drawing and fill colors, alter the shape of the brush, and customize the snap of the crosshair cursor.

YOUR MICROCOMPUTER SKETCH PAD contains powerful routines to save your drawings on disk as image files. You can retrieve your illustrations from disk for later editing. The images created can be printed by dot matrix printers or ink jet printers using third-party graphics-printing utilities.

YOUR MICROCOMPUTER SKETCH PAD gives you high-performance artwork at your fingertips, using your standard keyboard.

SYSTEM REQUIREMENTS

To run the program, you need an IBM PC, XT, AT, RT, PS/2, or any IBM-compatible personal computer equipped with an EGA or VGA graphics adapter. Also required is a standard color display (SCD), enhanced color display (ECD), analog display (PS/2 or equivalent), or variable frequency display (Multisync, Multiscan, or equivalent).

You will need IBM PC-DOS or Microsoft MS-DOS. A version of BASIC which supports EGA graphics is required.

This version of *YOUR MICROCOMPUTER SKETCH PAD* is intended for BASIC interpreters which support EGA graphics, including IBM BASICA and GW-BASIC. You can easily modify this program for use with your QuickBASIC compiler. Refer to Appendix E for guidance.

YOUR MICROCOMPUTER SKETCH PAD runs on personal computers equipped with two disk drives. The program can be easily modified to use a hard disk or a simulated disk in RAM. Refer to Chapter 19 for guidance.

If you are using a CGA (color/graphics adapter) or MCGA, you can adapt this program for your personal computer, but the lack of 16 colors on CGAs will severely limit the program's usefulness. Refer to Appendix G for guidance in program conversions. (If you want to jump right in with a high-performance interactive graphics program already modified to run on the CGA and MCGA, skip ahead to Chapter 26.)

STARTING AND STOPPING THE PROGRAM

This section explains running the program.

Back-up Copies

Before you use the program you should create a back-up copy of it on a separate disk. Use the back-up disk. Store the original disk in a safe place. Remember the old adage, "Anything which you do not have backed up you are going to lose eventually."

Starting The Program

YOUR MICROCOMPUTER SKETCH PAD is comprised of two separate programs. SKETCH-A.BAS is the start-up module. SKETCH-B.BAS is the runtime module. To start using the program, load SKETCH-A.BAS under your BASIC interpreter. At the OK prompt, press F2 to run the program.

Using Disk Drives

The start-up module creates the menu system, the on-screen user interface, and initializes some variables that the program will use. When finished, it pauses and waits for you to press Enter. After you press Enter, the start-up module will attempt to load the runtime module from drive A. You should ensure that the disk containing SKETCH-B.BAS is in drive A. If it is in another drive, you should modify the drive assignment in line 1150 of SKETCH-A.BAS. If you have installed the two modules for *YOUR MICROCOMPUTER SKETCH PAD* on a hard drive, for example, you would change line 1150 in SKETCH-A.BAS to read: **1150 CHAIN "C:SKETCH-B.BAS",160,ALL**.

The runtime module, SKETCH-B.BAS, expects to use drive B to save image files and to retrieve image files. Image files contain your drawings and your illustrations. When first using the program, you should place a blank disk in drive B. If you wish to use a hard disk for this purpose, you should change the BSAVE drive letter in lines 1340, 1350, 1360, and 1370 in SKETCH-B.BAS. You should also change the BLOAD drive letter in lines 1450, 1460, 1470, and 1480.

Using A Simulated Disk

YOUR MICROCOMPUTER SKETCH PAD will run much more quickly if you use a simulated disk with your personal computer. If you have two disk drives, then your simulated disk will be drive C. If you have a hard disk, then your simulated disk will be drive D. You should change line 1150 to reflect this new drive letter.

Stopping The Program

There are three different ways to cleanly exit the program. Each method cleanly returns you to the 80-column text mode of the BASIC editor.

First Method: At any time and in any routine during the program you can press F2 to exit the program. F2 is a hot key which is managed by BASIC itself.

Second Method: When you are located anywhere on the main menu bar, you can press Alt-Q to exit the program. Alt-Q is a hot key which is managed by the program. (Hold down the Alt key and press Q.)

Third Method: Use the arrow keys to select the Quit pull-down menu. Select the Quit function from the menu to exit the program. This method is managed by the menu system of the program.

HOW TO USE THE PROGRAM

The keyboard controls for *YOUR MICROCOMPUTER SKETCH PAD* are annotated in Fig. 18-1. The Enter key is used to implement a function or command. The arrow keys are used to navigate through the menu system. The Esc key is used to discard the current menu and return to the previous level in the menu system.

Using the Menu System

When you are on the main menu bar, use the left-arrow and right-arrow keys to move the panning cursor to the desired selection. Then press Enter to invoke the pull-down menu. Use the down-arrow key to move the scrolling cursor through the selections on the pull-down menu. The cursor will wrap back around to the top selection after passing the bottom selection. Use the Enter key to implement your selection. Select Cancel or use the Esc key to discard the pull-down menu and to return to the main menu bar. The on-screen Draw icons work in the same manner.

To move from one pull-down menu to another, you must first return to the main menu bar and then use the panning cursor to select another pull-down menu. You cannot jump immediately from one pull-down menu to another.

To begin drawing, choose Draw from the main menu bar. Next, use the scrolling icon cursor to select the drawing function desired. Pressing Enter places you in the active

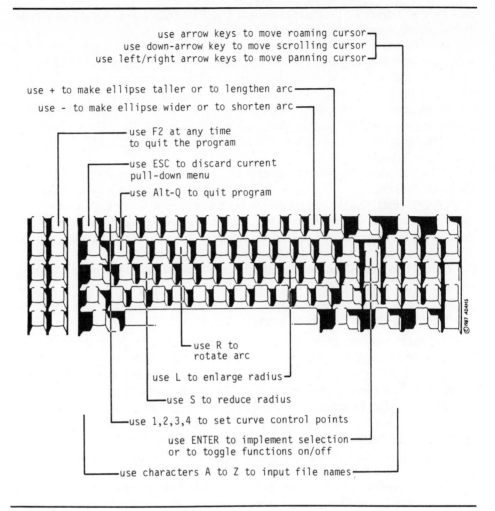

use arrow keys to move roaming cursor

use down-arrow key to move scrolling cursor

use left/right arrow keys to move panning cursor

use + to make ellipse taller or to lengthen arc

use - to make ellipse wider or to shorten arc

use F2 at any time
to quit the program

use ESC to discard current
pull-down menu

use Alt-Q to quit program

use R to
rotate arc

use L to enlarge radius

use S to reduce radius

use 1,2,3,4 to set curve control points

use ENTER to implement selection
or to toggle functions on/off

use characters A to Z to input file names

Fig. 18-1. Keystroke controls for the interactive paintbrush program listing in Chapter 17.

drawing area, where you can use the arrow keys to control the roaming crosshair cursor. To return to the Draw icons, simply press Esc.

Using the File Menu

The File Menu has several functions.

Save Function. The Save function in the File menu saves your current drawing on disk as a binary image file. Five full-screen images can be saved on a 5.25-inch diskette. More images can be saved on a hard disk. The Save function expects to use drive B. You must alter lines 1340, 1350, 1360, and 1370 in the program source code if you wish to use another drive. (See Chapter 17.)

When using Save, you must exercise caution not to overwrite any existing image files on your disk. The Save function is not error-trapped. A disk I/O error caused by an empty disk drive will crash the program and your current drawing will be lost. (See Chapter 19 for making source code revisions.)

Load Function. The Load function in the File menu downloads a previously saved image file from disk and display it on the screen. The Load function expects to find the image file in drive B. If you wish to use another drive, you must alter lines 1450, 1460, 1470, and 1480 in the program source code. (See Chapter 17.)

When using Load, you must ensure that a disk containing the desired image file is present in the drive. The Load function is not error-trapped. A disk I/O error caused by an empty disk drive or a missing file will crash the program. (See Chapter 19 for making source code revisions.)

Name Function. The Name function in the File menu allows you to create your own file names for image files. When you use Enter to select the Name function, a dialog box is displayed, containing the current file name. You may type in any eight character file name, using uppercase letters from A to Z. When you type the eighth character, the file name in the file name bar at the top of the screen is changed. During the input process, you may press Esc at any time to keep the original file name.

Cancel Function. The Cancel function in the File menu returns you to the main menu bar.

Using the Draw On-Screen Menu

The functions of the Draw on-screen menu are accessed by using the down-arrow key to move the scrolling cursor to the desired icon. Press Enter to go into the active drawing area. The roaming crosshair cursor is controlled by the arrow keys. The drawing functions are described as they appear in the Draw icon menu, from top to bottom.

Plastic Polyline Function. The Plastic Polyline function allows you to create a single line or a continuous series of seamless lines. Press Enter to establish the starting point for the line. Use the arrow keys to move the crosshair cursor. Press Enter to draw a line to the current position from the last-referenced position. Use Esc at any time to return to the Draw icon menu.

Rubber Polyline Function. The Rubber Polyline function displays a phantom line while you move the crosshair cursor to create a single line or a continuous series of seamless lines. Press Enter to establish the starting point for the line. Use the arrow keys to move the crosshair cursor. As you move the cursor, the phantom line shows the tentative line which can be constructed. Press Enter to draw the line. Use Esc at any time to return to the Draw icon menu. Press Backspace at any time to restart the polyline process; the next Enter will set a new starting position.

Rubber Rectangle Function. The Rubber Rectangle function displays a phantom rectangle while you move the crosshair cursor on the active drawing area. Press Enter to set the starting corner for the rectangle. Use the left-right and up-down arrow keys to establish the size of the rectangle. Press Enter to draw the rectangle. Use the arrow keys to continue with another rectangle using the same starting point, or press Backspace to restart the process. Press Esc at any time to return to the Draw icon menu.

Rubber Circle Function. A phantom circle is displayed on the screen as you use the arrow keys to move the crosshair cursor about the active drawing area. Use the Enter key to draw the circle. Press <S> to reduce the radius of the circle. Press <L> to enlarge the radius of the circle. Use Esc at any time to return to the Draw icon menu.

Rubber Ellipse Function. As you use the arrow keys to move the crosshair cursor, a phantom ellipse is displayed, showing the current parameters. Press Enter to draw the ellipse. Use <S> to reduce the radius of the ellipse. Use <L> to enlarge the radius of the ellipse. Press < + > to make the ellipse taller. Press < − > to make the ellipse wider. Press Esc at any time to return to the Draw icon menu.

Rubber Arc Function. A phantom arc is displayed as you use the arrow keys to relocate the center of the circle upon whose circumference the arc is based. Press Enter to draw the arc. Use <S> and <L> to reduce and to enlarge the radius of the arc's circle. Press <R> to rotate the arc segment counterclockwise around the circumference of the imaginary circle. Press < + > to lengthen the arc. Press < − > to shorten the arc. Your computer will beep when the minimum and maximum allowable arc lengths have been reached. Use Esc at any time to return to the Draw icon menu.

Freeform Curve Function. Use the arrow keys to move the crosshair cursor about the active drawing area. Press <1> to set the starting point for the curve. Press <2> to set the first magnetic point. Press <3> to set the second magnetic point. Press <4> to set the ending point for the curve. Use Enter to construct the curve. The parametric formulas will create a curve which is attracted to the magnetic points and which touches the starting and ending points.

Because the creation of freeform curves is often an experimental process, you should be prepared to use the Undo function to erase any curve which is not satisfactory. Use Undo before attempting any further drawing functions.

Area Fill Function. Use the arrow keys to position the crosshair cursor at the starting point for the fill. Press Enter to begin the fill. Use Esc to return to the Draw icon menu.

You can set the fill color and the boundary color by using the Options menu. If you attempt to fill an unclosed polygon, other portions of the screen may be inadvertently filled. Use Undo to restore your drawing. Correct the polygon before attempting the area fill again.

Spray Function. Use the arrow keys to move the crosshair cursor. Press <Enter> to place a simulated airbrush splatter on the screen. Change the color of the splatter by using the Options menu.

Rubber Burst Function. The Rubber Burst creates starburst effects. Press <Enter> to establish a starting point. Each subsequent Enter will create a line from the starting point to the current cursor position. The starting point remains constant. Press Esc at any time to return to the Draw icon menu.

Brush Function. Use the arrow keys to move the crosshair cursor. Use the Home, PgDn, PgUp, and End keys to snap the crosshair cursor to the corresponding corner of the drawing area. Use Enter to toggle the brush on and off. When on, the brush will smear color on the screen when the crosshair cursor is moved by the arrow keys. Press <Esc> to return to the Draw icon menu.

Sketch Function. Use the arrow keys to move the crosshair cursor. Use the Home, PgDn, PgUp, and End keys to snap the crosshair cursor to the corresponding corner of the drawing area. Press Enter to toggle the pencil sketch on and off. When sketch is toggled on, a line will be drawn on the screen as the crosshair cursor is moved by the arrow keys. Use Esc to return to the Draw icon menu.

Undo Function. Select the Undo function to erase the graphics which you created during your last foray on the active drawing area. On each occasion when you enter the active drawing area, the existing graphics are saved on a hidden graphics page. The most recent hidden graphics page is copied to the screen buffer when you select Undo from the Draw icon menu.

Return To Menu Bar Function. Select the Return function from the Draw icon menu to return to the main menu bar.

Using the Edit Menu

Use the down-arrow key to move the scrolling cursor to the desired selection in the Edit menu. Press Enter to implement the function.

Eraser Function. The eraser function uses a brush-like utility to paint a black smear across your drawing. Use the Enter key to toggle the eraser on and off. Use the arrow keys to move the crosshair cursor and the eraser about the active drawing area. Use Esc to return to the Edit menu.

Halftone Function. The Halftone function is used to fill a polygon with the current halftone pattern, which is displayed in the swatch at the lower left corner of the screen. The halftone shade can be changed to any one of the shades shown in the swatches displayed beside the Draw icons. Use the Options menu to change the halftone shade. Use the arrow keys to move the crosshair cursor to the starting location for the fill function. Press Enter to start the halftone fill. Press Esc to return to the Edit menu.

Clear Function. The Clear function clears the active drawing area to black. The Undo function can be used to restore the previous drawing, provided that you have not yet left the Edit menu. Once you leave the Edit menu, the Clear function is permanent.

Undo Function. The Undo function erases the effects of the previous Edit function. You must invoke Undo before you leave the Edit menu; otherwise, the changes produced by your most recent Edit function are permanent.

Cancel Function. Use the Cancel function to discard the Edit menu and to return to the main menu bar.

Using the Options Menu

Use the down-arrow key to move the scrolling cursor through the selections on the Options menu. Press Enter to implement the desired selection.

Active Color Function. The active color can be set to any of the colors displayed in the hue swatches located along the right side of the screen. Use the down-arrow key to scroll through the selections. Press Enter to implement the new color, which is displayed in the current color swatches at the lower left corner of the user interface.

Fill Color Function. The fill color can be set to any of the colors displayed in the hue swatches located along the right side of the screen. Use the down-arrow key to scroll through the selections. Press Enter to implement the new fill color, which is displayed in the current color swatches at the lower left corner of the screen.

Brush Color Function. The color of the brush can be set to any of the colors displayed in the hue swatches located along the right side of the screen. Use the down-arrow key to scroll through the selections. Press Enter to implement the new brush color, which is displayed in the current color swatches at the lower left corner of the screen.

Halftone Shade Function. The shade used by the halftone fill function (in the Edit menu) can be set to any of the shades shown in the swatches near the left side of the screen. Use the down-arrow key to scroll through the selections. Press Enter to implement the new halftone shade, which is displayed in the current color swatches at the lower left corner of the screen.

Snap Size Function. Use the plus and minus keys to increase or decrease the amount of movement that each press of an arrow key produces on the crosshair cursor. A numeric readout of the current snap size is displayed while you are using this function. Press plus or minus once to change the snap factor. If further changes are required, press Enter again and then press plus or minus. Repeat as required.

Brush Width Function. Use the plus key to make the brush wider. Use the minus key to make the brush narrower. Your computer beeps when you attempt to exceed the maximum or minimum allowable widths. Press plus or minus once to change the brush width. If further changes are required, press Enter again and then press plus or minus. Repeat as required.

Cancel Function. Use the Cancel function to discard the Options menu and to return to the main menu bar.

Using the Quit Menu

Use the down-arrow key to move the scrolling cursor through the selections in the Quit menu. Press Enter to implement your selection.

Quit Function. The Quit function terminates *YOUR MICROCOMPUTER SKETCH PAD*. Your current drawing is not saved before the program is ended. There is no way to recover your drawing after you exit.

Save + Quit Function. The Save + Quit function saves the current drawing on disk before ending the program. The drawing is saved to drive B. Disk I/O is not error-trapped; an empty disk drive will cause the program to crash and your drawing will be lost. Make sure that there is a disk with sufficient disk space in drive B (unless you are using your hard disk, of course).

Cancel Function. Use the Cancel function to discard the Quit menu and to return to the main menu bar.

SAMPLE SESSIONS

YOUR MICROCOMPUTER SKETCH PAD is capable of creating highly sophisticated illustrations and drawings, using only your keyboard for input. The drawings may be stored on disk using the program, or you can use a third-party graphics printing utility (such as Pizazz; see Appendix F) to print your artwork on a dot-matrix or ink-jet printer.

Non-objective Art: Spotlight

The nonobjective artwork shown in Fig. 18-2 was created using *YOUR MICROCOMPUTER SKETCH PAD*. The circles were created using the Circle function in the Draw menu. The circles were originally created in dark blue and then painted in varying halftone shades using the Halftone Fill function in the Edit menu.

The circle outlines between the shaded areas were hidden by redrawing the circles in light blue, dark blue, or black. Drawing time was about 15 minutes.

Realistic Art: Eyes

The realistic artwork shown in Fig. 18-3 was created using the Sketch function of *YOUR MICROCOMPUTER SKETCH PAD*. First, the Area Fill function was used to set

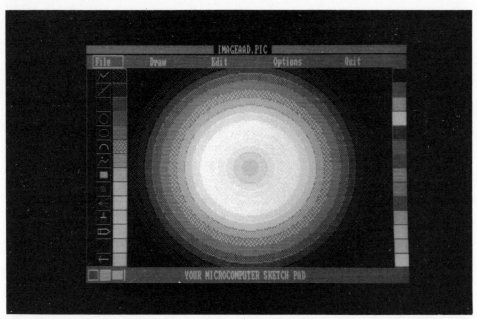

Fig. 18-2. The interactive paintbrush demo program listing in Chapter 17 can produce subtle gradations of color and efficient line dithering.

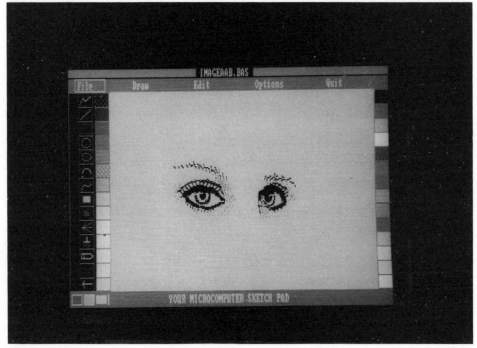

Fig. 18-3. Using the sketch function, the interactive paintbrush program listing in Chapter 17 can produce realistic drawings.

the background to white. Next, the Options menu was used to set the active drawing color to black. Then, the Sketch function in the Draw menu was used to create the eyes.

Mistakes were corrected during the preparation of this drawing by changing the active drawing color to white and using the Sketch function to cover the error. The active drawing color was then set back to black to continue work on the drawing. The main trick is to keep toggling the Sketch function on and off as you are working on realistic drawings like this illustration. Drawing time was 25 minutes.

Surrealistic Art: Chrome Sphere

The surrealistic artwork shown in Fig. 18-4 was created in approximately 50 minutes using *YOUR MICROCOMPUTER SKETCH PAD*. First, a horizon line was created. Then, the Area Fill function was used to paint the sky and terrain surfaces. The Spray function from the Draw menu was used to create the softened edges between sky and terrain. The active drawing color was set to black for this purpose.

The checkerboard pattern on the terrain was created in white using the Rubber Polyline function. The Area Fill function was used to fill the appropriate squares in white and red.

The active drawing color was set to black and the Rubber Ellipse function was used to create the shadow for the chrome sphere. Then, the active drawing color was set to light blue and the Circle function was used to create the chrome sphere. The Freeform Curve function was used to draw the line on the sphere which reflects the meeting of sky

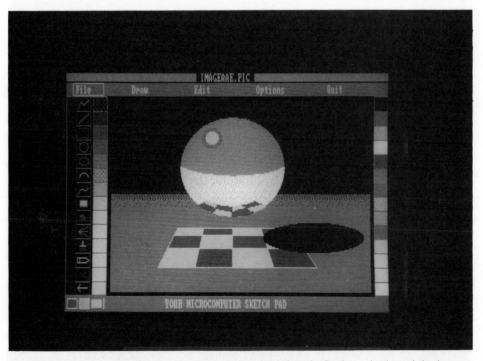

Fig. 18-4. By careful application of color, a convincing simulation of reflections, depth, and shadow can be created with the interactive paintbrush program listing in Chapter 17.

and terrain. The active drawing color was set to dark blue and the Rubber Arc function was used to re-outline the top half of the sphere. The Area Fill function was used to paint the top and bottom halves of the sphere.

The Spray function was used to dilute the terrain reflection on the sphere. The highlight was added using the Rubber Circle function. The checkerboard reflection was created using the same techniques used to draw the original checkerboard.

Objective Art: Paint Can

The objective artwork shown in Fig. 18-5 was created in about 40 minutes using *YOUR MICROCOMPUTER SKETCH PAD*.

First, the sprayed background was created by using the Spray function in the Draw menu. Both light gray and dark gray were used.

Next, the Rubber Ellipse function was used to create the top and bottom portions of the paint can. The Area Fill function was used to paint the can. The Plastic Polyline function was used to draw the shading on each side of the can.

The carrying handle for the paint can was created using the Freeform Curve function of the Draw menu. The outline for the red paint was drawn using the Sketch function. The fill color and boundary color were changed to red using the Options menu, and the Area Fill function was used to fill in the paint mass. The highlights on the wet paint were created using the Sketch function.

Art Nouveau: Prism and Light Rays

The artwork shown in Fig. 18-6 was created in 20 minutes using *YOUR MICROCOMPUTER SKETCH PAD*. The Rubber Polyline function was used to create the outlines for the prism and light swatches. The active color was changed at appropriate

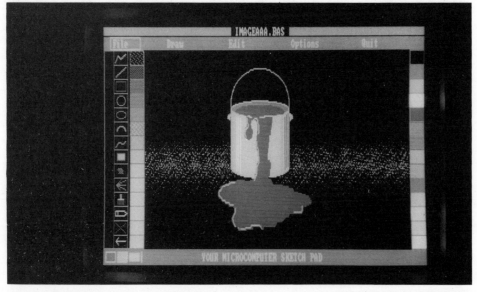

Fig. 18-5. Surrealism can be achieved by careful use of the graphics functions present in the interactive paintbrush program listing in Chapter 17.

Fig. 18-6. Pure hues can be used to generate symbolic illustrations in the interactive paintbrush program listing in Chapter 17.

times to re-outline the shapes after the Area Fill function had been used to fill in various colors.

The Spray function was employed to create the sparkles which surround the incoming beam of white light. The "Prism" title was created using the Sketch function of the Draw menu.

WORKING WITH THE PROGRAM

As you create drawings with the program, a special routine keeps track of available BASIC workspace. (See Chapter 19 for more on this.) If available memory falls below 1024 bytes, then a cautionary message is displayed, warning you to save your drawing on disk. After saving your image file, you can return to BASIC and restart *YOUR MICROCOMPUTER SKETCH PAD* with a fresh supply of memory in the BASIC workspace.

Unfortunately, BASIC interpreters use up a few bytes of memory every time a key is pressed. BASIC compilers such as QuickBASIC and Turbo BASIC do not suffer from this idiosyncracy.

It is wise to regularly save your drawing to disk while you are working. This practice gives you a fall-back position if your drawing isn't turning out the way you thought it would.

SUMMARY

This chapter provided a concise User's Guide for the multifunction paintbrush and drawing program, *YOUR MICROCOMPUTER SKETCH PAD*. The complete source code for this program appears in Chapter 17.

The next chapter provides a complete program analysis of the program, and discusses how it works.

19

Sketch Pad Analysis— How the Program Works

YOUR MICROCOMPUTER SKETCH PAD is a multifunction paintbrush and drawing program. The program is constructed according to sound fundamental concepts of modular programming. Once you understand how these modular concepts work, you can easily enhance the program with your own routines or adapt some of the program's algorithms to your own original interactive graphics programs. (You might want to refer to Chapter 17 for the complete program source code while you are reading this chapter.)

LOGIC FLOW

YOUR MICROCOMPUTER SKETCH PAD is comprised of two separate programs: a start-up module and a runtime module. The flow of logic for the start-up module is illustrated by Fig. 19-1.

THE START-UP MODULE

The Start-Up Module is called SKETCH-A.BAS.

Data Assignments

First, data is assigned to assorted variables and strings used by the program. Lines 230 through 670 assign values to variables. Note line 640, which assigns the file name string values. If you wish to use a default file name other than DRAWFILE.PIC, you can simply alter the string definitions in 640, provided that your new selections adhere to DOS file naming conventions.

Lines 680 through 790 contain the bit tiling codes which are used to create the half-tone shading swatches. A more detailed discussion of how these codes are derived is contained in Chapter 24, where fully-shaded 3D models are explored. (For a complete discussion of halftoning on personal computers using a CGA, MCGA, EGA, or VGA, refer to *High-Performance Interactive Graphics: Modeling, Rendering & Animating for IBM PCs and Compatibles,* TAB book 2879.)

Line 330 contains the color attribute assignments for EGA graphics. The values for C0, C1, C2, and C3 must remain as defined for the halftone area fill to function correctly. You may alter and experiment with the others. By changing the values in line 340, you can change the start-up default active colors for drawing, area fill, and so on.

Graphics Mode

As shown in Fig. 19-1, the start-up module next sets up the runtime environment for the graphics. Line 860 establishes the 640×200 16-color mode. This EGA graphics mode is fully compatible with the VGA on PS/2 computers. If you wished to use the 640×350 16-color mode instead, simply change **SCREEN 8** to **SCREEN 9** in line 870. The palette assignments in line 870 would then have to be changed to those described in Chapter 24 for the 640×350 mode. In addition, you would be required to experiment with the new xy coordinates needed to construct the on-screen user interface.

Hot Key

Line 880 installs the F2 hot key. When F2 is pressed, program control branches to the subroutine at line 1950, which provides a clean exit from the program. You can safely delete 880 if you are not planning to edit the program. Runtime performance is significantly improved if line 880 is removed, because the ON KEY instruction forces BASIC to check between each and every instruction to see if F2 has been pressed. The F2 hot key technique is invaluable during program testing and debugging, since it can cleanly bail you out of inadvertent endless loops.

Line 890 is a bulletproof method to ensure that the background remains pristine after any palette experimentation. It is based upon a hardware idiosyncracy found in IBM-compatible EGA boards.

Text Labels

As shown in Fig. 19-1, the start-up module next creates and saves a series of alphanumeric arrays. This occurs at lines 1200 through 1330 in SKETCH-A.BAS. These alphanumerics are used as labels on the main menu bar at the top of the screen and on the program name bar at the bottom of the screen. If the alphanumerics were placed directly on the menu bar and name bar, then the block rectangle containing the background for each character would obliterate the background graphics being overlaid. By using graphic arrays, the labels can be cleanly superimposed over the graphics background by using a variety of logical operators. You may wish to try changing the COLOR variable in 1210 to another value to see the effect of this graphic array labelling technique during runtime.

Note line 1290, which creates the panning cursor for the menu bar. It is saved in a graphic array named A7. Lines 1310 and 1320 create and save the crosshair cursor in a graphic array named A12.

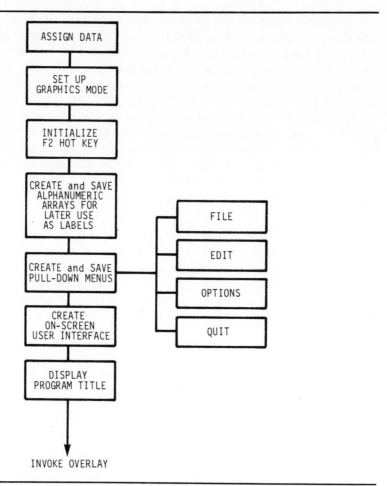

Fig. 19-1. Logic flowchart for the start-up module for the interactive paintbrush program listing in Chapter 17.

Pull-down Menus

Lines 1390 through 1690 create and save the images for the pull-down menus. These images are saved in graphic arrays named A9 through A14. First, the text material is created using BASIC's PRINT instruction. Next, LINE is used to create a border for the menu. Finally, GET is used to save the rectangular image for the menu in a graphic array. The image is then erased before the next menu image is created.

The code in this section of the program is closely linked with the DIM instructions near the beginning of the program. Try reducing a few of the DIM values in lines 260 through 320 and see how BASIC squawks when not enough memory has been reserved for a graphic array.

On-screen User Interface

As Fig. 19-1 illustrates, the start-up program next creates the on-screen graphics for the user interface. Line 960 creates the outside border graphics. Line 970 creates the program name banner. Note how the previously-saved graphic array containing the program name label is XORd into the graphics.

The file name bar is created using the same technique. Refer to line 980. The bar graphics for the menu bar is created by line 990. Line 1000 PUTs the graphic arrays containing the names of the pull-down menus onto the bar. Remember, these labels were previously saved as graphic arrays by lines 1200 through 1330.

Next, line 1010 uses the ERASE instruction to free up memory no longer needed, because the label graphic arrays will not be used again during runtime.

Program control then branches to the subroutine at line 1740, which creates the Draw icons. Then, the subroutine at line 2000 is called to create the halftone swatches along the left side of the screen. The subroutine at line 2090 creates the hue swatches along the right side of the screen. Finally, a subroutine at line 2180 installs the current active colors in a small series of swatches at the lower left corner of the screen.

Copyright Notice

The program then displays the mandatory copyright notice. First, line 1080 saves the clean screen image on a hidden page. Then, lines 1090 through 1110 write text on the screen. When the user presses Enter to continue, line 1130 restores the original clean graphics by copying the hidden page back into the screen buffer.

Overlay Code

The final task of the start-up module is to get rid of itself by loading the overlay runtime code. The CHAIN instruction in line 1150 loads the runtime module SKETCH-B.BAS into the memory space currently occupied by the start-up module, SKETCH-A.BAS. Program control is passed to line 160 of the runtime module, and all variables, arrays, and strings remain intact for the runtime module to use.

THE RUNTIME MODULE

The runtime module for *YOUR MICROCOMPUTER SKETCH PAD* is named SKETCH-B.BAS. It is loaded as a code overlay by the start-up module, SKETCH-A.BAS. The runtime module will not function correctly unless it has been chained to by the start-up module.

The logic flowchart for the runtime module is shown in Fig. 19-2. Although the flowchart might seem intimidating at first glance, it is a large chart only because of the numerous graphics functions provided by the program. The logic behind the paintbrush program is relatively straightforward. If only a few graphics functions were provided by each menu, the program flowchart would seem much simpler.

Having the flowchart for reference makes it an easier task to understand how the runtime module works. Source code and flowcharting go hand in hand, as discussed in Chapter 4.

Main Menu Bar

As Fig. 19-2 illustrates, the powerhouse behind the runtime module is the routine which provides control for the main menu bar. This loop routine is located at lines 230

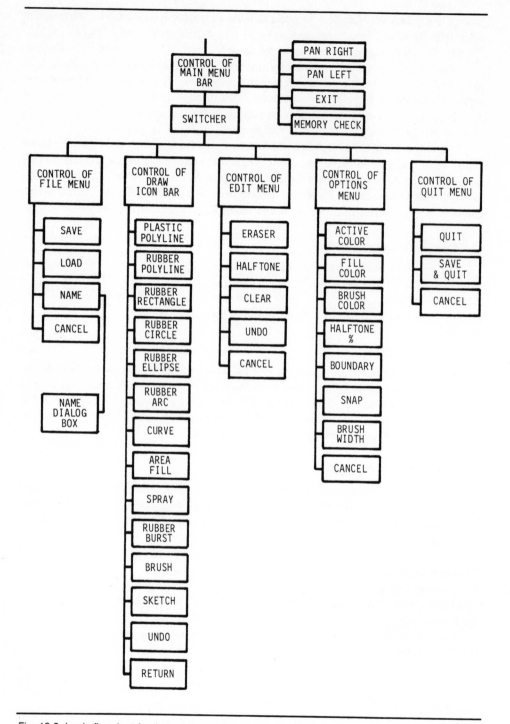

Fig. 19-2. Logic flowchart for the overlay runtime module for the interactive paintbrush program listing in Chapter 17.

through 300. The routine calls upon the module at lines 350 through 410 to move the panning cursor to the right. It then calls upon the module located at lines 450 through 510 to move the panning cursor to the left.

Note the use of the T1 runtime flag to keep track of the position of the cursor. The value of T1 is used to cleanly erase the previous cursor (using XOR) and to install the next cursor (using XOR). Note how the double use of XOR returns the screen to its original position.

Memory Check

Note the GOSUB 610 contained in line 240. This sends the program branching to a memory-checking subroutine. The FRE(0) instruction is used to find out how much memory is available in BASIC's workspace. It compares this value to the variable V1, which has been set by the start-up module to a value of 1024 bytes. If V is greater than V1, then the program returns to the main menu bar control routine. However, if memory availability is less than 1024 bytes, the program displays a warning message, urging you to save your current drawing before you run out of BASIC workspace.

Note the PCOPY instructions in lines 630 and 680, which save and restore the graphics while the warning message is being displayed. Line 650 generates a distinctive audio warning through the computer's speaker.

The memory-checking routine can be easily modified to display the remaining free memory on the display screen while you work on your drawing. Simply revise line 240 to read as follows: **240 K$=INKEY$:GOSUB 610:LOCATE 23,69:PRINT V" "**. Note the two spaces between the quotation marks. This ensures that the alphanumeric read-out will cleanly cover previous read-outs when the value and size of the value shrinks. By adding spaces, a four-digit value can cleanly cover a five-digit value, for example. As you strike various keys on the keyboard you will be able to observe BASIC's workspace shrinking by a few bytes for each keystroke.

Alt-Q Hot Key

Line 280 in the main menu bar control loop provides a hot key method for cleanly exiting the program. Pressing Alt-Q will send program control branching to the exit routine at line 560. You can easily add this Alt-Q function to all the pull-down menus by adding a line similar to line 280 to the keyboard control loop for each menu.

Enter

Line 290 in the main menu bar control routine checks to see if the Enter key, CHR$(13), has been pressed. If so, program flow jumps to the switcher routine at line 720.

Switcher Routine

The menu bar switcher is located at lines 720 through 780. Based upon the value stored in the T1 runtime flag (1 through 5 to represent the five possible positions of the panning cursor on the menu bar), line 730 sends the program to the appropriate line to jump to the corresponding pull-down menu subroutine. Refer to Fig. 19-2 to see how this switching logic works. It is an important concept which is integral to the efficient operation of a graphics menu system.

Draw Functions

Each of the 12 drawing functions contained in the Draw menu is a stand-alone routine, containing its own crosshair cursor control routine and graphics routine. This, in part, accounts for the length of the program listing in Chapter 17. Although a single crosshair cursor control routine could be used, it would make understanding of the program more difficult. The inefficient duplicated crosshair controls are used in *YOUR MICROCOMPUTER SKETCH PAD* to aid in learning. All future interactive demo programs will use a more efficient central routine to control the crosshair cursor on the active drawing area.

The main control loop for the Draw menu is located at lines 1730 through 2030. The switcher is located at line 1890. The switcher directs program control to the various graphics routines. Line 1940, for example, sends the program branching to the rubber ellipse subroutine located at line 3040. When control returns, the program circles back to line 1750 to complete the loop.

Note how the T7 runtime flag is checked in line 1860 to see if the undo function has been requested by the user. Note the previous line, which saves the existing graphics on a hidden page if undo has not been requested.

File Menu Control

The interactive control of the file name dialog box is located at lines 1530 through 1690. As Fig. 19-2 suggests, this dialog box is actually a nested menu, which can only be reached by first passing through the File pull-down menu. The Save, Load, and Name functions of the File pull-down menu follow the principles introduced previously in Chapter 13.

A Typical Graphics Function

The interactive control of the Plastic Polyline function is located at lines 2060 through 2340. By carefully studying this subroutine (as well as the other 11 graphics routines called by the Draw menu), you will be well on your way to acquiring real graphics expertise.

Line 2070 uses BASIC's VIEW SCREEN instruction to clip the graphics to fit the active drawing area. The values for J6, J7, J8, and J9 were defined by the start-up module. Note that the screen is returned to normal coordinates when this subroutine is exited in line 2290 (where the VIEW instruction without any parameters is used to disable the VIEW SCREEN mode.) Refer back to Chapter 5 for a discussion of the VIEW SCREEN instruction.

Note that only two lines (2330 and 2340) are needed to actually create the graphics on the screen. As is usually the case, most of the source code is used to handle the user interface. Graphics interactivity carries a high price in code length and in computing overhead.

PROGRAM TIPS AND TRICKS

A number of useful graphics tricks have been used to create *YOUR MICROCOMPUTER SKETCH PAD*.

Note line 5900, where BASIC's box fill instruction has been used to create the brush function using the J3 width variable and J4 depth variable. Also note line 6280, which uses offsets from the original x,y location to simulate the spray function.

It is worthwhile to study the Rubber Polyline function at lines 2370 through 2650. Note how the routine first sets up graphics page 2 as a refresh buffer. This buffer is used to restore the existing screen after the phantom line has been drawn after each movement of the crosshair cursor. This phantom line is called a rubber line. All the rubber functions (Polyline, Circle, Ellipse) use this refresh buffer technique to manage their phantoms.

Note how the Sketch function routine works. It is located at lines 4770 through 5020. Line 4810 saves the current snap value in JS and then changes the cursor snap to a value of one unit. This permits you to exercise precise control over the pencil sketcher. The previous value of snap is restored to J in line 5000 before the program exits the routine.

Note also how the diagonal cursor controls are kept within the legal screen range by the submodule located at lines 5170 through 5190.

A general-purpose routine to create smooth curves is located at lines 5500 through 5520. You can use this algorithm to create smooth 2D curves using two endpoints and two magnetic control points. (For a detailed discussion of the derivation of parametric curve formulas and for a programming example of 3D curves, see *High-performance Interactive Graphics: Modeling, Rendering & Animating for IBM PCs and Compatibles*, TAB book 2859.

It is interesting to observe how images are copied from graphics page 0 to page 1 to page 2 during management of the Edit menu at lines 6380 through 6610. Page 1 is used to set up a refresh buffer in case the Undo function is used for any of the Edit menu functions. Page 2 has been used to save the main menu bar graphics which are restored when the Edit menu is finally discarded and control passes back to the main menu bar. This fancy footwork with multiple graphics pages is not required when the Draw menu is being managed, mainly because the Draw menu is an on-screen icon system always being displayed.

Study the interactive color changer subroutine at lines 7710 through 8080. Note how the T9 runtime flag is used to identify which color parameter is being changed: active color, boundary color, fill color, et cetera. Also note that it is necessary to update the current color swatches located at the lower left corner of the screen. This is performed by the code at lines 8030 through 8070.

Closely related logically to the interactive color changer subroutine is the refresh routine at lines 8110 through 8170. This routine is used to update the current color swatches after a new drawing has been downloaded from disk. If not invoked, then the actual current colors may or may not match the swatches which were saved in the image file on disk.

MINOR BUGS

YOUR MICROCOMPUTER SKETCH PAD has a number of bugs. Many of these bugs are easy to live with and are nothing more than program idiosyncracies. Others, however, can produce serious consequences.

The following sections discuss some of the minor bugs.

Ellipse

The aspect ratio for the Rubber Ellipse function is not trapped. If it gets too small, BASIC will issue an error message, crashing the program. You can add IF . . . THEN instructions in the code at lines 3030 through 3370 to correct this.

Circle

The radius size for the Rubber Circle function is not trapped. If the radius gets too small, BASIC will squawk and crash the program. Add an IF . . . THEN instruction to the code at lines 2690 through 3000 to correct this oversight.

Curve

If you change your mind and enter a second set of magnetic control points when you are using the Freeform Curve function, those magnetic control points will not be cleanly erased from the screen after the curve is drawn. You can correct this by inserting a PSET instruction using color 0 when the X2 and X3 points are set. The code to change is located at lines 5240 through 5520.

Eraser

The Eraser function, located at lines 7250 through 7680, uses a brush which draws only in black. Clearly, such an eraser is useless if you are using a background other than black in your drawing. You could add a routine to the Options menu to overcome this deficiency. Model your new code on the code used to change the brush color.

MAJOR BUGS

Some of the more serious problems are discussed in the following paragraphs.

Disk Input/Output

Disk I/O functions are not error-trapped. For instance, if you attempt to save an image to disk and the disk drive is empty, BASIC will issue an error message and crash the program. Your current drawing will be lost.

Clearly, this is undesirable. To overcome this situation, use the ON ERROR GOTO . . . instruction to display a warning message. The code to change is located at lines 1310 through 1390. You might want to add a similar ON ERROR contingency line to the file loading code located at lines 1420 through 1500. Use the warning message handling routine at lines 630 through 640 as your model for this new code. Your warning message should be general, such as "**Disk Error. Correct and strike Enter.**" (For detailed examples of ON ERROR techniques, refer to the *High-Performance Interactive Graphics: Modeling, Rendering & Animation for IBM PCs and Compatibles,* TAB book 2879.)

Memory Check

Under certain circumstances, the memory-checking subroutine at lines 600 through 680 can put you into an endless loop from which there is no clean escape. You can use Ctrl-Break, but your drawing will be destroyed.

This messy bug is caused because the memory-checking subroutine is called only while you are in the main menu bar and in the Draw menu. If you spend a lot of time drawing in the active drawing area without returning to the Draw menu from time to time, available workspace can drop not only below 1024 bytes, but it can also drop below 256 bytes! If you refer to line 620, you will see that the threshold is lowered to 256 bytes after a memory check failure, in order to permit you to return to the main routine and invoke the File menu to save your current drawing. But if this 256-byte threshold has already been passed, your attempts to return to the main menu bar will only send you back to the memory-checking subroutine, where you are trapped.

To overcome this vicious trap, you must add workspace memory-checking to the graphics functions loops. In particular, the Sketch and Rubber Polyline functions eat up a lot of memory—and they eat it up fast. Holding down an arrow key (thereby invoking the automatic typematic function) will cause the cursor to clip along at over 10 times per second. Unfortunately, this speedy movement is also eating up available BASIC workspace at the rate of twenty bytes per second! (Compilers such as QuickBASIC and Turbo BASIC do not suffer from this idiosyncracy when keys are pressed during runtime.)

You should also follow the advice earlier in this chapter and add a read-out on the display screen so you can continually monitor the amount of free memory available.

SUMMARY

In this chapter you learned how the paintbrush program works. The next chapter introduces components of CADD drafting programs.

20

Components of CADD
Drafting Programs

Most drafting programs employ *entity-based algorithms,* as opposed to the *buffer-based algorithm* exhibited by the paintbrush program discussed in the previous four chapters. In particular, the graphics which are generated by a drafting program are dealt with on a primitive basis. It is the individual lines, ovals, pattern fill, and labels which are important, not necessarily the entire graphics page or screen buffer. These individual lines and so forth are called *graphics primitives.*

CADD (computer-assisted drafting and design) programs are useful for creating technical drawings, plans, electronic schematics, architectural floorplans, flowcharts, and related applications. Many of the advanced functions available in packaged drafting software programs can be easily encoded by you on your personal computer.

The photograph in Fig. 16-1 shows the start-up image produced by the drafting demonstration program listing provided in the next chapter. The program is entitled *YOUR MICROCOMPUTER DRAFTING TABLE.* It is capable of generating, saving, and editing complex graphics—and it can provide up to three levels of drawing overlay layers. Each layer can be displayed individually or in combination with other layers. Functions present in the demonstration program include set point, polyline, rectangle, parallelogram, circle, ellipse, arc, curve, fillet, eraser, hatch shading, regeneration, set text, leaderline, dimension lines, grid display, overlay selection, and more.

A complete User's Guide for the program appears in the chapter immediately following the program listing.

MENU MANAGEMENT

Drafting programs are often driven by graphics-oriented menu systems. The program listing for *YOUR MICROCOMPUTER DRAFTING TABLE* in the next chapter uses five pull-down menus to access the complete range of graphics functions provided by the program.

Drafting programs often provide mouse support and tablet support, where the intuitive nature of these input devices can be applied to the creative aspect of computer-assisted drafting and design. Because most personal computers are used without a mouse or tablet, however, the program listing for *YOUR MICROCOMPUTER DRAFTING TABLE* employs only keyboard input. By referring back to Chapter 11 you can readily add the mouse control routines which will make the program completely mouse-driven. Refer to Chapter 12 for further discussion of tablets.

The menu system for *YOUR MICROCOMPUTER DRAFTING TABLE* is based upon the algorithms discussed in Chapter 10. Five menus are used, including File, Draw, Edit, Label, and Options. The Draw menu is an on-screen, icon-based menu. The other four menus are pull-down menus which can be reached from the main menu bar at the top of the screen.

FILE MENU

The File menu provides the following selections: Name, Save, Load, Quit, and Menu Bar.

The Name function is used to specify file names for saving or loading images. It employs a dialog box to accept your keyboard input.

The Save function saves the current drawing on disk as a binary image file, using the name currently displayed in the file name bar at the top of the screen.

The Load function retrieves a previously saved binary image file from disk and displays it on the screen for editing or for printing.

The Quit function terminates the program. Your current drawing is not saved on disk before the program is ended.

The Menu Bar selection discards the File menu and returns you to the main menu bar at the top of the screen.

DRAW MENU

The on-screen Draw menu for *YOUR MICROCOMPUTER DRAFTING TABLE* is an icon-based menu. The desired graphics function is selected by using a scrolling cursor. Refer to Fig. 20-1 to see how the icons are arranged along the left side of the display screen.

The Set Point function places a single point on the drawing area.

The Polyline function can be used to create either a single line or a continuous length of connected line segments.

The Rectangle function will create a rectangle of any size. A rubber function shows a phantom rectangle while you are moving the crosshair cursor.

The Parallelogram function is used to draw a four-sided parallelogram, using any corner angle desired. A rubber function displays a phantom parallelogram while you move the crosshair cursor.

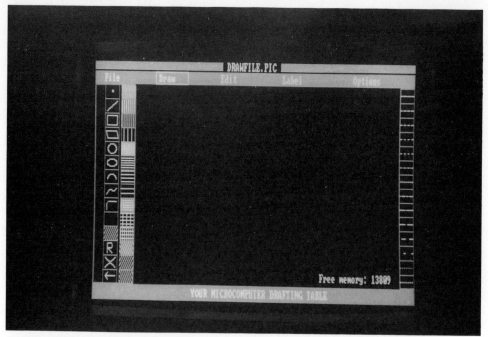

Fig. 20-1. The start-up display image generated by the interactive drafting program listing in Chapter 21.

The Circle function draws a circle of optional size, using the current position of the crosshair cursor as its center.

The Ellipse function draws an ellipse of optional radius and aspect ratio. A rubber function displays a phantom ellipse while you are moving the crosshair cursor and manipulating the ellipse parameters.

The Arc function uses a logical circle to create an arc of variable length. The arc's position on the logical circle may be rotated.

The Curve function uses cubic parametric curve formulas to create a smooth curve using two endpoints and two magnetic control points.

The Fillet function smoothly connects two lines. This function is useful for creating rounded corners and curved edges. Refer to Fig. 20-2.

The Eraser function uses a thin pencil-like utility to restore selected portions of the screen to black.

The Hatch function uses an area-fill algorithm to apply crosshatch shading patterns to your drawing. The available swatches are displayed next to the Draw icons. The current active hatch pattern is selected by using the Options menu. Refer to Fig. 20-3.

The Regen (regeneration) function is used to clear the screen and to automatically redraw your image. Your previous keystrokes during the current drawing session are saved in internal .CDF data files by the program. Regen simply retrieves these graphics primitives and uses them to redraw your design.

The Undo function permits you to erase your most recent graphics activity. On each occasion when you select an icon from the Draw menu, the existing graphics are saved on a hidden page before you begin to draw. When you select the Undo function from

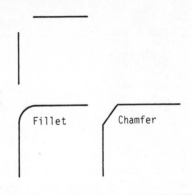

Fig. 20-2. A fillet produces a round corner where two lines would otherwise intersect. A chamfer uses a straight line to connect two primitives.

the Draw menu, this hidden page is copied back into the screen buffer, thereby restoring the original image.

The Menu Bar function returns control to the main menu bar.

EDIT MENU

Six selections are provided by the Edit menu: Define Entity, Move Entity, Copy Entity, Erase Entity, Undo, and Menu Bar.

The Define, Move, Copy, and Erase Entity functions are useful for duplicating an entity at different locations. The entity is created only once, and then moved using the graphic array techniques introduced in detail in Chapter 16. In its current version, these entity functions are inactive in *YOUR MICROCOMPUTER DRAFTING TABLE*. You can easily implement these functions by referring to the discussion in Chapter 23 and by reviewing the algorithm presented in Chapter 16.

The Undo function restores the graphics which existed before the previous Edit function.

The Menu Bar function discards the Edit menu and returns control to the main menu bar at the top of the screen.

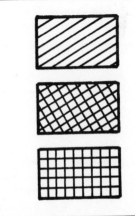

Fig. 20-3. Hatching, also called crosshatching, is used to represent texture or solidity in drafting program drawings.

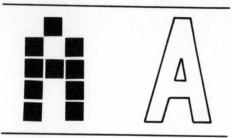

Fig. 20-4. Bit-mapped alphanumerics
vs. filled geometric outline characters.

LABEL MENU

The Label menu provides functions which add dimension lines, leaderlines, and text labels to your drafting drawings. Four functions are provided: Set Text, H-Dimension, V-Dimension, Leaderline, Undo, and Menu Bar.

The Set Text function gives you the ability to add text labels and descriptions to your drawings. By moving the crosshair cursor to the location where you wish the label to begin, you use characters from A to Z to annotate your drafting drawing. The Set Text function is used in cooperation with the Leaderline, H-Dimension, and V-Dimension functions. The Set Text function uses the bit-mapped character set provided by ROM BIOS. Commercial drafting software packages often provide their own character fonts, sometimes based upon the principle of filled geometric outline character sets. Refer to Fig. 20-4.

The H-Dimension function is used to add dimension lines which refer to horizontally measured entities in your drawing. Refer to Fig. 20-5.

The V-dimension is used to add dimension lines which reference vertically measured entities present in your drawing. Refer to Fig. 20-5.

The Leaderline function creates arrows which can point to selected portions of your drafting drawing. Refer to Fig. 20-5. The Leaderline function is often used in combination with the Set Text function.

The Undo function will restore the screen image which existed prior to your most recent labelling activity.

The Menu Bar function discards the Label menu and returns you to the main menu bar.

OPTIONS MENU

The Options menu is used to select functions that control the environment in which *YOUR MICROCOMPUTER DRAFTING TABLE* performs its activities. Functions include

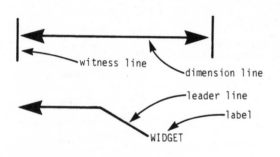

Fig. 20-5. Dimensioning primitives which are used in typical CADD (computer-aided design and drafting) programs.

Set Snap, Set Grid, Set Linestyle, Set Hatch, Zoom Image, Grid On/Off, Label On/Off, Key Layer $+/-$, Overlay 1 $+/-$, Overlay 2 $+/-$, and Menu Bar.

The Set Snap function adjusts the amount of movement exhibited by the crosshair cursor when an arrow key is pressed.

The Set Grid function is used to set the spacing between the horizontal and vertical lines which create the optional grid on the active drawing area. A special display is used to display your selection while you are using the Set Grid function.

The Set Linestyle function, inactive in this version of the program, is used to define the solid, dotted, or dashed attribute of the lines generated by various Draw functions.

The Set Hatch function is used to select the active hatch pattern for area fill. A scrolling cursor moves through the hatch swatches displayed near the left side of the screen.

The Zoom function, inactive in this version of the program, is used to enlarge or reduce your drawing.

The Grid On/Off function toggles the drawing grid on or off. The grid is useful for ensuring that your drawings are correctly dimensioned and that square corners are in fact square corners. The size of the grid is selected by using the Set Grid function.

The Label On/Off function, inactive in this version of the program, is used to toggle the labels on or off during regeneration.

The Key Layer $+/-$ function toggles the primary drawing layer on or off during regeneration. If toggled off, the graphics on the primary drawing layer are not redrawn during regen. If toggled on, they are recreated during regen.

The Overlay 1 $+/-$ function toggles the first overlay layer on or off during regeneration. If toggled off, the graphics on the first overlay layer are not redrawn during regen. If toggled on, the graphics on the first overlay layer are recreated during regen.

The Overlay 2 $+/-$ function toggles the second overlay layer on or off during regeneration. If toggled off, the graphics on the first overlay layer are not redrawn during regen. If toggled on, the graphics on the first overlay layer are recreated during regen.

The Menu Bar function discards the Options menu and returns control to the main menu bar at the top of the display screen.

POTENTIAL ENHANCEMENTS

Although *YOUR MICROCOMPUTER DRAFTING TABLE* provides a rich selection of drawing tools, you may wish to add even more drafting-related functions. By experimenting with the program and by carefully studying the runtime source code presented in Chapter 21, you will quickly acquire the expertise required to add further graphics functions to the program. (See the tutorial sessions in Chapter 22 for photographs of drawings created by this drafting program.)

Shear and rotate functions are often used by packaged drafting software to allow manipulation of individual entities in the drawing. Refer to Chapter 13 for further discussion. Stretch functions are ratio-based algorithms which simply enlarge or reduce certain dimensions of the entity.

Extend functions are often used to extend existing lines or curves. These algorithms are based upon a geometric analysis of the existing graphic, which is used to redraw the existing graphic with minor alterations (extensions). Trim functions are the logical opposites of extend functions. Existing entities are cut back using geometry-based algorithms.

The ability to rotate and scale text labels requires low level manipulation of bit-mapped or geometric outline-based character fonts. Refer to Fig. 20-4. The mathematics are based upon 2D matrices. 3D matrices can be employed to project the text labels in 3D space, providing an illusion of depth. Languages such as C or assembly language are usually used to perform advanced text manipulation.

Snap midpoints are subroutines which automatically move the crosshair cursor to the horizontal or vertical center of a particular entity. Snap tangents are routines which move the cursor to a position which reflects a true tangent (perpendicular) from a particular graphic entity.

Zoom functions can be used to enlarge or reduce the drawing recreated by a regen function. Associative dimensioning functions ensure that the labels and dimension lines are enlarged or reduced to match the new size of the drafting drawing.

SUMMARY

In this chapter you learned about the multitude of graphics functions present in typical CADD drafting programs, and you discovered the functions which have been coded into the program listing for *YOUR MICROCOMPUTER DRAFTING TABLE.*

The next chapter contains the complete source code listing for a multifunction drafting program, ready to run on your personal computer.

21

Program Listing— Your Microcomputer Drafting Table

This chapter contains the complete source code for *YOUR MICROCOMPUTER DRAFTING TABLE*, a multifunction drafting program. The photograph in Fig. 21-1 illustrates the start-up display produced by the program.

YOUR MICROCOMPUTER DRAFTING TABLE is composed of two modules. The program listing for CADD-1.BAS is the start-up module. The program listing for CADD-2.BAS is the runtime module which is loaded as an overlay by CADD-1.BAS. (Refer back to Chapter 15 for further discussion of code overlays.)

The start-up module creates and saves the graphic arrays which contain the various pull-down menus which the drafting program uses during runtime. The start-up module also assigns values to various variables, including the hatch area fill patterns. In addition, the start-up module creates the on-screen graphical user interface which the program uses.

After the start-up module has completed its tasks, it downloads CADD-2.BAS from disk. You should, therefore, ensure that CADD-2.BAS is present on a disk in drive A. If you are using a hard disk as drive C for this purpose, be sure to change the drive assignment in line 1230 of the CADD-1.BAS. (Refer to Chapter 23 for further guidance on modifying this program.)

The runtime module (CADD-2.BAS) contains the menu management system and the subroutines which implement the various graphics functions. The program is keyboard-controlled, although you can easily modify it to accept mouse input by applying the algorithms discussed in Chapter 11. Refer to Chapter 12 for information concerning graphics tablets.

The program listing for the start-up module (CADD-1.BAS) is contained in Fig. 21-2. The program listing for the runtime module, CADD-2.BAS, is contained in Fig. 21-3.

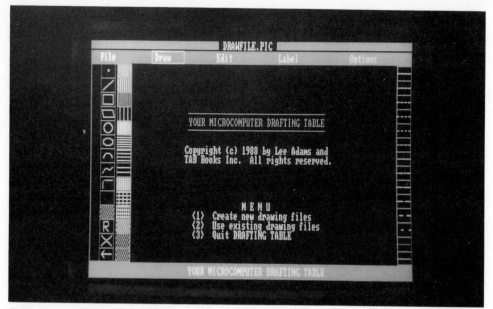

Fig. 21-1. The starting title image generated by the interactive drafting program listing in Fig. 21-2.

If you are using the companion disk to this book, all you need do to run *YOUR MICROCOMPUTER DRAFTING TABLE* is enter **LOAD "CADD-1.BAS",R**. (You should have the companion disk loaded in drive A.) If you are keying in the program listings from the book, be sure to key in and save the listings as two separate programs, of course.

YOUR MICROCOMPUTER DRAFTING TABLE is designed to run on IBM-compatible personal computers equipped with an EGA or a VGA graphics adapter. The program runs in the 640×200 16-color mode. The program can be easily modified to run on a CGA, MCGA, or PCjr. Refer to Appendix G for guidance concerning CGA and MCGA conversions. Refer to Appendix H for guidance concerning PCjr conversions.

If you are using a CGA and are anxious to skip ahead to program listings which can be run on a CGA, you might want to move directly ahead to Chapter 26, where a 3D CAD program is presented which has already been adapted in the appendices for both the CGA and the PCjr. The appendix programs are ready to run on a CGA or PCjr. The advanced regen functions and drawing layer functions provided by the drafting program are also present in the CGA and PCjr demonstration programs found in the appendices.

USER'S GUIDE

A detailed User's Guide for this program is contained in the next chapter, Chapter 22. The User's Guide contains sample sessions which include photographs of advanced drawings produced by the program listing in this chapter. A detailed analysis of how the program works is provided in Chapter 23.

HARDWARE/SOFTWARE COMPATIBILITY

The program listings in this chapter have been developed and tested on an IBM PC equipped with an EGA, using IBM BASICA 3.21. The program will run on a VGA-equipped PS/2 using IBM BASICA 3.30. The program will run on all IBM-compatible personal computers equipped with an EGA and which use a BASIC interpreter which can drive EGA graphics. If you are using QuickBASIC or Turbo BASIC with your EGA, you might want to read Appendix E. If you are using another BASIC interpreter which provides only CGA graphics, such as GW-BASIC or COMPAQ BASIC, you should read Appendix D.

If you are using a Color/Graphics Adapter (CGA) or a MCGA, you should read Appendix G. If you are using a PCjr or Tandy, you should read Appendix H.

```
100 'Program CADD-1.BAS:  YOUR MICROCOMPUTER DRAFTING TABLE
110 'Copyright (c) 1988 by Lee Adams and TAB Books Inc.
120 'All rights reserved.
130 'Version for EGA and VGA.  640x200 16-color mode.
140 'Use command line BASICA/F:4.  Ensure overlay program CADD-2.BAS is present
in drive A:
150 '
160 '_____INITIALIZE SYSTEM_____
170 '
180  KEY OFF:CLS:CLEAR:SCREEN 0,0,0,0:WIDTH 80:COLOR 7,0,0:CLS:LOCATE 10,20,0:PR
INT "Assigning memory space for graphic arrays"
190 '
200 '_____DATA ASSIGNMENTS_____
210 '
220 'module:  data assignments
230  DEFINT A,C,T,J
240  DIM A1(613):DIM A2(150):DIM A3(150):DIM A4(150):DIM A5(150):DIM A6(150)  't
emporary arrays for screen template
250  DIM A7(177)  'array for panning cursor
260  DIM A8(3073)  'array for Options menu
270  DIM A9(21)  'array for scrolling cursor
280  DIM A10(1057)  'array for File menu
290  DIM A11(953):DIM A11C(953)  'for Name dialog box
300  DIM A12(29)  'array for roaming crosshair cursor
310  DIM A13(1761)  'array for Edit menu
320  DIM A14(1651)  'array for Label menu
330  C0=1:C1=2:C2=9:C3=7:C4=11:C5=5:C6=6:C7=4:C8=8:C9=3:C10=10:C12=12:C13=13:C14
=14:C15=15 'software color codes
340  C=C7:CE=C7  'drawing, boundary colors
350  C16=C4  'temporary storage for hatch/style switcher
360  T=0  'loop counter
370  T1=2  'selection flag for menu bar
380  T2=25  'flag for echo position of file menu input
390  T3=0  'iterative flag for rubber functions
400  T5=0  'flag for function switcher
410  T6=0  'iterative flag for plastic functions
420  T7=1  'selection flag for Draw on-screen command menu
430  T8=1  'selection flag for menus
440  T9=0  'function flag for hatch/style changer
450  T10=1  'switcher for hatch/style changer
```

Fig. 21-2. Complete source code for the start-up module for a menu-driven, keyboard-controlled CADD drafting program. This version is for the EGA and VGA.

```
460  T11=1  'primitive attribute for .CDF file
470  T12=3  'active drawing layer
480  T13=0:T14=0:T15=1:T16=0:T17=0  'on/off toggle for regen
490  T18=0  '.CDF write toggle
500  T20=T12  'temporary storage of active drawing layer
510  J1=40  'radius for rubber circle, ellipse, arc
520  J2=4  'increment/decrement radius for rubber circles
530  J=2:JS=J  'snap, temporary storage of snap value
540  J6=85:J7=19:J8=608:J9=186  'viewport dimensions for active drawing surface
on 640x200 screen
550  JR=10:JC=10  'location of dimensioning text
560  H1=.16  'aspect ratio for rubber ellipse
570  H2=.04  'increment/decrement aspect ratio
580  H3=0:H4=1.57079  'start/end for rubber arc
590  H5=.39269  'increment/decrement rubber arc length
600  H6=1.57079  'length of rubber arc
610  SX=320:SY=100  'crosshair array location
620  XL=85:XR=594:YT=19:YB=180  'left, right, top, bottom range of roaming cross
hair cursor
630  SXC=SX+7:SYC=SY+3  'center of crosshair cursor
640  SXP=0:SYP=0  'last referenced drawing point
650  SXP1=0:SYP1=0:SXP2=0:SYP2=0:SXP3=0:SYP3=0  'corners of parallelogram
660  TX=7:TY=23  'location of Draw menu scrolling cursor
670  TYF=23  'erase position for Draw cursor
680  F$="DRAWFILE.PIC":F1$=F$:F2$="DRAWFILE"  'strings used to manipulate filena
me when saving images
690  V=0  'size of free memory in BASICA workspace
700  V1=1024  'threshold memory flag
710  B=0:B2=0:B3=0:D1=0:D2=0:D3=0:D4=0:X1=0:X2=0:X3=0:X4=0:Y1=0:Y2=0:Y3=0:Y4=0
'used in freeform curve routine
720  A1$=CHR$(&H0)+CHR$(&H0)+CHR$(&HAA)+CHR$(&H0)
730  A2$=CHR$(&H0)+CHR$(&H0)+CHR$(&HCC)+CHR$(&H0)
740  A3$=CHR$(&H0)+CHR$(&H0)+CHR$(&H88)+CHR$(&H0)
750  A4$=CHR$(&H0)+CHR$(&H0)+CHR$(&H8)+CHR$(&H0)
760  A5$=CHR$(&H0)+CHR$(&H0)+CHR$(&HEE)+CHR$(&H0)
770  A6$=CHR$(&H0)+CHR$(&H0)+CHR$(&H0)+CHR$(&H0)+CHR$(&H0)+CHR$(&H0)+CHR$(&HFF)+
CHR$(&H0)
780  A7$=CHR$(&H0)+CHR$(&H0)+CHR$(&H0)+CHR$(&H0)+CHR$(&H0)+CHR$(&H0)+CHR$(&H0)+C
HR$(&H0)+CHR$(&H0)+CHR$(&H0)+CHR$(&HFF)+CHR$(&H0)
790  A8$=CHR$(&H0)+CHR$(&H0)+CHR$(&H0)+CHR$(&H0)+CHR$(&H0)+CHR$(&H0)+CHR$(&H0)+C
HR$(&H0)+CHR$(&H0)+CHR$(&H0)+CHR$(&H0)+CHR$(&H0)+CHR$(&H0)+CHR$(&HFF)+
CHR$(&H0)
800  A9$=CHR$(&H0)+CHR$(&H0)+CHR$(&HCC)+CHR$(&H0)+CHR$(&H0)+CHR$(&H0)+CHR$(&HFF)
+CHR$(&H0)
810  A10$=CHR$(&H0)+CHR$(&H0)+CHR$(&H8)+CHR$(&H0)+CHR$(&H0)+CHR$(&H0)+CHR$(&H8)+
CHR$(&H0)+CHR$(&H0)+CHR$(&H0)+CHR$(&HFF)+CHR$(&H0)
820  A11$=CHR$(&H0)+CHR$(&H0)+CHR$(&H88)+CHR$(&H0)+CHR$(&H0)+CHR$(&H0)+CHR$(&H88
)+CHR$(&H0)+CHR$(&H0)+CHR$(&H0)+CHR$(&HFF)+CHR$(&H0)
830  A12$=CHR$(&H0)+CHR$(&H0)+CHR$(&HCC)+CHR$(&H0)+CHR$(&H0)+CHR$(&H0)+CHR$(&H66
)+CHR$(&H0)+CHR$(&H0)+CHR$(&H0)+CHR$(&H33)+CHR$(&H0)+CHR$(&H0)+CHR$(&H0)+CHR$(&H
99)+CHR$(&H0)
840  A13$=CHR$(&H0)+CHR$(&H0)+CHR$(&H11)+CHR$(&H0)+CHR$(&H0)+CHR$(&H0)+CHR$(&H22
)+CHR$(&H0)+CHR$(&H0)+CHR$(&H0)+CHR$(&H44)+CHR$(&H0)+CHR$(&H0)+CHR$(&H0)+CHR$(&H
```

Fig. 21-2. (Continued from page 209.)

```
88)+CHR$(&HO)
850   A14$=CHR$(&HO)+CHR$(&HO)+CHR$(&H88)+CHR$(&HO)+CHR$(&HO)+CHR$(&HO)+CHR$(&H44
)+CHR$(&HO)+CHR$(&HO)+CHR$(&HO)+CHR$(&H22)+CHR$(&HO)+CHR$(&HO)+CHR$(&HO)+CHR$(&H
11)+CHR$(&HO)
860   A$=A13$:T19=13   'active hatch pattern & flag
870   J10=25:J11=11   'horizontal, vertical spacing for grid
880   E1=320:E2=100:E3=0:E4=0:E5=0:E6=0:E7=0:E8=0:E9=0   'primitive parameters for
 .CDF file
890   '
900   '_____SET UP RUNTIME ENVIRONMENT_____
910   '
920   'module:  set up runtime environment
930   CLS:SCREEN 8,,0,0:COLOR C7,0:CLS   '640x200 16-clr mode
940   PALETTE 1,0:PALETTE 2,1:PALETTE 3,9:PALETTE 4,7:PALETTE 5,5:PALETTE 6,6:PAL
ETTE 7,3:PALETTE 8,8:PALETTE 9,2:PALETTE 10,10:PALETTE 11,4:PALETTE 12,12:PALETT
E 13,13:PALETTE 14,14:PALETTE 15,15
950   ON KEY(2) GOSUB 2040:KEY(2) ON   'install hot key
960   COLOR,0   'restore hardware color for background
970   '
980   '_____SET UP SCREEN DISPLAY_____
990   '
1000  'module:  set up screen template
1010  GOSUB 1290   'save alphanumeric graphic arrays
1020  GOSUB 1470   'create pull-down menus
1030  LINE (0,8)-(639,199),C8,B   'border
1040  LINE (0,187)-(639,187),C8:PAINT (320,190),C8,C8:PUT (198,189),A1,XOR   'ban
ner
1050  LINE (0,0)-(639,6),C2,B:PAINT (320,3),C2,C2:LOCATE 1,33:PRINT " DRAWFILE.C
DF ":LOCATE 1,34:PRINT F$   'filename bar
1060  LINE (1,8)-(639,18),C8,B:PAINT (320,10),C8,C8   'menu bar
1070  PUT (18,9),A2,XOR:PUT (130,9),A3,XOR:PUT (250,9),A4,XOR:PUT (370,9),A5,XOR
:PUT (510,9),A6,XOR   'selections for menu bar
1080  LOCATE 10,19:PRINT "Reclaiming memory used by temporary arrays":ERASE A1,A
2,A3,A4,A5,A6   'free up array memory
1090  LOCATE 10,19:PRINT "                                               "
1100  GOSUB 1830   'create on-screen command menu for Draw
1110  GOSUB 2090   'create on-screen menu for hatch patterns
1120  GOSUB 2180   'create on-screen menu for linestyle
1130  PUT (126,8),A7,XOR   'panning cursor for menu bar
1140  PCOPY 0,1:PCOPY 1,2   'establish refresh buffers
1150  LOCATE 9,26:COLOR C2:PRINT "YOUR MICROCOMPUTER DRAFTING TABLE":LOCATE 12,2
5:COLOR C7:PRINT "Copyright (c) 1988 by Lee Adams and":LOCATE 13,25:PRINT "TAB B
ooks Inc.  All rights reserved."
1160  LINE (198,60)-(464,60),C2:LINE (198,74)-(464,74),C2
1170  LOCATE 18,39:PRINT "M E N U":LOCATE 19,27:PRINT "<1>  Create new drawing f
iles":LOCATE 20,27:PRINT "<2>  Use existing drawing files":LOCATE 21,27:PRINT "<
3>  Quit DRAFTING TABLE":SOUND 860,2:SOUND 800,2
1180  K$=INKEY$:IF K$="1" THEN GOSUB 2380:GOTO 1220
1190  IF K$="2" THEN 1220
1200  IF K$="3" THEN GOTO 2040   'quit
1210  GOTO 1180
1220  PCOPY 1,0:SOUND 250,.7:LOCATE 23,57:PRINT "Free memory:"   'restore screen
1230  CHAIN "A:CADD-2.BAS",160,ALL   'load runtime module
```

Fig. 21-2. (Continued from page 210.)

```
1240   GOTO 1240  'bulletproof code barrier
1250 '
1260 '_____CREATE ALPHANUMERICS FOR TEMPLATE_____
1270 '
1280 'module: create alpha arrays for screen template
1290   COLOR C12:LOCATE 10,20:PRINT "YOUR MICROCOMPUTER DRAFTING TABLE"
1300   GET (150,71)-(416,79),A1:LOCATE 10,20:PRINT "
       "
1310   LOCATE 10,20:PRINT "File":GET (150,71)-(210,79),A2
1320   LOCATE 10,20:PRINT "Draw":GET (150,71)-(210,79),A3
1330   LOCATE 10,20:PRINT "Edit":GET (150,71)-(210,79),A4
1340   LOCATE 10,20:PRINT "Label":GET (150,71)-(210,79),A5
1350   LOCATE 10,20:PRINT "Options":GET (150,71)-(210,79),A6
1360   COLOR C7:LOCATE 10,20:PRINT "        "
1370   LINE (150,70)-(212,80),C12,B:GET (150,70)-(212,80),A7  'create panning cur
sor for menu bar
1380   LINE (150,70)-(212,80),0,B
1390   LINE (323,44)-(337,44),C7:LINE (330,41)-(330,47),C7:LINE (329,44)-(331,44)
,0  'create roaming crosshair cursor
1400   GET (323,41)-(337,47),A12:LINE (323,41)-(337,47),0,BF
1410   RETURN
1420 '
1430 '_____CREATE PULL-DOWN MENUS_____
1440 '
1450 'module:  create pull-down menus
1460 'submodule:  create Options menu
1470   COLOR C2:LOCATE 10,20:PRINT "Set snap":LOCATE 11,20:PRINT "Set grid":LOCAT
E 12,20:PRINT "Set linestyle":LOCATE 13,20:PRINT "Set hatch"
1480   LOCATE 14,20:PRINT "Zoom image":LOCATE 15,20:PRINT "Grid on/off":LOCATE 16
,20:PRINT "Label on/off":LOCATE 17,20:PRINT "Key layer +/-":LOCATE 18,20:PRINT "
Overlay 1 +/-"
1490   LOCATE 19,20:PRINT "Overlay 2 +/-":LOCATE 20,20:PRINT "Menu bar"
1500   LINE (138,67)-(264,162),C8,B
1510   GET (138,67)-(264,162),A8:LINE (138,67)-(264,162),0,BF  'save Options menu
1520   LOCATE 10,20:COLOR C7:PRINT CHR$(175):COLOR C7  'menu cursor >>
1530   GET (151,73)-(159,77),A9:LOCATE 10,20:PRINT " "
1540 '
1550 '_____
1560 'submodule:  create File menu
1570   COLOR C2:LOCATE 10,20:PRINT "Name":LOCATE 11,20:PRINT "Save":LOCATE 12,20:
PRINT "Load":LOCATE 13,20:PRINT "Quit":LOCATE 14,20:PRINT "Menu bar"
1580   LINE (138,67)-(220,114),C8,B
1590   GET (138,67)-(220,114),A10:LINE (138,67)-(220,114),0,BF  'save File menu
1600 '
1610 '_____
1620 'submodule:  create Name dialog box
1630   COLOR C2:LOCATE 10,20:PRINT "Enter new filename:            ":COLOR C7
1640   LINE (144,69)-(413,82),C8,B
1650   GET (144,69)-(413,82),A11:LINE (144,69)-(413,82),0,BF  'save Name dialog b
ox
1660 '_____
1670 '_____
1680 'submodule:  create Edit menu
```

Fig. 21-2. (Continued from page 211.)

```
1690   COLOR C2:LOCATE 4,20:PRINT "Define entity":LOCATE 5,20:PRINT "Move entity"
:LOCATE 6,20:PRINT "Copy entity":LOCATE 7,20:PRINT "Erase entity":LOCATE 8,20:PR
INT "Undo":LOCATE 9,20:PRINT "Menu bar"
1700   LINE (138,20)-(260,74),C8,B
1710   GET (138,20)-(260,74),A13:LINE (138,20)-(260,74),0,BF  'save Edit menu
1720   '_____
1730   '
1740   'submodule:  create Label menu
1750   LOCATE 4,20:PRINT "Set text":LOCATE 5,20:PRINT "H-dimension":LOCATE 6,20:P
RINT "V-dimension":LOCATE 7,20:PRINT "Leaderline":LOCATE 8,20:PRINT "Undo":LOCAT
E 9,20:PRINT "Menu bar"
1760   LINE (138,20)-(254,74),C8,B
1770   GET (138,20)-(254,74),A14:LINE (138,20)-(254,74),0,BF:COLOR C7   'save Labe
l menu
1780   RETURN
1790   '
1800   '_____CREATE ICONS FOR DRAW MENU_____
1810   '
1820   'module:  create icons for Draw on-screen menu
1830   LINE (1,19)-(50,186),C8,B:LINE (21,20)-(21,185),C8  'border around active
drawing area
1840   FOR T=31 TO 186 STEP 12:LINE (22,T)-(49,T),C8:NEXT T  'compartments
1850   LINE (35,24)-(37,24),C7:LINE (35,25)-(37,25),C7  'setpoint 1
1860   LINE (25,41)-(46,33),C7  'polyline 2
1870   LINE (25,45)-(46,53),C7,B  'rectangle 3
1880   LINE (23,58)-(45,58),C7:LINE-(48,64),C7:LINE-(26,64),C7:LINE-(23,58),C7
parallelogram 4
1890   CIRCLE (36,73),9,C7,,,.44  'circle 5
1900   CIRCLE (36,85),10,C7,,,,.3  'ellipse 6
1910   CIRCLE (36,99),9,C7,0,3.14159,.44  'arc 7
1920   LINE (25,112)-(31,108),C7:LINE-(35,108),C7:LINE-(39,109),C7:LINE-(41,109),
C7:LINE-(46,107),C7  'curve 8
1930   LINE (26,125)-(26,120),C7:PSET (27,119),C7:PSET (29,118),C7:LINE (31,118)-
(46,118),C7  'fillet 9
1940   PAINT (36,133),0,C8  'eraser 10
1950   PAINT (30,145),A13$,C8  'hatch 11
1960   LINE (29,161)-(29,153),C7:LINE-(38,153),C7:LINE (39,154)-(39,156),C7:LINE
(38,157)-(29,157),C7:LINE (31,157)-(39,161),C7  'regen 12
1970   LINE (25,165)-(46,173),C7:LINE (25,173)-(46,165),C7  'undo 13
1980   LINE (26,180)-(46,180),C7:LINE (26,180)-(31,177),C7:LINE (26,180)-(31,183)
,C7  'menu bar 14
1990   RETURN
2000   '
2010   '_____QUIT_____
2020   '
2030   'module:  exit routine
2040   CLS:SCREEN 0,0,0,0:WIDTH 80:COLOR 7,0,0:CLS:LOCATE 1,1,1:COLOR 2:PRINT "YO
UR MICROCOMPUTER DRAFTING TABLE":LOCATE 2,1:PRINT "is finished.":COLOR 7:SOUND 2
50,.7:END
2050   '
2060   '_____CREATE HATCH SWATCHES_____
2070   '
```

Fig. 21-2. (Continued from page 212.)

```
2080 'module:  create on-screen menu for hatch patterns
2090  LINE (55,20)-(55,186),C8:LINE (83,20)-(83,186),C8:FOR T=31 TO 186 STEP 12:
LINE (55,T)-(83,T),C8:NEXT T:LINE (50,19)-(83,19),C8:LINE (50,186)-(83,186),C8:L
INE (84,20)-(84,186),C8  'compartments
2100 Y=26:PAINT (65,Y),A1$,C8:Y=Y+12:PAINT (65,Y),A2$,C8:Y=Y+12:PAINT (65,Y),A3
$,C8:Y=Y+12:PAINT (65,Y),A4$,C8:Y=Y+12:PAINT (65,Y),A5$,C8:Y=Y+12:PAINT (65,Y),C
13,C8:PAINT (65,Y),A6$,C8
2110 Y=Y+12:PAINT (65,Y),C13,C8:PAINT (65,Y),A7$,C8:Y=Y+12:PAINT (65,Y),C13,C8:
PAINT (65,Y),A8$,C8:Y=Y+12:PAINT (65,Y),A9$,C8:Y=Y+12:PAINT (65,Y),A10$,C8:Y=Y+1
2:PAINT (65,Y),A11$,C8:Y=Y+12:PAINT (65,Y),A12$,C8
2120 Y=Y+12:PAINT (65,Y),A13$,C8:Y=Y+12:PAINT (65,Y),A14$,C8
2130 RETURN
2140 '
2150 '_____CREATE LINESTYLE SWATCHES_____
2160 '
2170 'module:  create on-screen menu for linestyle
2180  LINE (610,19)-(639,186),C8,B:LINE (609,19)-(609,186),C8:FOR T=31 TO 186 ST
EP 12:LINE (611,T)-(638,T),C8:NEXT T  'compartments
2190 T=25:LINE (611,T)-(638,T),C7,,&HFEFE
2200 T=T+12:LINE (611,T)-(638,T),C7,,&HFCFC
2210 T=T+12:LINE (611,T)-(638,T),C7,,&HF8F8
2220 T=T+12:LINE (611,T)-(638,T),C7,,&HF0F0
2230 T=T+12:LINE (611,T)-(638,T),C7,,&HE0E0
2240 T=T+12:LINE (611,T)-(638,T),C7,,&HE4E4
2250 T=T+12:LINE (611,T)-(638,T),C7,,&HEEEE
2260 T=T+12:LINE (611,T)-(638,T),C7,,&HFF3C
2270 T=T+12:LINE (611,T)-(638,T),C7,,&HFFFC
2280 T=T+12:LINE (611,T)-(638,T),C7,,&HFFF0
2290 T=T+12:LINE (611,T)-(638,T),C7,,&HFF00
2300 T=T+12:LINE (611,T)-(638,T),C7,,&HF000
2310 T=T+12:LINE (611,T)-(638,T),C7,,&H1111
2320 T=T+12:LINE (611,T)-(638,T),C7,,&H3333
2330 RETURN
2340 '
2350 '_____INITIALIZE DATA FILES_____
2360 '
2370 'module:  initialize .CDF data files
2380 T12=3:GOSUB 2410:T12=4:GOSUB 2410:T12=5:GOSUB 2410:T12=3:RETURN
2390 '
2400 '_____
2410  ON T12 GOTO 2420,2430,2440,2450,2460
2420  OPEN "A:GRID.CDF" FOR OUTPUT AS #1:WRITE #1,T11,E1,E2:CLOSE #1:RETURN
2430  SOUND 860,2:SOUND 800,2:RETURN  'label is inactive
2440  OPEN "A:KEYLAYER.CDF" FOR OUTPUT AS #2:WRITE #2,T11,E1,E2,E3,E4,E5,E6,E7,E
8,E9:CLOSE #2:RETURN
2450  OPEN "A:OVERLAY1.CDF" FOR OUTPUT AS #3:WRITE #3,T11,E1,E2,E3,E4,E5,E6,E7,E
8,E9:CLOSE #3:RETURN
2460  OPEN "A:OVERLAY2.CDF" FOR OUTPUT AS #4:WRITE #4,T11,E1,E2,E3,E4,E5,E6,E7,E
8,E9:CLOSE #4:RETURN
2470 '_____
2480 '_____
2490 END
```

Fig. 21-2. (Continued from page 213.)

```
100 'Program CADD-2.BAS:  YOUR MICROCOMPUTER DRAFTING TABLE
110 'Copyright (c) 1988 by Lee Adams and TAB Books Inc.
120 'All rights reserved.
130 'Overlay module.  Called by program CADD-1.BAS
140 'I/O Notes: Disk read/write is not error-trapped.
150 '_____
160 '
170  DEFINT A,C,T,J
180  SOUND 860,2:SOUND 800,2:ON KEY(2) GOSUB 240:KEY(2) ON
190  GOTO 290
200 '
210 '_____QUIT_____
220 '
230 'module:  exit routine
240  CLS:SCREEN 0,0,0,0:WIDTH 80:COLOR 7,0,0:CLS:LOCATE 1,1,1:COLOR 2:PRINT "YOU
R MICROCOMPUTER DRAFTING TABLE":LOCATE 2,1:PRINT "is finished.":COLOR 7:SOUND 25
0,.7:END
250 '
260 '_____MENU BAR CONTROL_____
270 '
280 'main module:  interactive control of menu bar
290  K$=INKEY$:GOSUB 610:LOCATE 23,69:PRINT V" "
300  IF LEN(K$)=2 THEN K$=RIGHT$(K$,1) ELSE 340
310  IF K$=CHR$(77) THEN T1=T1+1:GOSUB 400:GOTO 290
320  IF K$=CHR$(75) THEN T1=T1-1:GOSUB 500:GOTO 290
330  IF K$=CHR$(16) THEN GOTO 240  'Alt-Q to quit
340  IF K$=CHR$(13) THEN GOSUB 730  '<Enter> key
350  GOTO 290
360  GOTO 360  'bulletproof code barrier
370 '_____
380 '
390 'module:  pan right on menu bar
400  IF T1>5 THEN T1=1
410  ON T1 GOTO 420,430,440,450,460
420  PUT (506,8),A7,XOR:PUT (14,8),A7,XOR:RETURN  'File
430  PUT (14,8),A7,XOR:PUT (126,8),A7,XOR:RETURN  'Draw
440  PUT (126,8),A7,XOR:PUT (246,8),A7,XOR:RETURN 'Edit
450  PUT (246,8),A7,XOR:PUT (366,8),A7,XOR:RETURN 'Label
460  PUT (366,8),A7,XOR:PUT (506,8),A7,XOR:RETURN 'Options
470 '_____
480 '
490 'module:  pan left on menu bar
500  IF T1<1 THEN T1=5
510  ON T1 GOTO 520,530,540,550,560
520  PUT (126,8),A7,XOR:PUT (14,8),A7,XOR:RETURN  'File
530  PUT (246,8),A7,XOR:PUT (126,8),A7,XOR:RETURN 'Draw
540  PUT (366,8),A7,XOR:PUT (246,8),A7,XOR:RETURN 'Edit
550  PUT (506,8),A7,XOR:PUT (366,8),A7,XOR:RETURN 'Label
560  PUT (14,8),A7,XOR:PUT (506,8),A7,XOR:RETURN  'Options
570 '
580 '_____CHECK SIZE OF WORKSPACE_____
590 '
600 'module:  check if user is running out of memory
610  V=FRE(0):IF V>V1 THEN RETURN
```

Fig. 21-3. Complete source code for the runtime module for a menu-driven, keyboard-controlled CADD drafting program. This version is for the EGA and VGA.

```
620  V1=128  'lower threshold to permit return to pgm
630  PCOPY 0,1:CLS:COLOR C12:LOCATE 10,32:PRINT "W A R N I N G":COLOR C7:LOCATE
12,23:PRINT "Out of memory in BASIC workspace."
640  LOCATE 13,27:PRINT "Save your drawing on disk!":LOCATE 15,21:PRINT "Press <
Enter> to return to DRAFTING TABLE."
650  FOR T=1 TO 4 STEP 1:SOUND 250,3:SOUND 450,3:SOUND 650,3:NEXT T
660  K$=INKEY$:IF K$<>CHR$(13) THEN 660  'wait for <Enter>
670  K$=INKEY$:IF K$<>"" THEN 670  'empty keyboard buffer
680  PCOPY 1,0:SOUND 250,.7:RETURN
690  '
700  '_____MENU BAR SWITCHER_____
710  '
720  'module:  switcher to execute menu bar choices
730  ON T1 GOTO 740,750,760,770,780
740  GOSUB 830:RETURN  'invoke File menu
750  GOSUB 1510:RETURN  'invoke on-screen Draw menu
760  GOSUB 1900:RETURN  'invoke Edit menu
770  GOSUB 2190:RETURN  'invoke Label menu
780  GOSUB 2480:RETURN  'invoke Options menu
790  '
800  '_____FILE MENU CONTROL_____
810  '
820  'module:  interactive control of File menu
830  PCOPY 0,1  'save existing graphics
840  PUT (14,19),A10,PSET  'place menu on screen
850  PUT (16,25),A9,XOR  'place cursor >> on menu
860  T8=1  'reset flag
870  K$=INKEY$
880  IF LEN(K$)=2 THEN K$=RIGHT$(K$,1) ELSE 970
890  IF K$=CHR$(80) THEN T8=T8+1:GOTO 900 ELSE 870
900  IF T8>5 THEN T8=1
910  ON T8 GOTO 920,930,940,950,960
920  PUT (16,57),A9,XOR:PUT (16,25),A9,XOR:GOTO 870 'Name
930  PUT (16,25),A9,XOR:PUT (16,33),A9,XOR:GOTO 870 'Save
940  PUT (16,33),A9,XOR:PUT (16,41),A9,XOR:GOTO 870 'Load
950  PUT (16,41),A9,XOR:PUT (16,49),A9,XOR:GOTO 870 'Quit
960  PUT (16,49),A9,XOR:PUT (16,57),A9,XOR:GOTO 870 'Menu bar
970  IF K$=CHR$(13) THEN 1000  '<Enter> to implement
980  IF K$=CHR$(27) THEN 1050  '<ESC> to cancel
990  GOTO 870
1000  ON T8 GOTO 1010,1020,1030,1040,1050
1010  GOSUB 1310:PCOPY 1,0:LOCATE 1,34:PRINT F$:RETURN  'name change
1020  PCOPY 1,0:GOSUB 1090:RETURN  'save image
1030  PCOPY 1,0:GOSUB 1200:RETURN  'load image
1040  GOTO 240  'quit program
1050  PCOPY 1,0:RETURN  'menu bar
1060  '_____
1070  '
1080  'module: save 640x200 16-color image to disk
1090  MID$(F2$,1,8)=F$  'strip extension from file name
1100  SOUND 250,.7:DEF SEG=&HA000 'set up segment
1110  OUT &H3CE,4:OUT &H3CF,0:BSAVE "B:"+F2$+".BLU",0,16000 'bsave bit plane 0
1120  OUT &H3CE,4:OUT &H3CF,1:BSAVE "B:"+F2$+".GRN",0,16000 'bsave bit plane 1
1130  OUT &H3CE,4:OUT &H3CF,2:BSAVE "B:"+F2$+".RED",0,16000 'bsave bit plane 2
1140  OUT &H3CE,4:OUT &H3CF,3:BSAVE "B:"+F2$+".INT",0,16000 'bsave bit plane 3
1150  OUT &H3CE,4:OUT &H3CF,0:DEF SEG 'restore regs
```

Fig. 21-3. Continued from page 215.)

```
1160   SOUND 250,.7:RETURN
1170   '_____
1180   '
1190   'module: load 640x200 16-color image from disk
1200   MID$(F2$,1,8)=F$  'strip extension from file name
1210   SOUND 250,.7:DEF SEG=&HA000 'set up segment
1220   OUT &H3C4,2:OUT &H3C5,1:BLOAD "B:"+F2$+".BLU",0 'bload bit plane 0
1230   OUT &H3C4,2:OUT &H3C5,2:BLOAD "B:"+F2$+".GRN",0 'bload bit plane 1
1240   OUT &H3C4,2:OUT &H3C5,4:BLOAD "B:"+F2$+".RED",0 'bload bit plane 2
1250   OUT &H3C4,2:OUT &H3C5,8:BLOAD "B:"+F2$+".INT",0 'bload bit plane 3
1260   OUT &H3C4,2:OUT &H3C5,&HF:DEF SEG 'restore regs
1270   SOUND 250,.7:RETURN
1280   '_____
1290   '
1300   'module:  interactive control of Name dialog box
1310   GET (34,53)-(303,66),A11C  'save existing graphics
1320   PUT (34,53),A11,PSET  'display Name dialog box
1330   T2=25  'echo position flag
1340   F1$=F$  'temporary save of existing filename
1350   FOR T=1 TO 8 STEP 1
1360   K$=INKEY$
1370   IF K$="" THEN 1360  'wait for keystroke
1380   IF K$=CHR$(27) THEN F$=F1$:T=8:GOTO 1420   '<ESC> to cancel instructions an
d restore previous filename
1390   IF K$<"A" THEN SOUND 250,.7:GOTO 1360  'must be A-Z
1400   IF K$>"Z" THEN SOUND 250,.7:GOTO 1360  'must be A-Z
1410   T2=T2+1:LOCATE 8,T2:PRINT K$:MID$(F$,T,1)=K$  'echo user input and insert
character into F$
1420   NEXT T
1430   LOCATE 8,26:PRINT F$
1440   K$=INKEY$:IF K$<>CHR$(13) THEN 1440
1450   LOCATE 1,34:PRINT F$:SOUND 250,.7  'display on filename bar
1460   PUT (34,53),A11C,PSET:RETURN  'restore previous graphics
1470   '
1480   '_____DRAW MENU CONTROL_____
1490   '
1500   'module:  interactive controls for Draw menu
1510   PUT (TX,TY),A9,XOR  'install scrolling cursor
1520   LOCATE 23,69:PRINT FRE(0)" "
1530   K$=INKEY$:GOSUB 610
1540   IF LEN(K$)=2 THEN K$=RIGHT$(K$,1) ELSE 1620
1550   IF K$=CHR$(80) THEN TY=TY+12:T7=T7+1 ELSE 1530  'if cursor-down key
1560   IF TY>179 THEN TY=23  'inhibit scrolling range
1570   IF T7>14 THEN T7=1  'inhibit flag
1580   PUT (TX,TYF),A9,XOR  'erase previous cursor
1590   PUT (TX,TY),A9,XOR  'new cursor position
1600   TYF=TYF+12:IF TYF>179 THEN TYF=23  'update previous flag
1610   GOTO 1530
1620   IF K$=CHR$(13) THEN 1630 ELSE 1670   '<Enter>
1630   IF T7<>13 THEN 1640 ELSE 1660
1640   IF T18=1 THEN T18=0:GOSUB 4390
1650   PUT (TX,TY),A9,XOR:PCOPY 0,1:PUT (TX,TY),A9,XOR:GOTO 1710
1660   IF T7=13 THEN T18=0:GOTO 1840  'jump to undo function
1670   IF K$=CHR$(27) THEN PUT (TX,TY),A9,XOR:ELSE 1700
1680   IF T18=1 THEN T18=0:GOSUB 4390
1690   SOUND 250,.7:RETURN
```

Fig. 21-3. (Continued from page 216.)

```
1700  GOTO 1530
1710  ON T7 GOTO 1720,1730,1740,1750,1760,1770,1780,1790,1800,1810,1820,1830,184
0,1850  'jump to appropriate drawing function
1720  T5=1:GOSUB 2910:GOTO 1520  'setpoint
1730  T5=2:GOSUB 2910:GOTO 1520  'polyline
1740  T5=3:GOSUB 2910:GOTO 1520  'rectangle
1750  T5=4:GOSUB 2910:GOTO 1520  'parallelogram
1760  T5=5:GOSUB 3850:GOTO 1520  'circle
1770  T5=6:GOSUB 3850:GOTO 1520  'ellipse
1780  T5=7:GOSUB 3850:GOTO 1520  'arc
1790  T5=8:GOSUB 2910:GOTO 1520  'curve
1800  T5=9:GOSUB 2910:GOTO 1520  'fillet
1810  T5=10:GOSUB 2910:GOTO 1520  'eraser
1820  T5=11:GOSUB 2910:GOTO 1520  'hatch
1830  SOUND 860,2:SOUND 800,2:GOSUB 4500:LOCATE 23,57:PRINT "Free memory:":SOUND
 860,2:SOUND 800,2:GOTO 1520  'regen
1840  PCOPY 1,0:PUT (TX,TY),A9,XOR:SOUND 250,.7:GOTO 1520  'undo
1850  PUT (TX,TY),A9,XOR:SOUND 250,.7:RETURN  'menu bar
1860  '
1870  '_____EDIT MENU CONTROL_____
1880  '
1890  'module:  interactive control of Edit menu
1900  PCOPY 0,1  'save existing graphics
1910  PUT (246,19),A13,PSET  'place menu on screen
1920  PUT (248,24),A9,XOR  'place cursor >> on menu
1930  T8=1  'reset flag
1940  K$=INKEY$
1950  IF LEN(K$)=2 THEN K$=RIGHT$(K$,1) ELSE 2050
1960  IF K$=CHR$(80) THEN T8=T8+1:GOTO 1970 ELSE 1940
1970  IF T8>6 THEN T8=1
1980  ON T8 GOTO 1990,2000,2010,2020,2030,2040
1990  PUT (248,64),A9,XOR:PUT (248,24),A9,XOR:GOTO 1940 'Define entity
2000  PUT (248,24),A9,XOR:PUT (248,32),A9,XOR:GOTO 1940 'Move entity
2010  PUT (248,32),A9,XOR:PUT (248,40),A9,XOR:GOTO 1940 'Copy entity
2020  PUT (248,40),A9,XOR:PUT (248,48),A9,XOR:GOTO 1940 'Erase entity
2030  PUT (248,48),A9,XOR:PUT (248,56),A9,XOR:GOTO 1940 'Undo
2040  PUT (248,56),A9,XOR:PUT (248,64),A9,XOR:GOTO 1940 'Menu bar
2050  IF K$=CHR$(13) THEN 2080  '<Enter> to implement
2060  IF K$=CHR$(27) THEN 2140  '<ESC> to cancel
2070  GOTO 1940
2080  ON T8 GOTO 2090,2100,2110,2120,2130,2140
2090  PCOPY 1,2:PCOPY 1,0:GOSUB 2860:PCOPY 0,1:GOTO 1910  'define entity
2100  PCOPY 1,2:PCOPY 1,0:GOSUB 2860:PCOPY 0,1:GOTO 1910  'move entity
2110  PCOPY 1,2:PCOPY 1,0:GOSUB 2860:PCOPY 0,1:GOTO 1910  'copy entity
2120  PCOPY 1,2:PCOPY 1,0:GOSUB 2860:PCOPY 0,1:GOTO 1910  'erase entity
2130  PCOPY 2,1:PCOPY 1,0:SOUND 250,.7:RETURN  'undo
2140  PCOPY 1,0:RETURN  'menu bar
2150  '
2160  '_____LABEL MENU CONTROL_____
2170  '
2180  'module:  interactive control of Label menu
2190  PCOPY 0,1  'save existing graphics
2200  PUT (366,19),A14,PSET  'place menu on screen
2210  PUT (368,24),A9,XOR  'place cursor >> on menu
2220  T8=1  'reset flag
2230  K$=INKEY$
```

Fig. 21-3. (Continued from page 217.)

```
2240  IF LEN(K$)=2 THEN K$=RIGHT$(K$,1) ELSE 2340
2250  IF K$=CHR$(80) THEN T8=T8+1:GOTO 2260 ELSE 2230
2260  IF T8>6 THEN T8=1
2270  ON T8 GOTO 2280,2290,2300,2310,2320,2330
2280  PUT (368,64),A9,XOR:PUT (368,24),A9,XOR:GOTO 2230  'Set text
2290  PUT (368,24),A9,XOR:PUT (368,32),A9,XOR:GOTO 2230  'H-dimension
2300  PUT (368,32),A9,XOR:PUT (368,40),A9,XOR:GOTO 2230  'V-dimension
2310  PUT (368,40),A9,XOR:PUT (368,48),A9,XOR:GOTO 2230  'Leaderline
2320  PUT (368,48),A9,XOR:PUT (368,56),A9,XOR:GOTO 2230  'Undo
2330  PUT (368,56),A9,XOR:PUT (368,64),A9,XOR:GOTO 2230  'Menu bar
2340  IF K$=CHR$(13) THEN 2370  '<Enter> to implement
2350  IF K$=CHR$(27) THEN 2430  '<ESC> to cancel
2360  GOTO 2230
2370  ON T8 GOTO 2380,2390,2400,2410,2420,2430
2380  PCOPY 1,2:PCOPY 1,0:GOSUB 5630:PCOPY 0,1:GOTO 2200  'set text
2390  PCOPY 1,2:PCOPY 1,0:GOSUB 5630:PCOPY 0,1:GOTO 2200  'H-dimension
2400  PCOPY 1,2:PCOPY 1,0:GOSUB 5630:PCOPY 0,1:GOTO 2200  'V-dimension
2410  PCOPY 1,2:PCOPY 1,0:GOSUB 5630:PCOPY 0,1:GOTO 2200  'leaderline
2420  PCOPY 2,1:PCOPY 1,0:SOUND 250,.7:RETURN  'undo
2430  PCOPY 1,0:RETURN  'menu bar
2440  '
2450  '_____OPTIONS MENU CONTROL_____
2460  '
2470  'module:  interactive control of Options menu
2480  PCOPY 0,1  'save existing graphics
2490  PUT (505,19),A8,PSET  'place menu on screen
2500  PUT (507,25),A9,XOR  'place cursor >> on menu
2510  T8=1  'reset flag
2520  K$=INKEY$
2530  IF LEN(K$)=2 THEN K$=RIGHT$(K$,1) ELSE 2680
2540  IF K$=CHR$(80) THEN T8=T8+1:GOTO 2550 ELSE 2520
2550  IF T8>11 THEN T8=1
2560  ON T8 GOTO 2570,2580,2590,2600,2610,2620,2630,2640,2650,2660,2670
2570  PUT (507,105),A9,XOR:PUT (507,25),A9,XOR:GOTO 2520  'Set snap
2580  PUT (507,25),A9,XOR:PUT (507,33),A9,XOR:GOTO 2520  'Set grid
2590  PUT (507,33),A9,XOR:PUT (507,41),A9,XOR:GOTO 2520  'Set linestyle
2600  PUT (507,41),A9,XOR:PUT (507,49),A9,XOR:GOTO 2520  'Set hatch
2610  PUT (507,49),A9,XOR:PUT (507,57),A9,XOR:GOTO 2520  'Zoom image
2620  PUT (507,57),A9,XOR:PUT (507,65),A9,XOR:GOTO 2520  'Grid on/off
2630  PUT (507,65),A9,XOR:PUT (507,73),A9,XOR:GOTO 2520  'Label on/off
2640  PUT (507,73),A9,XOR:PUT (507,81),A9,XOR:GOTO 2520  'Key layer +/-
2650  PUT (507,81),A9,XOR:PUT (507,89),A9,XOR:GOTO 2520  'Overlay 1 +/-
2660  PUT (507,89),A9,XOR:PUT (507,97),A9,XOR:GOTO 2520  'Overlay 2 +/-
2670  PUT (507,97),A9,XOR:PUT (507,105),A9,XOR:GOTO 2520  'Menu bar
2680  IF K$=CHR$(13) THEN 2710  '<Enter> to implement
2690  IF K$=CHR$(27) THEN 2820  '<ESC> to cancel
2700  GOTO 2520
2710  ON T8 GOTO 2720,2730,2740,2750,2760,2770,2780,2790,2800,2810,2820
2720  GOSUB 5410:GOTO 2520  'set snap
2730  GOSUB 5220:GOTO 2520  'set grid spacing
2740  GOSUB 5540:GOTO 2520  'set linestyle
2750  GOSUB 5130:GOTO 2520  'set hatch
2760  GOSUB 5540:GOTO 2520  'zoom image
2770  GOSUB 5180:GOTO 2520  'grid on/off
2780  GOSUB 5540:GOTO 2520  'label on/off
2790  GOSUB 5350:GOTO 2520  'key layer +/-
```

Fig. 21-3. (Continued from page 218.)

```
2800  GOSUB 5360:GOTO 2520   'overlay 1 +/-
2810  GOSUB 5370:GOTO 2520   'overlay 2 +/-
2820  PCOPY 1,0:PAINT (30,145),C13,C8:PAINT (30,145),A$,C8:RETURN   'menu bar
2830  '
2840  '_____DO-NOTHING ROUTINE_____
2850  '
2860  SOUND 860,2:SOUND 800,2:RETURN   'do-nothing routine
2870  '
2880  '_____CROSSHAIR CURSOR CONTROL_____
2890  '
2900  'module:  interactive control of crosshair cursor
2910  SOUND 250,.7:VIEW SCREEN (J6,J7)-(J8,J9) 'clip canvas edges
2920  PUT (SX,SY),A12,XOR   'install crosshair cursor
2930  T6=0 'reset polyline flag
2940  T3=0 'reset iteration flag
2950  X1=100:X2=130:X3=160:X4=190:Y1=40:Y2=100:Y3=140:Y4=70   'reset control poin
ts for curve and fillet
2960  K$=INKEY$
2970  IF LEN(K$)=2 THEN K$=RIGHT$(K$,1) ELSE 3140
2980  IF K$=CHR$(77) THEN PUT (SX,SY),A12,XOR:SX=SX+J ELSE 3010
2990  IF SX>XR THEN SX=XR:SOUND 250,.7
3000  PUT (SX,SY),A12,XOR:GOTO 2960
3010  IF K$=CHR$(75) THEN PUT (SX,SY),A12,XOR:SX=SX-J ELSE 3040
3020  IF SX<XL THEN SX=XL:SOUND 250,.7
3030  PUT (SX,SY),A12,XOR:GOTO 2960
3040  IF K$=CHR$(72) THEN PUT (SX,SY),A12,XOR:SY=SY-J*.5 ELSE 3070
3050  IF SY<YT THEN SY=YT:SOUND 250,.7
3060  PUT (SX,SY),A12,XOR:GOTO 2960
3070  IF K$=CHR$(80) THEN PUT (SX,SY),A12,XOR:SY=SY+J*.5 ELSE 3100
3080  IF SY>YB THEN SY=YB:SOUND 250,.7
3090  PUT (SX,SY),A12,XOR:GOTO 2960
3100  IF K$=CHR$(71) THEN PUT (SX,SY),A12,XOR:SX=85:SY=19:PUT (SX,SY),A12,XOR:GO
TO 2960
3110  IF K$=CHR$(73) THEN PUT (SX,SY),A12,XOR:SX=594:SY=19:PUT (SX,SY),A12,XOR:G
OTO 2960
3120  IF K$=CHR$(81) THEN PUT (SX,SY),A12,XOR:SX=594:SY=180:PUT (SX,SY),A12,XOR:
GOTO 2960
3130  IF K$=CHR$(79) THEN PUT (SX,SY),A12,XOR:SX=85:SY=180:PUT (SX,SY),A12,XOR:G
OTO 2960
3140  IF K$=CHR$(27) THEN PUT (SX,SY),A12,XOR:VIEW:SOUND 250,.7:RETURN   '<ESC>
3150  IF K$=CHR$(13) THEN PUT (SX,SY),A12,XOR:GOSUB 3220:PUT (SX,SY),A12,XOR ELS
E 3160  '<Enter> to implement command
3160  GOTO 2960
3170  VIEW:SOUND 250,.7:RETURN
3180  '
3190  '_____SWITCHER TO INVOKE DRAWING FUNCTION_____
3200  '
3210  'module:  switcher for drawing functions
3220  ON T5 GOTO 3230,3240,3250,3260,3270,3280,3290,3300,3310,3320,3330
3230  GOSUB 3380:RETURN   'setpoint
3240  GOSUB 3420:RETURN   'polyline
3250  GOSUB 3470:RETURN   'rectangle
3260  GOSUB 3520:RETURN   'parallelogram
3270  GOSUB 2860:RETURN   'circle inactive
3280  GOSUB 2860:RETURN   'ellipse inactive
3290  GOSUB 2860:RETURN   'arc inactive
```

Fig. 21-3. (Continued from page 219.)

```
3300   GOSUB 3580:RETURN   'curve
3310   GOSUB 3670:RETURN   'fillet
3320   GOSUB 3750:RETURN   'eraser
3330   GOSUB 3800:RETURN   'hatch
3340   RETURN 3170
3350 '_____
3360 '
3370 'module:  setpoint function
3380   SXC=SX+7:SYC=SY+3:PSET (SXC,SYC),C:T11=1:E1=SXC:E2=SYC:E3=C:T18=1:RETURN 3
340
3390 '_____
3400 '_____
3410 'module:  polyline function
3420   IF T6=0 THEN SXC=SX+7:SYC=SY+3:PSET (SXC,SYC),C:T6=1:SXP=SXC:SYP=SYC:RETUR
N ELSE 3430
3430   SXC=SX+7:SYC=SY+3:LINE (SXP,SYP)-(SXC,SYC),C:T11=2:E1=SXP:E2=SYP:E3=SXC:E4
=SYC:E5=C:T18=1:SXP=SXC:SYP=SYC:RETURN 3340
3440 '_____
3450 '_____
3460 'module:  rectangle function
3470   IF T6=0 THEN SXC=SX+7:SYC=SY+3:PSET (SXC,SYC),C:T6=1:SXP=SXC:SYP=SYC:RETUR
N ELSE 3480
3480   SXC=SX+7:SYC=SY+3:LINE (SXP,SYP)-(SXC,SYC),C,B:T6=0:T11=3:E1=SXP:E2=SYP:E3
=SXC:E4=SYC:E5=C:T18=1:RETURN 3340
3490 '_____
3500 '_____
3510 'module:  parallelogram function
3520   IF T6=0 THEN SXP=SX+7:SYP=SY+3:PSET (SXP,SYP),C:T6=1:RETURN ELSE 3530
3530   IF T6=1 THEN SXP1=SX+7:SYP1=SY+3:LINE (SXP,SYP)-(SXP1,SYP1),C:T6=2:RETURN
ELSE 3540
3540   IF T6=2 THEN SXP2=SX+7:SYP2=SY+3:SXP3=SXP2+(SXP1-SXP):SYP3=SYP2+(SYP1-SYP)
:LINE (SXP,SYP)-(SXP2,SYP2),C:LINE-(SXP3,SYP3),C:LINE-(SXP1,SYP1),C:T6=0:T11=4:E
1=SXP:E2=SYP:E3=SXP2:E4=SYP2:E5=SXP3:E6=SYP3:E7=SXP1:E8=SYP1:E9=C:T18=1:RETURN 3
340
3550 '_____
3560 '_____
3570 'module:  curve function (cubic parametric)
3580   IF T6=0 THEN X1=SX+7:Y1=SY+3:PSET (X1,Y1),C:T6=1:RETURN ELSE 3590
3590   IF T6=1 THEN X2=SX+7:Y2=SY+3:PSET (X2,Y2),C:T6=2:RETURN ELSE 3600
3600   IF T6=2 THEN X3=SX+7:Y3=SY+3:PSET (X3,Y3),C:T6=3:RETURN ELSE 3610
3610   IF T6=3 THEN X4=SX+7:Y4=SY+3:PSET (X4,Y4),C:T6=0:GOSUB 3620:PSET (X2,Y2),0
:PSET (X3,Y3),0:SX=SX-7:SY=SY-3:T11=8:E1=X1:E2=Y1:E3=X2:E4=Y2:E5=X3:E6=Y3:E7=X4:
E8=Y4:E9=C:T18=1:RETURN 3340
3620   B=0:B2=B*B:B3=B*B*B:GOSUB 3630:PSET (SX,SY),C:FOR B=0 TO 1.01 STEP .05:B2=
B*B:B3=B*B*B:GOSUB 3630:LINE-(SX,SY),C:NEXT B:RETURN
3630   D1=X1*(-B3+3*B2-3*B+1):D2=X2*(3*B3-6*B2+3*B):D3=X3*(-3*B3+3*B2):D4=X4*B3:S
X=D1+D2+D3+D4:D1=Y1*(-B3+3*B2-3*B+1):D2=Y2*(3*B3-6*B2+3*B):D3=Y3*(-3*B3+3*B2):D4
=Y4*B3:SY=D1+D2+D3+D4:RETURN
3640 '_____
3650 '_____
3660 'module:  fillet function (round corner)
3670   IF T6=0 THEN X1=SX+7:Y1=SY+3:PSET (X1,Y1),C:T6=1:RETURN ELSE 3680
3680   IF T6=1 THEN X2=SX+7:Y2=SY+3:X3=X2:Y3=Y2:PSET (X2,Y2),C:T6=2:RETURN ELSE 3
690
3690   IF T6=2 THEN X4=SX+7:Y4=SY+3:PSET (X4,Y4),C:T6=0:GOSUB 3700:PSET (X2,Y2),0
:SX=SX-7:SY=SY-3:T11=9:E1=X1:E2=Y1:E3=X2:E4=Y2:E5=X3:E6=Y3:E7=X4:E8=Y4:E9=C:T18=
```

Fig. 21-3. (Continued from page 220.)

```
1:RETURN 3340
3700   B=0:B2=B*B:B3=B*B*B:GOSUB 3710:PSET (SX,SY),C:FOR B=0 TO 1.01 STEP .05:B2=
B*B:B3=B*B*B:GOSUB 3710:LINE-(SX,SY),C:NEXT B:RETURN
3710   D1=X1*(-B3+3*B2-3*B+1):D2=X2*(3*B3-6*B2+3*B):D3=X3*(-3*B3+3*B2):D4=X4*B3:S
X=D1+D2+D3+D4:D1=Y1*(-B3+3*B2-3*B+1):D2=Y2*(3*B3-6*B2+3*B):D3=Y3*(-3*B3+3*B2):D4
=Y4*B3:SY=D1+D2+D3+D4:RETURN
3720   '_____
3730   '_____
3740   'module:  eraser function
3750   IF T6=0 THEN SXC=SX+7:SYC=SY+3:PSET (SXC,SYC),0:T6=1:SXP=SXC:SYP=SYC:RETUR
N ELSE 3760
3760   SXC=SX+7:SYC=SY+3:LINE (SXP,SYP)-(SXC,SYC),0:T11=10:E1=SXP:E2=SYP:E3=SXC:E
4=SYC:T18=1:SXP=SXC:SYP=SYC:RETURN 3340
3770   '_____
3780   '_____
3790   'module:  crosshatch pattern fill function
3800   SXC=SX+7:SYC=SY+3:PAINT (SXC,SYC),C13,C:PAINT (SXC,SYC),A$,C:T11=11:E1=SXC
:E2=SYC:E3=T19:E4=C:T18=1:RETURN 3340
3810   '
3820   '_____RUBBER CROSSHAIR CURSOR CONTROL_____
3830   '
3840   'module:  interactive control of rubber circle
3850   PCOPY 0,2   'use page 2 as refresh buffer
3860   SOUND 250,.7:VIEW SCREEN (J6,J7)-(J8,J9) 'viewport
3870   PUT (SX,SY),A12,XOR  'install crosshair cursor
3880   SXC=SX+7:SYC=SY+3
3890   GOSUB 4290   'install rubber circle, ellipse, arc
3900   K$=INKEY$
3910   IF LEN(K$)=2 THEN K$=RIGHT$(K$,1) ELSE 4050
3920   IF K$=CHR$(77) THEN SX=SX+J ELSE 3950
3930   IF SX>XR THEN SX=XR:SOUND 250,.7
3940   GOTO 4030
3950   IF K$=CHR$(75) THEN SX=SX-J ELSE 3980
3960   IF SX<XL THEN SX=XL:SOUND 250,.7
3970   GOTO 4030
3980   IF K$=CHR$(72) THEN SY=SY-J ELSE 4010
3990   IF SY<YT THEN SY=YT:SOUND 250,.7
4000   GOTO 4030
4010   IF K$=CHR$(80) THEN SY=SY+J ELSE 4040
4020   IF SY>YB THEN SY=YB:SOUND 250,.7
4030   SXC=SX+7:SYC=SY+3:PCOPY 2,0:GOSUB 4290:PUT (SX,SY),A12,XOR:GOTO 3900
4040   SOUND 250,.7:GOTO 3900
4050   IF K$=CHR$(27) THEN T18=0:PCOPY 2,0:VIEW:SOUND 250,.7:RETURN   '<ESC> to re
turn to Draw menu
4060   IF K$="1" THEN J1=J1+J2:GOTO 4030 ELSE 4070   'increment radius
4070   IF K$="2" THEN J1=J1-J2 ELSE 4090   'decrement radius
4080   IF J1<8 THEN J1=8:SOUND 250,.7:GOTO 4030 ELSE 4030
4090   IF K$="3" THEN H1=H1+H2:GOTO 4030 ELSE 4100   'increment aspect ratio
4100   IF K$="4" THEN H1=H1-H2:GOTO 4030 ELSE 4110   'decrement aspect ratio
4110   IF K$="5" THEN H3=H3+H5:H4=H3+H6 ELSE 4140   'rotate arc
4120   IF H4>6.28318 THEN H4=6.28318:H3=H4-H6:SOUND 250,.7
4130   GOTO 4030
4140   IF K$="6" THEN H6=H6+H5 ELSE 4190   'lengthen arc
4150   IF H6>6.28318 THEN H6=6.28318:SOUND 250,.7
4160   H4=H3+H6
4170   IF H4>6.28318 THEN H4=6.28318:SOUND 250,.7
```

Fig. 21-3. (Continued from page 221.)

```
4180   GOTO 4030
4190   IF K$="7" THEN H6=H6-H5 ELSE 4230   'shorten arc
4200   IF H6<.39628 THEN H6=.39628:SOUND 250,.7
4210   H4=H3+H6:IF H4>6.28318 THEN H4=6.28318
4220   GOTO 4030
4230   IF K$="8" THEN J1=40:H1=.16:H3=0:H4=1.57079:H5=.39269:H6=1.57079:SX=320:SY
=100:GOTO 4030
4240   IF K$=CHR$(13) THEN PUT (SX,SY),A12,XOR:PCOPY 2,0:GOSUB 4290:PCOPY 0,2:VIE
W:SOUND 250,.7:RETURN   '<Enter>
4250   GOTO 3900
4260   '_____
4270   '
4280   'module:  switcher for rubber circle/ellipse/arc
4290   ON T5 GOTO 4300,4300,4300,4300,4310,4320,4330,4340
4300   SOUND 860,2:SOUND 800,2:RETURN   'dummy trap
4310   CIRCLE (SXC,SYC),J1,C:T11=5:E1=SXC:E2=SYC:E3=J1:E4=C:T18=1:RETURN   'circle
4320   CIRCLE (SXC,SYC),J1,C,,,H1:T11=6:E1=SXC:E2=SYC:E3=J1:E4=C:E5=H1:T18=1:RETU
RN   'ellipse
4330   CIRCLE (SXC,SYC),J1,C,H3,H4:T11=7:E1=SXC:E2=SYC:E3=J1:E4=C:E5=H3:E6=H4:T18
=1:RETURN   'arc
4340   SOUND 860,2:SOUND 800,2:RETURN   'dummy trap
4350   '
4360   '_____WRITE TO .CDF DATA FILE_____
4370   '
4380   'module:  storage of primitive attributes and parameters in data files
4390   ON T12 GOTO 4400,4410,4420,4430,4440
4400   OPEN "A:GRID.CDF" FOR OUTPUT AS #1:WRITE #1,T11,E1,E2:CLOSE #1:RETURN
4410   SOUND 860,2:SOUND 800,2:RETURN   'label is inactive
4420   OPEN "A:KEYLAYER.CDF" FOR APPEND AS #2:WRITE #2,T11,E1,E2,E3,E4,E5,E6,E7,E
8,E9:CLOSE #2:RETURN
4430   OPEN "A:OVERLAY1.CDF" FOR APPEND AS #3:WRITE #3,T11,E1,E2,E3,E4,E5,E6,E7,E
8,E9:CLOSE #3:RETURN
4440   OPEN "A:OVERLAY2.CDF" FOR APPEND AS #4:WRITE #4,T11,E1,E2,E3,E4,E5,E6,E7,E
8,E9:CLOSE #4:RETURN
4450   '
4460   '_____
4470   '_____READ .CDF DATA FILES_____
4480   '
4490   'module:  front end for regen function
4500   VIEW SCREEN (J6,J7)-(J8,J9):CLS:GOSUB 4540:VIEW:RETURN
4510   '_____
4520   '
4530   'module:  retrieval of graphics primitives from data files
4540   IF T13=1 THEN 4550 ELSE 4590 'check layer toggle
4550   OPEN "A:GRID.CDF" FOR INPUT AS #1
4560   IF EOF(1) THEN CLOSE #1:GOTO 4590
4570   INPUT #1,T11,E1,E2:GOSUB 4780
4580   GOTO 4560   'loop until end-of-file
4590   IF T15=1 THEN 4600 ELSE 4640
4600   OPEN "A:KEYLAYER.CDF" FOR INPUT AS #2
4610   IF EOF(2) THEN CLOSE #2:GOTO 4640
4620   INPUT #2,T11,E1,E2,E3,E4,E5,E6,E7,E8,E9:GOSUB 4780
4630   GOTO 4610
4640   IF T16=1 THEN 4650 ELSE 4690
4650   OPEN "A:OVERLAY1.CDF" FOR INPUT AS #3
4660   IF EOF(3) THEN CLOSE #3:GOTO 4690
```

Fig. 21-3.   (Continued from page 222.)

```
4670  INPUT #3,T11,E1,E2,E3,E4,E5,E6,E7,E8,E9:GOSUB 4780
4680  GOTO 4660
4690  IF T17=1 THEN 4700 ELSE 4740
4700  OPEN "A:OVERLAY2.CDF" FOR INPUT AS #4
4710  IF EOF(4) THEN CLOSE #4:RETURN
4720  INPUT #4,T11,E1,E2,E3,E4,E5,E6,E7,E8,E9:GOSUB 4780
4730  GOTO 4710
4740  RETURN
4750  '
4760  '_____
4770  'module:  regen of graphics on screen
4780  ON T11 GOTO 4790,4800,4810,4820,4830,4840,4850,4860,4870,4880,4890,4900
4790  PSET (E1,E2),E3:RETURN 'setpoint
4800  LINE (E1,E2)-(E3,E4),E5:RETURN 'polyline
4810  LINE (E1,E2)-(E3,E4),E5,B:RETURN 'rectangle
4820  LINE (E1,E2)-(E3,E4),E9:LINE-(E5,E6),E9:LINE-(E7,E8),E9:LINE-(E1,E2),E9:RE
TURN 'parallelogram
4830  CIRCLE (E1,E2),E3,E4:RETURN 'circle
4840  CIRCLE (E1,E2),E3,E4,,,E5:RETURN 'ellipse
4850  CIRCLE (E1,E2),E3,E4,E5,E6:RETURN 'arc
4860  X1=E1:Y1=E2:X2=E3:Y2=E4:X3=E5:Y3=E6:X4=E7:Y4=E8:C=E9:GOSUB 3620:RETURN 'cu
rve
4870  X1=E1:Y1=E2:X2=E3:Y2=E4:X3=E5:Y3=E6:X4=E7:Y4=E8:C=E9:GOSUB 3700:RETURN 'ar
c
4880  LINE (E1,E2)-(E3,E4),0:RETURN 'eraser
4890  T19=E3:GOSUB 4940:PAINT (E1,E2),C13,E4:PAINT (E1,E2),A$,E4:RETURN 'hatch
4900  T=85:WHILE T<609:LINE (T,19)-(T,186),C8:T=T+E1:WEND:T=19:WHILE T<187:LINE
(85,T)-(608,T),C8:T=T+E2:WEND:RETURN 'grid
4910  '_____
4920  '
4930  'module:  determine hatch pattern
4940  ON T19 GOTO 4950,4960,4970,4980,4990,5000,5010,5020,5030,5040,5050,5060,50
70,5080
4950  A$=A1$:RETURN
4960  A$=A2$:RETURN
4970  A$=A3$:RETURN
4980  A$=A4$:RETURN
4990  A$=A5$:RETURN
5000  A$=A6$:RETURN
5010  A$=A7$:RETURN
5020  A$=A8$:RETURN
5030  A$=A9$:RETURN
5040  A$=A10$:RETURN
5050  A$=A11$:RETURN
5060  A$=A12$:RETURN
5070  A$=A13$:RETURN
5080  A$=A14$:RETURN
5090  '
5100  '_____OPTIONS ROUTINES_____
5110  '
5120  'module:  set hatch pattern
5130  T19=T19+1:IF T19>14 THEN T19=1
5140  GOSUB 4940:PAINT (30,145),C13,C8:PAINT (30,145),A$,C8:RETURN
5150  '
5160  '_____
5170  'module:  toggle grid on/off
```

Fig. 21-3. (Continued from page 223.)

```
5180  IF T13=0 THEN T13=1:SOUND 250,.7:RETURN ELSE IF T13=1 THEN T13=0:SOUND 250
,.7:RETURN
5190  '_____
5200  '
5210  'module:  set grid spacing
5220  PCOPY 0,2
5230  CLS:LOCATE 1,12:PRINT "Press + or - to change grid spacing.":LOCATE 2,12:P
RINT "Press <Enter> to adopt spacing and return to Options menu."
5240  LINE (85,19)-(608,186),0,BF:T=85:WHILE T<609:LINE (T,19)-(T,186),C8:T=T+J1
0:WEND:T=19:WHILE T<187:LINE (85,T)-(608,T),C8:T=T+J11:WEND:SOUND 860,2:SOUND 80
0,2
5250  K$=INKEY$
5260  IF K$=CHR$(13) THEN T11=12:E1=J10:E2=J11:T20=T12:T12=1:GOSUB 4390:T12=T20:
PCOPY 2,0:SOUND 250,.7:RETURN
5270  IF K$="=" THEN J10=J10+5:J11=J10*.4 ELSE 5290
5280  IF J10>100 THEN SOUND 250,.7:J10=100:J11=J10*.44:GOTO 5240 ELSE 5240
5290  IF K$="-" THEN J10=J10-5:J11=J10*.4 ELSE 5310
5300  IF J10<5 THEN SOUND 250,.7:J10=5:J11=J10*.44:GOTO 5240 ELSE 5240
5310  GOTO 5250
5320  '_____
5330  '
5340  'module:  toggle drawing layers on/off
5350  T12=3:C=C7:IF T15=1 THEN T15=0:SOUND 250,.7:RETURN ELSE IF T15=0 THEN T15=
1:SOUND 250,.7:RETURN  'key layer
5360  T12=4:C=C4:IF T16=1 THEN T16=0:SOUND 250,.7:RETURN ELSE IF T16=0 THEN T16=
1:SOUND 250,.7:RETURN  'overlay 1
5370  T12=5:C=C1:IF T17=1 THEN T17=0:SOUND 250,.7:RETURN ELSE IF T17=0 THEN T17=
1:SOUND 250,.7:RETURN  'overlay 2
5380  '_____
5390  '
5400  'module:  set snap for crosshair cursor
5410  PCOPY 0,2
5420  CLS:LOCATE 10,12:PRINT "Press + or - to change snap for crosshair cursor."
:LOCATE 11,12:PRINT "Press <Enter> to adopt value and return to Options menu."
5430  LOCATE 13,30:PRINT "Current snap is"J
5440  K$=INKEY$
5450  IF K$="=" THEN J=J+2 ELSE 5470
5460  IF J>20 THEN J=20:SOUND 250,.7:GOTO 5430 ELSE 5430
5470  IF K$="-" THEN J=J-2 ELSE 5490
5480  IF J<2 THEN J=2:SOUND 250,.7:GOTO 5430 ELSE 5430
5490  IF K$=CHR$(13) THEN PCOPY 2,0:SOUND 860,2:SOUND 800,2:RETURN
5500  GOTO 5440
5510  '_____
5520  '
5530  'module:  announcement of inactive features
5540  PCOPY 0,2:CLS:LOCATE 10,10:PRINT "This feature is not available in this ve
rsion of the program."
5550  LOCATE 12,10:PRINT "You can easily write your own code to activate this fe
ature.":LOCATE 13,10:PRINT "If you require help, refer to the book for instructi
ons."
5560  LOCATE 17,26:PRINT "Press <Enter> to continue...":SOUND 860,2:SOUND 800,2
5570  K$=INKEY$:IF K$<>CHR$(13) THEN 5570
5580  PCOPY 2,0:SOUND 860,2:SOUND 800,2:RETURN
5590  '
5600  '_____LABEL CROSSHAIR CURSOR CONTROL_____
5610  '
```

Fig. 21-3. (Continued from page 224.)

```
5620  'module:  interactive control of crosshair cursor
5630   SOUND 250,.7:VIEW SCREEN (J6,J7)-(J8,J9)  'clip canvas edges
5640   PUT (SX,SY),A12,XOR  'install crosshair cursor
5650   T6=0  'reset iteration flag
5660   K$=INKEY$
5670   IF LEN(K$)=2 THEN K$=RIGHT$(K$,1) ELSE 5840
5680   IF K$=CHR$(77) THEN PUT (SX,SY),A12,XOR:SX=SX+J ELSE 5710
5690   IF SX>XR THEN SX=XR:SOUND 250,.7
5700   PUT (SX,SY),A12,XOR:GOTO 5660
5710   IF K$=CHR$(75) THEN PUT (SX,SY),A12,XOR:SX=SX-J ELSE 5740
5720   IF SX<XL THEN SX=XL:SOUND 250,.7
5730   PUT (SX,SY),A12,XOR:GOTO 5660
5740   IF K$=CHR$(72) THEN PUT (SX,SY),A12,XOR:SY=SY-J*.5 ELSE 5770
5750   IF SY<YT THEN SY=YT:SOUND 250,.7
5760   PUT (SX,SY),A12,XOR:GOTO 5660
5770   IF K$=CHR$(80) THEN PUT (SX,SY),A12,XOR:SY=SY+J*.5 ELSE 5800
5780   IF SY>YB THEN SY=YB:SOUND 250,.7
5790   PUT (SX,SY),A12,XOR:GOTO 5660
5800   IF K$=CHR$(71) THEN PUT (SX,SY),A12,XOR:SX=85:SY=19:PUT (SX,SY),A12,XOR:GO
TO 5660
5810   IF K$=CHR$(73) THEN PUT (SX,SY),A12,XOR:SX=594:SY=19:PUT (SX,SY),A12,XOR:G
OTO 5660
5820   IF K$=CHR$(81) THEN PUT (SX,SY),A12,XOR:SX=594:SY=180:PUT (SX,SY),A12,XOR:
GOTO 5660
5830   IF K$=CHR$(79) THEN PUT (SX,SY),A12,XOR:SX=85:SY=180:PUT (SX,SY),A12,XOR:G
OTO 5660
5840   IF K$=CHR$(27) THEN PUT (SX,SY),A12,XOR:VIEW:SOUND 250,.7:RETURN  '<ESC>
5850   IF K$=CHR$(13) THEN PUT (SX,SY),A12,XOR:GOSUB 5920:PUT (SX,SY),A12,XOR ELS
E 5860  '<Enter> to implement command
5860   GOTO 5660
5870   VIEW:SOUND 250,.7:RETURN
5880  '
5890  '_____SWITCHER TO INVOKE LABEL FUNCTION_____
5900  '
5910  'module:  switcher for drawing functions
5920   ON T8 GOTO 5930,5940,5950,5960
5930   GOSUB 6010:RETURN  'set text
5940   GOSUB 6170:RETURN  'set H-dimension
5950   GOSUB 6270:RETURN  'set V-dimension
5960   GOSUB 6370:RETURN  'set leaderline
5970   RETURN 5870
5980  '_____
5990  '
6000  'module:  set alphanumeric dimension text
6010   SXC=SX+7:SYC=SY+3:JR=SYC*.125:JC=SXC*.125
6020   IF JR<5 THEN SOUND 250,.7:RETURN
6030   IF JR>22 THEN SOUND 250,.7:RETURN
6040   IF JC<14 THEN SOUND 250,.7:RETURN
6050   IF JC>71 THEN SOUND 250,.7:RETURN
6060   LOCATE JR,JC:T2=1
6070   K$=INKEY$:IF K$="" THEN 6070
6080   IF K$="." THEN 6130 ELSE 6090
6090   IF K$>="0" AND K$<="9" THEN 6130 ELSE 6100
6100   IF K$>="A" AND K$<="Z" THEN 6130 ELSE 6110
6110   IF K$=CHR$(27) THEN RETURN 5970 ELSE 6120
6120   SOUND 250,.7:GOTO 6070
```

Fig. 21-3. (Continued from page 225.)

```
6130    PRINT K$:LOCATE JR,JC+T2:T2=T2+1:IF T2>5 THEN RETURN 5970 ELSE 6070
6140  '_____
6150  '
6160  'module:  horizontal dimension entity
6170   IF T6=0 THEN SXC=SX+7:SYC=SY+3:PSET (SXC,SYC),C:T6=1:SXP=SXC:SYP=SYC:RETUR
N ELSE 6180
6180    SXC=SX+7:SYC=SY+3
6190   IF SXC<(SXP+15) THEN SOUND 250,.7:RETURN
6200   LINE (SXP,SYP)-(SXC,SYP),C:LINE (SXP,SYP)-(SXP+5,SYP-2),C:LINE (SXP,SYP)-(
SXP+5,SYP+2),C
6210   LINE (SXC,SYP)-(SXC-5,SYP-2),C:LINE (SXC,SYP)-(SXC-5,SYP+2),C
6220   LINE (SXP,SYP-6)-(SXP,SYP+6),C:LINE (SXC,SYP-6)-(SXC,SYP+6),C
6230   RETURN 5970
6240  '_____
6250  '
6260  'module:  vertical dimension entity
6270   IF T6=0 THEN SXC=SX+7:SYC=SY+3:PSET (SXC,SYC),C:T6=1:SXP=SXC:SYP=SYC:RETUR
N ELSE 6280
6280    SXC=SX+7:SYC=SY+3
6290   IF SYC<(SYP+10) THEN SOUND 250,.7:RETURN
6300   LINE (SXP,SYP)-(SXP,SYC),C:LINE (SXP,SYP)-(SXP-3,SYP+3),C:LINE (SXP,SYP)-(
SXP+3,SYP+3),C
6310   LINE (SXP,SYC)-(SXP-3,SYC-3),C:LINE (SXP,SYC)-(SXP+3,SYC-3),C
6320   LINE (SXP-10,SYP)-(SXP+10,SYP),C:LINE (SXP-10,SYC)-(SXP+10,SYC),C
6330   RETURN 5970
6340  '_____
6350  '
6360  'module:  leaderline entity
6370   IF T6=0 THEN SXC=SX+7:SYC=SY+3:PSET (SXC,SYC),C:T6=1:SXP=SXC:SYP=SYC:RETUR
N ELSE 6380
6380    SXC=SX+7:SYC=SY+3:IF SXC<SXP THEN 6430 ELSE 6390
6390   IF SXC<(SXP+35) THEN SOUND 250,.7:RETURN
6400   LINE (SXP,SYP)-(SXP+30,SYP),C:LINE-(SXC,SYC),C
6410   LINE (SXP,SYP)-(SXP+5,SYP-2),C:LINE (SXP,SYP)-(SXP+5,SYP+2),C
6420   RETURN 5970
6430   IF SXP<(SXC+35) THEN SOUND 250,.7:RETURN
6440   LINE (SXP,SYP)-(SXP-30,SYP),C:LINE-(SXC,SYC),C
6450   LINE (SXP,SYP)-(SXP-5,SYP-2),C:LINE (SXP,SYP)-(SXP-5,SYP+2),C
6460   RETURN 5970
6470  '_____
6480  '
6490   END
```

Fig. 21-3. (Continued from page 226.)

22

Drafting Program Documentation— A User's Guide

This chapter contains the User's Guide for *YOUR MICROCOMPUTER DRAFTING TABLE,* a multifunction drafting program. The complete source code for this program appears in the previous chapter. The User's Guide in this chapter contains the following sections: Introduction, System Requirements, Starting And Stopping The Program, How To Use The Program, and Sample Sessions.

INTRODUCTION

YOUR MICROCOMPUTER DRAFTING TABLE gives you the drawing tools you need to create technical drawings and schematics with your personal computer. A rich selection of built-in functions gives you complete control over your creativity and talent. The comprehensive User's Guide gets you started right away by providing tutorial sessions complete with photographs of sample drawings created by the program.

Drawing tools include points, lines, rectangles, circles, ellipses, arcs, curves, fillets, crosshatch area fill, eraser, regen, and much more. A comprehensive set of Options features gives you the ability to define and toggle an optional grid, choose the hatch style, and toggle on and off the three drawing layers implemented by the regeneration function.

YOUR MICROCOMPUTER DRAFTING TABLE contains powerful routines to save your drawings on disk as image files. You can retrieve your drawings from disk for later editing. The images created can be printed by dot-matrix printers or ink-jet printers using third-party graphics printing utilities (such as Pizazz; refer to Appendix F).

YOUR MICROCOMPUTER DRAFTING TABLE gives you high-performance drafting drawing capabilities at your fingertips, using your standard keyboard.

SYSTEM REQUIREMENTS

To run the program, you need an IBM PC, XT, AT, RT, PS/2, or any IBM-compatible personal computer equipped with an EGA or VGA graphics adapter. Also required is a standard color display (SCD), enhanced color display (ECD), analog display (PS/2 or equivalent), or variable frequency display (Multisync, Multiscan, or equivalent).

You will need IBM PC-DOS or Microsoft MS-DOS. A version of BASIC which supports EGA graphics is required.

This version of *YOUR MICROCOMPUTER DRAFTING TABLE* is intended for BA-SIC interpreters which support EGA graphics, including IBM BASICA and Microsoft BASICA. You can easily modify this program for use with your QuickBASIC or Turbo BASIC compiler. Refer to Appendix E for guidance.

YOUR MICROCOMPUTER DRAFTING TABLE runs on personal computers equipped with two disk drives. The program can be easily modified to use a hard disk or a simulated disk in RAM. Refer to Chapter 23 for guidance.

If you are using a CGA (color/graphics adapter) or MCGA, you can adapt this program for your personal computer by referring to Appendix G. You might want to skip ahead to Chapter 26 to experiment with a high-performance interactive graphics program already modified to run on your CGA or MCGA.

STARTING AND STOPPING THE PROGRAM

Before you use the program, you should create a back-up copy of the program on a separate disk. Use the back-up disk. Store the original disk in a safe place. Remember the old adage: anything which you do not have backed up you are going to lose eventually.

Starting The Program

YOUR MICROCOMPUTER DRAFTING TABLE is comprised of two separate programs. CADD-1.BAS is the start-up module. CADD-2.BAS is the runtime module. To start using the program, load CADD-1.BAS under your BASIC interpreter. At the OK prompt, press F2 to run the program. (Ensure that you have initially loaded BASIC using the following syntax: **BASICA/F:4**. See Chapter 23 for more on this.)

At start-up, the program offers you three environment choices. If you press 1, then the program sets up a new set of data files (which are used during regen). You will normally use this option. If you select 2, the program will use the data files created by your last session. (Ensure these are loaded in the appropriate drive, usually A.) If you select 3, the program ends immediately.

Using Disk Drives

The start-up module creates the menu system, the on-screen user interface, and initializes some variables that the program will use. When finished, it pauses and waits for you to make a keystroke selection. After you press a key, the start-up module will attempt to load the runtime module from drive A. You should ensure that the disk containing CADD-2.BAS is in drive A. If it is in another drive, you should modify the drive assignment in line 1230 of CADD-1.BAS. If you have installed the two modules for the program on a hard drive, for example, you would change line 1230 in CADD-1.BAS to read: **1230 CHAIN "C:CADD-2.BAS",160,ALL**.

The runtime module, CADD-2.BAS, expects to use drive B to save image files and to retrieve image files. Image files contain your drawings and your illustrations. When first using the program, you should place a blank disk in drive B. If you wish to use a hard disk for this purpose, you should change the BSAVE drive letter in lines 1110, 1120, 1130, and 1140 in CADD-2.BAS. You should also change the BLOAD drive letter in lines 1220, 1230, 1240, and 1250.

Using A Simulated Disk

Because data is saved to a data file during the implementation of each graphics function, *YOUR MICROCOMPUTER DRAFTING TABLE* will run much quicker if you use a simulated disk with your personal computer. If you have two disk drives, then your simulated disk will be drive C. If you have a hard disk, then your simulated disk will be drive D. You should change line 1230 in CADD-1.BAS to reflect this new drive letter.

To write data files to the simulated disk, change the drive letter in lines 2420, 2440, 2450, and 2460 in CADD-1.BAS. Also modify lines 4400, 4420, 4430, and 4440 in CADD-2.BAS. The regen function uses lines 4550, 4600, 4650, and 4700 to retrieve data from the data files. Change the drive letter in these lines too.

To create the simulated disk in RAM memory, put the instruction **DEVICE=A:VDISK.SYS 360 512 16** in a CONFIG.SYS file on your boot disk. (See Chapter 15 for more on this.) Then, use either DOS or BASIC to copy both modules of *YOUR MICROCOMPUTER DRAFTING TABLE* onto the simulated disk.

Stopping The Program

There are three different ways to cleanly exit the program. Each method cleanly returns you to the 80-column text mode of the BASIC editor.

First Method. At any time and in any routine during the program you can press F2 to exit the program. F2 is a hot key which is managed by BASIC itself.

Second Method. When you are located anywhere on the main menu bar, you can press Alt-Q to exit the program. Alt-Q is a hot key which is managed by the program. (Hold down the Alt key and press Q.)

Third Method. Use the arrow keys to select the Quit pull-down menu. Select the Quit function from the menu to exit the program. This method is managed by the menu system of the program.

HOW TO USE THE PROGRAM

The keyboard controls for *YOUR MICROCOMPUTER DRAFTING TABLE* are annotated in Fig. 22-1. The Enter key is used to implement a function or command. The arrow keys are using to navigate through the menu system. The ESC key is used to discard the current menu and return to the previous level in the menu system.

Using the Menu System

When you are on the main menu bar, use the left-arrow and right-arrow keys to move the panning cursor to the desired selection. Then press Enter to invoke the pull-down menu. Use the down-arrow key to move the scrolling cursor through the selections on the pull-

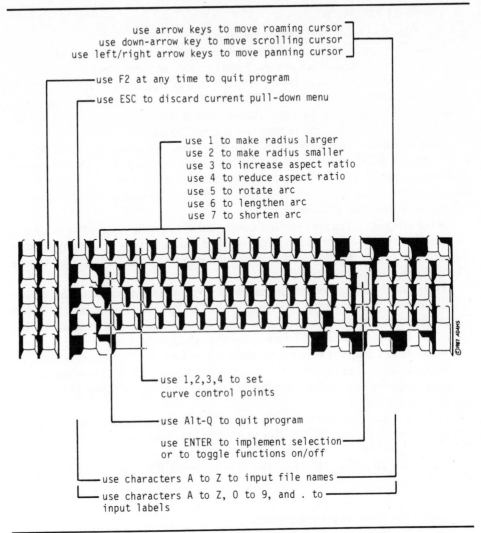

use arrow keys to move roaming cursor
use down-arrow key to move scrolling cursor
use left/right arrow keys to move panning cursor

use F2 at any time to quit program

use ESC to discard current pull-down menu

use 1 to make radius larger
use 2 to make radius smaller
use 3 to increase aspect ratio
use 4 to reduce aspect ratio
use 5 to rotate arc
use 6 to lengthen arc
use 7 to shorten arc

use 1,2,3,4 to set
curve control points

use Alt-Q to quit program

use ENTER to implement selection
or to toggle functions on/off

use characters A to Z to input file names

use characters A to Z, 0 to 9, and . to
input labels

Fig. 22-1. The keystroke controls used by the interactive drafting program listing in Chapter 21.

down menu. The cursor will wrap back around to the top selection after passing the bottom selection. Use the Enter key to implement your selection. Select Cancel or use the Esc key to discard the pull-down menu and to return to the main menu bar. The on-screen Draw icons work in the same manner.

To move from one pull-down menu to another, you must first return to the main menu bar and then use the panning cursor to select another pull-down menu. You cannot jump immediately from one pull-down menu to another.

To begin drawing, choose Draw from the main menu bar. Next, use the scrolling icon cursor to select the drawing function desired. Pressing <Enter> places you in the active drawing area, where you can use the arrow keys to control the roaming crosshair cursor. To return to the Draw icons, simply press Esc.

Using the File Menu

The File menu contains the following functions:

Name Function. The Name function in the File menu allows you to create your own file names for image files. When you use Enter to select the Name function, a dialog box is displayed, containing the current file name. You may type in any eight-character file name, using uppercase letters from A to Z. When you type the eighth character, the file name in the file name bar at the top of the screen is changed. During the input process, you may press Esc at any time to keep the original file name.

Save Function. The Save function in the File menu will save your current drawing on disk as a binary image file. Five full-screen images can be saved on a 5.25-inch diskette. More images can be saved on a hard disk. The Save function expects to use drive B. You must alter lines 1340, 1350, 1360, and 1370 in the program source code if you wish to use another drive. (See Chapter 21.)

When using Save, you must exercise caution not to overwrite any existing image files on your disk. The Save function is not error-trapped. A disk I/O error caused by an empty disk drive will crash the program and your current drawing will be lost. (See Chapter 23 for making source code revisions.)

Load Function. The Load function in the File menu will download a previously-saved image file from disk and display it on the screen. The Load function expects to find the image file in drive B. If you wish to use another drive, you must alter lines 1450, 1460, 1470, and 1480 in the program source code. (See Chapter 21.)

When using Load, you must ensure that a disk containing the desired image file is present in the drive. The Load function is not error-trapped. A disk I/O error caused by an empty disk drive or a missing file will crash the program. (See Chapter 23 for making source code revisions.)

Quit Function. The Quit function terminates the program. Your current drawing is not saved prior to the exit. If you wish to edit your drawing later, you should use the Save function before you invoke the Quit function.

Menu Bar Function. The Menu Bar function in the File menu returns you to the main menu bar.

Using the Draw On-Screen Menu

The functions of the Draw on-screen menu are accessed by using the down-arrow key to move the scrolling cursor to the desired icon. Press Enter places you in the active drawing area. The roaming crosshair cursor is controlled by the arrow keys. The drawing functions are described as they appear in the Draw icon menu, from top to bottom. You can use the Home, PgDn, PgUp, and End keys to snap the crosshair cursor to the corresponding corner of the drawing area when using the following functions: Set Point, Polyline, Rectangle, Parallelogram, Curve, Fillet, Eraser, and Area fill.

Set Point Function. Use the arrow keys to move the crosshair cursor to the desired location. Press Enter to set a single point on the active drawing area (and then automatically return you to the Draw menu). Press Esc at any time to return to the Draw menu.

Polyline Function. Use the arrow keys to move the crosshair cursor. Press Enter to establish the starting point for the polyline. Press Enter again to cause a line to be constructed from the last-referenced point to the current crosshair cursor location (and then automatically return you to the Draw menu). Press Esc at any time to return to the Draw menu.

Rectangle Function. Press Enter to set the starting corner for the rectangle. Use the arrow keys to set the diagonal corner and thereby establish the size of the rectangle. Press Enter to draw the rectangle (and then automatically returns you to the Draw menu). Press Esc at any time to return to the Draw icon menu.

Parallelogram Function. Press Enter to set the starting corner for the parallelogram. Move the crosshair cursor and press Enter to set the first side of the parallelogram. Then relocate the crosshair cursor and press Enter to set the second side of the parallelogram. The program immediately draws the complete parallelogram and then automatically returns you to the Draw menu. Strike Esc at any time to return to the Draw menu.

Circle Function. A phantom circle is displayed on the screen as you use the arrow keys to move the crosshair cursor about the active drawing area. Use the Enter key to draw the circle. Press <2> to reduce the radius of the circle. Press <1> to enlarge the radius of the circle. Press <8> to restore the default parameters. Use Esc at any time to return to the Draw icon menu.

Ellipse Function. As you use the arrow keys to move the crosshair cursor, a phantom ellipse is displayed, showing the current parameters. Press Enter to draw the ellipse. Use <2> to reduce the radius of the ellipse. Use <1> to enlarge the radius of the ellipse. Press <3> to make the ellipse taller. Press <4> to make the ellipse wider. Press <8> to restore the default parameters. Press Esc at any time to return to the Draw icon menu.

Arc Function. A phantom arc is displayed as you use the arrow keys to relocate the center of the circle upon whose circumference the arc is based. Press Enter to draw the arc. Use <1> and <2> to reduce and to enlarge the radius of the arc's circle. Press <5> to rotate the arc segment counterclockwise around the circumference of the imaginary circle. Press <6> to lengthen the arc. Press <7> to shorten the arc. Your computer will beep when the minimum and maximum allowable arc lengths have been reached. Press <8> to restore the default parameters. Use Esc at any time to return to the Draw icon menu.

Curve Function. Use the arrow keys to move the crosshair cursor about the active drawing area. Press <1> to set the starting point for the curve. Press <2> to set the first magnetic point. Press <3> to set the second magnetic point. Press <4> to set the ending point for the curve. Use Enter to construct the curve. The parametric formulas will create a curve which is attracted to the magnetic points and which touches the starting and ending points.

Because the creation of freeform curves is often an experimental process, you should be prepared to use the Undo function to erase any curve which is not satisfactory. Use Undo before attempting any further drawing functions.

Fillet Function. Use the Fillet function to create a smooth curve which connects the ends of two existing lines. Use the arrow keys to move the crosshair cursor. Press Enter at the endpoint of one of the existing lines. Press Enter a second time at the imaginary intersection of the two existing lines. Press Enter a third time at the endpoint of the other existing line. After the third Enter, a smooth fillet will be created. You can alter the curve of the fillet by experimenting with the location of the magnetic control point, which is established by the second Enter.

Eraser Function. Use the arrow keys to move the crosshair cursor. Use the Enter key to toggle the eraser on; continue using the arrow keys to move the eraser. Press Enter again or press Esc to return to the Draw icon menu.

Hatch Function. Use the arrow keys to position the crosshair cursor at the starting point for the fill. Press Enter to begin the fill. Use Esc to return to the Draw icon menu.

You can set the hatch pattern by using the Options menu. If you attempt to fill an unclosed polygon, other portions of the screen may be inadvertently filled. Use Undo to restore your drawing. Correct the polygon before attempting the hatch fill again.

Regen Function. Selecting the Regen function from the Draw menu causes the active drawing area to be cleared to black. The program then retrieves the graphics primitives created by your previous keystrokes from the .CDF data files and uses those primitives to redraw your drafting image. (NOTE: the labelling functions are not regenerated in this version of *YOUR MICROCOMPUTER DRAFTING TABLE.*)

Undo Function. Select the Undo function to erase the graphics which you created during your last foray on the active drawing area. On each occasion when you enter the active drawing area, the existing graphics are saved on a hidden graphics page. The most recent hidden graphics page is copied to the screen buffer when you select Undo from the Draw icon menu.

Return To Menu Bar Function. Select the Return function from the Draw icon menu to return to the main menu bar.

Using the Edit Menu

Use the down-arrow key to move the scrolling cursor through the selections on the Edit menu. Press Enter to implement the desired selection.

Define Entity Function. This function is inactive in this version of the program. You can readily add your own code to handle all the entity functions in this menu by referring to the algorithm provided in Chapter 16.

Move Entity Function. This function is inactive in this version of the program.

Copy Entity Function. This function is inactive in this version of the program.

Erase Entity Function. This function is inactive in this version of the program.

Undo Function. This function is not implemented in this pull-down menu, because the entity functions are inactive.

Menu Bar Function. The Menu Bar function is used to discard the Edit menu and to return to the main menu bar.

Using the Label Menu

Use the down-arrow key to move the scrolling cursor through the selection on the Label menu. Press Enter to implement the desired selection. You can use the Home, PgDn, PgUp, and End keys to snap the crosshair cursor to the corresponding corner of the drawing area when using the following functions: Set Text, H-Dimension, V-Dimension, and Leaderline.

Set Text Function. Use the arrow keys to move the crosshair cursor to the location where you wish the alphanumeric label to begin. Press Enter to enable keyboard input. Use uppercase characters A to Z, numerals 0 to 9, and the decimal point to create a label up to five characters in length. (To create longer labels, re-select the Set Text function and add the remainder of the label.) You are automatically returned to the Label menu after the fifth character is entered.

H-Dimension Function. Use the arrow keys to move the crosshair cursor about the active drawing area. Press Enter to first set the left-most dimension of the entity. Press Enter a second time to set the right-most dimension of the entity. The program will automatically generate a set of witness lines with a dimension arrow in a horizontal format. Press Esc at any time to return to the Label menu.

V-Dimension Function. Use the arrow keys to move the crosshair cursor about the active drawing area. Press Enter to first set the top-most dimension of the entity. Press Enter a second time to set the lowest dimension of the entity. The program will automatically generate a set of witness lines with a dimension arrow in a vertical format. Press Esc at any time to return to the Label menu.

Leaderline Function. Use the arrow keys to move the crosshair cursor. Press Enter to establish the tip of the arrow. Press Enter a second time to establish the labelling end of the leaderline. The program will automatically construct an arrow and leaderline. The labelling end of the leaderline does not have to be level with the arrow, because the Leaderline function will automatically insert an elbow at an appropriate location. Press Esc at any time to return to the Label menu.

Undo Function. The Undo function is used to restore the graphics which existed prior to a Label function. Once you leave the Label menu, your most recent Label function becomes permanent.

Menu Bar Function. Use the Menu Bar function to discard the Label menu and to return to the main menu bar at the top of the screen.

Using the Options Menu

Use the down-arrow key to move the scrolling cursor through the selections in the Options menu. Press Enter to implement the desired selection.

Set Snap Function. Use the plus and minus keys to increase or decrease the amount of movement that each press of an arrow key produces on the crosshair cursor. A help screen is displayed while you are using this function. Press Enter to adopt the currently displayed value and to return to the Options menu.

Set Grid Function. Use the plus and minus keys to set the spacing between the horizontal lines and the vertical lines which make up a grid. A separate help screen pops up during this function, showing you the grid which will be generated by your selection. Your computer beeps if you attempt to exceed the minimum or maximum spacing permitted by the program. Press Enter to adopt the currently displayed grid and to return to the Options menu.

Set Line Style Function. This function is inactive in this version of *YOUR MICROCOMPUTER DRAFTING TABLE.*

Set Hatch Function. Use the down-arrow key to display a series of hatch patterns in the hatch icon position of the Draw menu. Press Enter to make your selection, which will now be displayed as an icon in the Draw menu. Continue to press Enter until the desired pattern is obtained. Use Esc to return to the main menu bar.

Zoom Image Function. This function is inactive in this version of the program.

Grid On/Off Function. Selecting this function will toggle the grid on if it is off, and off if it is on. The Regen function will create a grid if this function is toggled on, otherwise no grid will be drawn during a regeneration of your drawing.

Label On/Off Function. This function is inactive in this version of the program.

Key Layer +/− Function. Selecting this function will toggle the primary drawing level. If toggled on, the graphics of the primary drawing level will be recreated during a Regen function. Otherwise, those graphics will not be displayed by a Regen procedure. All drawing functions will occur in the key layer when this function is toggled on.

Overlay 1 +/− Function. Selecting this function will toggle the first overlay drawing level. If toggled on, the graphics on the first overlay will be redrawn during a Regen function. Otherwise, those graphics will not be displayed during Regen. All drawing functions will occur in the overlay 1 drawing color while this function is toggled on.

Overlay 2 +/− Function. Selecting this function will toggle the second overlay drawing level. If toggled on, the graphics on the second overlay will be recreated during a Regen function. Otherwise, those graphics will not be drawn during Regen. All drawing functions will occur in the overlay 2 drawing color while this function is toggled on.

Menu Bar Function. You can use this selection to discard the Options menu and return to the main menu bar.

SAMPLE SESSIONS

YOUR MICROCOMPUTER DRAFTING TABLE is capable of creating highly sophisticated images, using only your keyboard for input. The drawings may be stored on disk using the program, or you can use a third-party graphics printing utility (such as Pizazz; see Appendix F) to print your drawings on a dot-matrix printer or ink-jet printer.

Available Tools: Primitives

The image shown in Fig. 22-2 illustrates the range of graphics functions available in this version of the program. The Fillet function was used to create the round cornered

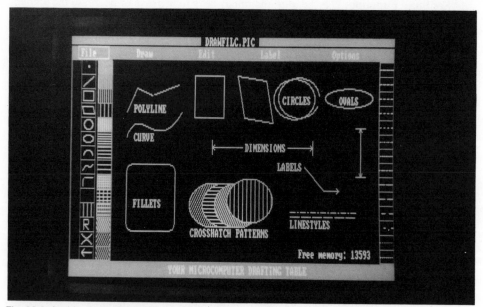

Fig. 22-2. A wide range of graphics primitives can be produced by the interactive drafting program listing in Chapter 21.

rectangle at lower left. The dotted and dashed lines were created by using the Eraser function to edit solid lines.

Multiple Elevations: Widget

The elevation views shown in Fig. 22-3 were created in about 40 minutes using *YOUR MICROCOMPUTER DRAFTING TABLE*. The side, front, and top elevation views were created with the Polyline function. The Hatch function was used to fill selected portions of the elevation views. The Set Text function was used to label the drawing.

The perspective view is a free-hand sketch. It is not real 3D. (Interactive graphics programs which create authentic 3D models are presented in Chapters 24 through 31.) During the drawing process for the perspective view, the Eraser function was occasionally used to correct mistakes.

Schematic: Diskette Design

The labelled diskette illustration shown in Fig. 22-4 was created in about 25 minutes. The Polyline function was used to create the diskette jacket. The Circle function was used to create the index window and disk hub. The Set Text function was employed to install the text labels, and the Leaderline function was used to create the arrow pointers.

During preparation of the labels, two or three passes through the Set Text function were used to achieve the desired results. The Eraser function from the Draw menu was used from time to time to delete unwanted characters and labels.

The layer functions from the Options menu were used in order to draw different parts of the illustration in different colors. The diskette schematic was created first. Then, the various labels and titles were added. Finally, the leaderlines were added.

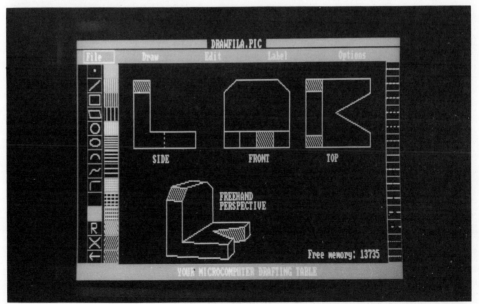

Fig. 22-3. Multiple elevation views can be easily outlined and hatched with the interactive drafting program listing in Chapter 21.

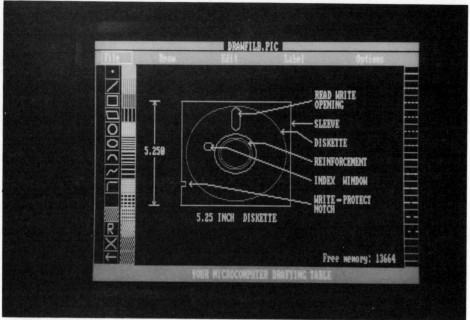

Fig. 22-4. Drawings can be enhanced with dimensioning lines, leader lines, and labels using the features of the interactive drafting program listing in Chapter 21.

WORKING WITH THE PROGRAM

As you create drawings with *YOUR MICROCOMPUTER DRAFTING TABLE,* a special subroutine keeps track of available BASIC workspace and displays the number of free bytes on the screen. If available memory falls below 1024 bytes, a caution message is displayed, urging you to save your drawing on disk. After doing so, you can then return to BASIC and restart the program with a fresh supply of memory in the BASIC workspace.

Unfortunately, BASIC interpreters insist on using a few bytes of memory each and every time a key is pressed. BASIC compilers such as QuickBASIC and Turbo BASIC do not exhibit this unfortunate idiosyncracy.

It is wise to regularly save your drawing on disk while you are working.

On many occasions, you might find it useful to toggle the grid and display it by using the Regen function before you begin your drawing. If your drawing becomes cluttered, you can eliminate the grid by going to the Options menu, toggling the grid off, and returning to the Draw menu and selecting Regen to redraw your drawing without the grid overlay.

I recommend that you add labels and dimension lines last, because these functions are not recreated during a regen procedure.

SUMMARY

This chapter provided you with a concise User's Guide for the multifunction CADD drafting program, *YOUR MICROCOMPUTER DRAFTING TABLE.* The complete source code for this program appears in Chapter 21.

The next chapter provides an analysis of how the program works.

23

Drafting
Program Analysis—
How the Program Works

*Y*OUR MICROCOMPUTER DRAFTING TABLE is a multifunction CADD drafting and drawing program. Because the program has been written in a modular format, you can easily improve the program by adding your own modules after you have learned how the original source code works. Refer to the program listing in Chapter 21 while you read this chapter.

LOGIC FLOW

YOUR MICROCOMPUTER DRAFTING TABLE is composed of two separate programs: a start-up module which initializes the system, and a runtime module. The logic flowchart for the start-up module, CADD-1.BAS, is shown in Fig. 23-1.

THE START-UP MODULE: CADD-1.BAS

The first task the start-up module performs is line 180, where the system is initialized to the 80-column text mode.

Data Assignments

Next, the DIM instruction is used to set aside memory for the graphic arrays which are used to store the interface labels and the pull-down menus. This occurs in lines 240 through 320.

Lines 330 through 710 assign values to assorted variables, runtime flags, and color codes used by the runtime module. Note line 680, which defines the default file name.

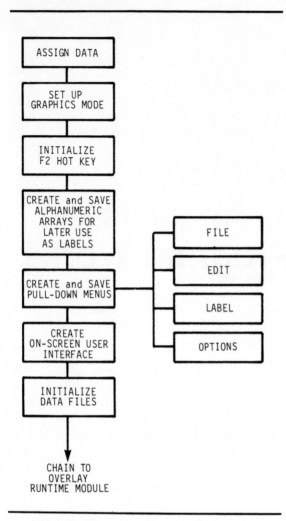

Fig. 23-1. Logic flowchart for the start-up module of the interactive drafting program listing in Chapter 21.

You can change F$ and F2$, if you wish to use another file name at program start-up. You can always use the File menu at runtime to change the image file names, as well.

Lines 720 through 860 define the pixel patterns for the hatch area fill. This function is based upon BASIC's bit tiling function. (Refer back to Chapter 6 for further discussion of this function.) By comparing the formulas in lines 720 through 860 with the results generated on the display screen, you can see how these bit patterns work during runtime.

Note line 880, which sets up a set of dummy values to be saved as the first entry in the data files.

Setting Up The Graphics Mode

The module at line 920 sets up the 640×200 16-color graphics mode. Line 950 installs the F2 hot key. You can strike this key at any time during program execution if you wish to halt the program and return cleanly to the BASIC editor.

Setting Up The User Interface

The module which runs from line 1000 to line 1230 sets up the graphical user interface. Line 1010 sends the program branching to a subroutine which creates and saves the text labels used on the user interface. The code is at lines 1280 through 1410. These labels are saved in graphic arrays in order that they can later be cleanly superimposed over the main menu bar and program name bar. If the text were simply PRINTed over the graphics, the block background for each character would obliterate the background graphics. Superimposition yields a more professional image. In addition, the XOR, OR, AND logical operators can be swapped during the PUT instruction to yield different colors during superimposition.

Line 1020 sends the program branching to a subroutine which creates and saves the pull-down menus in graphic arrays. The code in lines 1450 through 1780 performs this task. Note line 1770, for example, which saves the Label menu in a graphic array named A14, and then uses BASIC's BF parameter to the LINE instruction to quickly erase the menu graphics from the screen.

The code in lines 1450 through 1780 is dependent upon the DIM definitions in lines 250 through 320. Try reducing the value for DIM A14 in lines 320 to see how it affects program performance.

Returning to the main routine, lines 1030 through 1070 create the generic user interface. Note how line 1070 uses the previously saved graphic arrays to place the labels on the main menu bar. Line 1080 discards the memory which was set aside for these arrays. It is not required again during runtime.

Line 1100 sends the program to a subroutine at lines 1820 through 1990, which creates the various icons for the on-screen Draw menu. These lines have been liberally peppered with comments to aid your understanding of the code.

Next, line 1110 causes program execution to transfer to a subroutine at line 2090, which uses the previously defined bit tiling codes to draw the swatches for the hatch area fill function. Note line 2110, for example, where color C13 is used to paint the swatch magenta before the hatch fill is used. This preparatory PAINTing is required to avoid a failure of the area fill function where a pattern with large black areas is painted over a black area. Setting the polygon interior to magenta means that any black and white bit pattern can be PAINTed without error. Note also how the various string values (previously defined in lines 720 through 850) are used to select the hatch patterns for the swatches.

Session Selections

The code at lines 1150 through 1230 presents the user with the program's copyright notice and a display of options. You must press either <1>, <2>, or <3> to choose the program's course of action. Pressing key <1> sends the program branching to a subroutine which sets up the data files which the runtime module will use for the Regen function. Any files created by previous sessions will be overwritten. Pressing key <2> will not create any new files. This means you can use Regen to recreate a drawing which you built during a previous session with *YOUR MICROCOMPUTER DRAFTING TABLE.* Pressing key <3> exits the program.

This selection procedure means that you have two separate and distinct methods for saving your drawings. First, you can use the menu system to save your drawings as binary image files on disk. Second, you can use the data files automatically created during runtime to use Regen to recreate your drawing during a later session with the program.

Because this program uses four separate data files, you must load BASIC in a special way in order to avoid a program crash. BASIC, by default, provides support for only three data files during runtime. If you load and run the program without adjusting BASIC, it will halt and an error message will be displayed when BASIC attempts to open the fourth data file (in line 2460).

At the DOS prompt, you should load BASICA with the following command line: **BASICA/F:4.** This creates the potential to use up to four files for reading and writing sequential data during runtime. (Refer to Chapter 14 for further discussion about using sequential data files.)

The Code Overlay

Line 1230 merges the runtime module into memory and begins execution of the new code at line 160. If you have installed the two modules for *YOUR MICROCOMPUTER DRAFTING TABLE* on your hard disk, you must change the drive identifier in this line to C. Remember, the runtime module (CADD-2.BAS) must be saved on disk as an ASCII file using the A parameter with BASIC's SAVE instruction.

THE RUNTIME MODULE: CADD-2.BAS

CADD-2.BAS is the runtime module for the program. It will not run properly unless it has been loaded by the start-up module, CADD-1.BAS, because the assorted graphic arrays and variables must be pre-initialized by the start-up module.

Note how line 170 is needed to redefine the integer variables when a BASIC interpreter is used. In addition, the F2 hot key must be re-installed (see line 180).

The logic flowchart for the runtime module is shown in Fig. 23-2. The functioning of the on-screen Draw menu is shown separately in Fig. 23-3, because of the complicated flow of logic caused by the necessity to save and retrieve primitives to data files in order to support the Regen function.

Main Menu Bar

The module at line 280 controls the main menu bar, according to the programming principles introduced in Chapter 10. The subroutine at line 400 moves the panning cursor to the right on the menu bar. The subroutine at line 500 moves the cursor to the left.

The switcher for the main menu bar is located at lines 720 through 780. By tracing through the line numbers used in this routine, you can follow the program flow as a particular pull-down menu is invoked.

Memory Check

Line 290 in the main menu bar loop calls a subroutine which checks the amount of free memory available in the BASIC workspace. This routine is required because BASIC interpreters have the unpleasant habit of using up a few bytes of memory whenever a key is pressed.

When available memory drops below 1024 bytes, a warning message is displayed during runtime, encouraging you to save your drawing on disk. You can then return to

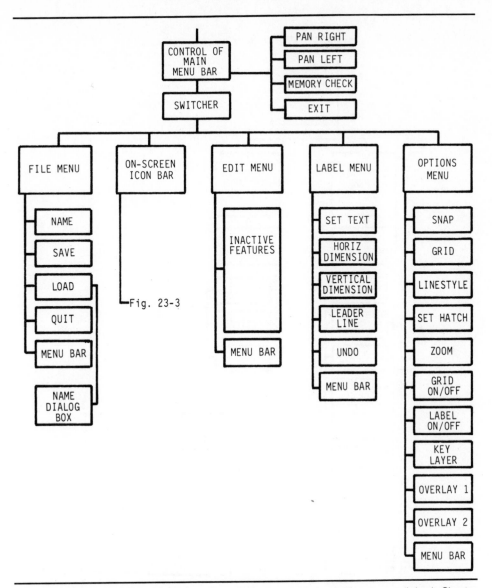

Fig. 23-2. Logic flowchart for the overlay runtime module of the interactive drafting program listing in Chapter 21.

BASIC and restart the program with a fresh supply of memory to work with. While you are using *YOUR MICROCOMPUTER DRAFTING TABLE,* a readout in the lower right corner of the screen keeps you advised on current memory available. The PRINT V instruction in line 290 creates the readout.

Draw Functions

A single subroutine controls movement of the crosshair cursor for most of the functions provided by the Draw menu. This is in contrast to the method used in *YOUR*

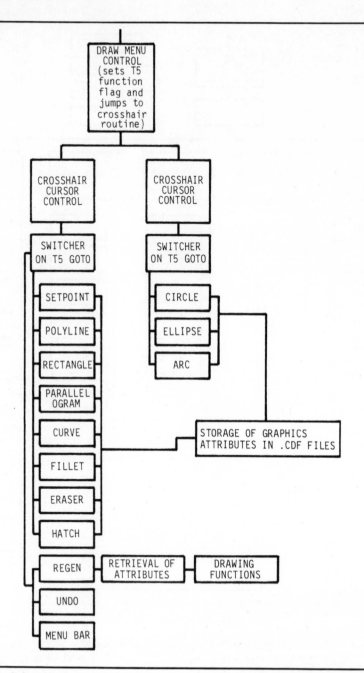

Fig. 23-3. Logic flowchart for the drawing routines in the interactive drafting program listing in Chapter 21.

MICROCOMPUTER SKETCH PAD, in which each Draw function contained its own crosshair cursor control routine.

The single controller means a considerable saving in code length and in the amount of memory required to hold the code in RAM during runtime.

The controller, located at lines 2900 through 3170, uses a runtime flag called T5 to keep track of which graphics function is being modeled. T5 is defined when the Draw function is selected by the user in lines 1720 through 1820. The runtime flag concept keeps this program running correctly.

The switcher for the crosshair cursor controller is located at lines 3210 through 3340. Using **ON T5 GOTO,** program flow branches to the desired graphics function.

By referring to Fig. 23-3, you can see that the previous explanation was a simplification. In actuality, two crosshair cursor control routines are used to support the functions provided by the Draw menu. This is because rubber functions use a different algorithm than do standard functions. The secondary cursor controller is located at lines 3840 through 4250.

Data Files

The module at lines 4380 through 4440 is responsible for storing graphics primitives in data files while you are creating your drawing. When you create a line on the screen, for example, the endpoints and color of the line are saved in the appropriate data file (depending upon which drawing layer you have selected from the Options menu).

Line 4390 jumps to the appropriate file-writing routine, based upon the value of T12. T12 is set when you select a drawing layer from the Options menu.

The module at lines 4530 through 4740 retrieves the data from the data files. This module calls the Regen routine at lines 4770 through 4900. The Regen routine contains code to draw every graphics function available in the Draw menu. Because the runtime flag T11, saved in the data file, contains the graphics function number, line 4780 can call the appropriate line to recreate the graphic on the screen. Check back to the module at lines 4380 through 4440 to review how the various attributes are saved.

Refer to Chapter 14 for a more detailed discussion of the syntax used when reading and writing fields to .CDF data files. You can easily add more drawing layers to this program if you want to use it to create drawings with multiple overlays (such as wiring schematics and so on).

Changing The Hatch Pattern

Note the module at lines 4930 through 5080. This routine uses runtime flag T19 to change the active hatch pattern for the area fill function. After calling this module, the module at lines 5120 through 5140 changes the appropriate icon in the Draw menu. You can use similar subroutines if you decide to add a linestyling capability to the program. The swatches for different line styles are already in place at the right side of the display screen. It has been left as an exercise for you to make this function active in any Draw functions which use BASIC's LINE instruction.

Choosing The Drawing Layers

The module at lines 5340 through 5370 determines the current active drawing layer (three are available; only one is active for drawing at any one time). The module also sets runtime flag T12, which is used by the Regen to determine which drawing layers are to be recreated during a regeneration. Any number (including nil) of the layers can be redrawn during regen.

Label Functions

The controller for the crosshair cursor for label functions is located at lines 5620 through 5870. The switcher, located at lines 5910 through 5970, uses runtime flag T8 to branch to the appropriate subroutine.

By changing lines 6080, 6090, and 6100, you can add lowercase characters to the range of legal letters for labelling. Note line 6010, where the statement JC=SXC*.125 is used to translate the x-coordinate of the crosshair cursor to the appropriate row number for 80×25 alphanumerics. (25 rows divided by 200 raster lines equals 0.125.) This translation does not always yield accurate results, so you may wish to fine-tune the formula.

The two modules at line 6160 and line 6260 are very similar. The first module generates a set of horizontal dimension lines. The second module generates a dimensioning construct for vertical measurements. Note how the witness lines and dimension lines are drawn by using offsets from the locations defined by the user.

PROGRAM TIPS AND TRICKS

Use the program flowcharts in Fig. 23-2 and Fig. 23-3 to assist your understanding of the program as you review the source code in Chapter 21. Flowcharts are just as helpful for learning what makes a program tick as they are during the original code-writing process.

At various points during runtime, the VIEW SCREEN instruction is used to ensure that graphics are clipped to fit the active drawing area. Then, when the graphic has been created, the VIEW instruction is used to return to full-screen clipping when program control returns to the Draw menu. Keep this clipping flipflop in mind if you intend to add your own drawing routines to the program.

With a bit of careful planning, and with a little work, you can add the full range of copy entity functions to the Edit menu. The algorithm that you need is discussed in Chapter 18. Be sure you set up a generic graphic array during the start-up module to hold the various images created during a move entity or copy entity process.

KNOWN BUGS

Disk input and output errors are not trapped by *YOUR MICROCOMPUTER DRAFT-ING TABLE*. You can use an ON ERROR GOTO instruction to gracefully handle situations where the user has neglected to insert a diskette into the drive or where the wrong disk is in place. Otherwise, in its current version, the program crashes during a disk error. (For numerous examples of advanced ON ERROR algorithms, see *High-Performance Interactive Graphics: Modeling, Rendering & Animating for IBM PCs and Compatibles*, TAB book 2879.

SUMMARY

In this chapter you learned some of the specific ways in which *YOUR MICROCOMPUTER DRAFTING TABLE* works. You read about suggested improvements to the program.

The next chapter discusses algorithms for 3D graphics on personal computers, which are useful for creating interactive 3D CAD programs.

24

Algorithms for 3D Graphics

Interactive graphics programs which can generate 3D models—whether as wire-frame models or as fully-shaded models—are well within your reach as a graphics programmer. The 3D perspective formulas and halftone shading algorithms which look so spectacular on graphics workstations are easily adapted to work on your personal computer. All that is required is an understanding of the programming concepts involved in 3D graphics.

This chapter presents an overview of important 3D concepts, algorithms, and formulas used in the two major demonstration 3D CAD programs presented later in the book.

Real objects possess the three dimensions of height, width, and depth. An image displayed on a microcomputer screen which simulates the height, width, and depth of the object is said to be three-dimensional, or 3D. In computer graphics, a 3D image is often called a 3D model. The generation of a 3D model is called *modeling*. The application of shading, highlights, textures, and shadows is called *rendering*.

WORLD COORDINATES

The fundamental shape of the model which you wish to display is expressed as xyz coordinates. Refer to Fig. 24-1. The three dimensions of height, width, and depth can be defined by using a coordinate axis system. The x-axis is often used to represent the left-right dimensions; the y-axis is used to represent the up-down dimensions; the z-axis is used to represent near-far dimensions. The viewpoint of you, the viewer, is located at position 0,0,0, as illustrated in Fig. 24-1.

Three sets of coordinates are used during the 3D modeling process. Refer to Fig. 24-2. The world coordinates are the true shape of the model in the 3D axis system. The

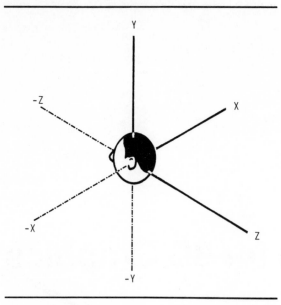

Fig. 24-1. The xyz axes used to plot 3D device-independent world coordinates.

view coordinates describe the position of the model after it has been rotated and moved to an appropriate location for viewing. The display coordinates are the xy coordinates used to draw the model on the microcomputer's 2D display screen.

CREATING A 3D MODEL

The first step in modeling an object is to define the *world coordinates* of the object. Refer to Fig. 24-3. These world coordinates are the fundamental shape or design of the model. World coordinates are also called *absolute coordinates, cartesian coordinates,* and *model space coordinates.* The xyz axis represents the real world, independent of your program and independent of your microcomputer. The xyz coordinates of the model are often termed *device-independent coordinates.*

The second step in modeling an object is to spin the object and move it to an appropriate viewing position. Spinning the object is called *rotation.* Moving the object is called *translation.* Refer to Fig. 24-3.

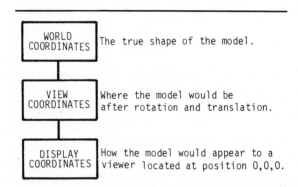

Fig. 24-2. Essential steps of 3D graphics for microcomputers.

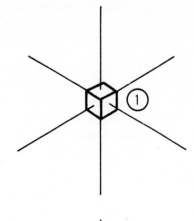

Fig. 24-3. The three steps of 3D modeling include (1) world coordinates, (2) view coordinates, and (3) display coordinates.

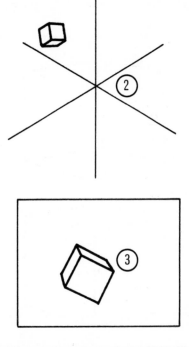

The rotation formulas are based upon matrix mathematics, which is expressed algebraically as sine and cosine in the formulas used with your personal computer. The translation formulas are based upon simple addition and subtraction. The xyz coordinates for various points which describe the model after rotation and translation are called view coordinates, because this is how the model will be viewed by an imaginary viewer in the 3D axis system.

The third step in modeling an object is to display it on the screen. The formulas which convert the xyz coordinates to xy display coordinates are called projection formulas.

DISPLAY OPTIONS

A number of different 3D displays can be created from the world coordinates of an object. Refer to Fig. 24-4. The simplest image is the transparent wire-frame model. This is the type of model generated by the program listing for *YOUR MICROCOMPUTER 3D CAD DESIGNER* in Chapter 26. The shape of the model is accurate, but no subroutines are provided to remove surfaces which should be hidden from view. (The CGA version of this program appears in Appendix G. The PCjr version appears in Appendix H. The Turbo BASIC version appears in Appendix E.)

Solid models are 3D images which have been subject to hidden-surface removal. The formulas which calculate whether a particular surface is hidden from view or not are usually based upon plane equation formulas. *Fully shaded models* are solid models which have been shaded using bit tiling area-fill patterns to represent different levels of brightness on the surface of the model. The formulas to calculate levels of illumination are usually based upon surface normals. Both solid models and fully shaded models are generated by the program listing for *YOUR MICROCOMPUTER 3D CAD MODELER* in Chapter 29. (A QuickBASIC version of this program appears in Appendix E.)

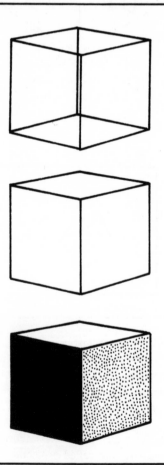

Fig. 24-4. Display options for 3D graphics on personal computers. Top: wire-frame. Center: solid model. Bottom: fully-shaded.

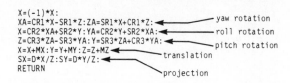

Fig. 24-5. Generic 3D formulas in BASIC for personal computers.

3D FORMULAS FOR PERSONAL COMPUTERS

The code fragment in Fig. 24-5 gives you complete control over the creation, rotation, translation, and display of a 3D model on your personal computer.

The formulas first perform the yaw, roll, and pitch rotations to the xyz world coordinates you have defined for the model. The SR and CR variables in the formulas are sine and cosine values of the appropriate angles, expressed as radians (6.28319 radians equals 360 degrees).

The formulas then perform the translation adjustments. During this process, the rotated model is moved left or right, up or down, or nearer or farther relative to the viewing position (at 0,0,0). To change the position of a model, it is the model itself that is always moved; the viewpoint remains constant.

Figure 24-6 shows how the three concepts of *yaw, roll,* and *pitch* fit into the 3D axis system. Yaw changes the compass heading of the model. Roll tilts the model clockwise or counterclockwise. Pitch tilts the model towards you or away from you.

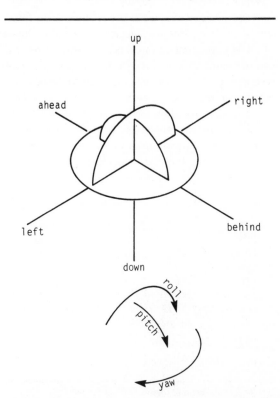

Fig. 24-6. The cartesian coordinate system used for 3D graphics on personal computers.

```
100 'Code fragment A-08.BAS   3D perspective formulas.
110 'Copyright (c) 1988 by Lee Adams and TAB Books Inc.
120 'All rights reserved.
130 '_____
140 '
150 'module:  perspective formulas
160  X=(-1)*X:XA=CR1*X-SR1*Z:ZA=SR1*X+CR1*Z:X=CR2*XA+SR2*Y:YA=CR2*Y-SR2*XA:Z=CR3
*ZA-SR3*YA:Y=SR3*ZA+CR3*YA:X=X+MX:Y=Y+MY:Z=Z+MZ:SXD=D*X/Z:SYD=D*Y/Z:RETURN
170 '_____
180 '_____
190  END
```

Fig. 24-7. The 3D perspective formulas in a subroutine format.

The last function provided by the 3D formulas is *projection*. Simple geometry is used to translate the 3D xyz view coordinates into 2D xy display coordinates which the microcomputer can plot onto the screen.

The code fragment in Fig. 24-7 shows the rotation, translation, and projection formulas in a subroutine format, ready for inclusion in any BASIC program.

HIDDEN SURFACE REMOVAL

The plane equation method of hidden surface removal uses vector mathematics to determine if a particular surface is visible or hidden from view. Refer to Fig. 24-8.

The plane equation method first determines the orientation of a plane in 3D space, by comparing at least three of its vertices. (A *vertex* is a corner of the plane.) Then, by comparing the orientation of the plane to the position of the viewpoint (at 0,0,0), the plane equation routine can discern if the surface of the plane is visible to the viewer or not.

The plane equation method provides a bullet-proof method for drawing solid models which are convex polygons. For more complex 3D models, where an extension or protrusion may obscure from view another portion of the model, it is important to construct the nearest portion of the model last. This ensures that the nearer parts of the 3D model will correctly hide the more distant parts of the model. (For an in-depth discussion of

```
100 'Code fragment A-09.BAS   Plane equation visibility test.
110 'Copyright (c) 1988 by Lee Adams and TAB Books Inc.
120 'All rights reserved.
130 '_____
140 '
150 'module:  plane equation method of hidden surface removal
160  SP1=X1*(Y2*Z3-Y3*Z2):SP1=(-1)*SP1:SP2=X2*(Y3*Z1-Y1*Z3):SP3=X3*(Y1*Z2-Y2*Z1)
:SP=SP1-SP2-SP3:RETURN
170 '_____
180 '_____
190  END
```

Fig. 24-8. The plane equation formula for removal of hidden surfaces.

this and other methods of hidden surface removal, refer to *High-Performance Interactive Graphics: Modeling, Rendering & Animating for IBM PCs and Compatibles*, TAB book 2879.

SHADING AND ILLUMINATION

Computer images begin to take on a life of their own when rendering techniques are used to add illumination and shading. The shading is applied using halftone shading techniques, based upon the bit tiling capabilities of BASIC introduced in Chapter 6. The algorithm which determines the style of halftone shading to be applied to a particular surface is based upon vector mathematics.

The brightness of a surface is determined by its orientation relative to the light source. Refer to Fig. 24-9. Specifically, the angle between the rays of light and the surface perpendicular will determine how bright the surface will appear to the viewer. This is often referred to as Lambert's Cosine Law, named after a mathematician. The *surface perpendicular* is a line (vector) coming out from the flat surface at a 90 degree angle to the surface. The surface perpendicular is often called a *surface normal*.

Figure 24-10 illustrates a subroutine which calculates the brightness of a particular surface, based upon a comparison between incoming light and the surface normal. The particular subroutine is suitable for the EGA's and VGA's 640×200 16-color mode, although it can be easily modified to work on the CGA's 320×200 four-color mode and the PCjr's 640×200 four-color mode.

The code fragment in Fig. 24-10 does three things. First, it calculates the illumination level of the surface, expressing the brightness as an integer in the range of 1 to 15. Second, it chooses an area fill pattern based on this level of brightness. The A$ strings for the bit tiling pattern have been defined in another part of the program. Third, it assigns

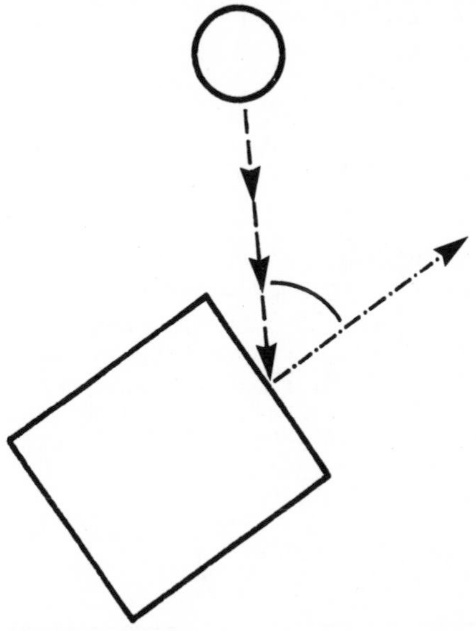

Fig. 24-9. The angle of incidence between the surface perpendicular and incoming rays of light will determine the perceived brightness of the surface.

```
100 'Code fragment A-10.BAS  Computer-controlled shading of 3D solid models.
110 'Copyright (c) 1988 by Lee Adams and TAB Books Inc.
120 'All rights reserved.
130 '_____
140 '
150 'module:  computer-controlled shading routine
160  XU=X2-X1:YU=Y2-Y1:ZU=Z2-Z1  'calculate vector from vertex 1 to vertex 2
170  XV=X3-X1:YV=Y3-Y1:ZV=Z3-Z1  'calculate vector from vertex 1 to vertex 3
180  XN=(YU*ZV)-(ZU*YV):YN=(ZU*XV)-(XU*ZV):ZN=(XU*YV)-(YU*XV)  'calculate surfac
e perpendicular vector
190  YN=YN*(-1):ZN=ZN*(-1)  'convert vector to cartesian system
200 'sub-module:  convert surface perpendicular vector to unit vector
210  V7=(XN*XN)+(YN*YN)+(ZN*ZN):V2=SQR(V7)  'magnitude of surface perpendicular
vector
220  V3=1/V2  'ratio of magnitude to unit vector magnitude
230  XW=V3*XN:YW=V3*YN:ZW=V3*ZN  'XYZ components of surface perpendicular unit v
ector
240  V4=(XW*XI)+(YW*YI)+(ZW*ZI)  'illumination factor 0 to 1
250  V4=V4*V6:V4=CINT(V4)  'set illumination range
260  V5=V4+1  'illumination factor from base 1
270  GOSUB 320
280  RETURN
290 '_____
300 '
310 'shading routine for EGA and VGA 640x200 mode
320  IF V5<1 THEN GOTO 350  'if light source is behind surface
330  ON V5 GOTO 350, 360, 370, 380, 390, 400, 410, 420, 430, 440, 450, 460, 470,
 480, 490
340  A$=CHR$(&HFF)+CHR$(&HO)+CHR$(&HO)+CHR$(&HO):C4=1:C5=1:C6=&HFFFF:RETURN  'so
lid black is unused
350  A$=A1$:CP=1:CC=2:CD=&H808:RETURN
360  A$=A2$:CP=1:CC=2:CD=&H4444:RETURN
370  A$=A3$:CP=1:CC=2:CD=&HAAAA:RETURN
380  A$=A4$:CP=2:CC=1:CD=&H4444:RETURN
390  A$=CHR$(&HO)+CHR$(&HFF)+CHR$(&HO)+CHR$(&HO):CP=2:CC=2:CD=&HFFFF:RETURN
400  A$=A5$:CP=2:CC=3:CD=&H808:RETURN
410  A$=A6$:CP=2:CC=3:CD=&H4444:RETURN
420  A$=A7$:CP=2:CC=3:CD=&HAAAA:RETURN
430  A$=A8$:CP=3:CC=2:CD=&H4444:RETURN
440  A$=CHR$(&HFF)+CHR$(&HFF)+CHR$(&HO)+CHR$(&HO):CP=3:CC=3:CD=&HFFFF:RETURN
450  A$=A9$:CP=3:CC=4:CD=&H8080:RETURN
460  A$=A10$:CP=3:CC=4:CD=&H4444:RETURN
470  A$=A11$:CP=3:CC=4:CD=&HAAAA:RETURN
480  A$=A12$:CP=4:CC=3:CD=&H4444:RETURN
490  A$=CHR$(&HO)+CHR$(&HO)+CHR$(&HFF)+CHR$(&HO):CP=4:CC=4:CD=&HFFFF:RETURN
500 '
510 '_____
520  END
```

Fig. 24-10. An illumination routine for personal computers.

a linestyling pattern which can be used to outline the filled area in a manner which closely matches the area fill halftone pattern. This outlining is called *line dithering*.

The area fill patterns for the EGA and VGA 640×200 16-color mode are given in Fig. 24-11. The patterns for the EGA and VGA 640×350 16-color mode are shown in Fig. 24-12. The halftone patterns for the CGA and PCjr 320×200 four-color mode and 640×200 four-color mode are provided in Fig. 24-13. The palette adjustments necessary to run the EGA and VGA patterns are provided in Fig. 24-14. (For a complete discussion of full shading capabilities for the EGA, CGA, and PCjr, consult *High-Performance Interactive Graphics: Modeling, Rendering & Animating for IBM PCs and Compatibles,* TAB book 2879.

```
100 'Code fragment A-11.BAS   Shading patterns and distribution matrix for EGA a
nd VGA 640x200 16-color mode.
110 'Copyright (c) 1988 by Lee Adams and TAB Books Inc.
120 'All rights reserved.
130 '_____
140 '
150 'module:  shading patterns
160  A1$=CHR$(&HDF)+CHR$(&H20)+CHR$(&HO)+CHR$(&HO)+CHR$(&HFD)+CHR$(&H2)+CHR$(&HO
)+CHR$(&HO)+CHR$(&H7F)+CHR$(&H80)+CHR$(&HO)+CHR$(&HO)+CHR$(&HF7)+CHR$(&H8)+CHR$(
&HO)+CHR$(&HO)
170  A2$=CHR$(&HBB)+CHR$(&H44)+CHR$(&HO)+CHR$(&HO)+CHR$(&HEE)+CHR$(&H11)+CHR$(&H
O)+CHR$(&HO)
180  A3$=CHR$(&HAA)+CHR$(&H55)+CHR$(&HO)+CHR$(&HO)+CHR$(&H55)+CHR$(&HAA)+CHR$(&H
O)+CHR$(&HO)
190  A4$=CHR$(&H44)+CHR$(&HBB)+CHR$(&HO)+CHR$(&HO)+CHR$(&H11)+CHR$(&HEE)+CHR$(&H
O)+CHR$(&HO)
200  A5$=CHR$(&H20)+CHR$(&HFF)+CHR$(&HO)+CHR$(&HO)+CHR$(&H2)+CHR$(&HFF)+CHR$(&HO
)+CHR$(&HO)+CHR$(&H80)+CHR$(&HFF)+CHR$(&HO)+CHR$(&HO)+CHR$(&H8)+CHR$(&HFF)+CHR$(
&HO)+CHR$(&HO)
210  A6$=CHR$(&H44)+CHR$(&HFF)+CHR$(&HO)+CHR$(&HO)+CHR$(&H11)+CHR$(&HFF)+CHR$(&H
O)+CHR$(&HO)
220  A7$=CHR$(&H55)+CHR$(&HFF)+CHR$(&HO)+CHR$(&HO)+CHR$(&HAA)+CHR$(&HFF)+CHR$(&H
O)+CHR$(&HO)
230  A8$=CHR$(&HBB)+CHR$(&HFF)+CHR$(&HO)+CHR$(&HO)+CHR$(&HEE)+CHR$(&HFF)+CHR$(&H
O)+CHR$(&HO)
240  A9$=CHR$(&HDF)+CHR$(&HDF)+CHR$(&H20)+CHR$(&HO)+CHR$(&HFD)+CHR$(&HFD)+CHR$(&
H2)+CHR$(&HO)+CHR$(&H7F)+CHR$(&H7F)+CHR$(&H80)+CHR$(&HO)+CHR$(&HF7)+CHR$(&HF7)+C
HR$(&H8)+CHR$(&HO)
250  A10$=CHR$(&HBB)+CHR$(&HBB)+CHR$(&H44)+CHR$(&HO)+CHR$(&HEE)+CHR$(&HEE)+CHR$(
&H11)+CHR$(&HO)
260  A11$=CHR$(&HAA)+CHR$(&HAA)+CHR$(&H55)+CHR$(&HO)+CHR$(&H55)+CHR$(&H55)+CHR$(
&HAA)+CHR$(&HO)
270  A12$=CHR$(&H44)+CHR$(&H44)+CHR$(&HBB)+CHR$(&HO)+CHR$(&H11)+CHR$(&H11)+CHR$(
&HEE)+CHR$(&HO)
280  A13$=CHR$(&H20)+CHR$(&HO)+CHR$(&HFF)+CHR$(&HO)+CHR$(&H2)+CHR$(&HO)+CHR$(&HF
F)+CHR$(&HO)+CHR$(&H80)+CHR$(&HO)+CHR$(&HFF)+CHR$(&HO)+CHR$(&H8)+CHR$(&HO)+CHR$(
&HFF)+CHR$(&HO)
290  A14$=CHR$(&H44)+CHR$(&HO)+CHR$(&HFF)+CHR$(&HO)+CHR$(&H11)+CHR$(&HO)+CHR$(&H
FF)+CHR$(&HO)
```

Fig. 24-11. An illumination matrix for the 640 × 200 16-color mode of the EGA and VGA.

```
300  A15$=CHR$(&H55)+CHR$(&HO)+CHR$(&HFF)+CHR$(&HO)+CHR$(&HAA)+CHR$(&HO)+CHR$(&H
FF)+CHR$(&HO)
310  A16$=CHR$(&HBB)+CHR$(&HO)+CHR$(&HFF)+CHR$(&HO)+CHR$(&HEE)+CHR$(&HO)+CHR$(&H
FF)+CHR$(&HO)
320  A$=CHR$(&HFF)+CHR$(&HO)+CHR$(&HO)+CHR$(&HO):C4=1:C5=1:C6=&HFFFF:RETURN  'so
lid black is unused
330  '
340  '_____
350  'module:  distribution matrix
360  A$=A1$:CP=1:CC=2:CD=&H808:RETURN
370  A$=A2$:CP=1:CC=2:CD=&H4444:RETURN
380  A$=A3$:CP=1:CC=2:CD=&HAAAA:RETURN
390  A$=A4$:CP=2:CC=1:CD=&H4444:RETURN
400  A$=CHR$(&HO)+CHR$(&HFF)+CHR$(&HO)+CHR$(&HO):CP=2:CC=2:CD=&HFFFF:RETURN
410  A$=A5$:CP=2:CC=3:CD=&H808:RETURN
420  A$=A6$:CP=2:CC=3:CD=&H4444:RETURN
430  A$=A7$:CP=2:CC=3:CD=&HAAAA:RETURN
440  A$=A8$:CP=3:CC=2:CD=&H4444:RETURN
450  A$=CHR$(&HFF)+CHR$(&HFF)+CHR$(&HO)+CHR$(&HO):CP=3:CC=3:CD=&HFFFF:RETURN
460  A$=A9$:CP=3:CC=4:CD=&H8080:RETURN
470  A$=A10$:CP=3:CC=4:CD=&H4444:RETURN
480  A$=A11$:CP=3:CC=4:CD=&HAAAA:RETURN
490  A$=A12$:CP=4:CC=3:CD=&H4444:RETURN
500  A$=CHR$(&HO)+CHR$(&HO)+CHR$(&HFF)+CHR$(&HO):CP=4:CC=4:CD=&HFFFF:RETURN
510  '
520  '_____
530  END
```

Fig. 24-11. (Continued from page 255.)

```
100  'Code fragment A-12.BAS   Shading pattern and distribution matrix for EGA an
d VGA 640x350 16-color mode.
110  'Copyright (c) 1988 by Lee Adams and TAB Books Inc.
120  'All rights reserved.
130  '
140  '_____
150  'module:  shading patterns
160  A1$=CHR$(&HDF)+CHR$(&H20)+CHR$(&HO)+CHR$(&HO)+CHR$(&HFD)+CHR$(&H2)+CHR$(&HO
)+CHR$(&HO)+CHR$(&H7F)+CHR$(&H80)+CHR$(&HO)+CHR$(&HO)+CHR$(&HF7)+CHR$(&H8)+CHR$(
&HO)+CHR$(&HO)
170  A2$=CHR$(&HBB)+CHR$(&H44)+CHR$(&HO)+CHR$(&HO)+CHR$(&HEE)+CHR$(&H11)+CHR$(&H
0)+CHR$(&HO)
180  A3$=CHR$(&HAA)+CHR$(&H55)+CHR$(&HO)+CHR$(&HO)+CHR$(&H55)+CHR$(&HAA)+CHR$(&H
0)+CHR$(&HO)
190  A4$=CHR$(&H44)+CHR$(&HBB)+CHR$(&HO)+CHR$(&HO)+CHR$(&H11)+CHR$(&HEE)+CHR$(&H
0)+CHR$(&HO)
200  A5$=CHR$(&H20)+CHR$(&HFF)+CHR$(&HO)+CHR$(&HO)+CHR$(&H2)+CHR$(&HFF)+CHR$(&HO
)+CHR$(&HO)+CHR$(&H80)+CHR$(&HFF)+CHR$(&HO)+CHR$(&HO)+CHR$(&H8)+CHR$(&HFF)+CHR$(
&HO)+CHR$(&HO)
210  A6$=CHR$(&H44)+CHR$(&HFF)+CHR$(&HO)+CHR$(&HO)+CHR$(&H11)+CHR$(&HFF)+CHR$(&H
0)+CHR$(&HO)
```

Fig. 24-12. An illumination matrix for the 640 × 350 16-color mode of the EGA and VGA.

```
220  A7$=CHR$(&H55)+CHR$(&HFF)+CHR$(&HO)+CHR$(&HO)+CHR$(&HAA)+CHR$(&HFF)+CHR$(&H
0)+CHR$(&HO)
230  A8$=CHR$(&HBB)+CHR$(&HFF)+CHR$(&HO)+CHR$(&HO)+CHR$(&HEE)+CHR$(&HFF)+CHR$(&H
0)+CHR$(&HO)
240  A9$=CHR$(&HDF)+CHR$(&HDF)+CHR$(&H20)+CHR$(&HO)+CHR$(&HFD)+CHR$(&HFD)+CHR$(&
H2)+CHR$(&HO)+CHR$(&H7F)+CHR$(&H7F)+CHR$(&H80)+CHR$(&HO)+CHR$(&HF7)+CHR$(&HF7)+C
HR$(&H8)+CHR$(&HO)
250  A10$=CHR$(&HBB)+CHR$(&HBB)+CHR$(&H44)+CHR$(&HO)+CHR$(&HEE)+CHR$(&HEE)+CHR$(
&H11)+CHR$(&HO)
260  A11$=CHR$(&HAA)+CHR$(&HAA)+CHR$(&H55)+CHR$(&HO)+CHR$(&H55)+CHR$(&H55)+CHR$(
&HAA)+CHR$(&HO)
270  A12$=CHR$(&H44)+CHR$(&H44)+CHR$(&HBB)+CHR$(&HO)+CHR$(&H11)+CHR$(&H11)+CHR$(
&HEE)+CHR$(&HO)
280  A13$=CHR$(&H20)+CHR$(&HO)+CHR$(&HFF)+CHR$(&HO)+CHR$(&H2)+CHR$(&HO)+CHR$(&HF
F)+CHR$(&HO)+CHR$(&H80)+CHR$(&HO)+CHR$(&HFF)+CHR$(&HO)+CHR$(&H8)+CHR$(&HO)+CHR$(
&HFF)+CHR$(&HO)
290  A14$=CHR$(&H44)+CHR$(&HO)+CHR$(&HFF)+CHR$(&HO)+CHR$(&H11)+CHR$(&HO)+CHR$(&H
FF)+CHR$(&HO)
300  A15$=CHR$(&H55)+CHR$(&HO)+CHR$(&HFF)+CHR$(&HO)+CHR$(&HAA)+CHR$(&HO)+CHR$(&H
FF)+CHR$(&HO)
310  A16$=CHR$(&HBB)+CHR$(&HO)+CHR$(&HFF)+CHR$(&HO)+CHR$(&HEE)+CHR$(&HO)+CHR$(&H
FF)+CHR$(&HO)
320  RETURN
330  '_____
340  '
350  'distribution matrix
360  A$=CHR$(&HFF)+CHR$(&HO)+CHR$(&HO)+CHR$(&HO):C4=1:C5=1:C6=&HFFFF:RETURN
370  A$=A1$:C4=1:C5=2:C6=&H808:RETURN
380  A$=A2$:C4=1:C5=2:C6=&H4444:RETURN
390  A$=CHR$(&HO)+CHR$(&HFF)+CHR$(&HO)+CHR$(&HO):C4=2:C5=2:C6=&HFFFF:RETURN
400  A$=A5$:C4=2:C5=3:C6=&H808:RETURN
410  A$=A6$:C4=2:C5=3:C6=&H4444:RETURN
420  A$=A7$:C4=2:C5=3:C6=&HAAAA:RETURN
430  A$=A8$:C4=3:C5=2:C6=&H4444:RETURN
440  A$=CHR$(&HFF)+CHR$(&HFF)+CHR$(&HO)+CHR$(&HO):C4=3:C5=3:C6=&HFFFF:RETURN
450  A$=A10$:C4=3:C5=4:C6=&H4444:RETURN
460  A$=A11$:C4=3:C5=4:C6=&HAAAA:RETURN
470  A$=A12$:C4=4:C5=3:C6=&H4444:RETURN
480  A$=CHR$(&HO)+CHR$(&HO)+CHR$(&HFF)+CHR$(&HO):C4=4:C5=4:C6=&HFFFF:RETURN
490  A$=A13$:C4=4:C5=5:C6=&H808:RETURN
500  A$=A14$:C4=4:C5=5:C6=&H4444:RETURN
510  A$=A15$:C4=4:C5=5:C6=&HAAAA:RETURN
520  '_____
530  '
540  END
```

Fig. 24-12. (Continued from page 256.)

The halftone fill patterns for full shading algorithms can be used by any programming language, although BASIC provides easiest access to these advanced graphics functions. If you are using C, you must either provide your own assembly language drivers or purchase a third-party graphics library which contains the area-fill bit tiling capability.

```
100 'Code fragment A-13.BAS   Shading patterns and distribution matrix for CGA a
nd MCGA 320x200 4-color mode, and PCjr 640x200 4-color mode.
110 'Copyright (c) 1988 by Lee Adams and TAB Books Inc.
120 'All rights reserved.
130 '_____
140 '
150 'module:   shading patterns
160   A1$=CHR$(&H40)+CHR$(&H0)+CHR$(&H4)+CHR$(&H0)
170   A2$=CHR$(&H40)+CHR$(&H4)+CHR$(&H40)+CHR$(&H4)
180   A3$=CHR$(&H44)+CHR$(&H10)+CHR$(&H11)+CHR$(&H1)+CHR$(&H44)+CHR$(&H4)+CHR$(&H
11)+CHR$(&H40)
190   A4$=CHR$(&H44)+CHR$(&H11)+CHR$(&H44)+CHR$(&H11)
200   A5$=CHR$(&H11)+CHR$(&H45)+CHR$(&H44)+CHR$(&H54)+CHR$(&H11)+CHR$(&H51)+CHR$(
&H44)+CHR$(&H15)
210   A6$=CHR$(&H15)+CHR$(&H51)+CHR$(&H15)+CHR$(&H51)
220   A7$=CHR$(&H15)+CHR$(&H55)+CHR$(&H51)+CHR$(&H55)
230   A9$=CHR$(&HD5)+CHR$(&H55)+CHR$(&H5D)+CHR$(&H55)
240   A10$=CHR$(&HD5)+CHR$(&H5D)+CHR$(&HD5)+CHR$(&H5D)
250   A12$=CHR$(&HDD)+CHR$(&H75)+CHR$(&H77)+CHR$(&H57)+CHR$(&HDD)+CHR$(&H5D)+CHR$
(&H77)+CHR$(&HD5)
260   A13$=CHR$(&HDD)+CHR$(&H77)+CHR$(&HDD)+CHR$(&H77)
270   A14$=CHR$(&H77)+CHR$(&HDF)+CHR$(&HDD)+CHR$(&HFD)+CHR$(&H77)+CHR$(&HF7)+CHR$
(&HDD)+CHR$(&H7F)
280   A15$=CHR$(&H7F)+CHR$(&HF7)+CHR$(&H7F)+CHR$(&HF7)
290   A16$=CHR$(&H7F)+CHR$(&HFF)+CHR$(&HF7)+CHR$(&HFF)
300   RETURN
310 '_____
320 '
330 'module:   distribution matrix
340   A$=CHR$(&H0):C4=0:C5=0:C6=&HFFFF:RETURN   'solid black -- unused
350   A$=A1$:C4=0:C5=1:C6=&H2108:RETURN
360   A$=A2$:C4=0:C5=1:C6=&H4444:RETURN
370   A$=A4$:C4=0:C5=1:C6=&HAAAA:RETURN
380   A$=A5$:C4=1:C5=0:C6=&H4924:RETURN
390   A$=A6$:C4=1:C5=0:C6=&H4444:RETURN
400   A$=A7$:C4=1:C5=0:C6=&H808:RETURN
410   A$=CHR$(&H55):C4=1:C5=1:C6=&HFFFF:RETURN
420   A$=A9$:C4=1:C5=3:C6=&H808:RETURN
430   A$=A10$:C4=1:C5=3:C6=&H4444:RETURN
440   A$=A12$:C4=1:C5=3:C6=&H4924:RETURN
450   A$=A13$:C4=1:C5=3:C6=&HAAAA:RETURN
460   A$=A14$:C4=3:C5=1:C6=&H4924:RETURN
470   A$=A15$:C4=3:C5=1:C6=&H4444:RETURN
480   A$=A16$:C4=3:C5=1:C6=&H808:RETURN
490   A$=CHR$(&HFF):C4=3:C5=3:C6=&HFFFF:RETURN
500 '
510 '_____
520   END
```

Fig. 24-13. An illumination matrix for the 320 × 200 4-color mode of the CGA and the 640 × 200 4-color mode of the PCjr.

```
100 'Code fragment A-19.BAS   EGA, VGA palettes.
110 'Copyright (c) 1988 by Lee Adams and TAB Books Inc.
120 'All rights reserved.
130 '_____
140 '
150 'module:  palette assignments for EGA and VGA 640x350 16-color mode.
160   SCREEN 9,,0,0:COLOR 7,0:PALETTE 1,8:PALETTE 2,1:PALETTE 3,9:PALETTE 4,11:PA
LETTE 5,7
170 '_____
180 '
190 'module:  palette assignments for EGA and VGA 640x200 16-color mode.
200   SCREEN 8,,0,0:COLOR 7,0:PALETTE 1,0:PALETTE 2,1:PALETTE 3,9:PALETTE 4,7
210 '_____
220 '
230   END
```

Fig. 24-14. Palette assignments for the shading matrix for the EGA and VGA.

SUMMARY

This chapter presented an overview of 3D concepts and algorithms for personal computers. You learned how accurate 3D models can be created, and how those models can be fully shaded.

The next chapter discusses components of interactive 3D CAD programs.

25

Components of
3D CAD Programs

3D CAD programs are useful for creating and experimenting with architectural designs, package designs, product designs. They are useful tools for manipulating any engineering or design work which will eventually yield a 3D product. Many of the advanced functions available in packaged 3D CAD software programs can be replicated on your personal computer using BASIC (or C, Ada, Modula-2, Pascal, or assembly language).

The photograph in Fig. 25-1 illustrates the start-up image produced by the 3D CAD demonstration program in the next chapter. The interactive program, which generates 3D wire-frame models, is called *YOUR MICROCOMPUTER 3D CAD DESIGNER*. It is capable of creating, saving, and editing complex 3D objects. (Chapter 26 contains the EGA and VGA version of the program. The CGA and MCGA version appears in Appendix G. The PCjr version appears in Appendix H. A Turbo BASIC version for the CGA is included in Appendix E.)

A complete User's Guide for *YOUR MICROCOMPUTER 3D CAD DESIGNER* appears in the chapter immediately following the program listing.

TYPICAL 3D CAD EDITORS

It is typical for a 3D CAD editor to operate through a menu system. After selecting the drawing mode, you normally create a 2D plan view (bird's eye view) of the model. By also providing elevation values (height) for each xy coordinate on the plan view, the program automatically generates a 3D model in another window on the display screen. By using the menu system to adjust the viewing parameters—yaw, roll, pitch, viewpoint distance, and so forth—you can observe your 3D model from different vantage points.

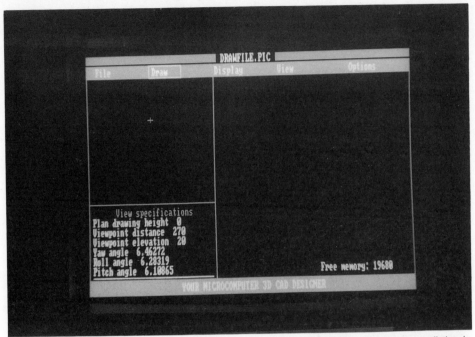

Fig. 25-1. Display image of the user interface for the interactive 3D wire-frame CAD program listing in Chapter 26.

Some 3D CAD editors are based on graphics primitives. In particular, you use simple functions such as lines, circles, and ovals to create complex 3D models. Other 3D CAD editors are based on graphics entities. These editors provide you with ready-formed 3D cubes, spheres, and planes, which you use to create your 3D model. By contrast, to create a sphere with a primitive-based CAD program, you would first create an arc and then rotate the arc around an axis.

It is commonplace for a 3D CAD program to continuously display the viewing parameters that are active. Parameters such as viewpoint distance and rotation can often apply to both the 2D plan view and the resulting 3D model.

The xyz axis system, often called a *gnomon*, is sometimes displayed as a part of the 3D viewing window. A variable grid is often provided for help in creating the 2D plan view.

The 3D CAD editors in this book adopt the primitive-based approach to 3D modeling and rendering, although there is nothing to prevent you from adding your own entity-based functions after you have become familiar with the programming algorithms. Figure 25-1 illustrates the 2D drawing area and the 3D window used by the 3D CAD programs in this book. The view specifications window contains the current viewing parameters.

MENU MANAGEMENT

The program listing for the program uses five pull-down menus to access the complete range of graphics functions provided by the program.

Packaged 3D CAD editors often provide mouse support and tablet support. The intuitive nature of these devices makes it easy to create the 2D plan view which the program will use to generate the 3D model. Because most personal computers are used without a mouse or tablet, however, the program listing for *YOUR MICROCOMPUTER 3D CAD DESIGNER* uses only keyboard input. By referring to Chapter 11, you can readily add the mouse control routines which will make the program completely mouse-driven. Refer to Chapter 12 for further discussion of tablets.

The interactive menu system for this program is based upon the principles discussed in Chapter 10. Five menus are employed, including File, Draw, Display, View, and Options. All menus are pull-down menus which are reached from the main menu bar at the top of the screen.

FILE MENU

The File menu provides the following selections: Name, Save, Load, Quit, and Menu Bar.

The Name function is used to specify file names for saving and loading images. It uses an interactive dialog box to accept your keyboard input. This is essentially the same algorithm employed by *YOUR MICROCOMPUTER SKETCH PAD* and *YOUR MICROCOMPUTER DRAFTING TABLE.*

The Save function saves the current drawing on disk as a binary image file, using the name currently displayed in the file name bar at the top of the screen.

The Load function fetches a previously saved binary image file from disk and displays your drawing on the screen for editing or for printing.

The Quit function ends the program. Your current drawing is not saved on disk before the program ends.

The Menu Bar selection discards the File menu and returns you to the main menu bar at the top of the screen.

DRAW MENU

The pull-down Draw menu provides the following selections: Line, Curve, Circle, Undo, and Menu Bar.

The Line function creates a polyline in the 2D drawing area which is automatically drawn in three dimensions in the 3D window.

The Curve function produces a parametric smooth curve in the 2D drawing area. A corresponding three-dimensional curve is generated in the 3D window.

The Circle function creates a circle in the 2D drawing area, which is automatically drawn in three dimensions in the 3D window.

The Undo function restores the graphics which existed before the previous Draw function.

The Menu Bar function discards the Draw menu and returns control to the main menu bar at the top of the screen.

DISPLAY MENU

The pull-down Display menu provides three functions. These are Regen, Clear, and Menu Bar.

The Regen function (for "regeneration") is used to clear both the 2D drawing area and the 3D window, and to automatically redraw your image. Your previous keystrokes during the drawing session were saved in internal .CDF data files by the program. Regen retrieves these graphics primitives from the data file and uses them to redraw the 2D plan view and the 3D model.

The Clear function is used to clear the 2D and 3D windows.

The Menu Bar functions discards the Display menu and returns you to the main menu bar at the top of the screen.

VIEW MENU

The pull-down View menu provides six functions: Distance, Elevation, Yaw, Roll, Pitch, and Menu Bar. These functions determine how the 3D model appears. You can rotate and translate your 3D model using the View menu. *YOUR MICROCOMPUTER 3D CAD DESIGNER* uses the existing 2D plan view to regenerate a new 3D model based upon the new parameters specified by the View menu. Changes made in the View menu affect only the 3D model, not the 2D plan.

The Distance +/− function is used to move the 3D model closer to the viewpoint or farther away from the viewpoint.

The Elevation +/− function adjusts the elevation height of the 3D model, relative to the viewing position.

The Yaw function adjusts the compass heading of the 3D model.

The Roll function is used to tilt the 3D model clockwise or counterclockwise.

The Pitch function tilts the 3D model towards you or away from you.

The Menu Bar function is used to discard the View menu and to return you to the main menu bar at the top of the screen.

OPTIONS MENU

The Options menu is used to control the working environment for the program. Six functions are provided by the Options menu: Set Snap, Set Grid, Grid On/Off, Gnomon On/Off, Set Color, and Menu Bar.

The Set Snap function is used to specify the amount of movement exhibited by the crosshair cursor in the 2D drawing area when an arrow key is depressed.

The Set Grid function is used to set the spacing between the horizontal and vertical lines which create the optional grid in the 2D drawing area.

The Grid On/Off function toggles the 2D drawing area grid on or off. The grid is useful for ensuring that your 2D plan view drawing is correctly dimensioned and aligned— ensuring for example, that square corners are really square corners. A subsequent regen function will produce a grid in the 2D drawing area if the grid function is toggled on. Refer to Fig. 25-2.

The Gnomon On/Off function toggles the 3D axis display on or off. The axis is displayed in the 3D model window. A subsequent regen function will produce an xyz axis in the 3D window if the Gnomon function is toggled on. Refer to Fig. 25-3.

The Set Color function changes the current drawing color. The current color is always displayed in the view specifications window. With an EGA or a VGA, 16 colors are available for 2D and 3D drawing. Fewer colors are available when a CGA or MCGA graphics adapter is being used.

The Menu Bar function discards the Options menu and returns control to the main menu bar.

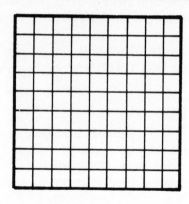

Fig. 25-2. A grid superimposed on the 2D drawing area provides accurate references.

POTENTIAL ENHANCEMENTS

Although *YOUR MICROCOMPUTER 3D CAD DESIGNER* provides a powerful set of tools for generating 3D wire-frame models, you might wish to add some functions found in high-end packaged software.

Extrusions

Often, a 3D CAD editor will permit you to generate an ordinary 2D drafting-like drawing. You can work with this image just as if you were using a drafting program like *YOUR MICROCOMPUTER DRAFTING TABLE* (in Chapter 21). At any later time, however, you can define elevation values and the program will automatically convert your 2D drawing in a 3D image. This process is called *extrusion.* Provided that the graphics primitives (the xy coordinates) have been stored in data files (as they are by *YOUR MICROCOMPUTER 3D CAD DESIGNER*), you can easily retrieve these values and manipulate them for your own purposes.

Sweeps

Packaged 3D CAD programs often allow you to create one 3D entity and then to use yaw, roll, or pitch to sweep the graphic around one of the axes. After you have studied

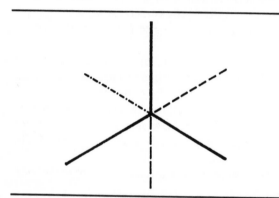

Fig. 25-3. A gnomon superimposed on the 3D viewing window provides easier visual interpretation of 3D wire-frame models.

the source code in the next chapter, you will be able to add your own sweep routine by simply leaving the existing image on the screen while you redraw the entity at a new location in the 3D window.

Surface Mapping

Professional 3D CAD editors often provide surface mapping facilities. These functions are useful for mapping 2D graphic designs onto the surfaces of 3D containers and packages. (For a detailed discussion of programming algorithms useful for surface mapping, consult *High-Performance Interactive Graphics: Modeling, Rendering & Animating for IBM PCs and Compatibles,* TAB book 2879.)

Full Shading

Subroutines to remove hidden surfaces and to add halftone shading are presented in the second 3D CAD program, in Chapter 29.

SUMMARY

In this chapter you learned about the graphics functions present in typical 3D CAD programs.

The next chapter contains the complete source code listing for *YOUR MICROCOMPUTER 3D CAD DESIGNER,* a powerful interactive 3D modeling program.

26

Program Listing—
Your Microcomputer
3D CAD Designer

This chapter contains the complete source code for *YOUR MICROCOMPUTER 3D CAD DESIGNER*, a powerful 3D modeling program. The photograph in Fig. 26-1 illustrates the start-up display produced by the program.

YOUR MICROCOMPUTER 3D CAD DESIGNER is designed to run on IBM-compatible personal computers equipped with an EGA or a VGA graphics adapter. The program runs in the 640×200 16-color mode. The complete program listing is presented in Fig. 26-2.

A version of the program for the color/graphics adapter (CGA) and the MCGA appears in Appendix G. The CGA version runs in the 640×200 two-color mode. A version for Turbo BASIC also appears in Appendix G.

A version of the program intended for the IBM PCjr (and for Tandy computers using GW-BASIC) is provided in Appendix H.

USER'S GUIDE

A detailed User's Guide for the program is provided in the next chapter. The User's Guide contains sample sessions which include photographs of advanced 3D models produced by the program listing in this chapter. An analysis of the program's algorithms appears in Chapter 28.

HARDWARE/SOFTWARE COMPATIBILITY

The program listing in this chapter was developed and tested on an IBM PC equipped with an EGA, using IBM BASICA 3.21. The program will run on VGA-equipped PS/2

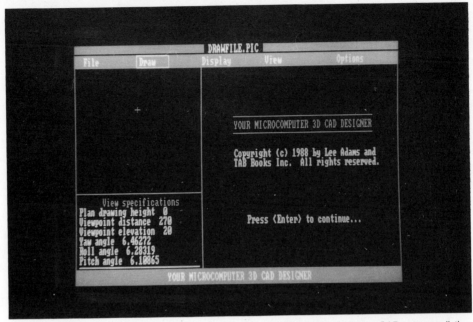

Fig. 26-1. The start-up display image generated by the interactive 3D wire-frame CAD program listing in Fig. 26-2.

computers using **IBM BASICA 3.30**. The program will run on any IBM-compatible personal computer equipped with an EGA and which uses a BASIC interpreter that supports EGA graphics.

　　If you are using QuickBASIC or Turbo BASIC, read Appendix E. A Turbo BASIC version of the program for CGA-equipped personal computers appears in that appendix.

```
100 'Program CAD-1.BAS:  YOUR MICROCOMPUTER 3D CAD DESIGNER
110 'Copyright (c) 1988 by Lee Adams and TAB Books Inc.
120 'All rights reserved.
130 'Version for EGA and VGA.  640x200 16-color mode.
140 '
150 '_____INITIALIZE SYSTEM_____
160 '
170  KEY OFF:CLS:CLEAR:SCREEN 0,0,0,0:WIDTH 80:COLOR 7,0,0:CLS:LOCATE 10,20,0:PR
INT "Assigning memory space for graphic arrays"
180 '
190 '_____DATA ASSIGNMENTS_____
200 '
210 'module:  data assignments
220  DEFINT A,T,J
230  DIM A1(631):DIM A2(150):DIM A3(150):DIM A4(150):DIM A5(150):DIM A6(150)   't
emporary arrays for screen template
```

Fig. 26-2. Complete source code for an interactive 3D wire-frame CAD program. This version is for the EGA and VGA. See Appendix G for the CGA and MCGA version. See Appendix H for the PCjr/Tandy version. See Appendix E for a Turbo BASIC version.

```
240   DIM A7(177)  'array for panning cursor
250   DIM A8(1793)  'array for Options menu
260   DIM A9(21)  'array for scrolling cursor
270   DIM A10(1057)  'array for File menu
280   DIM A11(953):DIM A11C(953)  'for Name dialog box
290   DIM A12(29)  'array for roaming crosshair cursor
300   DIM A13(683)  'array for Display menu
310   DIM A14(1321)  'array for View menu
320   DIM A15(1057)  'array for Draw menu
330   C0=1:C1=2:C2=9:C3=7:C4=11:C5=5:C6=6:C7=4:C8=8:C9=3:C10=10:C12=12:C13=13:C14
=14:C15=15  'software color codes
340   C=C7:CE=C7  'drawing, boundary colors
350   T=0  'loop counter
360   T1=2  'selection flag for menu bar
370   T2=25  'flag for echo position of file menu input
380   T3=0  '2D grid on/off toggle
390   T4=0  '3D gnomon on/off toggle
400   T5=0  'flag for function switcher
410   T6=0  'iterative flag for plastic functions
420   T8=1  'selection flag for menus
430   J=2:JS=J  'snap, temporary storage of snap value
440   J6=85:J7=19:J8=608:J9=186  'viewport dimensions for active drawing surface
on 640x200 screen
450   SX=122:SY=65  'crosshair array location
460   XL=2:XR=234:YT=19:YB=117  'left, right, top, bottom range of roaming crossh
air cursor
470   SXC=SX+7:SZC=SY+3:SYC=0  'center of crosshair cursor
480   SXP=0:SZP=0:SYP=0  'last referenced drawing point
490   F$="DRAWFILE.PIC":F1$=F$:F2$="DRAWFILE"  'strings used to manipulate filena
me when saving images
500   V=0  'size of free memory in BASICA workspace
510   V1=1024  'threshold memory flag
520   B=0:B2=0:B3=0:D1=0:D2=0:D3=0:D4=0:X1=0:X2=0:X3=0:X4=0:Y1=0:Y2=0:Y3=0:Y4=0
'used in freeform curve routine
530   D=1200!:R1=6.46272:R2=6.28319:R3=6.10865:MX=0!:MY=-20!:MZ=-270!:SR1=SIN(R1)
:SR2=SIN(R2):SR3=SIN(R3):CR1=COS(R1):CR2=COS(R2):CR3=COS(R3)  'variables used as
  input for perspective formulas
540   XA=0!:YA=0!:ZA=0!  'temporary variables used in perspective formulas
550   SX1=0!:SY1=0!  'output of perspective formulas
560   J10=25:J11=11  'horizontal, vertical spacing for grid
570   '
580   '_____SET UP RUNTIME ENVIRONMENT_____
590   '
600   'module:  set up runtime environment
610   CLS:SCREEN 8,,0,0:COLOR C7,0:CLS  '640x200 16-clr mode
620   PALETTE 1,0:PALETTE 2,1:PALETTE 3,9:PALETTE 4,7:PALETTE 5,5:PALETTE 6,6:PAL
ETTE 7,3:PALETTE 8,8:PALETTE 9,2:PALETTE 10,10:PALETTE 11,4:PALETTE 12,12:PALETT
E 13,13:PALETTE 14,14:PALETTE 15,15
630   ON KEY(2) GOSUB 1550:KEY(2) ON  'install hot key
640   COLOR,0  'restore hardware color for background
650   GOSUB 1600  'initialize .CDF data file
660   '
670   '_____SET UP SCREEN DISPLAY_____
```

Fig. 26-2. (Continued from page 267.)

```
680  '
690  'module:  set up screen template
700   GOSUB 960  'save alphanumeric graphic arrays
710   GOSUB 1140  'create pull-down menus
720   LINE (0,8)-(639,199),C8,B  'border
730   LINE (0,187)-(639,187),C8:PAINT (320,190),C8,C8:PUT (182,189),A1,XOR  'bann
er
740   LINE (0,0)-(639,6),C6,B:PAINT (320,3),C6,C6:LOCATE 1,33:PRINT " DRAWFILE.CD
F ":LOCATE 1,34:PRINT F$  'filename bar
750   LINE (1,8)-(639,18),C8,B:PAINT (320,10),C8,C8  'menu bar
760   PUT (18,9),A2,XOR:PUT (130,9),A3,XOR:PUT (250,9),A4,XOR:PUT (370,9),A5,XOR:
PUT (510,9),A6,XOR  'selections for menu bar
770   LOCATE 10,20:PRINT "Reclaiming memory used by temporary arrays":ERASE A1,A2
,A3,A4,A5,A6  'free up array memory
780   LOCATE 10,20:PRINT "                                                     "
790   LINE (250,19)-(250,186),C8:LINE (249,19)-(249,186),C8:LINE (1,19)-(1,186),C
8:LINE (638,19)-(638,186),C8:LINE (1,124)-(249,124),C8:LINE (122,53)-(132,53),C6
:LINE (127,51)-(127,55),C6  'split screen
800   LOCATE 18,2:PRINT "Plan drawing height":LOCATE 19,2:PRINT "Viewpoint distan
ce":LOCATE 20,2:PRINT "Viewpoint elevation":LOCATE 21,2:PRINT "Yaw angle":LOCATE
 22,2:PRINT "Roll angle":LOCATE 23,2:PRINT "Pitch angle"
810   LOCATE 17,8:COLOR C6:PRINT "View specifications":COLOR C7
820   GOSUB 5180  'alphanumeric readouts
830   PUT (126,8),A7,XOR  'panning cursor for menu bar
840   PCOPY 0,1:PCOPY 1,2  'establish refresh buffers
850   LOCATE 9,40:COLOR C6:PRINT "YOUR MICROCOMPUTER 3D CAD DESIGNER":LOCATE 12,4
0:COLOR C7:PRINT "Copyright (c) 1988 by Lee Adams and":LOCATE 13,40:PRINT "TAB B
ooks Inc.  All rights reserved."
860   LINE (310,60)-(584,60),C6:LINE (310,74)-(584,74),C6
870   LOCATE 19,43:PRINT "Press <Enter> to continue...":SOUND 860,2:SOUND 800,2
880   K$=INKEY$:IF K$<>CHR$(13) THEN 880
890   PCOPY 1,0:SOUND 250,.7:LOCATE 23,57:PRINT "Free memory:"FRE(0)  'restore sc
reen
900   GOTO 1650  'jump to runtime code
910   GOTO 910  'bulletproof code barrier
920  '
930  '_____CREATE ALPHANUMERICS FOR TEMPLATE_____
940  '
950  'module: create alpha arrays for screen template
960   COLOR C12:LOCATE 10,20:PRINT "YOUR MICROCOMPUTER 3D CAD DESIGNER"
970   GET (150,71)-(424,79),A1:LOCATE 10,20:PRINT "
                                                    "
980   LOCATE 10,20:PRINT "File":GET (150,71)-(210,79),A2
990   LOCATE 10,20:PRINT "Draw":GET (150,71)-(210,79),A3
1000   LOCATE 10,20:PRINT "Display":GET (150,71)-(210,79),A4
1010   LOCATE 10,20:PRINT "View   ":GET (150,71)-(210,79),A5
1020   LOCATE 10,20:PRINT "Options":GET (150,71)-(210,79),A6
1030   COLOR C7:LOCATE 10,20:PRINT "          "
1040   LINE (150,70)-(212,80),C12,B:GET (150,70)-(212,80),A7  'create panning cur
sor for menu bar
1050   LINE (150,70)-(212,80),0,B
1060   LINE (323,44)-(337,44),C7:LINE (330,41)-(330,47),C7:LINE (329,44)-(331,44)
,0  'create roaming crosshair cursor
```

Fig. 26-2. (Continued from page 268.)

```
1070  GET (323,41)-(337,47),A12:LINE (323,41)-(337,47),0,BF
1080  RETURN
1090  '
1100  '_____CREATE PULL-DOWN MENUS_____
1110  '
1120  'module:  create pull-down menus
1130  'submodule:  create Options menu
1140  COLOR C6:LOCATE 10,20:PRINT "Set snap":LOCATE 11,20:PRINT "Set grid":LOCAT
E 12,20:PRINT "Grid on/off":LOCATE 13,20:PRINT "Gnomon on/off"
1150  LOCATE 14,20:PRINT "Set color":LOCATE 15,20:PRINT "Menu bar"
1160  LINE (138,67)-(260,122),C8,B
1170  GET (138,67)-(260,122),A8:LINE (138,67)-(260,122),0,BF
1180  LOCATE 10,20:COLOR C7:PRINT CHR$(175):COLOR C7  'menu cursor >>
1190  GET (151,73)-(159,77),A9:LOCATE 10,20:PRINT " "
1200  '
1210  '_____
1220  'submodule:  create File menu
1230  COLOR C6:LOCATE 10,20:PRINT "Name":LOCATE 11,20:PRINT "Save":LOCATE 12,20:
PRINT "Load":LOCATE 13,20:PRINT "Quit":LOCATE 14,20:PRINT "Menu bar"
1240  LINE (138,67)-(220,114),C8,B
1250  GET (138,67)-(220,114),A10:LINE (138,67)-(220,114),0,BF
1260  '
1270  '_____
1280  'submodule:  create Draw menu
1290  COLOR C6:LOCATE 10,20:PRINT "Line":LOCATE 11,20:PRINT "Curve":LOCATE 12,20
:PRINT "Circle":LOCATE 13,20:PRINT "Undo":LOCATE 14,20:PRINT "Menu bar"
1300  LINE (138,67)-(220,114),C8,B
1310  GET (138,67)-(220,114),A15:LINE (138,67)-(220,114),0,BF
1320  '
1330  '_____
1340  'submodule:  create Name dialog box
1350  COLOR C6:LOCATE 10,20:PRINT "Enter new filename:          ":COLOR C7
1360  LINE (144,69)-(413,82),C8,B
1370  GET (144,69)-(413,82),A11:LINE (144,69)-(413,82),0,BF
1380  '
1390  '_____
1400  'submodule:  create Display menu
1410  COLOR C6:LOCATE 4,20:PRINT "Regen":LOCATE 5,20:PRINT "Clear":LOCATE 6,20:P
RINT "Menu bar"
1420  LINE (138,20)-(220,50),C8,B
1430  GET (138,20)-(220,50),A13:LINE (138,20)-(220,50),0,BF
1440  '
1450  '_____
1460  'submodule:  create View menu
1470  LOCATE 4,20:PRINT "Distance":LOCATE 5,20:PRINT "Elevation":LOCATE 6,20:PRI
NT "Yaw":LOCATE 7,20:PRINT "Roll":LOCATE 8,20:PRINT "Pitch":LOCATE 9,20:PRINT "M
enu bar"
1480  LINE (138,20)-(230,74),C8,B
1490  GET (138,20)-(230,74),A14:LINE (138,20)-(230,74),0,BF:COLOR C7
1500  RETURN
1510  '
1520  '_____QUIT_____
1530  '_____
```

Fig. 26-2. (Continued from page 269.)

```
1540 'module:  exit routine
1550  CLS:SCREEN 0,0,0,0:WIDTH 80:COLOR 7,0,0:CLS:LOCATE 1,1,1:COLOR 6:PRINT "YO
UR MICROCOMPUTER 3D CAD DESIGNER":LOCATE 2,1:PRINT "is finished.":COLOR 7:SOUND
250,.7:END
1560 '
1570 '_____INITIALIZE DATA FILES_____
1580 '
1590 'module:  initialize .CDF data files
1600  OPEN "A:KEYLAYER.CDF" FOR OUTPUT AS #1:WRITE #1,SXP,SZP,SXC,SZC,C,SYP,SYC:
CLOSE #1:RETURN
1610 '
1620 '_____MENU BAR CONTROL_____
1630 '
1640 'main module:  interactive control of menu bar
1650  K$=INKEY$:GOSUB 1970:LOCATE 23,69:PRINT V" "
1660  IF LEN(K$)=2 THEN K$=RIGHT$(K$,1) ELSE 1700
1670  IF K$=CHR$(77) THEN T1=T1+1:GOSUB 1760:GOTO 1650
1680  IF K$=CHR$(75) THEN T1=T1-1:GOSUB 1860:GOTO 1650
1690  IF K$=CHR$(16) THEN GOTO 1550   'Alt-Q to quit
1700  IF K$=CHR$(13) THEN GOSUB 2090  '<Enter> key
1710  GOTO 1650
1720  GOTO 1720   'bulletproof code barrier
1730 '_____
1740 '_____
1750 'module:  pan right on menu bar
1760  IF T1>5 THEN T1=1
1770  ON T1 GOTO 1780,1790,1800,1810,1820
1780  PUT (506,8),A7,XOR:PUT (14,8),A7,XOR:RETURN  'File
1790  PUT (14,8),A7,XOR:PUT (126,8),A7,XOR:RETURN  'Draw
1800  PUT (126,8),A7,XOR:PUT (246,8),A7,XOR:RETURN 'Display
1810  PUT (246,8),A7,XOR:PUT (366,8),A7,XOR:RETURN 'View
1820  PUT (366,8),A7,XOR:PUT (506,8),A7,XOR:RETURN 'Options
1830 '_____
1840 '_____
1850 'module:  pan left on menu bar
1860  IF T1<1 THEN T1=5
1870  ON T1 GOTO 1880,1890,1900,1910,1920
1880  PUT (126,8),A7,XOR:PUT (14,8),A7,XOR:RETURN  'File
1890  PUT (246,8),A7,XOR:PUT (126,8),A7,XOR:RETURN 'Draw
1900  PUT (366,8),A7,XOR:PUT (246,8),A7,XOR:RETURN 'Display
1910  PUT (506,8),A7,XOR:PUT (366,8),A7,XOR:RETURN 'View
1920  PUT (14,8),A7,XOR:PUT (506,8),A7,XOR:RETURN  'Options
1930 '
1940 '_____CHECK SIZE OF WORKSPACE_____
1950 '
1960 'module:  check if user is running out of memory
1970  V=FRE(0):IF V>V1 THEN RETURN
1980  V1=128  'lower threshold to permit return to pgm
1990  PCOPY 0,1:CLS:COLOR C12:LOCATE 10,32:PRINT "W A R N I N G":COLOR C7:LOCATE
 12,23:PRINT "Out of memory in BASIC workspace."
2000  LOCATE 13,27:PRINT "Save your drawing on disk!":LOCATE 15,21:PRINT "Press
<Enter> to return to 3D CAD DESIGNER."
2010  FOR T=1 TO 4 STEP 1:SOUND 250,3:SOUND 450,3:SOUND 650,3:NEXT T
```

Fig. 26-2 (Continued from page 270.)

```
2020  K$=INKEY$:IF K$<>CHR$(13) THEN 2020   'wait for <Enter>
2030  K$=INKEY$:IF K$<>"" THEN 2030   'empty keyboard buffer
2040  PCOPY 1,0:SOUND 250,.7:RETURN
2050  '
2060  '_____MENU BAR SWITCHER_____
2070  '
2080  'module:  switcher to execute menu bar choices
2090  ON T1 GOTO 2100,2110,2120,2130,2140
2100  GOSUB 2190:RETURN   'invoke File menu
2110  GOSUB 2870:RETURN   'invoke Draw menu
2120  GOSUB 3140:RETURN   'invoke Display menu
2130  GOSUB 3370:RETURN   'invoke View menu
2140  GOSUB 3660:RETURN   'invoke Options menu
2150  '
2160  '_____FILE MENU CONTROL_____
2170  '
2180  'module:  interactive control of File menu
2190  PCOPY 0,1   'save existing graphics
2200  PUT (14,19),A10,PSET   'place menu on screen
2210  PUT (16,25),A9,XOR   'place cursor >> on menu
2220  T8=1   'reset flag
2230  K$=INKEY$
2240  IF LEN(K$)=2 THEN K$=RIGHT$(K$,1) ELSE 2330
2250  IF K$=CHR$(80) THEN T8=T8+1:GOTO 2260 ELSE 2230
2260  IF T8>5 THEN T8=1
2270  ON T8 GOTO 2280,2290,2300,2310,2320
2280  PUT (16,57),A9,XOR:PUT (16,25),A9,XOR:GOTO 2230 'Name
2290  PUT (16,25),A9,XOR:PUT (16,33),A9,XOR:GOTO 2230 'Save
2300  PUT (16,33),A9,XOR:PUT (16,41),A9,XOR:GOTO 2230 'Load
2310  PUT (16,41),A9,XOR:PUT (16,49),A9,XOR:GOTO 2230 'Quit
2320  PUT (16,49),A9,XOR:PUT (16,57),A9,XOR:GOTO 2230 'Menu bar
2330  IF K$=CHR$(13) THEN 2360   '<Enter> to implement
2340  IF K$=CHR$(27) THEN 2410   '<ESC> to cancel
2350  GOTO 2230
2360  ON T8 GOTO 2370,2380,2390,2400,2410
2370  GOSUB 2670:PCOPY 1,0:LOCATE 1,34:PRINT F$:RETURN   'name change
2380  PCOPY 1,0:GOSUB 2450:RETURN   'save image
2390  PCOPY 1,0:GOSUB 2560:RETURN   'load image
2400  GOTO 1550   'quit program
2410  PCOPY 1,0:RETURN   'menu bar
2420  '_____
2430  '
2440  'module: save 640x200 16-color image to disk
2450  MID$(F2$,1,8)=F$   'strip extension from file name
2460  SOUND 250,.7:DEF SEG=&HA000 'set up segment
2470  OUT &H3CE,4:OUT &H3CF,0:BSAVE "B:"+F2$+".BLU",0,16000 'bsave bit plane 0
2480  OUT &H3CE,4:OUT &H3CF,1:BSAVE "B:"+F2$+".GRN",0,16000 'bsave bit plane 1
2490  OUT &H3CE,4:OUT &H3CF,2:BSAVE "B:"+F2$+".RED",0,16000 'bsave bit plane 2
2500  OUT &H3CE,4:OUT &H3CF,3:BSAVE "B:"+F2$+".INT",0,16000 'bsave bit plane 3
2510  OUT &H3CE,4:OUT &H3CF,0:DEF SEG 'restore regs
2520  SOUND 250,.7:RETURN
2530  '_____
2540  '
```

Fig. 26-2. (Continued from page 271.)

```
2550 'module: load 640x200 16-color image from disk
2560 MID$(F2$,1,8)=F$  'strip extension from file name
2570 SOUND 250,.7:DEF SEG=&HA000 'set up segment
2580 OUT &H3C4,2:OUT &H3C5,1:BLOAD "B:"+F2$+".BLU",0 'bload bit plane 0
2590 OUT &H3C4,2:OUT &H3C5,2:BLOAD "B:"+F2$+".GRN",0 'bload bit plane 1
2600 OUT &H3C4,2:OUT &H3C5,4:BLOAD "B:"+F2$+".RED",0 'bload bit plane 2
2610 OUT &H3C4,2:OUT &H3C5,8:BLOAD "B:"+F2$+".INT",0 'bload bit plane 3
2620 OUT &H3C4,2:OUT &H3C5,&HF:DEF SEG 'restore regs
2630 GOSUB 5180:SOUND 250,.7:RETURN
2640 '_____
2650 '
2660 'module:  interactive control of Name dialog box
2670 GET (34,53)-(303,66),A11C  'save existing graphics
2680 PUT (34,53),A11,PSET  'display Name dialog box
2690 T2=25  'echo position flag
2700 F1$=F$  'temporary save of existing filename
2710 FOR T=1 TO 8 STEP 1
2720 K$=INKEY$
2730 IF K$="" THEN 2720  'wait for keystroke
2740 IF K$=CHR$(27) THEN F$=F1$:T=8:GOTO 2780  '<ESC> to cancel instructions an
d restore previous filename
2750 IF K$<"A" THEN SOUND 250,.7:GOTO 2720  'must be A-Z
2760 IF K$>"Z" THEN SOUND 250,.7:GOTO 2720  'must be A-Z
2770 T2=T2+1:LOCATE 8,T2:PRINT K$:MID$(F$,T,1)=K$  'echo user input and insert
character into F$
2780 NEXT T
2790 LOCATE 8,26:PRINT F$
2800 K$=INKEY$:IF K$<>CHR$(13) THEN 2800
2810 LOCATE 1,34:PRINT F$:SOUND 250,.7 'display on filename bar
2820 PUT (34,53),A11C,PSET:RETURN  'restore previous graphics
2830 '
2840 '_____DRAW MENU CONTROL_____
2850 '
2860 'module:  interactive control of Draw menu
2870 PCOPY 0,1:PCOPY 0,2  'save existing graphics
2880 PUT (126,19),A15,PSET 'place menu on screen
2890 PUT (128,25),A9,XOR  'place cursor >> on menu
2900 T8=1  'reset flag
2910 K$=INKEY$
2920 IF LEN(K$)=2 THEN K$=RIGHT$(K$,1) ELSE 3010
2930 IF K$=CHR$(80) THEN T8=T8+1:GOTO 2940 ELSE 2910
2940 IF T8>5 THEN T8=1
2950 ON T8 GOTO 2960,2970,2980,2990,3000
2960 PUT (128,57),A9,XOR:PUT (128,25),A9,XOR:GOTO 2910 'Line
2970 PUT (128,25),A9,XOR:PUT (128,33),A9,XOR:GOTO 2910 'Curve
2980 PUT (128,33),A9,XOR:PUT (128,41),A9,XOR:GOTO 2910 'Circle
2990 PUT (128,41),A9,XOR:PUT (128,49),A9,XOR:GOTO 2910 'Undo
3000 PUT (128,49),A9,XOR:PUT (128,57),A9,XOR:GOTO 2910 'Menu bar
3010 IF K$=CHR$(13) THEN 3040  '<Enter> to implement
3020 IF K$=CHR$(27) THEN 3090  '<ESC> to cancel
3030 GOTO 2910
3040 ON T8 GOTO 3050,3060,3070,3080,3090
3050 T5=1:PCOPY 1,0:GOSUB 3990:GOTO 2880  'line
```

Fig. 26-2. (Continued from page 272.)

```
3060   T5=2:PCOPY 1,0:GOSUB 3990:GOTO 2880   'curve
3070   T5=3:PCOPY 1,0:GOSUB 3990:GOTO 2880   'circle
3080   PCOPY 2,0:LOCATE 18,22:PRINT SYC:SOUND 250,.7:RETURN   'undo
3090   PCOPY 1,0:RETURN   'menu bar
3100   '
3110   '_____DISPLAY MENU CONTROL_____
3120   '
3130   'module:  interactive control of Display menu
3140   PCOPY 0,1   'save existing graphics
3150   PUT (246,19),A13,PSET   'place menu on screen
3160   PUT (248,24),A9,XOR   'place cursor >> on menu
3170   T8=1   'reset flag
3180   K$=INKEY$
3190   IF LEN(K$)=2 THEN K$=RIGHT$(K$,1) ELSE 3260
3200   IF K$=CHR$(80) THEN T8=T8+1:GOTO 3210 ELSE 3180
3210   IF T8>3 THEN T8=1
3220   ON T8 GOTO 3230,3240,3250
3230   PUT (248,40),A9,XOR:PUT (248,24),A9,XOR:GOTO 3180 'Regen
3240   PUT (248,24),A9,XOR:PUT (248,32),A9,XOR:GOTO 3180 'Clear
3250   PUT (248,32),A9,XOR:PUT (248,40),A9,XOR:GOTO 3180 'Menu bar
3260   IF K$=CHR$(13) THEN 3290   '<Enter> to implement
3270   IF K$=CHR$(27) THEN 3320   '<ESC> to cancel
3280   GOTO 3180
3290   ON T8 GOTO 3300,3310,3320
3300   PCOPY 1,0:VIEW SCREEN (2,19)-(248,123):CLS:LINE (122,53)-(132,53),C6:LINE
(127,51)-(127,55),C6:VIEW SCREEN (251,19)-(637,186):CLS:VIEW:GOSUB 4590:GOSUB 51
80:LOCATE 23,57:PRINT "Free memory:":SOUND 860,2:SOUND 800,2:RETURN   'Regen
3310   PCOPY 1,0:VIEW SCREEN (2,19)-(248,123):CLS:LINE (122,53)-(132,53),C6:LINE
(127,51)-(127,55),C6:VIEW SCREEN (251,19)-(637,186):CLS:VIEW:GOSUB 1600:LOCATE 2
3,57:PRINT "Free memory:":SOUND 860,2:SOUND 800,2:RETURN   'Clear
3320   PCOPY 1,0:RETURN   'menu bar
3330   '
3340   '_____VIEW MENU CONTROL_____
3350   '
3360   'module:  interactive control of View menu
3370   PCOPY 0,1   'save existing graphics
3380   PUT (366,19),A14,PSET   'place menu on screen
3390   PUT (368,24),A9,XOR   'place cursor >> on menu
3400   T8=1   'reset flag
3410   K$=INKEY$
3420   IF LEN(K$)=2 THEN K$=RIGHT$(K$,1) ELSE 3520
3430   IF K$=CHR$(80) THEN T8=T8+1:GOTO 3440 ELSE 3410
3440   IF T8>6 THEN T8=1
3450   ON T8 GOTO 3460,3470,3480,3490,3500,3510
3460   PUT (368,64),A9,XOR:PUT (368,24),A9,XOR:GOTO 3410 'Distance
3470   PUT (368,24),A9,XOR:PUT (368,32),A9,XOR:GOTO 3410 'Elevation
3480   PUT (368,32),A9,XOR:PUT (368,40),A9,XOR:GOTO 3410 'Yaw
3490   PUT (368,40),A9,XOR:PUT (368,48),A9,XOR:GOTO 3410 'Roll
3500   PUT (368,48),A9,XOR:PUT (368,56),A9,XOR:GOTO 3410 'Pitch
3510   PUT (368,56),A9,XOR:PUT (368,64),A9,XOR:GOTO 3410 'Menu bar
3520   IF K$=CHR$(13) THEN 3550   '<Enter> to implement
3530   IF K$=CHR$(27) THEN 3610   '<ESC> to cancel
3540   GOTO 3410
```

Fig. 26-2. (Continued from page 273.)

```
3550   ON T8 GOTO 3560,3570,3580,3590,3600,3610
3560   GOSUB 4730:RETURN   'Distance
3570   GOSUB 4820:RETURN   'Elevation
3580   GOSUB 4910:RETURN   'Yaw
3590   GOSUB 5000:RETURN   'Roll
3600   GOSUB 5090:RETURN   'Pitch
3610   PCOPY 1,0:RETURN   'menu bar
3620   '
3630   '_____OPTIONS MENU CONTROL_____
3640   '
3650   'module:  interactive control of Options menu
3660   PCOPY 0,1  'save existing graphics
3670   PUT (505,19),A8,PSET  'place menu on screen
3680   PUT (507,25),A9,XOR  'place cursor >> on menu
3690   T8=1  'reset flag
3700   K$=INKEY$
3710   IF LEN(K$)=2 THEN K$=RIGHT$(K$,1) ELSE 3810
3720   IF K$=CHR$(80) THEN T8=T8+1:GOTO 3730 ELSE 3700
3730   IF T8>6 THEN T8=1
3740   ON T8 GOTO 3750,3760,3770,3780,3790,3800
3750   PUT (507,65),A9,XOR:PUT (507,25),A9,XOR:GOTO 3700  'Set snap
3760   PUT (507,25),A9,XOR:PUT (507,33),A9,XOR:GOTO 3700  'Set grid
3770   PUT (507,33),A9,XOR:PUT (507,41),A9,XOR:GOTO 3700  'Grid on/off
3780   PUT (507,41),A9,XOR:PUT (507,49),A9,XOR:GOTO 3700  'Gnomon on/off
3790   PUT (507,49),A9,XOR:PUT (507,57),A9,XOR:GOTO 3700  'Set color
3800   PUT (507,57),A9,XOR:PUT (507,65),A9,XOR:GOTO 3700  'Menu bar
3810   IF K$=CHR$(13) THEN 3840  '<Enter> to implement
3820   IF K$=CHR$(27) THEN 3900  '<ESC> to cancel
3830   GOTO 3700
3840   ON T8 GOTO 3850,3860,3870,3880,3890,3900
3850   GOSUB 3940:GOTO 3700  'Set snap
3860   GOSUB 3940:GOTO 3700  'Set grid spacing
3870   GOSUB 5420:GOTO 3700  'Grid on/off
3880   GOSUB 5500:GOTO 3700  'Gnomon on/off
3890   GOSUB 5230:GOTO 3700  'Set color
3900   PCOPY 1,0:GOSUB 5180:RETURN  'menu bar
3910   '
3920   '_____DO-NOTHING ROUTINE_____
3930   '
3940   SOUND 860,2:SOUND 800,2:RETURN   'do-nothing routine
3950   '
3960   '_____CROSSHAIR CURSOR CONTROL_____
3970   '
3980   'module:  interactive control of crosshair cursor
3990   SOUND 250,.7
4000   PUT (SX,SY),A12,XOR  'install crosshair cursor
4010   T6=0  'reset polyline flag
4020   X1=100:X2=130:X3=160:X4=190:Y1=40:Y2=100:Y3=140:Y4=70  'reset control poin
ts for curve and fillet
4030   K$=INKEY$
4040   IF LEN(K$)=2 THEN K$=RIGHT$(K$,1) ELSE 4210
4050   IF K$=CHR$(77) THEN PUT (SX,SY),A12,XOR:SX=SX+J ELSE 4080
4060   IF SX>XR THEN SX=XR:SOUND 250,.7
```

Fig. 26-2. (Continued from page 274.)

```
4070  PUT (SX,SY),A12,XOR:GOTO 4030
4080  IF K$=CHR$(75) THEN PUT (SX,SY),A12,XOR:SX=SX-J ELSE 4110
4090  IF SX<XL THEN SX=XL:SOUND 250,.7
4100  PUT (SX,SY),A12,XOR:GOTO 4030
4110  IF K$=CHR$(72) THEN PUT (SX,SY),A12,XOR:SY=SY-J*.5 ELSE 4140
4120  IF SY<YT THEN SY=YT:SOUND 250,.7
4130  PUT (SX,SY),A12,XOR:GOTO 4030
4140  IF K$=CHR$(80) THEN PUT (SX,SY),A12,XOR:SY=SY+J*.5 ELSE 4170
4150  IF SY>YB THEN SY=YB:SOUND 250,.7
4160  PUT (SX,SY),A12,XOR:GOTO 4030
4170  IF K$=CHR$(71) THEN PUT (SX,SY),A12,XOR:SX=XL:SY=YT:PUT (SX,SY),A12,XOR:GO
TO 4030
4180  IF K$=CHR$(73) THEN PUT (SX,SY),A12,XOR:SX=XR:SY=YT:PUT (SX,SY),A12,XOR:GO
TO 4030
4190  IF K$=CHR$(81) THEN PUT (SX,SY),A12,XOR:SX=XR:SY=YB:PUT (SX,SY),A12,XOR:GO
TO 4030
4200  IF K$=CHR$(79) THEN PUT (SX,SY),A12,XOR:SX=XL:SY=YB:PUT (SX,SY),A12,XOR:GO
TO 4030
4210  IF K$=CHR$(27) THEN PUT (SX,SY),A12,XOR:SOUND 250,.7:RETURN  '<ESC>
4220  IF K$=CHR$(13) THEN PUT (SX,SY),A12,XOR:GOSUB 4300:PCOPY 0,1:PUT (SX,SY),A
12,XOR:LOCATE 23,69:PRINT FRE(0):SOUND 250,.7:GOTO 4030  '<Enter> to implement c
ommand
4230  IF K$="1" THEN SYC=SYC+.25:LOCATE 18,22:PRINT SYC"  ":SOUND 250,.7:GOTO 40
30  'increment plan drawing height
4240  IF K$="2" THEN SYC=SYC-.25:LOCATE 18,22:PRINT SYC"  ":SOUND 250,.7:GOTO 40
30  'decrement plan drawing height
4250  GOTO 4030
4260  SOUND 250,.7:RETURN
4270  '_____
4280  '_____
4290  'module:  switcher for drawing functions
4300  ON T5 GOTO 4310,4320,4330
4310  GOSUB 4370:RETURN
4320  GOSUB 3940:RETURN
4330  GOSUB 3940:RETURN
4340  '_____
4350  '_____
4360  'module:  polyline function
4370  IF T6=0 THEN SXC=SX+7:SZC=SY+3:PSET (SXC,SZC),C:T6=1:SXP=SXC:SZP=SZC:SYP=S
YC:RETURN ELSE 4380
4380  SXC=SX+7:SZC=SY+3:LINE (SXP,SZP)-(SXC,SZC),C:GOSUB 4430:GOSUB 4550:SXP=SXC
:SZP=SZC:SYP=SYC:RETURN
4390  '
4400  '_____GENERATE 3D MODEL_____
4410  '
4420  'module:  generate 3D model
4430  WINDOW SCREEN (-399,-299)-(400,300):VIEW SCREEN (251,19)-(637,186)  'clip
3D viewing area
4440  X=(.404858*SXP)-51:Z=(.9523809*SZP)-51:Y=SYP:GOSUB 4500:SX1=SX1+125:SY1=SY
1+3:PSET (SX1,SY1),C
4450  X=(.404858*SXC)-51:Z=(.9523809*SZC)-51:Y=SYC:GOSUB 4500:SX1=SX1+125:SY1=SY
1+3:LINE-(SX1,SY1),C
4460  WINDOW SCREEN (0,0)-(639,199):VIEW:RETURN
```

Fig. 26-2. (Continued from page 275.)

```
4470 '_____
4480 '_____
4490 'module:  perspective formulas
4500  X=(-1)*X:XA=CR1*X-SR1*Z:ZA=SR1*X+CR1*Z:X=CR2*XA+SR2*Y:YA=CR2*Y-SR2*XA:Z=CR
3*ZA-SR3*YA:Y=SR3*ZA+CR3*YA:X=X+MX:Y=Y+MY:Z=Z+MZ:SX1=D*X/Z:SY1=D*Y/Z:RETURN
4510 '
4520 '_____DATA FILE INPUT/OUTPUT_____
4530 '
4540 'module:  storage of graphics attributes in data file
4550  OPEN "A:KEYLAYER.CDF" FOR APPEND AS #1:WRITE #1,SXP,SZP,SXC,SZC,C,SYP,SYC:
CLOSE #1:RETURN
4560 '_____
4570 '
4580 'module:  retrieval of graphics attributes from data file
4590  OPEN "A:KEYLAYER.CDF" FOR INPUT AS #1
4600  INPUT #1,SXP,SZP,SXC,SZC,C,SYP,SYC   'dummy pass
4610  IF T3=1 THEN GOSUB 5460  'is grid toggled on?
4620  IF T4=1 THEN GOSUB 5540  'is gnomon toggled on?
4630  IF EOF(1) THEN CLOSE #1:RETURN
4640  INPUT #1,SXP,SZP,SXC,SZC,C,SYP,SYC:GOSUB 4680:GOTO 4630
4650 '
4660 '_____
4670 'module:  regen function for 2D/3D modes
4680  LINE (SXP,SZP)-(SXC,SZC),C:GOSUB 4430:RETURN   'polyline regen
4690 '
4700 '_____ADJUST VIEW PARAMETERS_____
4710 '
4720 'module:  adjust Distance to viewpoint
4730  SOUND 250,.7
4740  K$=INKEY$
4750  IF K$="=" THEN MZ=MZ-10:GOSUB 5180:GOTO 4740
4760  IF K$="-" THEN MZ=MZ+10:GOSUB 5180:GOTO 4740
4770  IF K$=CHR$(13) THEN PCOPY 1,0:GOSUB 5180:VIEW SCREEN (2,19)-(248,123):CLS:
VIEW SCREEN (251,19)-(637,186):CLS:VIEW:GOSUB 4590:LOCATE 23,57:PRINT "Free memo
ry:":SOUND 860,2:SOUND 800,2:RETURN
4780  GOTO 4740
4790 '
4800 '_____
4810 'module:  adjust Elevation of viewpoint
4820  SOUND 250,.7
4830  K$=INKEY$
4840  IF K$="=" THEN MY=MY-2:GOSUB 5180:GOTO 4830
4850  IF K$="-" THEN MY=MY+2:GOSUB 5180:GOTO 4830
4860  IF K$=CHR$(13) THEN PCOPY 1,0:GOSUB 5180:VIEW SCREEN (2,19)-(248,123):CLS:
VIEW SCREEN (251,19)-(637,186):CLS:VIEW:GOSUB 4590:LOCATE 23,57:PRINT "Free memo
ry:":SOUND 860,2:SOUND 800,2:RETURN
4870  GOTO 4830
4880 '
4890 '_____
4900 'module:  adjust Yaw angle
4910  SOUND 250,.7
4920  K$=INKEY$:IF LEN(K$)=2 THEN K$=RIGHT$(K$,1) ELSE 4950
4930  IF K$=CHR$(77) THEN R1=R1-.17953:GOSUB 5180:GOTO 4920
```

Fig. 26-2. (Continued from page 276.)

```
4940    IF K$=CHR$(75) THEN R1=R1+.17953:GOSUB 5180:GOTO 4920
4950    IF K$=CHR$(13) THEN SR1=SIN(R1):CR1=COS(R1):PCOPY 1,0:GOSUB 5180:VIEW SCRE
EN (2,19)-(248,123):CLS:VIEW SCREEN (251,19)-(637,186):CLS:VIEW:GOSUB 4590:LOCAT
E 23,57:PRINT "Free memory:":SOUND 860,2:SOUND 800,2:RETURN
4960    GOTO 4920
4970   '_____
4980   '
4990   'module:  adjust Roll angle
5000    SOUND 250,.7
5010    K$=INKEY$:IF LEN(K$)=2 THEN K$=RIGHT$(K$,1) ELSE 5040
5020    IF K$=CHR$(77) THEN R2=R2+.08727:GOSUB 5180:GOTO 5010
5030    IF K$=CHR$(75) THEN R2=R2-.08727:GOSUB 5180:GOTO 5010
5040    IF K$=CHR$(13) THEN SR2=SIN(R2):CR2=COS(R2):PCOPY 1,0:GOSUB 5180:VIEW SCRE
EN (2,19)-(248,123):CLS:VIEW SCREEN (251,19)-(637,186):CLS:VIEW:GOSUB 4590:LOCAT
E 23,57:PRINT "Free memory:":SOUND 860,2:SOUND 800,2:RETURN
5050    GOTO 5010
5060   '_____
5070   '
5080   'module:  adjust Pitch angle
5090    SOUND 250,.7
5100    K$=INKEY$:IF LEN(K$)=2 THEN K$=RIGHT$(K$,1) ELSE 5130
5110    IF K$=CHR$(72) THEN R3=R3-.08727:GOSUB 5180:GOTO 5100
5120    IF K$=CHR$(80) THEN R3=R3+.08727:GOSUB 5180:GOTO 5100
5130    IF K$=CHR$(13) THEN SR3=SIN(R3):CR3=COS(R3):PCOPY 1,0:GOSUB 5180:VIEW SCRE
EN (2,19)-(248,123):CLS:VIEW SCREEN (251,19)-(637,186):CLS:VIEW:GOSUB 4590:LOCAT
E 23,57:PRINT "Free memory:":SOUND 860,2:SOUND 800,2:RETURN
5140    GOTO 5100
5150   '
5160   '_____REFRESH ALPHANUMERICS_____
5170   '
5180    LOCATE 18,22:PRINT SYC:LOCATE 19,21:PRINT (-1*MZ):LOCATE 20,22:PRINT (-1*M
Y):LOCATE 21,12:PRINT R1:LOCATE 22,13:PRINT R2:LOCATE 23,14:PRINT R3:LINE (8,185
)-(243,185),C:RETURN
5190   '
5200   '_____ADJUST OPTIONS_____
5210   '
5220   'module:  change the drawing color
5230    SOUND 250,.7
5240    IF C=C7 THEN C=C4:GOSUB 5180:RETURN
5250    IF C=C4 THEN C=C1:GOSUB 5180:RETURN
5260    IF C=C1 THEN C=C3:GOSUB 5180:RETURN
5270    IF C=C3 THEN C=C2:GOSUB 5180:RETURN
5280    IF C=C2 THEN C=C5:GOSUB 5180:RETURN
5290    IF C=C5 THEN C=C6:GOSUB 5180:RETURN
5300    IF C=C6 THEN C=C8:GOSUB 5180:RETURN
5310    IF C=C8 THEN C=C15:GOSUB 5180:RETURN
5320    IF C=C15 THEN C=C9:GOSUB 5180:RETURN
5330    IF C=C9 THEN C=C12:GOSUB 5180:RETURN
5340    IF C=C12 THEN C=C10:GOSUB 5180:RETURN
5350    IF C=C10 THEN C=C14:GOSUB 5180:RETURN
5360    IF C=C14 THEN C=C0:GOSUB 5180:RETURN
5370    IF C=C0 THEN C=C7:GOSUB 5180:RETURN
5380    GOSUB 5180:RETURN
```

Fig. 26-2.   (Continued from page 277.)

```
5390 '_____
5400 '
5410 'module:  toggle 2D grid on/off
5420  IF T3=0 THEN T3=1:SOUND 250,.7:RETURN ELSE IF T3=1 THEN T3=0:SOUND 250,.7:
RETURN
5430 '
5440 '_____
5450 'module:  create grid if toggled on
5460  T=1:WHILE T<249:LINE (T,19)-(T,123),C8:T=T+J10:WEND:T=19:WHILE T<123:LINE
(2,T)-(248,T),C8:T=T+J11:WEND:LINE (122,53)-(132,53),C6:LINE (127,51)-(127,55),C
6:RETURN
5470 '
5480 '_____
5490 'module:  toggle 3D gnomon on/off (x,y,z axis display)
5500  IF T4=0 THEN T4=1:SOUND 250,.7:RETURN ELSE IF T4=1 THEN T4=0:SOUND 250,.7:
RETURN
5510 '_____
5520 '
5530 'module:  create gnomon if toggled on
5540  WINDOW SCREEN (-399,-299)-(400,300):VIEW SCREEN (251,19)-(637,186)
5550  X=30:Z=0:Y=0:GOSUB 4500:SX1=SX1+125:SY1=SY1+3:PSET (SX1,SY1),C2:X=0:Z=0:Y=
0:GOSUB 4500:SX1=SX1+125:SY1=SY1+3:LINE-(SX1,SY1),C2:X=-30:Z=0:Y=0:GOSUB 4500:SX
1=SX1+125:SY1=SY1+3:LINE-(SX1,SY1),C8  'x-axis
5560  X=0:Z=0:Y=30:GOSUB 4500:SX1=SX1+125:SY1=SY1+3:PSET (SX1,SY1),C4:X=0:Z=0:Y=
0:GOSUB 4500:SX1=SX1+125:SY1=SY1+3:LINE-(SX1,SY1),C4:X=0:Z=0:Y=-30:GOSUB 4500:SX
1=SX1+125:SY1=SY1+3:LINE-(SX1,SY1),C8  'y-axis
5570  X=0:Z=30:Y=0:GOSUB 4500:SX1=SX1+125:SY1=SY1+3:PSET (SX1,SY1),C1:X=0:Z=0:Y=
0:GOSUB 4500:SX1=SX1+125:SY1=SY1+3:LINE-(SX1,SY1),C1:X=0:Z=-30:Y=0:GOSUB 4500:SX
1=SX1+125:SY1=SY1+3:LINE-(SX1,SY1),C8  'z-axis
5580  WINDOW SCREEN (0,0)-(639,199):VIEW:RETURN
5590 '_____
5600 '
5610  END
```

Fig. 26-2. (Continued from page 278.)

27

Wire-Frame CAD Documentation— A User's Guide

This chapter contains the User's Guide for *YOUR MICROCOMPUTER 3D CAD DESIGNER*, a multifunction 3D drawing and modeling program. The complete source code appears in the previous chapter. This chapter contains the following sections: Introduction, System Requirements, Starting And Stopping The Program, How to Use The Program, and Sample Sessions.

INTRODUCTION

YOUR MICROCOMPUTER 3D CAD DESIGNER gives you the tools you need to create actual 3D models with your personal computer. As you create a plan view in the 2D drawing area, the program automatically generates a 3D perspective view of the model in the 3D viewing window. The comprehensive User's Guide gets you started right away by providing tutorial sessions complete with photographs of sample drawings created by the program.

Drawing tools include a powerful 2D/3D polyline function, change color capability, rotation and zoom 3D capabilities, and a regen function (which provides regeneration). A comprehensive set of Options features gives you the ability to toggle an optional 2D drawing grid and a 3D gnomon (xyz axis system).

This program contains powerful routines to save your drawings on disk as binary image files. You can retrieve your drawings from disk for later editing or for printing with a third-party graphics printing utility.

YOUR MICROCOMPUTER 3D CAD DESIGNER gives you high-performance 3D modeling capabilities, using your standard keyboard for input.

SYSTEM REQUIREMENTS

To run the program, you need an IBM PC, XT, AT, RT, PS/2, or any IBM-compatible personal computer equipped with an EGA or VGA graphics adapter. Also required is either a standard color display (SCD), enhanced color display (ECD), analog display (PS/2 or equivalent), or variable frequency display (Multisync, Multiscan, or equivalent).

You also need IBM PC-DOS or Microsoft MS-DOS. A version of BASIC which supports EGA graphics is required. *YOUR MICROCOMPUTER 3D CAD DESIGNER* runs on personal computers equipped with two disk drives. The program can be easily modified to use a hard disk or a simulated disk in RAM. Refer to Chapter 28 for guidance.

This version of the program is intended for BASIC interpreters which support EGA graphics, including IBM BASICA and GW-BASIC. A Turbo BASIC version of the program appears in Appendix E.

If you are using a CGA (color/graphics adapter) or MCGA, a version of this program already modified to run on these adapters appears in Appendix G. If you are using an IBM PCjr or Tandy, use the version of the program which appears in Appendix H.

STARTING AND STOPPING THE PROGRAM

Before you use the program, you should create a back-up copy of the program on a separate disk. Use the back-up disk for your drawing sessions. Store the original disk in a safe place. Remember that anything you do not have backed up you are going to lose eventually.

Starting The Program

To start the program, load CAD-1.BAS under your BASIC interpreter. At the OK prompt, press F2 to run the program. (If you are using a CGA, load and run CAD-CGA1.BAS. If you are using a PCjr, load and run CAD-JR1.BAS.)

Using Disk Drives

YOUR MICROCOMPUTER 3D CAD DESIGNER expects to be loaded from drive A. During your drawing session, it saves your keystrokes in a data file using drive A. You can make the program run much quicker if you use a hard disk . . . even faster if you use a simulated disk in RAM.

To change the drive to which the data files are written, alter the drive letter in lines 1600, 4550, and 4590. (If you are using the CGA or PCjr version from the appendices, follow the instructions in the appendix.)

YOUR MICROCOMPUTER 3D CAD DESIGNER expects to use drive B to save image files and to retrieve image files. Image files contain your drawings. During your drawing session you should have a blank disk in drive B. If you wish to save and retrieve your drawings to/from another drive, you must change the drive letters in lines 2470, 2480, 2490, 2500, 2580, 2590, 2600, and 2610. (If you are using the CGA or PCjr version from the appendices, follow the instructions in the appendix.)

Refer back to Chapter 14 and Chapter 15 for further guidance in installing a simulated disk on your personal computer.

Stopping The Program

There are three different ways to cleanly exit the program. Each method returns you to the 80-column text mode of the BASIC editor.

Method One. At any time and in any routine during program execution, you can press F2 to exit the program. F2 is a hot key which is managed by BASIC itself.

Method Two. When you are located anywhere on the main menu bar, you can press Alt-Q to exit the program. Alt-Q is a hot key combination which is managed by the program, rather than by BASIC. Hold down the Alt key and press Q.

Method Three. Use the arrow keys to select the Quit pull-down menu. Select the Quit function from the menu to exit the program. This method is managed by the menu system of the program.

HOW TO USE THE PROGRAM

Refer to Fig. 27-1 for the keyboard layout used by *YOUR MICROCOMPUTER 3D CAD DESIGNER*. The Enter key is used to implement a function. The arrow keys are used to navigate the cursor around the 2D drawing area. The Esc key is used to discard the current function and to back up through the menu system.

Using the Menu System

When you are on the main menu bar, use the left-arrow and the right-arrow keys to move the panning cursor to the desired selection. Then press Enter to invoke the pull-down menu. Use the down-arrow key to move the scrolling cursor through the selections on the pull-down menu. The cursor will wrap back around to the top selection after passing the bottom selection. Use the Enter key to implement your selection. Select Menu Bar or use the Esc key to discard the pull-down menu and to return to the main menu bar.

To move from one pull-down menu to another, you must first return to the main menu bar and then use the panning cursor to select another pull-down menu. You cannot jump immediately from one pull-down menu to another.

To begin drawing, choose Line from the Draw menu. Use the arrow keys to move the cursor around the 2D drawing area in the upper left section of the screen. Use the <1> and <2> keys to set the current elevation, which is displayed in the view specifications section, located at the lower left corner of the screen. Use <Enter> to set the endpoints for the polyline. The 3D model is automatically constructed in the 3D window at the right side of the screen. Remember, the 2D drawing area gives you a bird's eye view of your drawing, looking straight down at it.

Using the File Menu

The File menu contains the following functions:

Name Function. The Name function in the File menu allows you to define your own file names for image files. When you use Enter to choose the Name function, a dialog box is displayed. You may type in any 8-character file name, using the uppercase letters from A to Z. When you type the eighth character, the new file name is displayed at the file name bar located at the top of the screen. During the input process, you may press Esc at any time to keep the original file name.

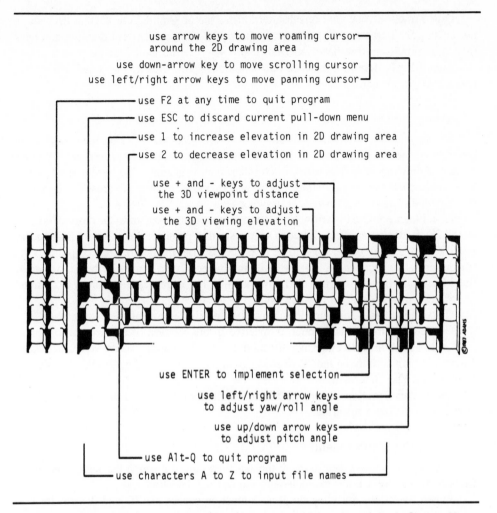

use arrow keys to move roaming cursor
around the 2D drawing area

use down-arrow key to move scrolling cursor

use left/right arrow keys to move panning cursor

use F2 at any time to quit program

use ESC to discard current pull-down menu

use 1 to increase elevation in 2D drawing area

use 2 to decrease elevation in 2D drawing area

use + and - keys to adjust
the 3D viewpoint distance

use + and - keys to adjust
the 3D viewing elevation

use ENTER to implement selection

use left/right arrow keys
to adjust yaw/roll angle

use up/down arrow keys
to adjust pitch angle

use Alt-Q to quit program

use characters A to Z to input file names

Fig. 27-1. Keystroke controls for the interactive 3D wire-frame CAD program listing in Chapter 26.

Save Function. The Save function is used to store your current drawing on disk as a binary image file. Five images can be saved on a 5.25-inch diskette. More images can be saved on a hard disk. Refer to the discussion earlier in this chapter if you wish to use a drive other than drive B for saving and retrieving image files.

The Save function is not error-trapped. A disk I/O error caused by an empty disk drive will crash the program and your current drawing will be lost.

Load Function. The Load function in the File menu will download a previously saved image file from disk and display it on the screen. The Load function expects to find the image file in drive B. Refer to the discussion earlier in this chapter if you wish to invoke a drive other than drive B for saving and retrieving image files.

When using the Load function, you must ensure that a disk containing the desired image file is present in the drive. The Load function is not error-trapped. A disk I/O error caused by an empty disk drive or a missing file will crash the program.

Quit Function. The Quit function terminates the program. Your current drawing is not saved prior to the exit. If you wish to display or edit your current drawing at a later time, you should use the Save function before you use the Quit function.

Menu Bar Function. The Menu Bar function discards the File menu and returns you to the main menu bar.

Using the Draw Menu

The functions of the Draw pull-down menu are accessed by using the down-arrow key to move the scrolling cursor to the desired selection. Press Enter to activate the cursor in the 2D drawing area. The roaming crosshair cursor is controlled by the arrow keys. You can also use the Home, PgDn, PgUp, and End keys to snap the crosshair cursor to the corresponding corner of the 2D drawing area.

Line Function. Use the arrow keys to move the crosshair cursor to the desired location on the 2D drawing area. Press Enter to set the starting point for the polyline. Subsequent Enter keystrokes will cause a line to be constructed from the last-referenced point to the current crosshair location. A 3D line will simultaneously be drawn in the 3D window. Press Esc at any time to return to the Draw menu. <1> increases elevation by 0.25 units. <2> decrements elevation by 0.25 units.

Curve Function. This function is inactive in this version of the program.

Circle Function. This function is inactive in this version of the program.

Undo Function. Select the Undo function to erase the graphics which you have created during your last activity on the 2D drawing area. The corresponding graphics on the 3D window will also be erased.

Menu Bar Function. Select the Menu Bar function to discard the Draw menu and to return to the main menu bar.

Using the Display Menu

Use the down-arrow key to move the scrolling cursor through the selections on the Display menu. Press Enter to implement the desired selection.

Regen Function. Selecting the Regen function causes the 2D and 3D windows to be cleared to black. The program then retrieves the graphics primitives created by your previous keystrokes from the .CDF data file and uses those primitives to redraw your 2D and 3D models. The 3D model is drawn in the position defined by the viewing parameters in the View menu.

Clear Function. The Clear function clears the 2D and 3D windows to black.

Menu Bar Function. The Menu Bar function discards the Display menu and returns you to the main menu bar.

Using the View Menu

Use the down-arrow key to move the scrolling cursor through the selections on the View menu. Press Enter to implement the desired selection.

Distance +/− Function. Press the plus or minus key to increase or decrease the distance from the 3D model to the viewpoint. The distance value is displayed in the view specifications window. Press Enter to regenerate your drawing using the new distance value and then return you to the main menu bar.

Elevation +/− Function. Press the plus or minus key to increase or decrease the elevation of the 3D model, relative to the viewpoint position. The elevation value is displayed in the view specifications window. Press Enter to regenerate your drawing using the new elevation value and then return you to the main menu bar.

Yaw Function. Press the left-arrow or right-arrow key to rotate the 3D model about the compass heading. The yaw value is displayed in the view specifications window. The yaw value is expressed in radians, not degrees. 6.28319 or 0 is due north. 1.57079 is east. 3.14159 is south. 4.71239 is west. Press Enter to regenerate your drawing using the new yaw value and then return you to the main menu bar.

Roll Function. Press the left-arrow or right-arrow key to rotate the 3D model clockwise or counterclockwise. The roll value is displayed in the view specifications window. The value is expressed in radians, not degrees. The value 6.28319, or 0, is zero degrees The value 1.57079 is 90 degrees. The value 3.14159 is 180 degrees, and 4.71239 is 270 degrees. Press Enter to regenerate your drawing using the new roll value and then return you to the main menu bar.

Pitch Function. Press the up-arrow or down-arrow key to tilt the 3D model towards you or away from you. The pitch value is displayed in the view specifications window. The value is expressed in radians, not degrees. Therefore, 6.28319 or 0 is due north, 1.57079 is east, 3.14159 is south, and 4.71239 is west. Press Enter to regenerate your drawing using the new pitch value and then return you to the main menu bar.

Menu Bar Function. Selecting the Menu Bar function discards the View menu and returns you to the main menu bar.

Using the Options Menu

Use the down-arrow key to move the scrolling cursor through the selections in the Options menu. Press Enter to implement the desired selection.

Set Snap Function. The Set Snap function is inactive.

Set Grid Function. The Set Grid function is inactive.

Grid On/Off Function. Selecting this function will toggle the grid on if it is off and will toggle the grid off if it is on. The Regen function will create a grid in the 2D drawing area if this function is toggled on, otherwise no grid will be drawn during a regeneration of your drawing.

Gnomon On/Off Function. Selecting this function will toggle the xyz axis system on and off. The Regen function will create a gnomon (xyz axis) in the 3D window if this function is toggled on, otherwise no gnomon will be created during a regeneration of your drawing. The xyz axis is drawn using the current view parameters defined by the View menu.

Set Color Function. Press Enter to cycle through the available drawing colors. The current drawing color is displayed as a line at the bottom of the view specifications panel at the lower left corner of the screen. Keep pressing Enter until the desired color is identified. Use the down-arrow key to leave this option.

Menu Bar Function. The Menu Bar function discards the Options menu and returns control to the main menu bar.

SAMPLE SESSIONS

YOUR MICROCOMPUTER 3D CAD DESIGNER is capable of creating complex 3D graphic images, using only your keyboard for input. Your drawings can be saved on disk using the program, or you can use a third-party graphics printing utility (such as Pizazz, see Appendix F) to print your drawings on a dot-matrix printer or an ink-jet printer.

Product Design: Office Chair

The image shown in Fig. 27-2 was created in about 40 minutes using *YOUR MICROCOMPUTER 3D CAD DESIGNER*. First, the seat of the chair was drawn. The plus key was used to increment the elevation slightly before a second outline was drawn in order to give the seat some thickness. Notice how vertical lines were used to connect the corners of the two levels of the seat to reduce ambiguity in the drawing.

Next, the View menu was used to adjust the viewing parameters until the chair's seat seemed appropriately rotated in the 3D window. The pedestal support was then constructed, making active use of the plus and minus elevation keys. Then the cross-braces were added. While the drawing was in progress, mistakes were corrected by changing the drawing color to black, covering the offending line, changing the drawing color back to white, and drawing the corrected line.

The backrest was tricky, calling for some artistic judgment. The rounded corners were created by simultaneously moving the cursor and adjusting the elevation. A notepad was used to keep track of how many cursor steps were needed with each elevation step; this information was used when creating the subsequent three rounded corners.

Architectural Design: House

The image shown in Fig. 27-3 was created in about 65 minutes using *YOUR MICROCOMPUTER 3D CAD DESIGNER*. Complicated drawings like this must be created

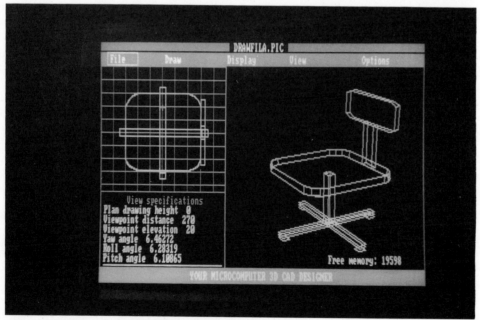

Fig. 27-2. Design and display of everyday items can be easily achieved with the interactive 3D wire-frame CAD program listing in Chapter 26.

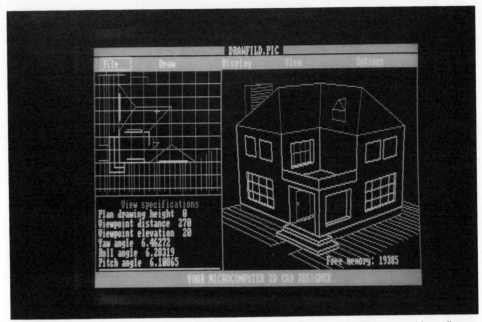

Fig. 27-3. Architectural design using the radial pre-sort method of hidden surface removal is easily accomplished using the interactive 3D wire-frame CAD program listing in Chapter 26.

using the block method. First, the major lines which define the major walls and other large surfaces are drawn. A notepad is kept nearby to keep track of elevation values for various windows, steps, and so on. The View menu is used to rotate the image to a pleasing viewpoint after the major lines have been blocked into place.

The roof details were then completed. Next, the handrail for the deck was finished. The meeting of the deck flooring and the far walls was created incrementally, inching along until the line just intersected the handrail. The same technique was used when creating the front door area.

The doors and windows were added next. Again, elevation values were jotted down on the notepad to ensure that windows and doors were placed at corresponding heights on the walls.

At numerous points during the drawing process the image was saved to disk. On more than one occasion, I was forced to retrieve the image from disk because of serious mistakes on the active drawing. Rather than spend time using black lines to erase the offending lines, it proved quicker to retrieve the earlier version from disk and continue work from that stage.

Engineering Design: Widget

The wireframe image in Fig. 27-4 was created in about 20 minutes using *YOUR MICROCOMPUTER 3D CAD DESIGNER*. Heavy use of the plus and minus keys was made while the surface planes that make up the widget were being created. No effort was made to remove the hidden lines or hidden surfaces.

The witness lines and dimension arrows were created manually, after the widget was complete.

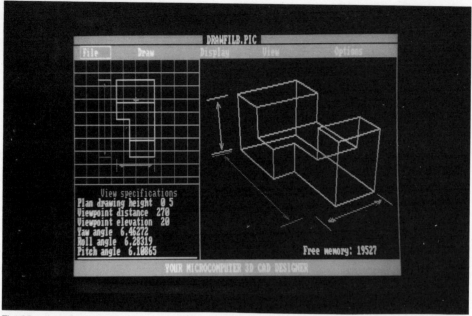

Fig. 27-4. A typical widget in 3D wire-frame form, created using the interactive 3D wire-frame CAD program listing in Chapter 26.

The image in Fig. 27-5 was modified from the previous image in about 10 minutes. The Options menu was used to change the active drawing color to black. The cursor was then inched along the appropriate lines in the 2D drawing, until the line had been clipped back or eliminated, as the case may be.

The resulting solid model is much easier to understand than the wireframe version, although wireframe versions are often essential during the preliminary design phase.

Graphics: Geometric Filled Characters

The image in Fig. 27-6 was created in about 30 minutes using *YOUR MICROCOMPUTER 3D CAD DESIGNER*. First, the outline for the characters was created in the 2D drawing area. Then the View menu was used to rotate the characters until a pleasing perspective was obtained.

The Options menu was used to change the active drawing color while the rainbow colored lines were drawn around the characters. Small errors where the colored lines clipped the geometric characters were corrected by redrawing the character outlines when the drawing was finished.

Similar techniques can be used to create simpler, line-based characters which can be used to label your drawings. The labels will be rotated along with your actual drawing, because they have been created in 3D space.

WORKING WITH THE PROGRAM

You might find it easier to work with *YOUR MICROCOMPUTER 3D CAD DESIGNER* if you use Regen to display a 2D drawing grid and a 3D xyz axis before you being creating

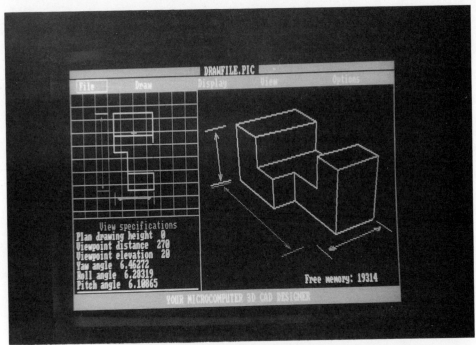

Fig. 27-5. A typical widget transformed from 3D wire-frame to 3D solid model by using intuitive line trimming. Image created by the interactive 3D wire-frame CAD program listing in Chapter 26.

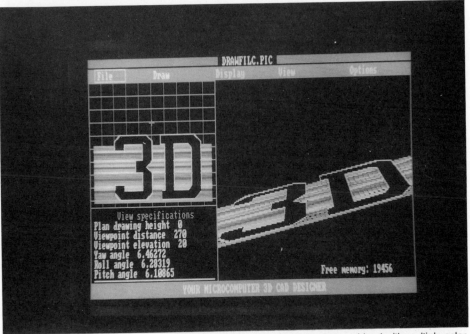

Fig. 27-6. Oversized alphanumerics (geometric filled outline fonts) can be combined with multiple-color graphics using the interactive 3D wire-frame CAD program listing in Chapter 26.

your model. When you first start up the program, use the Options menu to toggle on the Grid function and the Gnomon function. Then, go to the Display menu and select Regen. The program will use the regeneration routine to recreate your drawing (all black, so far) and to create a grid and xyz axis system. The grid provides a reference point for your 2D drawing and the gnomon makes it easier to understand where your first few lines are located in 3D space.

If you are planning a complicated 3D drawing, you should first define the scale of your model. You can do this by drawing a 3D cube which will just contain your proposed model. Then, use the View menu to rotate and scale the cube until you are satisfied with the 3D image on the screen. Jot down the values which are displayed in the view specifications window. Then exit the program and restart it, setting the view parameters before you being work on your actual model.

SUMMARY

This chapter provides a concise User's Guide for the powerful 3D modeling program, *YOUR MICROCOMPUTER 3D CAD MODELER*. The complete source code for this program appears in Chapter 26.

The next chapter provides an analysis of how the program works.

28

Wire-Frame CAD Analysis—How the Program Works

The source code for *YOUR MICROCOMPUTER 3D CAD DESIGNER*, presented in the preceding chapter, is based upon the drafting program in Chapter 21. The same menu system and function switching principles apply to both programs. The 3D modeling program, however, uses only the upper left corner of the screen for 2D drawing. Most of the rest of the screen is used for the 3D model, which the program automatically generates from the 2D drawing.

LOGIC FLOW

The logic flowchart for the start-up portion of *YOUR MICROCOMPUTER 3D CAD DESIGNER* is shown in Fig. 28-1. This flow of logic is similar to two previous demonstration programs, *YOUR MICROCOMPUTER SKETCH PAD* and *YOUR MICROCOMPUTER DRAFTING TABLE*. In this program, however, both the start-up module and the runtime module have been integrated into a single program.

The runtime module is depicted in Fig. 28-2. This flowchart is similar in layout and implementation to the runtime flowchart for the drafting program in Chapter 21. (Go back and review Chapter 23 to see how the drafting program works, if you have not already done so.) Note how the Regen function in the Display menu calls four routines to draw the grid and gnomon, retrieve primitives from the data file, generate the 2D drawing, and produce the 3D drawing. Note also how the Line function in the Draw menu calls two routines to produce the 3D drawing and to save the line's attributes in the data file.

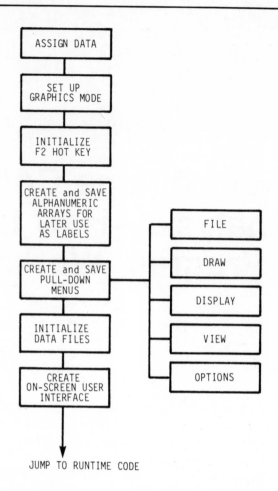

Fig. 28-1. Logic flowchart for the start-up section of the interactive 3D wire-frame CAD program listing in Chapter 26.

Drawing Functions

The Draw menu control routine is located at lines 2860 through 3090. The algorithm used is identical to previous programs. Refer back to Chapter 10 for detailed discussion of menu management. The crosshair cursor control routine is located at lines 3980 through 4260. The switcher is at lines 4290 through 4330.

Note the structure of the polyline routine at lines 4360 through 4380. In addition to creating the line on the 2D drawing area, the routine calls the subroutine at line 4420. This subroutine first uses the WINDOW SCREEN and VIEW instructions to clip the 3D window as a viewport of the screen, and then draws the 3D model. The 2D image is drawn with the x and z coordinates. The y-coordinate is used to add the element of elevation when the 3D model is drawn. (Note how these coordinates and the drawing color are saved in the data file in line 4550.)

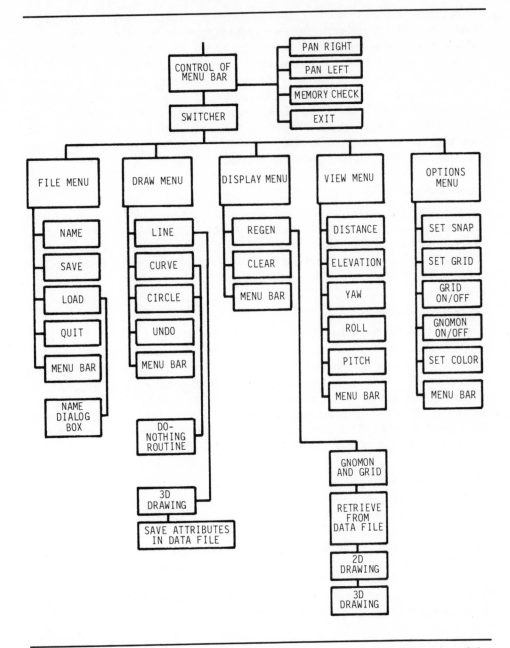

Fig. 28-2. Logic flowchart for the runtime section of the interactive 3D wire-frame CAD program listing in Chapter 26.

The math in line 4440 is used to translate the 2D coordinates to the world coordinates used by the 3D formulas. In concept, the 2D drawing which was created in the upper left corner of the screen must be logically moved to the center of the screen before it can be drawn in 3D.

Note how the SX1 and SY1 display coordinates are increased by 125 and 3, respectively. This moves them to the center of the 3D window, which itself is not centered on the screen. Try changing 125 to 50 and watch the result when you work on a 3D drawing.

After drawing the 3D line on the screen, the 3D subroutine uses the WINDOW SCREEN and VIEW instructions to return to the 2D clipping parameters. This occurs in line 4460. This is a key operating technique for this program. By carefully flipping back and forth between the 2D and 3D windows, a *dynamic graphics environment* (one that seems to be doing two things at once) can be maintained. (If you are using a programming language which does not provide window-mapping or viewport-mapping routines, you can refer to the mapping algorithms provided in Appendix A.)

VIEW PARAMETERS

The code which allows you to modify the rotation and translation parameters for the 3D model is located at lines 4720 through 5140. Notice how the keyboard loops are set up to permit continued adjustment of the R1, R2, or R3 factors until the Enter key is pressed. Each routine calls the subroutine at line 5180 which refreshes the values being displayed in the view specifications window on the screen.

GRID AND GNOMON

The routine that draws the 2D grid is located at lines 5450 through 5460. The WHILE . . . WEND construct is used to continue drawing the crosshatched lines until the limits of the 2D drawing area are reached. The variables J10 and J11, which define the spacing between the lines of the grid, were defined during program start-up in line 560.

The module that draws the gnomon is located at lines 5530 through 5580. Note how the T4 runtime flag was checked earlier in line 4620 during Regen to see if the gnomon was toggled on or off. The runtime flag was set at line 5500. This is the same technique used to control the display or non-display of the 2D grid.

GENERAL NOTES

When you start a new session with this program, the previous data file is overwritten. By referring to the source code for the drafting program in Chapter 21, you can easily add a routine during start-up to give the user a choice in this matter. If the previous data file is left intact, you can use Regen to recreate the drawing you were working on in a previous session.

If you wish to redirect input and output for the data file to a drive other than drive A, you can simply alter the drive letter in lines 1600, 4550, and 4590. Refer to Chapter 14 and Chapter 15 for further discussion of data files and simulated disks in RAM.

SUMMARY

In this chapter you learned about the 3D routines that differentiate this program from the drafting program discussed in earlier chapters. You saw how careful control of the windowing and viewport functions could sustain a dual 2D and 3D graphics environment on the display screen.

The next chapter provides the complete source code for a 3D CAD program which can produce solid, fully shaded 3D models, with automatic removal of hidden surfaces.

29

Program Listing—
Your Microcomputer 3D
CAD Modeler

This chapter contains the complete source code for *YOUR MICROCOMPUTER 3D CAD MODELER*, a powerful 3D modeling program capable of producing fully shaded, solid 3D models with automatic hidden surface removal. The photograph in Fig. 29-1 illustrates the start-up display produced by the program.

YOUR MICROCOMPUTER 3D CAD MODELER is designed to run on IBM-compatible personal computers equipped with an EGA or a VGA graphics adapter. The program listing in Fig. 29-2 runs in the 640×200 16-color mode. A QuickBASIC version of the program listing is provided in Appendix E.

USER'S GUIDE

A detailed User's Guide for *YOUR MICROCOMPUTER 3D CAD MODELER* is provided in the next chapter. The User's Guide includes photographs of advanced, fully shaded, solid 3D models produced by the program listing in this chapter. An analysis of the program's algorithms appears in Chapter 31.

HARDWARE/SOFTWARE COMPATIBILITY

The program listing in this chapter was developed and tested on an IBM PC equipped with an EGA, using IBM BASICA 3.21. The program will run on VGA-equipped PS/2 computers using IBM BASICA 3.30. The program will run on any IBM-compatible personal computer equipped with an EGA and which uses a BASIC interpreter that supports EGA graphics.

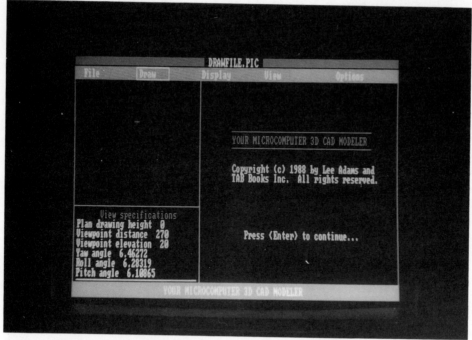

Fig. 29-1. Start-up display image generated by the interactive 3D solid model CAD program listing in Fig. 29-2.

If you are using QuickBASIC or Turbo BASIC, read Appendix E. A QuickBASIC version of the program appears in that appendix.

If you are using a CGA (color/graphics adapter) or an MCGA, you might want to read Appendix G for guidance in converting this program. If you are using an IBM PCjr or a Tandy, refer to Appendix H.

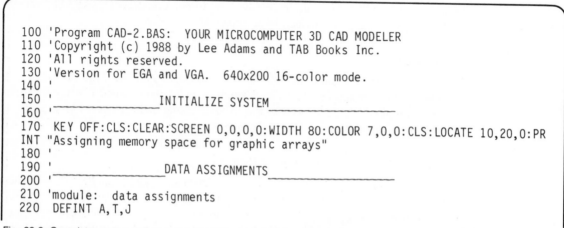

```
100 'Program CAD-2.BAS:  YOUR MICROCOMPUTER 3D CAD MODELER
110 'Copyright (c) 1988 by Lee Adams and TAB Books Inc.
120 'All rights reserved.
130 'Version for EGA and VGA.  640x200 16-color mode.
140 '
150 '_____INITIALIZE SYSTEM_____
160 '
170  KEY OFF:CLS:CLEAR:SCREEN 0,0,0,0:WIDTH 80:COLOR 7,0,0:CLS:LOCATE 10,20,0:PR
INT "Assigning memory space for graphic arrays"
180 '
190 '_____DATA ASSIGNMENTS_____
200 '
210 'module:  data assignments
220  DEFINT A,T,J
```

Fig. 29-2. Complete source code for an interactive, menu-driven, keyboard-controlled, 3D solid model CAD program. This version is for the EGA and VGA. See Appendix E for the QuickBASIC version.

```
230  DIM A1(631):DIM A2(150):DIM A3(150):DIM A4(150):DIM A5(150):DIM A6(150)  't
emporary arrays for screen template
240  DIM A7(177)  'array for panning cursor
250  DIM A8(1793)  'array for Options menu
260  DIM A9(21)  'array for scrolling cursor
270  DIM A10(1057)  'array for File menu
280  DIM A11(953):DIM A11C(953)  'for Name dialog box
290  DIM A12(29)  'array for roaming crosshair cursor
300  DIM A13(683)  'array for Display menu
310  DIM A14(1321)  'array for View menu
320  DIM A15(1057)  'array for Draw menu
330  C0=1:C1=2:C2=9:C3=7:C4=11:C5=5:C6=6:C7=4:C8=8:C9=3:C10=10:C12=12:C13=13:C14
=14:C15=15  'software color codes
340  C=C7:CE=C7  'drawing, boundary colors
350  CP=0  'preparatory color for line dithering
360  CC=0  'active color for line dithering
370  CD=&H0  'pattern for line dithering
380  T=0  'loop counter
390  T1=2  'selection flag for menu bar
400  T2=25  'flag for echo position of file menu input
410  T3=0  '2D grid on/off toggle
420  T4=0  '3D gnomon on/off toggle
430  T5=0  'flag for function switcher
440  T6=0  'iterative flag for plastic functions
450  T7=0  '3D shading on/off toggle
460  T8=1  'selection flag for menus
470  T9=0  'outlining on/off toggle
480  J=2:JS=J  'snap, temporary storage of snap value
490  J6=85:J7=19:J8=608:J9=186  'viewport dimensions for active drawing surface
on 640x200 screen
500  SX=122:SY=65  'crosshair array location
510  XL=2:XR=234:YT=19:YB=117  'left, right, top, bottom range of roaming crossh
air cursor
520  SXC=SX+7:SZC=SY+3:SYC=0  'center of crosshair cursor
530  SXP=0:SZP=0:SYP=0  'last referenced drawing point
540  SXF=0:SZF=0  'first drawing point for solid polygon
550  F$="DRAWFILE.PIC":F1$=F$:F2$="DRAWFILE"  'strings used to manipulate filena
me when saving images
560  V=0  'size of free memory in BASICA workspace
570  V1=1024  'threshold memory flag
580  SP=0:SP1=0:SP2=0:SP3=0  'used in plane equation formula for hidden surface
removal
590  SX1=0:SX2=0:SX3=0:SX4=0:SX5=0:SY1=0:SY2=0:SY3=0:SY4=0:SY5=0  'display coord
inates used in solid model polygon surface
600  X1=0:X2=0:X3=0:X4=0:X5=0:Y1=0:Y2=0:Y3=0:Y4=0:Y5=0:Z1=0:Z2=0:Z3=0:Z4=0:Z5=0
 'view coordinates used in solid model polygon surface
610  XN=0:YN=0:ZN=0:XU=0:YU=0:ZU=0:XV=0:YV=0:ZV=0:XW=0:YW=0:ZW=0  'used in shadi
ng routine
620  V2=0:V3=0:V4=0:V5=0:V7=0  'used to calculate shading matrix
630  V6=14  'range of shades available in 640x200 16-color mode
640  XI=.57735:YI=.57735:ZI=.57735  'xyz components of unit vector for angle of
incidence used in illumination algorithm
650  D=1200!:R1=6.46272:R2=6.28319:R3=6.10865:MX=0!:MY=-20!:MZ=-270!:SR1=SIN(R1)
```

Fig. 29-2. (Continued from page 296.)

```
  :SR2=SIN(R2):SR3=SIN(R3):CR1=COS(R1):CR2=COS(R2):CR3=COS(R3)  'variables used as
  input for perspective formulas
660   XA=0!:YA=0!:ZA=0!  'temporary variables used in perspective formulas
670   SXD=0:SYD=0  'output of perspective formulas
680   J10=25:J11=11  'horizontal, vertical spacing for grid
690   A1$=CHR$(&HDF)+CHR$(&H20)+CHR$(&H0)+CHR$(&H0)+CHR$(&HFD)+CHR$(&H2)+CHR$(&H0
  )+CHR$(&H0)+CHR$(&H7F)+CHR$(&H80)+CHR$(&H0)+CHR$(&H0)+CHR$(&HF7)+CHR$(&H8)+CHR$(
  &H0)+CHR$(&H0)
700   A2$=CHR$(&HBB)+CHR$(&H44)+CHR$(&H0)+CHR$(&H0)+CHR$(&HEE)+CHR$(&H11)+CHR$(&H
  0)+CHR$(&H0)
710   A3$=CHR$(&HAA)+CHR$(&H55)+CHR$(&H0)+CHR$(&H0)+CHR$(&H55)+CHR$(&HAA)+CHR$(&H
  0)+CHR$(&H0)
720   A4$=CHR$(&H44)+CHR$(&HBB)+CHR$(&H0)+CHR$(&H0)+CHR$(&H11)+CHR$(&HEE)+CHR$(&H
  0)+CHR$(&H0)
730   A5$=CHR$(&H20)+CHR$(&HFF)+CHR$(&H0)+CHR$(&H0)+CHR$(&H2)+CHR$(&HFF)+CHR$(&H0
  )+CHR$(&H0)+CHR$(&H80)+CHR$(&HFF)+CHR$(&H0)+CHR$(&H0)+CHR$(&H8)+CHR$(&HFF)+CHR$(
  &H0)+CHR$(&H0)
740   A6$=CHR$(&H44)+CHR$(&HFF)+CHR$(&H0)+CHR$(&H0)+CHR$(&H11)+CHR$(&HFF)+CHR$(&H
  0)+CHR$(&H0)
750   A7$=CHR$(&H55)+CHR$(&HFF)+CHR$(&H0)+CHR$(&H0)+CHR$(&HAA)+CHR$(&HFF)+CHR$(&H
  0)+CHR$(&H0)
760   A8$=CHR$(&HBB)+CHR$(&HFF)+CHR$(&H0)+CHR$(&H0)+CHR$(&HEE)+CHR$(&HFF)+CHR$(&H
  0)+CHR$(&H0)
770   A9$=CHR$(&HDF)+CHR$(&HDF)+CHR$(&H20)+CHR$(&H0)+CHR$(&HFD)+CHR$(&HFD)+CHR$(&
  H2)+CHR$(&H0)+CHR$(&H7F)+CHR$(&H7F)+CHR$(&H80)+CHR$(&H0)+CHR$(&HF7)+CHR$(&HF7)+C
  HR$(&H8)+CHR$(&H0)
780   A10$=CHR$(&HBB)+CHR$(&HBB)+CHR$(&H44)+CHR$(&H0)+CHR$(&HEE)+CHR$(&HEE)+CHR$(
  &H11)+CHR$(&H0)
790   A11$=CHR$(&HAA)+CHR$(&HAA)+CHR$(&H55)+CHR$(&H0)+CHR$(&H55)+CHR$(&H55)+CHR$(
  &HAA)+CHR$(&H0)
800   A12$=CHR$(&H44)+CHR$(&H44)+CHR$(&HBB)+CHR$(&H0)+CHR$(&H11)+CHR$(&H11)+CHR$(
  &HEE)+CHR$(&H0)
810   A13$=CHR$(&H20)+CHR$(&H0)+CHR$(&HFF)+CHR$(&H0)+CHR$(&H2)+CHR$(&H0)+CHR$(&HF
  F)+CHR$(&H0)+CHR$(&H80)+CHR$(&H0)+CHR$(&HFF)+CHR$(&H0)+CHR$(&H8)+CHR$(&H0)+CHR$(
  &HFF)+CHR$(&H0)
820   A14$=CHR$(&H44)+CHR$(&H0)+CHR$(&HFF)+CHR$(&H0)+CHR$(&H11)+CHR$(&H0)+CHR$(&H
  FF)+CHR$(&H0)
830   A15$=CHR$(&H55)+CHR$(&H0)+CHR$(&HFF)+CHR$(&H0)+CHR$(&HAA)+CHR$(&H0)+CHR$(&H
  FF)+CHR$(&H0)
840   A16$=CHR$(&HBB)+CHR$(&H0)+CHR$(&HFF)+CHR$(&H0)+CHR$(&HEE)+CHR$(&H0)+CHR$(&H
  FF)+CHR$(&H0)
850   A$=A10$  'generic shading code
860   '
870   '_____SET UP RUNTIME ENVIRONMENT_____
880   '
890   'module:  set up runtime environment
900   CLS:SCREEN 8,,0,0:COLOR C7,0:CLS  '640x200 16-clr mode
910   PALETTE 1,0:PALETTE 2,1:PALETTE 3,9:PALETTE 4,7:PALETTE 5,5:PALETTE 6,6:PAL
ETTE 7,3:PALETTE 8,8:PALETTE 9,2:PALETTE 10,10:PALETTE 11,4:PALETTE 12,12:PALETT
E 13,13:PALETTE 14,14:PALETTE 15,15
920   ON KEY(2) GOSUB 1840:KEY(2) ON  'install hot key
930   COLOR,0  'restore hardware color for background
940   GOSUB 1890  'initialize .CDF data file
```

Fig. 29-2. (Continued from page 297.)

```
950  '
960  '_____SET UP SCREEN DISPLAY_____
970  '
980  'module:  set up screen template
990   GOSUB 1250  'save alphanumeric graphic arrays
1000   GOSUB 1430   'create pull-down menus
1010   LINE (0,8)-(639,199),C8,B  'border
1020   LINE (0,187)-(639,187),C8:PAINT (320,190),C8,C8:PUT (182,189),A1,XOR  'ban
ner
1030   LINE (0,0)-(639,6),C4,B:PAINT (320,3),C4,C4:LOCATE 1,33:PRINT " DRAWFILE.C
DF ":LOCATE 1,34:PRINT F$  'filename bar
1040   LINE (1,8)-(639,18),C8,B:PAINT (320,10),C8,C8  'menu bar
1050   PUT (18,9),A2,XOR:PUT (130,9),A3,XOR:PUT (250,9),A4,XOR:PUT (370,9),A5,XOR
:PUT (510,9),A6,XOR  'selections for menu bar
1060   LOCATE 10,20:PRINT "Reclaiming memory used by temporary arrays":ERASE A1,A
2,A3,A4,A5,A6  'free up array memory                              "
1070   LOCATE 10,20:PRINT "
1080   LINE (250,19)-(250,186),C8:LINE (249,19)-(249,186),C8:LINE (1,19)-(1,186),
C8:LINE (638,19)-(638,186),C8:LINE (1,124)-(249,124),C8:LINE (122,53)-(132,53),C
4:LINE (127,51)-(127,55),C4  'split screen
1090   LOCATE 18,2:PRINT "Plan drawing height":LOCATE 19,2:PRINT "Viewpoint dista
nce":LOCATE 20,2:PRINT "Viewpoint elevation":LOCATE 21,2:PRINT "Yaw angle":LOCAT
E 22,2:PRINT "Roll angle":LOCATE 23,2:PRINT "Pitch angle"
1100   LOCATE 17,8:COLOR C4:PRINT "View specifications":COLOR C7
1110   GOSUB 5680  'alphanumeric readouts
1120   PUT (126,8),A7,XOR  'panning cursor for menu bar
1130   PCOPY 0,1:PCOPY 1,2  'establish refresh buffers
1140   LOCATE 9,40:COLOR C4:PRINT "YOUR MICROCOMPUTER 3D CAD MODELER":LOCATE 12,4
0:COLOR C7:PRINT "Copyright (c) 1988 by Lee Adams and":LOCATE 13,40:PRINT "TAB B
ooks Inc.  All rights reserved."
1150   LINE (310,60)-(584,60),C4:LINE (310,74)-(584,74),C4
1160   LOCATE 19,43:PRINT "Press <Enter> to continue...":SOUND 860,2:SOUND 800,2
1170   K$=INKEY$:IF K$<>CHR$(13) THEN 1170
1180   PCOPY 1,0:SOUND 250,.7:LOCATE 23,57:PRINT "Free memory:"FRE(0)  'restore s
creen
1190   GOTO 1940  'jump to runtime code
1200   GOTO 1200  'bulletproof code barrier
1210   '
1220   '_____CREATE ALPHANUMERICS FOR TEMPLATE_____
1230   '
1240   'module: create alpha arrays for screen template
1250   COLOR C12:LOCATE 10,20:PRINT "YOUR MICROCOMPUTER 3D CAD MODELER"
1260   GET (150,71)-(424,79),A1:LOCATE 10,20:PRINT "
                "
1270   LOCATE 10,20:PRINT "File":GET (150,71)-(210,79),A2
1280   LOCATE 10,20:PRINT "Draw":GET (150,71)-(210,79),A3
1290   LOCATE 10,20:PRINT "Display":GET (150,71)-(210,79),A4
1300   LOCATE 10,20:PRINT "View   ":GET (150,71)-(210,79),A5
1310   LOCATE 10,20:PRINT "Options":GET (150,71)-(210,79),A6
1320   COLOR C7:LOCATE 10,20:PRINT "         "
1330   LINE (150,70)-(212,80),C12,B:GET (150,70)-(212,80),A7  'create panning cur
sor for menu bar
1340   LINE (150,70)-(212,80),0,B
```

Fig. 29-2. (Continued from page 298.)

```
1350  LINE (323,44)-(337,44),C7:LINE (330,41)-(330,47),C7:LINE (329,44)-(331,44)
,0  'create roaming crosshair cursor
1360  GET (323,41)-(337,47),A12:LINE (323,41)-(337,47),0,BF
1370  RETURN
1380  '
1390  '                CREATE PULL-DOWN MENUS
1400  '
1410  'module:  create pull-down menus
1420  'submodule:  create Options menu
1430  COLOR C4:LOCATE 10,20:PRINT "Shading on/off":LOCATE 11,20:PRINT "Outline o
n/off":LOCATE 12,20:PRINT "Grid on/off":LOCATE 13,20:PRINT "Gnomon on/off"
1440  LOCATE 14,20:PRINT "Set color":LOCATE 15,20:PRINT "Menu bar"
1450  LINE (138,67)-(264,122),C8,B
1460  GET (138,67)-(264,122),A8:LINE (138,67)-(264,122),0,BF
1470  LOCATE 10,20:COLOR C7:PRINT CHR$(175):COLOR C7  'menu cursor >>
1480  GET (151,73)-(159,77),A9:LOCATE 10,20:PRINT " "
1490  '
1500  '_____
1510  'submodule:  create File menu
1520  COLOR C4:LOCATE 10,20:PRINT "Name":LOCATE 11,20:PRINT "Save":LOCATE 12,20:
PRINT "Load":LOCATE 13,20:PRINT "Quit":LOCATE 14,20:PRINT "Menu bar"
1530  LINE (138,67)-(220,114),C8,B
1540  GET (138,67)-(220,114),A10:LINE (138,67)-(220,114),0,BF
1550  '
1560  '_____
1570  'submodule:  create Draw menu
1580  COLOR C4:LOCATE 10,20:PRINT "3-edged":LOCATE 11,20:PRINT "4-edged":LOCATE
12,20:PRINT "Polyline":LOCATE 13,20:PRINT "Undo":LOCATE 14,20:PRINT "Menu bar"
1590  LINE (138,67)-(220,114),C8,B
1600  GET (138,67)-(220,114),A15:LINE (138,67)-(220,114),0,BF
1610  '
1620  '_____
1630  'submodule:  create Name dialog box
1640  COLOR C4:LOCATE 10,20:PRINT "Enter new filename:            ":COLOR C7
1650  LINE (144,69)-(413,82),C8,B
1660  GET (144,69)-(413,82),A11:LINE (144,69)-(413,82),0,BF
1670  '
1680  '_____
1690  'submodule:  create Display menu
1700  COLOR C4:LOCATE 4,20:PRINT "Regen":LOCATE 5,20:PRINT "Clear":LOCATE 6,20:P
RINT "Menu bar"
1710  LINE (138,20)-(220,50),C8,B
1720  GET (138,20)-(220,50),A13:LINE (138,20)-(220,50),0,BF
1730  '
1740  '_____
1750  'submodule:  create View menu
1760  LOCATE 4,20:PRINT "Distance":LOCATE 5,20:PRINT "Elevation":LOCATE 6,20:PRI
NT "Yaw":LOCATE 7,20:PRINT "Roll":LOCATE 8,20:PRINT "Pitch":LOCATE 9,20:PRINT "M
enu bar"
1770  LINE (138,20)-(230,74),C8,B
1780  GET (138,20)-(230,74),A14:LINE (138,20)-(230,74),0,BF:COLOR C7
1790  RETURN
1800  '
```

Fig. 29-2. (Continued from page 299.)

```
1810 '_____QUIT_____
1820 '
1830 'module:  exit routine
1840  CLS:SCREEN 0,0,0,0:WIDTH 80:COLOR 7,0,0:CLS:LOCATE 1,1,1:COLOR 4:PRINT "YO
UR MICROCOMPUTER 3D CAD MODELER":LOCATE 2,1:PRINT "is finished.":COLOR 7:SOUND 2
50,.7:END
1850 '
1860 '_____INITIALIZE DATA FILES_____
1870 '
1880 'module:  initialize .CDF data files
1890  OPEN "A:KEYLAYER.CDF" FOR OUTPUT AS #1:WRITE #1,SXP,SZP,SXC,SZC,C,SYP,SYC:
CLOSE #1:RETURN
1900 '
1910 '_____MENU BAR CONTROL_____
1920 '
1930 'main module:  interactive control of menu bar
1940  K$=INKEY$:GOSUB 2260:LOCATE 23,69:PRINT V" "
1950  IF LEN(K$)=2 THEN K$=RIGHT$(K$,1) ELSE 1990
1960  IF K$=CHR$(77) THEN T1=T1+1:GOSUB 2050:GOTO 1940
1970  IF K$=CHR$(75) THEN T1=T1-1:GOSUB 2150:GOTO 1940
1980  IF K$=CHR$(16) THEN GOTO 1840  'Alt-Q to quit
1990  IF K$=CHR$(13) THEN GOSUB 2380  '<Enter> key
2000  GOTO 1940
2010  GOTO 2010  'bulletproof code barrier
2020 '_____
2030 '
2040 'module:  pan right on menu bar
2050  IF T1>5 THEN T1=1
2060  ON T1 GOTO 2070,2080,2090,2100,2110
2070  PUT (506,8),A7,XOR:PUT (14,8),A7,XOR:RETURN   'File
2080  PUT (14,8),A7,XOR:PUT (126,8),A7,XOR:RETURN   'Draw
2090  PUT (126,8),A7,XOR:PUT (246,8),A7,XOR:RETURN  'Display
2100  PUT (246,8),A7,XOR:PUT (366,8),A7,XOR:RETURN  'View
2110  PUT (366,8),A7,XOR:PUT (506,8),A7,XOR:RETURN  'Options
2120 '_____
2130 '
2140 'module:  pan left on menu bar
2150  IF T1<1 THEN T1=5
2160  ON T1 GOTO 2170,2180,2190,2200,2210
2170  PUT (126,8),A7,XOR:PUT (14,8),A7,XOR:RETURN   'File
2180  PUT (246,8),A7,XOR:PUT (126,8),A7,XOR:RETURN  'Draw
2190  PUT (366,8),A7,XOR:PUT (246,8),A7,XOR:RETURN  'Edit
2200  PUT (506,8),A7,XOR:PUT (366,8),A7,XOR:RETURN  'Label
2210  PUT (14,8),A7,XOR:PUT (506,8),A7,XOR:RETURN   'Options
2220 '
2230 '_____CHECK SIZE OF WORKSPACE_____
2240 '
2250 'module:  check if user is running out of memory
2260  V=FRE(0):IF V>V1 THEN RETURN
2270  V1=128  'lower threshold to permit return to pgm
2280  PCOPY 0,1:CLS:COLOR C12:LOCATE 10,32:PRINT "W A R N I N G":COLOR C7:LOCATE
 12,23:PRINT "Out of memory in BASIC workspace."
2290  LOCATE 13,27:PRINT "Save your drawing on disk!":LOCATE 15,21:PRINT "Press
```

Fig. 29-2. (Continued from page 300.)

```
       <Enter> to return to 3D CAD MODELER."
2300   FOR T=1 TO 4 STEP 1:SOUND 250,3:SOUND 450,3:SOUND 650,3:NEXT T
2310   K$=INKEY$:IF K$<>CHR$(13) THEN 2310  'wait for <Enter>
2320   K$=INKEY$:IF K$<>"" THEN 2320  'empty keyboard buffer
2330   PCOPY 1,0:SOUND 250,.7:RETURN
2340   '
2350   '_____MENU BAR SWITCHER_____
2360   '
2370   'module:  switcher to execute menu bar choices
2380   ON T1 GOTO 2390,2400,2410,2420,2430
2390   GOSUB 2480:RETURN  'invoke File menu
2400   GOSUB 3160:RETURN  'invoke Draw menu
2410   GOSUB 3430:RETURN  'invoke Display menu
2420   GOSUB 3660:RETURN  'invoke View menu
2430   GOSUB 3950:RETURN  'invoke Options menu
2440   '
2450   '_____FILE MENU CONTROL_____
2460   '
2470   'module:  interactive control of File menu
2480   PCOPY 0,1  'save existing graphics
2490   PUT (14,19),A10,PSET  'place menu on screen
2500   PUT (16,25),A9,XOR  'place cursor >> on menu
2510   T8=1  'reset flag
2520   K$=INKEY$
2530   IF LEN(K$)=2 THEN K$=RIGHT$(K$,1)'ELSE 2620
2540   IF K$=CHR$(80) THEN T8=T8+1:GOTO 2550 ELSE 2520
2550   IF T8>5 THEN T8=1
2560   ON T8 GOTO 2570,2580,2590,2600,2610
2570   PUT (16,57),A9,XOR:PUT (16,25),A9,XOR:GOTO 2520 'Name
2580   PUT (16,25),A9,XOR:PUT (16,33),A9,XOR:GOTO 2520 'Save
2590   PUT (16,33),A9,XOR:PUT (16,41),A9,XOR:GOTO 2520 'Load
2600   PUT (16,41),A9,XOR:PUT (16,49),A9,XOR:GOTO 2520 'Quit
2610   PUT (16,49),A9,XOR:PUT (16,57),A9,XOR:GOTO 2520 'Menu bar
2620   IF K$=CHR$(13) THEN 2650  '<Enter> to implement
2630   IF K$=CHR$(27) THEN 2700  '<ESC> to cancel
2640   GOTO 2520
2650   ON T8 GOTO 2660,2670,2680,2690,2700
2660   GOSUB 2960:PCOPY 1,0:LOCATE 1,34:PRINT F$:RETURN   'name change
2670   PCOPY 1,0:GOSUB 2740:RETURN  'save image
2680   PCOPY 1,0:GOSUB 2850:RETURN  'load image
2690   GOTO 1840  'quit program
2700   PCOPY 1,0:RETURN  'menu bar
2710   '
2720   '_____
2730   'module: save 640x200 16-color image to disk
2740   MID$(F2$,1,8)=F$  'strip extension from file name
2750   SOUND 250,.7:DEF SEG=&HA000 'set up segment
2760   OUT &H3CE,4:OUT &H3CF,0:BSAVE "B:"+F2$+".BLU",0,16000 'bsave bit plane 0
2770   OUT &H3CE,4:OUT &H3CF,1:BSAVE "B:"+F2$+".GRN",0,16000 'bsave bit plane 1
2780   OUT &H3CE,4:OUT &H3CF,2:BSAVE "B:"+F2$+".RED",0,16000 'bsave bit plane 2
2790   OUT &H3CE,4:OUT &H3CF,3:BSAVE "B:"+F2$+".INT",0,16000 'bsave bit plane 3
2800   OUT &H3CE,4:OUT &H3CF,0:DEF SEG 'restore regs
2810   SOUND 250,.7:RETURN
```

Fig. 29-2. (Continued from page 301.)

```
2820 '_____
2830 '
2840 'module: load 640x200 16-color image from disk
2850 MID$(F2$,1,8)=F$  'strip extension from file name
2860 SOUND 250,.7:DEF SEG=&HA000 'set up segment
2870 OUT &H3C4,2:OUT &H3C5,1:BLOAD "B:"+F2$+".BLU",0 'bload bit plane 0
2880 OUT &H3C4,2:OUT &H3C5,2:BLOAD "B:"+F2$+".GRN",0 'bload bit plane 1
2890 OUT &H3C4,2:OUT &H3C5,4:BLOAD "B:"+F2$+".RED",0 'bload bit plane 2
2900 OUT &H3C4,2:OUT &H3C5,8:BLOAD "B:"+F2$+".INT",0 'bload bit plane 3
2910 OUT &H3C4,2:OUT &H3C5,&HF:DEF SEG 'restore regs
2920 GOSUB 5680:SOUND 250,.7:RETURN
2930 '_____
2940 '
2950 'module:  interactive control of Name dialog box
2960 GET (34,53)-(303,66),A11C  'save existing graphics
2970 PUT (34,53),A11,PSET  'display Name dialog box
2980 T2=25  'echo position flag
2990 F1$=F$  'temporary save of existing filename
3000 FOR T=1 TO 8 STEP 1
3010 K$=INKEY$
3020 IF K$="" THEN 3010  'wait for keystroke
3030 IF K$=CHR$(27) THEN F$=F1$:T=8:GOTO 3070  '<ESC> to cancel instructions an
d restore previous filename
3040 IF K$<"A" THEN SOUND 250,.7:GOTO 3010  'must be A-Z
3050 IF K$>"Z" THEN SOUND 250,.7:GOTO 3010  'must be A-Z
3060 T2=T2+1:LOCATE 8,T2:PRINT K$:MID$(F$,T,1)=K$  'echo user input and insert
character into F$
3070 NEXT T
3080 LOCATE 8,26:PRINT F$
3090 K$=INKEY$:IF K$<>CHR$(13) THEN 3090
3100 LOCATE 1,34:PRINT F$:SOUND 250,.7 'display on filename bar
3110 PUT (34,53),A11C,PSET:RETURN  'restore previous graphics
3120 '
3130 '_____DRAW MENU CONTROL_____
3140 '
3150 'module:  interactive control of Draw menu
3160 PCOPY 0,1:PCOPY 0,2  'save existing graphics
3170 PUT (126,19),A15,PSET 'place menu on screen
3180 PUT (128,25),A9,XOR  'place cursor >> on menu
3190 T8=1  'reset flag
3200 K$=INKEY$
3210 IF LEN(K$)=2 THEN K$=RIGHT$(K$,1) ELSE 3300
3220 IF K$=CHR$(80) THEN T8=T8+1:GOTO 3230 ELSE 3200
3230 IF T8>5 THEN T8=1
3240 ON T8 GOTO 3250,3260,3270,3280,3290
3250 PUT (128,57),A9,XOR:PUT (128,25),A9,XOR:GOTO 3200 '3-edged
3260 PUT (128,25),A9,XOR:PUT (128,33),A9,XOR:GOTO 3200 '4-edged
3270 PUT (128,33),A9,XOR:PUT (128,41),A9,XOR:GOTO 3200 'Polyline
3280 PUT (128,41),A9,XOR:PUT (128,49),A9,XOR:GOTO 3200 'Undo
3290 PUT (128,49),A9,XOR:PUT (128,57),A9,XOR:GOTO 3200 'Menu bar
3300 IF K$=CHR$(13) THEN 3330  '<Enter> to implement
3310 IF K$=CHR$(27) THEN 3380  '<ESC> to cancel
3320 GOTO 3200
```

Fig. 29-2. (Continued from page 302.)

```
3330   ON T8 GOTO 3340,3350,3360,3370,3380
3340   T5=1:PCOPY 1,0:GOSUB 4280:GOTO 3170    '3-edged
3350   T5=2:PCOPY 1,0:GOSUB 4280:GOTO 3170    '4-edged
3360   T5=3:PCOPY 1,0:GOSUB 4280:GOTO 3170    'Polyline
3370   PCOPY 2,0:LOCATE 18,22:PRINT SYC:SOUND 250,.7:RETURN   'undo
3380   PCOPY 1,0:RETURN  'menu bar
3390   '
3400   '_____DISPLAY MENU CONTROL_____
3410   '
3420   'module:  interactive control of Display menu
3430   PCOPY 0,1  'save existing graphics
3440   PUT (246,19),A13,PSET  'place menu on screen
3450   PUT (248,24),A9,XOR  'place cursor >> on menu
3460   T8=1  'reset flag
3470   K$=INKEY$
3480   IF LEN(K$)=2 THEN K$=RIGHT$(K$,1) ELSE 3550
3490   IF K$=CHR$(80) THEN T8=T8+1:GOTO 3500 ELSE 3470
3500   IF T8>3 THEN T8=1
3510   ON T8 GOTO 3520,3530,3540
3520   PUT (248,40),A9,XOR:PUT (248,24),A9,XOR:GOTO 3470 'Regen
3530   PUT (248,24),A9,XOR:PUT (248,32),A9,XOR:GOTO 3470 'Clear
3540   PUT (248,32),A9,XOR:PUT (248,40),A9,XOR:GOTO 3470 'Menu bar
3550   IF K$=CHR$(13) THEN 3580   '<Enter> to implement
3560   IF K$=CHR$(27) THEN 3610   '<ESC> to cancel
3570   GOTO 3470
3580   ON T8 GOTO 3590,3600,3610
3590   PCOPY 1,0:VIEW SCREEN (2,19)-(248,123):CLS:LINE (122,53)-(132,53),C4:LINE
(127,51)-(127,55),C4:VIEW SCREEN (251,19)-(637,186):CLS:VIEW:GOSUB 5090:GOSUB 56
80:LOCATE 23,57:PRINT "Free memory:":SOUND 860,2:SOUND 800,2:RETURN   'Regen
3600   PCOPY 1,0:VIEW SCREEN (2,19)-(248,123):CLS:LINE (122,53)-(132,53),C4:LINE
(127,51)-(127,55),C4:VIEW SCREEN (251,19)-(637,186):CLS:VIEW:GOSUB 1890:LOCATE 2
3,57:PRINT "Free memory:":SOUND 860,2:SOUND 800,2:RETURN   'Clear
3610   PCOPY 1,0:RETURN   'menu bar
3620   '
3630   '_____VIEW MENU CONTROL_____
3640   '
3650   'module:  interactive control of View menu
3660   PCOPY 0,1  'save existing graphics
3670   PUT (366,19),A14,PSET  'place menu on screen
3680   PUT (368,24),A9,XOR  'place cursor >> on menu
3690   T8=1  'reset flag
3700   K$=INKEY$
3710   IF LEN(K$)=2 THEN K$=RIGHT$(K$,1) ELSE 3810
3720   IF K$=CHR$(80) THEN T8=T8+1:GOTO 3730 ELSE 3700
3730   IF T8>6 THEN T8=1
3740   ON T8 GOTO 3750,3760,3770,3780,3790,3800
3750   PUT (368,64),A9,XOR:PUT (368,24),A9,XOR:GOTO 3700 'Distance
3760   PUT (368,24),A9,XOR:PUT (368,32),A9,XOR:GOTO 3700 'Elevation
3770   PUT (368,32),A9,XOR:PUT (368,40),A9,XOR:GOTO 3700 'Yaw
3780   PUT (368,40),A9,XOR:PUT (368,48),A9,XOR:GOTO 3700 'Roll
3790   PUT (368,48),A9,XOR:PUT (368,56),A9,XOR:GOTO 3700 'Pitch
3800   PUT (368,56),A9,XOR:PUT (368,64),A9,XOR:GOTO 3700 'Menu bar
3810   IF K$=CHR$(13) THEN 3840   '<Enter> to implement
```

Fig. 29-2. (Continued from page 303.)

```
3820   IF K$=CHR$(27) THEN 3900  '<ESC> to cancel
3830   GOTO 3700
3840   ON T8 GOTO 3850,3860,3870,3880,3890,3900
3850   GOSUB 5230:RETURN  'Distance
3860   GOSUB 5320:RETURN  'Elevation
3870   GOSUB 5410:RETURN  'Yaw
3880   GOSUB 5500:RETURN  'Roll
3890   GOSUB 5590:RETURN  'Pitch
3900   PCOPY 1,0:RETURN   'menu bar
3910   '
3920   '_____OPTIONS MENU CONTROL_____
3930   '
3940   'module:  interactive control of Options menu
3950   PCOPY 0,1  'save existing graphics
3960   PUT (505,19),A8,PSET  'place menu on screen
3970   PUT (507,25),A9,XOR  'place cursor >> on menu
3980   T8=1  'reset flag
3990   K$=INKEY$
4000   IF LEN(K$)=2 THEN K$=RIGHT$(K$,1) ELSE 4100
4010   IF K$=CHR$(80) THEN T8=T8+1:GOTO 4020 ELSE 3990
4020   IF T8>6 THEN T8=1
4030   ON T8 GOTO 4040,4050,4060,4070,4080,4090
4040   PUT (507,65),A9,XOR:PUT (507,25),A9,XOR:GOTO 3990  'Shading on/off
4050   PUT (507,25),A9,XOR:PUT (507,33),A9,XOR:GOTO 3990  'Outline on/off
4060   PUT (507,33),A9,XOR:PUT (507,41),A9,XOR:GOTO 3990  'Grid on/off
4070   PUT (507,41),A9,XOR:PUT (507,49),A9,XOR:GOTO 3990  'Gnomon on/off
4080   PUT (507,49),A9,XOR:PUT (507,57),A9,XOR:GOTO 3990  'Set color
4090   PUT (507,57),A9,XOR:PUT (507,65),A9,XOR:GOTO 3990  'Menu bar
4100   IF K$=CHR$(13) THEN 4130  '<Enter> to implement
4110   IF K$=CHR$(27) THEN 4190  '<ESC> to cancel
4120   GOTO 3990
4130   ON T8 GOTO 4140,4150,4160,4170,4180,4190
4140   GOSUB 5770:GOTO 3990  'Shading on/off
4150   GOSUB 5730:GOTO 3990  'Outline on/off
4160   GOSUB 6000:GOTO 3990  'Grid on/off
4170   GOSUB 6080:GOTO 3990  'Gnomon on/off
4180   GOSUB 5810:GOTO 3990  'Set color
4190   PCOPY 1,0:GOSUB 5680:RETURN  'menu bar
4200   '
4210   '_____DO-NOTHING ROUTINE_____
4220   '
4230   SOUND 860,2:SOUND 800,2:RETURN  'do-nothing routine
4240   '
4250   '_____CROSSHAIR CURSOR CONTROL_____
4260   '
4270   'module:  interactive control of crosshair cursor
4280   SOUND 250,.7
4290   PUT (SX,SY),A12,XOR  'install crosshair cursor
4300   T6=0  'reset polyline flag
4310   X1=100:X2=130:X3=160:X4=190:Y1=40:Y2=100:Y3=140:Y4=70  'reset control poin
ts for curve and fillet
4320   K$=INKEY$
4330   IF LEN(K$)=2 THEN K$=RIGHT$(K$,1) ELSE 4500
```

Fig. 29-2. (Continued from page 304.)

```
4340  IF K$=CHR$(77) THEN PUT (SX,SY),A12,XOR:SX=SX+J ELSE 4370
4350  IF SX>XR THEN SX=XR:SOUND 250,.7
4360  PUT (SX,SY),A12,XOR:GOTO 4320
4370  IF K$=CHR$(75) THEN PUT (SX,SY),A12,XOR:SX=SX-J ELSE 4400
4380  IF SX<XL THEN SX=XL:SOUND 250,.7
4390  PUT (SX,SY),A12,XOR:GOTO 4320
4400  IF K$=CHR$(72) THEN PUT (SX,SY),A12,XOR:SY=SY-J*.5 ELSE 4430
4410  IF SY<YT THEN SY=YT:SOUND 250,.7
4420  PUT (SX,SY),A12,XOR:GOTO 4320
4430  IF K$=CHR$(80) THEN PUT (SX,SY),A12,XOR:SY=SY+J*.5 ELSE 4460
4440  IF SY>YB THEN SY=YB:SOUND 250,.7
4450  PUT (SX,SY),A12,XOR:GOTO 4320
4460  IF K$=CHR$(71) THEN PUT (SX,SY),A12,XOR:SX=XL:SY=YT:PUT (SX,SY),A12,XOR:GO
TO 4320
4470  IF K$=CHR$(73) THEN PUT (SX,SY),A12,XOR:SX=XR:SY=YT:PUT (SX,SY),A12,XOR:GO
TO 4320
4480  IF K$=CHR$(81) THEN PUT (SX,SY),A12,XOR:SX=XR:SY=YB:PUT (SX,SY),A12,XOR:GO
TO 4320
4490  IF K$=CHR$(79) THEN PUT (SX,SY),A12,XOR:SX=XL:SY=YB:PUT (SX,SY),A12,XOR:GO
TO 4320
4500  IF K$=CHR$(27) THEN PUT (SX,SY),A12,XOR:SOUND 250,.7:RETURN   '<ESC>
4510  IF K$=CHR$(13) THEN PUT (SX,SY),A12,XOR:GOSUB 4610:PCOPY 0,1:PUT (SX,SY),A
12,XOR:LOCATE 23,69:PRINT FRE(0):SOUND 250,.7:GOTO 4320   '<Enter> to implement c
ommand
4520  IF K$="1" THEN SYC=SYC+.25:LOCATE 18,22:PRINT SYC"  ":SOUND 250,.7:GOTO 43
20  'increment plan drawing height
4530  IF K$="2" THEN SYC=SYC-.25:LOCATE 18,22:PRINT SYC"  ":SOUND 250,.7:GOTO 43
20  'decrement plan drawing height
4540  IF K$="3" THEN SYC=SYC+5:LOCATE 18,22:PRINT SYC"  ":SOUND 250,.7:GOTO 4320
  'mega-increment plant drawing height
4550  IF K$="4" THEN SYC=SYC-5:LOCATE 18,22:PRINT SYC"  ":SOUND 250,.7:GOTO 4320
  'mega-decrement plant drawing height
4560  GOTO 4320
4570  SOUND 250,.7:RETURN
4580  '_____
4590  '_____
4600  'module:  switcher for drawing functions
4610  ON T5 GOTO 4620,4630,4640
4620  GOSUB 4230:RETURN   '3-edged polygon
4630  GOSUB 4730:RETURN   '4-edged solid polygon plane surface
4640  GOSUB 4680:RETURN   'polyline
4650  '_____
4660  '_____
4670  'module:  polyline function
4680  IF T6=0 THEN SXC=SX+7:SZC=SY+3:PSET (SXC,SZC),C:T6=1:SXP=SXC:SZP=SZC:SYP=S
YC:RETURN ELSE 4690
4690  SXC=SX+7:SZC=SY+3:LINE (SXP,SZP)-(SXC,SZC),C:GOSUB 4930:GOSUB 5050:SXP=SXC
:SZP=SZC:SYP=SYC:RETURN
4700  '_____
4710  '_____
4720  'module:  4-edged solid polygon function
4730  IF T6=0 THEN T6=1:SXC=SX+7:SZC=SY+3:PSET (SXC,SZC),C:SXP=SXC:SZP=SZC:SYP=S
YC:SXF=SXC:SZF=SZC:GOSUB 4880:X1=X:Y1=Y:Z1=Z:SX1=SXD:SY1=SYD:RETURN ELSE 4740  '
```

Fig. 29-2. (Continued from page 305.)

```
vertex #1
4740  IF T6=1 THEN T6=2:SXC=SX+7:SZC=SY+3:LINE (SXP,SZP)-(SXC,SZC),C:SXP=SXC:SZP
=SZC:SYP=SYC:GOSUB 4880:X2=X:Y2=Y:Z2=Z:SX2=SXD:SY2=SYD:RETURN ELSE 4750  'vertex
 #2
4750  IF T6=2 THEN T6=3:SXC=SX+7:SZC=SY+3:LINE (SXP,SZP)-(SXC,SZC),C:SXP=SXC:SZP
=SZC:SYP=SYC:GOSUB 4880:X3=X:Y3=Y:Z3=Z:SX3=SXD:SY3=SYD:RETURN  ELSE 4760  'verte
x #3
4760  IF T6=3 THEN T6=0:SXC=SX+7:SZC=SY+3:LINE (SXP,SZP)-(SXC,SZC),C:LINE-(SXF,S
ZF),C:SXP=SXC:SZP=SZC:SYP=SYC:GOSUB 4880:X4=X:Y4=Y:Z4=Z:SX4=SXD:SY4=SYD  'vertex
 #4
4770  GOSUB 6210:IF SP>0 THEN SOUND 250,.7:RETURN ELSE 4780  'test for surface v
isibility;  if hidden then do not draw
4780  GOSUB 6750  'use geometric center of polygon as area fill seed point
4790  GOSUB 6260:IF T7=0 THEN WINDOW SCREEN (0,0)-(639,199):VIEW:RETURN ELSE 480
0  'draw solid polygon plane surface
4800  GOSUB 6320:PAINT (SX5,SY5),C13,C:PAINT (SX5,SY5),A$,C  'apply halftone sha
ding
4810  GOSUB 6690  'apply line dithering
4820  IF T9=0 THEN 4840  'is outlining toggle off?
4830  GOSUB 6810  'apply outlining
4840  RETURN  'solid polygon plane is completed
4850  '_____
4860  '
4870  'module:  prepare 2D plan coordinates for input to 3D formulas
4880  X=(.404858*SXC)-51:Z=(.9523809*SZC)-51:Y=SYC:GOSUB 5000:SXD=SXD+125:SYD=SY
D+3:RETURN
4890  '
4900  '_____GENERATE 3D MODEL_____
4910  '
4920  'module:  generate 3D model
4930  WINDOW SCREEN (-399,-299)-(400,300):VIEW SCREEN (251,19)-(637,186)  'clip
3D viewing area
4940  X=(.404858*SXP)-51:Z=(.9523809*SZP)-51:Y=SYP:GOSUB 5000:SXD=SXD+125:SYD=SY
D+3:PSET (SXD,SYD),C
4950  X=(.404858*SXC)-51:Z=(.9523809*SZC)-51:Y=SYC:GOSUB 5000:SXD=SXD+125:SYD=SY
D+3:LINE-(SXD,SYD),C
4960  WINDOW SCREEN (0,0)-(639,199):VIEW:RETURN
4970  '_____
4980  '
4990  'module:  perspective formulas
5000  X=(-1)*X:XA=CR1*X-SR1*Z:ZA=SR1*X+CR1*Z:X=CR2*XA+SR2*Y:YA=CR2*Y-SR2*XA:Z=CR
3*ZA-SR3*YA:Y=SR3*ZA+CR3*YA:X=X+MX:Y=Y+MY:Z=Z+MZ:SXD=D*X/Z:SYD=D*Y/Z:RETURN
5010  '
5020  '_____DATA FILE INPUT/OUTPUT_____
5030  '
5040  'module:  storage of graphics attributes in data file
5050  OPEN "A:KEYLAYER.CDF" FOR APPEND AS #1:WRITE #1,SXP,SZP,SXC,SZC,C,SYP,SYC:
CLOSE #1:RETURN
5060  '
5070  '_____
5080  'module:  retrieval of graphics attributes from data file
5090  OPEN "A:KEYLAYER.CDF" FOR INPUT AS #1
5100  INPUT #1,SXP,SZP,SXC,SZC,C,SYP,SYC  'dummy pass
```

Fig. 29-2. (Continued from page 306.)

```
5110  IF T3=1 THEN GOSUB 6040  'is grid toggled on?
5120  IF T4=1 THEN GOSUB 6120  'is gnomon toggled on?
5130  IF EOF(1) THEN CLOSE #1:RETURN
5140  INPUT #1,SXP,SZP,SXC,SZC,C,SYP,SYC:GOSUB 5180:GOTO 5130
5150  '_____
5160  '
5170  'module:  regen function for 2D/3D modes
5180  LINE (SXP,SZP)-(SXC,SZC),C:GOSUB 4930:RETURN  'polyline regen
5190  '
5200  '_____ADJUST VIEW PARAMETERS_____
5210  '
5220  'module:  adjust Distance to viewpoint
5230  SOUND 250,.7
5240  K$=INKEY$
5250  IF K$="=" THEN MZ=MZ-10:GOSUB 5680:GOTO 5240
5260  IF K$="-" THEN MZ=MZ+10:GOSUB 5680:GOTO 5240
5270  IF K$=CHR$(13) THEN PCOPY 1,0:GOSUB 5680:VIEW SCREEN (2,19)-(248,123):CLS:
VIEW SCREEN (251,19)-(637,186):CLS:VIEW:GOSUB 5090:LOCATE 23,57:PRINT "Free memo
ry:":SOUND 860,2:SOUND 800,2:RETURN
5280  GOTO 5240
5290  '_____ .
5300  '
5310  'module:  adjust Elevation of viewpoint
5320  SOUND 250,.7
5330  K$=INKEY$
5340  IF K$="=" THEN MY=MY-2:GOSUB 5680:GOTO 5330
5350  IF K$="-" THEN MY=MY+2:GOSUB 5680:GOTO 5330
5360  IF K$=CHR$(13) THEN PCOPY 1,0:GOSUB 5680:VIEW SCREEN (2,19)-(248,123):CLS:
VIEW SCREEN (251,19)-(637,186):CLS:VIEW:GOSUB 5090:LOCATE 23,57:PRINT "Free memo
ry:":SOUND 860,2:SOUND 800,2:RETURN
5370  GOTO 5330
5380  '_____
5390  '
5400  'module:  adjust Yaw angle
5410  SOUND 250,.7
5420  K$=INKEY$:IF LEN(K$)=2 THEN K$=RIGHT$(K$,1) ELSE 5450
5430  IF K$=CHR$(77) THEN R1=R1-.17953:GOSUB 5680:GOTO 5420
5440  IF K$=CHR$(75) THEN R1=R1+.17953:GOSUB 5680:GOTO 5420
5450  IF K$=CHR$(13) THEN SR1=SIN(R1):CR1=COS(R1):PCOPY 1,0:GOSUB 5680:VIEW SCRE
EN (2,19)-(248,123):CLS:VIEW SCREEN (251,19)-(637,186):CLS:VIEW:GOSUB 5090:LOCAT
E 23,57:PRINT "Free memory:":SOUND 860,2:SOUND 800,2:RETURN
5460  GOTO 5420
5470  '_____
5480  '
5490  'module:  adjust Roll angle
5500  SOUND 250,.7
5510  K$=INKEY$:IF LEN(K$)=2 THEN K$=RIGHT$(K$,1) ELSE 5540
5520  IF K$=CHR$(77) THEN R2=R2+.08727:GOSUB 5680:GOTO 5510
5530  IF K$=CHR$(75) THEN R2=R2-.08727:GOSUB 5680:GOTO 5510
5540  IF K$=CHR$(13) THEN SR2=SIN(R2):CR2=COS(R2):PCOPY 1,0:GOSUB 5680:VIEW SCRE
EN (2,19)-(248,123):CLS:VIEW SCREEN (251,19)-(637,186):CLS:VIEW:GOSUB 5090:LOCAT
E 23,57:PRINT "Free memory:":SOUND 860,2:SOUND 800,2:RETURN
5550  GOTO 5510
5560  '_____
```

Fig. 29-2. (Continued from page 307.)

```
5570 '
5580 'module:  adjust Pitch angle
5590  SOUND 250,.7
5600  K$=INKEY$:IF LEN(K$)=2 THEN K$=RIGHT$(K$,1) ELSE 5630
5610  IF K$=CHR$(72) THEN R3=R3-.08727:GOSUB 5680:GOTO 5600
5620  IF K$=CHR$(80) THEN R3=R3+.08727:GOSUB 5680:GOTO 5600
5630  IF K$=CHR$(13) THEN SR3=SIN(R3):CR3=COS(R3):PCOPY 1,0:GOSUB 5680:VIEW SCRE
EN (2,19)-(248,123):CLS:VIEW SCREEN (251,19)-(637,186):CLS:VIEW:GOSUB 5090:LOCAT
E 23,57:PRINT "Free memory:":SOUND 860,2:SOUND 800,2:RETURN
5640  GOTO 5600
5650 '
5660 '_____REFRESH ALPHANUMERICS_____
5670 '
5680  LOCATE 18,22:PRINT SYC:LOCATE 19,21:PRINT (-1*MZ):LOCATE 20,22:PRINT (-1*M
Y):LOCATE 21,12:PRINT R1:LOCATE 22,13:PRINT R2:LOCATE 23,14:PRINT R3:LINE (8,185
)-(243,185),C:RETURN
5690 '
5700 '_____ADJUST OPTIONS_____
5710 '
5720 'module:  toggle outlining on/off
5730  IF T9=0 THEN T9=1:SOUND 250,.7:RETURN ELSE IF T9=1 THEN T9=0:SOUND 250,.7:
RETURN
5740 '_____
5750 '_____
5760 'module:  toggle shading on/off
5770  IF T7=0 THEN T7=1:SOUND 250,.7:RETURN ELSE IF T7=1 THEN T7=0:SOUND 250,.7:
RETURN
5780 '_____
5790 '_____
5800 'module:  change the drawing color
5810  SOUND 250,.7
5820  IF C=C7 THEN C=C4:GOSUB 5680:RETURN
5830  IF C=C4 THEN C=C1:GOSUB 5680:RETURN
5840  IF C=C1 THEN C=C3:GOSUB 5680:RETURN
5850  IF C=C3 THEN C=C2:GOSUB 5680:RETURN
5860  IF C=C2 THEN C=C5:GOSUB 5680:RETURN
5870  IF C=C5 THEN C=C6:GOSUB 5680:RETURN
5880  IF C=C6 THEN C=C8:GOSUB 5680:RETURN
5890  IF C=C8 THEN C=C15:GOSUB 5680:RETURN
5900  IF C=C15 THEN C=C9:GOSUB 5680:RETURN
5910  IF C=C9 THEN C=C12:GOSUB 5680:RETURN
5920  IF C=C12 THEN C=C10:GOSUB 5680:RETURN
5930  IF C=C10 THEN C=C14:GOSUB 5680:RETURN
5940  IF C=C14 THEN C=C0:GOSUB 5680:RETURN
5950  IF C=C0 THEN C=C7:GOSUB 5680:RETURN
5960  GOSUB 5680:RETURN
5970 '_____
5980 '_____
5990 'module:  toggle 2D grid on/off
6000  IF T3=0 THEN T3=1:SOUND 250,.7:RETURN ELSE IF T3=1 THEN T3=0:SOUND 250,.7:
RETURN
6010 '_____
6020 '_____
6030 'module:  create grid if toggled on
```

Fig. 29-2. (Continued from page 308.)

```
6040  T=1:WHILE T<249:LINE (T,19)-(T,123),C8:T=T+J10:WEND:T=19:WHILE T<123:LINE
(2,T)-(248,T),C8:T=T+J11:WEND:LINE (122,53)-(132,53),C4:LINE (127,51)-(127,55),C
4:RETURN
6050  '_____
6060  '
6070  'module:  toggle 3D gnomon on/off (x,y,z axis display)
6080  IF T4=0 THEN T4=1:SOUND 250,.7:RETURN ELSE IF T4=1 THEN T4=0:SOUND 250,.7:
RETURN
6090  '_____
6100  '
6110  'module:  create gnomon if toggled on
6120  WINDOW SCREEN (-399,-299)-(400,300):VIEW SCREEN (251,19)-(637,186)
6130  X=30:Z=0:Y=0:GOSUB 5000:SXD=SXD+125:SYD=SYD+3:PSET (SXD,SYD),C2:X=0:Z=0:Y=
0:GOSUB 5000:SXD=SXD+125:SYD=SYD+3:LINE-(SXD,SYD),C2:X=-30:Z=0:Y=0:GOSUB 5000:SX
D=SXD+125:SYD=SYD+3:LINE-(SXD,SYD),C8  'x-axis
6140  X=0:Z=0:Y=30:GOSUB 5000:SXD=SXD+125:SYD=SYD+3:PSET (SXD,SYD),C5:X=0:Z=0:Y=
0:GOSUB 5000:SXD=SXD+125:SYD=SYD+3:LINE-(SXD,SYD),C5:X=0:Z=0:Y=-30:GOSUB 5000:SX
D=SXD+125:SYD=SYD+3:LINE-(SXD,SYD),C8   'y-axis
6150  X=0:Z=30:Y=0:GOSUB 5000:SXD=SXD+125:SYD=SYD+3:PSET (SXD,SYD),C1:X=0:Z=0:Y=
0:GOSUB 5000:SXD=SXD+125:SYD=SYD+3:LINE-(SXD,SYD),C1:X=0:Z=-30:Y=0:GOSUB 5000:SX
D=SXD+125:SYD=SYD+3:LINE-(SXD,SYD),C8   'z-axis
6160  WINDOW SCREEN (0,0)-(639,199):VIEW:RETURN
6170  '
6180  '_____HIDDEN SURFACE REMOVAL_____
6190  '
6200  'module:  plane equation method of hidden surface removal
6210  SP1=X1*(Y2*Z3-Y3*Z2):SP1=(-1)*SP1:SP2=X2*(Y3*Z1-Y1*Z3):SP3=X3*(Y1*Z2-Y2*Z1
):SP=SP1-SP2-SP3:RETURN
6220  '
6230  '_____DRAW 4-SIDED POLYGON_____
6240  '
6250  'module:  solid surface modeling of 4-sided polygon
6260  WINDOW SCREEN (-399,-299)-(400,300):VIEW SCREEN (251,19)-(637,186)  'clip
3D viewing area
6270  LINE (SX1,SY1)-(SX2,SY2),C13:LINE-(SX3,SY3),C13:LINE-(SX4,SY4),C13:LINE-(S
X1,SY1),C13:PAINT (SX5,SY5),C13,C13:LINE (SX1,SY1)-(SX2,SY2),C:LINE-(SX3,SY3),C:
LINE-(SX4,SY4),C:LINE-(SX1,SY1),C:PAINT (SX5,SY5),0,C:RETURN
6280  '
6290  '_____COMPUTER-CONTROLLED SHADING_____
6300  '
6310  'module:  computer-controlled shading routine
6320  XU=X2-X1:YU=Y2-Y1:ZU=Z2-Z1  'calculate vector from vertex 1 to vertex 2
6330  XV=X3-X1:YV=Y3-Y1:ZV=Z3-Z1  'calculate vector from vertex 1 to vertex 3
6340  XN=(YU*ZV)-(ZU*YV):YN=(ZU*XV)-(XU*ZV):ZN=(XU*YV)-(YU*XV)  'calculate surfa
ce perpendicular vector
6350  YN=YN*(-1):ZN=ZN*(-1)  'convert vector to cartesian system
6360  'sub-module:  convert surface perpendicular vector to unit vector
6370  V7=(XN*XN)+(YN*YN)+(ZN*ZN):V2=SQR(V7)  'magnitude of surface perpendicular
 vector
6380  V3=1/V2  'ratio of magnitude to unit vector magnitude
6390  XW=V3*XN:YW=V3*YN:ZW=V3*ZN  'XYZ components of surface perpendicular unit
vector
6400  V4=(XW*XI)+(YW*YI)+(ZW*ZI)  'illumination factor 0 to 1
6410  V4=V4*V6:V4=CINT(V4)  'set illumination range
```

Fig. 29-2. (Continued from page 309.)

```
6420   V5=V4+1  'illumination factor from base 1
6430   GOSUB 6480
6440   RETURN
6450 '_____
6460 '
6470 'shading routine for EGA and VGA 640x200 mode
6480   IF V5<1 THEN GOTO 6510  'if light source is behind surface
6490   ON V5 GOTO 6510, 6520, 6530, 6540, 6550, 6560, 6570, 6580, 6590, 6600, 661
0, 6620, 6630, 6640, 6650
6500   A$=CHR$(&HFF)+CHR$(&HO)+CHR$(&HO)+CHR$(&HO):C4=1:C5=1:C6=&HFFFF:RETURN    's
olid black is unused
6510   A$=A1$:CP=1:CC=2:CD=&H808:RETURN
6520   A$=A2$:CP=1:CC=2:CD=&H4444:RETURN
6530   A$=A3$:CP=1:CC=2:CD=&HAAAA:RETURN
6540   A$=A4$:CP=2:CC=1:CD=&H4444:RETURN
6550   A$=CHR$(&HO)+CHR$(&HFF)+CHR$(&HO)+CHR$(&HO):CP=2:CC=2:CD=&HFFFF:RETURN
6560   A$=A5$:CP=2:CC=3:CD=&H808:RETURN
6570   A$=A6$:CP=2:CC=3:CD=&H4444:RETURN
6580   A$=A7$:CP=2:CC=3:CD=&HAAAA:RETURN
6590   A$=A8$:CP=3:CC=2:CD=&H4444:RETURN
6600   A$=CHR$(&HFF)+CHR$(&HFF)+CHR$(&HO)+CHR$(&HO):CP=3:CC=3:CD=&HFFFF:RETURN
6610   A$=A9$:CP=3:CC=4:CD=&H8080:RETURN
6620   A$=A10$:CP=3:CC=4:CD=&H4444:RETURN
6630   A$=A11$:CP=3:CC=4:CD=&HAAAA:RETURN
6640   A$=A12$:CP=4:CC=3:CD=&H4444:RETURN
6650   A$=CHR$(&HO)+CHR$(&HO)+CHR$(&HFF)+CHR$(&HO):CP=4:CC=4:CD=&HFFFF:RETURN
6660 '_____
6670 '
6680 'module:  computer-controlled dithering routine
6690   LINE (SX1,SY1)-(SX2,SY2),CP:LINE (SX1,SY1)-(SX2,SY2),CC,,CD:LINE (SX2,SY2)
-(SX3,SY3),CP:LINE (SX2,SY2)-(SX3,SY3),CC,,CD:LINE (SX3,SY3)-(SX4,SY4),CP:LINE (
SX3,SY3)-(SX4,SY4),CC,,CD
6700   LINE (SX4,SY4)-(SX1,SY1),CP:LINE (SX4,SY4)-(SX1,SY1),CC,,CD
6710   WINDOW SCREEN (0,0)-(639,199):VIEW:RETURN
6720 '_____
6730 '
6740 'module:  determine area fill seed point
6750   X=X1+.5*(X3-X1):Y=Y1+.5*(Y3-Y1):Z=Z1+.5*(Z3-Z1)  'diagonal midpoint betwee
n polygon's view coordinates in 3D space
6760   SX5=D*X/Z:SY5=D*Y/Z:SX5=SX5+125:SY5=SY5+3  'display coordinates for seed
6770   RETURN
6780 '_____
6790 '
6800 'module:  outlining of solid polygon plane surface
6810   WINDOW SCREEN (-399,-299)-(400,300):VIEW SCREEN (251,19)-(637,186)  'clip
3D viewing area
6820   LINE (SX1,SY1)-(SX2,SY2),C:LINE-(SX3,SY3),C:LINE-(SX4,SY4),C:LINE-(SX1,SY1
),C
6830   WINDOW SCREEN (0,0)-(639,199):VIEW:RETURN
6840 '_____
6850 '_____
6860 '_____
6870   END
```

Fig. 29-2. (Continued from page 310.)

30

Solid CAD Documentation —A User's Guide

This chapter contains the User's Guide for *YOUR MICROCOMPUTER 3D CAD MODELER*, a 3D drawing and modeling program capable of generating fully shaded, solid 3D models with automatic hidden surface removal. The complete source code appears in the previous chapter. The User's Guide in this chapter contains the following sections: Introduction, System Requirements, Starting And Stopping The Program, How to Use The Program, and Sample Sessions.

INTRODUCTION

YOUR MICROCOMPUTER 3D CAD MODELER gives you the tools you need to create solid 3D models with your personal computer. As you use polygon planes to create a plan view in the 2D drawing area, the program automatically generates a fully-shaded 3D perspective view of the model in the 3D window. The comprehensive User's Guide provides a reference to the graphics functions and offers tutorial sessions complete with photographs of sample drawings created by the program.

Drawing tools include a powerful 2D/3D polyline function to generate four-sided plane surfaces, a color-changing capability, rotation and zoom 3D capabilities, a toggle for fully shaded or black-and-white models, and a color outline function. A comprehensive set of options gives you the ability to toggle an optional 2D drawing grid and a 3D gnomon (xyz axis system).

YOUR MICROCOMPUTER 3D CAD MODELER contains powerful routines to save your drawings on disk as binary image files. You can retrieve your drawings from disk for later editing or for printing with a third-party graphics printing utility (such as Pizazz; see Appendix F).

YOUR MICROCOMPUTER 3D CAD MODELER gives you fully-shaded 3D modeling capabilities just like those found in packaged software products, using your standard keyboard for input. By using the algorithms and routines presented in Chapter 11, you can readily add mouse control capabilities to the program.

SYSTEM REQUIREMENTS

To run the program, you need an IBM PC, XT, AT, RT, PS/2, or any IBM-compatible personal computer equipped with an EGA or VGA graphics adapter. Also required is either a standard color display (SCD), enhanced color display (ECD), analog display (PS/2 or equivalent), or variable frequency display (Multisync, Multiscan, or equivalent).

IBM PC-DOS or Microsoft MS-DOS is required. A version of BASIC which supports EGA graphics is required. *YOUR MICROCOMPUTER 3D CAD MODELER* is designed for personal computers equipped with two disk drives. The program can be easily modified to use a hard disk or a simulated disk in RAM. Refer to Chapter 31 for guidance.

The program is intended for BASIC interpreters which support EGA graphics, including IBM BASICA and Microsoft BASICA. A QuickBASIC version of the program appears in Appendix E. The shading codes which you would require to modify the program for a CGA or PCjr graphics adapter appear in Chapter 24.

STARTING AND STOPPING THE PROGRAM

Before you use the program, you should create a back-up copy of it. Store the original disk in a safe place and use the back-up copy for your drawing sessions. If you use the original copy, the question is not IF you will lose your only copy, but WHEN.

Starting The Program

To start the program, load CAD-2.BAS under your BASIC interpreter. At the OK prompt, press F2 to run the program. If you are using QuickBASIC, you can load, compile to RAM, and then run QB-001.BAS (presented in Appendix E).

Using Disk Drives

YOUR MICROCOMPUTER 3D CAD MODELER expects to be loaded from drive A. During your drawing session, it saves your keystrokes in a data file using drive A. You can make the program run much quicker if you use a hard disk. It will execute even faster if you use a simulated disk in RAM. You can change the drive to which the data files are written by altering the drive letter in lines 1890, 5050, and 5090.

The program uses drive B to save image files and to retrieve previously stored image files. During your drawing session, you should have a disk in drive B with enough storage space for at least one image file (64032 bytes for the 640×200 16-color screen mode). If you wish to save and retrieve your drawings to/from another drive, you must change the drive letters in lines 2760, 2770, 2780, 2790, 2870, 2880, 2890, and 2900.

Refer back to Chapter 14 and Chapter 15 for further guidance in installing a simulated disk on your personal computer.

Stopping The Program

There are three different ways to cleanly exit the program. Each method restores the 80-column text mode of the BASIC editor.

Method One. At any time and in any routine during program execution, you can press F2 to exit the program. F2 is a hot key which is managed by BASIC itself.

Method Two. When you are located anywhere on the main menu bar, you can press Alt-Q to exit the program. Alt-Q is a hot key combination which is managed by the program, rather than by BASIC. Hold down the Alt key and press Q.

Method Three. Use the arrow keys to select the Quit pull-down menu. Select the Quit function from the menu to exit the program. This method is managed by the menu system of the program.

HOW TO USE THE PROGRAM

Figure 30-1 contains the keyboard layout used by the program. The Enter key is used to implement a function. The arrow keys are used to navigate the cursor around the 2D

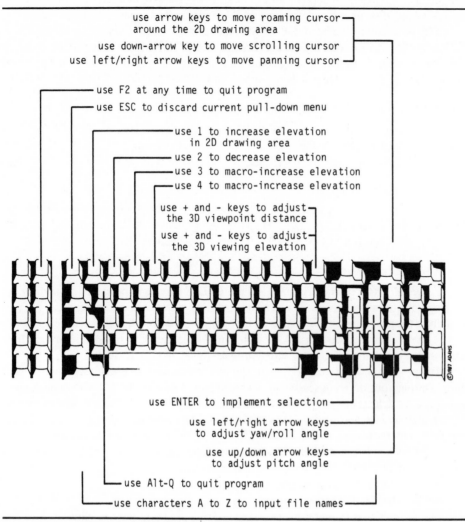

Fig. 30-1. Keystroke controls for the interactive 3D solid model CAD program listing in Chapter 29.

drawing area. The Esc is used to discard the current function and to back up through the menu system.

Fully shaded models are built from individual four-sided planes which you create in the 2D drawing area. Using the 4-Edged function in the Draw menu, use the arrow keys and Enter key to create a four-sided polygon. Use the <1> and <2> keys to define the elevation of each of the four points you are using to make the polygon.

Ensure that you have entered the points in a counterclockwise sequence as viewed from *outside* the model which you are building. When you press Enter for the fourth time, the program uses the standard plane equation to determine if the polygon will be visible or not. Vector math is then used to apply halftone shading to the polygon (if you have the Shading function toggled on in the Options menu).

Using the Menu System

When you are at the main menu bar, use the left-arrow and the right-arrow keys to move the panning cursor to the desired selection. Then press Enter to invoke the pull-down menu. Use the down-arrow key to move the scrolling cursor through the selections on the pull-down menu. The cursor will wrap back around to the top selection after passing the bottom selection. Use the Enter key to implement your selection. Select Menu Bar or use the Esc key to discard the pull-down menu and to return to the main menu bar.

To move from one pull-down menu to another, you must first return to the main menu bar and then use the panning cursor to select another pull-down menu. You cannot jump immediately from one pull-down menu to another.

To begin drawing, choose the 4-Edged function from the Draw menu. Use the arrow keys to move the cursor around the 2D drawing area in the upper left section of the screen. Use the <1> and <2> keys to set the current elevation, which is displayed in the view specifications section, located at the lower left corner of the screen. Use Enter to set the four points for the polygon. The 3D model is automatically constructed in the 3D window at the right side of the screen. The 2D drawing area provides a plan view of your drawing, looking straight down at it from directly above.

Using the File Menu

Name Function. The Name function in the File menu allows you to define your own file names for image files. When you use Enter to choose the Name function, a dialog box is displayed. You may type in any eight-character file name, using the uppercase letters from A to Z. When you type the eighth character, the new file name is displayed at the file name bar located at the top of the screen. During the input process, you may press Esc at any time to keep the original file name.

Save Function. The Save function is used to store your current drawing on disk as a binary image file. Five images can be saved on a 5.25-inch diskette. Many more images can be saved on a hard disk. Each image requires 64032 bytes to store the four bit planes. Refer to the discussion earlier in this chapter if you wish to use a drive other than drive B for saving and retrieving image files.

The Save function is not error-trapped. An empty disk drive will crash the program and your current drawing will be lost. (You can readily add an ON ERROR GOTO . . . routine to gracefully handle this scenario.)

Load Function. The Load function in the File menu will download a previously saved .PIC image file from disk and display it on the screen. The Load function expects to find the image file in drive B. You can modify the program if you wish to invoke a drive other than drive B for saving and retrieving image files. Refer to the discussion earlier in this chapter.

When using the Load function, you must ensure that a disk containing the desired image file is present in the drive. The Load function is not error-trapped; an empty disk drive or a missing file will crash the program.

Quit Function. The Quit function terminates the program. Your current drawing is not saved prior to the exit. If you wish to display or edit your current drawing during a later session, you should use the Save function before you use the Quit function.

Menu Bar Function. The Menu Bar function discards the File menu and returns you to the main menu bar.

Using the Draw Menu

The functions of the Draw pull-down menu are accessed by using the down-arrow key to move the scrolling cursor to the desired selection. Press Enter to activate the cursor in the 2D drawing area. The roaming crosshair cursor is controlled by the arrow keys.

3-Edged Function. This function is inactive.

4-Edged Function. Use the arrow keys to move the crosshair cursor to the desired location on the 2D drawing area. Use the <1> and <2> keys to set the elevation of the point. The elevation value is displayed in the view specifications window. The <1> increases the elevation by 0.25 units. The <2> decrements the elevation by 0.25 units. (For high-speed elevation adjustment, use <3> to increase elevation by steps of 5.0 units; use <4> to decrease elevation by jumps of −5.0 units.)

Use Enter to set the four points which make up your four-sided polygon plane. The program will check to see if the plane is visible from your current viewpoint. If so, the plane will be drawn in the 3D window. If you have toggled the Shading function in the Options menu, the program will apply halftone shading to represent the proper light level on the surface of the plane.

The four points of the polygon should be entered in counterclockwise rotation, as viewed from outside the model you are constructing. If you enter the points in clockwise rotation, the program assumes that you wish the hidden and visible surfaces of the polygon to be swapped.

Polyline Function. The Polyline function can be used to create wireframe models. Use the arrow keys to move the crosshair cursor in the 2D drawing area. Use the <1> and <2> keys to define the elevation. The <1> increments elevation by 0.25 units. The <2> decrements elevation by 0.25 units. (For major changes in elevation, use <3> to increment by 5.0 units; use <4> to decrement by 5.0 units.)

Press Enter to set the starting point for the polyline. Subsequent entries of Enter will cause a line to be drawn from the last-referenced point to the current cursor position. The program will automatically generate a 3D polyline in the 3D window, using the current active color define by the Set Color function of the Options menu. No hidden surface removal or halftone shading is performed with this function. Use Esc to return to the Draw menu.

Undo Function. Select the Undo function to erase the graphics which you have created during your last activity on the 2D drawing area. The corresponding graphics on the 3D window will also be erased. Your most-recent graphics become permanent if you reenter the 2D drawing area or if you leave the Draw menu.

Menu Bar Function. Select the Menu Bar function to discard the Draw menu and to return to the main menu bar.

Using the Display Menu

Use the down-arrow key to move the scrolling cursor through the selections on the Display menu. Press Enter to implement the desired selection.

Regen Function. Selecting the Regen function causes the 2D and 3D windows to be cleared to black. The program then retrieves the graphics primitives created by your previous keystrokes from the .CDF data file and uses those primitives to redraw your 2D and 3D models. The 3D model is drawn in the position defined by the viewing parameters in the View menu.

(The Regen function works only with the Polyline function of the Draw menu. By following the existing algorithm of saving graphics primitives, you can easily build your own modules to regenerate the fully shaded polygons of the 4-Edged function.)

Clear Function. The Clear function clears the 2D and 3D windows to black.

Menu Bar Function. The Menu Bar function discards the Display menu and returns you to the main menu bar.

Using the View Menu

Use the down-arrow key to move the scrolling cursor through the selections on the View menu. Press Enter to implement the desired selection.

Distance +/− Function. Press the plus or minus key to increase or decrease the distance from the 3D model to the viewpoint. The distance value is displayed in the view specifications window. Press Enter to regenerate your drawing using the new distance value and return you to the main menu bar. (Refer to the documentation for the Regen function.)

Elevation +/− Function. Press the plus or minus key to increase or decrease the elevation of the 3D model, relative to the viewpoint position. The elevation value is displayed in the view specifications window. Press Enter to regenerate your drawing using the new elevation value and return you to the main menu bar. (Refer to the documentation for the Regen function.)

Yaw Function. Press the left-arrow or right-arrow key to rotate the 3D model about the compass heading. The yaw value is displayed in the view specifications window. The yaw value is expressed in radians, not degrees; therefore, 6.28319 or 0 is due north, 1.57079 is east, 3.14159 is south, and 4.71239 is west. Press Enter to regenerate your drawing using the new yaw value and return you to the main menu bar. (Refer to the documentation for the Regen function.)

Roll Function. Press the left-arrow or right-arrow key to rotate the 3D model clockwise or counterclockwise. The roll value is displayed in the view specifications window. The value is expressed in radians, not degrees; therefore, 6.28319 or 0 is zero degrees, 1.57079 is 90 degrees, 3.14159 is 180 degrees, and 4.71239 is 270 degrees. Press Enter to regenerate your drawing using the new roll value and return you to the main menu bar. (Refer to the documentation for the Regen function.)

Pitch Function. Press the up-arrow or down-arrow key to tilt the 3D model towards you or away from you. The pitch value is displayed in the view specifications window. The value is expressed in radians, not degrees; therefore, 6.28319 or 0 is due north, 1.57079 is east, 3.14159 is south, and 4.71239 is west. Press Enter to regenerate your drawing using the new pitch value and return you to the main menu bar. (Refer to the documentation for the Regen function.)

Menu Bar Function. Selecting the Menu Bar function discards the View menu and returns you to the main menu bar.

Using the Options Menu

Use the down-arrow key to move the scrolling cursor through the selections in the Options menu. Press Enter to implement the desired selection.

Shading On/Off Function. Select this function to toggle the Shading function. If toggled on, any four-sided polygons which you create (with the 4-Edged function of the Draw menu) will be automatically shaded to reflect the amount of light falling on the surface. If toggled off (the default position at program start-up), then no halftone shading will occur and the four-sided polygon will be drawn as a black-and-white solid surface.

Outline On/Off Function. Select this function to toggle the Outline function on or off. If toggled on, any four-sided polygons which you create (with the 4-Edged function of the Draw menu) will be automatically shaded and re-outlined using the current drawing color. The current drawing color is selected with the Set Color function of the Options menu. If toggled off (the default position at program start-up), the four-sided polygon will be shaded and the edges will be dithered to match the shading.

Grid On/Off Function. Selecting this function will toggle the grid on if it is off, and off if it is on. The Regen function will create a grid in the 2D drawing area if this function is toggled on, otherwise no grid will be drawn during a regeneration of your drawing. (Refer to the documentation for the Regen function.)

Gnomon On/Off Function. Selecting this function will toggle the xyz axis system on and off. The Regen function will create a gnomon (xyz axis) in the 3D window if this function is toggled on, otherwise no gnomon will be created during a regeneration of your drawing. The xyz axis is drawn using the current view parameters defined by the View menu. (Refer to the documentation for the Regen function.)

Set Color Function. Press Enter to cycle through the available drawing colors. The current drawing color is displayed as a line at the bottom of the view specifications panel at the lower left corner of the screen. Keep pressing Enter until the desired color is identified. Use the down-arrow key to leave this option.

The current drawing color defined by the Set Color function is used when the Polyline function is selected from the Draw menu. The current drawing color is used to re-outline any solid polygons in the 3D window when the Outline function in the Options menu has been toggled on.

Menu Bar Function. The Menu Bar function discards the Options menu and returns control to the main menu bar.

SAMPLE SESSIONS

Here are some samples of working with this program.

Graphical Entities: Fully-Shaded Cylinder

The image shown in Fig. 30-2 was created in 30 minutes using *YOUR MICROCOMPUTER 3D CAD MODELER*. The graphics in the 2D drawing area show the juxtaposition of the cylinder.

First, the Polyline function was used to create the end of the cylinder as shown in the 2D drawing area. Next, the View menu was used to rotate and scale the image in the 3D window.

Finally, the Options menu was used to toggle on the Shading function. The 4-Edged function of the Draw menu was used to create each of the four-sided polygons that makes up the cylinder. The four points of each polygon were set in a counterclockwise rotation, using the <1> and <2> keys to set the elevation.

The far side of the cylinder was drawn first, using counterclockwise point-setting as viewed from inside the cylinder. This ensured that the correct surfaces would be hidden. Then the near side of the cylinder was drawn, using counterclockwise point-setting as viewed from outside the cylinder.

Alphanumerics: Geometric Filled Characters

The image shown in Fig. 30-3 was generated in about 25 minutes using *YOUR MICROCOMPUTER 3D CAD MODELER*.

First, the Polyline function was used to create the characters in the 2D drawing area. Then the View menu was used to rotate and scale the graphics to give a pleasing appearance in the 3D window.

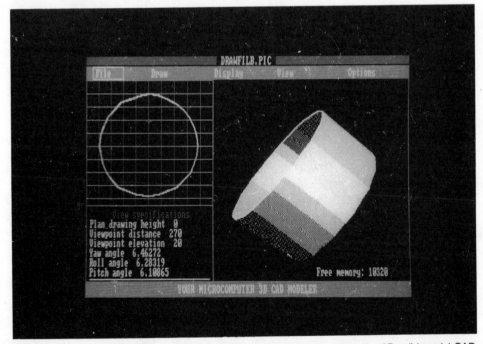

Fig. 30-2. Automatic, computer-controlled shading is provided by the interactive 3D solid model CAD program listing in Chapter 29.

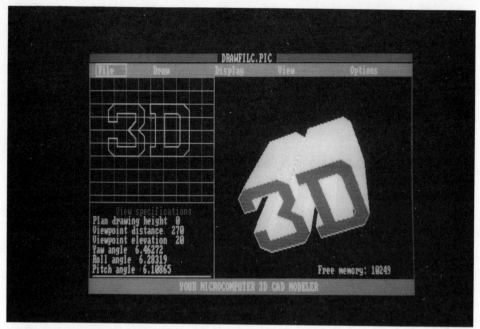

Fig. 30-3. Fully-shaded, solid alphanumerics can be easily created with the interactive 3D solid model CAD program listing in Chapter 29.

The 4-Edged function of the Draw menu was used to create the depth of the characters. Surfaces which would be obscured by nearer surfaces were drawn first, using the <3> and <4> keys to set the elevation. The program automatically added the proper shading to the surfaces.

After depth had been finished, the Polyline function of the Draw menu was again employed to touch up the outlines of the characters.

Backgrounds: Geometric Macro-Enitities

The image illustrated in Fig. 30-4 was created in 40 minutes using *YOUR MICROCOMPUTER 3D CAD MODELER*. First, the Polyline function was used to sketch a simple rectangle which defined the perimeter of the graphic. Then, the View menu was used to rotate and scale the blocked-out graphic. The viewing parameters were noted and the program was restarted. The parameters were reset and work was started on the geometric shape.

A single five-sided object (called a frustrum of a pyramid) was created first. The top of the entity was drawn, then the four sides. The object in the upper right corner of the macro-entity was the first to be drawn, ensuring that other nearer parts of the entity would cleanly cover it in the 3D image. Working from farthest to nearest, the other objects were created.

Geometric macro-entities such as this are useful as 3D backgrounds for presentation purposes.

Oblique Perspective: Checkerboard

The image in Fig. 30-5 was created in 15 minutes using *YOUR MICROCOMPUTER 3D CAD MODELER*. No hidden surface removal or shading was employed.

The Polyline function was used to generate the outline and crosshatches of the checkerboard. Then the View menu was used to rotate and scale the image.

To create the filled portions of the checkerboard, I added a simple area fill routine in place of the (inactive) 3-Edged function in the Draw menu. The routine simply uses BASIC's PAINT instruction to fill at the current cursor position using the current drawing color as the fill color and as the boundary color. The coordinates were passed through the 3D formulas to obtain the correct position on the 3D window, of course. It has been left as an exercise for you to add this routine to your own version of the program.

Multiple Objects: Stacked Cubes

The image illustrated in Fig. 30-6 was created in 15 minutes. The Shading function was toggled off. The Outline function was toggled on.

The cubes at the bottom of the screen were drawn first, to ensure that cubes above them would obscure areas which naturally would be hidden from the viewer. The Options menu was used to change the current drawing color (used by the Outline function) for each cube. Note how the WINDOW SCREEN and VIEW instructions in the program successfully clip the cube at the lower left corner of the 3D window.

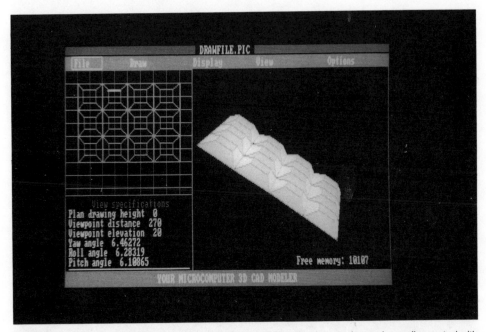

Fig. 30-4. Intricate solid geometric patterns, which are useful as backgrounds, can be easily created with the interactive 3D solid model CAD program listing in Chapter 29.

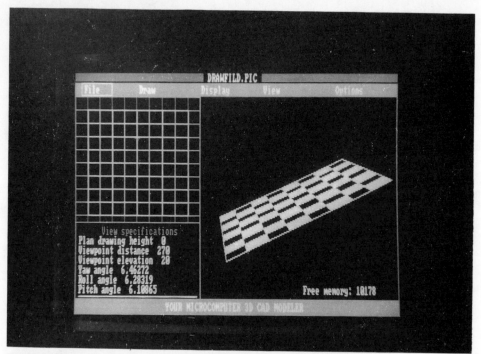

Fig. 30-5. Simple 2D models can be rotated using the interactive 3D solid model CAD program listing in Chapter 29.

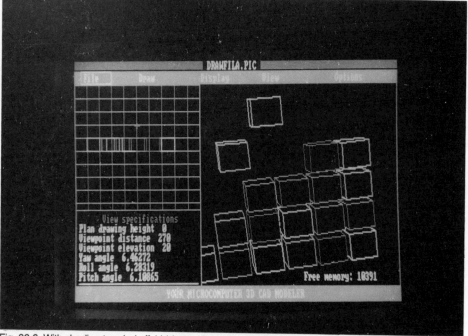

Fig. 30-6. With shading toggled off, hidden surface removal provides the ability to manipulate solid shapes using the interactive 3D solid model CAD program listing in Chapter 29.

Packaging Design: Carton

The image shown in Fig. 30-7 was created in about 45 minutes. First, the Polyline function was used to create a simple wireframe carton which was rotated and scaled using the View menu. The view specifications were noted and the program was restarted with these specifications.

The Shading function was toggled on in the Options menu. Then the three visible surfaces of the carton were created, using the 4-Edged function of the Draw menu. Note how the model has been aligned in the 2D drawing area. Because the front of the carton is fully visible, it will be easy to produce detailed graphics on that surface.

The Polyline function was used to create the alphanumerics on the front of the carton. The Set Color function was used, of course, to obtain the desired color.

The striped graphics on the front, side, and top of the carton were created by changing the active color appropriately and by using the Polyline function. The image was saved at numerous times to disk, and I experimented with different stripes, often retrieving the image from disk to eliminate designs which were not aesthetically pleasing.

This particular sample illustrates the importance of the light source location, which can be changed, of course. (Simply alter the values in line 640, whose square roots must add up to a value of one.) In this sample, the model is backlit, which adds to the dramatic visual impact of the image. (For a detailed discussion of the 3D geometric analysis used to move the location of the light source to a specific location, refer to *High-Performance Interactive Graphics: Modeling, Rendering & Animating for IBM PCs and Compatibles*,

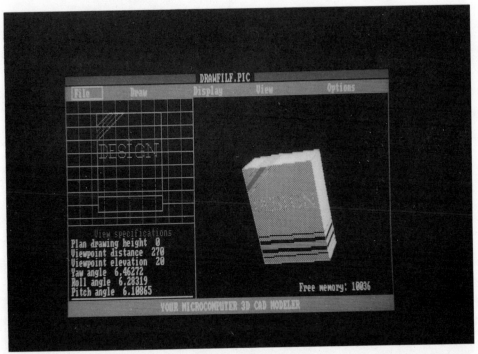

Fig. 30-7. Packaging design and product design can be easily achieved using the color select capabilities of the interactive 3D solid model CAD program listing in Chapter 29.

TAB book 2879. The book also provides source code which will map 2D graphic designs onto 3D cartons, spheres, and cylinders.)

Engineering Design: Aerospace Vehicle

The image in Fig. 30-8 was created in about 55 minutes using *YOUR MICROCOMPUTER 3D CAD DESIGNER*. No hidden surface removal or shading was used. The Polyline function in the Draw menu was used to create the lines in differing colors in the 2D drawing area.

As Fig. 30-8 shows, the space vehicle was drawn from a frontal view. This means that the <1> and <2> keys could be used to define the depth of the model while the vehicle outline was retraced by the crosshair cursor. The Undo function was used repeatedly while I experimented with the shape of the leading edge of the wings and the curvature of the engine pods.

Because the Polyline function was used throughout, the finished image can be rotated and scaled using the Regen function.

WORKING WITH THE PROGRAM

As the sample sessions illustrate, *YOUR MICROCOMPUTER 3D CAD MODELER* is capable of producing some very complex 3D graphics, including fully shaded 3D models with hidden surface removal. To get the best results from the program, use the Polyline function to block out a rough sketch of your model first. Then use the View menu to rotate

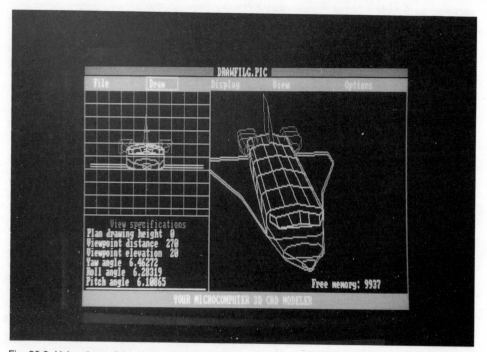

Fig. 30-8. Using the radial pre-sort method of hidden surface removal, the line function can be used to create complex models using the interactive 3D solid model CAD program listing in Chapter 29.

and scale your blocked-out image. Take note of the view parameters, then restart the program using those parameters.

While you are drawing, remember that Regen will recreate your polylines, but it will not regenerate the solid 3D polygons. Use the File menu to frequently save your image to disk. You can use this image as a fall-back position if you make a blunder while preparing your model.

It is helpful to have a firm idea of the model you are trying to create. As you work, use a notepad to jot down elevation values. These values are helpful when you are connecting other polygons to your current work at a later point in the session.

To get the best performance out of the program, use the QuickBASIC version presented in Appendix E. Alter the program to use a simulated disk in RAM for the data file. Revise the program to use drive B for storage of image files.

SUMMARY

In this chapter you reviewed the User's Guide for the 3D solid modeling program, *YOUR MICROCOMPUTER 3D CAD MODELER*. You saw how advanced, fully shaded, solid models with automatic hidden surface removal could be generated.

The next chapter discusses how the program works.

31

Solid CAD Analysis—
How the Program Works

YOUR MICROCOMPUTER 3D CAD MODELER is a 3D modeling program capable of generating solid, fully shaded 3D objects with automatic hidden surface removal. The complete source code for the program was given in Chapter 29. You might want to refer to the program listing as you read this chapter.

Few, if any, of the subroutines in the program will appear new to you if you have read through the earlier chapters. The menu system introduced in Chapter 10 is used in YOUR MICROCOMPUTER 3D CAD MODELER. The structuring of the cursor control routines and functions switchers is the same technique used in the drafting program and the 3D CAD wireframe program.

LOGIC FLOW

A chart of program flow gives you the overview you need to be able to intimately understand the program at the line-by-line level. The flowchart for the start-up section of the program is shown in Fig. 31-1. The modules and their functions are essentially identical to the paintbrush, drafting, and wireframe CAD programs presented earlier in the book.

The flowchart for the runtime section of the program is depicted in Fig. 31-2. Of particular interest are the shading matrix and line dithering modules. In fact, it is these two routines plus the outlining function that differentiates this program from the 3D wireframe CAD program presented in an earlier chapter.

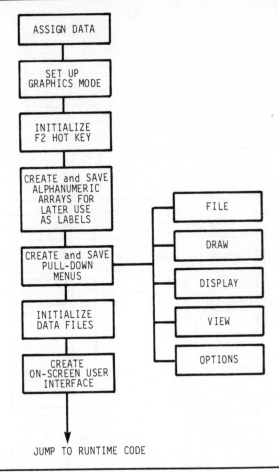

Fig. 31-1. Logic flowchart for the start-up section of the interactive 3D solid model CAD program listing in Chapter 29.

HALFTONE PATTERNS

During start-up, the hexadecimal tiling codes for the halftone patterns are defined at lines 690 through 850. These string codes provide a gradient set of fill patterns which can be used to depict various levels of illumination upon a surface. The bit tiling techniques used were introduced in Chapter 6.

CROSSHAIR CURSOR CONTROL

The module that controls the crosshair cursor on the 2D drawing area is located at lines 4270 through 4570. Note in particular lines 4520 through 4550, which provide keyboard control for the elevation values and display the value in the view specifications window.

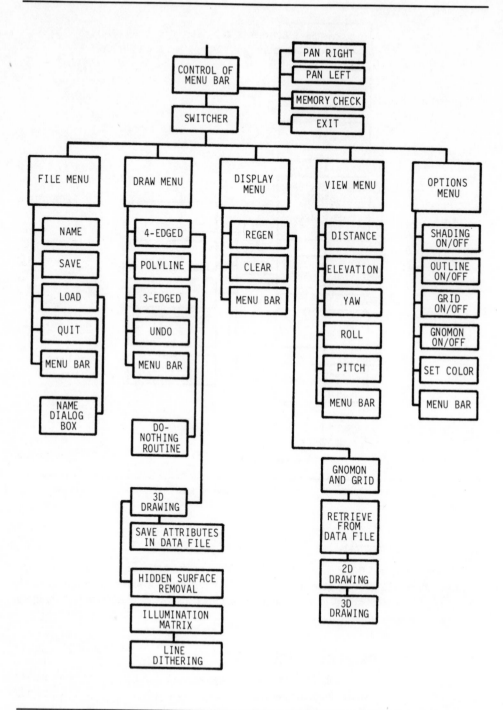

Fig. 31-2. Logic flowchart for the runtime section of the interactive 3D solid model CAD program listing in Chapter 29.

SWITCHER

The switcher for the drawing functions is located at lines 4600 through 4640. Line 4620, which controls the three-edged polygon, simply calls a do-nothing routine at line 4230. If you decide to add the area fill routine discussed in the previous chapter, simply change GOSUB 4230 to the line number at the start of your new routine. The do-nothing subroutine technique of building programs makes it a simple matter to add enhancements to the source code.

FOUR-SIDED POLYGON

The module that creates the four-sided polygon on the 2D drawing area is located at lines 4720 through 4840. Note how the T6 runtime flag, which is set by the crosshair cursor control routine (lines 4270 through 4570) is used to keep track of which corner of the polygon is being worked upon.

After all four sets of xz coordinates have been entered by the user, line 4770 sends program control branching to the subroutine at line 6210. This subroutine uses the standard plane equation formula to determine if the four-edged polygon is visible or not. Provided that the four vertices of the polygon have been entered in counterclockwise sequence as viewed from outside the model being drawn, then any surface which is facing away from the viewpont will be classified as hidden by the routine at line 6210. Because the hidden surface routine requires only three vertices to make its assessment, any polygon of three, four, five, or more edges can be tested.

In line 4770, **IF SP > 0** tests for visibility. If SP is greater than zero, then the surface is hidden and program control returns to the cursor control routine without the polygon being drawn.

If the surface is visible, however, line 4780 jumps to a subroutine which uses common trigonometry to determine the geometric center of the polygon. This center will be used later as the fill start-point for the halftone routine. (If you decide to add the area fill subroutine discussed in the previous chapter, you can use the output of the subroutine at line 6750 as your seed point.)

RENDERING THE SURFACE

Line 4790 calls the module at line 6260 to construct a four-sided polygon in the 3D window. Next, the program tests the T7 flag to see if the user has toggled the Shading function in the Options menu. If T7 is zero, then no shading is required. If T7 is one, then program control falls through to line 4800.

Line 4800 calls the halftone shading routine at line 6320.

HALFTONE SHADING

The halftone shading routine is located at lines 6310 through 6440. Line 6320 calculates the 3D vector from vertex 1 to vertex 2. Line 6330 computes the vector from vertex 1 to vertex 3. Line 6340 uses these two vectors to calculate the surface perpendicular vector, sometimes called a surface normal. The next few lines convert this value to a unit vector, whose length equals one unit.

Line 6400 uses a vector cross product to determine the relationship between the surface perpendicular and the unit vector described by the location of the light source (defined in line 640). The next few lines modify this factor to fit the range of area fill patterns provided in the 640×200 16-color mode.

The module then calls the subroutine at lines 6470 through 6650 to assign the proper shading and dithering values for the halftoning process. The correct A$ string is assigned and the correct &H hex linestyling pattern is prescribed. (For a detailed discussion of halftone patterns and dithering techniques for the EGA and CGA, consult *High-Performance Interactive Graphics: Modeling, Rendering & Animating for IBM PCs and Compatibles,* TAB book 2879.

When control returns to line 4800, the PAINT instruction is used to apply the C13 key matte color and then to apply the appropriate A$ halftone area fill.

Line 4810 then sends the program branching to the line dithering routine at line 6690, which simply uses BASIC's **LINE,,,&Hnnnn** linestyling parameter to draw the four lines which make up the polygon plane.

OUTLINING

Line 4820 then checks to see if the Outline function is toggled on. The T9 runtime flag keeps track of Outline status. If on, the program jumps to the module at line 6810, which uses the current drawing color to re-outline the polygon.

RUNTIME FLAGS

The essential ingredient of the ability of the menu system to control this program is the use of runtime flags. Runtime flags track which corner of the four-sided polygon is being entered by the user. Runtime flags keep track of which rendering options have been requested by the user . . . shading, outlining, and so forth.

KNOWN BUGS

Here are a few minor bugs to be found in the Solid CAD program.

Disk I/O

Like the previous demonstration programs, disk I/O is not error-trapped. It has been left as an exercise for you to add the appropriate ON ERROR GOTO . . . instructions to gracefully handle these error conditions (which will crash the program).

Clipping

The 3D window is clipped by the WINDOW SCREEN and VIEW instructions which are invoked before each drawing foray into the 3D area. Therefore, any polylines or polygons or halftone shading or line dithering will stop at the limits of the 3D window.

The Outline function, however, suffers from a more serious bug in this regard. It will continue to draw even outside the edges of the 3D window. The function has not been clipped by any WINDOW SCREEN or VIEW instructions. It has been left as an exercise for you to track down and correct this bug by adding the WINDOW SCREEN and VIEW instructions at entry into the outline module.

POTENTIAL IMPROVEMENTS

In its present format, the data produced by the 4-Edged function in the Draw menu is not saved in the .CDF data file. This means that the Regen function will not recreate any fully shaded surfaces which you create. However, because all the necessary building blocks are already present in the program, you can readily add this enhancement.

Use the following modules as guides for writing your own routine to save and retrieve graphical primitives, and to use that data to generate fully-shaded surfaces in the 3D window: the data file manager at lines 5020 through 5140; the regeneration manager at lines 5170 through 5180. For further general discussion of data files, refer to Chapter 14. For program-oriented discussion, see Chapter 23.

SUMMARY

In this chapter you explored the shading enhancements which separate *YOUR MICROCOMPUTER 3D CAD MODELER* from the earlier 3D wireframe CAD program.

The next chapter discusses important fundamentals of animation on personal computers.

32

Fundamentals of Animation

No matter what type of graphics adapter you use with your personal computer, you can use three different methods to produce high-speed animation. These methods are graphic array animation, frame animation, and real-time animation. Each method has its advantages and disadvantages. Each technique can be implemented on an EGA, a VGA, a color/graphics adapter (CGA), an MCGA, and a PCjr video subsystem (and Tandy).

GRAPHIC ARRAY ANIMATION

Graphic array animation is also called *bitblt animation, block graphics, software sprite animation,* and *partial-screen animation.* Refer to Fig. 32-1. (Bitblt is an acroynym for *bit boundary block transfer.*)

By using BASIC's DIM, PUT, and GET instructions, you can save a rectangular image from the screen buffer and store it as a graphic array (in BASIC's workspace). You can then create animation by placing the graphic array back into the screen buffer at appropriate locations and at appropriate times.

Graphic array animation is supported by all versions of IBM BASIC, IBM Cartridge BASIC, COMPAQ BASIC, GW-BASIC, Microsoft BASICA, Microsoft QuickBASIC, and Borland Turbo BASIC. Graphic array animation is also supported by BetterBASIC, True BASIC, and a number of third-party graphics drivers for C and Pascal (such as MetaWINDOWS, for example), where it is usually known as bitblt graphics. Graphic array animation is not supported by ZBasic 1.0.

Graphic array animation is supported by the following screen modes: SCREEN 1, SCREEN 2, SCREEN 4, SCREEN 5, SCREEN 6, SCREEN 7, SCREEN 8, SCREEN

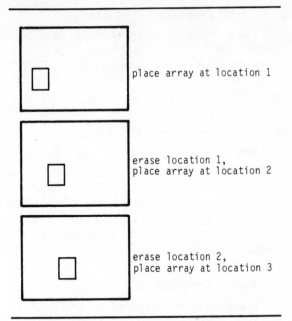

Fig. 32-1. The fundamental methodology of graphic array animation, also called bitblt and block graphics.

9, SCREEN 11, and SCREEN 12. Graphic arrays are supported by the standard color/graphics adapter, by the EGA, by the VGA, by the MCGA, and by the PCjr video subsystem.

Chapter 34 provides a detailed discussion of graphic array animation, including a demonstration program which illustrates arcade-style animation techniques.

FRAME ANIMATION

Frame animation is also called full-screen animation and iterative animation. Refer to Fig. 32-2. The animation program draws a series of full-screen images, and saves each image in a separate page buffer. When all the pages have been stored, a separate routine in the program flips through the pages in the proper sequence in order to create animation.

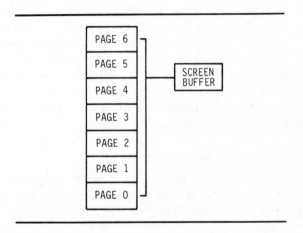

Fig. 32-2. Frame animation is produced by the quick, successive display of previously-displayed images held in page buffers.

Frame Animation On The EGA

Frame animation is supported on the EGA by IBM BASICA 3.21, Microsoft QuickBASIC 2.0 and 3.0 (and newer), and by Borland Turbo BASIC 1.0 (and newer). Eight graphics pages are available in the SCREEN 7 320×200 16-color mode; four pages are available in the SCREEN 8 640×200 16-color mode; two pages are available in the SCREEN 9 640×350 16-color mode.

Frame Animation On The VGA

Frame animation is supported on the VGA by IBM BASICA 3.21/3.30 and by Borland Turbo BASIC 1.0 (and newer). Eight graphics pages are available in the SCREEN 7 320×200 16-color mode; four pages are available in the SCREEN 8 640×200 16-color mode; two pages are available in the SCREEN 9 640×350 16-color mode. One page is available in the SCREEN 12 640×480 16-color mode; six pages are available in the SCREEN 11 640×480 2-color mode. QuickBASIC version 4.0 and newer support VGA graphics.

Frame Animation On The PCjr

Frame animation is supported on the IBM PCjr by IBM Cartridge BASIC J1.00. Frame animation is supported on Tandy microcomputers by GW-BASIC. On the PCjr, six pages are available in the 320×200 four-color mode. On the Tandy, eight pages are available in this screen mode. On the PCjr, three pages are available in the 640×200 four-color mode, while four pages are available on the Tandy.

Frame Animation On The CGA

Frame animation is not directly supported on the standard CGA (color/graphics adapter) by any version of BASIC. In addition, because most CGAs carry only 16384 bytes of display memory, there is simply no room for more than one page. (A 320×200 four-color image requires 16384 bytes, as does a 640×200 two-color image.) There is, however, a way around this limitation.

By using a short assembly language routine to set up graphics pages in RAM, high-speed frame animation can be implemented with a CGA. While each frame is being drawn in the screen buffer at B80000 hex, the assembly language subroutine moves the 16384 bytes of data to a designated area in RAM. After all the frames have been prepared, the assembly language subroutine is used to quickly move the pages back onto the display screen, thereby creating animation. Because the graphics pages in RAM are not corrupted during this process, the animation can be cycled over and over again by the assembly language graphics driver.

Chapter 33 provides a full discussion of frame animation, in addition to a demonstration program for the EGA and VGA.

REAL-TIME ANIMATION

Unlike graphic array animation and frame animation, in which all the images are drawn and saved before starting the animation sequence, real-time animation draws the images as it animates them. During real-time animation, the microprocessor must split its computing power between creating the images and animating them. During graphic array animation and frame animation, the microprocessor can focus its full computing power to animation, because all the images have already been drawn and exist in memory.

Real-time animation is also called *live animation, ping-pong animation,* and *dynamic page-flipping animation.* A minimum of two separate graphics pages is required. While your personal computer is drawing an image on one page, the other page is being displayed. When an image is completed, it is displayed on the screen and the computer begins preparing the next image on the other page. The observer never sees the images being drawn, only the completed images. The speed of the animation is limited only by the complexity of the image to be drawn.

Real-Time Animation on the EGA and VGA

Real-time animation is supported on the EGA by IBM BASICA 3.21, by Microsoft QuickBASIC 2.0 and 3.0 (and newer), and by Borland Turbo BASIC 1.0 (and newer). Real-time animation is supported on the VGA by IBM BASICA 3.30 and by Borland Turbo BASIC 1.0 (and newer). The **[SCREEN,, written-to-page, displayed-page]** syntax is used to swap the written-to hidden page and the page being displayed on the monitor. Refer to Fig. 32-3. On the EGA and VGA, animation speeds of one frame per second to six seconds per frame per second are normal with interpreted BASIC. Compiled BASIC can produce real-time animation programs running at a respectable two frames per second to four frames per second.

Real-Time Animation on the PCjr

Real-time animation is supported on the PCjr video subsystem by IBM Cartridge BASIC J1.00. Refer to Fig. 19-4. Real-time animation is supported on the Tandy by GW-BASIC. Again, the **SCREEN,,p1,p2** syntax is used to control the mechanics of animation. Real-time animation speeds on the PCjr and Tandy are comparable to speeds which can be achieved on an EGA or VGA.

Real-Time Animation on the CGA

Real-time animation is not supported on the standard CGA. Two factors are relevant. First, there is simply not enough display memory on the adapter to permit storage of more than one graphics page. Second, there is no version of BASIC which will draw to a hidden

Fig. 32-3. The fundamental methodology of real-time animation. The microprocessor draws on a hidden page while the hardware displays an already-completed image on a visible page.

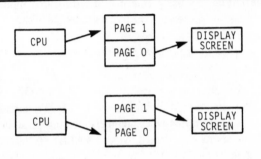

page other than the page which is located on the adapter. There is, however, a method to countermand these difficulties.

By using the POKE instruction, you can physically alter whatever version of BASIC you are using and make it send all graphics output to a memory location of your choosing. Then, by using the assembly language subroutine introduced in Chapter 15, you can move the image from the artificial hidden page onto the display screen.

The POKE routines for versions 2.0, 2.1, 3.0, and 3,1 of IBM BASICA are discussed in detail in *High-Performance Interactive Graphics: Modeling, Rendering & Animating for IBM PCs and Compatibles,* TAB book 2879. If your programming emphasis is on animation, you might want to consult *High-Speed Animation & Simulation for Microcomputers,* TAB book 2859.

STRENGTHS AND WEAKNESSES

Each method for producing animation has its strengths and weaknesses. By carefully defining the results you are seeking, you can make an informed decision regarding which technique is the best animation method for a particular project.

Frame Animation: Best Speed But Large Memory Requirements

Frame animation produces the quickest animation, but because all the images have been created in advance, you are limited to those images during the animation sequence. You cannot change horses midstream, so to speak. Chapter 33 contains a programming example of frame animation.

Bitblt Animation: Good Speed With No Wasted Memory

Graphic array animation (bitblt animation) is not quite as quick as frame animation, but it conserves memory because only selected areas of the screen are being manipulated. Graphic array animation will preserve complicated backgrounds, thereby saving you the time and memory required to redraw the background graphics. Again, however, you are limited to using images which you have already saved in your graphic arrays.

Real-Time Animation: Speed Is Dependent On Graphics

Real-time animation is the most versatile method, but it is also the slowest. Because you are drawing each frame as you animate, you can change the contents of the next frame in the animation sequence. Real-time animation is interactive in the true sense of the definition. By using transparent wire-frame models you can keep drawing time down, animation speeds up, and visual content high.

OTHER ANIMATION TECHNIQUES

Other animation techniques which you can use with your personal computer include color cycling. If you are using an EGA or VGA with a version of BASIC which supports those adapters, you can use the PALETTE instruction to invoke animation.

Color cycling works on the following principles. First, a single version of the image being animated is drawn. Next, a PALETTE instruction is used to redefine the color codes of the image to match the background colors of the screen graphics. This makes the image effectively disappear.

Then, a second version of the image being animated is drawn. The stage is now set for simple animation. By using PALETTE to cause the visible image to disappear into the background and then immediately using a second PALETTE instruction to restore the correct colors of the other image, the two images can be flipped. By repeating this process, short bursts of animation can be created.

The primary limitation of color cycling is the restrictions imposed by color available, by trying to preserve the background when overlapping images are being animated, and by the static nature of the process itself.

SUMMARY

In this chapter you learned about three different ways to generate high-speed animation on your personal computer. You saw that the EGA, the VGA, and the PCjr support all three methods of animation. You saw that the CGA requires some innovative programming in order to produce real-time animation and frame animation. Graphic array animation is available on all graphics adapters.

The next chapter discusses techniques for managing animation programs.

33

Animation of a 3D Entity

This chapter provides a programming demonstration of high-speed frame animation on your personal computer. A complex 3D model is created in the form of four slightly different versions and then subjected to high-speed animation. The demonstration program provides a template which you can use to animate your own 2D or 3D drawings.

The photograph shown in Fig. 33-1 illustrates a display image produced at runtime by the demonstration program in Fig. 33-2. To run the program from the companion disk, type **LOAD "FRAME.BAS",R.**

The program listing in Fig. 33-2 is intended for the EGA and the VGA, using either IBM BASICA 3.21, IBM BASICA 3.30, Microsoft QuickBASIC 2.0 (and newer), and Borland Turbo BASIC 1.0 (and newer).

If you are using a CGA (color/graphics adapter) or an MCGA, you should refer to Appendix G for the converted program FRAME1.BAS. The CGA version of the program uses an assembly language graphics driver to invoke the frame animation.

If you are using a PCjr or a Tandy, you should refer to Appendix H for the program listing FRAMEJR.BAS.

HOW THE PROGRAM WORKS

The program first draws four different versions of a 3D wire-frame mesh. During the drawing process, the PCOPY instruction is used to move each completed image to a hidden page. When the drawing process is completed, the **[SCREEN,, written-to page, displayed page]** instruction is used to flip the pages onto the screen in sequence, thereby creating the high-speed animation.

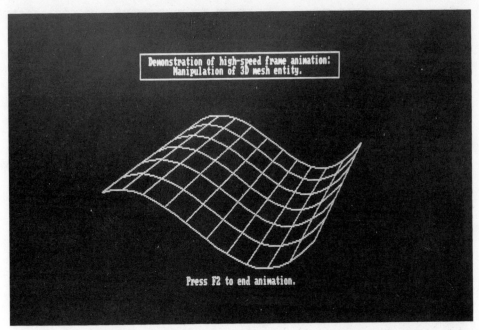

Fig. 33-1. The runtime display image generated by the frame animation demonstration program listing in Fig. 33-2.

The program uses a cubic parametric curve formula to create the smooth curves which make up the 3D wire-frame mesh. One of the magnetic control points for the formula is slightly altered before each version of the model is created. Refer to Fig. 33-3. The resulting animation is of a 3D mesh being subjected to moderate distortion, much like a piece of thin sheet metal being flexed under stress.

PROGRAM ANALYSIS

Variables are defined at lines 170 through 230. Note line 210, which specifies the endpoints and the magnetic control points for the cubic parametric curve routine. The first control point, at $X2$ and $Y2$, will be altered during later stages of the program in order to distort the 3D model.

Lines 270 through 290 set up the runtime graphics environment. The WINDOW SCREEN instruction in line 290 is required to ensure that the 4:3 ratio of the display screen is preserved when the world coordinates are eventually mapped to the screen. Without this instruction, the model would appear too thin.

The Main Routine

The main routine is located at lines 330 through 480. The first part of the main routine, located at lines 330 through 380, is responsible for creating the images of the 3D mesh and for saving them in separate graphics pages.

The main routine calls a subroutine at line 530 to create each version of the 3D wire-frame mesh. This subroutine in turn calls the free-form curve driver at line 860 and the standard perspective formulas at line 930.

```
100 'Program FRAME.BAS    Frame animation demonstration.
110 'Copyright (c) 1988 by Lee Adams and TAB Books Inc.
120 'All rights reserved.
130 'Version for EGA and VGA.  640x200 16-color mode.
140 '
150 '_____DATA ASSIGNMENTS_____
160 '
170 DEFINT H:H=0
180 DIM B11(20,1)   '21 sets sx,sy coordinates near curve
190 DIM B12(20,1)   '21 sets sx,sy coordinates far curve
200 D=1200:R1=5.88319:R2=6.28319:R3=5.79778:MX=0:MY=0:MZ=-150   '3D parameters
210 X1=-30:Y1=0:X4=30:Y4=0:X2=-5:Y2=15:X3=10:Y3=-35   'control points for cubic
parametric curve routine
220 X=0:Y=0:Z=0
230 SR1=SIN(R1):CR1=COS(R1):SR2=SIN(R2):CR2=COS(R2):SR3=SIN(R3):CR3=COS(R3)
240 '
250 '_____SET UP RUNTIME ENVIRONMENT_____
260 '
270 KEY OFF:CLS:SCREEN 8,,0,0:COLOR 7,0:PALETTE 1,0:PALETTE 2,1:PALETTE 3,9:PAL
ETTE 4,7:PALETTE 8,4:PALETTE 9,2:C0=0:C1=8:C2=9:C3=7
280 ON KEY(2) GOSUB 990:KEY(2) ON  'install hot key
290 WINDOW SCREEN (-399,-299)-(400,300)
300 '
310 '_____MAIN ROUTINE_____
320 '
330 'MAIN ROUTINE:  manages the creation of 4 separate graphics pages and then i
nvokes high-speed frame animation.
340 CLS:GOSUB 530:PCOPY 0,3  'store graphics page 3
350 CLS:X2=X2-2:Y2=Y2+2:GOSUB 530:PCOPY 0,2   'store graphics page 2
360 CLS:X2=X2-2:Y2=Y2+2:GOSUB 530:PCOPY 0,1   'store graphics page 1
370 CLS:X2=X2-2:Y2=Y2+2:GOSUB 530   'store graphics page 0
380 FOR T=1 TO 5 STEP 1:SOUND 860,2:SOUND 800,2:NEXT T
390 '_____
400 '_____
410 'module:  animation manager
420 SCREEN,,1,1:FOR T=1 TO 70 STEP 1:NEXT T
430 SCREEN,,2,2:FOR T=1 TO 70 STEP 1:NEXT T
440 SCREEN,,3,3:FOR T=1 TO 200 STEP 1:NEXT T
450 SCREEN,,2,2:FOR T=1 TO 70 STEP 1:NEXT T
460 SCREEN,,1,1:FOR T=1 TO 70 STEP 1:NEXT T
470 SCREEN,,0,0:FOR T=1 TO 200 STEP 1:NEXT T
480 GOTO 420
490 '
500 '_____CREATE A SINGLE FRAME_____
510 '
520 'module:  create a single frame for the animation sequence
530 LOCATE 25,27:PRINT "Press F2 to end animation.":LOCATE 2,18:PRINT "Demonstr
ation of high-speed frame animation:":LOCATE 3,24:PRINT "Manipulation of 3D mesh
 entity."
540 LINE (-250,-285)-(230,-220),C3,B
550 '_____
```

Fig. 33-2. Complete source code for a frame animation demonstration program. This version is for the EGA and VGA. See Appendix G for the CGA and MCGA version. See Appendix H for the PCjr/Tandy version.

```
560 '
570 'module:  create near edge curve and save vertices
580 T=0:T2=T*T:T3=T*T*T:GOSUB 880:Z=30:GOSUB 940:PSET (SX,SY),C3  'establish st
art point
590 H=0:FOR T=0 TO 1.01 STEP .05:T2=T*T:T3=T*T*T:GOSUB 880:Z=30:GOSUB 940:LINE-
(SX,SY),C3:B11(H,0)=SX:B11(H,1)=SY:H=H+1:NEXT T
600 '_____
610 '
620 'module:  create far edge curve and save vertices
630 T=0:T2=T*T:T3=T*T*T:GOSUB 880:Z=-30:GOSUB 940:PSET (SX,SY),C3  'establish s
tart point
640 H=0:FOR T=0 TO 1.01 STEP .05:T2=T*T:T3=T*T*T:GOSUB 880:Z=-30:GOSUB 940:LINE
-(SX,SY),C3:B12(H,0)=SX:B12(H,1)=SY:H=H+1:NEXT T
650 '_____
660 '
670 'module:  draw central curves
680 FOR H=-20 TO 20 STEP 10
690 T=0:T2=T*T:T3=T*T*T:GOSUB 880:Z=H:GOSUB 940:PSET (SX,SY),C3  'establish sta
rt point
700 FOR T=0 TO 1.01 STEP .05:T2=T*T:T3=T*T*T:GOSUB 880:Z=H:GOSUB 940:LINE-(SX,S
Y),C3:NEXT T
710 NEXT H
720 '_____
730 '
740 'module:  connect the saved vertices
750 FOR H=0 TO 20 STEP 2
760 SX1=B11(H,0):SY1=B11(H,1):SX2=B12(H,0):SY2=B12(H,1)
770 LINE (SX1,SY1)-(SX2,SY2),C3
780 NEXT H
790 '_____
800 '
810 SOUND 860,2:SOUND 800,2:RETURN  'this frame completed
820 GOTO 820
830 '
840 '_____CUBIC PARAMETRIC CURVE_____
850 '
860 'module:  FREE-FORM curve driver
870 'calculates location of point on cubic parametric curve
880 J1=X1*(-T3+3*T2-3*T+1):J2=X2*(3*T3-6*T2+3*T):J3=X3*(-3*T3+3*T2):J4=X4*T3:X=
J1+J2+J3+J4
890 J1=Y1*(-T3+3*T2-3*T+1):J2=Y2*(3*T3-6*T2+3*T):J3=Y3*(-3*T3+3*T2):J4=Y4*T3:Y=
J1+J2+J3+J4:RETURN
900 '
910 '_____PERSPECTIVE FORMULAS_____
920 '
930 'module:  perspective calculations
940 X=(-1)*X:XA=CR1*X-SR1*Z:ZA=SR1*X+CR1*Z:X=CR2*XA+SR2*Y:YA=CR2*Y-SR2*XA:Z=CR3
*ZA-SR3*YA:Y=SR3*ZA+CR3*YA:X=X+MX:Y=Y+MY:Z=Z+MZ:SX=D*X/Z:SY=D*Y/Z:RETURN
950 '
960 '_____QUIT_____
970 '
980 'module:  quit program
990 CLS:SCREEN 0,0,0,0:WIDTH 80:COLOR 7,0,0:CLS:COLOR 2:LOCATE 1,1,1:PRINT "Fra
```

Fig. 33-2. (Continued from page 340.)

```
me animation demo finished.":COLOR 7:LOCATE 3,1:SOUND 860,2:SOUND 800,2:END
1000 '
1010 '_____
1020 '
1030  END
```

Fig. 33-2. (Continued from page 341.)

When control returns to the main routine, a PCOPY instruction is used to save the completed version of the 3D model in a hidden page. For example, **PCOPY 0,2** saves the image from page 0 to page 2. The four pages used in this demonstration program are page 0, page 1, page 2, and page 3. (Remember, computer numbering starts at zero, not at one.)

Note how X2 and Y2 are decremented and incremented in lines 350, 360, and 370. Manipulation of these magnetic control points serves to distort the 3D mesh. (For a detailed discussion of cubic parametric curve routines, consult *High-Performance Interactive Graphics: Modeling, Rendering & Animating for IBM PCs and Compatibles,* TAB book 2879.)

The Animation Manager

The second part of the main routine contains the animation manager, located at lines 420 through 480.

The SCREEN instruction is used to switch the display page, creating the actual animation. Provided that the visual difference between different versions of the 3D model is not too extreme, this form of animation can produce extremely smooth and subtle results.

The FOR . . . NEXT loop in each line of the animation manager is required to slow down the animation speed. Otherwise, runtime performance is so fast that the animation appears like a fast-forward videotape. Note how the pause is increased for line 470, where the movement of the 3D mesh is reversed during its return to a normal shape.

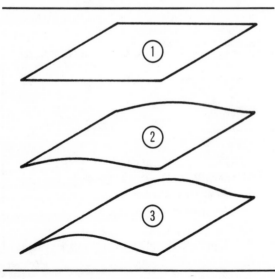

Fig. 33-3. The subtle high-speed animation of a flexing 3D mesh produced by the frame animation demonstration program in Fig. 33-2.

EXPERIMENTING WITH THE PROGRAM

To introduce a slight rotation to the model during animation, add the instruction **R1 = R1 − .08727** to lines 350, 360, and 370. This will alter the yaw value for the viewpoint for each of the versions of the 3D model.

To induce a more dramatic flexing movement into the animation, try increasing the amount of change to the X2 and Y2 variables in lines 350 through 370. For example, **X2 = X2 − 4:Y2 = Y2 + 4** will double the stress on the 3D mesh.

You can adjust the animation rate by tinkering with the FOR . . . NEXT delays in lines 420 through 470. Try changing **FOR T = 1 to 70** to read **FOR T = 1 to 40**. The results will be quicker, but the new impression provided by the animation might surprise you.

These line changes will produce similar results on the CGA version in Appendix G and on the PCjr/Tandy version in Appendix H.

OTHER OPTIONS

The frame generator at lines 520 through 820 could just as easily have been written to draw a simple 3D cube or even a two-dimensional object. You might want to modify this demonstration program to create personalized animation routines of your own. As you can see, the essential ingredients of this form of animation, contained in lines 330 through 480, are not very complicated. Deciding what to animate—choosing the subject of the animation—is as important as the programming algorithms used to invoke the animation.

34

Arcade Animation

Graphic array animation, also called bitblt animation, can be used to create high-performance, arcade-style programs. The trick resides not so much in the actual manipulation of the graphic array on the screen, but in the mating of the animated shape with the keyboard controls. As you learned during your study of the drafting, paintbrush, and 3D CAD demonstration programs in earlier chapters, the routines which control the crosshair cursor are not particularly difficult, especially when the shape of the cursor does not change. In an arcade-style program, however, the contents of the graphic array do change (to match the direction of movement).

The photograph in Fig. 34-1 shows a typical image produced during runtime animation by the demonstration program in Fig. 34-3. The photograph in Fig. 34-2 shows the screen generated by a crash scenario.

The program listing in Fig. 34-3 is intended for the EGA and VGA. To run the program from the companion disk to this book, type **LOAD "ARCADE.BAS",R**. A version of the program suitable for use with a color/graphics adapter and an MCGA is presented as ARCADE1.BAS in Appendix G. The PCjr version of the program listing appears in Appendix H as ARCADEJR.BAS.

The program uses the keyboard to steer an arrow-shaped graphic array (a software sprite) around the screen. The arrow is rotated in order to point in the same direction it is heading. . . and therein lies the main trick to this program: the careful management of different graphic arrays with different keystrokes on the keyboard. Because the arrow can be pointed in eight different directions, eight different graphic arrays must be used at runtime.

Although a simple arrow is used in this program, you could easily use an aircraft, car, spaceship, robot, or other interesting graphic in its place.

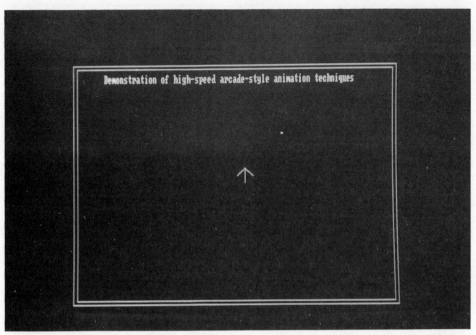

Fig. 34-1. The runtime display image generated by the arcade-style animation demonstration program in Fig. 34-3.

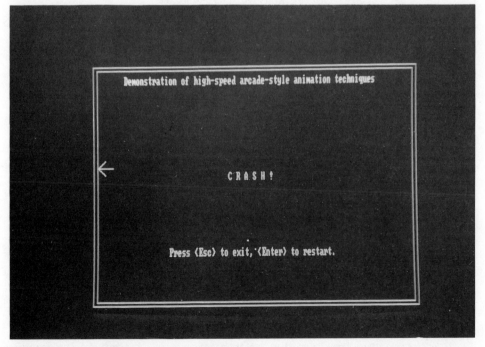

Fig. 34-2. The crash display image generated by the arcade-style animation demonstration program in Fig. 34-3.

```
100 'Program ARCADE.BAS    Arcade animation manager.
110 'Copyright (c) 1988 by Lee Adams and TAB Books Inc.
120 'All rights reserved.
130 'Version for EGA and VGA.  640x200 16-color mode.
140 '
150 '_____INITIALIZE SYSTEM_____
160 '
170  KEY OFF:CLS:SCREEN 0,0,0,0:WIDTH 80:COLOR 7,0,0:CLS
180  ON KEY(2) GOSUB 190:KEY(2) ON:GOTO 230
190  CLS:SCREEN 0,0,0,0:WIDTH 80:COLOR 7,0,0:CLS:COLOR 2:LOCATE 1,1,1:PRINT "Arc
ade animation manager finished.":COLOR 7:LOCATE 3,1:SOUND 250,.7:END
200 '
210 '_____DATA ASSIGNMENTS_____
220 '
230  DEFINT A,C,M,T,X,Y
240  DIM A1(105):DIM A2(105):DIM A3(105):DIM A4(105):DIM A5(105):DIM A6(105):DIM
 A7(105):DIM A8(105)  'reserve space for graphic arrays
250  C4=12:C7=7:C14=14  'color codes
260  X=320:Y=100  'write position of graphic array
270  XP=X:YP=Y  'erase position of graphic array
280  XL=9:XR=599:YU=4:YD=183  'boundary limits for entity movement
290  MX1=5  'horizontal x-movement factor
300  MX2=3  'diagonal x-movement factor
310  MY1=2  'vertical y-movement factor
320  MY2=1  'diagonal y-movement factor
330 '
340 '_____SET UP RUNTIME ENVIRONMENT_____
350 '
360  SCREEN 8,,0,0:COLOR 7,0:CLS
370 '_____
380 '
390 'module:  create 8 versions of entity to be animated
400  LINE (63,20)-(63,32),C4:LINE (48,26)-(63,20),C4:LINE-(79,26),C4  'entity fo
r heading 0 degrees
410  LINE (57,43)-(79,34),C4:LINE (57,34)-(79,34),C4:LINE-(79,42),C4  'entity fo
r heading 45 degrees
420  LINE (48,54)-(79,54),C4:LINE (63,48)-(79,54),C4:LINE-(63,60),C4  'entity fo
r heading 90 degrees
430  LINE (57,65)-(79,74),C4:LINE (79,66)-(79,74),C4:LINE-(57,74),C4  'entity fo
r heading 135 degrees
440  LINE (63,76)-(63,88),C4:LINE (48,82)-(63,88),C4:LINE-(79,82),C4  'entity fo
r heading 180 degrees
450  LINE (70,93)-(48,102),C4:LINE (48,93)-(48,102),C4:LINE-(70,102),C4  'entity
 for 235 degrees
460  LINE (48,110)-(79,110),C4:LINE (63,116)-(48,110),C4:LINE-(63,104),C4  'enti
ty for heading 270 degrees
470  LINE (48,118)-(70,127),C4:LINE (48,127)-(48,118),C4:LINE-(70,118),C4  'enti
ty for heading 315 degrees
480 '_____
490 '_____
500 'module:  save 8 versions of entity as graphic arrays
```

Fig. 34-3. Complete source code for an interactive, keyboard-controlled, arcade-style animation program. This version is for the EGA and VGA. See Appendix G for the CGA and MCGA version. See Appendix H for the PCjr/Tandy version.

```
510   GET (48,20)-(79,32),A1:GET (48,34)-(79,46),A2:GET (48,48)-(79,60),A3:GET (4
8,62)-(79,74),A4:GET (48,76)-(79,88),A5:GET (48,90)-(79,102),A6:GET (48,104)-(79
,116),A7:GET (48,118)-(79,130),A8
520   '
530   '_____SET UP ARCADE TEMPLATE_____
540   '
550   CLS:LINE (0,0)-(639,199),7,B:LINE (8,3)-(631,196),7,B
560   LOCATE 2,9:PRINT "Demonstration of high-speed arcade-style animation techni
ques"
570   PUT (X,Y),A1,XOR:SOUND 460,2:SOUND 400,2
580   '
590   '_____INTERACTIVE KEYBOARD CONTROLS_____
600   '
610   'module:  array A1
620   Y=YP-MY1  'calculate next position
630   IF Y<YU THEN GOSUB 2170 'test for crash
640   PUT (XP,YP),A1,XOR:PUT (X,Y),A1,XOR  'animate
650   XP=X:YP=Y  'update coordinates
660   K$=INKEY$  'check the keyboard buffer
670   IF K$="Y" THEN 700  'is it a turn-right?
680   IF K$="R" THEN 740  'is it a turn-left?
690   GOTO 620  'loop
700   X=XP+MX2:Y=YP-MY2  'calculate next position
710   IF (Y<YU) OR (X>XR) THEN GOSUB 2170  'test for crash
720   PUT (XP,YP),A1,XOR:PUT (X,Y),A2,XOR  'change entity
730   GOTO 840  'jump to A2 routine
740   X=XP-MX2:Y=YP-MY2  'calculate next position
750   IF (X<XL) OR (Y<YU) THEN GOSUB 2170  'test for crash
760   PUT (XP,YP),A1,XOR:PUT (X,Y),A8,XOR  'change entity
770   GOTO 1980  'jump to A8 routine
780   '_____
790   '_____
800   'module:  array A2
810   X=XP+MX2:Y=YP-MY2  'calculate next position
820   IF (Y<YU) OR (X>XR) THEN GOSUB 2170  'test for crash
830   PUT (XP,YP),A2,XOR:PUT (X,Y),A2,XOR  'animate
840   XP=X:YP=Y  'update coordinates
850   K$=INKEY$  'check the keyboard buffer
860   IF K$="H" THEN 890  'is it a turn-right?
870   IF K$="T" THEN 930  'is it a turn-left?
880   GOTO 810  'loop
890   X=XP+MX1  'calculate next position
900   IF X>XR THEN GOSUB 2170  'test for crash
910   PUT (XP,YP),A2,XOR:PUT (X,Y),A3,XOR  'change entity
920   GOTO 1030  'jump to A3 routine
930   Y=YP-MY1  'calculate next position
940   IF Y<YU THEN GOSUB 2170  'test for crash
950   PUT (XP,YP),A2,XOR:PUT (X,Y),A1,XOR  'change entity
960   GOTO 650  'jump to A1 routine
970   '_____
980   '_____
990   'module:  array A3
1000   X=XP+MX1  'calculate next position
```

Fig. 34-3. (Continued from page 346.)

```
1010   IF X>XR THEN GOSUB 2170  'test for crash
1020   PUT (XP,YP),A3,XOR:PUT (X,Y),A3,XOR  'animate
1030   XP=X:YP=Y  'update coordinates
1040   K$=INKEY$  'check the keyboard buffer
1050   IF K$="N" THEN 1080  'is it a turn-right?
1060   IF K$="Y" THEN 1120  'is it a turn-left?
1070   GOTO 1000  'loop
1080   X=XP+MX2:Y=YP+MY2  'calculate next position
1090   IF (Y>YD) OR (X>XR) THEN GOSUB 2170  'test for crash
1100   PUT (XP,YP),A3,XOR:PUT (X,Y),A4,XOR  'change entity
1110   GOTO 1220  'jump to A4 routine
1120   X=XP+MX2:Y=YP-MY2  'calculate next position
1130   IF (X>XR) OR (Y<YU) THEN GOSUB 2170  'test for crash
1140   PUT (XP,YP),A3,XOR:PUT (X,Y),A2,XOR  'change entity
1150   GOTO 840  'jump to A2 routine
1160   '——————
1170   '
1180   'module:  array A4
1190   X=XP+MX2:Y=YP+MY2  'calculate next position
1200   IF (X>XR) OR (Y>YD) THEN GOSUB 2170  'test for crash
1210   PUT (XP,YP),A4,XOR:PUT (X,Y),A4,XOR  'animate
1220   XP=X:YP=Y  'update coordinates
1230   K$=INKEY$  'check the keyboard buffer
1240   IF K$="B" THEN 1270  'is it a turn-right?
1250   IF K$="H" THEN 1310  'is it a turn-left?
1260   GOTO 1190  'loop
1270   Y=YP+MY1  'calculate next position
1280   IF Y>YD THEN GOSUB 2170  'test for crash
1290   PUT (XP,YP),A4,XOR:PUT (X,Y),A5,XOR  'change entity
1300   GOTO 1410  'jump to A5 routine
1310   X=XP+MX1  'calculate next position
1320   IF X>XR THEN GOSUB 2170  'test for crash
1330   PUT (XP,YP),A4,XOR:PUT (X,Y),A3,XOR  'change entity
1340   GOTO 1030  'jump to A3 routine
1350   '——————
1360   '
1370   'module:  array A5
1380   Y=YP+MY1  'calculate next position
1390   IF Y>YD THEN GOSUB 2170  'test for crash
1400   PUT (XP,YP),A5,XOR:PUT (X,Y),A5,XOR  'animate
1410   XP=X:YP=Y  'update coordinates
1420   K$=INKEY$  'check the keyboard buffer
1430   IF K$="V" THEN 1460  'is it a turn-right?
1440   IF K$="N" THEN 1500  'is it a turn-left?
1450   GOTO 1380  'loop
1460   X=XP-MX2:Y=YP+MY2  'calculate next position
1470   IF (Y>YD) OR (X<XL) THEN GOSUB 2170  'test for crash
1480   PUT (XP,YP),A5,XOR:PUT (X,Y),A6,XOR  'change entity
1490   GOTO 1600  'jump to A6 routine
1500   X=XP+MX2:Y=YP+MY2  'calculate next position
1510   IF (X>XR) OR (Y>YD) THEN GOSUB 2170  'test for crash
1520   PUT (XP,YP),A5,XOR:PUT (X,Y),A4,XOR  'change entity
1530   GOTO 1220  'jump to A4 routine
```

Fig. 34-3. (Continued from page 347.)

```
1540 '_____
1550 '
1560 'module:  array A6
1570 X=XP-MX2:Y=YP+MY2  'calculate next position
1580 IF (Y>YD) OR (X<XL) THEN GOSUB 2170 'test for crash
1590 PUT (XP,YP),A6,XOR:PUT (X,Y),A6,XOR  'animate
1600 XP=X:YP=Y  'update coordinates
1610 K$=INKEY$  'check the keyboard buffer
1620 IF K$="F" THEN 1650 'is it a turn-right?
1630 IF K$="B" THEN 1690 'is it a turn-left?
1640 GOTO 1570  'loop
1650 X=XP-MX1  'calculate next position
1660 IF X<XL THEN GOSUB 2170 'test for crash
1670 PUT (XP,YP),A6,XOR:PUT (X,Y),A7,XOR  'change entity
1680 GOTO 1790  'jump to A7 routine
1690 Y=YP+MY1  'calculate next position
1700 IF Y>YD THEN GOSUB 2170 'test for crash
1710 PUT (XP,YP),A6,XOR:PUT (X,Y),A5,XOR  'change entity
1720 GOTO 1410  'jump to A5 routine
1730 '_____
1740 '
1750 'module:  array A7
1760 X=XP-MX1  'calculate next position
1770 IF X<XL THEN GOSUB 2170 'test for crash
1780 PUT (XP,YP),A7,XOR:PUT (X,Y),A7,XOR  'animate
1790 XP=X:YP=Y  'update coordinates
1800 K$=INKEY$  'check the keyboard buffer
1810 IF K$="R" THEN 1840 'is it a turn-right?
1820 IF K$="V" THEN 1880 'is it a turn-left?
1830 GOTO 1760  'loop
1840 X=XP-MX2:Y=YP-MY2  'calculate next position
1850 IF (X<XL) OR (Y<YU) THEN GOSUB 2170 'check for crash
1860 PUT (XP,YP),A7,XOR:PUT (X,Y),A8,XOR  'change entity
1870 GOTO 1980  'jump to A8 routine
1880 X=XP-MX2:Y=YP+MY2  'calculate next position
1890 IF (Y>YD) OR (X<XL) THEN GOSUB 2170 'test for crash
1900 PUT (XP,YP),A7,XOR:PUT (X,Y),A6,XOR  'change entity
1910 GOTO 1600  'jump to A6 routine
1920 '_____
1930 '
1940 'module:  array A8
1950 X=XP-MX2:Y=YP-MY2  'calculate next position
1960 IF (X<XL) OR (Y<YU) THEN GOSUB 2170 'test for crash
1970 PUT (XP,YP),A8,XOR:PUT (X,Y),A8,XOR  'animate
1980 XP=X:YP=Y  'update coordinates
1990 K$=INKEY$  'check the keyboard buffer
2000 IF K$="T" THEN 2030 'is it a turn-right?
2010 IF K$="F" THEN 2070 'is it a turn-left?
2020 GOTO 1950  'loop
2030 Y=YP-MY1  'calculate next position
2040 IF Y<YU THEN GOSUB 2170 'test for crash
2050 PUT (XP,YP),A8,XOR:PUT (X,Y),A1,XOR  'change entity
2060 GOTO 650  'jump to A1 routine
```

Fig. 34-3. (Continued from page 348.)

```
2070   X=XP-MX1  'calculate next position
2080   IF X<XL THEN GOSUB 2170  'test for crash
2090   PUT (XP,YP),A8,XOR:PUT (X,Y),A7,XOR  'change entity
2100   GOTO 1790  'jump to A7 routine
2110  '
2120  '_____
2130  '
2140  '_____BOUNDARY CRASH_____
2150  '
2160  'module:  crash routine
2170   LOCATE 12,34:COLOR C14:PRINT "C R A S H !":FOR T=1 TO 10 STEP 1:SOUND 560,
1:SOUND 500,1:NEXT T
2180   COLOR 7:LOCATE 20,20:PRINT "Press <Esc> to exit, <Enter> to restart."
2190   K$=INKEY$
2200   IF K$=CHR$(27) THEN 190
2210   IF K$=CHR$(13) THEN X=320:Y=100:XP=X:YP=Y:RETURN 550
2220   GOTO 2190
2230  '
2240  '_____
2250  '
2260   END
```

Fig. 34-3. (Continued from page 349.)

HOW THE PROGRAM WORKS

The program first creates the eight different versions of the sprite that will be moved around the screen by the user. Refer to Fig. 34-4. These versions are stored as graphic arrays in the BASIC workspace. Next, the program sets up a playing field and waits for the user to begin play. During the arcade animation, the program carefully chooses a graphic array which corresponds to the direction selected by the player. A control yoke, centered around the G key, gives the player full control over the sprite. Refer to Fig. 34-5. In addition, the program continually checks to determine if the sprite has collided with the edge of the playing field. If so, a crash routine is invoked.

PROGRAM ANALYSIS

Assorted variables are defined in lines 230 through 320. The space is set aside for the graphic arrays in line 240. Note line 260, which defines the starting position for the graphic array. Line 270 defines two variables which will erase the current graphic array before installing the next array to create animation. Lines 290 through 320 establish the amount of vertical and horizontal movement that will be required in order for the sprite to appear to be moving at uniform speed, no matter which direction is being invoked.

The proper graphics mode is established by line 360.

Preparation

The module which creates the eight versions of the graphic array is located at lines 390 through 470. The comments in the section of code relate to the particular arrow being drawn. Refer to Fig. 34-4. The module at lines 500 through 510 stores the images in graphic arrays. The space required to store these arrays had been previously specified in line 240.

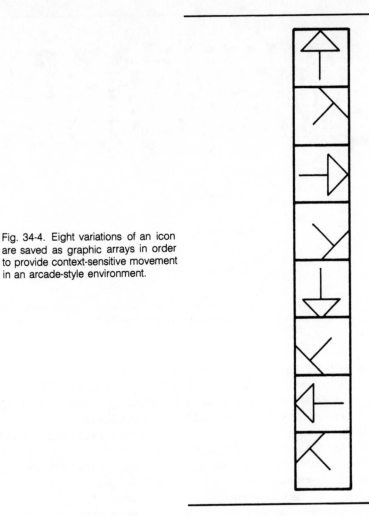

Fig. 34-4. Eight variations of an icon are saved as graphic arrays in order to provide context-sensitive movement in an arcade-style environment.

The playing field for the animation is created at lines 550 and 560. Line 570 places the first graphic array onto the screen.

The Animation Manager

The animation manager is located at lines 610 through 2100. This section of code is somewhat lengthy because each direction of movement requires its own control module. The individual modules in themselves are neither lengthy nor complex.

A typical example is found at lines 1180 through 1340. Line 1190 calculates the next position for the graphic array. The variables XP and YP refer to the previous position. The variables MX2 and MY2 are the movement factors, which are different for each direction, of course. Refer back to the data assignment module to see how these values are defined.

Line 1200 uses standard IF. . . THEN instructions to test if the graphic array has exceeded the legal range. The playing field is distorted for the graphic arrays, because

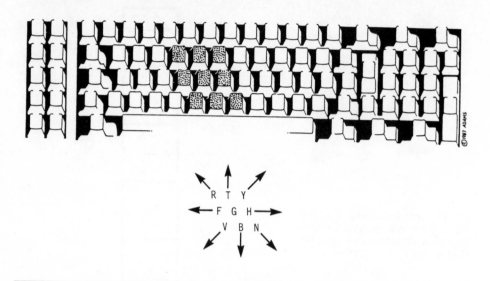

© 1987 ADAMS

Fig. 34-5. Keystroke controls for the interactive arcade-style animation demonstration program listing in Fig. 35-3.

the hot spot of an array is the upper left corner, not the center of the array. Refer to Fig. 34-6. Basically, the width of the array is subtracted from the right-most edge of the playing field. BASIC will generate an error message and will crash the program if an attempt is made to install a graphic array past the physical edge of the screen.

Line 1210 uses PUT to erase the current image and to install the next graphic array. This process creates the animation. The XOR logical operator ensures that the next time the array is placed at the current location, it will effectively erase the image by restoring the screen to its previously-existing condition. Line 1220 then updates the XP and YP variables, which contain the current location of the graphic array.

The keyboard loop starts at line 1230, when a character is retrieved from the keyboard buffer. Lines 1240 and 1250 check for the specific keystrokes which will turn the sprite towards the left or towards the right. Compare these two lines with their counterparts

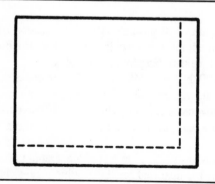

Fig. 34-6. The actual range of screen coordinates available for a graphic array whose focus is located in the upper-left corner of the bitblt rectangle.

in the other seven modules which steer the graphic arrays, keeping in mind the keyboard yoke shown in Fig. 34-5.

Lines 1270 through 1300 handle the turn-right scenario. Note how graphic array A4 is discarded and graphic array A5 is adopted. The PUT instruction is used to place the new array on the screen and program control then jumps to the appropriate control routine. Remember, each direction scenario uses its own control routine.

Lines 1310 through 1340 use the same algorithm to handle the turn-left scenario.

Boundary Crash

The module which manages a boundary crash is located at lines 2160 through 2220. Note line 2210, which reassigns the variables which control the location of the graphic array, and which sends the program looping back to line 550 to restart the arcade game.

A

Dictionary of Variables

The variable names used throughout this book were organized and categorized as follows:

A1, A2, A3 . . . graphic arrays used to hold labels and pull-down menus in major interactive demo programs

A$ hexadecimal bit tiling code for current halftone pattern

A1$,A2$,A3$ . . . strings which hold hexadecimal bit tiling codes for halftone shading functions

A: drive letter used to CHAIN to overlay code (runtime module)

B: drive letter used for storage and retrieval of image files

B1,B2,B3 used in cubic parametric curve formulas

B11,B12 arrays used to hold display coordinates for 3D mesh in frame animation demo program

.BLU file name extension used to save bit plane 0 (blue) of EGA and VGA

C active drawing color

CC active color for line dithering functions

CD hexadecimal value for line dithering binary pattern

CE boundary color for area fill functions

CP preparatory color for line dithering functions

CR1,CR2,CR3 cosine values of yaw, roll, and pitch used in 3D perspective formulas

C0, C1, C2 . . . software color codes used to represent hardware colors

D angular perspective factor for 3D perspective formulas

D1,D2,D3,D4 used in cubic parametric curve formulas

E1,E2,E3 . . . E9 attributes for graphical primitives which are stored in .CDF data files for later retrieval during a Regen function

F$ start-up file name and extension

F1$ temporary storage of file name during name change routine

F2$ file name used to save and retrieve image files

.GRN file name extension used to save bit plane 1 (green) for EGA and VGA

H1 aspect ratio for ellipse

H2 value to increment or decrement aspect ratio for ellipse

H3,H4 radian value to define starting angle and ending angle for arc

H5 value to increment or decrement length of arc

H6 length of arc

.INT file name extension used to save bit plane 3 (intensity) of EGA and VGA

J snap factor

JR crosshair cursor location for text labelling routine

JS temporary storage of snap factor

J1 radius of circle, ellipse, arc

J2 value to increment or decrement radius of circle, ellipse, arc

J6,J7,J8,J9 viewport dimensions for active drawing area on 640x200 screen

J10,J11 horizontal and vertical spacing factors for grid

MX,MY,MZ translation factors for calculating view coordinates of 3D model

MX1,MY1,MX2,MY2 horizontal and vertical movement factors for arcade animation demo program

R1,R2,R3 yaw, roll, and pitch angles (expressed in radians)

RSP,SP1,SP2,SP3 used in plane equation formula for hidden surface removal

.RED file name extension used to save bit plane 2 (red) of EGA and VGA

SR1,SR2,SR3 sine values of yaw, roll, and pitch

SX,SY current location of crosshair cursor

SX+7,SY+3 hot spot (center) of crosshair cursor

SX1,SY1,SX2,SY2,SX3,SY3,SX4,SY4,SX5,SY5 display coordinates used in modeling of a solid model polygon

SXF,SYF first user-defined location used in 4-edged polygon routine

SXM,SYM erase position for crosshair cursor for rubber functions in paintbrush program

SXP,SYP last-referenced drawing location

SXP1,SYP1,SXP2,SYP2,SXP3,SYP3 user-defined corners of parallelogram

SX1,SY1 display coordinates (output of 3D perspective formulas in wire-frame modeling program)

SXD,SYD display coordinates (output of 3D perspective formulas in full shading demonstration program)

T loop counter

TX,TY location of scrolling cursor for Draw on-screen menu

TYF erase location for Draw on-screen scrolling cursor

T1, T2, T3 . . . runtime flags, used to pass values between modules and subroutines; also used as temporary storage of values.

V amount of free memory in BASIC workspace

V1 threshold value to trigger memory warning routine

V2,V3,V4,V5,V7 used to calculate the correct halftone value in the shading matrix

V6 range of available halftone shades

XA,YA,ZA temporary variables used in 3D perspective formulas

XI,YI,ZI components of unit vector which describes the location of the light source for fully-shaded solid models

X1,Y1,X4,Y4 endpoints for cubic parametric curves

X2,Y2,X3,Y3 control points for cubic parametric curves

X1,X2,X3,X4,Y1,Y2,Y3,Y4,Z1,Z2,Z3,Z4 view coordinates (rotated and translated) used in the solid model polygon routine

XL,XR left and right maximum legal range for crosshair cursor (also used as boundary limits for arcade animation)

XN,YN,ZN,XU,YU,ZU,XV,YV,ZV,XW,YW,ZW used in the computer-controlled shading routine

XP,YP current position (erase position) of graphic array in arcade animation demo program

YT,YB top and bottom maximum legal range for crosshair cursor (also used as boundary limits for arcade animation)

B

Mathematics for Computer Graphics

A variety of different mathematical concepts are used in the generation of modeling, rendering, and animation displays on microcomputers. These include geometry, trigonometry, cubic parametrics, vector dot products, vector cross products, matrix multiplication, and others.

Although no single appendix can ever replace a good mathematics text, this appendix presents an overview of important formulas and concepts for your quick reference.

MOVING THE LIGHT SOURCE

You can move the location of the light source for the fully shaded solid models in *YOUR MICROCOMPUTER 3D CAD MODELER*. The complete source code for this demonstration program appears in Chapter 29.

Because the vector which describes the incoming light is a unit vector where vector length equals one unit, a simple formula can be used to derive the xyz components of the vector. In any two-dimensional, right-angle triangle, the square of the hypotenuse is equal to the sum of the squares of the other two sides. The same concept applies to the xyz descriptors of a unit vector in 3D space. That is, the sum of the squares of the xyz components equals the square of the hypotenuse, where the hypotenuse is the length of the vector. Because the length of the vector is one unit, one squared equals one. Therefore, the sum of the squares of the xyz descriptors equals one.

To move the light source to a position of 45 degrees inclination (up) located directly behind the viewpont (due south), it follows that XL would equal 0, the z-displacement would be 0.5, and the y-displacement would be 0.5. Because $XL^2+YL^2+ZL^2=1$, you know that $0+YL^2+ZL^2=1$. The square root of 0.5 is 0.7071068. Therefore, you would define XL as 0, YL as 0.7071068, and ZL as 0.7071068 in your program.

To move the light source to a position behind your right shoulder at east-southeast and approximately 30 degrees inclination (up), you should ensure that each component of the vector is equal. In other words, $3.333+3.333+3.333=1$. Because the square root of 3.333 is 0.5773503, you would define XL,YL, and ZL as each being 0.5773503 in your program.

You can experiment with different light source locations by using the following variable assignments in line 640 of *YOUR MICROCOMPUTER 3D CAD MODELER*:

Directly behind you at due south at 45 degrees inclination:

    XL=0:YL=.7071068:ZL=.7071068

To your right at due east at 45 degrees inclination:

    XL=.7071068:YL=.7071068:ZL=0

To your left at due west at 45 degrees inclination:

    XL=.7071068:YL=.7071068:ZL=0

Directly in front of you at due north at 45 degrees inclination:

    XL=0:YL=.7071068:ZL=-.7071068

Behind your right shoulder at east-southeast (from heading 135) at 45 degrees inclination:

    XL=.5773503:YL=.5773503:ZL=.5773503

Behind your right shoulder at east-southeast (from heading 135) at 30 degrees inclination:

    XL=.5477225:YL=.5477226:ZL=.6324555

Behind your left shoulder at west-southwest (from heading 225) at 45 degrees inclination:

    XL=-.5773503:YL=.5773503:ZL=.5773503

Behind your left shoulder at west-southwest (from heading 225) at 30 degrees inclination:

    XL=-.5477225:YL=.5477226:ZL=.6324555

PRINCIPLES OF TRIGONOMETRY

Trignometric formulas are concerned with the relationships between an angle and the sides of a right-angle triangle. The sine of angle R is equal to the result of the length of the opposite side, B, divided by the length of the hypotenuse, A. The cosine of angle R is equal to the result of the length of the adjacent side, C, divided by the length of the hypotenuse, A.

If you know the size of the angle and the length of one side, you can quickly calculate the length of the other two sides. If you know the length of two or three sides, you can quickly calculate the sine and cosine values. Sine and cosine are the fundamental functions used in the 3D perspective formulas in order to rotate the model through different angles in each axis, thereby creating *View Coordinates*.

The relationship of the lengths of the three sides in a right-angle triangle is also useful for some programming applications. The square of hypotenuse A equals the sum of the squares of the other two sides.

PRINCIPLES OF GEOMETRY

Geometric formulas are concerned with common ratios between the sides of different right-angle triangles which share a common oblique angle. The ratio of any two sides in one triangle is equal to the ratio of the corresponding two sides in the other triangle. These ratios are the fundamental building blocks for 2D line-clipping routines. Geometric ratios are also used in the projection formulas used to place the 3D View Coordinates onto the 2D display screen.

RADIAN MEASUREMENTS

When dealing with circles and angles, computers do not usually use *degrees* for making their calculations. Degrees in a circle are not based upon any scientific or geometric logic. The choice of 360 degrees to represent a full sweep around a circle is an arbitrary one; there is nothing preventing the adoption of 345 degrees to describe a circle, for example.

Radians, on the other hand, are based upon geometric principles. A unit circle has a radius of one unit. The circumference of a circle can be found by the formula **circumference=2(pi)radius**, where pi equals approximately 3.14159. Because the radius is one unit, the circumference can be described as 6.28319 radians. In other words, the arc produced by any angle can be expressed as radians.

WINDOWING FORMULAS

The WINDOW and WINDOW SCREEN statements in BASIC can be used to map positive and negative world coordinates onto the display screen. Although this ability seems almost like magic to many computer-users, the mathematics involved are relatively straightforward.

If you prefer to perform these calculations yourself, or if you are using a programming language which does not support a graphical windowing function (such as C, Pascal, Ada, Modula-2, or assembly language), you can use the window mapping utility shown in Fig. B-1. The routine accepts SX,SY display coordinates in the range of $(-399, -299)-(400,300)$ and maps them onto the 640×200 display screen.

The algorithm follows three steps. First, simple addition is used to translate the low limits of the world coordinates so they match the low limits of the physical screen. Second, the ratio of world coordinates gross size to physical screen coordinates gross size is calculated. Third, the world coordinates to be mapped are multiplied by this ratio to yield the proper xy coordinates for the physical screen.

```
100 'Code fragment A-14.BAS   Window mapping utility.
110 'Copyright (c) 1988 by Lee Adams and TAB Books Inc.
120 'All rights reserved.
130 '_____
140 '_____
150 'module:  map graphics to a specified window
160 'Places world coordinates on the physical 640x200 screen.  Simulates a WINDO
W SCREEN (-399,-299)-(400,300) instruction in BASIC.
170 'INPUT:  Enter with SX,SY world coordinates.  X must be within range -399 to
 +400.  Y must be within range -299 to +300.
180 'OUTPUT:  Exit with SX,SY coordinates which fit 640x200 screen.
190 '_____
200 '_____
210  SX=SX+399:SY=SY+299   'convert low end to 0,0
220  RX=639/799  'calculate ratio to convert X high end to 639
230  RY=199/599  'calculate ratio to convert Y high end to 199
240  SX=SX*RX    'calculate physical display coordinate for X
250  SY=SY*RY    'calculate physical display coordinate for Y
260  RETURN
270 '_____
280 '_____
290  END
```

Fig. B-1. A code fragment which demonstrates window mapping.

Translate To Low End Range

Line 210 adds 399 to SX in order to shift the low end of the world coordinates x-range (−399) over to the low end of the screen coordinates x-range (0). Then, 299 is added to the SY coordinate to shift the low end of the world coordinates y-range (−299) over to the low end of the screen coordinates y-range (0). The world coordinates now fall in an effective range of (0,0)−(799,599). The problem now becomes that of converting (0,0)−(799,599) to (0,0)−(639,199).

Determine The Conversion Ratio

Line 220 divides the x-length of the physical screen by the x-length of the world coordinates range to determine an x-conversion ratio RX. Line 230 divides the y-length of the physical screen by the y-length of the world coordinates range to determine a y-conversion ratio RY.

Calculate The Screen Coordinates

Line 240 multiplies the SX world coordinate by the x-conversion ratio RX to generate the correct SX physical screen coordinate. Line 250 multiplies the SY world coordinate by the y-conversion ratio RY to generate the correct SY physical screen coordinate.

Mapping To The 320×200 Mode

You can easily modify this algorithm to map world coordinates to the 320×200 display screen. Simply change the constant 639 in line 220 to 319. You can also easily change the range of legal world coordinates by modifying the constants in line 230 and by changing the divisors in lines 240 and 250.

VIEWPORT FORMULAS

The VIEW statement in BASIC can be used to map graphics onto a small portion (subset) of the display screen. The effect is similar to creating a small display screen inside the larger whole display screen. Again, the math involved is relatively straightforward.

Many programming languages (such as C, Pascal, Ada, Modula-2, and assembly language) do not directly support a VIEW function. You can do the math calculations yourself by using the viewport utility in Fig. B-2.

In its current format, the utility accepts SX,SY coordinates for the 640×200 screen and maps them into a viewport located in the lower right quadrant at (319,199)−(620,190). In other words, the entire screen is condensed to fit into the lower right hand corner.

Viewport Mapping Algorithm

The algorithm follows three steps. First, addition is used to translate the 0,0 low end of the physical screen coordinates to the low end coordinates of the viewport (in this case 319,99). Second, the ratios of the x-length and y-length of the full screen and the viewport are calculated. Third, the ratios are used to multiply the SX,SY screen coordinates to produce the SX,SY viewport coordinates.

```
100 'Code fragment A-15.BAS   Viewport mapping utility.
110 'Copyright (c) 1988 by Lee Adams and TAB Books Inc.
120 'All rights reserved.
130 '_____
140 '
150 'module:  maps graphics onto a viewport placed at any location on the 640x20
0 physical screen.
160 'INPUT:  Enter with SX,SY coordinates within range 0,0 to 639,199.
170 'OUTPUT:  Exit with SX,SY coordinates mapped to a viewport located within th
e rectangle bounded by (319,99)-(620,140).
180 '_____
190 '
200   SX=SX+319:SY=SY+99
210   RX=301/639  'X conversion ratio is length of viewport divided by length of
physical screen
220   RY=91/199   'Y conversion ratio is height of viewport divided by height of
physical screen
230   SX=SX*RX    'calculate SX within viewport
240   SY=SY*RY    'calculate SY within viewport
250   RETURN
260 '_____
270 '
280   END
```

Fig. B-2. A code fragment which demonstrates viewport mapping.

Translate To Low End Range

Line 200 adds 319 to the SX physical screen coordinate and adds 99 to the SY physical screen coordinate. This moves the low end of the (0,0)−(639,199) range to (319,99), which is the low end of the viewport range (319,199)−(620,190).

Determine The Conversion Ratio

Line 210 divides the gross x-length of the viewport by the gross x-length of the physical screen in order to generate an x-conversion ratio RX. Line 220 divides the gross y-length of the viewport by the gross y-length of the physical screen in order to generate a y-conversion ratio RY.

Calculate The Screen Coordinates

Line 230 multiplies the SX input coordinate by the x-conversion ratio RX to generate the proper coordinate within the logical viewport. Line 240 multiplies the SY input coordinate by the y-conversion ratio RY to produce the proper coordinate with the viewport.

Mapping Other Viewports

You can easily modify the utility to map to different viewports. The value of 301 in line 210 is found by subtracting 319 from 620. The value of 91 in line 220 is derived by subtracting 99 from 190. The comments in the source code are self-explanatory.

HIDDEN SURFACE REMOVAL

The hidden surface routines in the 3D CAD solid model demonstration program (Chapter 29) use the standard equation for a plane to test for visibility. The viewpoint for 3D computer graphics is always located at 0,0,0 so the location of this viewpoint relative to the orientation of the surface of a plane can be used to determine if the plane is visible or hidden.

Matrix math is used to calculate the constants for the plane equation. The xyz coordinates used to compute the constants must be plotted in a counterclockwise direction around the perimeter of the plane when the surface is being viewed from outside the model.

Then, if the equation produces zero when a set of xyz coordinates are used, the point defined by those coordinates resides on the surface of the plane. If the equation produces a result greater than zero, the point is on the inside of a convex polyhedron. (The surface is hidden.) If the result is less than zero, the point is on the outside surface of a convex polyhedron. (The surface is visible.)

VECTOR MULTIPLICATION

Vector multiplication is used in this book for calculating the brightness level of a surface. Two forms of vector multiplication are invoked: *vector dot products* and *vector cross-products*.

Vector Dot Products

By definition, **N^L^COS(angle)**= **N** • **L**, where N • L is algebraic notation for the dot product of vectors N and L. The length of vector N is expressed as N^. The length of vector L is expressed as L^.

If vector U equals (a,b,c) and if vector V equals (d,e,f), then the dot product **U • V=(a,b,c)*(d,e,f)=(ad+be+cf)**, which equals a numerical value (not a vector).

If the vectors are unit vectors, then the length of each vector is one unit. Therefore, **1*1*COS(angle)=N • L**. This, of course, reduces to **COS(angle)=N • L**. In other words, the cosine of the angle between the two vectors N and L is equal to the dot product of the vectors N and L.

Vector dot products are used in this book to invoke computer-controlled shading of solid models. The dot product of two vectors (XW,YW,ZW) • (XL,YL,ZL) can be expressed in algebraic notation as (XW*XL)+(YW*YL)+(ZW*ZL), where XW,YW,ZW is a surface perpendicular vector and XL,YL,ZL represents a vector of the incoming light rays. Refer to Chapter 31 for an explanation of the shading algorithm.

Vector Cross-Products

By definition, the cross-product of two vectors produces a vector which is perpendicular to the plane of the two vectors. If vector U equals (a,b,c) and if vector V equals (d,e,f), then the cross-product **U*V=(a,b,c)*(d,e,f)=(bf−ce,cd−af,ae−bd)**, which equals a vector (i.e. not a numerical value).

In 3D space, vector U can be described as (x2−x1,y2−y1,z2−z1). The computer code is written as **XU=X2−X1:YU=Y2−Y1:ZU=Z2−Z1**. Vector V can be described by (x3−x1,y3−y1,z3−z1). The computer code is written as **XV=X3−X1:YV=Y3−Y1: ZV=Z3−Z1**.

The surface perpendicular can be calculated thus: vector N equals the cross-product of vector U and vector V. That is, N=U*V, where vector U and vector V are written in the computer code previously described. The surface perpendicular can be described, therefore, in computer code as follows:

XN=(YU*ZV)−(ZU*YV):YN=(ZU*XV)−(XU*ZV):ZN=(XU*YV)−(YU*XV)

Scalar Multiplication of Vectors

Multiplying a vector by a positive scalar will change the length of the vector, but will not affect its direction.

If vector U equals (a,b), then the multiplication of vector U by T will yield T*(a,b), which is the same as (T*a,T*b).

COMPUTER-CONTROLLED SHADING

A surface normal is a vector which is perpendicular to the surface of a plane. Provided that the points on perimeter of a plane have been described in a counterclockwise order as viewed from the outside of the polyhedron, then the cross-product of two vectors on the surface of the plane will produce a vector which is an outside perpendicular to the surface of the plane. If the points are clockwise, the result will be a perpendicular which points to the inside of the model containing the plane.

The computer-controlled shading routines in this book operate by comparing the angle between the surface perpendicular of the plane and the angle of incidence of incoming light. The comparison is made by converting the vectors to unit vectors.

3D ROTATION FORMULAS

The rotation of a point in 3D space is best implemented by matrix multiplication. The three rotations of yaw, roll, and pitch are controlled by a separate set of formulas.

Yaw: Rotation Around the Y-Axis

$$(X,Y,Z,1) \begin{matrix} \text{COS} & \text{SIN} & 0 & 0 \\ -\text{SIN} & \text{COS} & 0 & 0 \\ 0 & 0 & 1 & 0 \\ 0 & 0 & 0 & 1 \end{matrix}$$

The resulting computer code is XA=CR1*X−SR1*Z:ZA=SR1*X+CR1*Z, where SR1 refers to the sine of the yaw viewing angle R1 and CR1 refers to the cosine of the yaw viewing angle R1.

Roll: Rotation Around the Z-Axis

$$(X,Y,Z,1) \begin{matrix} \text{COS} & 0 & -\text{SIN} & 0 \\ 0 & 1 & 0 & 0 \\ \text{SIN} & 0 & \text{COS} & 0 \\ 0 & 0 & 0 & 1 \end{matrix}$$

The resulting computer code is X=CR2*XA+SR2*Y:YA=CR2*Y−SR2*XA.

Pitch: Rotation Around the X-Axis

$$(X,Y,Z,1) \begin{matrix} 1 & 0 & 0 & 0 \\ 0 & \text{COS} & \text{SIN} & 0 \\ 0 & -\text{SIN} & \text{COS} & 0 \\ 0 & 0 & 0 & 1 \end{matrix}$$

The resulting computer code is Z=CR3*ZA−SR3*YA:Y=SR3*ZA+CR3*YA. After the point has been rotated through the yaw, roll, and pitch planes, simple addition and subtraction along the xyz axes will translate the rotated model to an appropriate location. The finished formulas are presented in Fig. B-3. The formulas accept the XYZ world coordinates as input and return as output the SXD and SYD display coordinates.

CUBIC PARAMETRIC CURVES

During generation of computer graphics, matrix math finds its most useful implementation in the generation of free-form curves. Refer to Fig. B-4. The formula will generate the x-coordinate for a single point on the free-form curve. The y-coordinate can be derived by swapping Y for X in the formula. (For detailed discussion of cubic parametric curve formulas, consult *High-Performance Interactive Graphics: Modeling, Rendering & Animating for IBM PCs and Compatibles*, TAB book 2879.)

2D LINE-CLIPPING

Lines whose endpoints are located outside the display screen limits must be *clipped*. A point located to the right of the display screen must be pushed left, so to speak. Simple

```
100 'Code fragment A-16.BAS   3D perspective formulas.
110 'Copyright (c) 1988 by Lee Adams and TAB Books Inc.
120 'All rights reserved.
130 '_____
140 '
150 'module:  perspective formulas
160  X=(-1)*X:XA=CR1*X-SR1*Z:ZA=SR1*X+CR1*Z:X=CR2*XA+SR2*Y:YA=CR2*Y-SR2*XA:Z=CR3
*ZA-SR3*YA:Y=SR3*ZA+CR3*YA:X=X+MX:Y=Y+MY:Z=Z+MZ:SXD=D*X/Z:SYD=D*Y/Z:RETURN
170 '_____
180 '
190  END
```

Fig. B-3. A code fragment which demonstrates 3D perspective formulas for personal computers.

```
100 'Code fragment A-17.BAS   Cubic parametric curve.
110 'Copyright (c) 1988 by Lee Adams and TAB Books Inc.
120 'All rights reserved.
130 '_____
140 '
150 'module:  curve controller
160  T=0:T2=T*T:T3=T*T*T:GOSUB 220:Z=30:GOSUB 270:PSET (SX,SY),C3  'establish st
art point
170  H=0:FOR T=0 TO 1.01 STEP .05:T2=T*T:T3=T*T*T:GOSUB 220:Z=30:GOSUB 270:LINE-
(SX,SY),C3:B11(H,0)=SX:B11(H,1)=SY:H=H+1:NEXT T
180 '_____
190 '
200 'module:  free-form curve driver
210 'calculates location of point on cubic parametric curve
220  J1=X1*(-T3+3*T2-3*T+1):J2=X2*(3*T3-6*T2+3*T):J3=X3*(-3*T3+3*T2):J4=X4*T3:X=
J1+J2+J3+J4
230  J1=Y1*(-T3+3*T2-3*T+1):J2=Y2*(3*T3-6*T2+3*T):J3=Y3*(-3*T3+3*T2):J4=Y4*T3:Y=
J1+J2+J3+J4:RETURN
240 '_____
250 '
260 'module:  perspective calculations
270  X=(-1)*X:XA=CR1*X-SR1*Z:ZA=SR1*X+CR1*Z:X=CR2*XA+SR2*Y:YA=CR2*Y-SR2*XA:Z=CR3
*ZA-SR3*YA:Y=SR3*ZA+CR3*YA:X=X+MX:Y=Y+MY:Z=Z+MZ:SX=D*X/Z:SY=D*Y/Z:RETURN
280 '_____
290 '
300  END
```

Fig. B-4. A code fragment which demonstrates a free-form curve driver for personal computers.

geometry is used to compare the ratios of right-angled triangles in order to accomplish this pushing operation.

Although BASIC automatically clips lines which fall outside the physical boundaries of the display screen, it will produce a math overflow condition if the coordinates to be clipped are smaller than -32768 or larger than $+32767$. You can easily modify the window mapping utility in Fig. B-1 to perform general 2D clipping in your programs. (For a ready-to-use line-clipping routine, see the appendices in, *High-Performance Interactive Graphics: Modeling, Rendering & Animating for IBM PCs and Compatibles*.

C

Algorithms for Computer Graphics

The challenges of programming high-performance graphics on a personal computer often extend beyond the task of merely using the language correctly. As the old saying goes, it's not what you've got that counts, but what you do with it. Although an exhaustive understanding of any language—BASIC, C, Pascal, Ada, Modula-2, or assembly language—will make your programming task much easier, it is the algorithms that make or break a program.

Many languages (including some versions of BASIC) do not provide a high-quality area-fill routine, for example. Such a routine is vital to the graphics programmer. Also of importance is the ability to save images from the screen to disk—not always an easy task with an EGA or a VGA.

AREA FILL ROUTINES

The advanced area-fill algorithm presented in this appendix is provided in BASIC, although it can easily be translated into your favorite programming language because it has been written in a modular format.

The algorithm is based on a high-performance first-in first-out queue (FIFO). As the routine runs, the program is continually checking up and down to see if another area needs to be filled. If so, a *seed point* (a new starting point for additional fill) is stored in the queue. After the routine has filled the current scan line, a seed point is retrieved from the queue. This process continues until the queue is empty, thereby ensuring that polygons of any shape—no matter how complex—will be cleanly filled.

The photographs in Figs. C-1 through C-4 show the area fill routine at work. Peninsulas and islands located inside the polygon present no difficulty whatsoever for the algorithm, which is provided in Fig. C-5. If you intend to write serious graphics programs, you should understand the principles behind area fill, because sooner or later there is a good chance that you will find yourself using a language that does not offer a good fill routine.

HOW THE FILL ROUTINE WORKS

The program listing in Fig. C-5 will run in the 320×200 four-color mode on any CGA, MCGA, EGA, VGA, and PCjr. To run the program from the companion disk, type **LOAD "AREAFILL.BAS",R**. If you are using QuickBASIC or Turbo BASIC, you will have to use BASICA to resave the program as an ASCII file before you can load, compile, and run the fill routine under your compiler. (Refer to Appendix E for further discussion of BASIC compilers.)

The main routine for the area fill algorithm is located at lines 520 through 610. Lines 530 and 540 ensure that the initial seed point (defined in line 190) is legal for the 320×200 screen. Line 550 sends program control branching to a subroutine at line 640 that fills one scan line. The subroutine also checks up and down to see if area fill is required on the scan line immediately above and immediately below the current scan line.

When control returns to the main routine, line 560 checks the write pointer variable to see if any seeds were placed in the queue. This pointer is incremented with each new seed store, so if the pointer is still zero, no seeds were stored during the filling of the first scan line. Line 570 resets the read pointer to the start of the queue. If any seeds were stored, this ensures that the first seed stored will be the first seed retrieved.

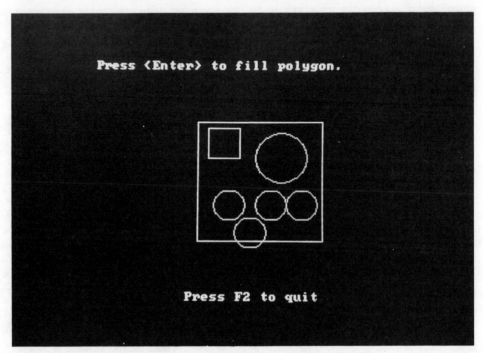

Fig. C-1. The complex polygon which will be filled by the algorithm in Fig. C-5.

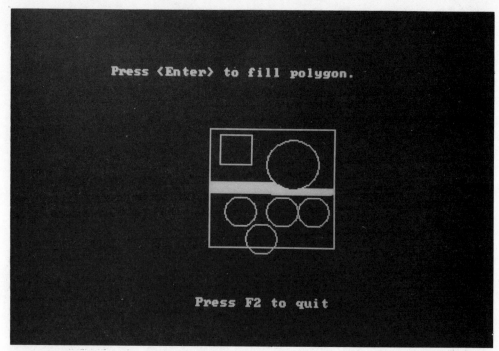

Fig. C-2. The first few raster lines of the area fill routine.

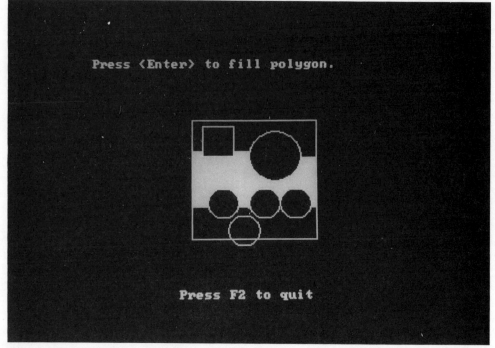

Fig. C-3. The area fill routine begins to fill multiple peninsulas.

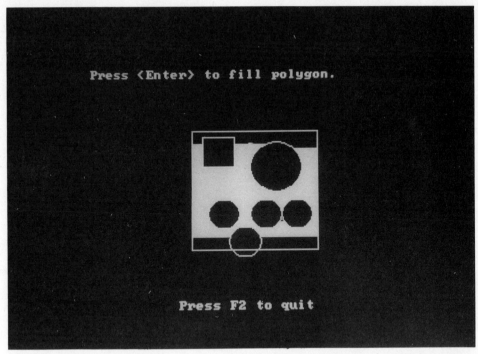

Fig. C-4. The area fill algorithm has successfully filled the isolated, inverted peninsula located between the two rightmost circles.

```
100 'Program title:  AREAFILL.BAS
110 'Demonstrates algorithm for filling complex polygons.
120 'Copyright (c) 1987 by Lee Adams and TAB Books Inc.
130 'All rights reserved.
140 '
150 '_____DATA ASSIGNMENTS_____
160 '
170  DEFINT A,V,X,Y  'integer variables
180  DIM A1(1000,1) 'initialize array for 1001 seeds
190  X1=160:Y1=100  'current position [global]
200  X2=0:Y2=0  'position above or below current position [static]
210  X3=0:Y3=0  'temporary storage of current position [static]
220  V=0    'color attribute of current position [static]
230  V1=0   'write flag for upward seeds [global]
240  V2=0   'write pointer for seed array [global]
250  V3=0   'write flag for downward seeds [global]
260  V4=0   'read pointer for seed array [static]
270  CF=2   'fill color 0-3 [global]
280  CB=3   'boundary color 0-3 [global]
290  '
300  '_____SET UP RUNTIME MODE_____
```

Fig. C-5. Complete source code for an area fill algorithm capable of painting complex, random polygons containing multiple peninsulas and islands.

```
310  '
320  KEY OFF:CLS:SCREEN 1,0:COLOR 0,1:CLS   '320x200 4-clr mode
330  LOCATE 25,12:PRINT "Press F2 to quit"
340  ON KEY(2) GOSUB 350:KEY(2) ON:GOTO 390 'set up hot key
350  CLS:SCREEN 0,0,0,0:WIDTH 80:COLOR 7,0,0:CLS:LOCATE 1,1:COLOR 2:PRINT "Area
fill prototype finished.":SOUND 250,.7:COLOR 7:LOCATE 3,1:END
360  '
370  '_____CREATE RANDOM POLYGON_____
380  '
390  LINE (100,50)-(220,150),CB,B:CIRCLE (180,80),25,CB:CIRCLE (130,120),15,CB:C
IRCLE (170,120),15,CB:CIRCLE (200,120),15,CB:CIRCLE (150,143),15,CB:LINE (110,55
)-(140,80),CB,B
400  '
410  '_____USER INTERFACE_____
420  '
430  LOCATE 1,1:PRINT "Press <Enter> to fill polygon.      ":SOUND 860,2:SOUND 80
0,2
440  K$=INKEY$:IF K$<>CHR$(13) THEN 440
450  GOSUB 520  'call the area fill routine
460  LOCATE 1,1:PRINT "Press <Enter> to create next shape.":SOUND 860,2:SOUND 80
0,2
470  K$=INKEY$:IF K$<>CHR$(13) THEN 470
480  X1=160:Y1=100:LINE (0,10)-(319,189),0,BF:GOTO 390
490  '
500  '_____AREA FILL ALGORITHM_____
510  '
520  'module:  area fill controller
530  IF X1<0 OR X1>319 THEN RETURN 'screen limit trap.
540  IF Y1<0 OR Y1>199 THEN RETURN 'screen limit trap.
550  GOSUB 640  'jump to subroutine to fill one line.
560  IF V2=0 THEN RETURN 'if write pointer equals 0, then no seeds were placed
into array, so return to caller.
570  V4=0  'reset read pointer to start of seed array.
580  X1=A1(V4,0):Y1=A1(V4,1)  'retrieve seed from array.
590  GOSUB 640 'jump to subroutine to fill one line.
600  V4=V4+1  'increment read pointer for array.
610  IF V4>(V2-1) THEN V2=0:RETURN ELSE 580 'loop until all seeds have been retr
ieved from array.
620  '
630  '_____
640  'module:  fill one line
650  V=POINT(X1,Y1)  'what is color of seed position?
660  IF V=CF THEN RETURN  'if it is fill color, then abort.
670  IF V=CB THEN RETURN   'if it is boundary color, then abort.
680  V1=0:V3=0  'reset up/down flags to write state.
690  X3=X1:Y3=Y1:GOTO 710  'save initial seed position.
700  IF V=CB THEN 770 ELSE 710 'if current position is boundary color then jump
 to fill-towards-left code.
710  PSET (X1,Y1),CF  'fill one pixel.
720  GOSUB 880:GOSUB 1010  'check up and down for seed positions and store seeds
 in array A1.
730  X1=X1+1  'move one pixel position to the right.
```

Fig. C-5. (Continued from page 369.)

```
740  IF X1>319 THEN 770 ELSE 750  'if current position exceeds screen limits the
n jump to fill-towards-left code.
750  V=POINT (X1,Y1) 'what is color of new current position?
760  GOTO 700  'loop until boundary color is encountered or until screen limit i
s exceeded.
770  X1=X3:Y1=Y3  'restore initial seed position.
780  V=POINT (X1,Y1)  'what is color of seed position?
790  IF V=CB THEN RETURN  'if it is boundary color, then this line is finished.
800  PSET (X1,Y1),CF  'fill one pixel.
810  GOSUB 880:GOSUB 1010  'check up and down for seed positions and store seeds
 in array A1.
820  X1=X1-1  'move one pixel position to the left.
830  IF X1<0 THEN RETURN ELSE 840  'if current position exceeds screen limits th
en this line is finished.
840  V=POINT(X1,Y1) 'what is color of new current position?
850  GOTO 790  'loop until boundary color is encountered or until screen limit i
s exceeded.
860  '_____
870  '_____
880  'module:  check upward
890  IF Y1<1 THEN RETURN  'abort if on top line.
900  X2=X1:Y2=Y1-1  'X2,Y2 is pixel directly above current position.
910  V=POINT(X2,Y2)  'what is color of position above current position?
920  IF V=CB THEN V1=0:RETURN  'if it is boundary color then set flag to write s
tate and return to caller.
930  IF V=CF THEN RETURN  'if it is fill color then return to caller.
940  IF V1=1 THEN RETURN  'if flag is not in write state then return to caller.
950  A1(V2,0)=X2:A1(V2,1)=Y2  'save X2,Y2 seed coordinates in the seed array.
960  V2=V2+1  'increment the seed array write pointer.
970  V1=1  'set flag to non-write state to indicate that a seed has already been
 planted.
980  RETURN
990  '_____
1000 '_____
1010 'module:  check downward
1020  IF Y1>198 THEN RETURN  'abort if on bottom line.
1030  X2=X1:Y2=Y1+1  'X2,Y2 is pixel directly below current position.
1040  V=POINT(X2,Y2)  'what is color of position below current position?
1050  IF V=CB THEN V3=0:RETURN  'if it is boundary color then set flag to write
state and return to caller.
1060  IF V=CF THEN RETURN  'if it is fill color then return to caller.
1070  IF V3=1 THEN RETURN  'if flag is not in write state then return to caller.
1080  A1(V2,0)=X2:A1(V2,1)=Y2  'save X2,Y2 seed coordinates in the seed array.
1090  V2=V2+1  'increment the seed array write pointer.
1100  V3=1  'set flag to non-write state to indicate that a seed has already bee
n planted.
1110  RETURN
1120 '_____
1130 '
1140 '
1150  END
```

Fig. C-5. (Continued from page 370.)

Line 580 retrieves one seed from the queue. The read pointer, V4, is incremented at line 600 to ensure that any subsequent retrievals will capture the correct seed. Line 590, of course, calls the subroutine that fills one scan line using the freshly retrieved seed. The subroutine will store more seeds during its fill, if necessary.

Line 610 compares the read pointer and write pointer. If the read pointer has caught up to the write pointer, then there are no more seeds in the queue and the area fill is complete.

FILLING ONE SCAN LINE

The module at lines 640 through 850 fills a single scan line within the polygon. The first three lines of the routine check the color of the seed position and then abort the fill if the color is the same as either the boundary color or the fill color.

Line 680 contains the essential ingredient of this module. V1 and V3 are used as runtime flags for the up and down write pointers. If a seed has already been stored for the scan line immediately above the current line, then there is no need to store any more seeds for that line. If the runtime flag is set when a seed is stored, the module will store no more seeds. On the other hand, if the routine encounters the boundary color while it is checking upward and downward (while it fills pixels along the scan line), it will reset the runtime flag (because any future seed requirement would obviously be a peninsula).

Line 720 calls the two modules which check upward and downward. The module at line 880 checks up; the module at line 1010 checks down.

At start-up, the routine saves the initial seed position (line 690) and begins filling towards the right on the scan line. It checks to see if the boundary has been met (line 700) or if the edge of the screen has been met (line 730) and, if so, retrieves the seed point and begins to fill towards the left (line 770).

As you can readily discern while you watch this program executing on your personal computer, it is impossible to defeat the algorithm. No matter how convoluted or complicated the polygon to be filled, the algorithm will function correctly, eventually filling every pixel inside the shape. The only limitation is the amount of space reserved for storing seeds (in this case, room for 1001 xy coordinates has been reserved by line 180).

SAVING SCREEN IMAGES ON DISK

The code fragment in Fig. C-6 can be used to save and retrieve screen images to and from disk as binary image files. Because of the multiplane-per-pixel layout of the EGA and VGA (see Chapter 2), each bit plane of the graphics adapter must be saved individually. The display memory of the CGA, MCGA, and PCjr, on the other hand, can be saved with a simple BSAVE instruction (see Chapter 13).

The code fragment in Fig. C-6 will correctly handle full screen images in the 640×200 16-color mode, provided that you have defined F2$ as a legal file name. The constant value 16000 used in lines 170 through 200 is the length of the bit plane. The OUT instructions are used to modify the latching registers of the EGA and VGA in order to isolate the bit plane being read or written.

If you wish to use the 640×350 16-color mode, change the constant 16000 to 28000. If you wish to BSAVE and BLOAD the 320×200 16-color mode, use 8000. If you wish to manipulate the 640×480 16-color mode, replace 16000 with 38400.

```
100 'Code fragment A-18.BAS   BSAVE/BLOAD EGA-VGA graphics.
110 'Copyright (c) 1988 by Lee Adams and TAB Books Inc.
120 'All rights reserved.
130 '_____
140 '
150 'module: save 640x200 16-color image to disk
160  SOUND 250,.7:DEF SEG=&HA000 'set up segment
170  OUT &H3CE,4:OUT &H3CF,0:BSAVE "B:"+F2$+".BLU",0,16000 'bsave bit plane 0
180  OUT &H3CE,4:OUT &H3CF,1:BSAVE "B:"+F2$+".GRN",0,16000 'bsave bit plane 1
190  OUT &H3CE,4:OUT &H3CF,2:BSAVE "B:"+F2$+".RED",0,16000 'bsave bit plane 2
200  OUT &H3CE,4:OUT. &H3CF,3:BSAVE "B:"+F2$+".INT",0,16000 'bsave bit plane 3
210  OUT &H3CE,4:OUT &H3CF,0:DEF SEG 'restore regs
220  SOUND 250,.7:RETURN
230 '_____
240 '
250 'module: load 640x200 16-color image from disk
260  SOUND 250,.7:DEF SEG=&HA000 'set up segment
270  OUT &H3C4,2:OUT &H3C5,1:BLOAD "B:"+F2$+".BLU",0 'bload bit plane 0
280  OUT &H3C4,2:OUT &H3C5,2:BLOAD "B:"+F2$+".GRN",0 'bload bit plane 1
290  OUT &H3C4,2:OUT &H3C5,4:BLOAD "B:"+F2$+".RED",0 'bload bit plane 2
300  OUT &H3C4,2:OUT &H3C5,8:BLOAD "B:"+F2$+".INT",0 'bload bit plane 3
310  OUT &H3C4,2:OUT &H3C5,&HF:DEF SEG 'restore regs
320  SOUND 250,.7:RETURN
330 '_____
340 '
350  END
```

Fig. C-6. A code fragment which demonstrates algorithms for saving and retrieving binary images in the EGA and VGA modes.

Note how lines 160 and 260 set the target address for the BSAVE and BLOAD to the start of EGA/VGA display memory. The routine in Fig. C-6 will read and write graphics page 0. If you wish to manipulate one of the other pages on your EGA or VGA, you must change the value &HA000 to one of the addresses provided on the memory map in Chapter 2. To read/write page 1, for example, the correct address is &HA400 if you are using the 640×200 16-color mode.

D
BASIC Interpreters

Microsoft Corporation licenses its BASIC interpreter to a number of *OEMs* (original equipment manufacturers), including Tandy, COMPAQ, Panasonic, and many others. If you use an IBM-compatible personal computer, chances are that the BASIC interpreter provided by the manufacturer is in fact a Microsoft product.

Sometimes the interpreter is called GW-BASIC, or Microsoft BASIC, or COMPAQ BASIC, or some other nomenclature, but the software often originates with Microsoft and is being used under license. Even IBM BASICA was initially developed by the programmers at Microsoft Corporation (although more recent versions contain a sizeable percentage of IBM proprietary code).

IS YOUR BASIC A MICROSOFT VERSION?

To determine if your BASIC interpreter is a Microsoft product, check the first few pages of your user's manual for the standard copyright notice. The copyright notice or licensing notice is de facto proof of Microsoft's presence and is clear evidence that the BASIC interpreter adheres to the accepted syntax in use today. Even highly specialized functions like line dithering and halftone fill are uniform in their application across a wide range of BASIC interpreters, thanks to a common geneological background.

Another clue to the origins of your BASIC is the banner which is displayed when you first load BASIC. The technically correct version number and the legally required copyright notice almost always are displayed at start-up.

GRAPHICS CAPABILITIES

Most BASIC interpreters offer standard CGA compatibility, meaning that the following graphics modes are supported: 320×200 four-color SCREEN 1 and 640×200 two-color SCREEN 2. Versions of GW-BASIC intended for Tandy microcomputers offer graphics modes which closely mimic those found on the PCjr: 320×200 four-color SCREEN 1, 640×200 two-color SCREEN 2, 320×200 four-color SCREEN 4, 320×200 16-color SCREEN 5, and 640×200 four-color SCREEN 6.

If your BASIC interpreter offers EGA compatibility, then it supports the CGA modes plus the following EGA modes: 320×200 16-color SCREEN 7, 640×200 16-color SCREEN 8, and 640×350 16-color SCREEN 9. Such an interpreter provides capabilities equivalent to IBM BASICA 3.21, which was the first version of BASIC to provide full support for the EGA. (IBM BASICA 3.30 supports the EGA modes on the VGA.)

If your BASIC interpreter offers only screen modes 1 and 2, you should refer to the program listings in Appendix G for demonstration programs which will run on your personal computer. (It does not matter whether you use an EGA or a CGA with your computer if your version of BASIC supports only the CGA graphics modes. In that case, you are limited to those modes, even though your EGA can produce more colors at higher resolution.)

VERSION IDIOSYNCRACIES

Some versions of GW-BASIC contain minor idiosyncracies which differentiate them from the IBM BASICA syntax standard. When using the PUT instruction to place a graphic array on the screen, for example, GW-BASIC insists that the xy coordinates being used are actual physical screen coordinates. On the other hand, IBM BASICA allows you to use world coordinates established by a WINDOW SCREEN instruction.

No version of IBM BASICA can be run on a non-IBM personal computer. The reasons for this reside in ROM (read-only memory). Part of BASIC's kernel code has been magnetically encoded into the ROM chips. This means that in order to run BASIC, authentic IBM ROM chips must be installed—and IBM does not sell these chips to independent computer manufacturers. You can, however, run many different versions of third-party BASIC on your IBM personal computer.

The CLEAR instruction in GW-BASIC (and in IBM Cartridge BASIC for the PCjr) offers an additional parameter not found in other versions of BASIC. For example, **CLEAR,,,32768** reserves 32768 bytes of memory for display purposes. If you are using the 320×200 four-color mode (which requires 16384 bytes of memory), you could then use two graphics pages because 16384×2=32768. Up to eight pages, are available in some graphics modes, giving computers such as the Tandy 1000 SX multiple page capabilities rivaling those of an EGA and VGA.

E

BASIC Compilers

There are six major BASIC compilers in use today. Of the group, Microsoft QuickBASIC and Borland Turbo BASIC are the most popular. The other four are IBM BASIC Compiler, BetterBASIC, True BASIC, and ZBasic.

Many programmers seem to hold the view that QuickBASIC and Turbo BASIC offer the best mix of easy program development and compatibility with IBM BASICA syntax. In this appendix, sample program conversions are presented in their complete format for both QuickBASIC and Turbo BASIC.

QUICKBASIC AND TURBO BASIC

If you are using QuickBASIC or Turbo BASIC with your personal computer, you should take into consideration a number of factors when running the demonstration programs in this book:

- The CHAIN instruction can be used only to chain to a disk file which has been previously compiled as an .EXE program. The CHAIN instruction is used to load code overlays in the drafting and paintbrush demonstration programs in this book.
- Because of the amount of memory used by QuickBASIC and Turbo BASIC, you might want to use a smaller simulated disk in RAM than the 360K specified in earlier chapters. QuickBASIC and Turbo BASIC each require nearly 200K. In addition, your original program and the compiled code must both exist in RAM simultaneously, which can eat up a lot of memory fast.

- QuickBASIC and Turbo BASIC sometimes will not accept expressions as lengthy as those accepted by many BASIC interpreters. You can solve this situation by breaking lengthy expressions into chunks.
- The FRE(0) instruction does not return the size of free memory like it does in interpreted BASIC. The memory check performed by the drafting, paintbrush, and 3D CAD demonstration programs is unnecessary if you are using QuickBASIC or Turbo BASIC.
- Some early versions of QuickBASIC have suffered from quirks when attempting to write to a hidden page on an EGA or when flipping pages. More recent versions appear to have overcome these bugs. Likewise, some early versions of Turbo BASIC suffered from similar quirks.
- Turbo BASIC does not provide a PCOPY instruction. A short assembly language routine can be used to compensate for this situation.
- Although QuickBASIC can compile programs to run efficiently on personal computers either with or without a math coprocessor, Turbo BASIC uses a math format which will produce the fastest performance only when a math coprocessor is present. A typical real-time animation program written in BASIC yielded the following results: IBM BASICA 4.3 seconds per frame; QuickBASIC .725 seconds per frame; Turbo BASIC 1.8 seconds per frame. These benchmarks represent performance achieved on an IBM PC with no math coprocessor installed.

A SAMPLE CONVERSION FOR QUICKBASIC

The program listing in Fig. E-1 contains the complete source code for *YOUR MICROCOMPUTER 3D CAD MODELER,* a program capable of generating fully shaded solid 3D models with automatic hidden surface removal. This version has been adapted from the listing in Chapter 29 and is fully compatible with QuickBASIC 2.0 and 3.0 using an EGA. To compile this program under QuickBASIC from the companion disk to this book, load QB-001.BAS.

Note line 690, which splits a lengthy expression into two shorter expressions which the QuickBASIC compiler can digest. Note also line 1940, which does not call any memory-checking subroutine. Unlike BASIC interpreters, a compiled program does not generate garbage (which uses up memory) during keystrokes.

Refer to Chapters 30 and 31 for detailed discussion of how this program works. By reviewing the material in this appendix and throughout the book, you can readily convert most of the demonstration programs for use with your QuickBASIC compiler.

```
100 'Program QB-001.BAS:  YOUR MICROCOMPUTER 3D CAD MODELER
110 'Copyright (c) 1988 by Lee Adams and TAB Books Inc.
120 'All rights reserved.
130 'Version for QuickBASIC.  EGA-VGA 640x200 16-color mode.
140 '
150 '_____INITIALIZE SYSTEM_____
160 '
170  KEY OFF:CLS:CLEAR:SCREEN 0,0,0,0:WIDTH 80:COLOR 7,0,0:CLS
180 '
```

Fig. E-1. Complete source code for the QuickBASIC version of the interactive 3D solid model CAD program from Chapter 29.

```
190 '_____DATA ASSIGNMENTS_____
200 '
210 'module:  data assignments
220  DEFINT A,T,J
230  DIM A1(631):DIM A2(150):DIM A3(150):DIM A4(150):DIM A5(150):DIM A6(150)  't
emporary arrays for screen template
240  DIM A7(177)  'array for panning cursor
250  DIM A8(1793)  'array for Options menu
260  DIM A9(21)  'array for scrolling cursor
270  DIM A10(1057)  'array for File menu
280  DIM A11(953):DIM A11C(953)  'for Name dialog box
290  DIM A12(29)  'array for roaming crosshair cursor
300  DIM A13(683)  'array for Display menu
310  DIM A14(1321)  'array for View menu
320  DIM A15(1057)  'array for Draw menu
330  C0=1:C1=2:C2=9:C3=7:C4=11:C5=5:C6=6:C7=4:C8=8:C9=3:C10=10:C12=12:C13=13:C14
=14:C15=15  'software color codes
340  C=C7:CE=C7  'drawing, boundary colors
350  CP=0  'preparatory color for line dithering
360  CC=0  'active color for line dithering
370  CD=&H0  'pattern for line dithering
380  T=0  'loop counter
390  T1=2  'selection flag for menu bar
400  T2=25  'flag for echo position of file menu input
410  T3=0  '2D grid on/off toggle
420  T4=0  '3D gnomon on/off toggle
430  T5=0  'flag for function switcher
440  T6=0  'iterative flag for plastic functions
450  T7=0  '3D shading on/off toggle
460  T8=1  'selection flag for menus
470  T9=0  'outlining on/off toggle
480  J=2:JS=J  'snap, temporary storage of snap value
490  J6=85:J7=19:J8=608:J9=186  'viewport dimensions for active drawing surface
on 640x200 screen
500  SX=122:SY=65  'crosshair array location
510  XL=2:XR=234:YT=19:YB=117  'left, right, top, bottom range of roaming crossh
air cursor
520  SXC=SX+7:SZC=SY+3:SYC=0  'center of crosshair cursor
530  SXP=0:SZP=0:SYP=0  'last referenced drawing point
540  SXF=0:SZF=0  'first drawing point for solid polygon
550  F$="DRAWFILE.PIC":F1$=F$:F2$="DRAWFILE"  'strings used to manipulate filena
me when saving images
580  SP=0:SP1=0:SP2=0:SP3=0  'used in plane equation formula for hidden surface
removal
590  SX1=0:SX2=0:SX3=0:SX4=0:SX5=0:SY1=0:SY2=0:SY3=0:SY4=0:SY5=0  'display coord
inates used in solid model polygon surface
600  X1=0:X2=0:X3=0:X4=0:X5=0:Y1=0:Y2=0:Y3=0:Y4=0:Y5=0:Z1=0:Z2=0:Z3=0:Z4=0:Z5=0
 'view coordinates used in solid model polygon surface
610  XN=0:YN=0:ZN=0:XU=0:YU=0:ZU=0:XV=0:YV=0:ZV=0:XW=0:YW=0:ZW=0  'used in shadi
ng routine
620  V2=0:V3=0:V4=0:V5=0:V7=0  'used to calculate shading matrix
630  V6=14  'range of shades available in 640x200 16-color mode
```

Fig. E-1. (Continued from page 377.)

```
640  XI=.57735:YI=.57735:ZI=.57735   'xyz components of unit vector for angle of
incidence used in illumination algorithm
650  D=1200!:R1=6.46272:R2=6.28319:R3=6.10865:MX=0!:MY=-20!:MZ=-270!:SR1=SIN(R1)
:SR2=SIN(R2):SR3=SIN(R3):CR1=COS(R1):CR2=COS(R2):CR3=COS(R3)   'variables used as
input for perspective formulas
660  XA=0!:YA=0!:ZA=0!   'temporary variables used in perspective formulas
670  SXD=0:SYD=0  'output of perspective formulas
680  J10=25:J11=11   'horizontal, vertical spacing for grid
690  AA$=CHR$(&HDF)+CHR$(&H20)+CHR$(&H0)+CHR$(&H0)+CHR$(&HFD)+CHR$(&H2)+CHR$(&H0
)+CHR$(&H0)+CHR$(&H7F):A1$=AA$+CHR$(&H80)+CHR$(&H0)+CHR$(&H0)+CHR$(&HF7)+CHR$(&H
8)+CHR$(&H0)+CHR$(&H0)
700  A2$=CHR$(&HBB)+CHR$(&H44)+CHR$(&H0)+CHR$(&H0)+CHR$(&HEE)+CHR$(&H11)+CHR$(&H
0)+CHR$(&H0)
710  A3$=CHR$(&HAA)+CHR$(&H55)+CHR$(&H0)+CHR$(&H0)+CHR$(&H55)+CHR$(&HAA)+CHR$(&H
0)+CHR$(&H0)
720  A4$=CHR$(&H44)+CHR$(&HBB)+CHR$(&H0)+CHR$(&H0)+CHR$(&H11)+CHR$(&HEE)+CHR$(&H
0)+CHR$(&H0)
730  AB$=CHR$(&H20)+CHR$(&HFF)+CHR$(&H0)+CHR$(&H0)+CHR$(&H2)+CHR$(&HFF)+CHR$(&H0
)+CHR$(&H0)+CHR$(&H80):A5$=AB$+CHR$(&HFF)+CHR$(&H0)+CHR$(&H0)+CHR$(&H8)+CHR$(&HF
F)+CHR$(&H0)+CHR$(&H0)
740  A6$=CHR$(&H44)+CHR$(&HFF)+CHR$(&H0)+CHR$(&H0)+CHR$(&H11)+CHR$(&HFF)+CHR$(&H
0)+CHR$(&H0)
750  A7$=CHR$(&H55)+CHR$(&HFF)+CHR$(&H0)+CHR$(&H0)+CHR$(&HAA)+CHR$(&HFF)+CHR$(&H
0)+CHR$(&H0)
760  A8$=CHR$(&HBB)+CHR$(&HFF)+CHR$(&H0)+CHR$(&H0)+CHR$(&HEE)+CHR$(&HFF)+CHR$(&H
0)+CHR$(&H0)
770  AC$=CHR$(&HDF)+CHR$(&HDF)+CHR$(&H20)+CHR$(&H0)+CHR$(&HFD)+CHR$(&HFD)+CHR$(&
H2)+CHR$(&H0)+CHR$(&H7F):A9$=AC$+CHR$(&H7F)+CHR$(&H80)+CHR$(&H0)+CHR$(&HF7)+CHR$
(&HF7)+CHR$(&H8)+CHR$(&H0)
780  A10$=CHR$(&HBB)+CHR$(&HBB)+CHR$(&H44)+CHR$(&H0)+CHR$(&HEE)+CHR$(&HEE)+CHR$(
&H11)+CHR$(&H0)
790  A11$=CHR$(&HAA)+CHR$(&HAA)+CHR$(&H55)+CHR$(&H0)+CHR$(&H55)+CHR$(&H55)+CHR$(
&HAA)+CHR$(&H0)
800  A12$=CHR$(&H44)+CHR$(&H44)+CHR$(&HBB)+CHR$(&H0)+CHR$(&H11)+CHR$(&H11)+CHR$(
&HEE)+CHR$(&H0)
810  AD$=CHR$(&H20)+CHR$(&H0)+CHR$(&HFF)+CHR$(&H0)+CHR$(&H2)+CHR$(&H0)+CHR$(&HFF
)+CHR$(&H0)+CHR$(&H80):A13$=AD$+CHR$(&H0)+CHR$(&HFF)+CHR$(&H0)+CHR$(&H8)+CHR$(&H
0)+CHR$(&HFF)+CHR$(&H0)
820  A14$=CHR$(&H44)+CHR$(&H0)+CHR$(&HFF)+CHR$(&H0)+CHR$(&H11)+CHR$(&H0)+CHR$(&H
FF)+CHR$(&H0)
830  A15$=CHR$(&H55)+CHR$(&H0)+CHR$(&HFF)+CHR$(&H0)+CHR$(&HAA)+CHR$(&H0)+CHR$(&H
FF)+CHR$(&H0)
840  A16$=CHR$(&HBB)+CHR$(&H0)+CHR$(&HFF)+CHR$(&H0)+CHR$(&HEE)+CHR$(&H0)+CHR$(&H
FF)+CHR$(&H0)
850  A$=A10$   'generic shading code
860  '
870  '_____SET UP RUNTIME ENVIRONMENT_____
880  '
890  'module:  set up runtime environment
900  CLS:SCREEN 8,,0,0:COLOR C7,0:CLS   '640x200 16-clr mode
910  PALETTE 1,0:PALETTE 2,1:PALETTE 3,9:PALETTE 4,7:PALETTE 5,5:PALETTE 6,6:PAL
ETTE 7,3:PALETTE 8,8:PALETTE 9,2:PALETTE 10,10:PALETTE 11,4:PALETTE 12,12:PALETT
E 13,13:PALETTE 14,14:PALETTE 15,15
```

Fig. E-1. (Continued from page 378.)

```
930   COLOR,0   'restore hardware color for background
940   GOSUB 1890   'initialize .CDF data file
950 '
960 '_____SET UP SCREEN DISPLAY_____
970 '
980 'module:  set up screen template
990   GOSUB 1250   'save alphanumeric graphic arrays
1000  GOSUB 1430   'create pull-down menus
1010  LINE (0,8)-(639,199),C8,B   'border
1020  LINE (0,187)-(639,187),C8:PAINT (320,190),C8,C8:PUT (182,189),A1,XOR   'ban
ner
1030  LINE (0,0)-(639,6),C4,B:PAINT (320,3),C4,C4:LOCATE 1,33:PRINT " DRAWFILE.C
DF ":LOCATE 1,34:PRINT F$   'filename bar
1040  LINE (1,8)-(639,18),C8,B:PAINT (320,10),C8,C8   'menu bar
1050  PUT (18,9),A2,XOR:PUT (130,9),A3,XOR:PUT (250,9),A4,XOR:PUT (370,9),A5,XOR
:PUT (510,9),A6,XOR   'selections for menu bar
1070  LOCATE 10,20:PRINT "                                    "
1080  LINE (250,19)-(250,186),C8:LINE (249,19)-(249,186),C8:LINE (1,19)-(1,186),
C8:LINE (638,19)-(638,186),C8:LINE (1,124)-(249,124),C8:LINE (122,53)-(132,53),C
4:LINE (127,51)-(127,55),C4   'split screen
1090  LOCATE 18,2:PRINT "Plan drawing height":LOCATE 19,2:PRINT "Viewpoint dista
nce":LOCATE 20,2:PRINT "Viewpoint elevation":LOCATE 21,2:PRINT "Yaw angle":LOCAT
E 22,2:PRINT "Roll angle":LOCATE 23,2:PRINT "Pitch angle"
1100  LOCATE 17,8:COLOR C4:PRINT "View specifications":COLOR C7
1110  GOSUB 5680   'alphanumeric readouts
1120  PUT (126,8),A7,XOR   'panning cursor for menu bar
1130  PCOPY 0,1:PCOPY 1,2   'establish refresh buffers
1140  LOCATE 9,40:COLOR C4:PRINT "YOUR MICROCOMPUTER 3D CAD MODELER":LOCATE 12,4
0:COLOR C7:PRINT "Copyright (c) 1988 by Lee Adams and":LOCATE 13,40:PRINT "TAB B
ooks Inc.  All rights reserved."
1150  LINE (310,60)-(584,60),C4:LINE (310,74)-(584,74),C4
1160  LOCATE 19,43:PRINT "Press <Enter> to continue...":SOUND 860,2:SOUND 800,2
1170  K$=INKEY$:IF K$<>CHR$(13) THEN 1170
1180  PCOPY 1,0:SOUND 250,.7   'restore screen
1190  GOTO 1940   'jump to runtime code
1200  GOTO 1200   'bulletproof code barrier
1210 '
1220 '_____CREATE ALPHANUMERICS FOR TEMPLATE_____
1230 '
1240 'module: create alpha arrays for screen template
1250  COLOR C12:LOCATE 10,20:PRINT "YOUR MICROCOMPUTER 3D CAD MODELER"
1260  GET (150,71)-(424,79),A1:LOCATE 10,20:PRINT "
                  "
1270  LOCATE 10,20:PRINT "File":GET (150,71)-(210,79),A2
1280  LOCATE 10,20:PRINT "Draw":GET (150,71)-(210,79),A3
1290  LOCATE 10,20:PRINT "Display":GET (150,71)-(210,79),A4
1300  LOCATE 10,20:PRINT "View   ":GET (150,71)-(210,79),A5
1310  LOCATE 10,20:PRINT "Options":GET (150,71)-(210,79),A6
1320  COLOR C7:LOCATE 10,20:PRINT "           "
1330  LINE (150,70)-(212,80),C12,B:GET (150,70)-(212,80),A7   'create panning cur
sor for menu bar
1340  LINE (150,70)-(212,80),0,B
1350  LINE (323,44)-(337,44),C7:LINE (330,41)-(330,47),C7:LINE (329,44)-(331,44)
```

Fig. E-1. (Continued from page 379.)

```
,0  'create roaming crosshair cursor
1360  GET (323,41)-(337,47),A12:LINE (323,41)-(337,47),0,BF
1370  RETURN
1380  '
1390  '_____CREATE PULL-DOWN MENUS_____
1400  '
1410  'module:  create pull-down menus
1420  'submodule:  create Options menu
1430  COLOR C4:LOCATE 10,20:PRINT "Shading on/off":LOCATE 11,20:PRINT "Outline o
n/off":LOCATE 12,20:PRINT "Grid on/off":LOCATE 13,20:PRINT "Gnomon on/off"
1440  LOCATE 14,20:PRINT "Set color":LOCATE 15,20:PRINT "Menu bar"
1450  LINE (138,67)-(264,122),C8,B
1460  GET (138,67)-(264,122),A8:LINE (138,67)-(264,122),0.BF
1470  LOCATE 10,20:COLOR C7:PRINT CHR$(175):COLOR C7   'menu cursor >>
1480  GET (151,73)-(159,77),A9:LOCATE 10,20:PRINT " "
1490  '_____
1500  '
1510  'submodule:  create File menu
1520  COLOR C4:LOCATE 10,20:PRINT "Name":LOCATE 11,20:PRINT "Save":LOCATE 12,20:
PRINT "Load":LOCATE 13,20:PRINT "Quit":LOCATE 14,20:PRINT "Menu bar"
1530  LINE (138,67)-(220,114),C8,B
1540  GET (138,67)-(220,114),A10:LINE (138,67)-(220,114),0,BF
1550  '_____
1560  '
1570  'submodule:  create Draw menu
1580  COLOR C4:LOCATE 10,20:PRINT "3-edged":LOCATE 11,20:PRINT "4-edged":LOCATE
12,20:PRINT "Polyline":LOCATE 13,20:PRINT "Undo":LOCATE 14,20:PRINT "Menu bar"
1590  LINE (138,67)-(220,114),C8,B
1600  GET (138,67)-(220,114),A15:LINE (138,67)-(220,114),0,BF
1610  '_____
1620  '
1630  'submodule:  create Name dialog box
1640  COLOR C4:LOCATE 10,20:PRINT "Enter new filename:            ":COLOR C7
1650  LINE (144,69)-(413,82),C8,B
1660  GET (144,69)-(413,82),A11:LINE (144,69)-(413,82),0,BF
1670  '_____
1680  '
1690  'submodule:  create Display menu
1700  COLOR C4:LOCATE 4,20:PRINT "Regen":LOCATE 5,20:PRINT "Clear":LOCATE 6,20:P
RINT "Menu bar"
1710  LINE (138,20)-(220,50),C8,B
1720  GET (138,20)-(220,50),A13:LINE (138,20)-(220,50),0,BF
1730  '_____
1740  '
1750  'submodule:  create View menu
1760  LOCATE 4,20:PRINT "Distance":LOCATE 5,20:PRINT "Elevation":LOCATE 6,20:PRI
NT "Yaw":LOCATE 7,20:PRINT "Roll":LOCATE 8,20:PRINT "Pitch":LOCATE 9,20:PRINT "M
enu bar"
1770  LINE (138,20)-(230,74),C8,B
1780  GET (138,20)-(230,74),A14:LINE (138,20)-(230,74),0,BF:COLOR C7
1790  RETURN
1800  '
1810  '_____QUIT_____
```

Fig. E-1. (Continued from page 380.)

```
1820 '
1830 'module:  exit routine
1840   CLS:SCREEN 0,0,0,0:WIDTH 80:COLOR 7,0,0:CLS:LOCATE 1,1,1:COLOR 4:PRINT "YO
UR MICROCOMPUTER 3D CAD MODELER":LOCATE 2,1:PRINT "is finished.":COLOR 7:SOUND 2
50,.7:END
1850 '
1860 '_____INITIALIZE DATA FILES_____
1870 '
1880 'module:  initialize .CDF data files
1890   OPEN "A:KEYLAYER.CDF" FOR OUTPUT AS #1:WRITE #1,SXP,SZP,SXC,SZC,C,SYP,SYC:
CLOSE #1:RETURN
1900 '
1910 '_____MENU BAR CONTROL_____
1920 '
1930 'main module:  interactive control of menu bar
1940   K$=INKEY$
1950   IF LEN(K$)=2 THEN K$=RIGHT$(K$,1) ELSE 1990
1960   IF K$=CHR$(77) THEN T1=T1+1:GOSUB 2050:GOTO 1940
1970   IF K$=CHR$(75) THEN T1=T1-1:GOSUB 2150:GOTO 1940
1980   IF K$=CHR$(16) THEN GOTO 1840  'Alt-Q to quit
1990   IF K$=CHR$(13) THEN GOSUB 2380  '<Enter> key
2000   GOTO 1940
2010   GOTO 2010  'bulletproof code barrier
2020 '
2030 '_____
2040 'module:  pan right on menu bar
2050   IF T1>5 THEN T1=1
2060   ON T1 GOTO 2070,2080,2090,2100,2110
2070   PUT (506,8),A7,XOR:PUT (14,8),A7,XOR:RETURN  'File
2080   PUT (14,8),A7,XOR:PUT (126,8),A7,XOR:RETURN  'Draw
2090   PUT (126,8),A7,XOR:PUT (246,8),A7,XOR:RETURN 'Display
2100   PUT (246,8),A7,XOR:PUT (366,8),A7,XOR:RETURN 'View
2110   PUT (366,8),A7,XOR:PUT (506,8),A7,XOR:RETURN 'Options
2120 '
2130 '_____
2140 'module:  pan left on menu bar
2150   IF T1<1 THEN T1=5
2160   ON T1 GOTO 2170,2180,2190,2200,2210
2170   PUT (126,8),A7,XOR:PUT (14,8),A7,XOR:RETURN   'File
2180   PUT (246,8),A7,XOR:PUT (126,8),A7,XOR:RETURN  'Draw
2190   PUT (366,8),A7,XOR:PUT (246,8),A7,XOR:RETURN  'Edit
2200   PUT (506,8),A7,XOR:PUT (366,8),A7,XOR:RETURN  'Label
2210   PUT (14,8),A7,XOR:PUT (506,8),A7,XOR:RETURN   'Options
2220 '
2350 '_____MENU BAR SWITCHER_____
2360 '
2370 'module:  switcher to execute menu bar choices
2380   ON T1 GOTO 2390,2400,2410,2420,2430
2390   GOSUB 2480:RETURN  'invoke File menu
2400   GOSUB 3160:RETURN  'invoke Draw menu
2410   GOSUB 3430:RETURN  'invoke Display menu
2420   GOSUB 3660:RETURN  'invoke View menu
2430   GOSUB 3950:RETURN  'invoke Options menu
```

Fig. E-1. (Continued from page 381.)

```
2440 '
2450 '_____FILE MENU CONTROL_____
2460 '
2470 'module:  interactive control of File menu
2480 PCOPY 0,1  'save existing graphics
2490 PUT (14,19),A10,PSET  'place menu on screen
2500 PUT (16,25),A9,XOR  'place cursor >> on menu
2510 T8=1  'reset flag
2520 K$=INKEY$
2530 IF LEN(K$)=2 THEN K$=RIGHT$(K$,1) ELSE 2620
2540 IF K$=CHR$(80) THEN T8=T8+1:GOTO 2550 ELSE 2520
2550 IF T8>5 THEN T8=1
2560 ON T8 GOTO 2570,2580,2590,2600,2610
2570 PUT (16,57),A9,XOR:PUT (16,25),A9,XOR:GOTO 2520 'Name
2580 PUT (16,25),A9,XOR:PUT (16,33),A9,XOR:GOTO 2520 'Save
2590 PUT (16,33),A9,XOR:PUT (16,41),A9,XOR:GOTO 2520 'Load
2600 PUT (16,41),A9,XOR:PUT (16,49),A9,XOR:GOTO 2520 'Quit
2610 PUT (16,49),A9,XOR:PUT (16,57),A9,XOR:GOTO 2520 'Menu bar
2620 IF K$=CHR$(13) THEN 2650  '<Enter> to implement
2630 IF K$=CHR$(27) THEN 2700  '<ESC> to cancel
2640 GOTO 2520
2650 ON T8 GOTO 2660,2670,2680,2690,2700
2660 GOSUB 2960:PCOPY 1,0:LOCATE 1,34:PRINT F$:RETURN   'name change
2670 PCOPY 1,0:GOSUB 2740:RETURN  'save image
2680 PCOPY 1,0:GOSUB 2850:RETURN  'load image
2690 GOTO 1840  'quit program
2700 PCOPY 1,0:RETURN  'menu bar
2710 '_____
2720 '_____
2730 'module: save 640x200 16-color image to disk
2740 MID$(F2$,1,8)=F$  'strip extension from file name
2750 SOUND 250,.7:DEF SEG=&HA000 'set up segment
2760 OUT &H3CE,4:OUT &H3CF,0:BSAVE "B:"+F2$+".BLU",0,16000 'bsave bit plane 0
2770 OUT &H3CE,4:OUT &H3CF,1:BSAVE "B:"+F2$+".GRN",0,16000 'bsave bit plane 1
2780 OUT &H3CE,4:OUT &H3CF,2:BSAVE "B:"+F2$+".RED",0,16000 'bsave bit plane 2
2790 OUT &H3CE,4:OUT &H3CF,3:BSAVE "B:"+F2$+".INT",0,16000 'bsave bit plane 3
2800 OUT &H3CE,4:OUT &H3CF,0:DEF SEG 'restore regs
2810 SOUND 250,.7:RETURN
2820 '_____
2830 '_____
2840 'module: load 640x200 16-color image from disk
2850 MID$(F2$,1,8)=F$  'strip extension from file name
2860 SOUND 250,.7:DEF SEG=&HA000 'set up segment
2870 OUT &H3C4,2:OUT &H3C5,1:BLOAD "B:"+F2$+".BLU",0 'bload bit plane 0
2880 OUT &H3C4,2:OUT &H3C5,2:BLOAD "B:"+F2$+".GRN",0 'bload bit plane 1
2890 OUT &H3C4,2:OUT &H3C5,4:BLOAD "B:"+F2$+".RED",0 'bload bit plane 2
2900 OUT &H3C4,2:OUT &H3C5,8:BLOAD "B:"+F2$+".INT",0 'bload bit plane 3
2910 OUT &H3C4,2:OUT &H3C5,&HF:DEF SEG 'restore regs
2920 GOSUB 5680:SOUND 250,.7:RETURN
2930 '_____
2940 '_____
2950 'module:  interactive control of Name dialog box
2960 GET (34,53)-(303,66),A11C  'save existing graphics
```

Fig. E-1. (Continued from page 382.)

```
2970  PUT (34,53),A11,PSET  'display Name dialog box
2980  T2=25  'echo position flag
2990  F1$=F$  'temporary save of existing filename
3000  FOR T=1 TO 8 STEP 1
3010  K$=INKEY$
3020  IF K$="" THEN 3010  'wait for keystroke
3030  IF K$=CHR$(27) THEN F$=F1$:T=8:GOTO 3070  '<ESC> to cancel instructions an
d restore previous filename
3040  IF K$<"A" THEN SOUND 250,.7:GOTO 3010  'must be A-Z
3050  IF K$>"Z" THEN SOUND 250,.7:GOTO 3010  'must be A-Z
3060  T2=T2+1:LOCATE 8,T2:PRINT K$:MID$(F$,T,1)=K$  'echo user input and insert
character into F$
3070  NEXT T
3080  LOCATE 8,26:PRINT F$
3090  K$=INKEY$:IF K$<>CHR$(13) THEN 3090
3100  LOCATE 1,34:PRINT F$:SOUND 250,.7  'display on filename bar
3110  PUT (34,53),A11C,PSET:RETURN  'restore previous graphics
3120  '
3130  '_____DRAW MENU CONTROL_____
3140  '
3150  'module:  interactive control of Draw menu
3160  PCOPY 0,1:PCOPY 0,2  'save existing graphics
3170  PUT (126,19),A15,PSET  'place menu on screen
3180  PUT (128,25),A9,XOR  'place cursor >> on menu
3190  T8=1  'reset flag
3200  K$=INKEY$
3210  IF LEN(K$)=2 THEN K$=RIGHT$(K$,1) ELSE 3300
3220  IF K$=CHR$(80) THEN T8=T8+1:GOTO 3230 ELSE 3200
3230  IF T8>5 THEN T8=1
3240  ON T8 GOTO 3250,3260,3270,3280,3290
3250  PUT (128,57),A9,XOR:PUT (128,25),A9,XOR:GOTO 3200 '3-edged
3260  PUT (128,25),A9,XOR:PUT (128,33),A9,XOR:GOTO 3200 '4-edged
3270  PUT (128,33),A9,XOR:PUT (128,41),A9,XOR:GOTO 3200 'Polyline
3280  PUT (128,41),A9,XOR:PUT (128,49),A9,XOR:GOTO 3200 'Undo
3290  PUT (128,49),A9,XOR:PUT (128,57),A9,XOR:GOTO 3200 'Menu bar
3300  IF K$=CHR$(13) THEN 3330  '<Enter> to implement
3310  IF K$=CHR$(27) THEN 3380  '<ESC> to cancel
3320  GOTO 3200
3330  ON T8 GOTO 3340,3350,3360,3370,3380
3340  T5=1:PCOPY 1,0:GOSUB 4280:GOTO 3170  '3-edged
3350  T5=2:PCOPY 1,0:GOSUB 4280:GOTO 3170  '4-edged
3360  T5=3:PCOPY 1,0:GOSUB 4280:GOTO 3170  'Polyline
3370  PCOPY 2,0:LOCATE 18,22:PRINT SYC:SOUND 250,.7:RETURN  'undo
3380  PCOPY 1,0:RETURN  'menu bar
3390  '
3400  '_____DISPLAY MENU CONTROL_____
3410  '
3420  'module:  interactive control of Display menu
3430  PCOPY 0,1  'save existing graphics
3440  PUT (246,19),A13,PSET  'place menu on screen
3450  PUT (248,24),A9,XOR  'place cursor >> on menu
3460  T8=1  'reset flag
3470  K$=INKEY$
```

Fig. E-1. (Continued from page 383.)

```
3480   IF LEN(K$)=2 THEN K$=RIGHT$(K$,1) ELSE 3550
3490   IF K$=CHR$(80) THEN T8=T8+1:GOTO 3500 ELSE 3470
3500   IF T8>3 THEN T8=1
3510   ON T8 GOTO 3520,3530,3540
3520   PUT (248,40),A9,XOR:PUT (248,24),A9,XOR:GOTO 3470 'Regen
3530   PUT (248,24),A9,XOR:PUT (248,32),A9,XOR:GOTO 3470 'Clear
3540   PUT (248,32),A9,XOR:PUT (248,40),A9,XOR:GOTO 3470 'Menu bar
3550   IF K$=CHR$(13) THEN 3580  '<Enter> to implement
3560   IF K$=CHR$(27) THEN 3610  '<ESC> to cancel
3570   GOTO 3470
3580   ON T8 GOTO 3590,3600,3610
3590   PCOPY 1,0:VIEW SCREEN (2,19)-(248,123):CLS:LINE (122,53)-(132,53),C4:LINE
(127,51)-(127,55),C4:VIEW SCREEN (251,19)-(637,186):CLS:VIEW:GOSUB 5090:GOSUB 56
80:SOUND 860,2:SOUND 800,2:RETURN  'Regen
3600   PCOPY 1,0:VIEW SCREEN (2,19)-(248,123):CLS:LINE (122,53)-(132,53),C4:LINE
(127,51)-(127,55),C4:VIEW SCREEN (251,19)-(637,186):CLS:VIEW:GOSUB 1890:SOUND 86
0,2:SOUND 800,2:RETURN  'Clear
3610   PCOPY 1,0:RETURN  'menu bar
3620   '
3630   '_____VIEW MENU CONTROL_____
3640   '
3650   'module:  interactive control of View menu
3660   PCOPY 0,1  'save existing graphics
3670   PUT (366,19),A14,PSET  'place menu on screen
3680   PUT (368,24),A9,XOR  'place cursor >> on menu
3690   T8=1  'reset flag
3700   K$=INKEY$
3710   IF LEN(K$)=2 THEN K$=RIGHT$(K$,1) ELSE 3810
3720   IF K$=CHR$(80) THEN T8=T8+1:GOTO 3730 ELSE 3700
3730   IF T8>6 THEN T8=1
3740   ON T8 GOTO 3750,3760,3770,3780,3790,3800
3750   PUT (368,64),A9,XOR:PUT (368,24),A9,XOR:GOTO 3700 'Distance
3760   PUT (368,24),A9,XOR:PUT (368,32),A9,XOR:GOTO 3700 'Elevation
3770   PUT (368,32),A9,XOR:PUT (368,40),A9,XOR:GOTO 3700 'Yaw
3780   PUT (368,40),A9,XOR:PUT (368,48),A9,XOR:GOTO 3700 'Roll
3790   PUT (368,48),A9,XOR:PUT (368,56),A9,XOR:GOTO 3700 'Pitch
3800   PUT (368,56),A9,XOR:PUT (368,64),A9,XOR:GOTO 3700 'Menu bar
3810   IF K$=CHR$(13) THEN 3840  '<Enter> to implement
3820   IF K$=CHR$(27) THEN 3900  '<ESC> to cancel
3830   GOTO 3700
3840   ON T8 GOTO 3850,3860,3870,3880,3890,3900
3850   GOSUB 5230:RETURN  'Distance
3860   GOSUB 5320:RETURN  'Elevation
3870   GOSUB 5410:RETURN  'Yaw
3880   GOSUB 5500:RETURN  'Roll
3890   GOSUB 5590:RETURN  'Pitch
3900   PCOPY 1,0:RETURN  'menu bar
3910   '
3920   '_____OPTIONS MENU CONTROL_____
3930   '
3940   'module:  interactive control of Options menu
3950   PCOPY 0,1  'save existing graphics
3960   PUT (505,19),A8,PSET  'place menu on screen
```

Fig. E-1. (Continued from page 384.)

```
3970  PUT (507,25),A9,XOR   'place cursor >> on menu
3980  T8=1  'reset flag
3990  K$=INKEY$
4000  IF LEN(K$)=2 THEN K$=RIGHT$(K$,1) ELSE 4100
4010  IF K$=CHR$(80) THEN T8=T8+1:GOTO 4020 ELSE 3990
4020  IF T8>6 THEN T8=1
4030  ON T8 GOTO 4040,4050,4060,4070,4080,4090
4040  PUT (507,65),A9,XOR:PUT (507,25),A9,XOR:GOTO 3990   'Shading on/off
4050  PUT (507,25),A9,XOR:PUT (507,33),A9,XOR:GOTO 3990   'Outline on/off
4060  PUT (507,33),A9,XOR:PUT (507,41),A9,XOR:GOTO 3990   'Grid on/off
4070  PUT (507,41),A9,XOR:PUT (507,49),A9,XOR:GOTO 3990   'Gnomon on/off
4080  PUT (507,49),A9,XOR:PUT (507,57),A9,XOR:GOTO 3990   'Set color
4090  PUT (507,57),A9,XOR:PUT (507,65),A9,XOR:GOTO 3990   'Menu bar
4100  IF K$=CHR$(13) THEN 4130   '<Enter> to implement
4110  IF K$=CHR$(27) THEN 4190   '<ESC> to cancel
4120  GOTO 3990
4130  ON T8 GOTO 4140,4150,4160,4170,4180,4190
4140  GOSUB 5770:GOTO 3990   'Shading on/off
4150  GOSUB 5730:GOTO 3990   'Outline on/off
4160  GOSUB 6000:GOTO 3990   'Grid on/off
4170  GOSUB 6080:GOTO 3990   'Gnomon on/off
4180  GOSUB 5810:GOTO 3990   'Set color
4190  PCOPY 1,0:GOSUB 5680:RETURN   'menu bar
4200  '
4210  '_____DO-NOTHING ROUTINE_____
4220  '
4230  SOUND 860,2:SOUND 800,2:RETURN   'do-nothing routine
4240  '
4250  '_____CROSSHAIR CURSOR CONTROL_____
4260  '
4270  'module:  interactive control of crosshair cursor
4280  SOUND 250,.7
4290  PUT (SX,SY),A12,XOR   'install crosshair cursor
4300  T6=0  'reset polyline flag
4310  X1=100:X2=130:X3=160:X4=190:Y1=40:Y2=100:Y3=140:Y4=70   'reset control poin
ts for curve and fillet
4320  K$=INKEY$
4330  IF LEN(K$)=2 THEN K$=RIGHT$(K$,1) ELSE 4500
4340  IF K$=CHR$(77) THEN PUT (SX,SY),A12,XOR:SX=SX+J ELSE 4370
4350  IF SX>XR THEN SX=XR:SOUND 250,.7
4360  PUT (SX,SY),A12,XOR:GOTO 4320
4370  IF K$=CHR$(75) THEN PUT (SX,SY),A12,XOR:SX=SX-J ELSE 4400
4380  IF SX<XL THEN SX=XL:SOUND 250,.7
4390  PUT (SX,SY),A12,XOR:GOTO 4320
4400  IF K$=CHR$(72) THEN PUT (SX,SY),A12,XOR:SY=SY-J*.5 ELSE 4430
4410  IF SY<YT THEN SY=YT:SOUND 250,.7
4420  PUT (SX,SY),A12,XOR:GOTO 4320
4430  IF K$=CHR$(80) THEN PUT (SX,SY),A12,XOR:SY=SY+J*.5 ELSE 4460
4440  IF SY>YB THEN SY=YB:SOUND 250,.7
4450  PUT (SX,SY),A12,XOR:GOTO 4320
4460  IF K$=CHR$(71) THEN PUT (SX,SY),A12,XOR:SX=XL:SY=YT:PUT (SX,SY),A12,XOR:GO
TO 4320
4470  IF K$=CHR$(73) THEN PUT (SX,SY),A12,XOR:SX=XR:SY=YT:PUT (SX,SY),A12,XOR:GO
```

Fig. E-1. (Continued from page 385.)

```
TO 4320
4480  IF K$=CHR$(81) THEN PUT (SX,SY),A12,XOR:SX=XR:SY=YB:PUT (SX,SY),A12,XOR:GO
TO 4320
4490  IF K$=CHR$(79) THEN PUT (SX,SY),A12,XOR:SX=XL:SY=YB:PUT (SX,SY),A12,XOR:GO
TO 4320
4500  IF K$=CHR$(27) THEN PUT (SX,SY),A12,XOR:SOUND 250,.7:RETURN   '<ESC>
4510  IF K$=CHR$(13) THEN PUT (SX,SY),A12,XOR:GOSUB 4610:PCOPY 0,1:PUT (SX,SY),A
12,XOR:SOUND 250,.7:GOTO 4320   '<Enter> to implement command
4520  IF K$="1" THEN SYC=SYC+.25:LOCATE 18,22:PRINT SYC" ":SOUND 250,.7:GOTO 43
20  'increment plan drawing height
4530  IF K$="2" THEN SYC=SYC-.25:LOCATE 18,22:PRINT SYC" ":SOUND 250,.7:GOTO 43
20  'decrement plan drawing height
4540  IF K$="3" THEN SYC=SYC+5:LOCATE 18,22:PRINT SYC"  ":SOUND 250,.7:GOTO 4320
  'mega-increment plant drawing height
4550  IF K$="4" THEN SYC=SYC-5:LOCATE 18,22:PRINT SYC"  ":SOUND 250,.7:GOTO 4320
  'mega-decrement plant drawing height
4560  GOTO 4320
4570  SOUND 250,.7:RETURN
4580  '_____
4590  '
4600  'module:  switcher for drawing functions
4610  ON T5 GOTO 4620,4630,4640
4620  GOSUB 4230:RETURN   '3-edged polygon
4630  GOSUB 4730:RETURN   '4-edged solid polygon plane surface
4640  GOSUB 4680:RETURN   'polyline
4650  '_____
4660  '
4670  'module:  polyline function
4680  IF T6=0 THEN SXC=SX+7:SZC=SY+3:PSET (SXC,SZC),C:T6=1:SXP=SXC:SZP=SZC:SYP=S
YC:RETURN ELSE 4690
4690  SXC=SX+7:SZC=SY+3:LINE (SXP,SZP)-(SXC,SZC),C:GOSUB 4930:GOSUB 5050:SXP=SXC
:SZP=SZC:SYP=SYC:RETURN
4700  '_____
4710  '
4720  'module:  4-edged solid polygon function
4730  IF T6=0 THEN T6=1:SXC=SX+7:SZC=SY+3:PSET (SXC,SZC),C:SXP=SXC:SZP=SZC:SYP=S
YC:SXF=SXC:SZF=SZC:GOSUB 4880:X1=X:Y1=Y:Z1=Z:SX1=SXD:SY1=SYD:RETURN ELSE 4740  '
vertex #1
4740  IF T6=1 THEN T6=2:SXC=SX+7:SZC=SY+3:LINE (SXP,SZP)-(SXC,SZC),C:SXP=SXC:SZP
=SZC:SYP=SYC:GOSUB 4880:X2=X:Y2=Y:Z2=Z:SX2=SXD:SY2=SYD:RETURN ELSE 4750  'vertex
 #2
4750  IF T6=2 THEN T6=3:SXC=SX+7:SZC=SY+3:LINE (SXP,SZP)-(SXC,SZC),C:SXP=SXC:SZP
=SZC:SYP=SYC:GOSUB 4880:X3=X:Y3=Y:Z3=Z:SX3=SXD:SY3=SYD:RETURN  ELSE 4760  'verte
x #3
4760  IF T6=3 THEN T6=0:SXC=SX+7:SZC=SY+3:LINE (SXP,SZP)-(SXC,SZC),C:LINE-(SXF,S
ZF),C:SXP=SXC:SZP=SZC:SYP=SYC:GOSUB 4880:X4=X:Y4=Y:Z4=Z:SX4=SXD:SY4=SYD  'vertex
 #4
4770  GOSUB 6210:IF SP>0 THEN SOUND 250,.7:RETURN ELSE 4780  'test for surface v
isibility;  if hidden then do not draw
4780  GOSUB 6750   'use geometric center of polygon as area fill seed point
4790  GOSUB 6260:IF T7=0 THEN WINDOW SCREEN (0,0)-(639,199):VIEW:RETURN ELSE 480
0  'draw solid polygon plane surface
4800  GOSUB 6320:PAINT (SX5,SY5),C13,C:PAINT (SX5,SY5),A$,C  'apply halftone sha
```

Fig. E-1. (Continued from page 386.)

```
       ding
4810   GOSUB 6690  'apply line dithering
4820   IF T9=0 THEN 4840  'is outlining toggle off?
4830   GOSUB 6810  'apply outlining
4840   RETURN  'solid polygon plane is completed
4850   '_____
4860   '_____
4870   'module:  prepare 2D plan coordinates for input to 3D formulas
4880   X=(.404858*SXC)-51:Z=(.9523809*SZC)-51:Y=SYC:GOSUB 5000:SXD=SXD+125:SYD=SY
D+3:RETURN
4890   '
4900   '_____GENERATE 3D MODEL_____
4910   '
4920   'module:  generate 3D model
4930   WINDOW SCREEN (-399,-299)-(400,300):VIEW SCREEN (251,19)-(637,186)  'clip
3D viewing area
4940   X=(.404858*SXP)-51:Z=(.9523809*SZP)-51:Y=SYP:GOSUB 5000:SXD=SXD+125:SYD=SY
D+3:PSET (SXD,SYD),C
4950   X=(.404858*SXC)-51:Z=(.9523809*SZC)-51:Y=SYC:GOSUB 5000:SXD=SXD+125:SYD=SY
D+3:LINE-(SXD,SYD),C
4960   WINDOW SCREEN (0,0)-(639,199):VIEW:RETURN
4970   '
4980   '_____
4990   'module:  perspective formulas
5000   X=(-1)*X:XA=CR1*X-SR1*Z:ZA=SR1*X+CR1*Z:X=CR2*XA+SR2*Y:YA=CR2*Y-SR2*XA:Z=CR
3*ZA-SR3*YA:Y=SR3*ZA+CR3*YA:X=X+MX:Y=Y+MY:Z=Z+MZ:SXD=D*X/Z:SYD=D*Y/Z:RETURN
5010   '
5020   '_____DATA FILE INPUT/OUTPUT_____
5030   '
5040   'module:  storage of graphics attributes in data file
5050   OPEN "A:KEYLAYER.CDF" FOR APPEND AS #1:WRITE #1,SXP,SZP,SXC,SZC,C,SYP,SYC:
CLOSE #1:RETURN
5060   '
5070   '_____
5080   'module:  retrieval of graphics attributes from data file
5090   OPEN "A:KEYLAYER.CDF" FOR INPUT AS #1
5100   INPUT #1,SXP,SZP,SXC,SZC,C,SYP,SYC  'dummy pass
5110   IF T3=1 THEN GOSUB 6040  'is grid toggled on?
5120   IF T4=1 THEN GOSUB 6120  'is gnomon toggled on?
5130   IF EOF(1) THEN CLOSE #1:RETURN
5140   INPUT #1,SXP,SZP,SXC,SZC,C,SYP,SYC:GOSUB 5180:GOTO 5130
5150   '
5160   '_____
5170   'module:  regen function for 2D/3D modes
5180   LINE (SXP,SZP)-(SXC,SZC),C:GOSUB 4930:RETURN  'polyline regen
5190   '
5200   '_____ADJUST VIEW PARAMETERS_____
5210   '
5220   'module:  adjust Distance to viewpoint
5230   SOUND 250,.7
5240   K$=INKEY$
5250   IF K$="=" THEN MZ=MZ-10:GOSUB 5680:GOTO 5240
5260   IF K$="-" THEN MZ=MZ+10:GOSUB 5680:GOTO 5240
```

Fig. E-1. (Continued from page 387.)

```
5270  IF K$=CHR$(13) THEN PCOPY 1,0:GOSUB 5680:VIEW SCREEN (2,19)-(248,123):CLS:
VIEW SCREEN (251,19)-(637,186):CLS:VIEW:GOSUB 5090:SOUND 860,2:SOUND 800,2:RETUR
N
5280  GOTO 5240
5290  '_____
5300  '
5310  'module:  adjust Elevation of viewpoint
5320  SOUND 250,.7
5330  K$=INKEY$
5340  IF K$="=" THEN MY=MY-2:GOSUB 5680:GOTO 5330
5350  IF K$="-" THEN MY=MY+2:GOSUB 5680:GOTO 5330
5360  IF K$=CHR$(13) THEN PCOPY 1,0:GOSUB 5680:VIEW SCREEN (2,19)-(248,123):CLS:
VIEW SCREEN (251,19)-(637,186):CLS:VIEW:GOSUB 5090:SOUND 860,2:SOUND 800,2:RETUR
N
5370  GOTO 5330
5380  '_____
5390  '
5400  'module:  adjust Yaw angle
5410  SOUND 250,.7
5420  K$=INKEY$:IF LEN(K$)=2 THEN K$=RIGHT$(K$,1) ELSE 5450
5430  IF K$=CHR$(77) THEN R1=R1-.17953:GOSUB 5680:GOTO 5420
5440  IF K$=CHR$(75) THEN R1=R1+.17953:GOSUB 5680:GOTO 5420
5450  IF K$=CHR$(13) THEN SR1=SIN(R1):CR1=COS(R1):PCOPY 1,0:GOSUB 5680:VIEW SCRE
EN (2,19)-(248,123):CLS:VIEW SCREEN (251,19)-(637,186):CLS:VIEW:GOSUB 5090:SOUND
 860,2:SOUND 800,2:RETURN
5460  GOTO 5420
5470  '_____
5480  '
5490  'module:  adjust Roll angle
5500  SOUND 250,.7
5510  K$=INKEY$:IF LEN(K$)=2 THEN K$=RIGHT$(K$,1) ELSE 5540
5520  IF K$=CHR$(77) THEN R2=R2+.08727:GOSUB 5680:GOTO 5510
5530  IF K$=CHR$(75) THEN R2=R2-.08727:GOSUB 5680:GOTO 5510
5540  IF K$=CHR$(13) THEN SR2=SIN(R2):CR2=COS(R2):PCOPY 1,0:GOSUB 5680:VIEW SCRE
EN (2,19)-(248,123):CLS:VIEW SCREEN (251,19)-(637,186):CLS:VIEW:GOSUB 5090:SOUND
 860,2:SOUND 800,2:RETURN
5550  GOTO 5510
5560  '_____
5570  '
5580  'module:  adjust Pitch angle
5590  SOUND 250,.7
5600  K$=INKEY$:IF LEN(K$)=2 THEN K$=RIGHT$(K$,1) ELSE 5630
5610  IF K$=CHR$(72) THEN R3=R3-.08727:GOSUB 5680:GOTO 5600
5620  IF K$=CHR$(80) THEN R3=R3+.08727:GOSUB 5680:GOTO 5600
5630  IF K$=CHR$(13) THEN SR3=SIN(R3):CR3=COS(R3):PCOPY 1,0:GOSUB 5680:VIEW SCRE
EN (2,19)-(248,123):CLS:VIEW SCREEN (251,19)-(637,186):CLS:VIEW:GOSUB 5090:SOUND
 860,2:SOUND 800,2:RETURN
5640  GOTO 5600
5650  '
5660  '_____REFRESH ALPHANUMERICS_____
5670  '
5680  LOCATE 18,22:PRINT SYC:LOCATE 19,21:PRINT (-1*MZ):LOCATE 20,22:PRINT (-1*M
Y):LOCATE 21,12:PRINT R1:LOCATE 22,13:PRINT R2:LOCATE 23,14:PRINT R3:LINE (8,185
```

Fig. E-1. (Continued from page 388.)

```
                )-(243,185),C:RETURN
5690 '
5700 '_____ADJUST OPTIONS_____
5710 '
5720 'module:  toggle outlining on/off
5730  IF T9=0 THEN T9=1:SOUND 250,.7:RETURN ELSE IF T9=1 THEN T9=0:SOUND 250,.7:
RETURN
5740 '_____
5750 '
5760 'module:  toggle shading on/off
5770  IF T7=0 THEN T7=1:SOUND 250,.7:RETURN ELSE IF T7=1 THEN T7=0:SOUND 250,.7:
RETURN
5780 '_____
5790 '
5800 'module:  change the drawing color
5810  SOUND 250,.7
5820  IF C=C7 THEN C=C4:GOSUB 5680:RETURN
5830  IF C=C4 THEN C=C1:GOSUB 5680:RETURN
5840  IF C=C1 THEN C=C3:GOSUB 5680:RETURN
5850  IF C=C3 THEN C=C2:GOSUB 5680:RETURN
5860  IF C=C2 THEN C=C5:GOSUB 5680:RETURN
5870  IF C=C5 THEN C=C6:GOSUB 5680:RETURN
5880  IF C=C6 THEN C=C8:GOSUB 5680:RETURN
5890  IF C=C8 THEN C=C15:GOSUB 5680:RETURN
5900  IF C=C15 THEN C=C9:GOSUB 5680:RETURN
5910  IF C=C9 THEN C=C12:GOSUB 5680:RETURN
5920  IF C=C12 THEN C=C10:GOSUB 5680:RETURN
5930  IF C=C10 THEN C=C14:GOSUB 5680:RETURN
5940  IF C=C14 THEN C=C0:GOSUB 5680:RETURN
5950  IF C=C0 THEN C=C7:GOSUB 5680:RETURN
5960  GOSUB 5680:RETURN
5970 '_____
5980 '
5990 'module:  toggle 2D grid on/off
6000  IF T3=0 THEN T3=1:SOUND 250,.7:RETURN ELSE IF T3=1 THEN T3=0:SOUND 250,.7:
RETURN
6010 '_____
6020 '
6030 'module:  create grid if toggled on
6040  T=1:WHILE T<249:LINE (T,19)-(T,123),C8:T=T+J10:WEND:T=19:WHILE T<123:LINE
(2,T)-(248,T),C8:T=T+J11:WEND:LINE (122,53)-(132,53),C4:LINE (127,51)-(127,55),C
4:RETURN
6050 '_____
6060 '
6070 'module:  toggle 3D gnomon on/off (x,y,z axis display)
6080  IF T4=0 THEN T4=1:SOUND 250,.7:RETURN ELSE IF T4=1 THEN T4=0:SOUND 250,.7:
RETURN
6090 '_____
6100 '
6110 'module:  create gnomon if toggled on
6120  WINDOW SCREEN (-399,-299)-(400,300):VIEW SCREEN (251,19)-(637,186)
6130  X=30:Z=0:Y=0:GOSUB 5000:SXD=SXD+125:SYD=SYD+3:PSET (SXD,SYD),C2:X=0:Z=0:Y=
0:GOSUB 5000:SXD=SXD+125:SYD=SYD+3:LINE-(SXD,SYD),C2:X=-30:Z=0:Y=0:GOSUB 5000:SX
```

Fig. E-1. (Continued from page 389.)

```
D=SXD+125:SYD=SYD+3:LINE-(SXD,SYD),C8    'x-axis
6140  X=0:Z=0:Y=30:GOSUB 5000:SXD=SXD+125:SYD=SYD+3:PSET (SXD,SYD),C5:X=0:Z=0:Y=
0:GOSUB 5000:SXD=SXD+125:SYD=SYD+3:LINE-(SXD,SYD),C5:X=0:Z=0:Y=-30:GOSUB 5000:SX
D=SXD+125:SYD=SYD+3:LINE-(SXD,SYD),C8    'y-axis
6150  X=0:Z=30:Y=0:GOSUB 5000:SXD=SXD+125:SYD=SYD+3:PSET (SXD,SYD),C1:X=0:Z=0:Y=
0:GOSUB 5000:SXD=SXD+125:SYD=SYD+3:LINE-(SXD,SYD),C1:X=0:Z=-30:Y=0:GOSUB 5000:SX
D=SXD+125:SYD=SYD+3:LINE-(SXD,SYD),C8    'z-axis
6160  WINDOW SCREEN (0,0)-(639,199):VIEW:RETURN
6170  '
6180  '_____HIDDEN SURFACE REMOVAL_____
6190  '
6200  'module:   plane equation method of hidden surface removal
6210  SP1=X1*(Y2*Z3-Y3*Z2):SP1=(-1)*SP1:SP2=X2*(Y3*Z1-Y1*Z3):SP3=X3*(Y1*Z2-Y2*Z1
):SP=SP1-SP2-SP3:RETURN
6220  '
6230  '_____DRAW 4-SIDED POLYGON_____
6240  '
6250  'module:   solid surface modeling of 4-sided polygon
6260  WINDOW SCREEN (-399,-299)-(400,300):VIEW SCREEN (251,19)-(637,186)    'clip
3D viewing area
6270  LINE (SX1,SY1)-(SX2,SY2),C13:LINE-(SX3,SY3),C13:LINE-(SX4,SY4),C13:LINE-(S
X1,SY1),C13:PAINT (SX5,SY5),C13,C13:LINE (SX1,SY1)-(SX2,SY2),C:LINE-(SX3,SY3),C:
LINE-(SX4,SY4),C:LINE-(SX1,SY1),C:PAINT (SX5,SY5),0,C:RETURN
6280  '
6290  '_____COMPUTER-CONTROLLED SHADING_____
6300  '
6310  'module:   computer-controlled shading routine
6320  XU=X2-X1:YU=Y2-Y1:ZU=Z2-Z1    'calculate vector from vertex 1 to vertex 2
6330  XV=X3-X1:YV=Y3-Y1:ZV=Z3-Z1    'calculate vector from vertex 1 to vertex 3
6340  XN=(YU*ZV)-(ZU*YV):YN=(ZU*XV)-(XU*ZV):ZN=(XU*YV)-(YU*XV)    'calculate surfa
ce perpendicular vector
6350  YN=YN*(-1):ZN=ZN*(-1)  'convert vector to cartesian system
6360  'sub-module:   convert surface perpendicular vector to unit vector
6370  V7=(XN*XN)+(YN*YN)+(ZN*ZN):V2=SQR(V7)    'magnitude of surface perpendicular
 vector
6380  V3=1/V2  'ratio of magnitude to unit vector magnitude
6390  XW=V3*XN:YW=V3*YN:ZW=V3*ZN  'XYZ components of surface perpendicular unit
vector
6400  V4=(XW*XI)+(YW*YI)+(ZW*ZI)  'illumination factor 0 to 1
6410  V4=V4*V6:V4=CINT(V4)  'set illumination range
6420  V5=V4+1  'illumination factor from base 1
6430  GOSUB 6480
6440  RETURN
6450  '_____
6460  '
6470  'shading routine for EGA and VGA 640x200 mode
6480  IF V5<1 THEN GOTO 6510  'if light source is behind surface
6490  ON V5 GOTO 6510, 6520, 6530, 6540, 6550, 6560, 6570, 6580, 6590, 6600, 661
0, 6620, 6630, 6640, 6650
6500  A$=CHR$(&HFF)+CHR$(&HO)+CHR$(&HO)+CHR$(&HO):C4=1:C5=1:C6=&HFFFF:RETURN    's
olid black is unused
6510  A$=A1$:CP=1:CC=2:CD=&H808:RETURN
6520  A$=A2$:CP=1:CC=2:CD=&H4444:RETURN
```

Fig. E-1. (Continued from page 390.)

```
6530   A$=A3$:CP=1:CC=2:CD=&HAAAA:RETURN
6540   A$=A4$:CP=2:CC=1:CD=&H4444:RETURN
6550   A$=CHR$(&HO)+CHR$(&HFF)+CHR$(&HO)+CHR$(&HO):CP=2:CC=2:CD=&HFFFF:RETURN
6560   A$=A5$:CP=2:CC=3:CD=&H808:RETURN
6570   A$=A6$:CP=2:CC=3:CD=&H4444:RETURN
6580   A$=A7$:CP=2:CC=3:CD=&HAAAA:RETURN
6590   A$=A8$:CP=3:CC=2:CD=&H4444:RETURN
6600   A$=CHR$(&HFF)+CHR$(&HFF)+CHR$(&HO)+CHR$(&HO):CP=3:CC=3:CD=&HFFFF:RETURN
6610   A$=A9$:CP=3:CC=4:CD=&H8080:RETURN
6620   A$=A10$:CP=3:CC=4:CD=&H4444:RETURN
6630   A$=A11$:CP=3:CC=4:CD=&HAAAA:RETURN
6640   A$=A12$:CP=4:CC=3:CD=&H4444:RETURN
6650   A$=CHR$(&HO)+CHR$(&HO)+CHR$(&HFF)+CHR$(&HO):CP=4:CC=4:CD=&HFFFF:RETURN
6660   '
6670   '_____
6680   'module:   computer-controlled dithering routine
6690   LINE (SX1,SY1)-(SX2,SY2),CP:LINE (SX1,SY1)-(SX2,SY2),CC,,CD:LINE (SX2,SY2)
       -(SX3,SY3),CP:LINE (SX2,SY2)-(SX3,SY3),CC,,CD:LINE (SX3,SY3)-(SX4,SY4),CP:LINE (
       SX3,SY3)-(SX4,SY4),CC,,CD
6700   LINE (SX4,SY4)-(SX1,SY1),CP:LINE (SX4,SY4)-(SX1,SY1),CC,,CD
6710   WINDOW SCREEN (0,0)-(639,199):VIEW:RETURN
6720   '
6730   '_____
6740   'module:   determine area fill seed point
6750   X=X1+.5*(X3-X1):Y=Y1+.5*(Y3-Y1):Z=Z1+.5*(Z3-Z1)   'diagonal midpoint betwee
       n polygon's view coordinates in 3D space
6760   SX5=D*X/Z:SY5=D*Y/Z:SX5=SX5+125:SY5=SY5+3   'display coordinates for seed
6770   RETURN
6780   '
6790   '_____
6800   'module:   outlining of solid polygon plane surface
6810   WINDOW SCREEN (-399,-299)-(400,300):VIEW SCREEN (251,19)-(637,186)   'clip
       3D viewing area
6820   LINE (SX1,SY1)-(SX2,SY2),C:LINE-(SX3,SY3),C:LINE-(SX4,SY4),C:LINE-(SX1,SY1
       ),C
6830   WINDOW SCREEN (0,0)-(639,199):VIEW:RETURN
6840   '
6850   '
6860   '_____
6870   END
```

Fig. E-1. (Continued from page 391.)

A SAMPLE CONVERSION FOR TURBO BASIC

If you are using Turbo BASIC with your personal computer, you might want to experiment with the program listing in Fig. E-2. This program is a CGA-compatible version of the 3D wire-frame CAD program listing from Chapter 26. To compile the program under Turbo BASIC from the companion disk to this book, load TB-001.BAS.

Because Turbo BASIC does not provide a PCOPY instruction to copy graphics from one page to another, a series of assembly language routines have been added to provide this capability. (Refer to Chapter 15 for further discussion of performance boosters.) The program in Fig. E-2 will run on CGA-equipped personal computers.

Note lines 325, 326, and 327 which make data assignments for the assembly language subroutine. Note also line 640, which calls a subroutine to install the hexadecimal opcodes for the assembly language subroutine. This routine is placed into a linear array by Turbo BASIC.

Of particular importance are the emulation routines at lines 5760 through 5970. Each of these routines uses a POKE instruction to modify the source and target addresses in the assembly language routine in order to faithfully emulate the PCOPY instruction. By using this approach, the menu code and the graphics code earlier in the program can be kept simpler and easier to understand.

Refer to Chapters 27 and 28 for a detailed discussion of how this program works. For further discussion concerning the changes made for the purpose of CGA compatibility, consult Appendix G. You can readily convert most of the demonstration programs in this book for your Turbo BASIC compiler.

```
100 'Program TB-001.BAS   YOUR MICROCOMPUTER 3D CAD DESIGNER
110 'Copyright (c) 1988 by Lee Adams and TAB Books Inc.
120 'All rights reserved.
130 'Version for TURBO BASIC.  640x200 2-color mode.
140 '
150 '_____INITIALIZE SYSTEM_____
160 '
170  KEY OFF:CLS:CLEAR:SCREEN 0,0,0,0:WIDTH 80:COLOR 7,0,0:CLS:LOCATE 10,20,0:PR
INT "Assigning memory space for graphic arrays"
180 '
190 '_____DATA ASSIGNMENTS_____
200 '
210 'module:  data assignments
220  DEFINT A,T,J,H,P
230  DIM A1(631):DIM A2(150):DIM A3(150):DIM A4(150):DIM A5(150):DIM A6(150)   't
emporary arrays for screen template
240  DIM A7(177)  'array for panning cursor
250  DIM A8(1793)  'array for Options menu
260  DIM A9(21)  'array for scrolling cursor
270  DIM A10(1057)  'array for File menu
280  DIM A11(953):DIM A11C(953)  'for Name dialog box
290  DIM A12(29)  'array for roaming crosshair cursor
300  DIM A13(683)  'array for Display menu
310  DIM A14(1321)  'array for View menu
320  DIM A15(1057)  'array for Draw menu
325  DIM A99(18)  'scalar array for machine code subroutine
326  HEX=0  'variable to migrate contents of hex database
327  PCOPY=0  'address of machine code subroutine
330  C0=0:C1=1:C2=1:C3=1:C4=1:C5=1:C6=1:C7=1:C8=1:C9=1:C10=1:C12=1:C13=1:C14=1:C
15=1  'software color codes
340  C=C7:CE=C7  'drawing, boundary colors
350  T=0  'loop counter
360  T1=2  'selection flag for menu bar
370  T2=25  'flag for echo position of file menu input
380  T3=0  '2D grid on/off toggle
```

Fig. E-2. Complete source code for the Turbo BASIC version of the interactive 3D wire-frame CAD program from Chapter 26.

```
390  T4=0   '3D gnomon on/off toggle
400  T5=0   'flag for function switcher
410  T6=0   'iterative flag for plastic functions
420  T8=1   'selection flag for menus
430  J=2:JS=J   'snap, temporary storage of snap value
440  J6=85:J7=19:J8=608:J9=186   'viewport dimensions for active drawing surface
on 640x200 screen
450  SX=122:SY=65   'crosshair array location
460  XL=2:XR=234:YT=19:YB=117   'left, right, top, bottom range of roaming crossh
air cursor
470  SXC=SX+7:SZC=SY+3:SYC=0   'center of crosshair cursor
480  SXP=0:SZP=0:SYP=0   'last referenced drawing point
490  F$="DRAWFILE.PIC":F1$=F$:F2$="DRAWFILE"   'strings used to manipulate filena
me when saving images
500  V=0   'size of free memory in BASICA workspace
510  V1=1024   'threshold memory flag
520  B=0:B2=0:B3=0:D1=0:D2=0:D3=0:D4=0:X1=0:X2=0:X3=0:X4=0:Y1=0:Y2=0:Y3=0:Y4=0
'used in freeform curve routine
530  D=1200!:R1=6.46272:R2=6.28319:R3=6.10865:MX=0!:MY=-20!:MZ=-270!:SR1=SIN(R1)
:SR2=SIN(R2):SR3=SIN(R3):CR1=COS(R1):CR2=COS(R2):CR3=COS(R3)   'variables used as
   input for perspective formulas
540  XA=0:YA=0:ZA=0   'temporary variables used in perspective formulas
550  SX1=0:SY1=0   'output of perspective formulas
560  J10=25:J11=11   'horizontal, vertical spacing for grid
570  '
580  '_____SET UP RUNTIME ENVIRONMENT_____
590  '
600  'module:  set up runtime environment
610  CLS:SCREEN 2   '640x200 2-clr mode
620  CLS
640  GOSUB 5620   'install PCOPY machine code subroutine
650  GOSUB 1600   'initialize .CDF data file
660  '
670  '_____SET UP SCREEN DISPLAY_____
680  '
690  'module:  set up screen template
700  GOSUB 960   'save alphanumeric graphic arrays
710  GOSUB 1140   'create pull-down menus
720  LINE (0,8)-(639,199),C8,B   'border
730  LINE (0,187)-(639,187),C8:PAINT (320,190),C8,C8:PUT (182,189),A1,XOR  'bann
er
740  LINE (0,0)-(639,6),C6,B:PAINT (320,3),C6,C6:LOCATE 1,33:PRINT " DRAWFILE.CD
F ":LOCATE 1,34:PRINT F$   'filename bar
750  LINE (1,8)-(639,18),C8,B:PAINT (320,10),C8,C8   'menu bar
760  PUT (18,9),A2,XOR:PUT (130,9),A3,XOR:PUT (250,9),A4,XOR:PUT (370,9),A5,XOR:
PUT (510,9),A6,XOR   'selections for menu bar
770  LOCATE 10,20:PRINT "Reclaiming memory used by temporary arrays":ERASE A1,A2
,A3,A4,A5,A6   'free up array memory
780  LOCATE 10,20:PRINT "                                                      "
790  LINE (250,19)-(250,186),C8:LINE (249,19)-(249,186),C8:LINE (1,19)-(1,186),C
8:LINE (638,19)-(638,186),C8:LINE (1,124)-(249,124),C8:LINE (122,53)-(132,53),C6
:LINE (127,51)-(127,55),C6   'split screen
800  LOCATE 18,2:PRINT "Plan drawing height":LOCATE 19,2:PRINT "Viewpoint distan
```

Fig. E-2. (Continued from page 393.)

```
ce":LOCATE 20,2:PRINT "Viewpoint elevation":LOCATE 21,2:PRINT "Yaw angle":LOCATE
 22,2:PRINT "Roll angle":LOCATE 23,2:PRINT "Pitch angle"
810   LOCATE 17,8:PRINT "View specifications"
820   GOSUB 5180   'alphanumeric readouts
830   PUT (126,8),A7,XOR  'panning cursor for menu bar
840   GOSUB 5810:GOSUB 5930   'establish refresh buffers
850   LOCATE 9,40:PRINT "YOUR MICROCOMPUTER 3D CAD DESIGNER":LOCATE 12,40:PRINT "
Copyright (c) 1988 by Lee Adams and":LOCATE 13,40:PRINT "TAB Books Inc.  All rig
hts reserved."
860   LINE (310,60)-(584,60),C6:LINE (310,74)-(584,74),C6
870   LOCATE 19,43:PRINT "Press <Enter> to continue...":SOUND 860,2:SOUND 800,2
880   K$=INKEY$:IF K$<>CHR$(13) THEN 880
890   GOSUB 5770:SOUND 250,.7   'restore screen
900   GOTO 1650   'jump to runtime code
910   GOTO 910   'bulletproof code barrier
920   '
930   '_____CREATE ALPHANUMERICS FOR TEMPLATE_____
940   '
950  'module: create alpha arrays for screen template
960   LOCATE 10,20:PRINT "YOUR MICROCOMPUTER 3D CAD DESIGNER"
970   GET (150,71)-(424,79),A1:LOCATE 10,20:PRINT "
      "
980   LOCATE 10,20:PRINT "File":GET (150,71)-(210,79),A2
990   LOCATE 10,20:PRINT "Draw":GET (150,71)-(210,79),A3
1000   LOCATE 10,20:PRINT "Display":GET (150,71)-(210,79),A4
1010   LOCATE 10,20:PRINT "View    ":GET (150,71)-(210,79),A5
1020   LOCATE 10,20:PRINT "Options":GET (150,71)-(210,79),A6
1030   LOCATE 10,20:PRINT "        "
1040   LINE (150,70)-(212,80),C12,B:GET (150,70)-(212,80),A7   'create panning cur
sor for menu bar
1050   LINE (150,70)-(212,80),0,B
1060   LINE (323,44)-(337,44),C7:LINE (330,41)-(330,47),C7:LINE (329,44)-(331,44)
,0  'create roaming crosshair cursor
1070   GET (323,41)-(337,47),A12:LINE (323,41)-(337,47),0,BF
1080   RETURN
1090   '
1100   '_____CREATE PULL-DOWN MENUS_____
1110   '
1120  'module:  create pull-down menus
1130  'submodule:  create Options menu
1140   LOCATE 10,20:PRINT "Set snap":LOCATE 11,20:PRINT "Set grid":LOCATE 12,20:P
RINT "Grid on/off":LOCATE 13,20:PRINT "Gnomon on/off"
1150   LOCATE 14,20:PRINT "Set color":LOCATE 15,20:PRINT "Menu bar"
1160   LINE (138,67)-(260,122),C8,B
1170   GET (138,67)-(260,122),A8:LINE (138,67)-(260,122),0,BF
1180   LOCATE 10,20:PRINT CHR$(175)  'menu cursor >>
1190   GET (151,73)-(159,77),A9:LOCATE 10,20:PRINT " "
1200   '_____
1210   '
1220  'submodule:  create File menu
1230   LOCATE 10,20:PRINT "Name":LOCATE 11,20:PRINT "Save":LOCATE 12,20:PRINT "Lo
ad":LOCATE 13,20:PRINT "Quit":LOCATE 14,20:PRINT "Menu bar"
1240   LINE (138,67)-(220,114),C8,B
```

Fig. E-2. (Continued from page 394.)

```
1250  GET (138,67)-(220,114),A10:LINE (138,67)-(220,114),0,BF
1260  '_____
1270  '
1280  'submodule:  create Draw menu
1290  LOCATE 10,20:PRINT "Line":LOCATE 11,20:PRINT "Curve":LOCATE 12,20:PRINT "C
ircle":LOCATE 13,20:PRINT "Undo":LOCATE 14,20:PRINT "Menu bar"
1300  LINE (138,67)-(220,114),C8,B
1310  GET (138,67)-(220,114),A15:LINE (138,67)-(220,114),0,BF
1320  '_____
1330  '
1340  'submodule:  create Name dialog box
1350  LOCATE 10,20:PRINT "Enter new filename:            "
1360  LINE (144,69)-(413,82),C8,B
1370  GET (144,69)-(413,82),A11:LINE (144,69)-(413,82),0,BF
1380  '_____
1390  '
1400  'submodule:  create Display menu
1410  LOCATE 4,20:PRINT "Regen":LOCATE 5,20:PRINT "Clear":LOCATE 6,20:PRINT "Men
u bar"
1420  LINE (138,20)-(220,50),C8,B
1430  GET (138,20)-(220,50),A13:LINE (138,20)-(220,50),0,BF
1440  '_____
1450  '
1460  'submodule:  create View menu
1470  LOCATE 4,20:PRINT "Distance":LOCATE 5,20:PRINT "Elevation":LOCATE 6,20:PRI
NT "Yaw":LOCATE 7,20:PRINT "Roll":LOCATE 8,20:PRINT "Pitch":LOCATE 9,20:PRINT "M
enu bar"
1480  LINE (138,20)-(230,74),C8,B
1490  GET (138,20)-(230,74),A14:LINE (138,20)-(230,74),0,BF
1500  RETURN
1510  '
1520  '_____QUIT_____
1530  '
1540  'module:  exit routine
1550  DEF SEG:CLS:SCREEN 0,0,0,0:WIDTH 80:COLOR 7,0,0:CLS:LOCATE 1,1,1:COLOR 6:P
RINT "YOUR MICROCOMPUTER 3D CAD DESIGNER":LOCATE 2,1:PRINT "is finished.":COLOR
7:SOUND 250,.7:END
1560  '
1570  '_____INITIALIZE DATA FILES_____
1580  '
1590  'module:  initialize .CDF data files
1600  OPEN "A:KEYLAYER.CDF" FOR OUTPUT AS #1:WRITE #1,SXP,SZP,SXC,SZC,C,SYP,SYC:
CLOSE #1:RETURN
1610  '
1620  '_____MENU BAR CONTROL_____
1630  '
1640  'main module:  interactive control of menu bar
1650  K$=INKEY$
1660  IF LEN(K$)=2 THEN K$=RIGHT$(K$,1) ELSE 1700
1670  IF K$=CHR$(77) THEN T1=T1+1:GOSUB 1760:GOTO 1650
1680  IF K$=CHR$(75) THEN T1=T1-1:GOSUB 1860:GOTO 1650
1690  IF K$=CHR$(16) THEN GOTO 1550   'Alt-Q to quit
1700  IF K$=CHR$(13) THEN GOSUB 2090   '<Enter> key
```

Fig. E-2. (Continued from page 395.)

```
1710  GOTO 1650
1720  GOTO 1720   'bulletproof code barrier
1730  '_____
1740  '
1750  'module:  pan right on menu bar
1760  IF T1>5 THEN T1=1
1770  ON T1 GOTO 1780,1790,1800,1810,1820
1780  PUT (506,8),A7,XOR:PUT (14,8),A7,XOR:RETURN   'File
1790  PUT (14,8),A7,XOR:PUT (126,8),A7,XOR:RETURN   'Draw
1800  PUT (126,8),A7,XOR:PUT (246,8),A7,XOR:RETURN  'Display
1810  PUT (246,8),A7,XOR:PUT (366,8),A7,XOR:RETURN  'View
1820  PUT (366,8),A7,XOR:PUT (506,8),A7,XOR:RETURN  'Options
1830  '_____
1840  '
1850  'module:  pan left on menu bar
1860  IF T1<1 THEN T1=5
1870  ON T1 GOTO 1880,1890,1900,1910,1920
1880  PUT (126,8),A7,XOR:PUT (14,8),A7,XOR:RETURN   'File
1890  PUT (246,8),A7,XOR:PUT (126,8),A7,XOR:RETURN  'Draw
1900  PUT (366,8),A7,XOR:PUT (246,8),A7,XOR:RETURN  'Edit
1910  PUT (506,8),A7,XOR:PUT (366,8),A7,XOR:RETURN  'Label
1920  PUT (14,8),A7,XOR:PUT (506,8),A7,XOR:RETURN   'Options
1930  '
2060  '_____MENU BAR SWITCHER_____
2070  '
2080  'module:  switcher to execute menu bar choices
2090  ON T1 GOTO 2100,2110,2120,2130,2140
2100  GOSUB 2190:RETURN   'invoke File menu
2110  GOSUB 2870:RETURN   'invoke Draw menu
2120  GOSUB 3140:RETURN   'invoke Display menu
2130  GOSUB 3370:RETURN   'invoke View menu
2140  GOSUB 3660:RETURN   'invoke Options menu
2150  '
2160  '_____FILE MENU CONTROL_____
2170  '
2180  'module:  interactive control of File menu
2190  GOSUB 5810   'save existing graphics
2200  PUT (14,19),A10,PSET  'place menu on screen
2210  PUT (16,25),A9,XOR   'place cursor >> on menu
2220  T8=1  'reset flag
2230  K$=INKEY$
2240  IF LEN(K$)=2 THEN K$=RIGHT$(K$,1) ELSE 2330
2250  IF K$=CHR$(80) THEN T8=T8+1:GOTO 2260 ELSE 2230
2260  IF T8>5 THEN T8=1
2270  ON T8 GOTO 2280,2290,2300,2310,2320
2280  PUT (16,57),A9,XOR:PUT (16,25),A9,XOR:GOTO 2230 'Name
2290  PUT (16,25),A9,XOR:PUT (16,33),A9,XOR:GOTO 2230 'Save
2300  PUT (16,33),A9,XOR:PUT (16,41),A9,XOR:GOTO 2230 'Load
2310  PUT (16,41),A9,XOR:PUT (16,49),A9,XOR:GOTO 2230 'Quit
2320  PUT (16,49),A9,XOR:PUT (16,57),A9,XOR:GOTO 2230 'Menu bar
2330  IF K$=CHR$(13) THEN 2360   '<Enter> to implement
2340  IF K$=CHR$(27) THEN 2410   '<ESC> to cancel
2350  GOTO 2230
```

Fig. E-2. (Continued from page 396.)

```
2360   ON T8 GOTO 2370,2380,2390,2400,2410
2370   GOSUB 2670:GOSUB 5770:LOCATE 1,34:PRINT F$:RETURN   'name change
2380   GOSUB 5770:GOSUB 2450:RETURN   'save image
2390   GOSUB 5770:GOSUB 2560:RETURN   'load image
2400   GOTO 1550   'quit program
2410   GOSUB 5770:RETURN   'menu bar
2420   '
2430   '_____
2440   'module: save 640x200 2-color image to disk
2450   MID$(F2$,1,8)=F$   'strip extension from file name
2460   SOUND 250,.7:DEF SEG=&HB800 'set up segment
2470   BSAVE "B:"+F2$+".PIC",0,&H4000
2510   DEF SEG=VARSEG(A99(0))   'restore ES register
2520   SOUND 250,.7:RETURN
2530   '
2540   '_____
2550   'module: load 640x200 2-color image from disk
2560   MID$(F2$,1,8)=F$   'strip extension from file name
2570   SOUND 250,.7:DEF SEG=&HB800 'set up segment
2580   BLOAD "B:"+F2$+".PIC",0
2620   DEF SEG=VARSEG(A99(0))   'restore ES register
2630   GOSUB 5180:SOUND 250,.7:RETURN
2640   '
2650   '_____
2660   'module:  interactive control of Name dialog box
2670   GET (34,53)-(303,66),A11C  'save existing graphics
2680   PUT (34,53),A11,PSET  'display Name dialog box
2690   T2=25  'echo position flag
2700   F1$=F$  'temporary save of existing filename
2710   FOR T=1 TO 8 STEP 1
2720   K$=INKEY$
2730   IF K$="" THEN 2720  'wait for keystroke
2740   IF K$=CHR$(27) THEN F$=F1$:T=8:GOTO 2780  '<ESC> to cancel instructions an
d restore previous filename
2750   IF K$<"A" THEN SOUND 250,.7:GOTO 2720  'must be A-Z
2760   IF K$>"Z" THEN SOUND 250,.7:GOTO 2720  'must be A-Z
2770   T2=T2+1:LOCATE 8,T2:PRINT K$:MID$(F$,T,1)=K$  'echo user input and insert
character into F$
2780   NEXT T
2790   LOCATE 8,26:PRINT F$
2800   K$=INKEY$:IF K$<>CHR$(13) THEN 2800
2810   LOCATE 1,34:PRINT F$:SOUND 250,.7  'display on filename bar
2820   PUT (34,53),A11C,PSET:RETURN  'restore previous graphics
2830   '
2840   '_____DRAW MENU CONTROL_____
2850   '
2860   'module:  interactive control of Draw menu
2870   GOSUB 5810:GOSUB 5930  'save existing graphics
2880   PUT (126,19),A15,PSET  'place menu on screen
2890   PUT (128,25),A9,XOR  'place cursor >> on menu
2900   T8=1  'reset flag
2910   K$=INKEY$
2920   IF LEN(K$)=2 THEN K$=RIGHT$(K$,1) ELSE 3010
```

Fig. E-2. (Continued from page 397.)

```
2930   IF K$=CHR$(80) THEN T8=T8+1:GOTO 2940 ELSE 2910
2940   IF T8>5 THEN T8=1
2950   ON T8 GOTO 2960,2970,2980,2990,3000
2960   PUT (128,57),A9,XOR:PUT (128,25),A9,XOR:GOTO 2910 'Line
2970   PUT (128,25),A9,XOR:PUT (128,33),A9,XOR:GOTO 2910 'Curve
2980   PUT (128,33),A9,XOR:PUT (128,41),A9,XOR:GOTO 2910 'Circle
2990   PUT (128,41),A9,XOR:PUT (128,49),A9,XOR:GOTO 2910 'Undo
3000   PUT (128,49),A9,XOR:PUT (128,57),A9,XOR:GOTO 2910 'Menu bar
3010   IF K$=CHR$(13) THEN 3040  '<Enter> to implement
3020   IF K$=CHR$(27) THEN 3090  '<ESC> to cancel
3030   GOTO 2910
3040   ON T8 GOTO 3050,3060,3070,3080,3090
3050   T5=1:GOSUB 5770:GOSUB 3990:GOTO 2880  'line
3060   T5=2:GOSUB 5770:GOSUB 3990:GOTO 2880  'curve
3070   T5=3:GOSUB 5770:GOSUB 3990:GOTO 2880  'circle
3080   GOSUB 5970:LOCATE 18,22:PRINT SYC:SOUND 250,.7:RETURN  'undo
3090   GOSUB 5770:RETURN  'menu bar
3100   '
3110   '_____DISPLAY MENU CONTROL_____
3120   '
3130   'module:  interactive control of Display menu
3140   GOSUB 5810  'save existing graphics
3150   PUT (246,19),A13,PSET 'place menu on screen
3160   PUT (248,24),A9,XOR 'place cursor >> on menu
3170   T8=1  'reset flag
3180   K$=INKEY$
3190   IF LEN(K$)=2 THEN K$=RIGHT$(K$,1) ELSE 3260
3200   IF K$=CHR$(80) THEN T8=T8+1:GOTO 3210 ELSE 3180
3210   IF T8>3 THEN T8=1
3220   ON T8 GOTO 3230,3240,3250
3230   PUT (248,40),A9,XOR:PUT (248,24),A9,XOR:GOTO 3180 'Regen
3240   PUT (248,24),A9,XOR:PUT (248,32),A9,XOR:GOTO 3180 'Clear
3250   PUT (248,32),A9,XOR:PUT (248,40),A9,XOR:GOTO 3180 'Menu bar
3260   IF K$=CHR$(13) THEN 3290  '<Enter> to implement
3270   IF K$=CHR$(27) THEN 3320  '<ESC> to cancel
3280   GOTO 3180
3290   ON T8 GOTO 3300,3310,3320
3300   GOSUB 5770:VIEW SCREEN (2,19)-(248,123):CLS:LINE (122,53)-(132,53),C6:LINE
  (127,51)-(127,55),C6:VIEW SCREEN (251,19)-(637,186):CLS:VIEW:GOSUB 4590:GOSUB 5
180:SOUND 860,2:SOUND 800,2:RETURN  'Regen
3310   GOSUB 5770:VIEW SCREEN (2,19)-(248,123):CLS:LINE (122,53)-(132,53),C6:LINE
  (127,51)-(127,55),C6:VIEW SCREEN (251,19)-(637,186):CLS:VIEW:GOSUB 1600:SOUND 8
60,2:SOUND 800,2:RETURN  'Clear
3320   GOSUB 5770:RETURN  'menu bar
3330   '
3340   '_____VIEW MENU CONTROL_____
3350   '
3360   'module:  interactive control of View menu
3370   GOSUB 5810  'save existing graphics
3380   PUT (366,19),A14,PSET 'place menu on screen
3390   PUT (368,24),A9,XOR  'place cursor >> on menu
3400   T8=1  'reset flag
3410   K$=INKEY$
```

Fig. E-2. (Continued from page 398.)

```
3420  IF LEN(K$)=2 THEN K$=RIGHT$(K$,1) ELSE 3520
3430  IF K$=CHR$(80) THEN T8=T8+1:GOTO 3440 ELSE 3410
3440  IF T8>6 THEN T8=1
3450  ON T8 GOTO 3460,3470,3480,3490,3500,3510
3460  PUT (368,64),A9,XOR:PUT (368,24),A9,XOR:GOTO 3410  'Distance
3470  PUT (368,24),A9,XOR:PUT (368,32),A9,XOR:GOTO 3410  'Elevation
3480  PUT (368,32),A9,XOR:PUT (368,40),A9,XOR:GOTO 3410  'Yaw
3490  PUT (368,40),A9,XOR:PUT (368,48),A9,XOR:GOTO 3410  'Roll
3500  PUT (368,48),A9,XOR:PUT (368,56),A9,XOR:GOTO 3410  'Pitch
3510  PUT (368,56),A9,XOR:PUT (368,64),A9,XOR:GOTO 3410  'Menu bar
3520  IF K$=CHR$(13) THEN 3550  '<Enter> to implement
3530  IF K$=CHR$(27) THEN 3610  '<ESC> to cancel
3540  GOTO 3410
3550  ON T8 GOTO 3560,3570,3580,3590,3600,3610
3560  GOSUB 4730:RETURN  'Distance
3570  GOSUB 4820:RETURN  'Elevation
3580  GOSUB 4910:RETURN  'Yaw
3590  GOSUB 5000:RETURN  'Roll
3600  GOSUB 5090:RETURN  'Pitch
3610  GOSUB 5770:RETURN  'menu bar
3620  '
3630  '_____OPTIONS MENU CONTROL_____
3640  '
3650  'module:  interactive control of Options menu
3660  GOSUB 5810  'save existing graphics
3670  PUT (505,19),A8,PSET  'place menu on screen
3680  PUT (507,25),A9,XOR  'place cursor >> on menu
3690  T8=1  'reset flag
3700  K$=INKEY$
3710  IF LEN(K$)=2 THEN K$=RIGHT$(K$,1) ELSE 3810
3720  IF K$=CHR$(80) THEN T8=T8+1:GOTO 3730 ELSE 3700
3730  IF T8>6 THEN T8=1
3740  ON T8 GOTO 3750,3760,3770,3780,3790,3800
3750  PUT (507,65),A9,XOR:PUT (507,25),A9,XOR:GOTO 3700  'Set snap
3760  PUT (507,25),A9,XOR:PUT (507,33),A9,XOR:GOTO 3700  'Set grid
3770  PUT (507,33),A9,XOR:PUT (507,41),A9,XOR:GOTO 3700  'Grid on/off
3780  PUT (507,41),A9,XOR:PUT (507,49),A9,XOR:GOTO 3700  'Gnomon on/off
3790  PUT (507,49),A9,XOR:PUT (507,57),A9,XOR:GOTO 3700  'Set color
3800  PUT (507,57),A9,XOR:PUT (507,65),A9,XOR:GOTO 3700  'Menu bar
3810  IF K$=CHR$(13) THEN 3840  '<Enter> to implement
3820  IF K$=CHR$(27) THEN 3900  '<ESC> to cancel
3830  GOTO 3700
3840  ON T8 GOTO 3850,3860,3870,3880,3890,3900
3850  GOSUB 3940:GOTO 3700  'Set snap
3860  GOSUB 3940:GOTO 3700  'Set grid spacing
3870  GOSUB 5420:GOTO 3700  'Grid on/off
3880  GOSUB 5500:GOTO 3700  'Gnomon on/off
3890  GOSUB 5230:GOTO 3700  'Set color
3900  GOSUB 5770:GOSUB 5180:RETURN  'menu bar
3910  '
3920  '_____DO-NOTHING ROUTINE_____
3930  '
3940  SOUND 860,2:SOUND 800,2:RETURN  'do-nothing routine
```

Fig. E-2. (Continued from page 399.)

```
3950 '
3960 '_____CROSSHAIR CURSOR CONTROL_____
3970 '
3980 'module:  interactive control of crosshair cursor
3990 SOUND 250,.7
4000 PUT (SX,SY),A12,XOR  'install crosshair cursor
4010 T6=0 'reset polyline flag
4020 X1=100:X2=130:X3=160:X4=190:Y1=40:Y2=100:Y3=140:Y4=70 'reset control poin
ts for curve and fillet
4030 K$=INKEY$
4040 IF LEN(K$)=2 THEN K$=RIGHT$(K$,1) ELSE 4210
4050 IF K$=CHR$(77) THEN PUT (SX,SY),A12,XOR:SX=SX+J ELSE 4080
4060 IF SX>XR THEN SX=XR:SOUND 250,.7
4070 PUT (SX,SY),A12,XOR:GOTO 4030
4080 IF K$=CHR$(75) THEN PUT (SX,SY),A12,XOR:SX=SX-J ELSE 4110
4090 IF SX<XL THEN SX=XL:SOUND 250,.7
4100 PUT (SX,SY),A12,XOR:GOTO 4030
4110 IF K$=CHR$(72) THEN PUT (SX,SY),A12,XOR:SY=SY-J*.5 ELSE 4140
4120 IF SY<YT THEN SY=YT:SOUND 250,.7
4130 PUT (SX,SY),A12,XOR:GOTO 4030
4140 IF K$=CHR$(80) THEN PUT (SX,SY),A12,XOR:SY=SY+J*.5 ELSE 4170
4150 IF SY>YB THEN SY=YB:SOUND 250,.7
4160 PUT (SX,SY),A12,XOR:GOTO 4030
4170 IF K$=CHR$(71) THEN PUT (SX,SY),A12,XOR:SX=XL:SY=YT:PUT (SX,SY),A12,XOR:GO
TO 4030
4180 IF K$=CHR$(73) THEN PUT (SX,SY),A12,XOR:SX=XR:SY=YT:PUT (SX,SY),A12,XOR:GO
TO 4030
4190 IF K$=CHR$(81) THEN PUT (SX,SY),A12,XOR:SX=XR:SY=YB:PUT (SX,SY),A12,XOR:GO
TO 4030
4200 IF K$=CHR$(79) THEN PUT (SX,SY),A12,XOR:SX=XL:SY=YB:PUT (SX,SY),A12,XOR:GO
TO 4030
4210 IF K$=CHR$(27) THEN PUT (SX,SY),A12,XOR:SOUND 250,.7:RETURN  '<ESC>
4220 IF K$=CHR$(13) THEN PUT (SX,SY),A12,XOR:GOSUB 4300:GOSUB 5810:PUT (SX,SY),
A12,XOR:LOCATE 23,69:SOUND 250,.7:GOTO 4030  '<Enter> to implement command
4230 IF K$="1" THEN SYC=SYC+.25:LOCATE 18,22:PRINT SYC" ":SOUND 250,.7:GOTO 40
30 'increment plan drawing height
4240 IF K$="2" THEN SYC=SYC-.25:LOCATE 18,22:PRINT SYC" ":SOUND 250,.7:GOTO 40
30 'decrement plan drawing height
4250 GOTO 4030
4260 SOUND 250,.7:RETURN
4270 '_____
4280 '_____
4290 'module:  switcher for drawing functions
4300 ON T5 GOTO 4310,4320,4330
4310 GOSUB 4370:RETURN
4320 GOSUB 3940:RETURN
4330 GOSUB 3940:RETURN
4340 '_____
4350 '_____
4360 'module:  polyline function
4370 IF T6=0 THEN SXC=SX+7:SZC=SY+3:PSET (SXC,SZC),C:T6=1:SXP=SXC:SZP=SZC:SYP=S
YC:RETURN ELSE 4380
4380 SXC=SX+7:SZC=SY+3:LINE (SXP,SZP)-(SXC,SZC),C:GOSUB 4430:GOSUB 4550:SXP=SXC
```

Fig. E-2. (Continued from page 400.)

```
    :SZP=SZC:SYP=SYC:RETURN
4390 '
4400 '_____GENERATE 3D MODEL_____
4410 '
4420 'module:  generate 3D model
4430  WINDOW SCREEN (-399,-299)-(400,300):VIEW SCREEN (251,19)-(637,186)  'clip
3D viewing area
4440  X=(.404858*SXP)-51:Z=(.9523809*SZP)-51:Y=SYP:GOSUB 4500:SX1=SX1+125:SY1=SY
1+3:PSET (SX1,SY1),C
4450  X=(.404858*SXC)-51:Z=(.9523809*SZC)-51:Y=SYC:GOSUB 4500:SX1=SX1+125:SY1=SY
1+3:LINE-(SX1,SY1),C
4460  WINDOW SCREEN (0,0)-(639,199):VIEW:RETURN
4470 '
4480 '‾‾‾‾‾‾‾
4490 'module:  perspective formulas
4500  X=(-1)*X:XA=CR1*X-SR1*Z:ZA=SR1*X+CR1*Z:X=CR2*XA+SR2*Y:YA=CR2*Y-SR2*XA:Z=CR
3*ZA-SR3*YA:Y=SR3*ZA+CR3*YA:X=X+MX:Y=Y+MY:Z=Z+MZ:SX1=D*X/Z:SY1=D*Y/Z:RETURN
4510 '
4520 '_____DATA FILE INPUT/OUTPUT_____
4530 '
4540 'module:  storage of graphics attributes in data file
4550  OPEN "A:KEYLAYER.CDF" FOR APPEND AS #1:WRITE #1,SXP,SZP,SXC,SZC,C,SYP,SYC:
CLOSE #1:RETURN
4560 '
4570 '‾‾‾‾‾‾‾
4580 'module:  retrieval of graphics attributes from data file
4590  OPEN "A:KEYLAYER.CDF" FOR INPUT AS #1
4600  INPUT #1,SXP,SZP,SXC,SZC,C,SYP,SYC  'dummy pass
4610  IF T3=1 THEN GOSUB 5460  'is grid toggled on?
4620  IF T4=1 THEN GOSUB 5540  'is gnomon toggled on?
4630  IF EOF(1) THEN CLOSE #1:RETURN
4640  INPUT #1,SXP,SZP,SXC,SZC,C,SYP,SYC:GOSUB 4680:GOTO 4630
4650 '
4660 '‾‾‾‾‾‾‾
4670 'module:  regen function for 2D/3D modes
4680  LINE (SXP,SZP)-(SXC,SZC),C:GOSUB 4430:RETURN  'polyline regen
4690 '
4700 '_____ADJUST VIEW PARAMETERS_____
4710 '
4720 'module:  adjust Distance to viewpoint
4730  SOUND 250,.7
4740  K$=INKEY$
4750  IF K$="=" THEN MZ=MZ-10:GOSUB 5180:GOTO 4740
4760  IF K$="-" THEN MZ=MZ+10:GOSUB 5180:GOTO 4740
4770  IF K$=CHR$(13) THEN GOSUB 5770:GOSUB 5180:VIEW SCREEN (2,19)-(248,123):CLS
:VIEW SCREEN (251,19)-(637,186):CLS:VIEW:GOSUB 4590:SOUND 860,2:SOUND 800,2:RETU
RN
4780  GOTO 4740
4790 '
4800 '‾‾‾‾‾‾‾
4810 'module:  adjust Elevation of viewpoint
4820  SOUND 250,.7
4830  K$=INKEY$
```

Fig. E-2. (Continued from page 401.)

```
4840   IF K$="=" THEN MY=MY-2:GOSUB 5180:GOTO 4830
4850   IF K$="-" THEN MY=MY+2:GOSUB 5180:GOTO 4830
4860   IF K$=CHR$(13) THEN GOSUB 5770:GOSUB 5180:VIEW SCREEN (2,19)-(248,123):CLS
:VIEW SCREEN (251,19)-(637,186):CLS:VIEW:GOSUB 4590:SOUND 860,2:SOUND 800,2:RETU
RN
4870   GOTO 4830
4880   '_____
4890   '
4900   'module:  adjust Yaw angle
4910   SOUND 250,.7
4920   K$=INKEY$:IF LEN(K$)=2 THEN K$=RIGHT$(K$,1) ELSE 4950
4930   IF K$=CHR$(77) THEN R1=R1-.17953:GOSUB 5180:GOTO 4920
4940   IF K$=CHR$(75) THEN R1=R1+.17953:GOSUB 5180:GOTO 4920
4950   IF K$=CHR$(13) THEN SR1=SIN(R1):CR1=COS(R1):GOSUB 5770:GOSUB 5180:VIEW SCR
EEN (2,19)-(248,123):CLS:VIEW SCREEN (251,19)-(637,186):CLS:VIEW:GOSUB 4590:SOUN
D 860,2:SOUND 800,2:RETURN
4960   GOTO 4920
4970   '_____
4980   '
4990   'module:  adjust Roll angle
5000   SOUND 250,.7
5010   K$=INKEY$:IF LEN(K$)=2 THEN K$=RIGHT$(K$,1) ELSE 5040
5020   IF K$=CHR$(77) THEN R2=R2+.08727:GOSUB 5180:GOTO 5010
5030   IF K$=CHR$(75) THEN R2=R2-.08727:GOSUB 5180:GOTO 5010
5040   IF K$=CHR$(13) THEN SR2=SIN(R2):CR2=COS(R2):GOSUB 5770:GOSUB 5180:VIEW SCR
EEN (2,19)-(248,123):CLS:VIEW SCREEN (251,19)-(637,186):CLS:VIEW:GOSUB 4590:SOUN
D 860,2:SOUND 800,2:RETURN
5050   GOTO 5010
5060   '_____
5070   '
5080   'module:  adjust Pitch angle
5090   SOUND 250,.7
5100   K$=INKEY$:IF LEN(K$)=2 THEN K$=RIGHT$(K$,1) ELSE 5130
5110   IF K$=CHR$(72) THEN R3=R3-.08727:GOSUB 5180:GOTO 5100
5120   IF K$=CHR$(80) THEN R3=R3+.08727:GOSUB 5180:GOTO 5100
5130   IF K$=CHR$(13) THEN SR3=SIN(R3):CR3=COS(R3):GOSUB 5770:GOSUB 5180:VIEW SCR
EEN (2,19)-(248,123):CLS:VIEW SCREEN (251,19)-(637,186):CLS:VIEW:GOSUB 4590:SOUN
D 860,2:SOUND 800,2:RETURN
5140   GOTO 5100
5150   '
5160   '_____REFRESH ALPHANUMERICS_____
5170   '
5180   LOCATE 18,22:PRINT SYC:LOCATE 19,21:PRINT (-1*MZ):LOCATE 20,22:PRINT (-1*M
Y):LOCATE 21,12:PRINT R1:LOCATE 22,13:PRINT R2:LOCATE 23,14:PRINT R3:LINE (8,185
)-(243,185),C:RETURN
5190   '
5200   '_____ADJUST OPTIONS_____
5210   '
5220   'module:  change the drawing color
5230   SOUND 250,.7
5240   IF C=C7 THEN C=C0:GOSUB 5180:RETURN
5250   IF C=C0 THEN C=C7:GOSUB 5180:RETURN
5380   GOSUB 5180:RETURN
```

Fig. E-2. (Continued from page 402.)

```
5390 '_____
5400 '
5410 'module:  toggle 2D grid on/off
5420  IF T3=0 THEN T3=1:SOUND 250,.7:RETURN ELSE IF T3=1 THEN T3=0:SOUND 250,.7:
RETURN
5430 '
5440 '_____
5450 'module:  create grid if toggled on
5460  T=1:WHILE T<249:LINE (T,19)-(T,123),C8,,&HAAAA:T=T+J10:WEND:T=19:WHILE T<1
23:LINE (2,T)-(248,T),C8,,&H8888:T=T+J11:WEND:LINE (122,53)-(132,53),C6:LINE (12
7,51)-(127,55),C6:RETURN
5470 '
5480 '_____
5490 'module:  toggle 3D gnomon on/off (x,y,z axis display)
5500  IF T4=0 THEN T4=1:SOUND 250,.7:RETURN ELSE IF T4=1 THEN T4=0:SOUND 250,.7:
RETURN
5510 '
5520 '_____
5530 'module:  create gnomon if toggled on
5540  WINDOW SCREEN (-399,-299)-(400,300):VIEW SCREEN (251,19)-(637,186)
5550  X=30:Z=0:Y=0:GOSUB 4500:SX1=SX1+125:SY1=SY1+3:PSET (SX1,SY1),C2:X=0:Z=0:Y=
0:GOSUB 4500:SX1=SX1+125:SY1=SY1+3:LINE-(SX1,SY1),C2,,&H9249:X=-30:Z=0:Y=0:GOSUB
 4500:SX1=SX1+125:SY1=SY1+3:LINE-(SX1,SY1),C8,,&H9249  'x-axis
5560  X=0:Z=0:Y=30:GOSUB 4500:SX1=SX1+125:SY1=SY1+3:PSET (SX1,SY1),C4:X=0:Z=0:Y=
0:GOSUB 4500:SX1=SX1+125:SY1=SY1+3:LINE-(SX1,SY1),C4,,&H9249:X=0:Z=0:Y=-30:GOSUB
 4500:SX1=SX1+125:SY1=SY1+3:LINE-(SX1,SY1),C8,,&H9249  'y-axis
5570  X=0:Z=30:Y=0:GOSUB 4500:SX1=SX1+125:SY1=SY1+3:PSET (SX1,SY1),C1:X=0:Z=0:Y=
0:GOSUB 4500:SX1=SX1+125:SY1=SY1+3:LINE-(SX1,SY1),C1,,&H9249:X=0:Z=-30:Y=0:GOSUB
 4500:SX1=SX1+125:SY1=SY1+3:LINE-(SX1,SY1),C8,,&H9249  'z-axis
5580  WINDOW SCREEN (0,0)-(639,199):VIEW:RETURN
5585 '
5590 '_____PCOPY MACHINE CODE LOADER_____
5600 '
5610 'module:  load hex opcodes into scalar array A99 inside BASIC's workspace
5620  RESTORE 5690  'set data pointer
5630  DEF SEG=VARSEG(A99(0)):PCOPY=VARPTR(A99(0))  'define PCOPY as address of a
rray
5640  FOR T=0 TO 34 STEP 1:READ HEX:POKE (PCOPY+T),HEX:NEXT T  'move hex opcode
values from database into array A99
5650  RETURN
5660 '
5670 '_____
5680 'module:  database of hex opcodes for PCOPY machine code routine to move gr
aphics page from 3C000 hex to B8000 hex
5690  DATA  &H51,&H1E,&H06,&H56,&H57,&H9C,&HB9,&H00,&H3C
5700  DATA  &H8E,&HD9,&HB9,&H00,&HB8,&H8E,&HC1,&HFC
5710  DATA  &HBE,&H00,&H00,&HBF,&H00,&H00,&HB9,&H00,&H40
5720  DATA  &HF3,&HA4,&H9D,&H5F,&H5E,&H07,&H1F,&H59,&HCB
5730 '
5740 '_____PCOPY EMULATION ROUTINES_____
5750 '
5760 'module:  emulate PCOPY 0,1 function
5770  POKE (PCOPY+8),&H3C:POKE (PCOPY+13),&HB8:CALL ABSOLUTE PCOPY:RETURN
```

Fig. E-2. (Continued from page 403.)

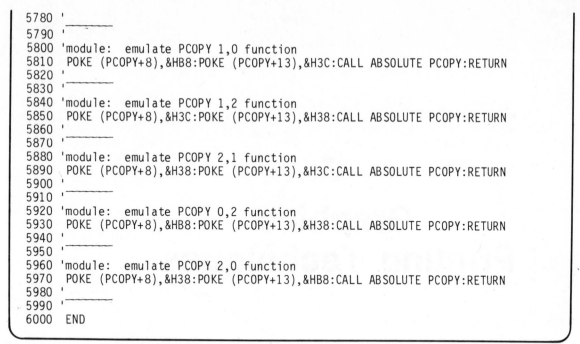

```
5780 '_____
5790 '
5800 'module:  emulate PCOPY 1,0 function
5810  POKE (PCOPY+8),&HB8:POKE (PCOPY+13),&H3C:CALL ABSOLUTE PCOPY:RETURN
5820 '
5830 '_____
5840 'module:  emulate PCOPY 1,2 function
5850  POKE (PCOPY+8),&H3C:POKE (PCOPY+13),&H38:CALL ABSOLUTE PCOPY:RETURN
5860 '
5870 '_____
5880 'module:  emulate PCOPY 2,1 function
5890  POKE (PCOPY+8),&H38:POKE (PCOPY+13),&H3C:CALL ABSOLUTE PCOPY:RETURN
5900 '
5910 '_____
5920 'module:  emulate PCOPY 0,2 function
5930  POKE (PCOPY+8),&HB8:POKE (PCOPY+13),&H38:CALL ABSOLUTE PCOPY:RETURN
5940 '
5950 '_____
5960 'module:  emulate PCOPY 2,0 function
5970  POKE (PCOPY+8),&H38:POKE (PCOPY+13),&HB8:CALL ABSOLUTE PCOPY:RETURN
5980 '
5990 '_____
6000  END
```

Fig. E-2. (Continued from page 404.)

BETTERBASIC, TRUE BASIC, AND ZBASIC

Other BASIC compilers often do not provide the syntax compatibilities provided by QuickBASIC and Turbo BASIC. Although BetterBASIC, True BASIC, and ZBasic each offer powerful capabilities, especially in data management and file management, some programmers place high emphasis on IBM BASICA graphics compatibility—a compatability which is not always present in these three compilers.

True BASIC, for example, uses the statement **BOX SHOW S\$ AT X,Y USING "XOR"** to accomplish the graphics function defined by BASICA's statement **PUT (X,Y),A1,XOR**. By way of further example, BASICA's statement **LINE (X1,Y1)−(X2,Y2),C** translates in True BASIC as **PLOT X1,Y1;X2,Y2** and requires that you have previously invoked SET COLOR to set the drawing color. Versions of ZBasic offer no graphic arrays capabilities. Line styling and area-fill bit tiling functions are also lacking.

F

Graphics Printing Techniques

You can use your dot-matrix or ink-jet printer to transfer a screen image to a sheet of paper. This provides a permanent record of your graphics, which does not require the presence of a computer for viewing. It is also an economical substitute for the expensive plotters used by professional graphics workstations.

USING DOS

If you are using a CGA or an MCGA, you can use DOS to provide a graphics print-out of either the 320×200 four-color mode or the 640×200 two-color mode. The program listing for YOUR MICROCOMPUTER 3D CAD DESIGNER in Appendix G is intended for the 640×200 two-color mode of the color/graphics adapter using interpreted BASIC. (If you are using Turbo BASIC, use the program listing provided in Appendix E.) To generate a graphics print-out of your 3D drawing, follow these steps:

1. After you have booted DOS, but before you load BASIC, use your keyboard to enter A > **GRAPHICS** (or C > **GRAPHICS** if you are using a hard disk). This will instruct DOS to load a short subroutine as a memory resident program. The GRAPHICS subroutine contains the printer drivers required to print either the 320×200 four-color screen or the 640×200 two-color screen on most dot matrix printers. (Refer to your DOS manual if you are using some other type of printer.) If your DOS program disk is not in the current drive, then you must tell DOS where to find the GRAPHICS utility. If it is in drive B, for example, you would type **B:GRAPHICS**.
2. Load BASIC (either your interpreter or your compiler).

3. Load and run *YOUR MICROCOMPUTER 3D CAD DESIGNER* (or any other graphics program that uses either the 320×200 four-color screen mode or the 640×200 two-color screen mode).

4. At an appropriate time, press Shift-PrtSc to produce a graphics print-out on your printer. (Hold down the Shift key while you press the PrtSc key.) Be sure that your printer is turned on, it is on-line, and it is loaded with paper.

5. The printer will print one scan line at a time, often taking two minutes or more to produce the graphics print-out. White pixels will be printed as black images on the paper. Black pixels will print as white. Cyan and magenta will be printed as dithered (patterned) lines.

Depending upon which graphics mode you are using, the image will be printed either lengthwise or sideways on the paper. Note, however, that the DOS graphics printing utility works only with the 320×200 four-color mode and the 640×200 two-color mode. If you have an EGA and you wish to produce a graphics print-out of any of the EGA modes, you cannot use DOS for that purpose.

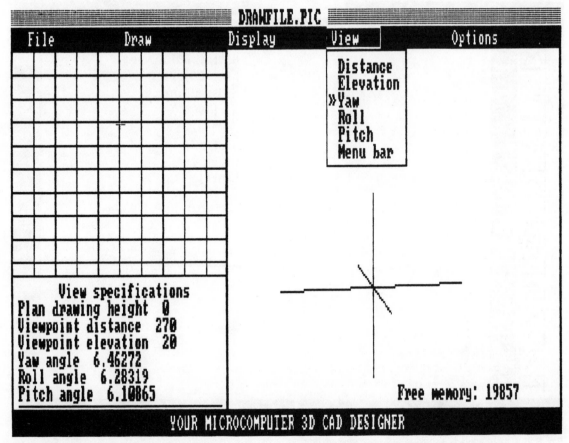

Fig. F-1. A black on white graphics print-out generated on a dot-matrix printer using third-party utility software.

USING OTHER METHODS

In order to generate a graphics print-out of any EGA or VGA mode, you require a specialty program (such as *Pizazz* from Application Techniques, although others are available).

Figure F-1 shows a typical graphics print-out using the 640×200 16-color mode of the EGA. This image is taken from *YOUR MICROCOMPUTER 3D CAD DESIGNER*, the wire-frame modeling program whose listing appears in Chapter 26. The graphics print-out was produced on a Panasonic KX-P1091 dot-matrix printer. The graphics printing program was Pizazz. The graphics adapter was a QuadEGA+ enhanced graphics adapter from Quadram Corporation.

Third-party graphics printing utilities are loaded in much the same manner as the DOS utility. At the DOS prompt, type the name of the utility, which is then loaded as a memory resident program. (See your graphics printing manual for full instructions, of course.) Then, when your graphics program is running on your EGA or VGA, all you need do is strike Shift-PrtSc to produce a paper copy of the screen image.

Third-party utilities like Pizazz are very powerful, but you might not be satisfied with their default printing parameters. The image in Fig. F-2 shows a print-out taken from

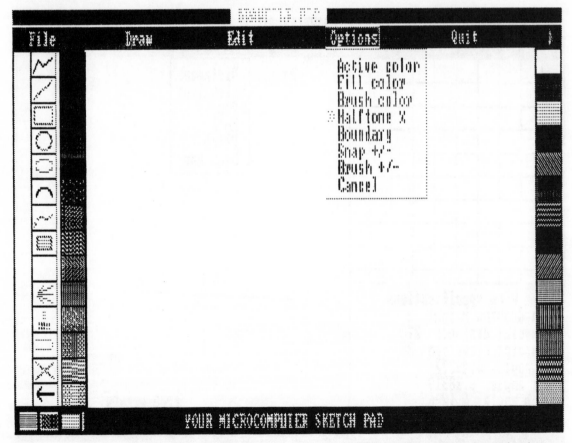

Fig. F-2. Without attribute tweaking, full-color images tend to produce unsatisfactory print-outs on a dot-matrix printer.

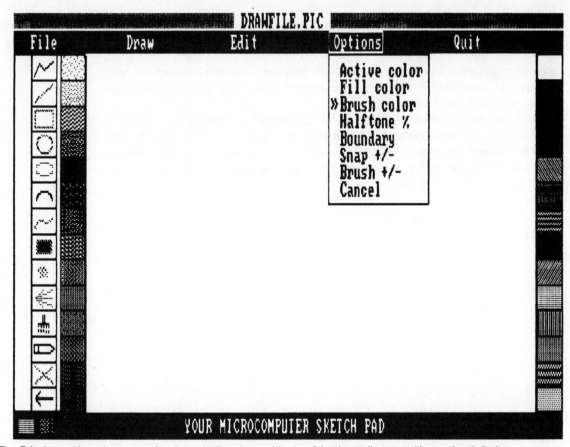

Fig. F-3. A graphics print-out can be dramatically enhanced by careful color attribute tweaking and anti-aliasing.

YOUR MICROCOMPUTER SKETCH PAD, which uses the 640×200 16-color mode. Note how the file name at the top of the image is nearly invisible. The border which surrounds the pull-down menu is difficult to see. The scrolling cursor is pale. Many of the Draw icons at the left of the screen are fragmented.

These printing characteristics are caused by the utility program's use of dithering (patterning) to represent different colors generated by your EGA. Remember, your EGA or VGA can produce 16 colors, but your dot-matrix printer can only generate two colors (black and white). Shades of black are used by the graphics printing utility to represent other colors.

Most graphics printing programs, including Pizazz, provide a menu system which permits you to change the patterns used to print different colors. By invoking these changes, the image in Fig. F-3 was produced. Note the improvement in legibility, even though it was produced from the same screen image as the print-out in Fig. F-2. Even the half-tone swatches, which were inverted in Fig. F-2, have been printed correctly in Fig. F-3.

To get the most out of your third-party graphics printing utility, you must personalize it to suit your needs. Quite often this means experimenting until you obtain the results you seek on the printed page.

AVOIDING PRINTER BURN-OUT

Dot-matrix printers were simply not engineered to handle the stress of graphics printing. The tiny wire pins that strike the ribbon and produce those miniscule dots on the paper were designed with the expectation of frequent momentary pauses (between alphanumeric characters, for example). These frequent pauses allow the pins to cool down, thereby preventing overheating.

If you are printing large areas of solid black, however, the pins in your dot-matrix printer do not have any opportunity to cool down between strikes. If enough sheets of solid black images are printed, the pins will heat up and expand to the point where the print head will seize up. Be forewarned: use caution and judgment if you must print images containing large areas of black.

G

Additional Program Listings for Color/Graphics Adapter

The program listings in this appendix have been specially converted for the CGA (the color graphics adapter found on IBM PC, XT, and compatible personal computers) and the MCGA (found on 8086-based IBM Personal System/2 computers). You can also use these program listings on an EGA or VGA, but they will only run in CGA modes.

The program listing in Fig. G-1 is the CGA version of *YOUR MICROCOMPUTER 3D CAD DESIGNER,* a wire-frame modeling program found in Chapters 26, 27, and 28. If you are using the companion disk to this book, type **LOAD "CAD-CGA1.BAS",R.** (For a Turbo BASIC version for your CGA, see Appendix E.)

The program listing in Fig. G-2 is the CGA version of the interactive, arcade-style animation program found in Chapter 34. If you are using the companion disk to this book, type **LOAD "ARCADE1.BAS",R.**

The program listing in Fig. G-3 is the CGA version of the high-speed frame animation program found in Chapter 33. If you are using the companion disk to this book, type **LOAD "FRAME1.BAS",R.**

The three program listings in this appendix are presented as ready-to-run, stand-alone programs. No further conversion or adaptation is required. The complete source code is given. Simply type them in and they are ready to execute. (Consult the List of Demonstration Programs, located after the Table of Contents, for a complete list of programs from the main body of the book which run on computers equipped with a CGA or an MCGA.)

HOW THE PROGRAMS WERE CONVERTED

By adhering to the modular programming techniques presented in the demonstration programs in this appendix, you can readily convert most of the programs from the main body of the book to run on your CGA or MCGA. A number of simple program changes should be kept in mind:

1. Alter the syntax of the BSAVE and BLOAD instructions. BASIC can save and retrieve an entire CGA screen with a single command. Refer to lines 2470 and 2580 in Fig. G-1.
2. Add the short assembly language routine which is needed to emulate the PCOPY instruction used with the EGA and VGA. See lines 5590 through 5720 in Fig. G-1 for the machine code loader. Refer to lines 5740 through 5970 for the emulation routines in Fig. G-1. The frame animation program in Fig. G-3 also uses the PCOPY assembly language routine.
3. Change all drawing colors to either 1 or 0, because only two colors are available in the 640×200 mode on a CGA.
4. Delete all COLOR instructions from the code.
5. Reduce the size of any DIM instructions, because you need 75% less space to store graphic arrays. (The 640×200 two-color mode uses one bit-per-pixel; the 640×200 16-color mode requires four bits-per-pixel.)
6. In frame animation programs, slow down the animation speed in order to compensate for the slower PCOPY emulation being used. To do this, simply increase the length of the FOR . . . NEXT timing loops.
7. Remember that the CGA cannot compete successfully against the multiplane-per-pixel graphics capabilities of the EGA and the VGA.

The program listings in this appendix push the CGA to its maximum limits in terms of resolution, menu management, 3D modeling capabilities, and animation. (The CGA is also capable of producing fully-shaded 3D models with hidden surface removal. Consult *High-Performance Interactive Graphics: Modeling, Rendering & Animating for IBM PCs and Compatibles,* TAB book 2879.)

```
100 'Program CAD-CGA1.BAS   YOUR MICROCOMPUTER 3D CAD DESIGNER
110 'Copyright (c) 1988 by Lee Adams and TAB Books Inc.
120 'All rights reserved.
130 'Version for CGA and MCGA.  640x200 2-color mode.
140 '
150 '_____INITIALIZE SYSTEM_____
160 '
170  KEY OFF:CLS:CLEAR:SCREEN 0,0,0,0:WIDTH 80:COLOR 7,0,0:CLS:LOCATE 10,20,0:PR
INT "Assigning memory space for graphic arrays"
180 '
190 '_____DATA ASSIGNMENTS_____
200 '
210 'module:  data assignments
220  DEFINT A,T,J,H,P
```

Fig. G-1. Complete source code for the CGA and MCGA version of the interactive 3D wire-frame CAD program from Chapter 26.

```
230   DIM A1(631):DIM A2(150):DIM A3(150):DIM A4(150):DIM A5(150):DIM A6(150)   't
emporary arrays for screen template
240   DIM A7(177)   'array for panning cursor
250   DIM A8(1793)   'array for Options menu
260   DIM A9(21)   'array for scrolling cursor
270   DIM A10(1057)   'array for File menu
280   DIM A11(953):DIM A11C(953)   'for Name dialog box
290   DIM A12(29)   'array for roaming crosshair cursor
300   DIM A13(683)   'array for Display menu
310   DIM A14(1321)   'array for View menu
320   DIM A15(1057)   'array for Draw menu
325   DIM A99(18)   'scalar array for machine code subroutine
326   HEX=0   'variable to migrate contents of hex database
327   PCOPY=0   'address of machine code subroutine
330   C0=0:C1=1:C2=1:C3=1:C4=1:C5=1:C6=1:C7=1:C8=1:C9=1:C10=1:C12=1:C13=1:C14=1:C
15=1   'software color codes
340   C=C7:CE=C7   'drawing, boundary colors
350   T=0   'loop counter
360   T1=2   'selection flag for menu bar
370   T2=25   'flag for echo position of file menu input
380   T3=0   '2D grid on/off toggle
390   T4=0   '3D gnomon on/off toggle
400   T5=0   'flag for function switcher
410   T6=0   'iterative flag for plastic functions
420   T8=1   'selection flag for menus
430   J=2:JS=J   'snap, temporary storage of snap value
440   J6=85:J7=19:J8=608:J9=186   'viewport dimensions for active drawing surface
on 640x200 screen
450   SX=122:SY=65   'crosshair array location
460   XL=2:XR=234:YT=19:YB=117   'left, right, top, bottom range of roaming crossh
air cursor
470   SXC=SX+7:SZC=SY+3:SYC=0   'center of crosshair cursor
480   SXP=0:SZP=0:SYP=0   'last referenced drawing point
490   F$="DRAWFILE.PIC":F1$=F$:F2$="DRAWFILE"   'strings used to manipulate filena
me when saving images
500   V=0   'size of free memory in BASICA workspace
510   V1=1024   'threshold memory flag
520   B=0:B2=0:B3=0:D1=0:D2=0:D3=0:D4=0:X1=0:X2=0:X3=0:X4=0:Y1=0:Y2=0:Y3=0:Y4=0
'used in freeform curve routine
530   D=1200!:R1=6.46272:R2=6.28319:R3=6.10865:MX=0!:MY=-20!:MZ=-270!:SR1=SIN(R1)
:SR2=SIN(R2):SR3=SIN(R3):CR1=COS(R1):CR2=COS(R2):CR3=COS(R3)   'variables used as
 input for perspective formulas
540   XA=0:YA=0:ZA=0   'temporary variables used in perspective formulas
550   SX1=0:SY1=0   'output of perspective formulas
560   J10=25:J11=11   'horizontal, vertical spacing for grid
570   '
580   '_____SET UP RUNTIME ENVIRONMENT_____
590   '
600   'module:  set up runtime environment
610   CLS:SCREEN 2   '640x200 2-clr mode
620   CLS
630   ON KEY(2) GOSUB 1550:KEY(2) ON   'install hot key
640   GOSUB 5620   'install PCOPY machine code subroutine
```

Fig. G-1. (Continued from page 412.)

```
650   GOSUB 1600   'initialize .CDF data file
660 '
670 '_____SET UP SCREEN DISPLAY_____
680 '
690 'module:  set up screen template
700   GOSUB 960   'save alphanumeric graphic arrays
710   GOSUB 1140  'create pull-down menus
720   LINE (0,8)-(639,199),C8,B  'border
730   LINE (0,187)-(639,187),C8:PAINT (320,190),C8,C8:PUT (182,189),A1,XOR  'bann
er
740   LINE (0,0)-(639,6),C6,B:PAINT (320,3),C6,C6:LOCATE 1,33:PRINT " DRAWFILE.CD
F ":LOCATE 1,34:PRINT F$  'filename bar
750   LINE (1,8)-(639,18),C8,B:PAINT (320,10),C8,C8  'menu bar
760   PUT (18,9),A2,XOR:PUT (130,9),A3,XOR:PUT (250,9),A4,XOR:PUT (370,9),A5,XOR:
PUT (510,9),A6,XOR  'selections for menu bar
770   LOCATE 10,20:PRINT "Reclaiming memory used by temporary arrays":ERASE A1,A2
,A3,A4,A5,A6  'free up array memory
780   LOCATE 10,20:PRINT "                                            "
790   LINE (250,19)-(250,186),C8:LINE (249,19)-(249,186),C8:LINE (1,19)-(1,186),C
8:LINE (638,19)-(638,186),C8:LINE (1,124)-(249,124),C8:LINE (122,53)-(132,53),C6
:LINE (127,51)-(127,55),C6  'split screen
800   LOCATE 18,2:PRINT "Plan drawing height":LOCATE 19,2:PRINT "Viewpoint distan
ce":LOCATE 20,2:PRINT "Viewpoint elevation":LOCATE 21,2:PRINT "Yaw angle":LOCATE
 22,2:PRINT "Roll angle":LOCATE 23,2:PRINT "Pitch angle"
810   LOCATE 17,8:PRINT "View specifications"
820   GOSUB 5180   'alphanumeric readouts
830   PUT (126,8),A7,XOR  'panning cursor for menu bar
840   GOSUB 5810:GOSUB 5930  'establish refresh buffers
850   LOCATE 9,40:PRINT "YOUR MICROCOMPUTER 3D CAD DESIGNER":LOCATE 12,40:PRINT "
Copyright (c) 1988 by Lee Adams and":LOCATE 13,40:PRINT "TAB Books Inc.  All rig
hts reserved."
860   LINE (310,60)-(584,60),C6:LINE (310,74)-(584,74),C6
870   LOCATE 19,43:PRINT "Press <Enter> to continue...":SOUND 860,2:SOUND 800,2
880   K$=INKEY$:IF K$<>CHR$(13) THEN 880
890   GOSUB 5770:SOUND 250,.7:LOCATE 23,57:PRINT "Free memory:"FRE(0)  'restore s
creen
900   GOTO 1650   'jump to runtime code
910   GOTO 910   'bulletproof code barrier
920 '
930 '_____CREATE ALPHANUMERICS FOR TEMPLATE_____
940 '
950 'module: create alpha arrays for screen template
960   LOCATE 10,20:PRINT "YOUR MICROCOMPUTER 3D CAD DESIGNER"
970   GET (150,71)-(424,79),A1:LOCATE 10,20:PRINT "
       "
980   LOCATE 10,20:PRINT "File":GET (150,71)-(210,79),A2
990   LOCATE 10,20:PRINT "Draw":GET (150,71)-(210,79),A3
1000   LOCATE 10,20:PRINT "Display":GET (150,71)-(210,79),A4
1010   LOCATE 10,20:PRINT "View   ":GET (150,71)-(210,79),A5
1020   LOCATE 10,20:PRINT "Options":GET (150,71)-(210,79),A6
1030   LOCATE 10,20:PRINT "       "
1040   LINE (150,70)-(212,80),C12,B:GET (150,70)-(212,80),A7  'create panning cur
sor for menu bar
```

Fig. G-1. (Continued from page 413.)

```
1050   LINE (150,70)-(212,80),0,B
1060   LINE (323,44)-(337,44),C7:LINE (330,41)-(330,47),C7:LINE (329,44)-(331,44)
,0   'create roaming crosshair cursor
1070   GET (323,41)-(337,47),A12:LINE (323,41)-(337,47),0,BF
1080   RETURN
1090 '
1100 '_____CREATE PULL-DOWN MENUS_____
1110 '
1120 'module:  create pull-down menus
1130 'submodule:  create Options menu
1140   LOCATE 10,20:PRINT "Set snap":LOCATE 11,20:PRINT "Set grid":LOCATE 12,20:P
RINT "Grid on/off":LOCATE 13,20:PRINT "Gnomon on/off"
1150   LOCATE 14,20:PRINT "Set color":LOCATE 15,20:PRINT "Menu bar"
1160   LINE (138,67)-(260,122),C8,B
1170   GET (138,67)-(260,122),A8:LINE (138,67)-(260,122),0,BF
1180   LOCATE 10,20:PRINT CHR$(175)   'menu cursor >>
1190   GET (151,73)-(159,77),A9:LOCATE 10,20:PRINT " "
1200 '_____
1210 '
1220 'submodule:  create File menu
1230   LOCATE 10,20:PRINT "Name":LOCATE 11,20:PRINT "Save":LOCATE 12,20:PRINT "Lo
ad":LOCATE 13,20:PRINT "Quit":LOCATE 14,20:PRINT "Menu bar"
1240   LINE (138,67)-(220,114),C8,B
1250   GET (138,67)-(220,114),A10:LINE (138,67)-(220,114),0,BF
1260 '_____
1270 '
1280 'submodule:  create Draw menu
1290   LOCATE 10,20:PRINT "Line":LOCATE 11,20:PRINT "Curve":LOCATE 12,20:PRINT "C
ircle":LOCATE 13,20:PRINT "Undo":LOCATE 14,20:PRINT "Menu bar"
1300   LINE (138,67)-(220,114),C8,B
1310   GET (138,67)-(220,114),A15:LINE (138,67)-(220,114),0,BF
1320 '_____
1330 '
1340 'submodule:  create Name dialog box
1350   LOCATE 10,20:PRINT "Enter new filename:                    "
1360   LINE (144,69)-(413,82),C8,B
1370   GET (144,69)-(413,82),A11:LINE (144,69)-(413,82),0,BF
1380 '_____
1390 '
1400 'submodule:  create Display menu
1410   LOCATE 4,20:PRINT "Regen":LOCATE 5,20:PRINT "Clear":LOCATE 6,20:PRINT "Men
u bar"
1420   LINE (138,20)-(220,50),C8,B
1430   GET (138,20)-(220,50),A13:LINE (138,20)-(220,50),0,BF
1440 '_____
1450 '
1460 'submodule:  create View menu
1470   LOCATE 4,20:PRINT "Distance":LOCATE 5,20:PRINT "Elevation":LOCATE 6,20:PRI
NT "Yaw":LOCATE 7,20:PRINT "Roll":LOCATE 8,20:PRINT "Pitch":LOCATE 9,20:PRINT "M
enu bar"
1480   LINE (138,20)-(230,74),C8,B
1490   GET (138,20)-(230,74),A14:LINE (138,20)-(230,74),0,BF
1500   RETURN
```

Fig. G-1. (Continued from page 414.)

```
1510 '
1520 '_____QUIT_____
1530 '
1540 'module:  exit routine
1550   CLS:SCREEN 0,0,0,0:WIDTH 80:COLOR 7,0,0:CLS:LOCATE 1,1,1:COLOR 6:PRINT "YO
UR MICROCOMPUTER 3D CAD DESIGNER":LOCATE 2,1:PRINT "is finished.":COLOR 7:SOUND
250,.7:END
1560 '
1570 '_____INITIALIZE DATA FILES_____
1580 '
1590 'module:  initialize .CDF data files
1600   OPEN "A:KEYLAYER.CDF" FOR OUTPUT AS #1:WRITE #1,SXP,SZP,SXC,SZC,C,SYP,SYC:
CLOSE #1:RETURN
1610 '
1620 '_____MENU BAR CONTROL_____
1630 '
1640 'main module:  interactive control of menu bar
1650   K$=INKEY$:GOSUB 1970:LOCATE 23,69:PRINT V" "
1660   IF LEN(K$)=2 THEN K$=RIGHT$(K$,1) ELSE 1700
1670   IF K$=CHR$(77) THEN T1=T1+1:GOSUB 1760:GOTO 1650
1680   IF K$=CHR$(75) THEN T1=T1-1:GOSUB 1860:GOTO 1650
1690   IF K$=CHR$(16) THEN GOTO 1550 'Alt-Q to quit
1700   IF K$=CHR$(13) THEN GOSUB 2090  '<Enter> key
1710   GOTO 1650
1720   GOTO 1720  'bulletproof code barrier
1730 '
1740 '_____
1750 'module:  pan right on menu bar
1760   IF T1>5 THEN T1=1
1770   ON T1 GOTO 1780,1790,1800,1810,1820
1780   PUT (506,8),A7,XOR:PUT (14,8),A7,XOR:RETURN   'File
1790   PUT (14,8),A7,XOR:PUT (126,8),A7,XOR:RETURN   'Draw
1800   PUT (126,8),A7,XOR:PUT (246,8),A7,XOR:RETURN  'Display
1810   PUT (246,8),A7,XOR:PUT (366,8),A7,XOR:RETURN  'View
1820   PUT (366,8),A7,XOR:PUT (506,8),A7,XOR:RETURN  'Options
1830 '
1840 '_____
1850 'module:  pan left on menu bar
1860   IF T1<1 THEN T1=5
1870   ON T1 GOTO 1880,1890,1900,1910,1920
1880   PUT (126,8),A7,XOR:PUT (14,8),A7,XOR:RETURN   'File
1890   PUT (246,8),A7,XOR:PUT (126,8),A7,XOR:RETURN  'Draw
1900   PUT (366,8),A7,XOR:PUT (246,8),A7,XOR:RETURN  'Edit
1910   PUT (506,8),A7,XOR:PUT (366,8),A7,XOR:RETURN  'Label
1920   PUT (14,8),A7,XOR:PUT (506,8),A7,XOR:RETURN   'Options
1930 '
1940 '_____CHECK SIZE OF WORKSPACE_____
1950 '
1960 'module:  check if user is running out of memory
1970   V=FRE(0):IF V>V1 THEN RETURN
1980   V1=128  'lower threshold to permit return to pgm
1990   GOSUB 5810:CLS:COLOR C12:LOCATE 10,32:PRINT "W A R N I N G":COLOR C7:LOCAT
E 12,23:PRINT "Out of memory in BASIC workspace."
```

Fig. G-1. (Continued from page 415.)

```
2000  LOCATE 13,27:PRINT "Save your drawing on disk!":LOCATE 15,21:PRINT "Press
<Enter> to return to 3D CAD DESIGNER."
2010  FOR T=1 TO 4 STEP 1:SOUND 250,3:SOUND 450,3:SOUND 650,3:NEXT T
2020  K$=INKEY$:IF K$<>CHR$(13) THEN 2020  'wait for <Enter>
2030  K$=INKEY$:IF K$<>"" THEN 2030  'empty keyboard buffer
2040  GOSUB 5770:SOUND 250,.7:RETURN
2050  '
2060  '_____MENU BAR SWITCHER_____
2070  '
2080  'module:  switcher to execute menu bar choices
2090  ON T1 GOTO 2100,2110,2120,2130,2140
2100  GOSUB 2190:RETURN  'invoke File menu
2110  GOSUB 2870:RETURN  'invoke Draw menu
2120  GOSUB 3140:RETURN  'invoke Display menu
2130  GOSUB 3370:RETURN  'invoke View menu
2140  GOSUB 3660:RETURN  'invoke Options menu
2150  '
2160  '_____FILE MENU CONTROL_____
2170  '
2180  'module:  interactive control of File menu
2190  GOSUB 5810   'save existing graphics
2200  PUT (14,19),A10,PSET  'place menu on screen
2210  PUT (16,25),A9,XOR  'place cursor >> on menu
2220  T8=1  'reset flag
2230  K$=INKEY$
2240  IF LEN(K$)=2 THEN K$=RIGHT$(K$,1) ELSE 2330
2250  IF K$=CHR$(80) THEN T8=T8+1:GOTO 2260 ELSE 2230
2260  IF T8>5 THEN T8=1
2270  ON T8 GOTO 2280,2290,2300,2310,2320
2280  PUT (16,57),A9,XOR:PUT (16,25),A9,XOR:GOTO 2230 'Name

2290  PUT (16,25),A9,XOR:PUT (16,33),A9,XOR:GOTO 2230 'Save
2300  PUT (16,33),A9,XOR:PUT (16,41),A9,XOR:GOTO 2230 'Load
2310  PUT (16,41),A9,XOR:PUT (16,49),A9,XOR:GOTO 2230 'Quit
2320  PUT (16,49),A9,XOR:PUT (16,57),A9,XOR:GOTO 2230 'Menu bar
2330  IF K$=CHR$(13) THEN 2360  '<Enter> to implement
2340  IF K$=CHR$(27) THEN 2410  '<ESC> to cancel
2350  GOTO 2230
2360  ON T8 GOTO 2370,2380,2390,2400,2410
2370  GOSUB 2670:GOSUB 5770:LOCATE 1,34:PRINT F$:RETURN   'name change
2380  GOSUB 5770:GOSUB 2450:RETURN  'save image
2390  GOSUB 5770:GOSUB 2560:RETURN  'load image
2400  GOTO 1550  'quit program
2410  GOSUB 5770:RETURN  'menu bar
2420  '_____
2430  '_____
2440  'module: save 640x200 2-color image to disk
2450  MID$(F2$,1,8)=F$  'strip extension from file name
2460  SOUND 250,.7:DEF SEG=&HB800 'set up segment
2470  BSAVE "B:"+F2$+".PIC",0,&H4000
2510  DEF SEG  'restore ES register
2520  SOUND 250,.7:RETURN
2530  '_____
2540  '_____
```

Fig. G-1. (Continued from page 416.)

```
2550  'module: load 640x200 2-color image from disk
2560  MID$(F2$,1,8)=F$  'strip extension from file name
2570  SOUND 250,.7:DEF SEG=&HB800 'set up segment
2580  BLOAD "B:"+F2$+".PIC",0
2620  DEF SEG   'restore ES register
2630  GOSUB 5180:SOUND 250,.7:RETURN
2640  '_____
2650  '_____
2660  'module:  interactive control of Name dialog box
2670  GET (34,53)-(303,66),A11C  'save existing graphics
2680  PUT (34,53),A11,PSET  'display Name dialog box
2690  T2=25  'echo position flag
2700  F1$=F$  'temporary save of existing filename
2710  FOR T=1 TO 8 STEP 1
2720  K$=INKEY$
2730  IF K$="" THEN 2720  'wait for keystroke
2740  IF K$=CHR$(27) THEN F$=F1$:T=8:GOTO 2780  '<ESC> to cancel instructions an
d restore previous filename
2750  IF K$<"A" THEN SOUND 250,.7:GOTO 2720  'must be A-Z
2760  IF K$>"Z" THEN SOUND 250,.7:GOTO 2720  'must be A-Z
2770  T2=T2+1:LOCATE 8,T2:PRINT K$:MID$(F$,T,1)=K$  'echo user input and insert
character into F$
2780  NEXT T
2790  LOCATE 8,26:PRINT F$
2800  K$=INKEY$:IF K$<>CHR$(13) THEN 2800
2810  LOCATE 1,34:PRINT F$:SOUND 250,.7  'display on filename bar
2820  PUT (34,53),A11C,PSET:RETURN  'restore previous graphics
2830  '
2840  '_____DRAW MENU CONTROL_____
2850  '
2860  'module:  interactive control of Draw menu
2870  GOSUB 5810:GOSUB 5930  'save existing graphics
2880  PUT (126,19),A15,PSET  'place menu on screen
2890  PUT (128,25),A9,XOR  'place cursor >> on menu
2900  T8=1  'reset flag
2910  K$=INKEY$
2920  IF LEN(K$)=2 THEN K$=RIGHT$(K$,1) ELSE 3010
2930  IF K$=CHR$(80) THEN T8=T8+1:GOTO 2940 ELSE 2910
2940  IF T8>5 THEN T8=1
2950  ON T8 GOTO 2960,2970,2980,2990,3000
2960  PUT (128,57),A9,XOR:PUT (128,25),A9,XOR:GOTO 2910 'Line
2970  PUT (128,25),A9,XOR:PUT (128,33),A9,XOR:GOTO 2910 'Curve
2980  PUT (128,33),A9,XOR:PUT (128,41),A9,XOR:GOTO 2910 'Circle
2990  PUT (128,41),A9,XOR:PUT (128,49),A9,XOR:GOTO 2910 'Undo
3000  PUT (128,49),A9,XOR:PUT (128,57),A9,XOR:GOTO 2910 'Menu bar
3010  IF K$=CHR$(13) THEN 3040  '<Enter> to implement
3020  IF K$=CHR$(27) THEN 3090  '<ESC> to cancel
3030  GOTO 2910
3040  ON T8 GOTO 3050,3060,3070,3080,3090
3050  T5=1:GOSUB 5770:GOSUB 3990:GOTO 2880  'line
3060  T5=2:GOSUB 5770:GOSUB 3990:GOTO 2880  'curve
3070  T5=3:GOSUB 5770:GOSUB 3990:GOTO 2880  'circle
3080  GOSUB 5970:LOCATE 18,22:PRINT SYC:SOUND 250,.7:RETURN  'undo
```

Fig. G-1. (Continued from page 417.)

```
3090  GOSUB 5770:RETURN  'menu bar
3100  '
3110  '_____DISPLAY MENU CONTROL_____
3120  '
3130  'module:  interactive control of Display menu
3140  GOSUB 5810  'save existing graphics
3150  PUT (246,19),A13,PSET  'place menu on screen
3160  PUT (248,24),A9,XOR  'place cursor >> on menu
3170  T8=1  'reset flag
3180  K$=INKEY$
3190  IF LEN(K$)=2 THEN K$=RIGHT$(K$,1) ELSE 3260
3200  IF K$=CHR$(80) THEN T8=T8+1:GOTO 3210 ELSE 3180
3210  IF T8>3 THEN T8=1
3220  ON T8 GOTO 3230,3240,3250
3230  PUT (248,40),A9,XOR:PUT (248,24),A9,XOR:GOTO 3180 'Regen
3240  PUT (248,24),A9,XOR:PUT (248,32),A9,XOR:GOTO 3180 'Clear
3250  PUT (248,32),A9,XOR:PUT (248,40),A9,XOR:GOTO 3180 'Menu bar
3260  IF K$=CHR$(13) THEN 3290  '<Enter> to implement
3270  IF K$=CHR$(27) THEN 3320  '<ESC> to cancel
3280  GOTO 3180
3290  ON T8 GOTO 3300,3310,3320
3300  GOSUB 5770:VIEW SCREEN (2,19)-(248,123):CLS:LINE (122,53)-(132,53),C6:LINE
(127,51)-(127,55),C6:VIEW SCREEN (251,19)-(637,186):CLS:VIEW:GOSUB 4590:GOSUB 5
180:LOCATE 23,57:PRINT "Free memory:":SOUND 860,2:SOUND 800,2:RETURN  'Regen

3310  GOSUB 5770:VIEW SCREEN (2,19)-(248,123):CLS:LINE (122,53)-(132,53),C6:LINE
(127,51)-(127,55),C6:VIEW SCREEN (251,19)-(637,186):CLS:VIEW:GOSUB 1600:LOCATE
23,57:PRINT "Free memory:":SOUND 860,2:SOUND 800,2:RETURN  'Clear
3320  GOSUB 5770:RETURN  'menu bar
3330  '
3340  '_____VIEW MENU CONTROL_____
3350  '
3360  'module:  interactive control of View menu
3370  GOSUB 5810  'save existing graphics
3380  PUT (366,19),A14,PSET  'place menu on screen
3390  PUT (368,24),A9,XOR  'place cursor >> on menu
3400  T8=1  'reset flag
3410  K$=INKEY$
3420  IF LEN(K$)=2 THEN K$=RIGHT$(K$,1) ELSE 3520
3430  IF K$=CHR$(80) THEN T8=T8+1:GOTO 3440 ELSE 3410
3440  IF T8>6 THEN T8=1
3450  ON T8 GOTO 3460,3470,3480,3490,3500,3510
3460  PUT (368,64),A9,XOR:PUT (368,24),A9,XOR:GOTO 3410 'Distance
3470  PUT (368,24),A9,XOR:PUT (368,32),A9,XOR:GOTO 3410 'Elevation
3480  PUT (368,32),A9,XOR:PUT (368,40),A9,XOR:GOTO 3410 'Yaw
3490  PUT (368,40),A9,XOR:PUT (368,48),A9,XOR:GOTO 3410 'Roll
3500  PUT (368,48),A9,XOR:PUT (368,56),A9,XOR:GOTO 3410 'Pitch
3510  PUT (368,56),A9,XOR:PUT (368,64),A9,XOR:GOTO 3410 'Menu bar
3520  IF K$=CHR$(13) THEN 3550  '<Enter> to implement
3530  IF K$=CHR$(27) THEN 3610  '<ESC> to cancel
3540  GOTO 3410
3550  ON T8 GOTO 3560,3570,3580,3590,3600,3610
3560  GOSUB 4730:RETURN  'Distance
3570  GOSUB 4820:RETURN  'Elevation
```

Fig. G-1. (Continued from page 418.)

```
3580    GOSUB 4910:RETURN    'Yaw
3590    GOSUB 5000:RETURN    'Roll
3600    GOSUB 5090:RETURN    'Pitch
3610    GOSUB 5770:RETURN    'menu bar
3620    '
3630    '_____OPTIONS MENU CONTROL_____
3640    '
3650    'module:  interactive control of Options menu
3660    GOSUB 5810  'save existing graphics
3670    PUT (505,19),A8,PSET  'place menu on screen
3680    PUT (507,25),A9,XOR  'place cursor >> on menu
3690    T8=1  'reset flag
3700    K$=INKEY$
3710    IF LEN(K$)=2 THEN K$=RIGHT$(K$,1) ELSE 3810
3720    IF K$=CHR$(80) THEN T8=T8+1:GOTO 3730 ELSE 3700
3730    IF T8>6 THEN T8=1
3740    ON T8 GOTO 3750,3760,3770,3780,3790,3800
3750    PUT (507,65),A9,XOR:PUT (507,25),A9,XOR:GOTO 3700  'Set snap
3760    PUT (507,25),A9,XOR:PUT (507,33),A9,XOR:GOTO 3700  'Set grid
3770    PUT (507,33),A9,XOR:PUT (507,41),A9,XOR:GOTO 3700  'Grid on/off
3780    PUT (507,41),A9,XOR:PUT (507,49),A9,XOR:GOTO 3700  'Gnomon on/off
3790    PUT (507,49),A9,XOR:PUT (507,57),A9,XOR:GOTO 3700  'Set color
3800    PUT (507,57),A9,XOR:PUT (507,65),A9,XOR:GOTO 3700  'Menu bar
3810    IF K$=CHR$(13) THEN 3840   '<Enter> to implement
3820    IF K$=CHR$(27) THEN 3900   '<ESC> to cancel
3830    GOTO 3700
3840    ON T8 GOTO 3850,3860,3870,3880,3890,3900
3850    GOSUB 3940:GOTO 3700   'Set snap
3860    GOSUB 3940:GOTO 3700   'Set grid spacing
3870    GOSUB 5420:GOTO 3700   'Grid on/off
3880    GOSUB 5500:GOTO 3700   'Gnomon on/off
3890    GOSUB 5230:GOTO 3700   'Set color
3900    GOSUB 5770:GOSUB 5180:RETURN   'menu bar
3910    '
3920    '_____DO-NOTHING ROUTINE_____
3930    '
3940    SOUND 860,2:SOUND 800,2:RETURN  'do-nothing routine
3950    '
3960    '_____CROSSHAIR CURSOR CONTROL_____
3970    '
3980    'module:  interactive control of crosshair cursor
3990    SOUND 250,.7
4000    PUT (SX,SY),A12,XOR  'install crosshair cursor
4010    T6=0  'reset polyline flag
4020    X1=100:X2=130:X3=160:X4=190:Y1=40:Y2=100:Y3=140:Y4=70  'reset control poin
ts for curve and fillet
4030    K$=INKEY$
4040    IF LEN(K$)=2 THEN K$=RIGHT$(K$,1) ELSE 4210
4050    IF K$=CHR$(77) THEN PUT (SX,SY),A12,XOR:SX=SX+J ELSE 4080
4060    IF SX>XR THEN SX=XR:SOUND 250,.7
4070    PUT (SX,SY),A12,XOR:GOTO 4030
4080    IF K$=CHR$(75) THEN PUT (SX,SY),A12,XOR:SX=SX-J ELSE 4110
```

Fig. G-1. (Continued from page 419.)

```
4090  IF SX<XL THEN SX=XL:SOUND 250,.7
4100  PUT (SX,SY),A12,XOR:GOTO 4030
4110  IF K$=CHR$(72) THEN PUT (SX,SY),A12,XOR:SY=SY-J*.5 ELSE 4140
4120  IF SY<YT THEN SY=YT:SOUND 250,.7
4130  PUT (SX,SY),A12,XOR:GOTO 4030
4140  IF K$=CHR$(80) THEN PUT (SX,SY),A12,XOR:SY=SY+J*.5 ELSE 4170
4150  IF SY>YB THEN SY=YB:SOUND 250,.7
4160  PUT (SX,SY),A12,XOR:GOTO 4030
4170  IF K$=CHR$(71) THEN PUT (SX,SY),A12,XOR:SX=XL:SY=YT:PUT (SX,SY),A12,XOR:GO
TO 4030
4180  IF K$=CHR$(73) THEN PUT (SX,SY),A12,XOR:SX=XR:SY=YT:PUT (SX,SY),A12,XOR:GO
TO 4030
4190  IF K$=CHR$(81) THEN PUT (SX,SY),A12,XOR:SX=XR:SY=YB:PUT (SX,SY),A12,XOR:GO
TO 4030
4200  IF K$=CHR$(79) THEN PUT (SX,SY),A12,XOR:SX=XL:SY=YB:PUT (SX,SY),A12,XOR:GO
TO 4030
4210  IF K$=CHR$(27) THEN PUT (SX,SY),A12,XOR:SOUND 250,.7:RETURN  '<ESC>
4220  IF K$=CHR$(13) THEN PUT (SX,SY),A12,XOR:GOSUB 4300:GOSUB 5810:PUT (SX,SY),
A12,XOR:LOCATE 23,69:PRINT FRE(0):SOUND 250,.7:GOTO 4030  '<Enter> to implement
command
4230  IF K$="1" THEN SYC=SYC+.25:LOCATE 18,22:PRINT SYC"  ":SOUND 250,.7:GOTO 40
30  'increment plan drawing height
4240  IF K$="2" THEN SYC=SYC-.25:LOCATE 18,22:PRINT SYC"  ":SOUND 250,.7:GOTO 40
30  'decrement plan drawing height
4250  GOTO 4030
4260  SOUND 250,.7:RETURN
4270  '_____
4280  '
4290  'module:  switcher for drawing functions
4300  ON T5 GOTO 4310,4320,4330
4310  GOSUB 4370:RETURN
4320  GOSUB 3940:RETURN
4330  GOSUB 3940:RETURN
4340  '_____
4350  '
4360  'module:  polyline function
4370  IF T6=0 THEN SXC=SX+7:SZC=SY+3:PSET (SXC,SZC),C:T6=1:SXP=SXC:SZP=SZC:SYP=S
YC:RETURN ELSE 4380
4380  SXC=SX+7:SZC=SY+3:LINE (SXP,SZP)-(SXC,SZC),C:GOSUB 4430:GOSUB 4550:SXP=SXC
:SZP=SZC:SYP=SYC:RETURN
4390  '
4400  '_____GENERATE 3D MODEL_____
4410  '
4420  'module:  generate 3D model
4430  WINDOW SCREEN (-399,-299)-(400,300):VIEW SCREEN (251,19)-(637,186)  'clip
3D viewing area
4440  X=(.404858*SXP)-51:Z=(.9523809*SZP)-51:Y=SYP:GOSUB 4500:SX1=SX1+125:SY1=SY
1+3:PSET (SX1,SY1),C
4450  X=(.404858*SXC)-51:Z=(.9523809*SZC)-51:Y=SYC:GOSUB 4500:SX1=SX1+125:SY1=SY
1+3:LINE-(SX1,SY1),C
4460  WINDOW SCREEN (0,0)-(639,199):VIEW:RETURN
4470  '
4480  '_____
```

Fig. G-1. (Continued from page 420.)

```
4490 'module:  perspective formulas
4500  X=(-1)*X:XA=CR1*X-SR1*Z:ZA=SR1*X+CR1*Z:X=CR2*XA+SR2*Y:YA=CR2*Y-SR2*XA:Z=CR
3*ZA-SR3*YA:Y=SR3*ZA+CR3*YA:X=X+MX:Y=Y+MY:Z=Z+MZ:SX1=D*X/Z:SY1=D*Y/Z:RETURN
4510 '
4520 '_____DATA FILE INPUT/OUTPUT_____
4530 '
4540 'module:  storage of graphics attributes in data file
4550  OPEN "A:KEYLAYER.CDF" FOR APPEND AS #1:WRITE #1,SXP,SZP,SXC,SZC,C,SYP,SYC:
CLOSE #1:RETURN
4560 '_____
4570 '_____
4580 'module:  retrieval of graphics attributes from data file
4590  OPEN "A:KEYLAYER.CDF" FOR INPUT AS #1
4600  INPUT #1,SXP,SZP,SXC,SZC,C,SYP,SYC  'dummy pass
4610  IF T3=1 THEN GOSUB 5460  'is grid toggled on?
4620  IF T4=1 THEN GOSUB 5540  'is gnomon toggled on?
4630  IF EOF(1) THEN CLOSE #1:RETURN
4640  INPUT #1,SXP,SZP,SXC,SZC,C,SYP,SYC:GOSUB 4680:GOTO 4630
4650 '
4660 '_____
4670 'module:  regen function for 2D/3D modes
4680  LINE (SXP,SZP)-(SXC,SZC),C:GOSUB 4430:RETURN   'polyline regen
4690 '
4700 '_____ADJUST VIEW PARAMETERS_____
4710 '_____
4720 'module:  adjust Distance to viewpoint
4730  SOUND 250,.7
4740  K$=INKEY$
4750  IF K$="=" THEN MZ=MZ-10:GOSUB 5180:GOTO 4740
4760  IF K$="-" THEN MZ=MZ+10:GOSUB 5180:GOTO 4740
4770  IF K$=CHR$(13) THEN GOSUB 5770:GOSUB 5180:VIEW SCREEN (2,19)-(248,123):CLS
:VIEW SCREEN (251,19)-(637,186):CLS:VIEW:GOSUB 4590:LOCATE 23,57:PRINT "Free mem
ory:":SOUND 860,2:SOUND 800,2:RETURN
4780  GOTO 4740
4790 '
4800 '_____
4810 'module:  adjust Elevation of viewpoint
4820  SOUND 250,.7
4830  K$=INKEY$
4840  IF K$="=" THEN MY=MY-2:GOSUB 5180:GOTO 4830
4850  IF K$="-" THEN MY=MY+2:GOSUB 5180:GOTO 4830
4860  IF K$=CHR$(13) THEN GOSUB 5770:GOSUB 5180:VIEW SCREEN (2,19)-(248,123):CLS
:VIEW SCREEN (251,19)-(637,186):CLS:VIEW:GOSUB 4590:LOCATE 23,57:PRINT "Free mem
ory:":SOUND 860,2:SOUND 800,2:RETURN
4870  GOTO 4830
4880 '
4890 '_____
4900 'module:  adjust Yaw angle
4910  SOUND 250,.7
4920  K$=INKEY$:IF LEN(K$)=2 THEN K$=RIGHT$(K$,1) ELSE 4950
4930  IF K$=CHR$(77) THEN R1=R1-.17953:GOSUB 5180:GOTO 4920
4940  IF K$=CHR$(75) THEN R1=R1+.17953:GOSUB 5180:GOTO 4920
4950  IF K$=CHR$(13) THEN SR1=SIN(R1):CR1=COS(R1):GOSUB 5770:GOSUB 5180:VIEW SCR
```

Fig. G-1. (Continued from page 421.)

```
EEN (2,19)-(248,123):CLS:VIEW SCREEN (251,19)-(637,186):CLS:VIEW:GOSUB 4590:LOCA
TE 23,57:PRINT "Free memory:":SOUND 860,2:SOUND 800,2:RETURN
4960  GOTO 4920
4970  '_____
4980  '
4990  'module:  adjust Roll angle
5000  SOUND 250,.7
5010  K$=INKEY$:IF LEN(K$)=2 THEN K$=RIGHT$(K$,1) ELSE 5040
5020  IF K$=CHR$(77) THEN R2=R2+.08727:GOSUB 5180:GOTO 5010
5030  IF K$=CHR$(75) THEN R2=R2-.08727:GOSUB 5180:GOTO 5010
5040  IF K$=CHR$(13) THEN SR2=SIN(R2):CR2=COS(R2):GOSUB 5770:GOSUB 5180:VIEW SCR
EEN (2,19)-(248,123):CLS:VIEW SCREEN (251,19)-(637,186):CLS:VIEW:GOSUB 4590:LOCA
TE 23,57:PRINT "Free memory:":SOUND 860,2:SOUND 800,2:RETURN
5050  GOTO 5010
5060  '_____
5070  '
5080  'module:  adjust Pitch angle
5090  SOUND 250,.7
5100  K$=INKEY$:IF LEN(K$)=2 THEN K$=RIGHT$(K$,1) ELSE 5130
5110  IF K$=CHR$(72) THEN R3=R3-.08727:GOSUB 5180:GOTO 5100
5120  IF K$=CHR$(80) THEN R3=R3+.08727:GOSUB 5180:GOTO 5100
5130  IF K$=CHR$(13) THEN SR3=SIN(R3):CR3=COS(R3):GOSUB 5770:GOSUB 5180:VIEW SCR
EEN (2,19)-(248,123):CLS:VIEW SCREEN (251,19)-(637,186):CLS:VIEW:GOSUB 4590:LOCA
TE 23,57:PRINT "Free memory:":SOUND 860,2:SOUND 800,2:RETURN
5140  GOTO 5100
5150  '
5160  '_____REFRESH ALPHANUMERICS_____
5170  '
5180  LOCATE 18,22:PRINT SYC:LOCATE 19,21:PRINT (-1*MZ):LOCATE 20,22:PRINT (-1*M
Y):LOCATE 21,12:PRINT R1:LOCATE 22,13:PRINT R2:LOCATE 23,14:PRINT R3:LINE (8,185
)-(243,185),C:RETURN
5190  '
5200  '_____ADJUST OPTIONS_____
5210  '
5220  'module:  change the drawing color
5230  SOUND 250,.7
5240  IF C=C7 THEN C=C0:GOSUB 5180:RETURN
5250  IF C=C0 THEN C=C7:GOSUB 5180:RETURN
5380  GOSUB 5180:RETURN
5390  '_____
5400  '
5410  'module:  toggle 2D grid on/off
5420  IF T3=0 THEN T3=1:SOUND 250,.7:RETURN ELSE IF T3=1 THEN T3=0:SOUND 250,.7:
RETURN
5430  '_____
5440  '
5450  'module:  create grid if toggled on
5460  T=1:WHILE T<249:LINE (T,19)-(T,123),C8,,&HAAAA:T=T+J10:WEND:T=19:WHILE T<1
23:LINE (2,T)-(248,T),C8,,&H8888:T=T+J11:WEND:LINE (122,53)-(132,53),C6:LINE (12
7,51)-(127,55),C6:RETURN
5470  '_____
5480  '
5490  'module:  toggle 3D gnomon on/off (x,y,z axis display)
```

Fig. G-1. (Continued from page 422.)

```
5500  IF T4=0 THEN T4=1:SOUND 250,.7:RETURN ELSE IF T4=1 THEN T4=0:SOUND 250,.7:
RETURN
5510  '_____
5520  '_____
5530  'module:  create gnomon if toggled on
5540  WINDOW SCREEN (-399,-299)-(400,300):VIEW SCREEN (251,19)-(637,186)
5550  X=30:Z=0:Y=0:GOSUB 4500:SX1=SX1+125:SY1=SY1+3:PSET (SX1,SY1),C2:X=0:Z=0:Y=
0:GOSUB 4500:SX1=SX1+125:SY1=SY1+3:LINE-(SX1,SY1),C2,,&H9249:X=-30:Z=0:Y=0:GOSUB
 4500:SX1=SX1+125:SY1=SY1+3:LINE-(SX1,SY1),C8,,&H9249  'x-axis
5560  X=0:Z=0:Y=30:GOSUB 4500:SX1=SX1+125:SY1=SY1+3:PSET (SX1,SY1),C4:X=0:Z=0:Y=
0:GOSUB 4500:SX1=SX1+125:SY1=SY1+3:LINE-(SX1,SY1),C4,,&H9249:X=0:Z=0:Y=-30:GOSUB
 4500:SX1=SX1+125:SY1=SY1+3:LINE-(SX1,SY1),C8,,&H9249  'y-axis
5570  X=0:Z=30:Y=0:GOSUB 4500:SX1=SX1+125:SY1=SY1+3:PSET (SX1,SY1),C1:X=0:Z=0:Y=
0:GOSUB 4500:SX1=SX1+125:SY1=SY1+3:LINE-(SX1,SY1),C1,,&H9249:X=0:Z=-30:Y=0:GOSUB
 4500:SX1=SX1+125:SY1=SY1+3:LINE-(SX1,SY1),C8,,&H9249  'z-axis
5580  WINDOW SCREEN (0,0)-(639,199):VIEW:RETURN
5585  '
5590  '_____PCOPY MACHINE CODE LOADER_____
5600  '
5610  'module:  load hex opcodes into scalar array A99 inside BASIC's workspace
5620  RESTORE 5690  'set data pointer
5630  PCOPY=VARPTR(A99(0))  'define PCOPY as address of array
5640  FOR T=0 TO 34 STEP 1:READ HEX:POKE (PCOPY+T),HEX:NEXT T  'move hex opcode
values from database into array A99
5650  RETURN
5660  '
5670  '_____
5680  'module:  database of hex opcodes for PCOPY machine code routine to move gr
aphics page from 3C000 hex to B8000 hex
5690  DATA  &H51,&H1E,&H06,&H56,&H57,&H9C,&HB9,&H00,&H3C
5700  DATA  &H8E,&HD9,&HB9,&H00,&HB8,&H8E,&HC1,&HFC
5710  DATA  &HBE,&H00,&H00,&HBF,&H00,&H00,&HB9,&H00,&H40
5720  DATA  &HF3,&HA4,&H9D,&H5F,&H5E,&H07,&H1F,&H59,&HCB
5730  '
5740  '_____PCOPY EMULATION ROUTINES_____
5750  '
5760  'module:  emulate PCOPY 0,1 function
5770  PCOPY=VARPTR(A99(0)):POKE (PCOPY+8),&H3C:POKE (PCOPY+13),&HB8:CALL PCOPY:R
ETURN
5780  '_____
5790  '
5800  'module:  emulate PCOPY 1,0 function
5810  PCOPY=VARPTR(A99(0)):POKE (PCOPY+8),&HB8:POKE (PCOPY+13),&H3C:CALL PCOPY:R
ETURN
5820  '_____
5830  '
5840  'module:  emulate PCOPY 1,2 function
5850  PCOPY=VARPTR(A99(0)):POKE (PCOPY+8),&H3C:POKE (PCOPY+13),&H38:CALL PCOPY:R
ETURN
5860  '_____
5870  '
5880  'module:  emulate PCOPY 2,1 function
```

Fig. G-1. (Continued from page 423.)

```
5890  PCOPY=VARPTR(A99(0)):POKE (PCOPY+8),&H38:POKE (PCOPY+13),&H3C:CALL PCOPY:R
ETURN
5900 '_____
5910 '
5920 'module:  emulate PCOPY 0,2 function
5930  PCOPY=VARPTR(A99(0)):POKE (PCOPY+8),&HB8:POKE (PCOPY+13),&H38:CALL PCOPY:R
ETURN
5940 '_____
5950 '
5960 'module:  emulate PCOPY 2,0 function
5970  PCOPY=VARPTR(A99(0)):POKE (PCOPY+8),&H38:POKE (PCOPY+13),&HB8:CALL PCOPY:R
ETURN
5980 '_____
5990 '
6000  END
```

Fig. G-1. (Continued from page 424.)

```
100 'Program ARCADE1.BAS     Arcade animation manager.
110 'Copyright (c) 1988 by Lee Adams and TAB Books Inc.
120 'All rights reserved.
130 'Version for CGA and MCGA.  640x200 2-color mode.
140 '
150 '_____INITIALIZE SYSTEM_____
160 '
170  KEY OFF:CLS:SCREEN 0,0,0,0:WIDTH 80:COLOR 7,0,0:CLS
180  ON KEY(2) GOSUB 190:KEY(2) ON:GOTO 230
190  CLS:SCREEN 0,0,0,0:WIDTH 80:COLOR 7,0,0:CLS:COLOR 2:LOCATE 1,1,1:PRINT "Arc
ade animation manager finished.":COLOR 7:LOCATE 3,1:SOUND 250,.7:END
200 '
210 '_____DATA ASSIGNMENTS_____
220 '
230  DEFINT A,C,M,T,X,Y
240  DIM A1(105):DIM A2(105):DIM A3(105):DIM A4(105):DIM A5(105):DIM A6(105):DIM
 A7(105):DIM A8(105)  'reserve space for graphic arrays
250  C4=1:C7=1:C14=1  'color codes
260  X=320:Y=100  'write position of graphic array
270  XP=X:YP=Y  'erase position of graphic array
280  XL=9:XR=599:YU=4:YD=183 'boundary limits for entity movement
290  MX1=5  'horizontal x-movement factor
300  MX2=3  'diagonal x-movement factor
310  MY1=2  'vertical y-movement factor
320  MY2=1  'diagonal y-movement factor
330 '
340 '_____SET UP RUNTIME ENVIRONMENT_____
350 '
360  SCREEN 2:CLS
370 '_____
380 '
390 'module:  create 8 versions of entity to be animated
400  LINE (63,20)-(63,32),C4:LINE (48,26)-(63,20),C4:LINE-(79,26),C4  'entity fo
r heading 0 degrees
```

Fig. G-2. Complete source code for the CGA and MCGA version of the interactive arcade-style animation program from Chapter 35.

```
410  LINE (57,43)-(79,34),C4:LINE (57,34)-(79,34),C4:LINE-(79,42),C4  'entity fo
r heading 45 degrees
420  LINE (48,54)-(79,54),C4:LINE (63,48)-(79,54),C4:LINE-(63,60),C4  'entity fo
r heading 90 degrees
430  LINE (57,65)-(79,74),C4:LINE (79,66)-(79,74),C4:LINE-(57,74),C4  'entity fo
r heading 135 degrees
440  LINE (63,76)-(63,88),C4:LINE (48,82)-(63,88),C4:LINE-(79,82),C4  'entity fo
r heading 180 degrees
450  LINE (70,93)-(48,102),C4:LINE (48,93)-(48,102),C4:LINE-(70,102),C4  'entity
 for 235 degrees
460  LINE (48,110)-(79,110),C4:LINE (63,116)-(48,110),C4:LINE-(63,104),C4  'enti
ty for heading 270 degrees
470  LINE (48,118)-(70,127),C4:LINE (48,127)-(48,118),C4:LINE-(70,118),C4  'enti
ty for heading 315 degrees
480  '_____
490  '_____
500  'module:  save 8 versions of entity as graphic arrays
510  GET (48,20)-(79,32),A1:GET (48,34)-(79,46),A2:GET (48,48)-(79,60),A3:GET (4
8,62)-(79,74),A4:GET (48,76)-(79,88),A5:GET (48,90)-(79,102),A6:GET (48,104)-(79
,116),A7:GET (48,118)-(79,130),A8
520  '
530  '_____SET UP ARCADE TEMPLATE_____
540  '
550  CLS:LINE (0,0)-(639,199),7,B:LINE (8,3)-(631,196),7,B
560  LOCATE 2,9:PRINT "Demonstration of high-speed arcade-style animation techni
ques"
570  PUT (X,Y),A1,XOR:SOUND 460,2:SOUND 400,2
580  '
590  '_____INTERACTIVE KEYBOARD CONTROLS_____
600  '
610  'module:  array A1
620  Y=YP-MY1   'calculate next position
630  IF Y<YU THEN GOSUB 2170  'test for crash
640  PUT (XP,YP),A1,XOR:PUT (X,Y),A1,XOR  'animate
650  XP=X:YP=Y  'update coordinates
660  K$=INKEY$  'check the keyboard buffer
670  IF K$="Y" THEN 700  'is it a turn-right?
680  IF K$="R" THEN 740  'is it a turn-left?
690  GOTO 620  'loop
700  X=XP+MX2:Y=YP-MY2   'calculate next position
710  IF (Y<YU) OR (X>XR) THEN GOSUB 2170  'test for crash
720  PUT (XP,YP),A1,XOR:PUT (X,Y),A2,XOR  'change entity
730  GOTO 840  'jump to A2 routine
740  X=XP-MX2:Y=YP-MY2   'calculate next position
750  IF (X<XL) OR (Y<YU) THEN GOSUB 2170  'test for crash
760  PUT (XP,YP),A1,XOR:PUT (X,Y),A8,XOR  'change entity
770  GOTO 1980  'jump to A8 routine
780  '_____
790  '_____
800  'module:  array A2
810  X=XP+MX2:Y=YP-MY2   'calculate next position
820  IF (Y<YU) OR (X>XR) THEN GOSUB 2170  'test for crash
830  PUT (XP,YP),A2,XOR:PUT (X,Y),A2,XOR  'animate
```

Fig. G-2. Continued from page 425.)

```
840   XP=X:YP=Y  'update coordinates
850   K$=INKEY$  'check the keyboard buffer
860   IF K$="H" THEN 890  'is it a turn-right?
870   IF K$="T" THEN 930  'is it a turn-left?
880   GOTO 810  'loop
890   X=XP+MX1  'calculate next position
900   IF X>XR THEN GOSUB 2170  'test for crash
910   PUT (XP,YP),A2,XOR:PUT (X,Y),A3,XOR  'change entity
920   GOTO 1030  'jump to A3 routine
930   Y=YP-MY1  'calculate next position
940   IF Y<YU THEN GOSUB 2170  'test for crash
950   PUT (XP,YP),A2,XOR:PUT (X,Y),A1,XOR  'change entity
960   GOTO 650  'jump to A1 routine
970   '_____
980   '
990   'module:  array A3
1000   X=XP+MX1  'calculate next position
1010   IF X>XR THEN GOSUB 2170  'test for crash
1020   PUT (XP,YP),A3,XOR:PUT (X,Y),A3,XOR  'animate
1030   XP=X:YP=Y  'update coordinates
1040   K$=INKEY$  'check the keyboard buffer
1050   IF K$="N" THEN 1080  'is it a turn-right?
1060   IF K$="Y" THEN 1120  'is it a turn-left?
1070   GOTO 1000  'loop
1080   X=XP+MX2:Y=YP+MY2  'calculate next position
1090   IF (Y>YD) OR (X>XR) THEN GOSUB 2170  'test for crash
1100   PUT (XP,YP),A3,XOR:PUT (X,Y),A4,XOR  'change entity
1110   GOTO 1220  'jump to A4 routine
1120   X=XP+MX2:Y=YP-MY2  'calculate next position
1130   IF (X>XR) OR (Y<YU) THEN GOSUB 2170  'test for crash
1140   PUT (XP,YP),A3,XOR:PUT (X,Y),A2,XOR  'change entity
1150   GOTO 840  'jump to A2 routine
1160   '_____
1170   '
1180   'module:  array A4
1190   X=XP+MX2:Y=YP+MY2  'calculate next position
1200   IF (X>XR) OR (Y>YD) THEN GOSUB 2170  'test for crash
1210   PUT (XP,YP),A4,XOR:PUT (X,Y),A4,XOR  'animate
1220   XP=X:YP=Y  'update coordinates
1230   K$=INKEY$  'check the keyboard buffer
1240   IF K$="B" THEN 1270  'is it a turn-right?
1250   IF K$="H" THEN 1310  'is it a turn-left?
1260   GOTO 1190  'loop
1270   Y=YP+MY1  'calculate next position
1280   IF Y>YD THEN GOSUB 2170  'test for crash
1290   PUT (XP,YP),A4,XOR:PUT (X,Y),A5,XOR  'change entity
1300   GOTO 1410  'jump to A5 routine
1310   X=XP+MX1  'calculate next position
1320   IF X>XR THEN GOSUB 2170  'test for crash
1330   PUT (XP,YP),A4,XOR:PUT (X,Y),A3,XOR  'change entity
1340   GOTO 1030  'jump to A3 routine
1350   '_____
1360   '
```

Fig. G-2. Continued from page 426.)

```
1370  'module:  array A5
1380  Y=YP+MY1  'calculate next position
1390  IF Y>YD THEN GOSUB 2170  'test for crash
1400  PUT (XP,YP),A5,XOR:PUT (X,Y),A5,XOR  'animate
1410  XP=X:YP=Y  'update coordinates
1420  K$=INKEY$  'check the keyboard buffer
1430  IF K$="V" THEN 1460  'is it a turn-right?
1440  IF K$="N" THEN 1500  'is it a turn-left?
1450  GOTO 1380  'loop
1460  X=XP-MX2:Y=YP+MY2  'calculate next position
1470  IF (Y>YD) OR (X<XL) THEN GOSUB 2170  'test for crash
1480  PUT (XP,YP),A5,XOR:PUT (X,Y),A6,XOR  'change entity
1490  GOTO 1600  'jump to A6 routine
1500  X=XP+MX2:Y=YP+MY2  'calculate next position
1510  IF (X>XR) OR (Y>YD) THEN GOSUB 2170  'test for crash
1520  PUT (XP,YP),A5,XOR:PUT (X,Y),A4,XOR  'change entity
1530  GOTO 1220  'jump to A4 routine
1540  '_____
1550  '
1560  'module:  array A6
1570  X=XP-MX2:Y=YP+MY2  'calculate next position
1580  IF (Y>YD) OR (X<XL) THEN GOSUB 2170  'test for crash
1590  PUT (XP,YP),A6,XOR:PUT (X,Y),A6,XOR  'animate
1600  XP=X:YP=Y  'update coordinates
1610  K$=INKEY$  'check the keyboard buffer
1620  IF K$="F" THEN 1650  'is it a turn-right?
1630  IF K$="B" THEN 1690  'is it a turn-left?
1640  GOTO 1570  'loop
1650  X=XP-MX1  'calculate next position
1660  IF X<XL THEN GOSUB 2170  'test for crash
1670  PUT (XP,YP),A6,XOR:PUT (X,Y),A7,XOR  'change entity
1680  GOTO 1790  'jump to A7 routine
1690  Y=YP+MY1  'calculate next position
1700  IF Y>YD THEN GOSUB 2170  'test for crash
1710  PUT (XP,YP),A6,XOR:PUT (X,Y),A5,XOR  'change entity
1720  GOTO 1410  'jump to A5 routine
1730  '_____
1740  '
1750  'module:  array A7
1760  X=XP-MX1  'calculate next position
1770  IF X<XL THEN GOSUB 2170  'test for crash
1780  PUT (XP,YP),A7,XOR:PUT (X,Y),A7,XOR  'animate
1790  XP=X:YP=Y  'update coordinates
1800  K$=INKEY$  'check the keyboard buffer
1810  IF K$="R" THEN 1840  'is it a turn-right?
1820  IF K$="V" THEN 1880  'is it a turn-left?
1830  GOTO 1760  'loop
1840  X=XP-MX2:Y=YP-MY2  'calculate next position
1850  IF (X<XL) OR (Y<YU) THEN GOSUB 2170  'check for crash
1860  PUT (XP,YP),A7,XOR:PUT (X,Y),A8,XOR  'change entity
1870  GOTO 1980  'jump to A8 routine
1880  X=XP-MX2:Y=YP+MY2  'calculate next position
1890  IF (Y>YD) OR (X<XL) THEN GOSUB 2170  'test for crash
```

Fig. G-2. Continued from page 427.)

```
1900  PUT (XP,YP),A7,XOR:PUT (X,Y),A6,XOR  'change entity
1910  GOTO 1600  'jump to A6 routine
1920  '_____
1930  '
1940  'module:  array A8
1950  X=XP-MX2:Y=YP-MY2  'calculate next position
1960  IF (X<XL) OR (Y<YU) THEN GOSUB 2170  'test for crash
1970  PUT (XP,YP),A8,XOR:PUT (X,Y),A8,XOR  'animate
1980  XP=X:YP=Y  'update coordinates
1990  K$=INKEY$  'check the keyboard buffer
2000  IF K$="T" THEN 2030  'is it a turn-right?
2010  IF K$="F" THEN 2070  'is it a turn-left?
2020  GOTO 1950  'loop
2030  Y=YP-MY1  'calculate next position
2040  IF Y<YU THEN GOSUB 2170  'test for crash
2050  PUT (XP,YP),A8,XOR:PUT (X,Y),A1,XOR  'change entity
2060  GOTO 650  'jump to A1 routine
2070  X=XP-MX1  'calculate next position
2080  IF X<XL THEN GOSUB 2170  'test for crash
2090  PUT (XP,YP),A8,XOR:PUT (X,Y),A7,XOR  'change entity
2100  GOTO 1790  'jump to A7 routine
2110  '_____
2120  '_____
2130  '
2140  '_____BOUNDARY CRASH_____
2150  '
2160  'module:  crash routine
2170  LOCATE 12,34:PRINT "C R A S H !":FOR T=1 TO 10 STEP 1:SOUND 560,1:SOUND 50
0,1:NEXT T
2180  LOCATE 20,20:PRINT "Press <Esc> to exit, <Enter> to restart."
2190  K$=INKEY$
2200  IF K$=CHR$(27) THEN 190
2210  IF K$=CHR$(13) THEN X=320:Y=100:XP=X:YP=Y:RETURN 550
2220  GOTO 2190
2230  '
2240  '_____
2250  '
2260  END
```

Fig. G-2. Continued from page 428.)

```
100  'Program FRAME1.BAS    Frame animation demonstration.
110  'Copyright (c) 1988 by Lee Adams and TAB Books Inc.
120  'All rights reserved.
130  'Version for CGA and MCGA.  640x200 2-color mode.
140  '
150  '_____DATA ASSIGNMENTS_____
160  '
170  DEFINT A,H,P
180  DIM B11(20,1)  '21 sets sx,sy coordinates near curve
190  DIM B12(20,1)  '21 sets sx,sy coordinates far curve
200  DIM A99(18)  'scalar array to store hex opcodes
210  H=0
220  HEX=0  'variable to migrate hex opcodes
```

Fig. G-3. Complete source code for the CGA and MCGA version of the frame animation program from Chapter 34.

```
230  PCOPY=0  'address of machine code subroutine
240  D=1200:R1=5.88319:R2=6.28319:R3=5.79778:MX=0:MY=0:MZ=-150   '3D parameters
250  X1=-30:Y1=0:X4=30:Y4=0:X2=-5:Y2=15:X3=10:Y3=-35  'control points for cubic
parametric curve routine
260  X=0:Y=0:Z=0
270  SR1=SIN(R1):CR1=COS(R1):SR2=SIN(R2):CR2=COS(R2):SR3=SIN(R3):CR3=COS(R3)
280  '
290  '_____SET UP RUNTIME ENVIRONMENT_____
300  '
310  KEY OFF:CLS:SCREEN 2:CLS
320  C0=0:C1=1:C2=1:C3=1  'color codes
330  ON KEY(2) GOSUB 1060:KEY(2) ON  'install hot key
340  GOSUB 1110  'load machine code into memory
350  WINDOW SCREEN (-399,-299)-(400,300)
360  '
370  '_____MAIN ROUTINE_____
380  '
390  'MAIN ROUTINE:  manages the creation of 4 separate graphics pages and then i
nvokes high-speed frame animation.
400  CLS:GOSUB 600:GOSUB 1380  'store graphics page 4
410  CLS:X2=X2-2:Y2=Y2+2:GOSUB 600:GOSUB 1340   'store graphics page 3
420  CLS:X2=X2-2:Y2=Y2+2:GOSUB 600:GOSUB 1300   'store graphics page 2
430  CLS:X2=X2-2:Y2=Y2+2:GOSUB 600:GOSUB 1260   'store graphics page 1
440  FOR H=1 TO 5 STEP 1:SOUND 860,2:SOUND 800,2:NEXT H
450  '_____
460  '_____
470  'module:  animation manager
480  GOSUB 1420:FOR H=1 TO 40 STEP 1:NEXT H
490  GOSUB 1460:FOR H=1 TO 40 STEP 1:NEXT H
500  GOSUB 1500:FOR H=1 TO 40 STEP 1:NEXT H
510  GOSUB 1540:FOR H=1 TO 300 STEP 1:NEXT H
520  GOSUB 1500:FOR H=1 TO 40 STEP 1:NEXT H
530  GOSUB 1460:FOR H=1 TO 40 STEP 1:NEXT H
540  GOSUB 1420:FOR H=1 TO 300 STEP 1:NEXT H
550  GOTO 490
560  '
570  '_____CREATE A SINGLE FRAME_____
580  '
590  'module:  create a single frame for the animation sequence
600  LOCATE 25,27:PRINT "Press F2 to end animation.":LOCATE 2,18:PRINT "Demonstr
ation of high-speed frame animation:":LOCATE 3,24:PRINT "Manipulation of 3D mesh
 entity."
610  LINE (-250,-285)-(230,-220),C3,B
620  '_____
630  '_____
640  'module:  create near edge curve and save vertices
650  T=0:T2=T*T:T3=T*T*T:GOSUB 950:Z=30:GOSUB 1010:PSET (SX,SY),C3  'establish s
tart point
660  H=0:FOR T=0 TO 1.01 STEP .05:T2=T*T:T3=T*T*T:GOSUB 950:Z=30:GOSUB 1010:LINE
-(SX,SY),C3:B11(H,0)=SX:B11(H,1)=SY:H=H+1:NEXT T
670  '_____
680  '_____
690  'module:  create far edge curve and save vertices
```

Fig. G-3. (Continued from page 429.)

```
700   T=0:T2=T*T:T3=T*T*T:GOSUB 950:Z=-30:GOSUB 1010:PSET (SX,SY),C3  'establish
start point
710   H=0:FOR T=0 TO 1.01 STEP .05:T2=T*T:T3=T*T*T:GOSUB 950:Z=-30:GOSUB 1010:LIN
E-(SX,SY),C3:B12(H,0)=SX:B12(H,1)=SY:H=H+1:NEXT T
720   '_____
730   '
740   'module:  draw central curves
750   FOR H=-20 TO 20 STEP 10
760   T=0:T2=T*T:T3=T*T*T:GOSUB 950:Z=H:GOSUB 1010:PSET (SX,SY),C3   'establish st
art point
770   FOR T=0 TO 1.01 STEP .05:T2=T*T:T3=T*T*T:GOSUB 950:Z=H:GOSUB 1010:LINE-(SX,
SY),C3:NEXT T
780   NEXT H
790   '_____
800   '
810   'module:  connect the saved vertices
820   FOR H=0 TO 20 STEP 2
830   SX1=B11(H,0):SY1=B11(H,1):SX2=B12(H,0):SY2=B12(H,1)
840   LINE (SX1,SY1)-(SX2,SY2),C3
850   NEXT H
860   '_____
870   '
880   SOUND 860,2:SOUND 800,2:RETURN   'this frame completed
890   GOTO 890
900   '
910   '_____CUBIC PARAMETRIC CURVE_____
920   '
930   'module:  FREE-FORM curve driver
940   'calculates location of point on cubic parametric curve
950   J1=X1*(-T3+3*T2-3*T+1):J2=X2*(3*T3-6*T2+3*T):J3=X3*(-3*T3+3*T2):J4=X4*T3:X=
J1+J2+J3+J4
960   J1=Y1*(-T3+3*T2-3*T+1):J2=Y2*(3*T3-6*T2+3*T):J3=Y3*(-3*T3+3*T2):J4=Y4*T3:Y=
J1+J2+J3+J4:RETURN
970   '
980   '_____PERSPECTIVE FORMULAS_____
990   '
1000  'module:  perspective calculations
1010  X=(-1)*X:XA=CR1*X-SR1*Z:ZA=SR1*X+CR1*Z:X=CR2*XA+SR2*Y:YA=CR2*Y-SR2*XA:Z=CR
3*ZA-SR3*YA:Y=SR3*ZA+CR3*YA:X=X+MX:Y=Y+MY:Z=Z+MZ:SX=D*X/Z:SY=D*Y/Z:RETURN
1020  '
1030  '_____QUIT_____
1040  '
1050  'module:  quit program
1060  CLS:SCREEN 0,0,0,0:WIDTH 80:COLOR 7,0,0:CLS:COLOR 2:LOCATE 1,1,1:PRINT "Fr
ame animation demo finished.":COLOR 7:LOCATE 3,1:SOUND 860,2:SOUND 800,2:END
1070  '
1080  '_____PCOPY MACHINE CODE LOADER_____
1090  '
1100  'module:  load hex opcodes into scalar array A99 inside BASIC's workspace
1110  RESTORE 1180   'set data pointer
1120  PCOPY=VARPTR(A99(0))   'define PCOPY as address of array
1130  FOR T=0 TO 34 STEP 1:READ HEX:POKE (PCOPY+T),HEX:NEXT T   'move hex opcode
values from database into array A99
```

Fig. G-3. (Continued from page 430.)

```
1140  RETURN
1150  '_____
1160  '
1170  'module:  database of hex opcodes for PCOPY machine code routine to move gr
aphics page from 3C000 hex to B8000 hex
1180  DATA  &H51,&H1E,&H06,&H56,&H57,&H9C,&HB9,&H00,&H3C
1190  DATA  &H8E,&HD9,&HB9,&H00,&HB8,&H8E,&HC1,&HFC
1200  DATA  &HBE,&H00,&H00,&HBF,&H00,&H00,&HB9,&H00,&H40
1210  DATA  &HF3,&HA4,&H9D,&H5F,&H5E,&H07,&H1F,&H59,&HCB
1220  '
1230  '_____PCOPY EMULATION ROUTINES_____
1240  '
1250  'module:  emulate PCOPY 0,1 function
1260  PCOPY=VARPTR(A99(0)):POKE (PCOPY+8),&HB8:POKE (PCOPY+13),&H3C:CALL PCOPY:R
ETURN
1270  '_____
1280  '
1290  'module:  emulate PCOPY 0,2 function
1300  PCOPY=VARPTR(A99(0)):POKE (PCOPY+8),&HB8:POKE (PCOPY+13),&H38:CALL PCOPY:R
ETURN
1310  '_____
1320  '
1330  'module:  emulate PCOPY 0,3 function
1340  PCOPY=VARPTR(A99(0)):POKE (PCOPY+8),&HB8:POKE (PCOPY+13),&H34:CALL PCOPY:R
ETURN
1350  '_____
1360  '
1370  'module:  emulate PCOPY 0,4 function
1380  PCOPY=VARPTR(A99(0)):POKE (PCOPY+8),&HB8:POKE (PCOPY+13),&H30:CALL PCOPY:R
ETURN
1390  '_____
1400  '
1410  'module:  emulate PCOPY 1,0 function
1420  PCOPY=VARPTR(A99(0)):POKE (PCOPY+8),&H3C:POKE (PCOPY+13),&HB8:CALL PCOPY:R
ETURN
1430  '_____
1440  '
1450  'module:  emulate PCOPY 2,0 function
1460  PCOPY=VARPTR(A99(0)):POKE (PCOPY+8),&H38:POKE (PCOPY+13),&HB8:CALL PCOPY:R
ETURN
1470  '_____
1480  '
1490  'module:  emulate PCOPY 3,0 function
1500  PCOPY=VARPTR(A99(0)):POKE (PCOPY+8),&H34:POKE (PCOPY+13),&HB8:CALL PCOPY:R
ETURN
1510  '_____
1520  '
1530  'module:  emulate PCOPY 4,0 function
1540  PCOPY=VARPTR(A99(0)):POKE (PCOPY+8),&H30:POKE (PCOPY+13),&HB8:CALL PCOPY:R
ETURN
1550  '_____
1560  '
1570  END
```

Fig. G-3. (Continued from page 431.)

H

Additional Program Listings for IBM PCjr and Tandy

The program listings in this appendix have been specially converted for an IBM PCjr using Cartridge BASIC. You can also use these program listings on a Tandy 1000 SX (and compatibles) using GW-BASIC.

The program listing in Fig. H-1 is the PCjr version of *YOUR MICROCOMPUTER 3D CAD DESIGNER,* a wire-frame modeling program found in Chapters 26, 27, and 28. If you are using the companion disk to this book, type **LOAD "CAD-JR1.BAS",R.**

The program listing in Fig. H-2 is the PCjr version of the arcade-style animation program found in Chapter 34. If you are using the companion disk to this book, type **LOAD "ARCADEJR.BAS",R.**

The program listing in Fig. H-3 is the PCjr version of the high-speed frame animation program found in Chapter 33. If you are using the companion disk to this book, type **LOAD "FRAMEJR.BAS",R.**

The three program listings in this appendix are presented as ready-to-run, stand-alone programs. No further conversion or adaptation is required. The complete source code is given. Simply type them in and they are ready to execute on your IBM PCjr. (Consult the List of Demonstration Programs, located after the Introduction, for a complete list of programs from the main body of the book which run on the IBM PCjr.)

HOW THE PROGRAMS WERE CONVERTED

By using the programming techniques presented in the demonstration programs in this appendix, you can readily convert most of the programs from the main body of the book to run on your IBM PCjr or Tandy. Keep the following techniques in mind:

1. Alter the syntax of the BSAVE and BLOAD instructions. BASIC can save and retrieve an entire PCjr screen with a single instruction. Refer to lines 2470 and 2580 in Fig. H-1.
2. Modify the drawing colors to 0 or 1, because only two colors are available in the PCjr/'s 640×200 SCREEN 2 mode. The program listing in Fig. H-1 uses the 640×200 two-color mode. The program listing in Fig. H-2 uses the 640×200 four-color mode. The program listing in Fig. H-3 uses the 640×200 two-color mode.
3. Use the **CLEAR,,,n** instruction to set up the required number of pages. In addition, remember that your ability to convert some programs from the main body of the book may be inhibited by the PCjr's limited memory. As you invoke more graphics pages, less memory is available for your BASIC program. Because multiple pages are available on the PCjr (and on the Tandy), hidden page techniques and animation techniques like those found on the EGA and the VGA are possible on a PCjr.
4. Be sure to use a CLEAR instruction in the quit subroutine, in order to restore your system to a single page.
5. Reduce the size of any DIM instructions, because you need less space to store graphic arrays. Whereas the 640×200 16-color mode of the EGA requires four bits-per-pixel, the 640×200 two-color mode of the PCjr needs only one bit-per-pixel and the 640×200 four-color mode requires only two bits-per-pixel.
6. The IBM PCjr (and Tandy) is capable of generating fully shaded solid 3D models with automatic hidden surface removal. For specific programming examples, refer to *High-Performance Interactive Graphics: Modeling, Rendering & Animating for IBM PCs and Compatibles,* TAB book 2879.

```
100 'Program CAD-JR1.BAS:  YOUR MICROCOMPUTER 3D CAD DESIGNER
110 'Copyright (c) 1988 by Lee Adams and TAB Books Inc.
120 'All rights reserved.
130 'Version for PCjr & Tandy.  640x200 2-color mode.
140 '
150 '_____INITIALIZE SYSTEM_____
160 '
170  KEY OFF:CLS:CLEAR,,,49152!:SCREEN 0,0,0,0:WIDTH 80:COLOR 7,0,0:CLS:LOCATE 1
0,20,0:PRINT "Assigning memory space for graphic arrays"
180 '
190 '_____DATA ASSIGNMENTS_____
200 '
210 'module:  data assignments
220  DEFINT A,T,J
230  DIM A1(631):DIM A2(150):DIM A3(150):DIM A4(150):DIM A5(150):DIM A6(150)  't
emporary arrays for screen template
240  DIM A7(177)  'array for panning cursor
250  DIM A8(1793)  'array for Options menu
260  DIM A9(21)  'array for scrolling cursor
270  DIM A10(1057)  'array for File menu
280  DIM A11(953):DIM A11C(953)  'for Name dialog box
```

Fig. H-1. Complete source code for the PCjr and Tandy version of the interactive 3D wire-frame CAD program from Chapter 26.

```
290  DIM A12(29)   'array for roaming crosshair cursor
300  DIM A13(683)  'array for Display menu
310  DIM A14(1321) 'array for View menu
320  DIM A15(1057) 'array for Draw menu
330  C0=0:C1=1:C2=1:C3=1:C4=1:C5=1:C6=1:C7=1:C8=1:C9=1:C10=1:C12=1:C13=1:C14=1:C
15=1  'software color codes
340  C=C7:CE=C7  'drawing, boundary colors
350  T=0  'loop counter
360  T1=2  'selection flag for menu bar
370  T2=25  'flag for echo position of file menu input
380  T3=0  '2D grid on/off toggle
390  T4=0  '3D gnomon on/off toggle
400  T5=0  'flag for function switcher
410  T6=0  'iterative flag for plastic functions
420  T8=1  'selection flag for menus
430  J=2:JS=J  'snap, temporary storage of snap value
440  J6=85:J7=19:J8=608:J9=186  'viewport dimensions for active drawing surface
on 640x200 screen
450  SX=122:SY=65  'crosshair array location
460  XL=2:XR=234:YT=19:YB=117  'left, right, top, bottom range of roaming crossh
air cursor
470  SXC=SX+7:SZC=SY+3:SYC=0  'center of crosshair cursor
480  SXP=0:SZP=0:SYP=0  'last referenced drawing point
490  F$="DRAWFILE.PIC":F1$=F$:F2$="DRAWFILE"  'strings used to manipulate filena
me when saving images
500  V=0  'size of free memory in BASICA workspace
510  V1=1024  'threshold memory flag
520  B=0:B2=0:B3=0:D1=0:D2=0:D3=0:D4=0:X1=0:X2=0:X3=0:X4=0:Y1=0:Y2=0:Y3=0:Y4=0
'used in freeform curve routine
530  D=1200!:R1=6.46272:R2=6.28319:R3=6.10865:MX=0!:MY=-20!:MZ=-270!:SR1=SIN(R1)
:SR2=SIN(R2):SR3=SIN(R3):CR1=COS(R1):CR2=COS(R2):CR3=COS(R3)  'variables used as
 input for perspective formulas
540  XA=0!:YA=0!:ZA=0!  'temporary variables used in perspective formulas
550  SX1=0!:SY1=0!  'output of perspective formulas
560  J10=25:J11=11  'horizontal, vertical spacing for grid
570  '
580  '_____SET UP RUNTIME ENVIRONMENT_____
590  '
600  'module:  set up runtime environment
610  CLS:SCREEN 2:CLS  '640x200 2-clr mode
630  ON KEY(2) GOSUB 1550:KEY(2) ON  'install hot key
650  GOSUB 1600  'initialize .CDF data file
660  '
670  '_____SET UP SCREEN DISPLAY_____
680  '
690  'module:  set up screen template
700  GOSUB 960  'save alphanumeric graphic arrays
710  GOSUB 1140  'create pull-down menus
720  LINE (0,8)-(639,199),C8,B  'border
730  LINE (0,187)-(639,187),C8:PAINT (320,190),C8,C8:PUT (182,189),A1,XOR  'bann
er
740  LINE (0,0)-(639,6),C6,B:PAINT (320,3),C6,C6:LOCATE 1,33:PRINT " DRAWFILE.CD
F ":LOCATE 1,34:PRINT F$  'filename bar
```

Fig. H-1. (Continued from page 434.)

```
750    LINE (1,8)-(639,18),C8,B:PAINT (320,10),C8,C8  'menu bar
760    PUT (18,9),A2,XOR:PUT (130,9),A3,XOR:PUT (250,9),A4,XOR:PUT (370,9),A5,XOR:
PUT (510,9),A6,XOR  'selections for menu bar
770    LOCATE 10,20:PRINT "Reclaiming memory used by temporary arrays":ERASE A1,A2
,A3,A4,A5,A6  'free up array memory
780    LOCATE 10,20:PRINT "                                              "
790    LINE (250,19)-(250,186),C8:LINE (249,19)-(249,186),C8:LINE (1,19)-(1,186),C
8:LINE (638,19)-(638,186),C8:LINE (1,124)-(249,124),C8:LINE (122,53)-(132,53),C6
:LINE (127,51)-(127,55),C6  'split screen
800    LOCATE 18,2:PRINT "Plan drawing height":LOCATE 19,2:PRINT "Viewpoint distan
ce":LOCATE 20,2:PRINT "Viewpoint elevation":LOCATE 21,2:PRINT "Yaw angle":LOCATE
 22,2:PRINT "Roll angle":LOCATE 23,2:PRINT "Pitch angle"
810    LOCATE 17,8:PRINT "View specifications"
820    GOSUB 5180  'alphanumeric readouts
830    PUT (126,8),A7,XOR  'panning cursor for menu bar
840    PCOPY 0,1:PCOPY 1,2  'establish refresh buffers
850    LOCATE 9,40:PRINT "YOUR MICROCOMPUTER 3D CAD DESIGNER":LOCATE 12,40:PRINT "
Copyright (c) 1988 by Lee Adams and":LOCATE 13,40:PRINT "TAB Books Inc.  All rig
hts reserved."
860    LINE (310,60)-(584,60),C6:LINE (310,74)-(584,74),C6
870    LOCATE 19,43:PRINT "Press <Enter> to continue...":SOUND 860,2:SOUND 800,2
880    K$=INKEY$:IF K$<>CHR$(13) THEN 880
890    PCOPY 1,0:SOUND 250,.7:LOCATE 23,57:PRINT "Free memory:"FRE(0)  'restore sc
reen
900    GOTO 1650  'jump to runtime code
910    GOTO 910  'bulletproof code barrier
920    '
930    '_____CREATE ALPHANUMERICS FOR TEMPLATE_____
940    '
950    'module: create alpha arrays for screen template
960    LOCATE 10,20:PRINT "YOUR MICROCOMPUTER 3D CAD DESIGNER"
970    GET (150,71)-(424,79),A1:LOCATE 10,20:PRINT "
                   "
980    LOCATE 10,20:PRINT "File":GET (150,71)-(210,79),A2
990    LOCATE 10,20:PRINT "Draw":GET (150,71)-(210,79),A3
1000   LOCATE 10,20:PRINT "Display":GET (150,71)-(210,79),A4
1010   LOCATE 10,20:PRINT "View    ":GET (150,71)-(210,79),A5
1020   LOCATE 10,20:PRINT "Options":GET (150,71)-(210,79),A6
1030   LOCATE 10,20:PRINT "       "
1040   LINE (150,70)-(212,80),C12,B:GET (150,70)-(212,80),A7  'create panning cur
sor for menu bar
1050   LINE (150,70)-(212,80),0,B
1060   LINE (323,44)-(337,44),C7:LINE (330,41)-(330,47),C7:LINE (329,44)-(331,44)
,0  'create roaming crosshair cursor
1070   GET (323,41)-(337,47),A12:LINE (323,41)-(337,47),0,BF
1080   RETURN
1090   '
1100   '_____CREATE PULL-DOWN MENUS_____
1110   '
1120   'module:  create pull-down menus
1130   'submodule:  create Options menu
1140   LOCATE 10,20:PRINT "Set snap":LOCATE 11,20:PRINT "Set grid":LOCATE 12,20:P
RINT "Grid on/off":LOCATE 13,20:PRINT "Gnomon on/off"
```

Fig. H-1. (Continued from page 435.)

```
1150   LOCATE 14,20:PRINT "Set color":LOCATE 15,20:PRINT "Menu bar"
1160   LINE (138,67)-(260,122),C8,B
1170   GET (138,67)-(260,122),A8:LINE (138,67)-(260,122),0,BF
1180   LOCATE 10,20:PRINT CHR$(175)  'menu cursor >>
1190   GET (151,73)-(159,77),A9:LOCATE 10,20:PRINT " "
1200  '_____
1210  '
1220  'submodule:  create File menu
1230   LOCATE 10,20:PRINT "Name":LOCATE 11,20:PRINT "Save":LOCATE 12,20:PRINT "Lo
ad":LOCATE 13,20:PRINT "Quit":LOCATE 14,20:PRINT "Menu bar"
1240   LINE (138,67)-(220,114),C8,B
1250   GET (138,67)-(220,114),A10:LINE (138,67)-(220,114),0,BF
1260  '_____
1270  '
1280  'submodule:  create Draw menu
1290   LOCATE 10,20:PRINT "Line":LOCATE 11,20:PRINT "Curve":LOCATE 12,20:PRINT "C
ircle":LOCATE 13,20:PRINT "Undo":LOCATE 14,20:PRINT "Menu bar"
1300   LINE (138,67)-(220,114),C8,B
1310   GET (138,67)-(220,114),A15:LINE (138,67)-(220,114),0,BF
1320  '_____
1330  '
1340  'submodule:  create Name dialog box
1350   LOCATE 10,20:PRINT "Enter new filename:            "
1360   LINE (144,69)-(413,82),C8,B
1370   GET (144,69)-(413,82),A11:LINE (144,69)-(413,82),0,BF
1380  '_____
1390  '
1400  'submodule:  create Display menu
1410   LOCATE 4,20:PRINT "Regen":LOCATE 5,20:PRINT "Clear":LOCATE 6,20:PRINT "Men
u bar"
1420   LINE (138,20)-(220,50),C8,B
1430   GET (138,20)-(220,50),A13:LINE (138,20)-(220,50),0,BF
1440  '_____
1450  '
1460  'submodule:  create View menu
1470   LOCATE 4,20:PRINT "Distance":LOCATE 5,20:PRINT "Elevation":LOCATE 6,20:PRI
NT "Yaw":LOCATE 7,20:PRINT "Roll":LOCATE 8,20:PRINT "Pitch":LOCATE 9,20:PRINT "M
enu bar"
1480   LINE (138,20)-(230,74),C8,B
1490   GET (138,20)-(230,74),A14:LINE (138,20)-(230,74),0,BF
1500   RETURN
1510  '
1520  '_____QUIT_____
1530  '
1540  'module:  exit routine
1550   CLS:SCREEN 0,0,0,0:WIDTH 80:COLOR 7,0,0:CLS:LOCATE 1,1,1:COLOR 6:PRINT "YO
UR MICROCOMPUTER 3D CAD DESIGNER":LOCATE 2,1:PRINT "is finished.":COLOR 7:SOUND
250,.7:CLEAR:END
1560  '
1570  '_____INITIALIZE DATA FILES_____
1580  '
1590  'module:  initialize .CDF data files
1600   OPEN "A:KEYLAYER.CDF" FOR OUTPUT AS #1:WRITE #1,SXP,SZP,SXC,SZC,C,SYP,SYC:
```

Fig. H-1. (Continued from page 436.)

```
      CLOSE #1:RETURN
1610 '
1620 '_____MENU BAR CONTROL_____
1630 '
1640 'main module:  interactive control of menu bar
1650  K$=INKEY$:GOSUB 1970:LOCATE 23,69:PRINT V" "
1660  IF LEN(K$)=2 THEN K$=RIGHT$(K$,1) ELSE 1700
1670  IF K$=CHR$(77) THEN T1=T1+1:GOSUB 1760:GOTO 1650
1680  IF K$=CHR$(75) THEN T1=T1-1:GOSUB 1860:GOTO 1650
1690  IF K$=CHR$(16) THEN GOTO 1550   'Alt-Q to quit
1700  IF K$=CHR$(13) THEN GOSUB 2090  '<Enter> key
1710  GOTO 1650
1720  GOTO 1720  'bulletproof code barrier
1730 '_____
1740 '
1750 'module:  pan right on menu bar
1760  IF T1>5 THEN T1=1
1770  ON T1 GOTO 1780,1790,1800,1810,1820
1780  PUT (506,8),A7,XOR:PUT (14,8),A7,XOR:RETURN   'File
1790  PUT (14,8),A7,XOR:PUT (126,8),A7,XOR:RETURN   'Draw
1800  PUT (126,8),A7,XOR:PUT (246,8),A7,XOR:RETURN  'Display
1810  PUT (246,8),A7,XOR:PUT (366,8),A7,XOR:RETURN  'View
1820  PUT (366,8),A7,XOR:PUT (506,8),A7,XOR:RETURN  'Options
1830 '_____
1840 '
1850 'module:  pan left on menu bar
1860  IF T1<1 THEN T1=5
1870  ON T1 GOTO 1880,1890,1900,1910,1920
1880  PUT (126,8),A7,XOR:PUT (14,8),A7,XOR:RETURN   'File
1890  PUT (246,8),A7,XOR:PUT (126,8),A7,XOR:RETURN  'Draw
1900  PUT (366,8),A7,XOR:PUT (246,8),A7,XOR:RETURN  'Display
1910  PUT (506,8),A7,XOR:PUT (366,8),A7,XOR:RETURN  'View
1920  PUT (14,8),A7,XOR:PUT (506,8),A7,XOR:RETURN   'Options
1930 '
1940 '_____CHECK SIZE OF WORKSPACE_____
1950 '
1960 'module:  check if user is running out of memory
1970  V=FRE(0):IF V>V1 THEN RETURN
1980  V1=128  'lower threshold to permit return to pgm
1990  PCOPY 0,1:CLS:LOCATE 10,32:PRINT "W A R N I N G":LOCATE 12,23:PRINT "Out o
f memory in BASIC workspace."
2000  LOCATE 13,27:PRINT "Save your drawing on disk!":LOCATE 15,21:PRINT "Press
<Enter> to return to 3D CAD DESIGNER."
2010  FOR T=1 TO 4 STEP 1:SOUND 250,3:SOUND 450,3:SOUND 650,3:NEXT T
2020  K$=INKEY$:IF K$<>CHR$(13) THEN 2020  'wait for <Enter>
2030  K$=INKEY$:IF K$<>"" THEN 2030  'empty keyboard buffer
2040  PCOPY 1,0:SOUND 250,.7:RETURN
2050 '
2060 '_____MENU BAR SWITCHER_____
2070 '
2080 'module:  switcher to execute menu bar choices
2090  ON T1 GOTO 2100,2110,2120,2130,2140
2100  GOSUB 2190:RETURN  'invoke File menu
```

Fig. H-1. (Continued from page 437.)

```
2110   GOSUB 2870:RETURN   'invoke Draw menu
2120   GOSUB 3140:RETURN   'invoke Display menu
2130   GOSUB 3370:RETURN   'invoke View menu
2140   GOSUB 3660:RETURN   'invoke Options menu
2150   '
2160   '_____FILE MENU CONTROL_____
2170   '
2180   'module:  interactive control of File menu
2190   PCOPY 0,1  'save existing graphics
2200   PUT (14,19),A10,PSET  'place menu on screen
2210   PUT (16,25),A9,XOR  'place cursor >> on menu
2220   T8=1  'reset flag
2230   K$=INKEY$
2240   IF LEN(K$)=2 THEN K$=RIGHT$(K$,1) ELSE 2330
2250   IF K$=CHR$(80) THEN T8=T8+1:GOTO 2260 ELSE 2230
2260   IF T8>5 THEN T8=1
2270   ON T8 GOTO 2280,2290,2300,2310,2320
2280   PUT (16,57),A9,XOR:PUT (16,25),A9,XOR:GOTO 2230 'Name
2290   PUT (16,25),A9,XOR:PUT (16,33),A9,XOR:GOTO 2230 'Save
2300   PUT (16,33),A9,XOR:PUT (16,41),A9,XOR:GOTO 2230 'Load
2310   PUT (16,41),A9,XOR:PUT (16,49),A9,XOR:GOTO 2230 'Quit
2320   PUT (16,49),A9,XOR:PUT (16,57),A9,XOR:GOTO 2230 'Menu bar
2330   IF K$=CHR$(13) THEN 2360   '<Enter> to implement
2340   IF K$=CHR$(27) THEN 2410   '<ESC> to cancel
2350   GOTO 2230
2360   ON T8 GOTO 2370,2380,2390,2400,2410
2370   GOSUB 2670:PCOPY 1,0:LOCATE 1,34:PRINT F$:RETURN   'name change
2380   PCOPY 1,0:GOSUB 2450:RETURN   'save image
2390   PCOPY 1,0:GOSUB 2560:RETURN   'load image
2400   GOTO 1550   'quit program
2410   PCOPY 1,0:RETURN   'menu bar
2420   '
2430   '_____
2440   'module: save 640x200 2-color image to disk
2450   MID$(F2$,1,8)=F$  'strip extension from file name
2460   SOUND 250,.7:DEF SEG=&HB800 'set up segment
2470   BSAVE "A:"+F2$+".PIC",0,&H4000
2510   DEF SEG   'restore ES register
2520   SOUND 250,.7:RETURN
2530   '
2540   '_____
2550   'module: load 640x200 2-color image from disk
2560   MID$(F2$,1,8)=F$  'strip extension from file name
2570   SOUND 250,.7:DEF SEG=&HB800 'set up segment
2580   BLOAD "A:"+F2$+".PIC",0
2620   DEF SEG   'restore ES register
2630   GOSUB 5180:SOUND 250,.7:RETURN
2640   '
2650   '_____
2660   'module:  interactive control of Name dialog box
2670   GET (34,53)-(303,66),A11C  'save existing graphics
2680   PUT (34,53),A11,PSET   'display Name dialog box
2690   T2=25   'echo position flag
```

Fig. H-1. (Continued from page 438.)

```
2700   F1$=F$   'temporary save of existing filename
2710   FOR T=1 TO 8 STEP 1
2720   K$=INKEY$
2730   IF K$="" THEN 2720   'wait for keystroke
2740   IF K$=CHR$(27) THEN F$=F1$:T=8:GOTO 2780   '<ESC> to cancel instructions an
d restore previous filename
2750   IF K$<"A" THEN SOUND 250,.7:GOTO 2720   'must be A-Z
2760   IF K$>"Z" THEN SOUND 250,.7:GOTO 2720   'must be A-Z
2770   T2=T2+1:LOCATE 8,T2:PRINT K$:MID$(F$,T,1)=K$   'echo user input and insert
character into F$
2780   NEXT T
2790   LOCATE 8,26:PRINT F$
2800   K$=INKEY$:IF K$<>CHR$(13) THEN 2800
2810   LOCATE 1,34:PRINT F$:SOUND 250,.7   'display on filename bar
2820   PUT (34,53),A11C,PSET:RETURN   'restore previous graphics
2830   '
2840   '_____DRAW MENU CONTROL_____
2850   '
2860   'module:  interactive control of Draw menu
2870   PCOPY 0,1:PCOPY 0,2   'save existing graphics
2880   PUT (126,19),A15,PSET   'place menu on screen
2890   PUT (128,25),A9,XOR   'place cursor >> on menu
2900   T8=1   'reset flag
2910   K$=INKEY$
2920   IF LEN(K$)=2 THEN K$=RIGHT$(K$,1) ELSE 3010
2930   IF K$=CHR$(80) THEN T8=T8+1:GOTO 2940 ELSE 2910
2940   IF T8>5 THEN T8=1
2950   ON T8 GOTO 2960,2970,2980,2990,3000
2960   PUT (128,57),A9,XOR:PUT (128,25),A9,XOR:GOTO 2910 'Line
2970   PUT (128,25),A9,XOR:PUT (128,33),A9,XOR:GOTO 2910 'Curve
2980   PUT (128,33),A9,XOR:PUT (128,41),A9,XOR:GOTO 2910 'Circle
2990   PUT (128,41),A9,XOR:PUT (128,49),A9,XOR:GOTO 2910 'Undo
3000   PUT (128,49),A9,XOR:PUT (128,57),A9,XOR:GOTO 2910 'Menu bar
3010   IF K$=CHR$(13) THEN 3040   '<Enter> to implement
3020   IF K$=CHR$(27) THEN 3090   '<ESC> to cancel
3030   GOTO 2910
3040   ON T8 GOTO 3050,3060,3070,3080,3090
3050   T5=1:PCOPY 1,0:GOSUB 3990:GOTO 2880   'line
3060   T5=2:PCOPY 1,0:GOSUB 3990:GOTO 2880   'curve
3070   T5=3:PCOPY 1,0:GOSUB 3990:GOTO 2880   'circle
3080   PCOPY 2,0:LOCATE 18,22:PRINT SYC:SOUND 250,.7:RETURN   'undo
3090   PCOPY 1,0:RETURN   'menu bar
3100   '
3110   '_____DISPLAY MENU CONTROL_____
3120   '
3130   'module:  interactive control of Display menu
3140   PCOPY 0,1   'save existing graphics
3150   PUT (246,19),A13,PSET   'place menu on screen
3160   PUT (248,24),A9,XOR   'place cursor >> on menu
3170   T8=1   'reset flag
3180   K$=INKEY$
3190   IF LEN(K$)=2 THEN K$=RIGHT$(K$,1) ELSE 3260
3200   IF K$=CHR$(80) THEN T8=T8+1:GOTO 3210 ELSE 3180
```

Fig. H-1. (Continued from page 439.)

```
3210   IF T8>3 THEN T8=1
3220   ON T8 GOTO 3230,3240,3250
3230   PUT (248,40),A9,XOR:PUT (248,24),A9,XOR:GOTO 3180 'Regen
3240   PUT (248,24),A9,XOR:PUT (248,32),A9,XOR:GOTO 3180 'Clear
3250   PUT (248,32),A9,XOR:PUT (248,40),A9,XOR:GOTO 3180 'Menu bar
3260   IF K$=CHR$(13) THEN 3290  '<Enter> to implement
3270   IF K$=CHR$(27) THEN 3320  '<ESC> to cancel
3280   GOTO 3180
3290   ON T8 GOTO 3300,3310,3320
3300   PCOPY 1,0:VIEW SCREEN (2,19)-(248,123):CLS:LINE (122,53)-(132,53),C6:LINE
(127,51)-(127,55),C6:VIEW SCREEN (251,19)-(637,186):CLS:VIEW:GOSUB 4590:LOCATE 2
3,57:PRINT "Free memory:":SOUND 860,2:SOUND 800,2:RETURN  'Regen
3310   PCOPY 1,0:VIEW SCREEN (2,19)-(248,123):CLS:LINE (122,53)-(132,53),C6:LINE
(127,51)-(127,55),C6:VIEW SCREEN (251,19)-(637,186):CLS:VIEW:GOSUB 1600:LOCATE 2
3,57:PRINT "Free memory:":SOUND 860,2:SOUND 800,2:RETURN  'Clear
3320   PCOPY 1,0:RETURN  'menu bar
3330   '
3340   '_____VIEW MENU CONTROL_____
3350   '
3360   'module:  interactive control of View menu
3370   PCOPY 0,1  'save existing graphics
3380   PUT (366,19),A14,PSET  'place menu on screen
3390   PUT (368,24),A9,XOR  'place cursor >> on menu
3400   T8=1  'reset flag
3410   K$=INKEY$
3420   IF LEN(K$)=2 THEN K$=RIGHT$(K$,1) ELSE 3520
3430   IF K$=CHR$(80) THEN T8=T8+1:GOTO 3440 ELSE 3410
3440   IF T8>6 THEN T8=1
3450   ON T8 GOTO 3460,3470,3480,3490,3500,3510
3460   PUT (368,64),A9,XOR:PUT (368,24),A9,XOR:GOTO 3410 'Distance
3470   PUT (368,24),A9,XOR:PUT (368,32),A9,XOR:GOTO 3410 'Elevation
3480   PUT (368,32),A9,XOR:PUT (368,40),A9,XOR:GOTO 3410 'Yaw
3490   PUT (368,40),A9,XOR:PUT (368,48),A9,XOR:GOTO 3410 'Roll
3500   PUT (368,48),A9,XOR:PUT (368,56),A9,XOR:GOTO 3410 'Pitch
3510   PUT (368,56),A9,XOR:PUT (368,64),A9,XOR:GOTO 3410 'Menu bar
3520   IF K$=CHR$(13) THEN 3550  '<Enter> to implement
3530   IF K$=CHR$(27) THEN 3610  '<ESC> to cancel
3540   GOTO 3410
3550   ON T8 GOTO 3560,3570,3580,3590,3600,3610
3560   GOSUB 4730:RETURN   'Distance
3570   GOSUB 4820:RETURN   'Elevation
3580   GOSUB 4910:RETURN   'Yaw
3590   GOSUB 5000:RETURN   'Roll
3600   GOSUB 5090:RETURN   'Pitch
3610   PCOPY 1,0:RETURN   'menu bar
3620   '
3630   '_____OPTIONS MENU CONTROL_____
3640   '
3650   'module:  interactive control of Options menu
3660   PCOPY 0,1  'save existing graphics
3670   PUT (505,19),A8,PSET  'place menu on screen
3680   PUT (507,25),A9,XOR  'place cursor >> on menu
3690   T8=1  'reset flag
```

Fig. H-1. (Continued from page 440.)

```
3700    K$=INKEY$
3710    IF LEN(K$)=2 THEN K$=RIGHT$(K$,1) ELSE 3810
3720    IF K$=CHR$(80) THEN T8=T8+1:GOTO 3730 ELSE 3700
3730    IF T8>6 THEN T8=1
3740    ON T8 GOTO 3750,3760,3770,3780,3790,3800
3750    PUT (507,65),A9,XOR:PUT (507,25),A9,XOR:GOTO 3700    'Set snap
3760    PUT (507,25),A9,XOR:PUT (507,33),A9,XOR:GOTO 3700    'Set grid
3770    PUT (507,33),A9,XOR:PUT (507,41),A9,XOR:GOTO 3700    'Grid on/off
3780    PUT (507,41),A9,XOR:PUT (507,49),A9,XOR:GOTO 3700    'Gnomon on/off
3790    PUT (507,49),A9,XOR:PUT (507,57),A9,XOR:GOTO 3700    'Set color
3800    PUT (507,57),A9,XOR:PUT (507,65),A9,XOR:GOTO 3700    'Menu bar
3810    IF K$=CHR$(13) THEN 3840    '<Enter> to implement
3820    IF K$=CHR$(27) THEN 3900    '<ESC> to cancel
3830    GOTO 3700
3840    ON T8 GOTO 3850,3860,3870,3880,3890,3900
3850    GOSUB 3940:GOTO 3700    'Set snap
3860    GOSUB 3940:GOTO 3700    'Set grid spacing
3870    GOSUB 5420:GOTO 3700    'Grid on/off
3880    GOSUB 5500:GOTO 3700    'Gnomon on/off
3890    GOSUB 5230:GOTO 3700    'Set color
3900    PCOPY 1,0:GOSUB 5180:RETURN    'menu bar
3910    '
3920    '_____DO-NOTHING ROUTINE_____
3930    '
3940    SOUND 860,2:SOUND 800,2:RETURN    'do-nothing routine
3950    '
3960    '_____CROSSHAIR CURSOR CONTROL_____
3970    '
3980    'module:  interactive control of crosshair cursor
3990    SOUND 250,.7
4000    PUT (SX,SY),A12,XOR    'install crosshair cursor
4010    T6=0    'reset polyline flag
4020    X1=100:X2=130:X3=160:X4=190:Y1=40:Y2=100:Y3=140:Y4=70    'reset control poin
ts for curve and fillet
4030    K$=INKEY$
4040    IF LEN(K$)=2 THEN K$=RIGHT$(K$,1) ELSE 4210
4050    IF K$=CHR$(77) THEN PUT (SX,SY),A12,XOR:SX=SX+J ELSE 4080
4060    IF SX>XR THEN SX=XR:SOUND 250,.7
4070    PUT (SX,SY),A12,XOR:GOTO 4030
4080    IF K$=CHR$(75) THEN PUT (SX,SY),A12,XOR:SX=SX-J ELSE 4110
4090    IF SX<XL THEN SX=XL:SOUND 250,.7
4100    PUT (SX,SY),A12,XOR:GOTO 4030
4110    IF K$=CHR$(72) THEN PUT (SX,SY),A12,XOR:SY=SY-J*.5 ELSE 4140
4120    IF SY<YT THEN SY=YT:SOUND 250,.7
4130    PUT (SX,SY),A12,XOR:GOTO 4030
4140    IF K$=CHR$(80) THEN PUT (SX,SY),A12,XOR:SY=SY+J*.5 ELSE 4170
4150    IF SY>YB THEN SY=YB:SOUND 250,.7
4160    PUT (SX,SY),A12,XOR:GOTO 4030
4170    IF K$=CHR$(71) THEN PUT (SX,SY),A12,XOR:SX=XL:SY=YT:PUT (SX,SY),A12,XOR:GO
TO 4030
4180    IF K$=CHR$(73) THEN PUT (SX,SY),A12,XOR:SX=XR:SY=YT:PUT (SX,SY),A12,XOR:GO
TO 4030
4190    IF K$=CHR$(81) THEN PUT (SX,SY),A12,XOR:SX=XR:SY=YB:PUT (SX,SY),A12,XOR:GO
```

Fig. H-1. (Continued from page 441.)

```
TO 4030
4200  IF K$=CHR$(79) THEN PUT (SX,SY),A12,XOR:SX=XL:SY=YB:PUT (SX,SY),A12,XOR:GO
TO 4030
4210  IF K$=CHR$(27) THEN PUT (SX,SY),A12,XOR:SOUND 250,.7:RETURN  '<ESC>
4220  IF K$=CHR$(13) THEN PUT (SX,SY),A12,XOR:GOSUB 4300:PCOPY 0,1:PUT (SX,SY),A
12,XOR:LOCATE 23,69:PRINT FRE(0):SOUND 250,.7:GOTO 4030  '<Enter> to implement c
ommand
4230  IF K$="1" THEN SYC=SYC+.25:LOCATE 18,22:PRINT SYC"  ":SOUND 250,.7:GOTO 40
30  'increment plan drawing height
4240  IF K$="2" THEN SYC=SYC-.25:LOCATE 18,22:PRINT SYC"  ":SOUND 250,.7:GOTO 40
30  'decrement plan drawing height
4250  GOTO 4030
4260  SOUND 250,.7:RETURN
4270  '_____
4280  '_____
4290  'module:  switcher for drawing functions
4300  ON T5 GOTO 4310,4320,4330
4310  GOSUB 4370:RETURN
4320  GOSUB 3940:RETURN
4330  GOSUB 3940:RETURN
4340  '_____
4350  '_____
4360  'module:  polyline function
4370  IF T6=0 THEN SXC=SX+7:SZC=SY+3:PSET (SXC,SZC),C:T6=1:SXP=SXC:SZP=SZC:SYP=S
YC:RETURN ELSE 4380
4380  SXC=SX+7:SZC=SY+3:LINE (SXP,SZP)-(SXC,SZC),C:GOSUB 4430:GOSUB 4550:SXP=SXC
:SZP=SZC:SYP=SYC:RETURN
4390  '
4400  '_____GENERATE 3D MODEL_____
4410  '
4420  'module:  generate 3D model
4430  WINDOW SCREEN (-399,-299)-(400,300):VIEW SCREEN (251,19)-(637,186)  'clip
3D viewing area
4440  X=(.404858*SXP)-51:Z=(.9523809*SZP)-51:Y=SYP:GOSUB 4500:SX1=SX1+125:SY1=SY
1+3:PSET (SX1,SY1),C
4450  X=(.404858*SXC)-51:Z=(.9523809*SZC)-51:Y=SYC:GOSUB 4500:SX1=SX1+125:SY1=SY
1+3:LINE-(SX1,SY1),C
4460  WINDOW SCREEN (0,0)-(639,199):VIEW:RETURN
4470  '_____
4480  '_____
4490  'module:  perspective formulas
4500  X=(-1)*X:XA=CR1*X-SR1*Z:ZA=SR1*X+CR1*Z:X=CR2*XA+SR2*Y:YA=CR2*Y-SR2*XA:Z=CR
3*ZA-SR3*YA:Y=SR3*ZA+CR3*YA:X=X+MX:Y=Y+MY:Z=Z+MZ:SX1=D*X/Z:SY1=D*Y/Z:RETURN
4510  '
4520  '_____DATA FILE INPUT/OUTPUT_____
4530  '
4540  'module:  storage of graphics attributes in data file
4550  OPEN "A:KEYLAYER.CDF" FOR APPEND AS #1:WRITE #1,SXP,SZP,SXC,SZC,C,SYP,SYC:
CLOSE #1:RETURN
4560  '_____
4570  '_____
4580  'module:  retrieval of graphics attributes from data file
4590  OPEN "A:KEYLAYER.CDF" FOR INPUT AS #1
```

Fig. H-1. (Continued from page 442.)

```
4600   INPUT #1,SXP,SZP,SXC,SZC,C,SYP,SYC   'dummy pass
4610   IF T3=1 THEN GOSUB 5460   'is grid toggled on?
4620   IF T4=1 THEN GOSUB 5540   'is gnomon toggled on?
4630   IF EOF(1) THEN CLOSE #1:RETURN
4640   INPUT #1,SXP,SZP,SXC,SZC,C,SYP,SYC:GOSUB 4680:GOTO 4630
4650   '_____
4660   '
4670   'module:  regen function for 2D/3D modes
4680   LINE (SXP,SZP)-(SXC,SZC),C:GOSUB 4430:RETURN   'polyline regen
4690   '
4700   '_____ADJUST VIEW PARAMETERS_____
4710   '
4720   'module:  adjust Distance to viewpoint
4730   SOUND 250,.7
4740   K$=INKEY$
4750   IF K$="=" THEN MZ=MZ-10:GOSUB 5180:GOTO 4740
4760   IF K$="-" THEN MZ=MZ+10:GOSUB 5180:GOTO 4740
4770   IF K$=CHR$(13) THEN PCOPY 1,0:GOSUB 5180:VIEW SCREEN (2,19)-(248,123):CLS:
VIEW SCREEN (251,19)-(637,186):CLS:VIEW:GOSUB 4590:LOCATE 23,57:PRINT "Free memo
ry:":SOUND 860,2:SOUND 800,2:RETURN
4780   GOTO 4740
4790   '_____
4800   '
4810   'module:  adjust Elevation of viewpoint
4820   SOUND 250,.7
4830   K$=INKEY$
4840   IF K$="=" THEN MY=MY-2:GOSUB 5180:GOTO 4830
4850   IF K$="-" THEN MY=MY+2:GOSUB 5180:GOTO 4830
4860   IF K$=CHR$(13) THEN PCOPY 1,0:GOSUB 5180:VIEW SCREEN (2,19)-(248,123):CLS:
VIEW SCREEN (251,19)-(637,186):CLS:VIEW:GOSUB 4590:LOCATE 23,57:PRINT "Free memo
ry:":SOUND 860,2:SOUND 800,2:RETURN
4870   GOTO 4830
4880   '_____
4890   '
4900   'module:  adjust Yaw angle
4910   SOUND 250,.7
4920   K$=INKEY$:IF LEN(K$)=2 THEN K$=RIGHT$(K$,1) ELSE 4950
4930   IF K$=CHR$(77) THEN R1=R1-.17953:GOSUB 5180:GOTO 4920
4940   IF K$=CHR$(75) THEN R1=R1+.17953:GOSUB 5180:GOTO 4920
4950   IF K$=CHR$(13) THEN SR1=SIN(R1):CR1=COS(R1):PCOPY 1,0:GOSUB 5180:VIEW SCRE
EN (2,19)-(248,123):CLS:VIEW SCREEN (251,19)-(637,186):CLS:VIEW:GOSUB 4590:LOCAT
E 23,57:PRINT "Free memory:":SOUND 860,2:SOUND 800,2:RETURN
4960   GOTO 4920
4970   '_____
4980   '
4990   'module:  adjust Roll angle
5000   SOUND 250,.7
5010   K$=INKEY$:IF LEN(K$)=2 THEN K$=RIGHT$(K$,1) ELSE 5040
5020   IF K$=CHR$(77) THEN R2=R2+.08727:GOSUB 5180:GOTO 5010
5030   IF K$=CHR$(75) THEN R2=R2-.08727:GOSUB 5180:GOTO 5010
5040   IF K$=CHR$(13) THEN SR2=SIN(R2):CR2=COS(R2):PCOPY 1,0:GOSUB 5180:VIEW SCRE
EN (2,19)-(248,123):CLS:VIEW SCREEN (251,19)-(637,186):CLS:VIEW:GOSUB 4590:LOCAT
E 23,57:PRINT "Free memory:":SOUND 860,2:SOUND 800,2:RETURN
```

Fig. H-1. (Continued from page 443.)

```
5050  GOTO 5010
5060  '_____
5070  '
5080  'module:  adjust Pitch angle
5090  SOUND 250,.7
5100  K$=INKEY$:IF LEN(K$)=2 THEN K$=RIGHT$(K$,1) ELSE 5130
5110  IF K$=CHR$(72) THEN R3=R3-.08727:GOSUB 5180:GOTO 5100
5120  IF K$=CHR$(80) THEN R3=R3+.08727:GOSUB 5180:GOTO 5100
5130  IF K$=CHR$(13) THEN SR3=SIN(R3):CR3=COS(R3):PCOPY 1,0:GOSUB 5180:VIEW SCRE
EN (2,19)-(248,123):CLS:VIEW SCREEN (251,19)-(637,186):CLS:VIEW:GOSUB 4590:LOCAT
E 23,57:PRINT "Free memory:":SOUND 860,2:SOUND 800,2:RETURN
5140  GOTO 5100
5150  '
5160  '_____REFRESH ALPHANUMERICS_____
5170  '
5180  LOCATE 18,22:PRINT SYC:LOCATE 19,21:PRINT (-1*MZ):LOCATE 20,22:PRINT (-1*M
Y):LOCATE 21,12:PRINT R1:LOCATE 22,13:PRINT R2:LOCATE 23,14:PRINT R3:LINE (8,185
)-(243,185),C:RETURN
5190  '
5200  '_____ADJUST OPTIONS_____
5210  '
5220  'module:  change the drawing color
5230  SOUND 250,.7
5240  IF C=C7 THEN C=C0:GOSUB 5180:RETURN
5250  IF C=C0 THEN C=C7:GOSUB 5180:RETURN
5380  GOSUB 5180:RETURN
5390  '_____
5400  '
5410  'module:  toggle 2D grid on/off
5420  IF T3=0 THEN T3=1:SOUND 250,.7:RETURN ELSE IF T3=1 THEN T3=0:SOUND 250,.7:
RETURN
5430  '_____
5440  '
5450  'module:  create grid if toggled on
5460  T=1:WHILE T<249:LINE (T,19)-(T,123),C8,,&HAAAA:T=T+J10:WEND:T=19:WHILE T<1
23:LINE (2,T)-(248,T),C8,,&H8888:T=T+J11:WEND:LINE (122,53)-(132,53),C6:LINE (12
7,51)-(127,55),C6:RETURN
5470  '_____
5480  '
5490  'module:  toggle 3D gnomon on/off (x,y,z axis display)
5500  IF T4=0 THEN T4=1:SOUND 250,.7:RETURN ELSE IF T4=1 THEN T4=0:SOUND 250,.7:
RETURN
5510  '_____
5520  '
5530  'module:  create gnomon if toggled on
5540  WINDOW SCREEN (-399,-299)-(400,300):VIEW SCREEN (251,19)-(637,186)
5550  X=30:Z=0:Y=0:GOSUB 4500:SX1=SX1+125:SY1=SY1+3:PSET (SX1,SY1),C2:X=0:Z=0:Y=
0:GOSUB 4500:SX1=SX1+125:SY1=SY1+3:LINE-(SX1,SY1),C2,,&H9249:X=-30:Z=0:Y=0:GOSUB
 4500:SX1=SX1+125:SY1=SY1+3:LINE-(SX1,SY1),C8,,&H9249  'x-axis
5560  X=0:Z=0:Y=30:GOSUB 4500:SX1=SX1+125:SY1=SY1+3:PSET (SX1,SY1),C4:X=0:Z=0:Y=
0:GOSUB 4500:SX1=SX1+125:SY1=SY1+3:LINE-(SX1,SY1),C4,,&H9249:X=0:Z=0:Y=-30:GOSUB
 4500:SX1=SX1+125:SY1=SY1+3:LINE-(SX1,SY1),C8,,&H9249  'y-axis
5570  X=0:Z=30:Y=0:GOSUB 4500:SX1=SX1+125:SY1=SY1+3:PSET (SX1,SY1),C1:X=0:Z=0:Y=
```

Fig. H-1. (Continued from page 444.)

```
    0:GOSUB 4500:SX1=SX1+125:SY1=SY1+3:LINE-(SX1,SY1),C1,,&H9249:X=0:Z=-30:Y=0:GOSUB
     4500:SX1=SX1+125:SY1=SY1+3:LINE-(SX1,SY1),C8,,&H9249  'z-axis
5580  WINDOW SCREEN (0,0)-(639,199):VIEW:RETURN
5590  '————
5600  '————
5610  END
```

Fig. H-1. (Continued from page 445.)

```
100 'Program ARCADEJR.BAS    Arcade animation manager.
110 'Copyright (c) 1988 by Lee Adams and TAB Books Inc.
120 'All rights reserved.
130 'Version for PCjr & Tandy.  640x200 4-color mode.
140 '
150 '_____INITIALIZE SYSTEM_____
160 '
170  KEY OFF:CLS:SCREEN 0,0,0,0:WIDTH 80:COLOR 7,0,0:CLS
175  CLEAR,,,32768! 'set up screen buffer
180  ON KEY(2) GOSUB 190:KEY(2) ON:GOTO 230
190  CLS:SCREEN 0,0,0,0:WIDTH 80:COLOR 7,0,0:CLS:COLOR 2:LOCATE 1,1,1:PRINT "Arc
ade animation manager finished.":COLOR 7:LOCATE 3,1:SOUND 250,.7:END
200 '
210 '_____DATA ASSIGNMENTS_____
220 '
230  DEFINT A,C,M,T,X,Y
240  DIM A1(105):DIM A2(105):DIM A3(105):DIM A4(105):DIM A5(105):DIM A6(105):DIM
 A7(105):DIM A8(105)  'reserve space for graphic arrays
250  C4=1:C7=3  'color codes
260  X=320:Y=100  'write position of graphic array
270  XP=X:YP=Y  'erase position of graphic array
280  XL=9:XR=599:YU=4:YD=183  'boundary limits for entity movement
290  MX1=5  'horizontal x-movement factor
300  MX2=3  'diagonal x-movement factor
310  MY1=2  'vertical y-movement factor
320  MY2=1  'diagonal y-movement factor
330 '
340 '_____SET UP RUNTIME ENVIRONMENT_____
350 '
360  SCREEN 6:PALETTE 1,12:PALETTE 3,7:CLS
370 '————
380 '
390 'module:  create 8 versions of entity to be animated
400  LINE (63,20)-(63,32),C4:LINE (48,26)-(63,20),C4:LINE-(79,26),C4  'entity fo
r heading 0 degrees
410  LINE (57,43)-(79,34),C4:LINE (57,34)-(79,34),C4:LINE-(79,42),C4  'entity fo
r heading 45 degrees
420  LINE (48,54)-(79,54),C4:LINE (63,48)-(79,54),C4:LINE-(63,60),C4  'entity fo
r heading 90 degrees
430  LINE (57,65)-(79,74),C4:LINE (79,66)-(79,74),C4:LINE-(57,74),C4  'entity fo
r heading 135 degrees
```

Fig. H-2. Complete source code for the PCjr and Tandy version of the interactive arcade-style animation program from Chapter 35.

```
440   LINE (63,76)-(63,88),C4:LINE (48,82)-(63,88),C4:LINE-(79,82),C4  'entity fo
r heading 180 degrees
450   LINE (70,93)-(48,102),C4:LINE (48,93)-(48,102),C4:LINE-(70,102),C4  'entity
 for 235 degrees
460   LINE (48,110)-(79,110),C4:LINE (63,116)-(48,110),C4:LINE-(63,104),C4  'enti
ty for heading 270 degrees
470   LINE (48,118)-(70,127),C4:LINE (48,127)-(48,118),C4:LINE-(70,118),C4  'enti
ty for heading 315 degrees
480   '_____
490   '
500   'module:  save 8 versions of entity as graphic arrays
510   GET (48,20)-(79,32),A1:GET (48,34)-(79,46),A2:GET (48,48)-(79,60),A3:GET (4
8,62)-(79,74),A4:GET (48,76)-(79,88),A5:GET (48,90)-(79,102),A6:GET (48,104)-(79
,116),A7:GET (48,118)-(79,130),A8
520   '
530   '_____SET UP ARCADE TEMPLATE_____
540   '
550   CLS:LINE (0,0)-(639,199),7,B:LINE (8,3)-(631,196),7,B
560   LOCATE 2,9:PRINT "Demonstration of high-speed arcade-style animation techni
ques"
570   PUT (X,Y),A1,XOR:SOUND 460,2:SOUND 400,2
580   '
590   '_____INTERACTIVE KEYBOARD CONTROLS_____
600   '
610   'module:  array A1
620   Y=YP-MY1  'calculate next position
630   IF Y<YU THEN GOSUB 2170  'test for crash
640   PUT (XP,YP),A1,XOR:PUT (X,Y),A1,XOR  'animate
650   XP=X:YP=Y  'update coordinates
660   K$=INKEY$  'check the keyboard buffer
670   IF K$="Y" THEN 700  'is it a turn-right?
680   IF K$="R" THEN 740  'is it a turn-left?
690   GOTO 620  'loop
700   X=XP+MX2:Y=YP-MY2  'calculate next position
710   IF (Y<YU) OR (X>XR) THEN GOSUB 2170  'test for crash
720   PUT (XP,YP),A1,XOR:PUT (X,Y),A2,XOR  'change entity
730   GOTO 840  'jump to A2 routine
740   X=XP-MX2:Y=YP-MY2  'calculate next position
750   IF (X<XL) OR (Y<YU) THEN GOSUB 2170  'test for crash
760   PUT (XP,YP),A1,XOR:PUT (X,Y),A8,XOR  'change entity
770   GOTO 1980  'jump to A8 routine
780   '_____
790   '
800   'module:  array A2
810   X=XP+MX2:Y=YP-MY2  'calculate next position
820   IF (Y<YU) OR (X>XR) THEN GOSUB 2170  'test for crash
830   PUT (XP,YP),A2,XOR:PUT (X,Y),A2,XOR  'animate
840   XP=X:YP=Y  'update coordinates
850   K$=INKEY$  'check the keyboard buffer
860   IF K$="H" THEN 890  'is it a turn-right?
870   IF K$="T" THEN 930  'is it a turn-left?
880   GOTO 810  'loop
890   X=XP+MX1  'calculate next position
```

Fig. H-2. (Continued from page 446.)

```
900   IF X>XR THEN GOSUB 2170  'test for crash
910   PUT (XP,YP),A2,XOR:PUT (X,Y),A3,XOR  'change entity
920   GOTO 1030  'jump to A3 routine
930   Y=YP-MY1  'calculate next position
940   IF Y<YU THEN GOSUB 2170  'test for crash
950   PUT (XP,YP),A2,XOR:PUT (X,Y),A1,XOR  'change entity
960   GOTO 650  'jump to A1 routine
970   '‾‾‾‾‾‾
980   '
990   'module:  array A3
1000  X=XP+MX1  'calculate next position
1010  IF X>XR THEN GOSUB 2170  'test for crash
1020  PUT (XP,YP),A3,XOR:PUT (X,Y),A3,XOR  'animate
1030  XP=X:YP=Y  'update coordinates
1040  K$=INKEY$  'check the keyboard buffer
1050  IF K$="N" THEN 1080  'is it a turn-right?
1060  IF K$="Y" THEN 1120  'is it a turn-left?
1070  GOTO 1000  'loop
1080  X=XP+MX2:Y=YP+MY2  'calculate next position
1090  IF (Y>YD) OR (X>XR) THEN GOSUB 2170  'test for crash
1100  PUT (XP,YP),A3,XOR:PUT (X,Y),A4,XOR  'change entity
1110  GOTO 1220  'jump to A4 routine
1120  X=XP+MX2:Y=YP-MY2  'calculate next position
1130  IF (X>XR) OR (Y<YU) THEN GOSUB 2170  'test for crash
1140  PUT (XP,YP),A3,XOR:PUT (X,Y),A2,XOR  'change entity
1150  GOTO 840  'jump to A2 routine
1160  '‾‾‾‾‾‾
1170  '
1180  'module:  array A4
1190  X=XP+MX2:Y=YP+MY2  'calculate next position
1200  IF (X>XR) OR (Y>YD) THEN GOSUB 2170  'test for crash
1210  PUT (XP,YP),A4,XOR:PUT (X,Y),A4,XOR  'animate
1220  XP=X:YP=Y  'update coordinates
1230  K$=INKEY$  'check the keyboard buffer
1240  IF K$="B" THEN 1270  'is it a turn-right?
1250  IF K$="H" THEN 1310  'is it a turn-left?
1260  GOTO 1190  'loop
1270  Y=YP+MY1  'calculate next position
1280  IF Y>YD THEN GOSUB 2170  'test for crash
1290  PUT (XP,YP),A4,XOR:PUT (X,Y),A5,XOR  'change entity
1300  GOTO 1410  'jump to A5 routine
1310  X=XP+MX1  'calculate next position
1320  IF X>XR THEN GOSUB 2170  'test for crash
1330  PUT (XP,YP),A4,XOR:PUT (X,Y),A3,XOR  'change entity
1340  GOTO 1030  'jump to A3 routine
1350  '‾‾‾‾‾‾
1360  '
1370  'module:  array A5
1380  Y=YP+MY1  'calculate next position
1390  IF Y>YD THEN GOSUB 2170  'test for crash
1400  PUT (XP,YP),A5,XOR:PUT (X,Y),A5,XOR  'animate
1410  XP=X:YP=Y  'update coordinates
1420  K$=INKEY$  'check the keyboard buffer
```

Fig. H-2. (Continued from page 447.)

```
1430   IF K$="V" THEN 1460  'is it a turn-right?
1440   IF K$="N" THEN 1500  'is it a turn-left?
1450   GOTO 1380  'loop
1460   X=XP-MX2:Y=YP+MY2  'calculate next position
1470   IF (Y>YD) OR (X<XL) THEN GOSUB 2170  'test for crash
1480   PUT (XP,YP),A5,XOR:PUT (X,Y),A6,XOR  'change entity
1490   GOTO 1600  'jump to A6 routine
1500   X=XP+MX2:Y=YP+MY2  'calculate next position
1510   IF (X>XR) OR (Y>YD) THEN GOSUB 2170  'test for crash
1520   PUT (XP,YP),A5,XOR:PUT (X,Y),A4,XOR  'change entity
1530   GOTO 1220  'jump to A4 routine
1540   '_____
1550   '
1560   'module:  array A6
1570   X=XP-MX2:Y=YP+MY2  'calculate next position
1580   IF (Y>YD) OR (X<XL) THEN GOSUB 2170  'test for crash
1590   PUT (XP,YP),A6,XOR:PUT (X,Y),A6,XOR  'animate
1600   XP=X:YP=Y  'update coordinates
1610   K$=INKEY$  'check the keyboard buffer
1620   IF K$="F" THEN 1650  'is it a turn-right?
1630   IF K$="B" THEN 1690  'is it a turn-left?
1640   GOTO 1570  'loop
1650   X=XP-MX1  'calculate next position
1660   IF X<XL THEN GOSUB 2170  'test for crash
1670   PUT (XP,YP),A6,XOR:PUT (X,Y),A7,XOR  'change entity
1680   GOTO 1790  'jump to A7 routine
1690   Y=YP+MY1  'calculate next position
1700   IF Y>YD THEN GOSUB 2170  'test for crash
1710   PUT (XP,YP),A6,XOR:PUT (X,Y),A5,XOR  'change entity
1720   GOTO 1410  'jump to A5 routine
1730   '_____
1740   '
1750   'module:  array A7
1760   X=XP-MX1  'calculate next position
1770   IF X<XL THEN GOSUB 2170  'test for crash
1780   PUT (XP,YP),A7,XOR:PUT (X,Y),A7,XOR  'animate
1790   XP=X:YP=Y  'update coordinates
1800   K$=INKEY$  'check the keyboard buffer
1810   IF K$="R" THEN 1840  'is it a turn-right?
1820   IF K$="V" THEN 1880  'is it a turn-left?
1830   GOTO 1760  'loop
1840   X=XP-MX2:Y=YP-MY2  'calculate next position
1850   IF (X<XL) OR (Y<YU) THEN GOSUB 2170  'check for crash
1860   PUT (XP,YP),A7,XOR:PUT (X,Y),A8,XOR  'change entity
1870   GOTO 1980  'jump to A8 routine
1880   X=XP-MX2:Y=YP+MY2  'calculate next position
1890   IF (Y>YD) OR (X<XL) THEN GOSUB 2170  'test for crash
1900   PUT (XP,YP),A7,XOR:PUT (X,Y),A6,XOR  'change entity
1910   GOTO 1600  'jump to A6 routine
1920   '_____
1930   '
1940   'module:  array A8
1950   X=XP-MX2:Y=YP-MY2  'calculate next position
```

Fig. H-2. (Continued from page 448.)

```
1960  IF (X<XL) OR (Y<YU) THEN GOSUB 2170   'test for crash
1970  PUT (XP,YP),A8,XOR:PUT (X,Y),A8,XOR   'animate
1980  XP=X:YP=Y  'update coordinates
1990  K$=INKEY$  'check the keyboard buffer
2000  IF K$="T" THEN 2030  'is it a turn-right?
2010  IF K$="F" THEN 2070  'is it a turn-left?
2020  GOTO 1950  'loop
2030  Y=YP-MY1  'calculate next position
2040  IF Y<YU THEN GOSUB 2170  'test for crash
2050  PUT (XP,YP),A8,XOR:PUT (X,Y),A1,XOR  'change entity
2060  GOTO 650  'jump to A1 routine
2070  X=XP-MX1  'calculate next position
2080  IF X<XL THEN GOSUB 2170  'test for crash
2090  PUT (XP,YP),A8,XOR:PUT (X,Y),A7,XOR  'change entity
2100  GOTO 1790  'jump to A7 routine
2110  '_____
2120  '
2130  '
2140  '_____BOUNDARY CRASH_____
2150  '
2160  'module:  crash routine
2170  LOCATE 12,34:PRINT "C R A S H !":FOR T=1 TO 10 STEP 1:SOUND 560,1:SOUND 50
0,1:NEXT T
2180  LOCATE 20,20:PRINT "Press <Esc> to exit, <Enter> to restart."
2190  K$=INKEY$
2200  IF K$=CHR$(27) THEN 190
2210  IF K$=CHR$(13) THEN X=320:Y=100:XP=X:YP=Y:RETURN 550
2220  GOTO 2190
2230  '
2240  '_____
2250  '
2260  END
```

Fig. H-2. (Continued from page 449.)

```
100  'Program FRAMEJR.BAS     Frame animation demonstration.
110  'Copyright (c) 1988 by Lee Adams and TAB Books Inc.
120  'All rights reserved.
130  'Version for PCjr & Tandy.  640x200 2-color mode.
140  '
150  '_____DATA ASSIGNMENTS_____
160  '
165  CLEAR,,,65536!  'set up 4 graphics pages
170  DEFINT H:H=0
180  DIM B11(20,1)  '21 sets sx,sy coordinates near curve
190  DIM B12(20,1)  '21 sets sx,sy coordinates far curve
200  D=1200:R1=5.88319:R2=6.28319:R3=5.79778:MX=0:MY=0:MZ=-150   '3D parameters
210  X1=-30:Y1=0:X4=30:Y4=0:X2=-5:Y2=15:X3=10:Y3=-35   'control points for cubic
parametric curve routine
220  X=0:Y=0:Z=0
230  SR1=SIN(R1):CR1=COS(R1):SR2=SIN(R2):CR2=COS(R2):SR3=SIN(R3):CR3=COS(R3)
240  '
```

Fig. H-3. Complete source code for the PCjr and Tandy version of the frame animation program from Chapter 34.

```
250 '_____SET UP RUNTIME ENVIRONMENT_____
260 '
270 KEY OFF:CLS:SCREEN 2:CLS:C0=0:C1=1:C2=1:C3=1
280 ON KEY(2) GOSUB 990:KEY(2) ON  'install hot key
290 WINDOW SCREEN (-399,-299)-(400,300)
300 '
310 '_____MAIN ROUTINE_____
320 '
330 'MAIN ROUTINE:  manages the creation of 4 separate graphics pages and then i
nvokes high-speed frame animation.
340 CLS:GOSUB 530:PCOPY 0,3  'store graphics page 3
350 CLS:X2=X2-2:Y2=Y2+2:GOSUB 530:PCOPY 0,2  'store graphics page 2
360 CLS:X2=X2-2:Y2=Y2+2:GOSUB 530:PCOPY 0,1  'store graphics page 1
370 CLS:X2=X2-2:Y2=Y2+2:GOSUB 530  'store graphics page 0
380 FOR T=1 TO 5 STEP 1:SOUND 860,2:SOUND 800,2:NEXT T
390 '_____
400 '
410 'module:  animation manager
420 SCREEN,,1,1:FOR T=1 TO 70 STEP 1:NEXT T
430 SCREEN,,2,2:FOR T=1 TO 70 STEP 1:NEXT T
440 SCREEN,,3,3:FOR T=1 TO 200 STEP 1:NEXT T
450 SCREEN,,2,2:FOR T=1 TO 70 STEP 1:NEXT T
460 SCREEN,,1,1:FOR T=1 TO 70 STEP 1:NEXT T
470 SCREEN,,0,0:FOR T=1 TO 200 STEP 1:NEXT T
480 GOTO 420
490 '
500 '_____CREATE A SINGLE FRAME_____
510 '
520 'module:  create a single frame for the animation sequence
530 LOCATE 25,27:PRINT "Press F2 to end animation.":LOCATE 2,18:PRINT "Demonstr
ation of high-speed frame animation:":LOCATE 3,24:PRINT "Manipulation of 3D mesh
 entity."
540 LINE (-250,-285)-(230,-220),C3,B
550 '_____
560 '
570 'module:  create near edge curve and save vertices
580 T=0:T2=T*T:T3=T*T*T:GOSUB 880:Z=30:GOSUB 940:PSET (SX,SY),C3  'establish st
art point
590 H=0:FOR T=0 TO 1.01 STEP .05:T2=T*T:T3=T*T*T:GOSUB 880:Z=30:GOSUB 940:LINE-
(SX,SY),C3:B11(H,0)=SX:B11(H,1)=SY:H=H+1:NEXT T
600 '_____
610 '
620 'module:  create far edge curve and save vertices
630 T=0:T2=T*T:T3=T*T*T:GOSUB 880:Z=-30:GOSUB 940:PSET (SX,SY),C3  'establish s
tart point
640 H=0:FOR T=0 TO 1.01 STEP .05:T2=T*T:T3=T*T*T:GOSUB 880:Z=-30:GOSUB 940:LINE
-(SX,SY),C3:B12(H,0)=SX:B12(H,1)=SY:H=H+1:NEXT T
650 '_____
660 '
670 'module:  draw central curves
680 FOR H=-20 TO 20 STEP 10
690 T=0:T2=T*T:T3=T*T*T:GOSUB 880:Z=H:GOSUB 940:PSET (SX,SY),C3  'establish sta
rt point
```

Fig. H-3. (Continued from page 450.)

```
700   FOR T=0 TO 1.01 STEP .05:T2=T*T:T3=T*T*T:GOSUB 880:Z=H:GOSUB 940:LINE-(SX,S
Y),C3:NEXT T
710   NEXT H
720   '_____
730   '_____
740   'module:  connect the saved vertices
750   FOR H=0 TO 20 STEP 2
760   SX1=B11(H,0):SY1=B11(H,1):SX2=B12(H,0):SY2=B12(H,1)
770   LINE (SX1,SY1)-(SX2,SY2),C3
780   NEXT H
790   '_____
800   '_____
810   SOUND 860,2:SOUND 800,2:RETURN   'this frame completed
820   GOTO 820
830   '
840   '_____CUBIC PARAMETRIC CURVE_____
850   '_____
860   'module:  FREE-FORM curve driver
870   'calculates location of point on cubic parametric curve
880   J1=X1*(-T3+3*T2-3*T+1):J2=X2*(3*T3-6*T2+3*T):J3=X3*(-3*T3+3*T2):J4=X4*T3:X=
J1+J2+J3+J4
890   J1=Y1*(-T3+3*T2-3*T+1):J2=Y2*(3*T3-6*T2+3*T):J3=Y3*(-3*T3+3*T2):J4=Y4*T3:Y=
J1+J2+J3+J4:RETURN
900   '
910   '_____PERSPECTIVE FORMULAS_____
920   '_____
930   'module:  perspective calculations
940   X=(-1)*X:XA=CR1*X-SR1*Z:ZA=SR1*X+CR1*Z:X=CR2*XA+SR2*Y:YA=CR2*Y-SR2*XA:Z=CR3
*ZA-SR3*YA:Y=SR3*ZA+CR3*YA:X=X+MX:Y=Y+MY:Z=Z+MZ:SX=D*X/Z:SY=D*Y/Z:RETURN
950   '_____
960   '_____QUIT_____
970   '_____
980   'module:  quit program
990   CLS:SCREEN 0,0,0,0:WIDTH 80:COLOR 7,0,0:CLS:COLOR 2:LOCATE 1,1,1:PRINT "Fra
me animation demo finished.":COLOR 7:LOCATE 3,1:SOUND 860,2:SOUND 800,2:CLEAR:EN
D
1000  '
1010  '
1020  '_____
1030  END
```

Fig. H-3. (Continued from page 451.)

Glossary

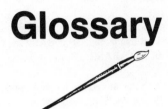

90/10 rule—Ten percent of the program code usually performs 90% of the computing during runtime.

3D—Three-dimensional graphics, consisting of width, depth, and height. In microcomputer graphics, 3D images are usually defined by xyz coordinates.

2D—Two-dimensional graphics, consisting of width and height. In microcomputer graphics, 2D images are usually defined by xy coordinates.

acronym—An abbreviation for a group of words.

active page—The graphics page to which the CPU is currently writing, also called the written-to page.

Ada—A compiled, high level, real-time language used by the U.S. military.

addressable—The ability to be addressed directly by a command from the keyboard or by an instruction in a program.

adversary—The computer-controlled opponent in adversarial games programming.

ALGOL—A compiled, high level language used for general numeric analysis in scientific computing.

algorithm—A method for solving a problem.

all-points-addressable—The ability of the microprocessor to read and write each separate pixel on the display monitor. Also called *APA*.

alphanumeric—A set of characters containing both letters and numbers.

analog—A signal or readout that varies continuously. A digital signal is either fully on or fully off.

animation—The quick display of separate graphic images in order to deceive the human eye into perceiving motion.

APA—An acronym for All-Points-Addressable, which refers to the ability of every pixel on the display monitor to be written to or read by the microprocessor.

APL—An interpreted, high-level language used for data processing.

application—Another way of saying software or program.

area fill—To fill a specified region of the display screen with a specified color or pattern. The attribute surrounding the region to be filled is generally called the boundary. Efficient area-fill routines employ a double-ended stack methodology. Refer to Appendix C for a BASIC algorithm which will fill complex irregular polygons.

argument—A parameter provided to a subroutine.

arithmetic operator—A mathematical operator such as addition (+), multiplication(*), and so on.

array—A set of data elements grouped together under a single name, usually arranged in rows and columns. Similar in concept to a collection of smaller groups. An array can be *scalar* (consisting of numeric or string data) or *graphic* (consisting of pixel attributes).

assembler—A program that converts assembly language source code into machine code. Sometimes called *MASM*. An assembler that works with syntax other than assembly language is usually called a *compiler*.

assembly language—A low-level language whose mnemonics and syntax closely reflect the internal workings of the microprocessor's registers.

back-up—A duplicate copy of software intended to protect the user from inadvertent damage to, or loss of, the original.

BASIC—A high-level general-purpose programming language, available in both interpreter and compiler versions. Common versions include IBM BASICA, GW-BASIC, COMPAQ BASIC, Microsoft BASICA, Microsoft QuickBASIC, Borland Turbo BASIC, True BASIC, and IBM BASIC Compiler.

BIOS—Assembly language subroutines stored as machine code in ROM which provide basic input/output services for DOS and applications programs. Also called *ROM BIOS*.

bit array—A graphic array.

bitblt—An acronym for *bit* boundary *block* transfer.

bit map—An arrangement of bytes in RAM whose bits correspond to the pixels on the display screen. Sometimes used to mean memory-mapped video. The bit map of a VGA is organized in a linear format distributed over four bit-planes. The bit map of a Color/graphics adapter is organized into two banks, one comprised of even-numbered rows, the other containing odd-numbered rows.

bit plane—One of four separate buffers which are sandwiched together by the VGA hardware to create the bit map on IBM Personal System/2 80286- and 80386-based microcomputers. Also called a *color plane*.

bit tiling—Mixing pixels of different colors to create patterns or shades. Also called *halftoning* and *patterning*.

block graphics—Same as *graphic array*.

buffer—An area of memory used for temporary storage.

bug—A programming mistake in the source code, usually an error in program logic flow.

byte—A group of eight adjacent bits.

C—A compiled, high-level programming language developed for systems programming (writing compilers, operating systems, text editors), but useful for high-performance graphics because of its low level functions. Also available in interpreter versions.

CAD—An acronym for *computer-aided-design* or *computer-assisted-design*.

CADD—An acronym for *computer-aided-design-and-drafting*.

CAE—An acronym for *computer-aided-engineering*.

call—A program instruction to transfer control to a routine, subroutine, or to another program.

CAM—An acronym for *computer-aided-manufacturing*.

CDF file—Comma delimited file. In graphics applications, used for storage of graphics primitives attributes.

CGA—An acronym for color/graphics adapter. A CGA which conforms to the IBM standard can display a 320×200 four-color graphics mode and a 640×200 monochrome graphics mode. Also called a C/GA, a Color/Graphics Card, and a color graphics board.

COBOL—A compiled, high-level language used for business applications.

color/graphics adapter—See *CGA*.

color cycling—Producing animation by swapping palette values.

command menu—A set of on-screen icons which represent the commands available to the CAD user.

compatible—Usually means a microcomputer which adheres closely to the hardware standards established by IBM. Compatibility can occur at the hardware level, at the ROM BIOS level, and at the software level.

compiler—A program that translates an entire source code into machine code prior to execution. The C programming language is usually provided as a compiler. QuickBASIC and Turbo BASIC are compilers; IBM BASICA and GW-BASIC are interpreters.

configure—To determine how the various parts of a microcomputer system are to be arranged.

constant—A value in a program which does not change during execution. For example, 23 is a constant, but X and Y are variables.

contour drawing—A drawing that represents the surface of an object. A wire-frame drawing is a skeletal drawing.

copyright—The right to copy an intellectual property such as a book, manuscript, software program, painting, photograph, and so forth.

coordinate system—The arrangement of xy axes in a 2D display or the arrangement of xyz axes in a 3D display. A number of contradictory coordinate systems are in use.

cosine—The cosine of an angle in a right-angle triangle defines the relationship between the hypotenuse and the adjacent side.

CPU—An acronym for *c*entral *p*rocessing *u*nit, the part of a microcomputer which actually does the computing. Also called the *microprocessor*.

crash—A program failure which causes control to return to DOS or to the BASIC editor. See also *hang* and *lock-up*.

crosshatch—Hatch.

CRT—Cathode ray tube, the displaying hardware of microcomputer monitors and television sets.

cubic parametric curve—A formula-generated smooth curve created by providing two endpoints and two control points as parameters for the formula.

cursor—The user-controlled symbol that identifies the active location on the display screen.

data file—In graphics programming, a CDF file used to store attributes of graphics primitives.

debug—To detect and correct errors in a program source code.

decrement—To decrease by a specified amount.

delete—To remove.

digital—A method of representing data whereby the individual components are either fully on or fully off.

dimension—The alphanumeric description of the size of an entity in a drafting program (CADD).

dimension line—The line and arrows which describe the entity to which a dimension refers.

display coordinates—Refers primarily to the converted view coordinates of a 3D modeling program. See also *view coordinates* and *world coordinates*.

distribution disk—The finished program disk which is distributed through marketing channels as commercial software, shareware, or freeware.

dither—Used in computer rendering. To dither a line is to modify a line to match the adjacent shading pattern.

do-nothing routine—A subroutine which merely returns control to the caller. Do-nothing routines are used during preliminary program development and debugging. Also called a *stub*.

DOS—Disk operating system. IBM DOS is often called PC-DOS. Microsoft DOS is often called

MS DOS. Both operating systems are nearly (but not exactly) identical and are authored by Microsoft Corporation.

double-buffer animation—Another name for *real-time animation, dynamic page flipping animation,* and *pingpong animation.*

drafting program—An interactive graphics program which performs many of the drawing functions a draftsperson would perform while creating an elevation drawing or technical drawing.

dynamic page flipping animation—Also called *real-time animation*; a technique involving display of a completed image while the microprocessor is drawing the next image on a hidden page. When the next image is complete, the graphics pages are flipped and the procedure is continued.

ECD—An acronym for *enhanced color display.* An ECD is a digital display capable of displaying the EGA's 640×350 16-color graphics mode.

editor—Generally refers to the interface which allows the user to create and modify text data. A graphics editor is the interface which permits the user to create and modify graphics.

EGA—An acronym for *enhanced graphics adapter.* An EGA which adheres to the IBM standard can display the following graphics modes: 640×350 16-color (out of 64 possible colors), 640×350 monochrome, 640×200 16-color, 320×200 16-color, 640×200 monochrome (same as CGA), and 320×200 four-color (same as CGA).

emulation—Simulation of unavailable hardware/software by available hardware/software. Example: the mathematical routines in Turbo BASIC provide emulation of a math coprocessor even when the math coprocessor is not present in the microcomputer.

enhanced graphics adapter—Same as *EGA.*

entity—In computer graphics, a cohesive graphical shape such as a rectangle, circle, or subassembly in a technical drawing.

ergonomics—Referring to compatibility with human psychology and physiology.

error trapping—Using a programmer-defined subroutine to respond to program flow errors caught by the interpreter or by the operating system during runtime.

extrusion—The act of converting a 2D graphic into a 3D model.

fillet—The round corner function in CAD and CADD programs.

firmware—Software which is stored in ROM.

floating point number—Generally, a number which contains a decimal point; specifically, a number expressed in scientific notation (which allows the decimal point to float). Floating point numbers in BASIC can range from 10E-38 to 10E+38 (for single-precision format, which is accurate to six digits).

FORTH—A high-level/low-level compiled/interpreter general-purpose language used mainly for robotics and graphics.

formatting—The general layout of a program listing, including tabs, spaces, indentations, and margins.

Fortran—A compiled, high-level programming language used for scientific and engineering applications. Fortran is an acronym for *for*mula *tra*nslator.

fps—An acronym for *f*rames *p*er *s*econd, used to measure the display rate of animation programs.

frame—A single image in an animation sequence.

frame grab—The act of capturing a graphic image and storing it in a buffer. The graphic image can be one which has been generated by the microcomputer itself or it can be a signal from a video camera, videocassette player, or television set.

frames per second—The rate of animation, expressed as new images per second. Also called *fps.*

function operator—A trigonometric, geometric, or mathematical function such as sine, cosine, and square root.

geometry—A branch of mathematics concerned with the relationship between two triangles possessing similar angles.

GET—The BASIC command which identifies a rectangular graphic on the display screen and saves the appropriate portion of the screen buffer in RAM as a graphic array.

global variable—A variable in a program which is available to all portions and subroutines of the program.

gnomon—A visual representation of the xyz axis system in a 3D CAD program.

graphic array—A rectangular portion of the display buffer which has been saved in RAM as a bit array for later retrieval.

graphic array animation—Placing one or more graphic arrays on the display screen (i.e., into the display buffer) in order to produce animation. Also called *software sprite animation*.

graphics driver—A module (usually written in assembly language) designed to create graphics in a particular screen mode.

graphics editor—The interface which allows the user to create and modify computer graphics. CAD programs can be considered to be graphics editors.

graphics programmer—An individual capable of creating, testing, debugging, maintaining, improving, and running graphics programs.

graphics page—An area of RAM containing the data to fill the display screen with graphics. The graphics page may or may not be the same as the screen buffer, which is the page being currently displayed.

GW-BASIC—A BASIC interpreter manufactured by Microsoft Corporation. GW-BASIC is licensed to various microcomputer manufacturers, most notably Tandy.

hacker—A person who is dedicated to high-quality microcomputer programming, especially programming performed for its own sake. By definition, good hackers are good programmers. In recent years the term has come to be associated with persons who attempt to penetrate computer security systems.

halftoning—Mixing pixels of different colors to simulate varying shades of a color. Also called *bit tiling*.

hang—A program failure resulting in an endless meaningless loop or execution of garbage code. The user can regain control with Ctrl-Break. See also *lock-up* and *crash*.

hardware—The physical and mechanical parts of a microcomputer system.

hatch—The area-fill pattern used to simulate the ink shading techniques used by many draftspersons.

hertz—One cycle per second.

heuristic—The use of random trial and error to solve a programming problem.

hex—Same as hexadecimal.

hexadecimal—The base 16 numbering system. The decimal system uses base 10. The base is also called the *radix*.

hidden line—In graphics programming, a line which should be hidden by another graphic.

hidden page—A graphics page which is not currently being displayed.

hidden surface—In graphics modeling, a polygonal surface which is hidden by other surfaces.

hidden surface removal—The algorithmic process of removing from the 3D model all surfaces which should be hidden from view. The formulas are usually based upon vector math.

high-performance graphics—Refers to graphics applications which stress speed and color complexity.

image file—A binary file on diskette, hard disk, or virtual disk, which contains a graphic image. In BASIC, the commands BSAVE and BLOAD are used to save and retrieve image files, respectively.

increment—To increase by a specified amount.

inline code—A section of computer code which does not jump to any subroutines to assist in completing its assigned tasks. Inline code generally executes quicker than modular code, but at the expense of legibility and maintainability.

instance—An occurrence of a graphical entity in a drawing.

instancing—Creating a complex 2D or 3D model by multiple occurrences of the same entity at different locations in the drawing.

integer—A whole number with no fractional parts or decimal point. An integer is normally considered to require two bytes of storage. BASIC integers range from -32768 to 32767.

interactive—Accepting input from, and returning feedback to, the user.

interactive graphics—Relating to a computer program which creates or modifies a graphical display in response to user input.

interpreter—A program that executes another program one line at a time. In this context IBM BASICA, Microsoft BASICA, GW-BASIC, and compatible editors are both a program and a programming language.

iterative—Repetitive.

iterative full screen animation—The rapid sequential display of previously-saved graphics pages for the purpose of producing animation. The number of pages available is limited by system RAM or graphics adapter display memory. Also called *frame animation* and *page animation*.

license—The right to use an intellectual property such as a book, software program, musical recording, painting. Copyright is the right to copy an intellectual property, which is rarely included in software licenses.

light pen—A pencil-shaped pointing device, through which the microprocessor reads a pixel location for use by the applications program.

line clipping—Deletion of a part of a line or graphic which exceeds the physical range of the display screen. .

line styling—Using a series of pixel attributes to generate dotted or dashed lines. Also refers to *dithering*.

LISP—An interpreted, high-level programming language used in artificial intelligence applications. LISP is an acronym for *list* processing language. LISP works on symbols rather than numbers.

local variable—Same as *static variable*.

lock-up—A program failure which results in execution of garbage code. The user can regain control only by a warm reboot (Ctrl-Alt-Del) or a cold restart (power off, then power on). See also *hang* and *crash*.

logical operator—An operator which compares bits to check for true and false conditions. Common logical operators include AND, OR, NOT, XOR. The results of logical operations can be used to produced advanced special effects during graphic array manipulation.

LOGO—An interpreted, high-level language used for educational purposes, especially the teaching of geometry and logical thinking.

loop—The iteration or repetition of a group of program instructions.

MASM—An acronym for *macro assembler*, an assembly language compiler capable of including separately created modules into the finished program. IBM Macro Assembler and Microsoft Macro Assembler are the industry standards.

MCGA—An acronym for *multicolor graphics array*, which is the proprietary graphics adapter used in the IBM Personal System/2 8086-based microcomputer.

memory-mapped video—An arrangement whereby the bit contents of an area of RAM correspond directly to the pixels on the display screen. Sometimes used to mean bit map.

menu—A series of options presented on the display screen from which the user is to choose.

menu bar—The horizontal graphic from which pull-down menus are positioned.

merge—To combine two or more diskette files, programs, or graphic images. See *overlay*.

mode—An operating form, format, or technique. A graphics mode refers to the pixel resolution and availability of colors in a hardware operating condition.

modeling—Creating the geometric shape which represents the 3D object on the display screen.

MODULA-2—A compiled, high-level/low-level language useful for systems programming and realtime programming.

modular—Comprised of individual modules, subroutines, or components.

modular programming—The design and creation of programs which use independent modules of code to accomplish specific tasks, thereby completing the overall task.

module—A subroutine in a program. Also called a subprogram by QuickBASIC, a procedure by assembly language, and a function by C.

mouse—A hand-held device designed to be rolled across a desktop in order to cause movement of cursors or graphics on the display screen. Called a pointing device by IBM.

mtbf—An acronym for *mean time between failures*, which is the average length of time that hardware or software will operate before failing.

multibuffer animation—Sometimes used as another name for dynamic page flipping animation, but more often employed to mean frame animation (iterative full screen animation).

nested loop—A program loop contained within a larger loop.

nondisclosure agreement—A contractual undertaking not to disclose proprietary information.

numeric expression—A number, either a numeric variable (such as X or SR3) or a numeric constant such as 4, -512, 6.28319, or 32767.

numeric operator—An operator which manipulates a numeric expression. The four types of numeric operators include relation operators, arithmetic operators, logical operators, and function operators.

object code—Machine code. A compiler or assembler takes source code (which can be understood by the programmer) and produces object code (which can be understood by the microprocessor).

OEM—Original equipment manufacturer.

op code—An acronym for *operational code*, which is comprised of the instructions recognized by the central processing unit.

optimize—To improve a program's speed of execution, while at the same time reducing the amount of memory it requires.

overlay—A section of program code which is loaded into RAM over an existing section of code, thereby replacing the previous code. BASIC supports code overlays to view its CHAIN and CHAIN MERGE statements.

page flipping—Quickly putting a different graphics page on display for the purpose of creating animation or simulation. Page flipping is used in frame animation and realtime animation.

paintbrush program—An interactive graphics program which emphasizes artistic creativity of design and color in the resultant image.

pan—To move a graphic to the left or to the right.

parameter—A variable which a subroutine expects to receive when it is called. Also called an *argument*.

Pascal—A compiled, high-level programming language used mainly for business applications. Pascal is noted for its highly structured programs and its ability to teach programming skills. Turbo Pascal, manufactured by Borland International, has created a large user base for the language on microcomputers.

PC—An acronym for *personal computer*. A personal computer is powerful enough for serious business, scientific, engineering, and graphics applications, yet inexpensive enough to permit individuals to purchase it. PC can mean a PC, an XT, an AT, or a PS/2.

pel— IBM 's acronym for *picture element*, called a *pixel* by nearly everyone else. A pixel is the smallest addressable graphic or dot on a display screen.

ping-pong animation—Another name for *dynamic page flipping animation.*

pixel—An acronym for picture element, called a *pel* by IBM. A pixel is the smallest addressable graphic or dot on a display screen. The medium resolution graphics mode on IBM personal computers contains 320 pixels across by 200 rows down. The enhanced high resolution graphics mode on an EGA contains 640 pixels across by 350 rows down. VGA graphics modes are available at even finer resolutions.

plane equation—A vector formula which describes the qualities of a plane surface, including the location of a given point relative to the surface of the plane. Plane equations are useful for hidden surface removal.

pop-up menu—A menu which is created as an island on the screen, unconnected to any other graphics.

PROLOG—An interpreted, high-level language used for artificial intelligence applications and database management systems.

pull-down menu—A menu which is appended to a menu bar, as if it were pulled down from the menu bar.

PUT—The BASIC command used to place a previously saved graphic array on the display screen.

QuickBASIC—An interactive, menu-driven BASIC compiler manufactured by Microsoft Corporation. QuickBASIC is compatible with IBM BASICA.

radian—A length of arc based upon the relationship between elements of a unit circle.

radix—The base of a numbering system. The radix of the hexadecimal numbering system is 16, of the decimal system is 10.

RAM—An acronym for random access memory, also called *user-memory*. It is the memory available for use by programs and graphics. When the microcomputer's power is shut off, the contents of RAM are obliterated.

RAM disk—A virtual disk which exists only in RAM memory. See *virtual disk.*

ray tracing—An algorithm which calculates the illumination level of a model by tracing a ray of light back from the eye to the model and beyond.

real-time—The actual time during which an event occurs.

real-time animation—Also called *double-buffer page-flipping animation.* The microprocessor displays a completed image while constructing the next image on a hidden page. The pages are flipped and the procedure continues.

redundancy—Unneeded duplication software or hardware, usually for the sake of protection against unexpected contingencies.

refresh buffer—The display buffer. The display hardware uses the display buffer to "refresh" the display monitor (at a rate of 60 times per second with a color/graphics adapter).

regen—Regeneration of a graphic entity. The term is used primarily in conjunction with CAD and CADD programs.

relation operator—A decision-making operator such as > (greater-than) or < = (less-than-or-equal-to).

rendering—Adding illumination, shading, and color to a 3D model. Personal computers using a CGA, an EGA, or a VGA can produce fully shaded 3D solid models by using an illumination matrix and vector math.

replay mode—Regeneration of a sequence of interactive events, especially in games programming and simulation programming.

ROM—An acronym for *read-only memory*, which cannot be changed by the user. Turning off the power supply has no effect on ROM.

ROM BIOS—Same as *BIOS.*

runtime—The time during which the program is executing.

scalar—A mathematical quantity that has quantity but not direction. A vector has quantity and direction.

SCD—An acronym for standard color display. An SCD is a digital monitor capable of displaying 16-colors at a maximum resolution of 640×200 pixels.

screen buffer—The area of memory which is being displayed on the screen, usually located at address B8000 hex on CGAs and at address A0000 hex on EGAs and VGAs. The location of the screen buffer can be changed on the EGA, the VGA, and the IBM PCjr. It cannot be changed on the color/graphics adapter.

scroll—To move a graphic or alphanumeric character upwards or downwards on the display screen.

SFX—Sound effects.

shading—Adding the effects of illumination, shadow, and color to a 3D model.

SIMULA—A compiled, high level language used for simulations. SIMULA is an acronym for *sim*ulation *la*nguage.

simulation—A programming attempt to imitate a real-world event in realtime mode.

simulator—A program that imitates a real-world event in realtime.

sine—The sine of an angle in a right-angle triangle defines the relationship between the hypotenuse and the side opposite.

SMALLTALK—A compiled, high-level language used for simulation and the teaching of thinking skills.

snap—The size of movement of a crosshair cursor in a CAD or CADD program.

SNOBOL—A compiled/interpreted, high-level language used for manipulating non-numerical characters.

software sprite—See *graphic array.*

software sprite animation—See *graphic array animation.*

source code—Program instructions written in the original programming language. A program listing is a print-out on paper of the program source code.

statement—An instruction in the program source code.

static variable—A variable which is available to only the subroutine in which it occurs. Also called a local variable. See also *global variable.* Both QuickBASIC and Turbo BASIC can differentiate between global variables and local variables. Interpreters use only global variables.

stub—See *do-nothing routine.*

subroutine—A subordinate, self-contained portion (or module) of a program designed to perform a specific task. A subroutine is called a procedure in assembly language, a subprogram in QuickBASIC, a function in C, and a module in Modula-2.

surface normal—A line which is perpendicular to the surface of a plane in a 3D environment. The illumination level of a surface can be derived by comparing the surface normal to the angle of incidence of incoming light rays.

syntax—The grammar to be used with a programming language.

system overhead—The amount of time the microcomputer allocates to general housekeeping functions instead of executing programs or generating graphics.

toggle—To change from one possible state to another, as in a program which defines a toggle key on the keyboard. Some programs define a variable as a flag which can be toggled on or off to indicate a specific condition during runtime.

touch-screen—A display screen which is made sensitive to finger touch by means of an electronic matrix.

trackball—A pointing device similar to a mouse, except the ball is located on the top surface of the device, meant to be activated by moving the palm of the hand over the ball.

trigonometry—A branch of mathematics concerned with the relationship of two sides opposite a specific angle in a right-angle triangle. Sine and cosine are particularly useful for 3D microcomputer graphics.

Turbo BASIC—An interactive, menu-driven BASIC compiler manufactured by Borland International Inc. Turbo BASIC is compatible with IBM BASICA. Turbo BASIC uses the IEEE mathematical standard exclusively.

utility program—A program used as a tool, designed to perform a utilitarian task or organizing type of function. A program which outputs the contents of a screen buffer to a printer is a utility program.

variable—A quantity whose value changes during program execution. X and Y are variables, but 23 is a constant.

vector—A mathematical value that has quantity and direction. A scalar value has only quantity.

VGA—The proprietary graphics adapter in the IBM Personal System/2 series of 80286 and 80386-based microcomputers. The VGA provides CGA, MCGA, and EGA graphics modes, in addition to its enhanced modes.

video gate array—The hardware in the PCjr which determines the area of RAM to be displayed or written to.

view coordinates—The xyz coordinates which describe how a 3D model will appear to a hypothetical viewer after rotation and translation. The view coordinates must be converted to display coordinates prior to being displayed on the monitor.

viewport—A rectangular portion of the display screen which becomes a mini-screen within the larger area of the whole display screen. A viewport is a subset of the display screen.

virtual disk—A simulated disk which exists only in RAM memory. Also called a *RAM disk*. Because no physical disk drives are involved, read/writes are much faster. All data contained in a virtual disk is obliterated when the microcomputer is turned off.

virtual screen—A written-to graphics buffer which is not the display buffer. A written-to, hidden graphics page is a virtual screen, although the term is usually reserved for buffers which are much larger than the screen buffer. Panning and scrolling of graphics can be achieved by sending selected portions of the virtual screen to the screen buffer.

visible page—The graphics page currently being displayed.

walk-through—Frame animation of a 3D architectural model which simulates a walk-through by the viewer.

window—Scaling of world coordinates to fit the display screen.

wire-frame drawing—A skeletal drawing of an object. The object is depicted as transparent. No surfaces or lines are hidden.

witness lines—Lines which connect a graphic entity to the dimension lines which describe it.

world coordinates—The raw xyz coordinates which describe the shape of an object. World coordinates are rotated and translated to produce view coordinates, which describe how a 3D model will appear to a hypothetical viewer. View coordinates are converted to 2D display coordinates before being displayed on the monitor.

written-to page—The graphics page to which the microprocessor is currently writing, also called the active page.

Bibliography

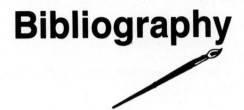

Iconsulted a great variety of texts, magazines, journals, and manuals during the preparation of this book. Some sources from which insight was derived are listed below:

Angermeyer, John and Jaeger, Kevin. *MS-DOS Developer's Guide*. Indianapolis: Howard W. Sams & Company, 1987.

Artwick, Bruce A. *Applied Concepts in Microcomputer Graphics*. Englewood Cliffs: Prentice-Hall, Inc., 1984. (Author's note—This book was republished in 1986 as *Microcomputer Displays, Graphics, and Animation.*)

Baker, M. Pauline and Hearn, Donald. *Computer Graphics*. Englewood Cliffs: Prentice-Hall, Inc., 1986.

Baron, Naomi S. *Computer Languages*. New York: Anchor Press/Doubleday, 1986.

Barr, Avron and Feigenbaum, Edward A. *The Handbook of Artificial Intelligence Vol. 1*. Los Altos: William Kaufmann, Inc., 1981.

Bowyer, Adrian and Woodwark, John. *A Programmer's Geometry*. London: Butterworths, 1985.

Chesley, Harry R. and Waite, Mitchell. *Supercharging C with Assembly Language*. Reading: Addison-Wesley Publishing Company, Inc., 1987.

Davies, Russ. *Mapping the IBM PC and PCjr*. Greensboro: Compute! Publications, Inc., 1985.

Duncan, Ray. *Advanced MS DOS*. Redmond: Microsoft Press, 1986.

Enderle, G. et al. *Computer Graphics Programming*. New York: Springer-Verlag, 1984.

Galitz, Wilbert O. *Handbook of Screen Format Design*. Wellesley Hills: QED Information Sciences, Inc., 1985.

Gellert, W. et al. *The VNR Concise Encyclopedia of Mathematics*. New York: Van Nostrand Reinhold Company, 1975.

Hergert, Douglas. *Microsoft QuickBASIC*. Redmond: Microsoft Press, 1987.

Holzner, Steven. *Advanced Assembly Language on the IBM PC*. New York: Brady Books, 1987.

Hoskins, Jim. *IBM Personal System/2: A Business Perspective*. New York: John Wiley & Sons, 1987.

Hyman, Michael J. *Advanced IBM PC Graphics*. New York: Brady Communications Company, Inc., 1985.

Jourdain, Robert. *Programmer's Problem Solver for the IBM PC, XT & AT*. New York: Prentice Hall Press, 1986.

Kelley, James. E. Jr. *Sound & Graphics for the IBM PCjr*. Wayne: Banbury Books, Inc., 1984.

Kemeny, John G. and Kurtz, Thomas E. *True BASIC Reference Manual*. Reading: Addison-Wesley Publishing Company, Inc., 1985.

Lafore, Robert. *Assembly Language Primer for the IBM PC & XT*. New York: New American Library,1984.

Lemone, Karen A. *Assembly Language & Systems Programming for the IBM PC and Compatibles*. Boston: Little, Brown and Company, 1985.

Liffick, Blaise W. *The Software Developer's Sourcebook*. Reading: Addison-Wesley Publishing Company, Inc., 1985.

Margolis, Art. *Computer Technician's Handbook, 2nd Edition*. Blue Ridge Summit: TAB BOOKS Inc., 1985.

McGregor, Jim and Watt, Alan. *The Art of Graphics for the IBM PC*. Reading: Addison-Wesley Publishing Company, Inc., 1986.

Meilach, Dona Z. *Dynamics of Presentation Graphics*. Homewood: Dow Jones-Irwin, 1986.

Morgan, Christopher L. *Bluebook of Assembly Routines for the IBM PC & XT*. New York: New American Library, 1984.

Myers, Roy E. *Microcomputer Graphics for the IBM PC*. Reading: Addison-Wesley Publishing Company, Inc., 1984.

Myers, Roy E. *Microcomputer Graphics for the Apple Computer.* Reading: Addison-Wesley Publishing Company, Inc., 1985.

Norton, Peter. *PC-DOS: Introduction to High-Performance Computing.* New York: Brady Communications Company, Inc., 1985.

Norton, Peter. *Programmer's Guide to the IBM PC.* Redmond: Microsoft Press, 1986.

Norton, Peter. *Inside the IBM PC.* New York: Brady Communications Company, Inc., 1986.

Norton, Peter and Socha, John. *Peter Norton's Assembly Language Book for the IBM PC.* New York: Brady Communications Company, Inc., 1986.

Pearson, Hilary E. *Computer Contracts.* New York: Chapman and Hall, 1985.

Sargent, Murray III and Shoemaker, Richard L. *The IBM PC from the Inside Out.* Reading: Addison-Wesley Publishing Company, Inc., 1986.

Scanlon, Leo J. *IBM PC & XT Assembly Language.* New York: Brady Communications Company, Inc., 1985.

Schildt, Herbert. *The Complete C Reference.* Berkeley: Osborne McGraw-Hill, 1987.

Tanimoto, Steven L. *The Elements of Artificial Intelligence.* Rockville: Computer Science Press Inc., 1987.

Trachtman, Michael G. *What Every Executive Better Know About The Law.* New York: Simon And Schuster, 1987.

Walker, Robert D. *Numerical Methods For Engineers And Scientists.* Blue Ridge Summit: TAB BOOKS Inc., 1987.

Walker, Roger S. *Understanding Computer Science.* Dallas: Texas Instruments Learning Center, 1981.

Weinstock, Neal. *Computer Animation.* Reading: Addison-Wesley Publishing Company, Inc., 1986.

Willen, David C. *IBM PCjr Assembler Language.* Indianapolis: Howard W. Sams & Co., Inc., 1984.

Williams, Gene B. *How to Repair and Maintain Your IBM PC.* Radnor: Chilton Book Company, 1984.

Wolverton, Van. *Supercharging MS DOS.* Redmond: Microsoft Press, 1986.

USER'S MANUALS AND TECHNICAL REFERENCES

BASIC Version 3.20 Reference. Computer Language Series. IBM, 1986.

BASIC Version 3.0 Reference. Personal Computer Hardware Reference Library. IBM, 1984.

BASIC Version 2.10 Reference. Personal Computer Hardware Reference Library. IBM, 1983.

BASIC by Microsoft Corp., PCjr Version 2.10 Reference. Personal Computer PCjr Hardware Reference Library. IBM, 1983.

COMPAQ BASIC Version 2 Reference Guide. COMPAQ Computer Corporation, 1984.

COMPAQ MS-DOS Version 2 Reference Guide. COMPAQ Computer Corporation, 1984.

Disk Operating System Version 3.20 Reference. IBM, 1986.

Disk Operating System by Microsoft Corp, Version 2.10 Reference. IBM, 1983.

Enhanced Graphics Adapter, Options and Adapters Technical Reference Update. IBM, 1986.

Guide To Operations. Personal Computer Hardware Reference Library. IBM, 1984.

Guide To Operations. Personal Computer PCjr Hardware Reference Library. IBM, 1984.

General Programming Information Handbook. BASIC Version 3.20, Computer Language Series. IBM, 1986.

Hardware Facts. IBM, 1985.

IBM Enhanced Color Display. Personal Computer Hardware Reference Library, IBM, 1984.

IBM Enhanced Color Display Installation and Operating Instructions. IBM, 1984.

IBM Enhanced Graphics Adapter. Personal Computer Hardware Reference Library, IBM, 1984.

IBM Macro Assembler Version 2.00 Manual. Programming Family. IBM, 1984.

IBM Macro Assembler Reference Version 2.00. Programming Family. IBM, 1984.

MetaWINDOW Reference Manual. C. Metagraphics Software Corporation, 1986.

Microsoft Mouse User's Guide. Microsoft Corporation, 1986.

Microsoft QuickBASIC 2.0 and 4.0 User's Guides. Microsoft Corporation, 1986–1988.

Pizazz User's Guide. Application Techniques, Inc., 1987.

QUADEGA+ Operations Manual. Quadram Corporation, 1985.

QuadEGA ProSync Operations Manual. Quadram Corporation, 1987.

Tandy 1000 BASIC Reference Manual. Tandy Corporation, 1985.

Technical Reference. Personal Computer Hardware Reference Library. IBM, 1986.

Turbo BASIC User's Manual. Borland International, Inc., 1987.

ZBasic Reference Manual. Zedcor, 1986.

Index

Supercharged Graphics:
A Programmer's Source Code Toolbox

If you are intrigued with the possibilities of the programs included in *Supercharged Graphics: A Programmer's Source Code Toolbox* (TAB Book No. 2959), you should definitely consider having the ready-to-run disk containing the software aplications. This software is guaranteed free of manufacturer's defects. (If you have any problems, return the disk within 30 days, and we'll send you a new one.) Not only will you save the time and effort of typing the programs, the disk eliminates the possibility of errors that can prevent the programs from functioning. Interested?

Available on disk for IBM PC/XT/AT/PCjr/PS-2 and Compatibles with CGA/EGA/VGA/MCGA adapters and BASICA or other BASIC at $24.95 for each disk plus $1.50 shipping and handling.